Show Me
Quicken 2006

Gina Carrillo

Que®

Que Publishing
800 East 96th Street
Indianapolis, IN 46240 USA

Show Me Quicken® 2006

Copyright © 2006 by Que Publishing

All rights reserved. No part of this book shall be reproduced, stored in a retrieval system, or transmitted by any means, electronic, mechanical, photocopying, recording, or otherwise, without written permission from the publisher. No patent liability is assumed with respect to the use of the information contained herein. Although every precaution has been taken in the preparation of this book, the publisher and author assume no responsibility for errors or omissions. Nor is any liability assumed for damages resulting from the use of the information contained herein.

International Standard Book Number: 0-7897-3433-8

Library of Congress Catalog Card Number: 2005905789

Printed in the United States of America

First Printing: November 2005

08 07 06 05   4 3 2 1

Trademarks

All terms mentioned in this book that are known to be trademarks or service marks have been appropriately capitalized. Que Publishing cannot attest to the accuracy of this information. Use of a term in this book should not be regarded as affecting the validity of any trademark or service mark.

Quicken is registered trademark of Intuit, Inc.

Warning and Disclaimer

Every effort has been made to make this book as complete and as accurate as possible, but no warranty or fitness is implied. The information provided is on an "as is" basis. The author and the publisher shall have neither liability nor responsibility to any person or entity with respect to any loss or damages arising from the information contained in this book.

Bulk Sales

Que Publishing offers excellent discounts on this book when ordered in quantity for bulk purchases or special sales. For more information, please contact

    U.S. Corporate and Government Sales

    1-800-382-3419

    corpsales@pearsontechgroup.com

For sales outside of the U.S., please contact

    International Sales

    international@pearsoned.com

Associate Publisher
Greg Wiegand

Acquisitions Editor
Michelle Newcomb

Development Editor
Kevin Howard

Managing Editor
Charlotte Clapp

Project Editor
Mandie Frank

Copy Editor
Kitty Jarrett

Indexer
Ken Johnson

Proofreader
Juli Cook

Technical Editor
Stacey Ammerman

Publishing Coordinator
Sharry Lee Gregory

Designer
Anne Jones

Page Layout
Michelle Mitchell
Nonie Ratcliff

Acknowledgements

Acknowledgments

Without a doubt, books like this could not materialize without a team of hard-working people to see this project from beginning to end. Thanks to Michelle and Kevin for quickly getting me acclimated and headed in the right direction with this book. Thank you to Kitty and Stacey for ensuring that the information is accurate and useful for those who invest their money and time in reading this book. I hope it is worthwhile and helpful. And thanks to the design, layout, and production folks for making everything look so good. And last but not least, thanks to my family and friends for supporting me and understanding when I fell off the radar during the time that I was hard at work writing this book into the wee hours of the night. Hard work indeed pays off when I see the end result. I am proud to have worked on this project.

About the Author

Gina Carrillo is a technical writer, an instructional designer, an instructor, an author, an editor, and a mother. She has worked in the technical communications and distance-learning industry for 13 years. She works full time developing online help systems, CBTs, training manuals, and user guides for software systems. The software systems Gina has worked with encompass a vast array of technological realms. These systems include many financial systems, ranging from consumer financial systems, such as Quicken and Microsoft Money, to corporate systems, such as PeopleSoft, and large government financial systems used by the Department of Veteran Affairs and the U.S. Treasury.

With a special interest in both education and technical communication, in 2000, Gina helped develop a certificate program for technical communicators at the University of South Florida, where she taught RoboHelp and technical editing for two years. In addition to her writing, editing, instructional design, and teaching endeavors, she also writes and edits for Que Publishing and Sams Publishing. Gina has written the books *Easy Microsoft Money 2004* and *Easy Web Pages,* 2nd Edition, and she was the technical editor for the books *Teach Yourself Microsoft FrontPage 2000 in 10 Minutes, Teach Yourself to Create Web Pages in 24 Hours,* and *Easy Microsoft FrontPage 2000.*

Dedication

I dedicate this book to Gabriela. Everything I do is for you.

We Want to Hear from You!

As the reader of this book, *you* are our most important critic and commentator. We value your opinion and want to know what we're doing right, what we could do better, what areas you'd like to see us publish in, and any other words of wisdom you're willing to pass our way.

As an associate publisher for Que Publishing, I welcome your comments. You can email or write me directly to let me know what you did or didn't like about this book—as well as what we can do to make our books better.

Please note that I cannot help you with technical problems related to the topic of this book. We do have a User Services group, however, where I will forward specific technical questions related to the book.

When you write, please be sure to include this book's title and author as well as your name, email address, and phone number. I will carefully review your comments and share them with the author and editors who worked on the book.

Email: feedback@quepublishing.com

Mail: Greg Wiegand
           Associate Publisher
           Que Publishing
           800 East 96th Street
           Indianapolis, IN 46240 USA

For more information about this book or another Que Publishing title, visit our website at www.quepublishing.com. Type the ISBN (excluding hyphens) or the title of a book in the Search field to find the page you're looking for.

Contents

Introduction   ix

1 Setting Up Quicken   1

Installing Quicken   3
Registering Quicken   8
Using Quicken Guided Setup   10
Entering Your Personal Information   11
Setting Your Financial Goals   12
Setting Up Your Bank Accounts   13
Setting Up Your Investments   19
Setting Up Property and Debt Accounts   23
Setting Up Your Paychecks   33
Setting Up Your Bills   36
Reviewing and Completing the Setup   38

2 Learning Quicken Basics   41

Customizing the Toolbar   42
Creating New Quicken Files   44
Backing Up Files   46
Importing and Exporting Files   48
Password-Protecting Your Files   51
Setting Quicken Preferences   53
Setting Up Remote Access to Your Accounts   61
Setting Up Your Internet Connection   63

3 Using Quicken Home Page Features   65

Using the Account Bar and Activity Centers   66
Getting the Big Picture   69
Selecting Accounts to Include in Your Net Worth   72
Using Alerts   74

Using Bills and Scheduled Transactions	76
Taking the Next Steps with Your Financial Goals	86
Using Online Updates	88
Using Tips and Services	93
Creating Links to Your Favorite Financial Websites	94

4 Managing Your Spending and Savings Accounts — 97

Setting Up New or Editing Existing Cash Flow Alerts	98
Updating Spending and Savings Account Balances	99
Reviewing, Adding, Editing, and Deleting Spending and Savings Accounts	101
Adding, Editing, and Deleting Spending and Savings Account Transactions	107
Searching for Spending and Savings Transactions	112
Transferring Funds Between Spending and Savings Accounts	113
Adding Scheduled Spending and Savings Transactions to Your Register	115
Managing All Your Scheduled Transactions	117
Viewing Spending and Savings Account Overviews	119
Balancing Your Spending and Savings Accounts	120

5 Managing Your Credit Card Accounts — 125

Setting Up New and Editing Existing Cash Flow Alerts	126
Updating Credit Card Account Balances and Transactions	127
Reviewing, Adding, Editing, and Deleting Credit Card Accounts	129
Adding, Editing, and Deleting Credit Card Account Transactions	135
Searching for Credit Card Transactions	142
Adding Scheduled Credit Card Transactions to Your Register	144
Managing All Your Scheduled Transactions	146
Viewing Credit Card Account Overviews	148
Balancing Your Credit Card Accounts	149

6 Managing Your Bills — 155

Setting Up New and Editing Existing Bill and Scheduled Transaction Alerts	156
Reviewing Your Bills and Scheduled Transactions	157
Adding, Editing, and Skipping Bills and Scheduled Transactions	160
Managing All Your Scheduled Transactions	162
Adding New Scheduled Transactions	164

Adding and Editing Paychecks	166
Viewing and Analyzing Income and Expenses	168
Using Quicken Bill Pay	170
Ordering and Printing Quicken Checks	176

7 Managing Your Investments and Retirement Information 181

Setting Up New and Editing Existing Investment Alerts	182
Updating Investment and Security Quotes and Transactions	183
Reviewing, Adding, Editing, and Deleting Investment Accounts	184
Tracking Investment Performances	191
Reviewing Investment and Retirement Account Summaries	193
Adding, Editing, and Deleting Investment and Retirement Transactions	195
Adding, Editing, and Deleting Scheduled Investment and Retirement Transactions	198
Managing All Your Scheduled Transactions	200
Reviewing Investment and Retirement Performance	202
Balancing Your Investment and Retirement Accounts	204

8 Analyzing Your Asset Allocations and Portfolio 207

Reviewing and Analyzing Your Asset Allocations	208
Getting Some Help with Asset Allocation	215
Estimating Capital Gains	218
Viewing Your Entire Portfolio	223
Analyzing Your Portfolio	229
Determining Whether You Need to Rebalance Your Portfolio	233

9 Managing Your Property and Debt 237

Setting Up New and Editing Existing Property and Debt Alerts	238
Reviewing, Adding, Editing, and Deleting Property and Debt Accounts	239
Updating Property and Debt Account Balances	244
Adding, Editing, and Deleting Property and Debt Transactions	245
Searching for Property and Debt Transactions	247
Transferring Funds Between Property and Debt Accounts	248
Viewing, Adding, Editing, and Deleting Scheduled Property and Debt Transactions	249
Managing All Your Scheduled Transactions	251
Viewing Property and Debt Account Overviews	253
Balancing Your Property and Debt Accounts	254

Contents vii

Reviewing and Adding Loans	256
Viewing Auto Expenses	269
Keeping Track of Your Home Inventory	270
Keeping Track of Your Emergency Records	278

10 Planning for the Future — 283

Setting Up New and Editing Existing Planning Alerts	284
Setting Up and Changing Your Planner Assumptions	285
Planning for Retirement	308
Planning for College	312
Planning to Purchase a Home	318
Getting Out of Debt	326
Planning for a Special Purchase	330
Setting Up a Budget	332
Reviewing and Editing Your Plans	336

11 Managing Your Tax Information — 337

Setting Up New and Editing Existing Tax Alerts	338
Importing and Exporting TurboTax Information	339
Creating Year-End Files	340
Reviewing and Editing Your Projected Tax by Using the Tax Planner	342
Reviewing and Editing Taxable Income	347
Assigning and Editing Tax Categories	349
Estimating Capital Gains	354
Estimating Tax Withholding	358
Finding Deductions	361

12 Working with Reports — 365

Viewing Reports	366
Customizing Reports	368
Setting Report Preferences	372
Exporting Reports	374
Saving and Viewing Saved Reports	375

Index	*377*

Introduction

What You'll Do

Welcome to *Show Me Quicken 2006,* a visual quick reference guide that shows you how you can take advantage of the nation's best-selling small business accounting program.

The Best Place to Start

The best place to start reading this book is with a question. What do you want to know? What's not working the way you expect it to work? What Quicken features do you think should provide you with more value? What kind of information are you trying to get from your Quicken program? Ask the question and then go to the table of contents or the index to find the area of the book that contains the answer.

Chances are, you'll begin by finding the answer to your question, and then you'll start paging through the book, discovering new features and learning tips for making your Quicken experience more worthwhile and efficient.

How This Book Works

Each task is presented on one page or two facing pages, with step-by-step instructions in the left column and screen illustrations on the right. This arrangement lets you focus on a single task without having to turn the page.

How You'll Learn

The Best Place to Start

How This Book Works

Step-by-Step Instructions

How This Book Is Organized

Step-by-Step Instructions

This book provides concise, step-by-step instructions that show you how to accomplish a task. Each set of instructions includes illustrations that directly correspond to the easy-to-follow steps. Also included in the text are timesavers, checklists, and sidebars to help you work more efficiently and to provide you with more in-depth information. A "Did You Know?" feature provides tips and techniques to help you work smarter, and a "See Also" feature directs you to other parts of the book that contain related information about the task.

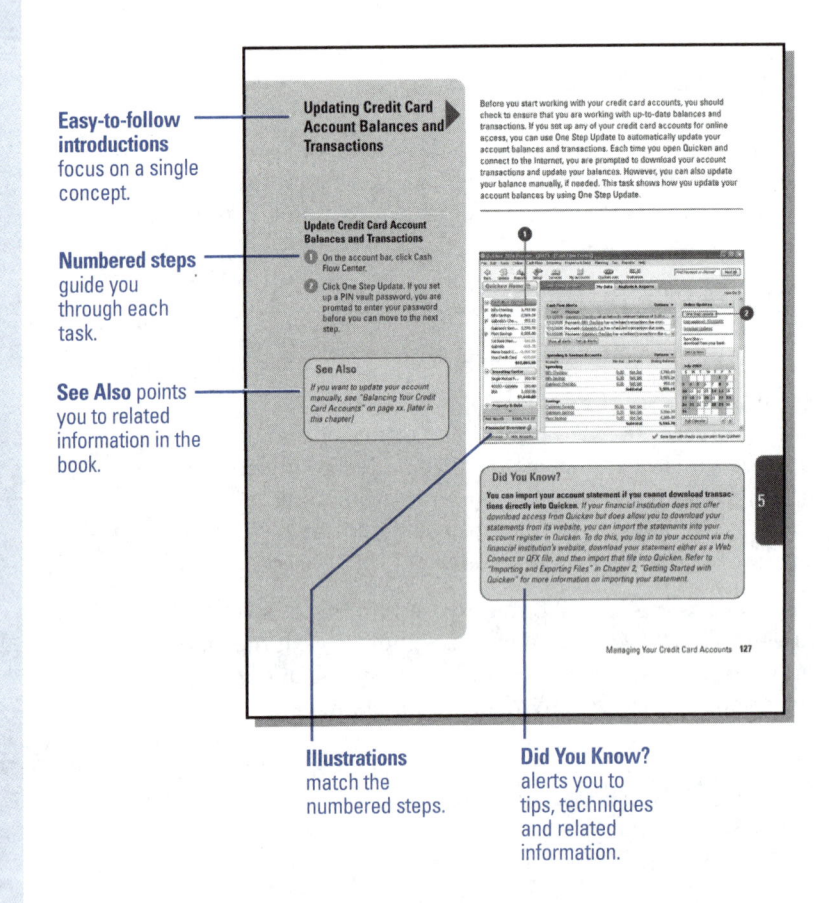

Easy-to-follow introductions focus on a single concept.

Numbered steps guide you through each task.

See Also points you to related information in the book.

Illustrations match the numbered steps.

Did You Know? alerts you to tips, techniques and related information.

How This Book Is Organized

Show Me Quicken 2006 is arranged in chapters that correspond with various features of the program. Although every chapter might not apply to your business, there's ample information about the Quicken program throughout the book, along with cross-references to other areas of the book, so after you find the answer to one question, you will likely be led to related information.

By chapter, these are the topics covered in this book:

- **Chapter 1, "Setting Up Quicken"**—This chapter provides step-by-step instructions on installing Quicken 2006 and upgrading to Quicken 2006 from a previous version. In addition, you will find tips on what information you need on hand before installing or upgrading the software, how to set up your personal information, financial goals, and all your banking, investment, property, debt, paycheck, and bill information. And because you might have a financial file that you want to import from another financial management software, there is information on how to pull that information into Quicken as well.

- **Chapter 2, "Learning Quicken Basics"**—This chapter provides an overview of basic Quicken functionality, including customizing the toolbar to include the buttons that you want to use, as well as creating, backing up, restoring, and importing Quicken files. You'll also learn how to set up remote access to your accounts and how to set up your Internet connection.

- **Chapter 3, "Using Quicken Home Page Features"**—Starting at home base, you'll learn to use the different features that the Quicken home page offers, such as the account bar, activity centers, alerts, and more. All these features help save you time in moving around the program and finding the information you need quickly. In addition, you will learn how to get a snapshot of your financial situation, review your financial goals, and find good resources.

- **Chapter 4, "Managing Your Spending and Savings Accounts"**—In this chapter, you will learn how to add account transactions to your spending and savings account registers, edit and delete transactions, add new accounts, set up scheduled transactions, and balance your accounts. In addition, you will learn how to download bank statements and reconcile your bank accounts by using Quicken.

- **Chapter 5, "Managing Your Credit Card Accounts"**—For your credit card accounts, you will learn how to manage your credit limits by using alerts, keep your credit card registers up-to-date, and review your overall credit situation. In addition, you can perform basic account functions, such as adding, editing, and deleting transactions; downloading statements; and reconciling your credit card accounts.

- **Chapter 6, "Managing Your Bills"**—This chapter shows you how to keep all your bills and scheduled transactions for all your accounts up-to-date. You will learn how to track your bills and how to pay your bills by using a manual method and by using Quicken Bill Pay, an online bill payment service.

- **Chapter 7, "Managing Your Investments and Retirement Information"**—Your investments and retirement accounts and information have their own section in Quicken. In this chapter, you will learn how to keep your investment and retirement information up-to-date by downloading quotes and statements. In addition, you'll learn how to set up watch lists to monitor the performance of both your own investments and those that are of interest to you.

- **Chapter 8, "Analyzing Your Asset Allocations and Portfolio"**—This chapter provides instruction on using some of Quicken's tools that help you analyze your portfolio and asset allocation. You will be able to determine whether you have your assets allocated appropriately, analyze potential capital gains and losses, and rebalance your portfolio.

- **Chapter 9, "Managing Your Property and Debt"**—For property and debt accounts, such as those for your home and car, you will learn some basic account features, such as managing transactions, keeping these accounts up-to-date, and keeping them balanced. You will also learn how to take inventory of your home and personal property and keep track of your emergency records.

- **Chapter 10, "Planning for the Future"**—This chapter will help you determine your financial needs for retirement, plan for college, figure out how much house you can afford, get out of debt, and set up a budget for yourself. You will also learn how to set savings goals for yourself to make your financial situation worry free.

- **Chapter 11, "Managing Your Tax Information"**—Some features in Quicken can really help you out at tax time. This chapter shows you what those features are and how to find deductions, estimate withholdings, and find reliable tax resources.

- **Chapter 12, "Working with Reports"**—Reports, reports, and more reports. There are endless possibilities for the reports that you can create in Quicken. You will learn how to pull out of Quicken the information you need to analyze your finances from just about any angle. You'll also learn the basics of using reports, such as how to view, customize, export, and save reports.

Setting Up Quicken

Introduction

This chapter provides detailed information on installing, registering, and setting up Quicken with all your financial and account information. If you have used Quicken before, you are already familiar with the Quicken Guided Setup. If you are a new Quicken user, you'll find that the Quicken Guided Setup steps you through adding all your financial information, from your bank accounts to your investment accounts.

The easiest way to get your financial information into Quicken is by downloading it. However, this requires that you have online access to your account(s) already, have an Internet connection, and have a valid login ID and password for your accounts. If you have all these things, then you are set. If not, that's okay; you can still enter the information. However, whether you're downloading the account information or entering it yourself, you need to gather your statements to ensure that you are providing Quicken with the latest information, such as your balances, interest rates, payment due dates, and so on. Quicken uses all this information to help manage your accounts, remind you when payments are due, and make projections for your taxes or for savings goals. It's like having an accountant at your fingertips, except all these services come at a much lower cost.

Be sure to review the "Quicken Setup Checklist" on page 2 before you get started with Quicken Guided Setup. Having all the information you need before you start will help save you some time and frustration.

What You'll Do

Install Quicken

Register Quicken

Use Quicken Guided Setup

Enter Your Personal Information

Set Your Financial Goals

Set Up Your Bank Accounts

Set Up Your Investments

Set Up Your Property and Debt Accounts

Set Up Your Paychecks

Set Up Your Bills

Review and Complete the Setup

Quicken Setup Checklist

Before you install Quicken and set up all your financial information, there are a few things you should gather to make the setup process as efficient and quick as possible. Review the following checklist and gather all the most recent information that is applicable to you:

- Bank statements for all your checking and savings accounts
- Credit card statements
- Investment and retirement statements
- Mortgage statement or rental agreement
- Loan statements (car loans, personal loans, student loans, and so on) and other liabilities information
- Information on any assets you own (antiques, art, jewelry, family heirlooms, and so on), including their value
- Paycheck stubs for you and/or your spouse, if applicable
- Statements for all your bills (utilities, insurance, and other non-debt expenses)
- Login IDs and passwords for all accounts (bank, credit card, utilities, and so on) that you access online

Installing Quicken

Before you install Quicken, if you are upgrading from an older version of Quicken, you need to ensure that you make a backup of your existing QIF or Quicken file. You also need to ensure that you save the file to a separate location from where all your Quicken software files are located. Also, you need to ensure that you have all your account information gathered, as indicated in the "Quicken Setup Checklist," and that you have your software ready to install. Depending on whether you downloaded the software or have a CD, your installation may look slightly different from what is shown here.

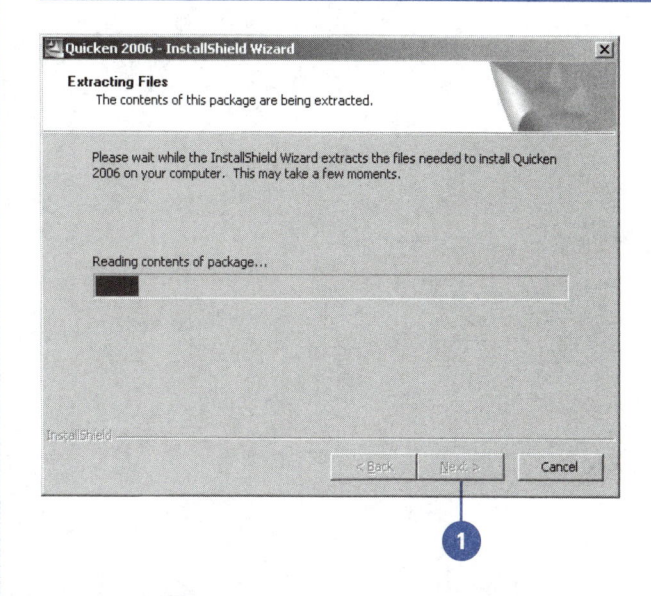

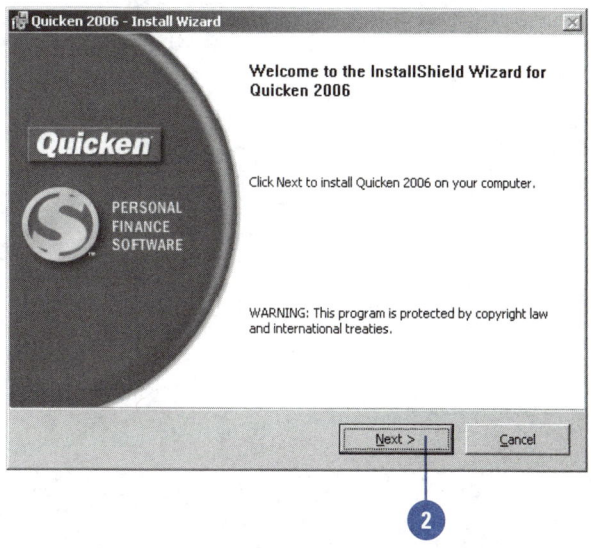

Perform a New Installation

1. When you first begin to install Quicken, the InstallShield Wizard prepares the files that are needed for the installation. When the wizard is ready to proceed, click Next.

2. Click Next to begin installing Quicken.

Setting Up Quicken **3**

3. Read the license agreement, select I accept the terms in the license agreement, and click Next.

4. It is recommended that you accept the destination folder (installation location) for the Quicken files. However, if you need to change it, click Change and locate the folder you want to use. Click Next to proceed.

5. If you need to go back and change any installation settings, click Back; otherwise, click Install.

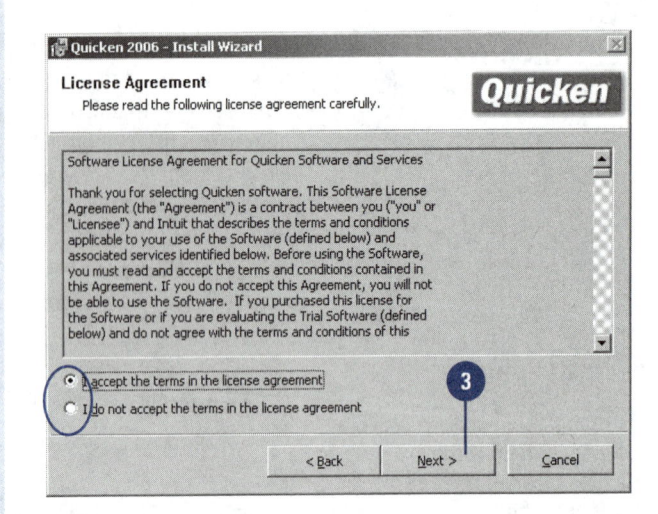

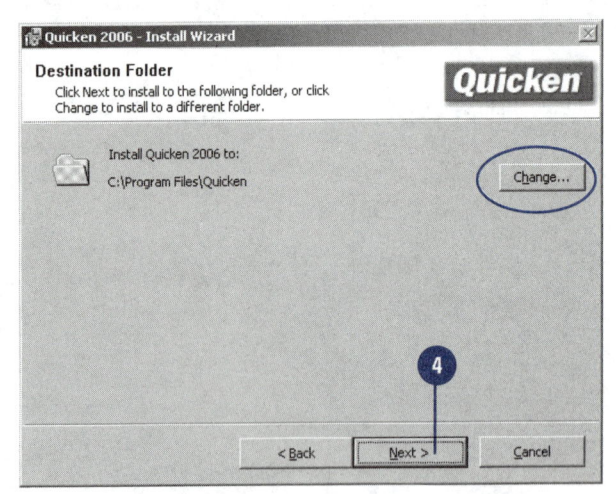

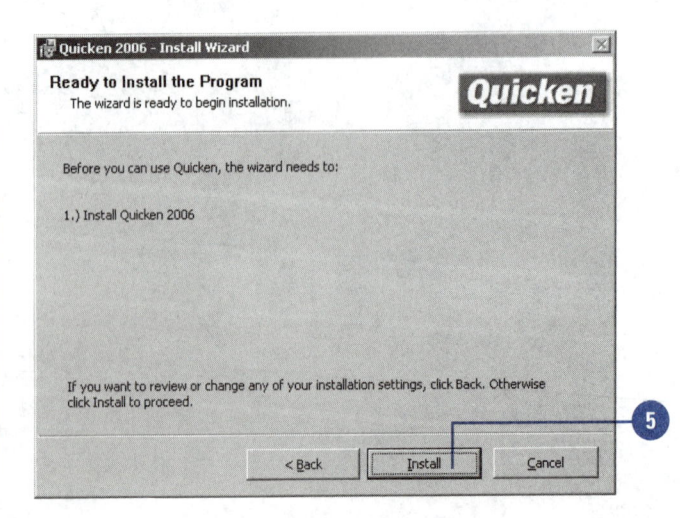

4

6. When Quicken is finished installing the required files, click Next.

7. Click Get Update to check for software updates or click Next to complete the installation.

8. Ensure that the Launch Quicken 2006 option is selected and click Done.

Did You Know?

You can get the latest updates to Quicken 2006. *If you are connected to the Internet, you can check for any updates to your Quicken 2006 software by selecting Get Update in step 7. This ensures that you have the latest files and helps ensure that your software runs as efficiently as possible. When Quicken is finished searching for and installing the updates, go to step 8.*

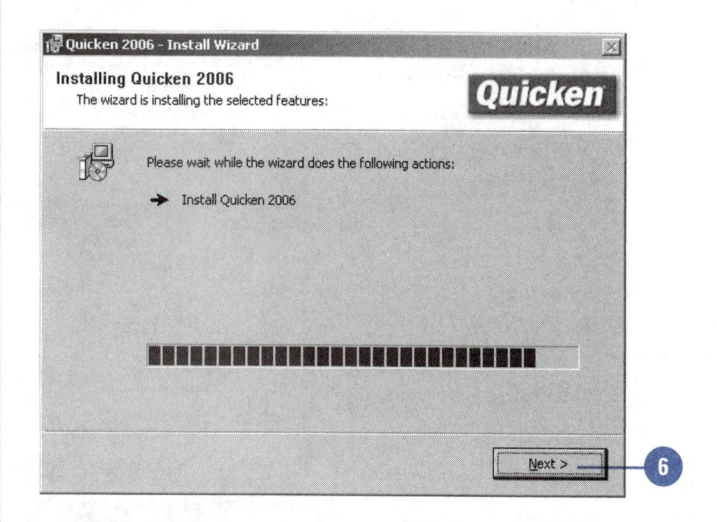

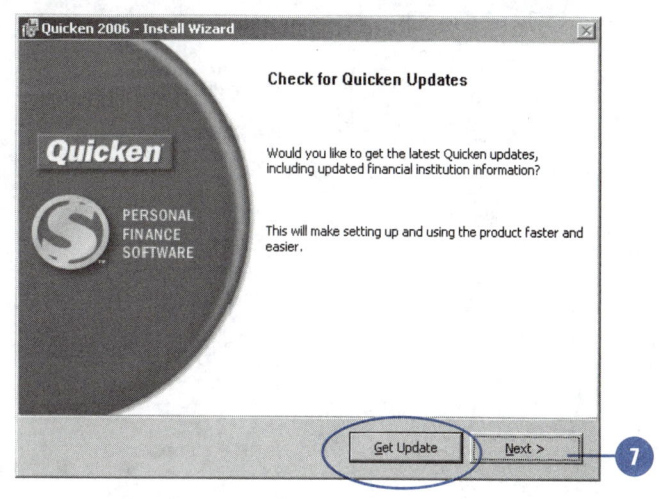

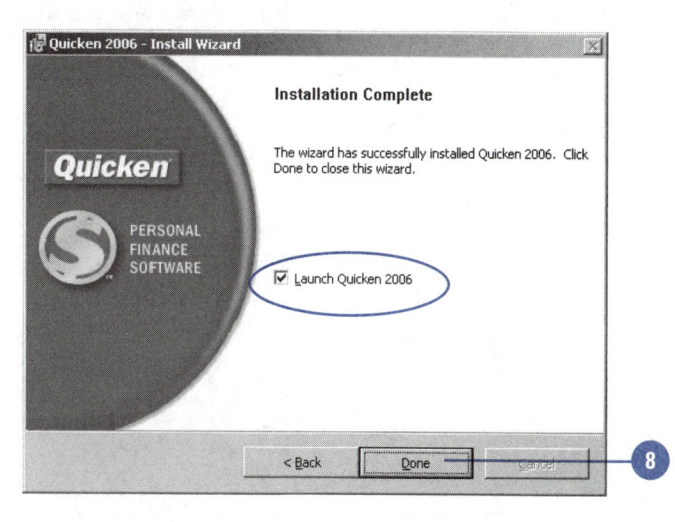

Setting Up Quicken **5**

Perform an Upgrade Installation

1. Refer to steps 1–8 from the task "Perform a New Installation" on pages 3, 4, and 5.

2. When the installation is complete, the Convert Your Data window opens to step you through converting all the information you had in your previous version of Quicken into this one. Click OK.

3. Review the information about upgrading to 2006 and then click Next.

4. If you are interested in Quicken Bill Pay, review the information and click Next.

Did You Know?

Upgrading your version of Quicken overwrites the existing one. When you upgrade your current version of Quicken to a new version of Quicken, the old version is overwritten. However, Quicken automatically backs up all of the information from your current version of Quicken in a Q05Files (where 05 represents the year) folder, and places it wherever your other Quicken files are located.

Did You Know?

Converting your old information into the new version of Quicken saves you time. When Quicken converts your information from a previous version of Quicken, it brings over all your accounts, payees, and so on. Therefore, when you open the new version of Quicken, all your information is there and you can start using the new version right away.

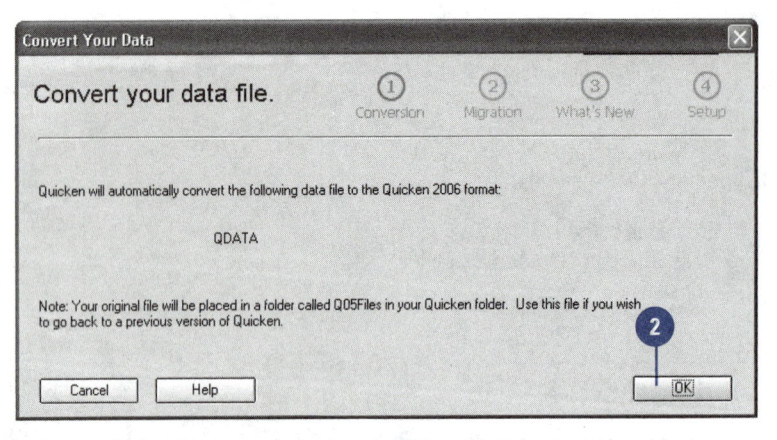

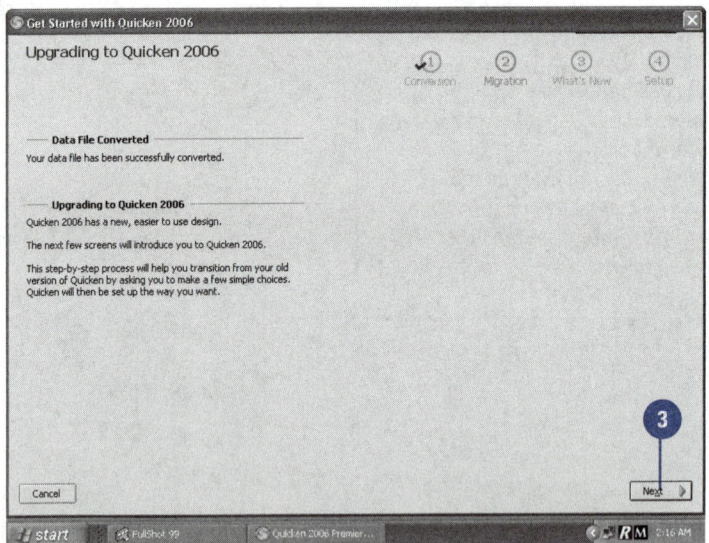

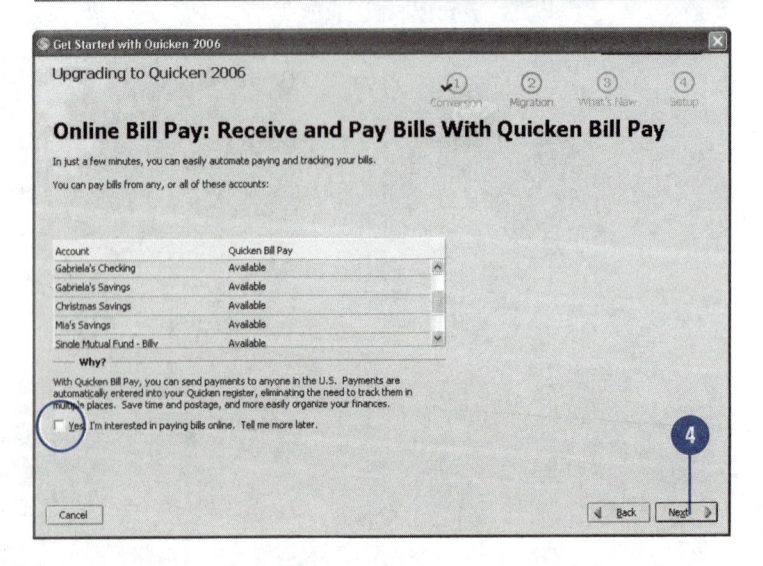

5. To learn more about what has changed in 2006, click a link. When you are ready to move on, click Next.

6. Select whether to use Guided Setup and then click Next.

See Also

Refer to "Using Quicken Bill Pay" on page 170 for more information on setting up and using Quicken's online bill payment service, called Quicken Bill Pay.

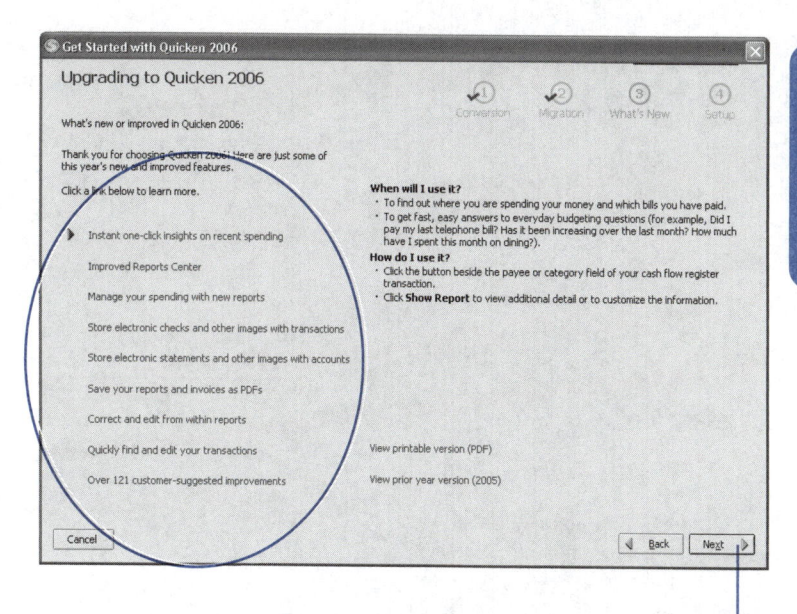

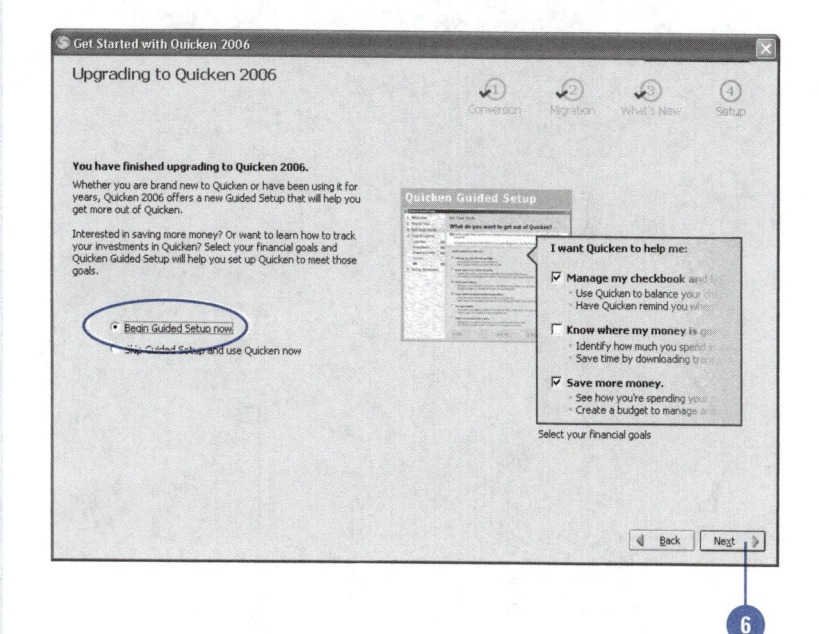

Setting Up Quicken 7

Registering Quicken

After you install Quicken, you should automatically be prompted to register it each time you open Quicken. If you are not automatically prompted to register Quicken and you have not used Quicken before, you can open the Registration window and register. If you have already used a previous version of Quicken, your information is transferred to the new version. You must register your version of Quicken before you can use any of the online features, such as online banking; downloading transactions for your investments, credit cards, and so on; or using Quicken.com features. As you use this version of Quicken, over time, you may also be prompted to install the free updates.

Register Quicken

1. Click Register Now.
2. Complete the required registration information and click Register at the bottom of the registration form. Required fields are indicated by a red dot next to the field title.

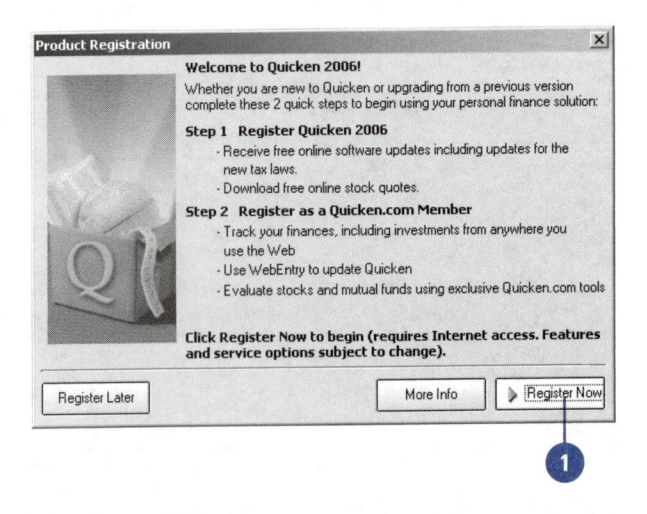

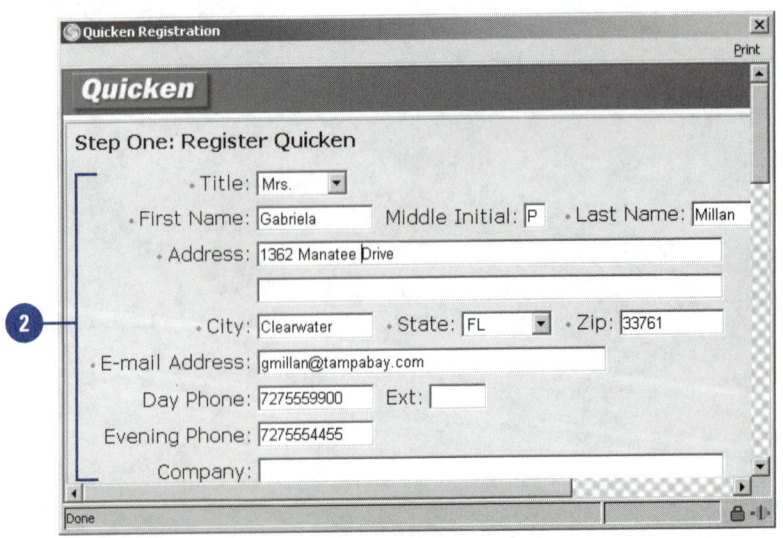

③ To register for Quicken.com, type your member ID and password and click Sign In. If you don't have a Quicken ID and password already, review the Create an Account section and follow the directions to obtain a Quicken ID and password.

④ Review the tools and features you will be able to use with Quicken and click Finished when you are done.

Did You Know?

Quicken.com allows remote access to your accounts. *Quicken.com is a secure Quicken site where you can access basic account information such as your balances. You can obtain a login ID and password to utilize this feature by referring to the Create an Account section shown in step 3. When you're set up, you can access your account information from anyplace where you have an Internet connection. Refer to "Setting Up Remote Access to Your Accounts" on page 61 for more information.*

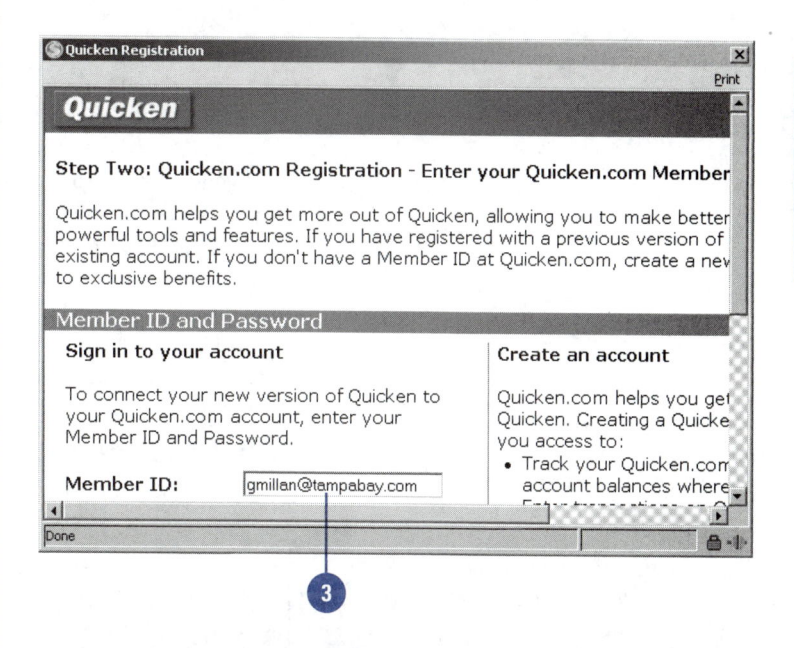

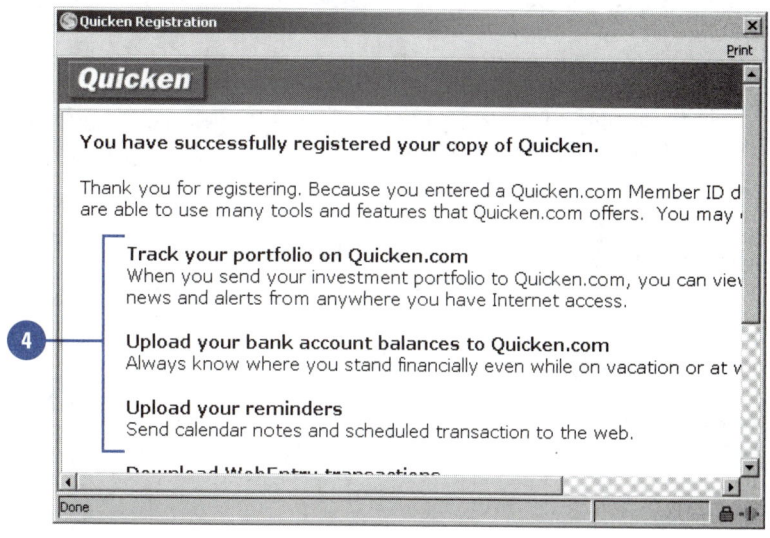

Setting Up Quicken **9**

Using Quicken Guided Setup

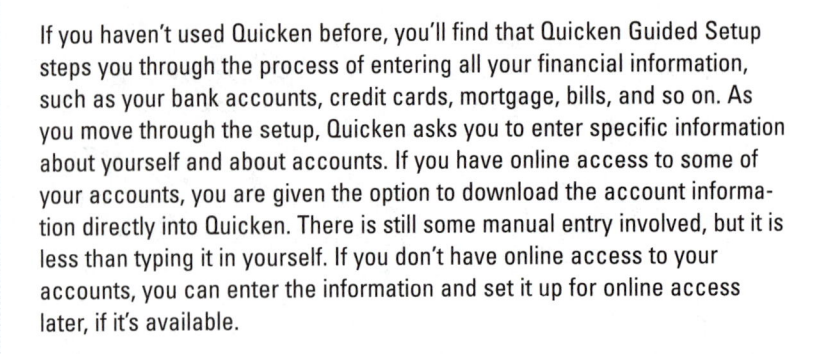

If you haven't used Quicken before, you'll find that Quicken Guided Setup steps you through the process of entering all your financial information, such as your bank accounts, credit cards, mortgage, bills, and so on. As you move through the setup, Quicken asks you to enter specific information about yourself and about accounts. If you have online access to some of your accounts, you are given the option to download the account information directly into Quicken. There is still some manual entry involved, but it is less than typing it in yourself. If you don't have online access to your accounts, you can enter the information and set it up for online access later, if it's available.

Use Quicken Guided Setup

1. Quicken Guided Setup is broken into five sections. Each section concentrates on specific information about you, your financial goals, or your accounts. Click any of the sections to go directly to that area.

2. Click Exit Setup if you want to set up your financial information later. When you open Quicken again, you are prompted to return to the setup.

3. Click Next Step to begin the guided setup.

Did You Know?

Your statements and financial documents can help you get through Quicken Guided Setup. You need to grab all your statements, paychecks, and so on to save some time and ensure that you enter accurate information during the setup process. Refer to the "Quicken Setup Checklist" checklist earlier in this chapter for a list of items you will most likely need during the setup.

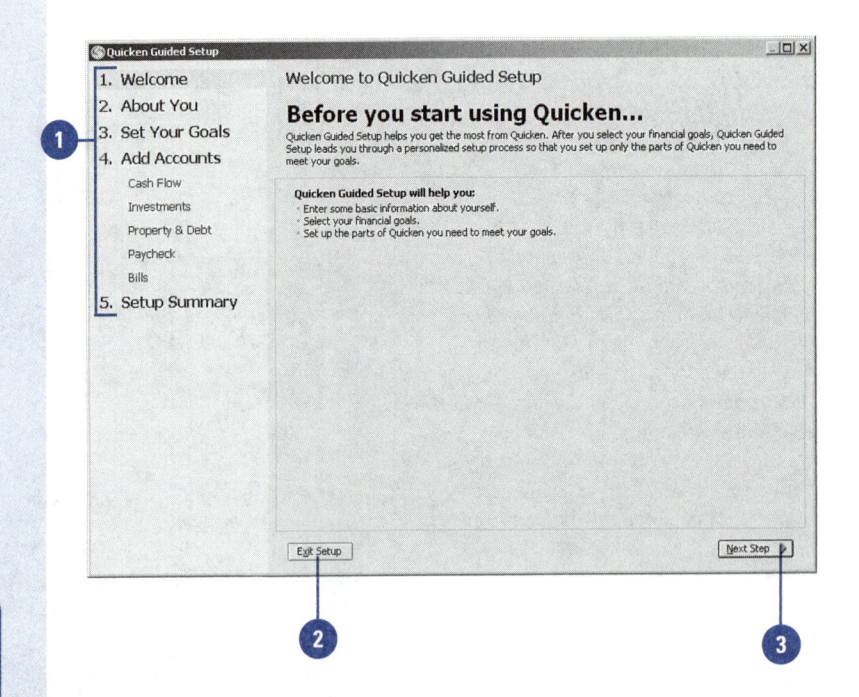

10

Entering Your Personal Information

The second section in the Quicken Guided Setup is the About You section. Quicken asks for some basic information, such as your name and birth date, and it asks some questions that help Quicken determine what information it needs to obtain in order to create the accounts that fit your needs.

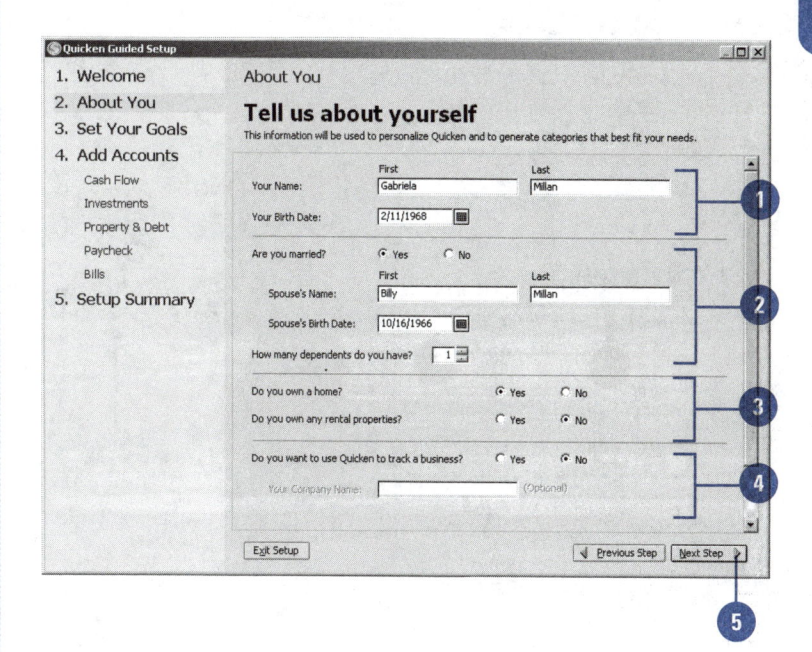

Enter Your Personal Information

1. Type your name and birth date. You can also use the calendar icon to select your birth date.

2. Provide information about your marital status, spouse, and dependents, if applicable.

3. Specify whether you own a home or rental property.

4. Specify whether you have a business for which you'd like to track finances.

5. Click Next Step to proceed.

Setting Up Quicken 11

Setting Your Financial Goals

By telling Quicken what your financial interests and goals are, it can determine which features to offer you. There are several options from which to choose, ranging from managing your bills to saving for retirement. You can select as many or as few goals as you like. The goals you select determine which accounts Quicken sets up for you.

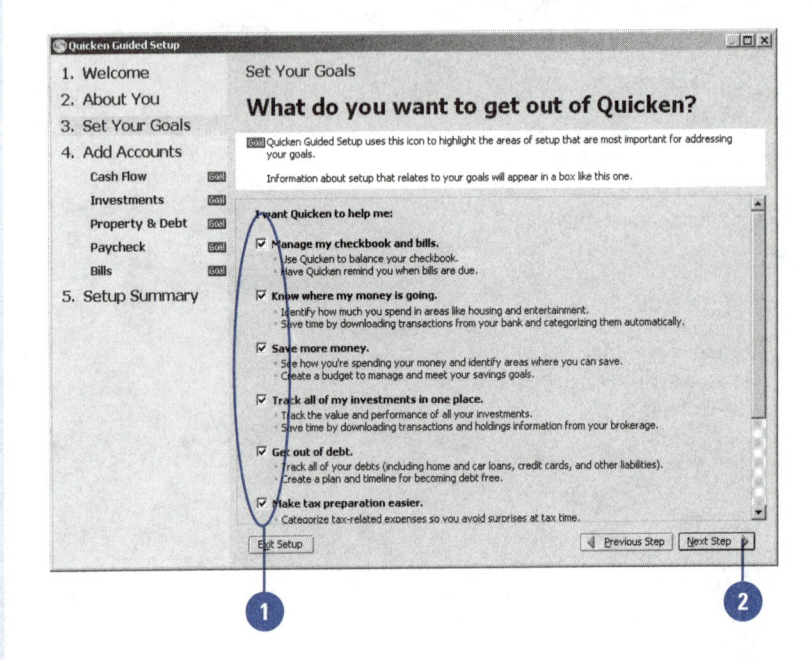

Set Your Financial Goals

1. Select a goal by clicking in the box next to the goal.
2. Click Next Step to proceed.

Did You Know?

You can finish the setup later. You don't have to complete the setup all in one sitting. On each section in the setup, there is a Finish Later button. Clicking this saves all the information you've entered to that point, and the next time you open Quicken, a message appears, asking if you want to continue with the setup. If you click OK, the setup opens right where you left off.

Setting Up Your Bank Accounts

The first accounts to set up are your bank accounts, or cash flow accounts, which include checking, savings, credit card, and any cash accounts you currently have. You need to pull out your bank and credit card statements for all your bank accounts in order to ensure that the latest information about these accounts is transferred to Quicken. Better yet, if you have online access to your bank accounts, retrieve your login IDs and passwords so that you can download the information into Quicken.

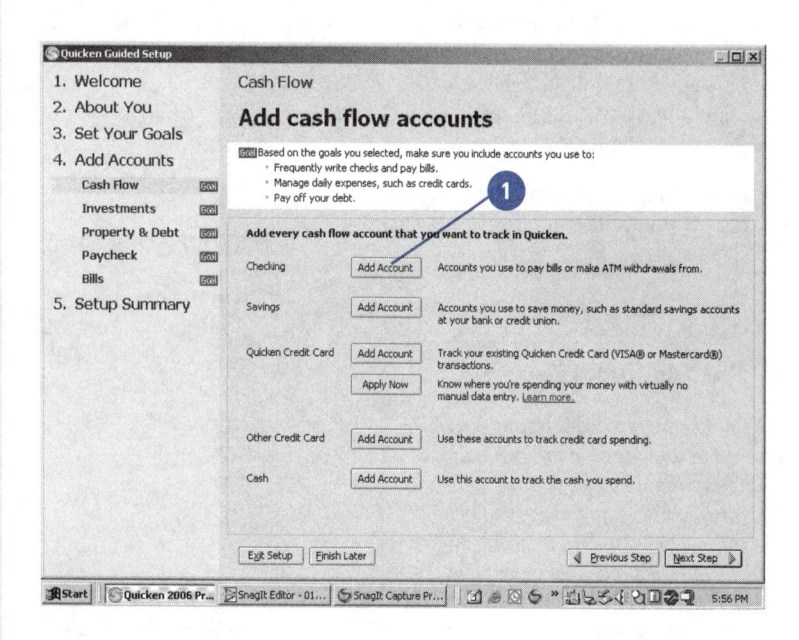

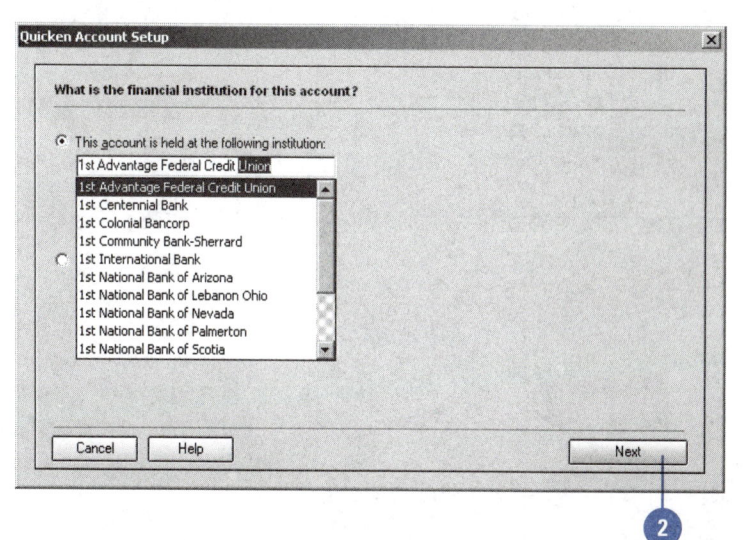

Set Up Checking and Savings Accounts

① To add a checking account, click Add Account next to Checking.

② Click in the This account is held at the following institute and start typing the name of your bank. A drop-down menu appears for you to select the name of the financial institute. If it is not listed, finish typing the name. Then, click Next.

Setting Up Quicken 13

③ Select Online if you can download the account information directly from your financial institution. Select Manual to enter the account information yourself. Then click Next.

④ If you are downloading your account information, skip to step 6. If you are entering the information manually, type the name you want to give this account. This name is used within Quicken only, to identify it and differentiate it from other accounts.

⑤ Type the date your statement cycle ends and your ending balance and then click Done.

Did You Know?

You must have a login ID and password to download your bank account information. In order to download your bank account information, you must already have a login ID and password from your financial institution. If you don't, click the Sign Up Now button to request the ID and password, or call your financial institution. If you don't have online access now, enter your bank information manually, and when you get your login ID and password, you can start downloading your account information from then on.

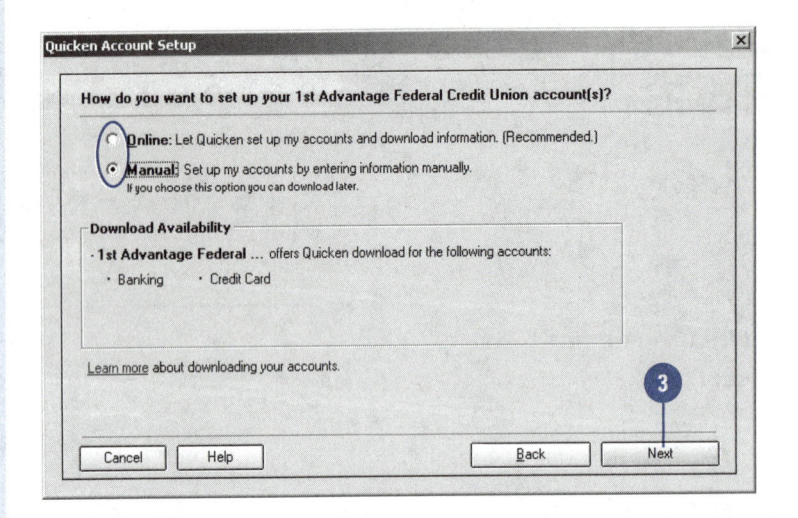

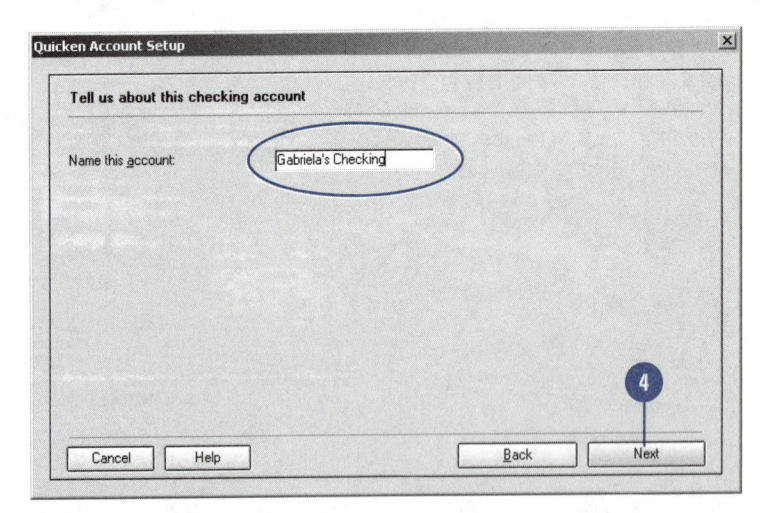

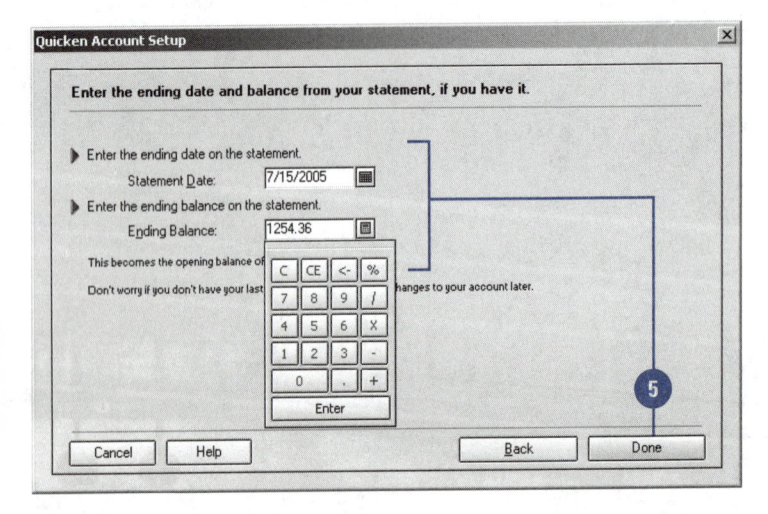

14

6. To download your account information, connect to the Internet, type your login ID (customer ID) and password (PIN), and click Next. Quicken connects to your financial institution and locates your account(s).

7. Select the accounts you want to download, type a name to use in Quicken for the account(s), and click Next.

8. Verify the account(s) you are about to download. If you need to make changes, click Back; if not, click Done. The Quicken One Step Update Status window shows you the progress of the download.

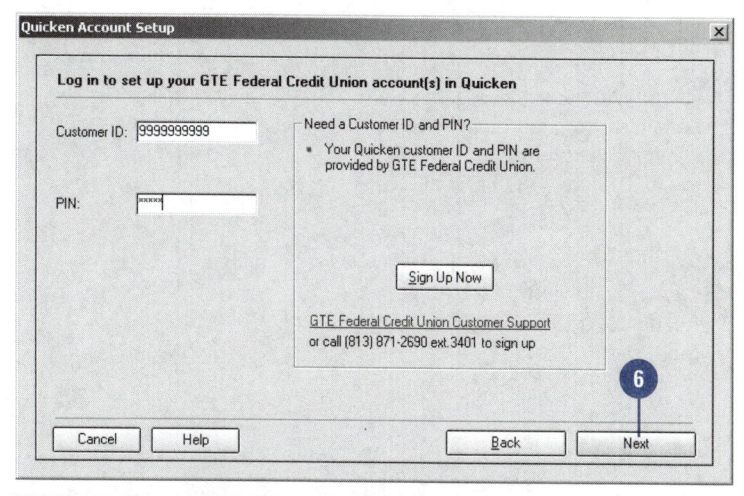

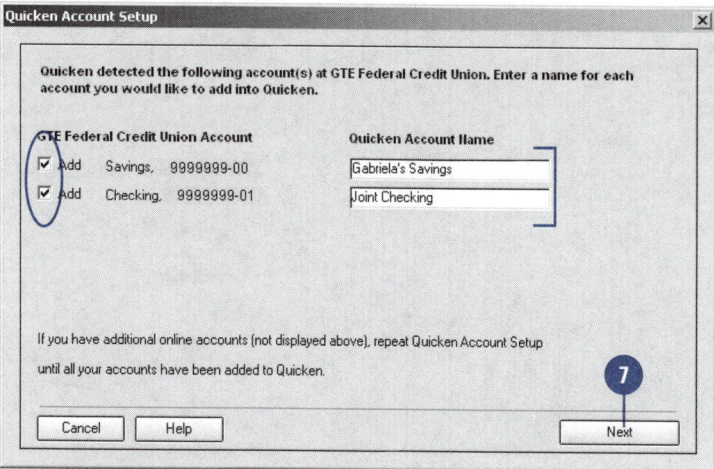

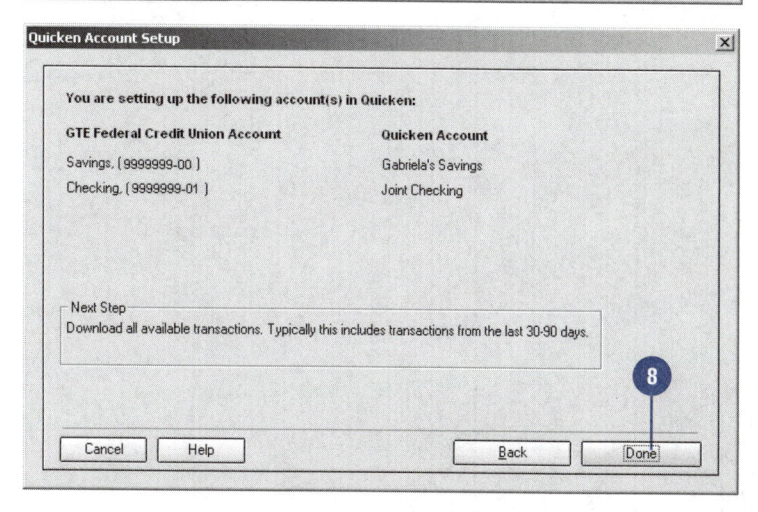

Setting Up Quicken **15**

9. Click Done.

10. To add additional savings accounts, from the Cash Flow window, click Add Account next to Checking and then repeat setps 2-9.

11. To add saving accounts, from the Cash Flow window, click Add Account next to Savings and then repeat steps 2-9.

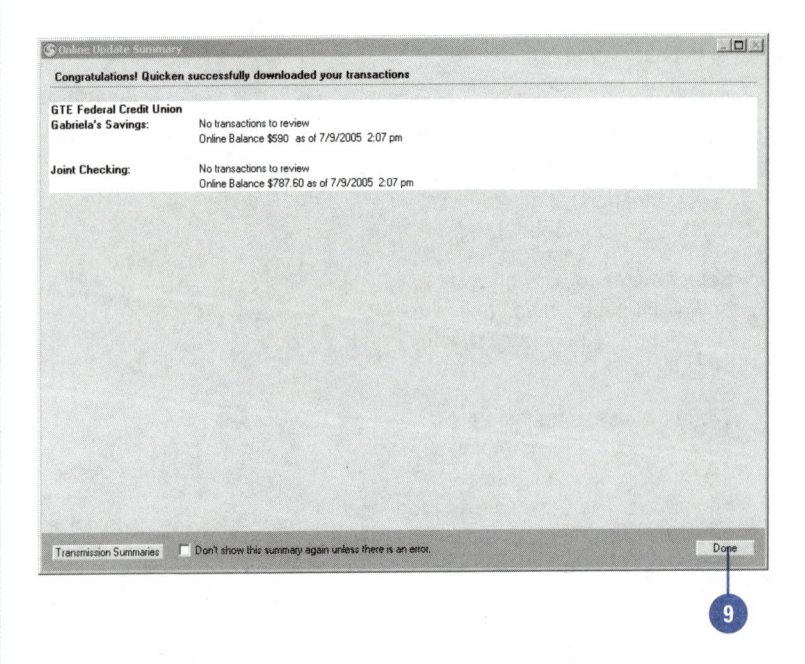

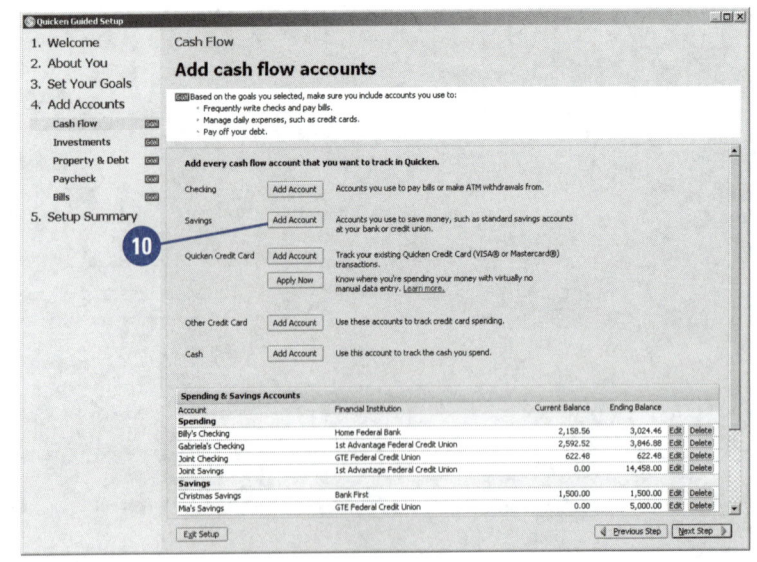

Set Up Credit Card Accounts

1. Click Add Account next to Quicken Credit Card, if you have a Quicken credit card, or click Other Credit Card for all other credit cards.

2. Type the name of the financial institution for your credit card and then click Next.

3. Select Online if you can download the account information directly from your financial institution. Select Manual to enter the account information yourself. Then click Next.

Did You Know?

You must have a login ID and password to download your credit card information. As with your checking and savings accounts, you must already have a login ID and password from your credit card company in order to access and download your credit card statements and transactions into Quicken. If you don't have a login ID and password, call your credit card company. Not all credit card companies offer the capability to download information into Quicken.

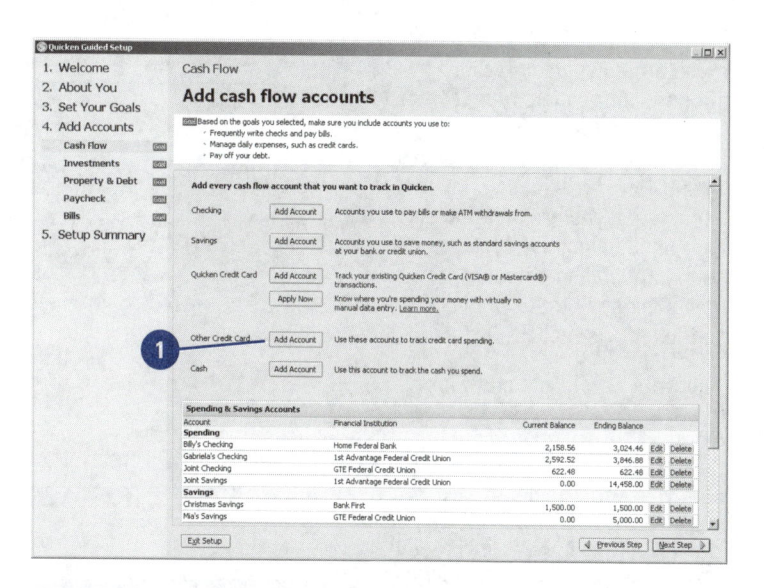

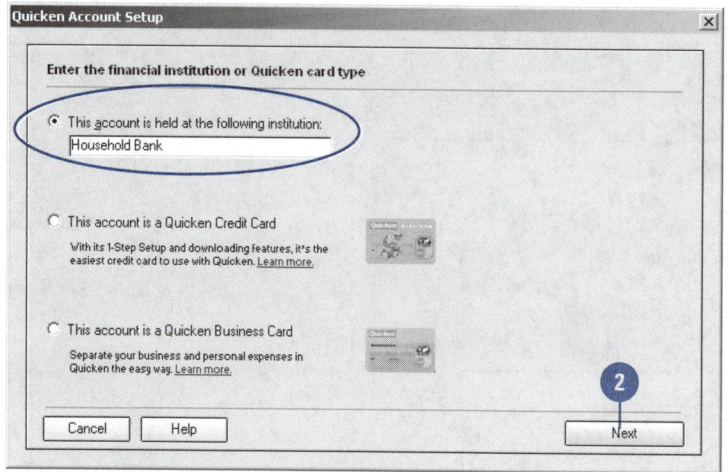

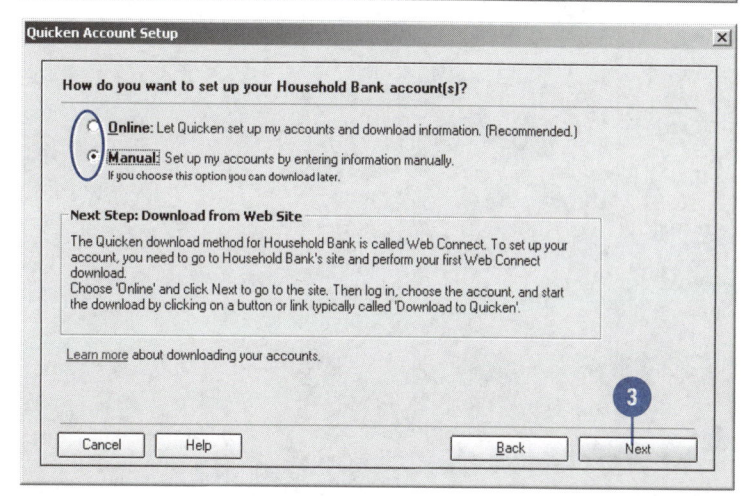

Setting Up Quicken 17

④ If you are downloading your account information, repeat steps 6–9 from the "Set Up Checking and Savings Accounts" task on pages 15 and 16 to download credit card accounts. If you are entering the information manually, type the statement ending date and the ending balance from your last statement. Then click Next.

⑤ Type your credit limit and click Done.

⑥ Repeat steps 1–5 for each credit card you want to add.

⑦ To add cash accounts, in the Cash Flow window, click Add Account next to Cash (visible in step 1) and then repeat steps 1–5.

> ### See Also
>
> *See "Set Up Checking and Savings Accounts" on page 13 for more information on downloading account information.*

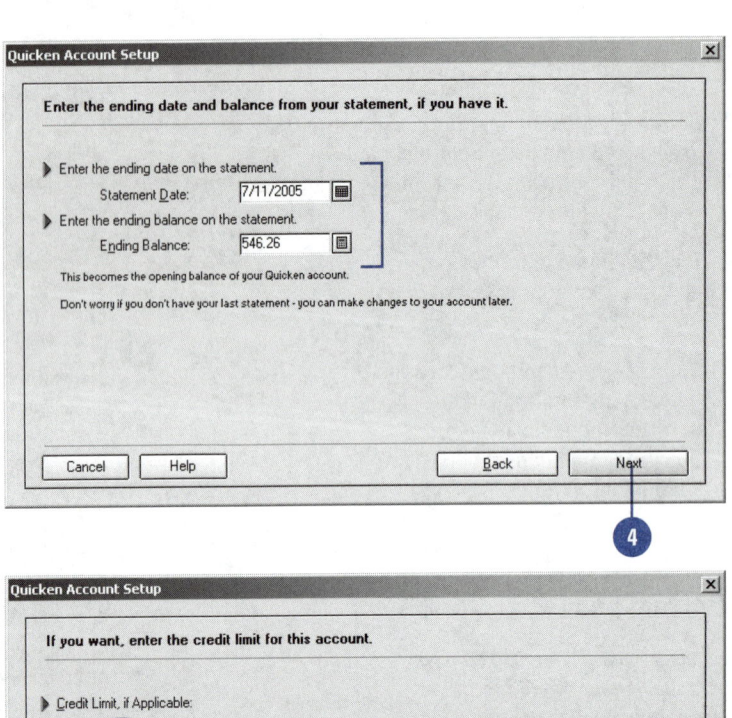

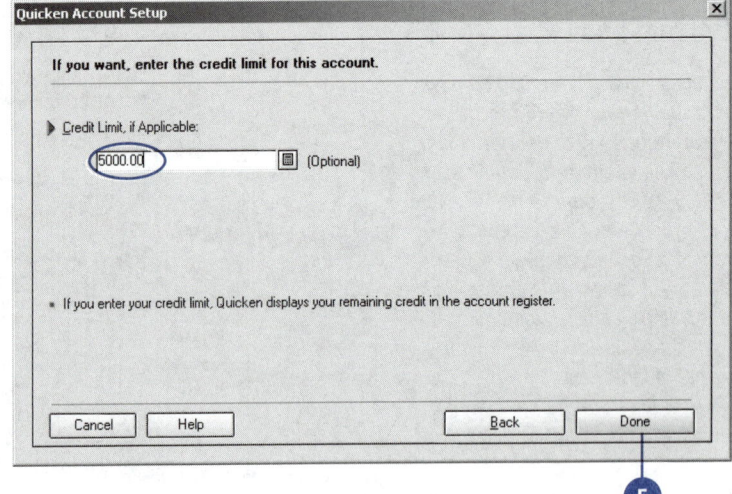

Setting Up Your Investments

You can set up brokerage, IRA, Keogh, 401(k), 403(b), and single mutual fund investment accounts in Quicken. You use brokerage type accounts to track employee Stock Option Grants (ESOGs), Employee Stock Purchase Plans (ESPPs), stocks, mutual funds, and bonds. For brokerage accounts, Quicken tracks the performance, capital gains, and more. You use the IRA and Keogh accounts for traditional Individual Retirement Accounts (IRA), Roth IRAs, Education IRAs, Keogh plans, and SEP-IRAs. You can also use the Roth IRA account type to track a 529 plan; however, the tax-related information for that account cannot be tracked in Quicken. Contributions to 401(k) and 403(b) retirement accounts can be tracked though. Single mutual funds can also be added and tracked in Quicken, as long as the mutual fund was purchased from a mutual fund company, have no cash balance, and have a separate account for each mutual fund.

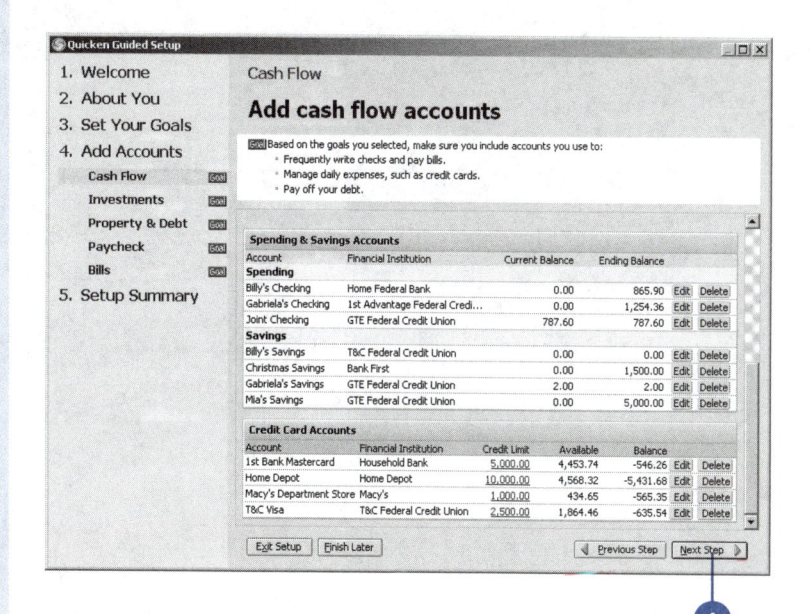

Add Brokerage Accounts

1. Click Next Step.

Setting Up Quicken   19

② Click Add Account next to Brokerage.

③ Type or select the name of the investment institution that holds the account and then click Next.

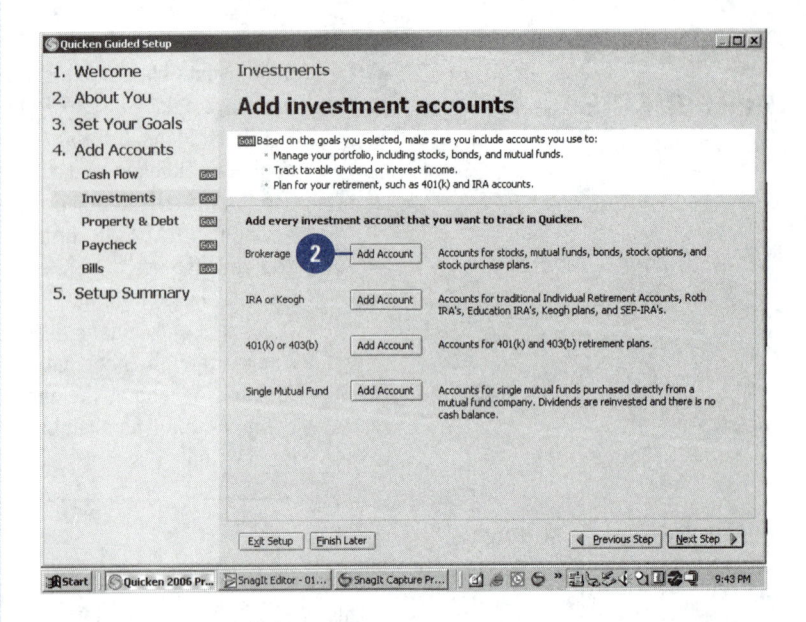

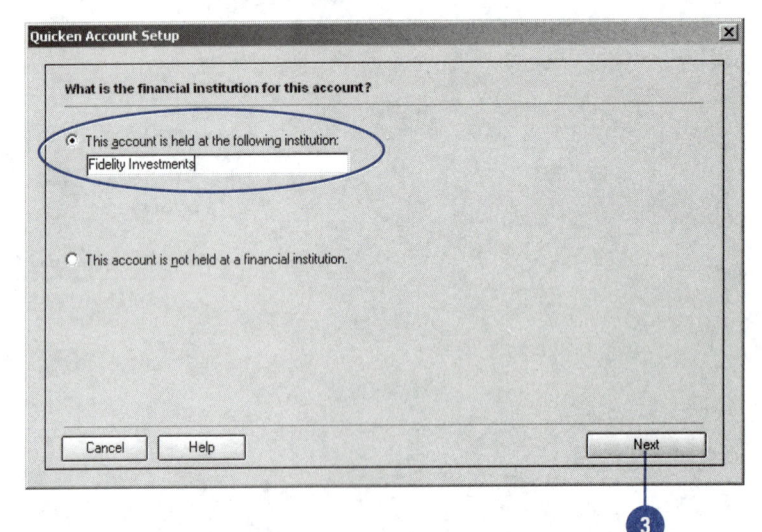

④ Select Online if you can download the account information directly from your investment institution. Select Manual to enter the account information yourself. Then click Next.

⑤ If you are downloading your account information, type your login ID (customer ID) and password (PIN) and then click Next. The rest of the download works just as it does for other accounts. Repeat steps 6–9 from the "Set Up Checking and Savings Accounts" task on pages 15 and 16 to download investment accounts.

Did You Know?

You must have a login ID and password to download your investment transactions. As with your other online accounts, you must already have a login ID and password from your investment company in order to access and download your investment statements and transactions into Quicken. If you don't have a login ID and password, call your investment company.

See Also

See "Set Up Checking and Savings Accounts" on page 13 for more information on downloading account information.

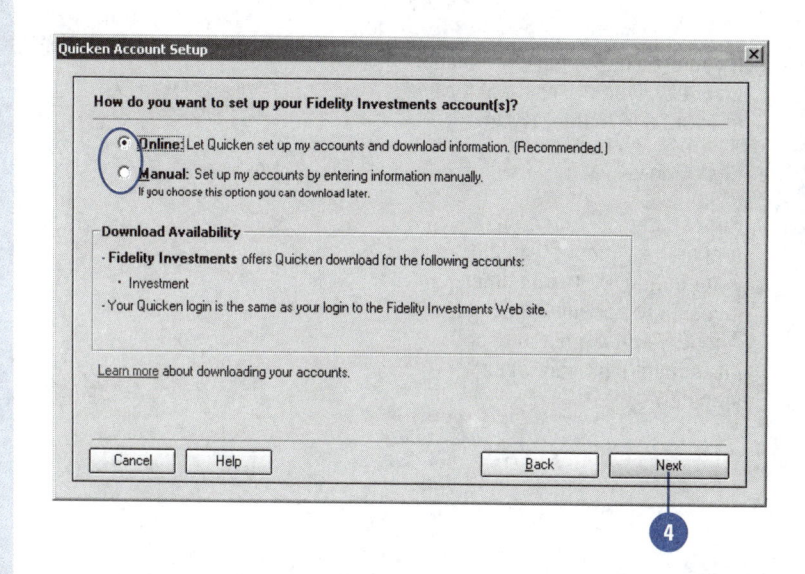

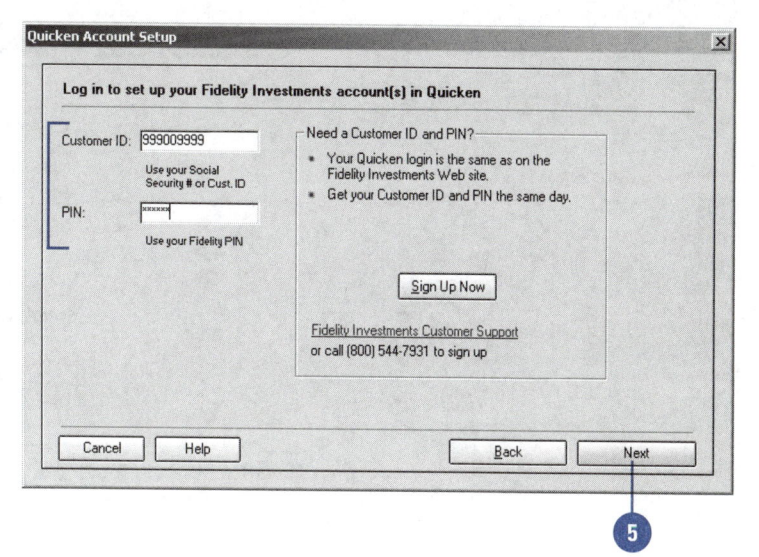

Setting Up Quicken **21**

6 If you are entering the information manually, type the name of the account and then click Next.

7 Click Done.

8 Repeat steps 2-7 for each brokerage account type that you want to add. Or, to add other investment accounts, click the Add Account button next to each investment type and repeat steps 2-7.

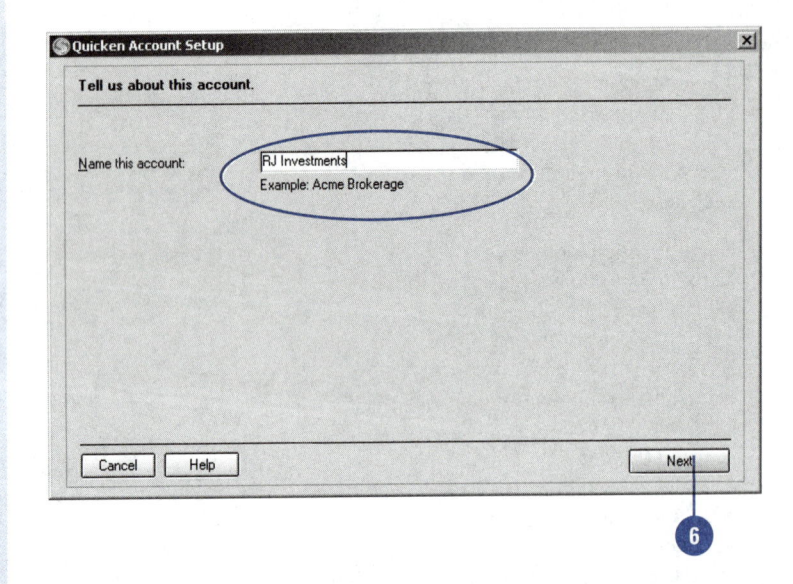

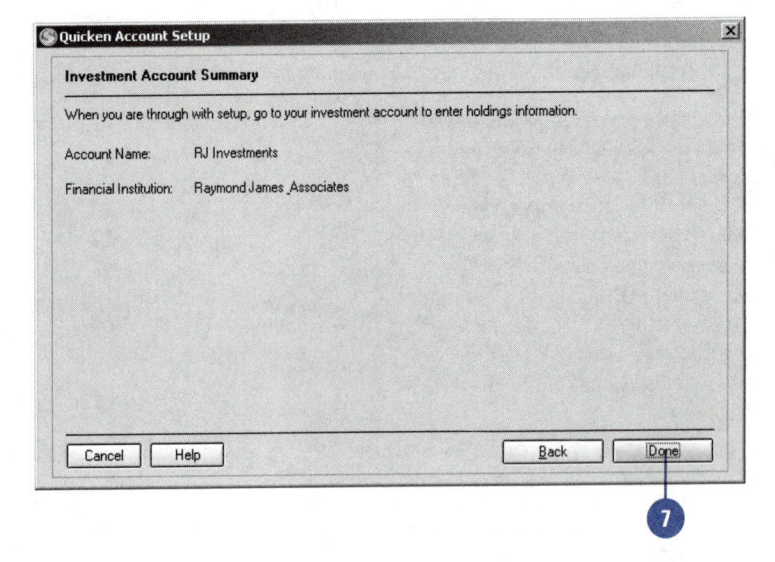

Setting Up Property and Debt Accounts

You can add accounts for your properties, such as your home or other real estate you own; vehicles; assets, such as antiques, art, or family heirlooms; and liabilities, such as your car or home loans. All these accounts are considered your property and debt.

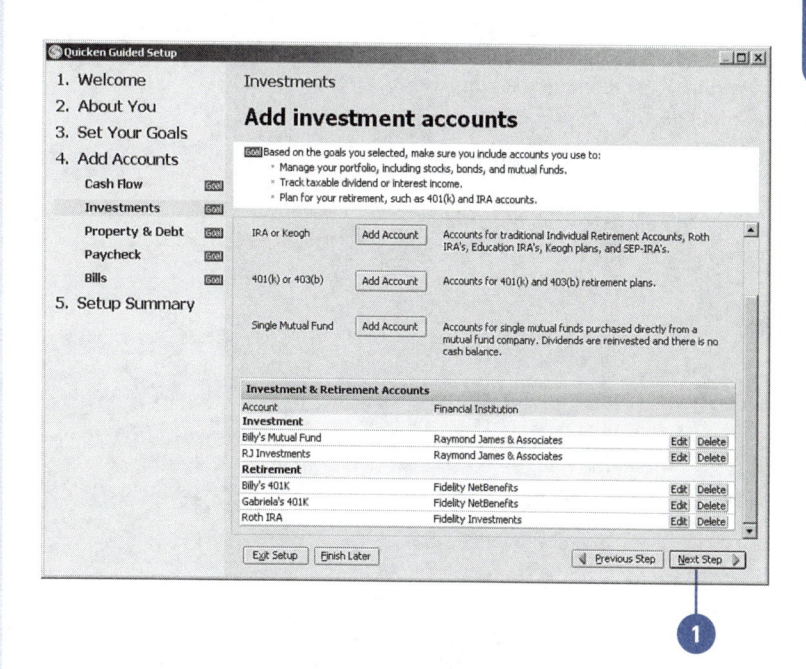

Set Up Home Property Accounts

1. Click Next Step.

2. To add an account for your house, click Add Account next to House.

Setting Up Quicken 23

3. Type the name of the house account and then click Next.

4. Type the date you bought or acquired the property, type the price you paid, and type the estimated value of the property. You don't have to have the exact value. You can update it later, if needed. Then click Next.

5. If you have a loan for this property, select Yes and then click Done. Quicken prompts you to enter the loan information.

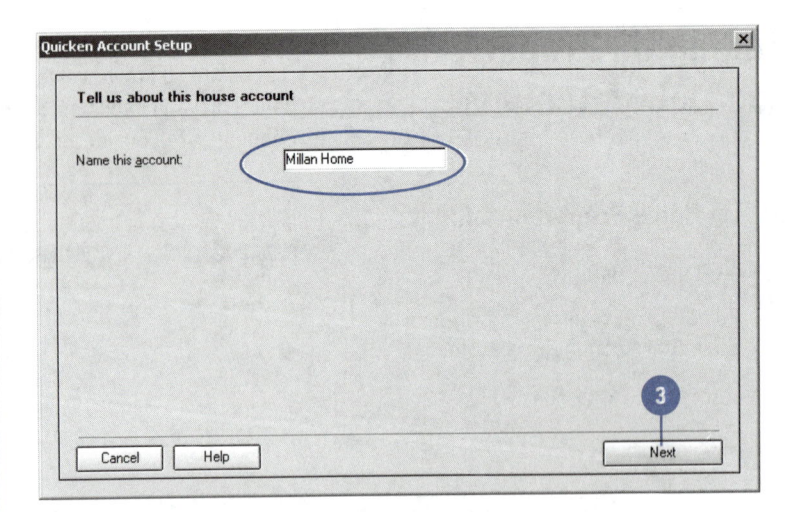

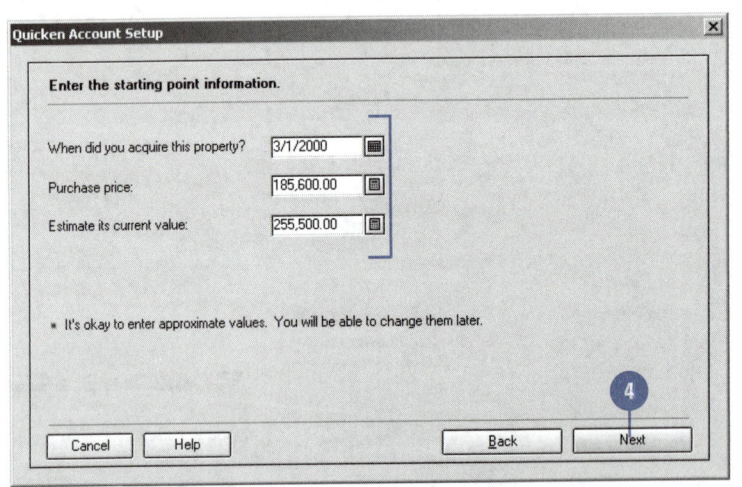

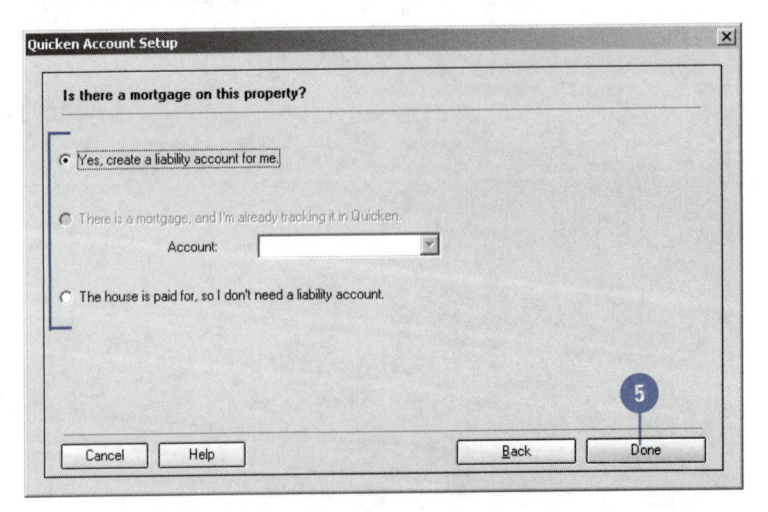

6 Type the date you obtained the loan, the original balance, the length of the loan, and the frequency of your payments. Then click Next.

7 Select the appropriate balloon payment information, if applicable, type the loan balance and date, and type the payment information. Then Click Done.

8 Review the loan information, select the type of payments you make, type the payee name, and type or select the date your payments are due.

9 Click Payment Method to set up a scheduled payment for the loan payment transaction.

Did You Know?

You can select the payment type you use to make your payments. You can use the Type drop-down menu to select the type of payment you make for your property. The Payment type is payment using your personal checks or online method. Print Check is payment using Quicken checks that you print from Quicken. These checks have to be purchased from Quicken. Online Pmt is payment made using an online method, such as through the lender's website or via an online bill payment tool. If you choose the Print Check type, you can click the Address button to enter the address and payee information.

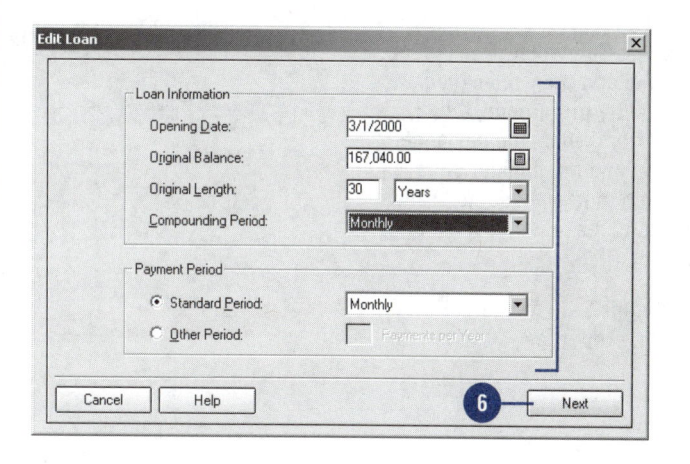

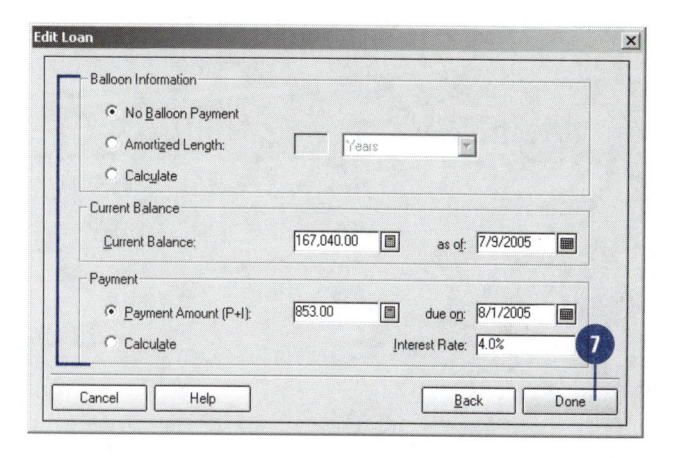

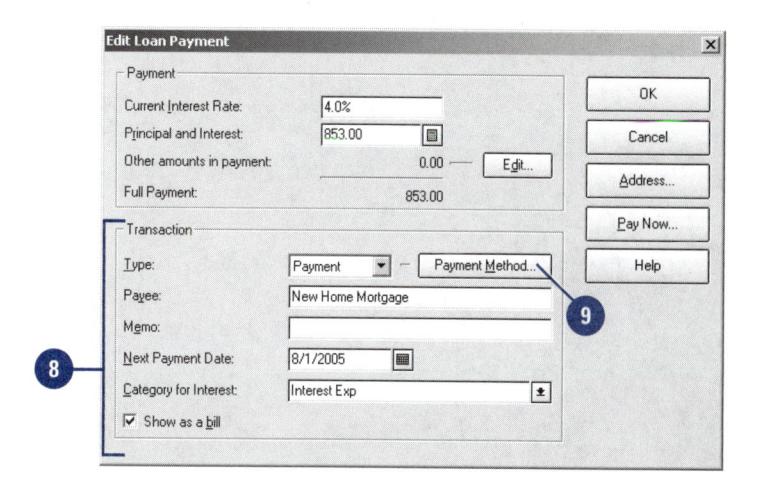

Setting Up Quicken **25**

10 Ensure that Scheduled Transaction is selected and then select your register entry preference, the account from which the payments are made, and the number of days in advance that you want to be reminded to make the payment. Then click OK.

11 Repeat steps 2–10 to add additional properties.

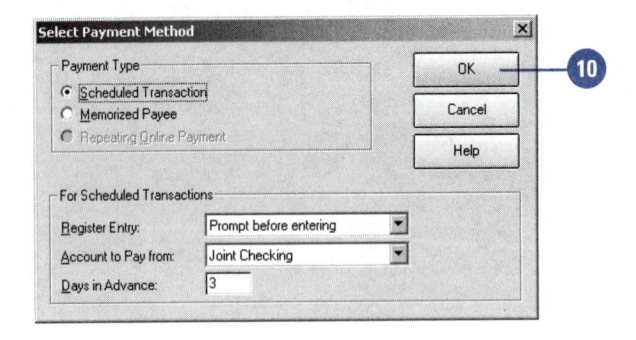

Set Up Auto Accounts

① Click Add Account next to Vehicle.

② Type a name for the account, and type the make, model, and year of the car. Then click Next.

③ Enter the date you purchased or acquired the vehicle, the price you paid for it, and the current value. Then click Next.

Did You Know?

You can find the value of your vehicle online. If you are unsure what the value of your vehicle is, visit the Kelley Blue Book website, at www.kbb.com, and look up the year, make, and model of your car.

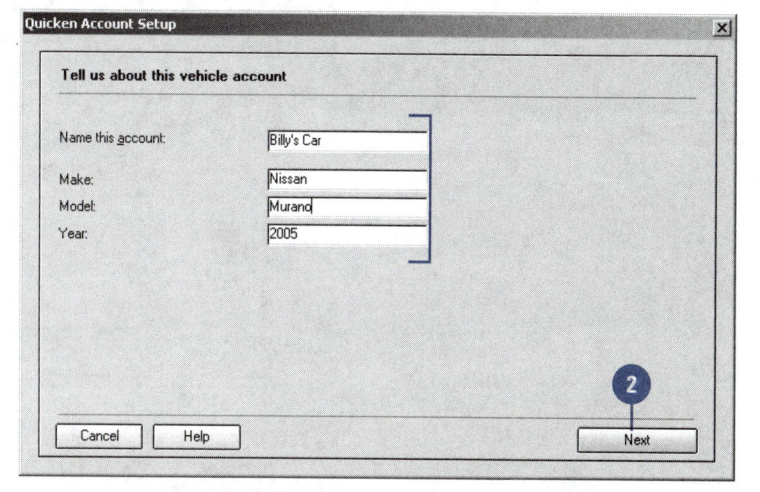

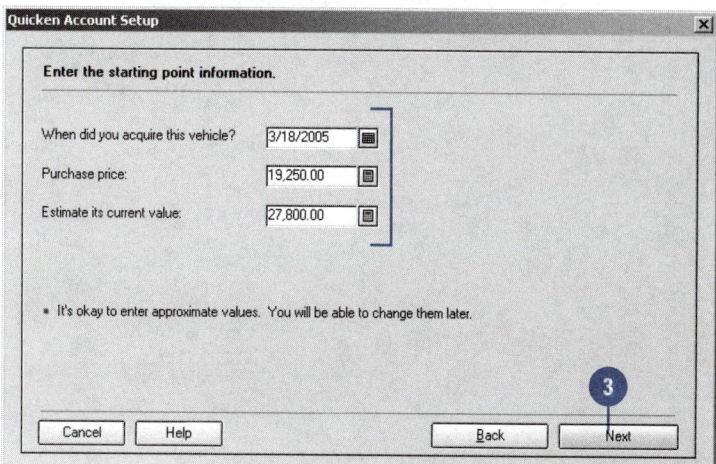

Setting Up Quicken 27

4. If you have a loan that you are currently paying for your vehicle, select Yes and then click Done. Quicken prompts you to enter the loan information.

5. Type the date you obtained the loan, the original balance, the length of the loan, how often interest is calculated, and the frequency of your payments. Then click Next.

6. Select the appropriate balloon information, type the current balance and date of this balance, and type the amount of your payment, the due date, and the interest rate. Then click Done.

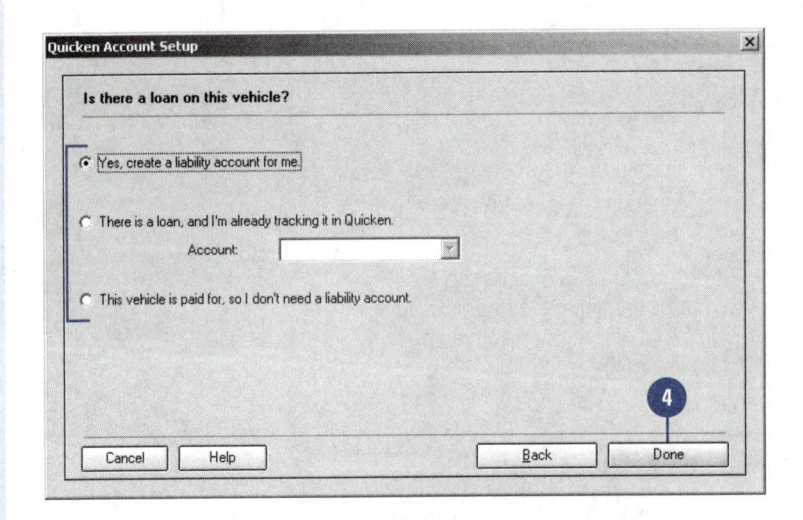

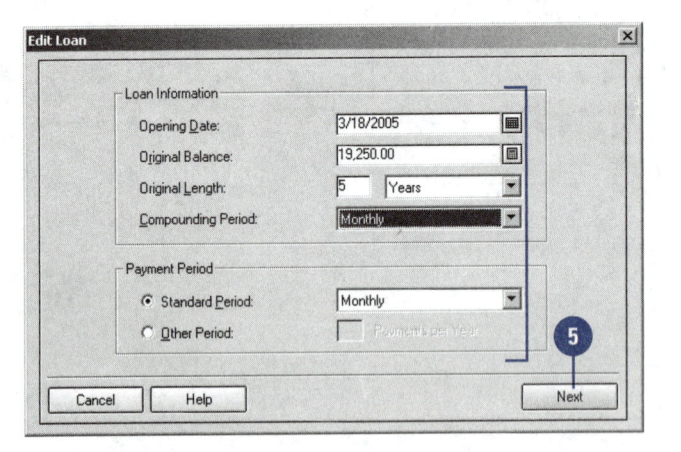

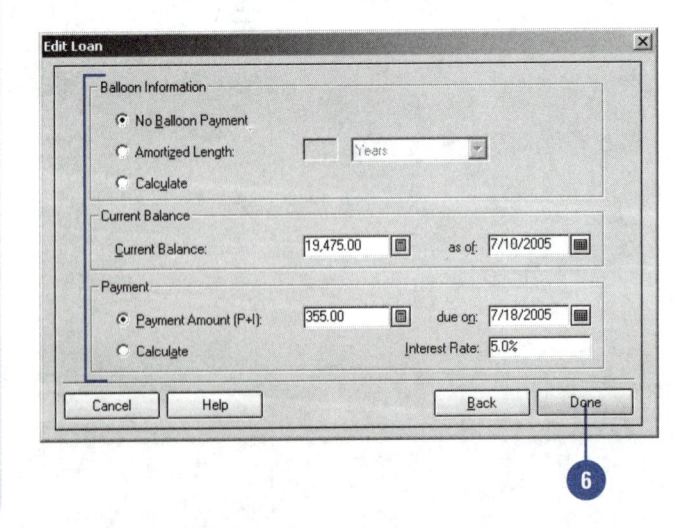

7 Review the loan information, select the type of payments you make, type the payee name, and type or select the date your payments are due.

> ### Did You Know?
>
> *You can select the payment type that you use to make your payments.* Use the Type drop-menu to select the type of payment. To use your personal checks or online payment, select Payment. To use Quicken checks, select Print Check. These checks have to be purchased from Quicken. If you choose the Print Check type, you can click the Address button to enter the address and payee information.

8 From the Category for Interest drop-down menu, select the category you want Quicken to use to track the interest, such as Interest Exp.

9 Click OK. Quicken prompts you to create a scheduled transaction for the loan so that you can be reminded of when you need to pay it. Quicken then reminds you when you need to make the payment and you enter the transaction in your register.

10 Select the payment type, when the transaction should be entered in your register, the account from which payments are made, and how many days in advance the transaction should take place. Then click OK.

11 A message appears, telling you that the transaction has been scheduled. Click OK.

12 Repeat steps 1–11 to add additional vehicles.

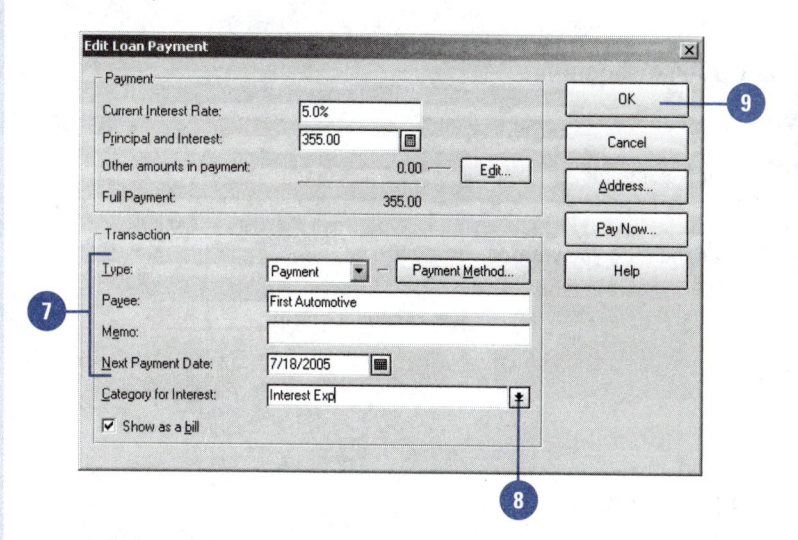

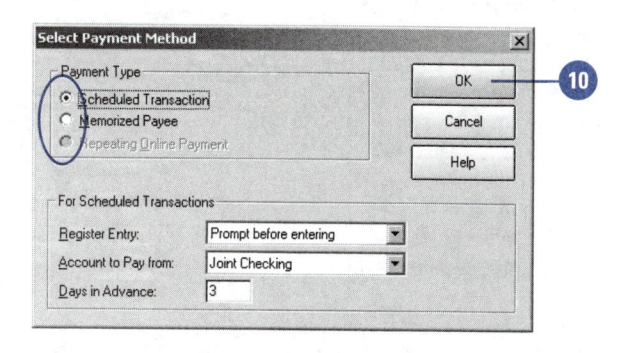

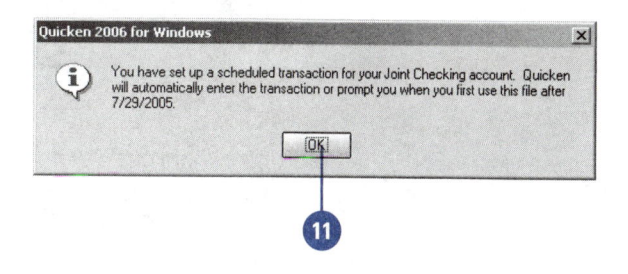

Setting Up Quicken 29

Set Up Asset Accounts

1 Click Add Account next to Asset.

2 Type a name for the account and then click Next.

3 Type the date you want to start tracking the asset and then type the value.

4 If the asset is tax deductible, click Tax.

Did You Know?

Be sure to enter all your assets. When you enter your assets, don't forget to enter those that are not tied to a financial account. For example, you can add antiques, jewelry, art, and so on. Not only is it a good idea to keep track of your valuables, but Quicken uses all your asset information to determine your net worth. Your total net worth is then used in reporting, forecasting, and so on.

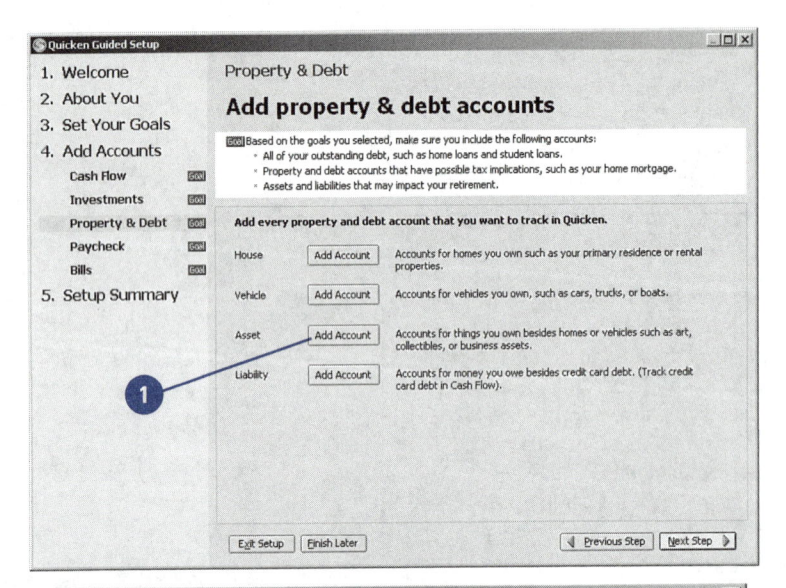

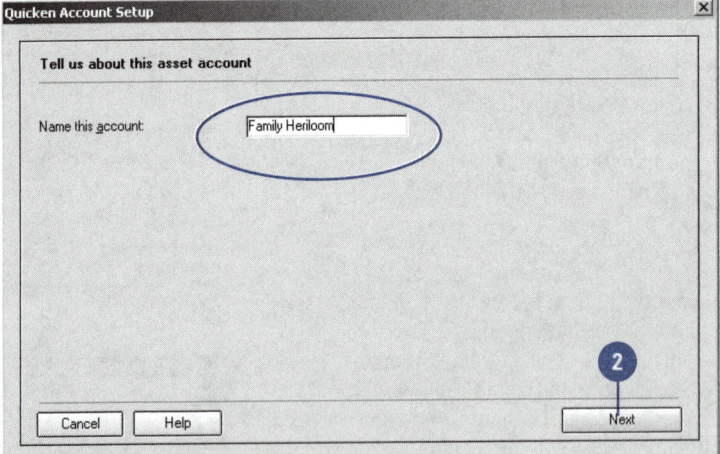

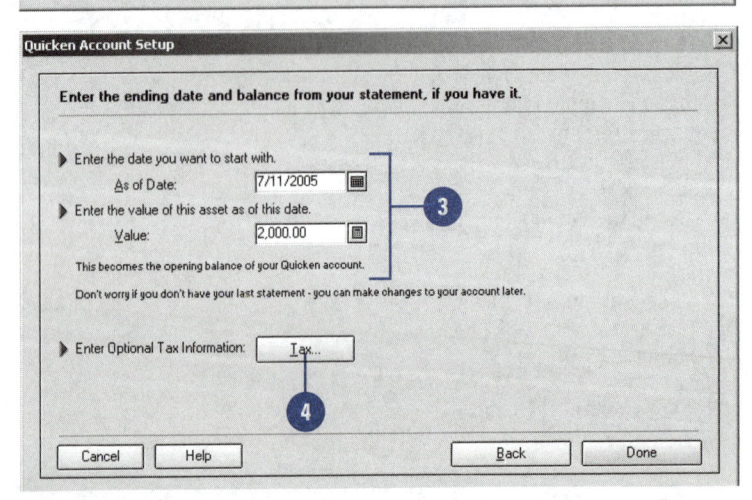

5. If the asset is tax-deductible, select the Tax-Deferred or Tax-Exempt Account option. If applicable, select the tax schedule forms you use for any incoming or outgoing account transfers. Then click OK.

6. Click Done.

7. Repeat steps 1–6 to add additional assets.

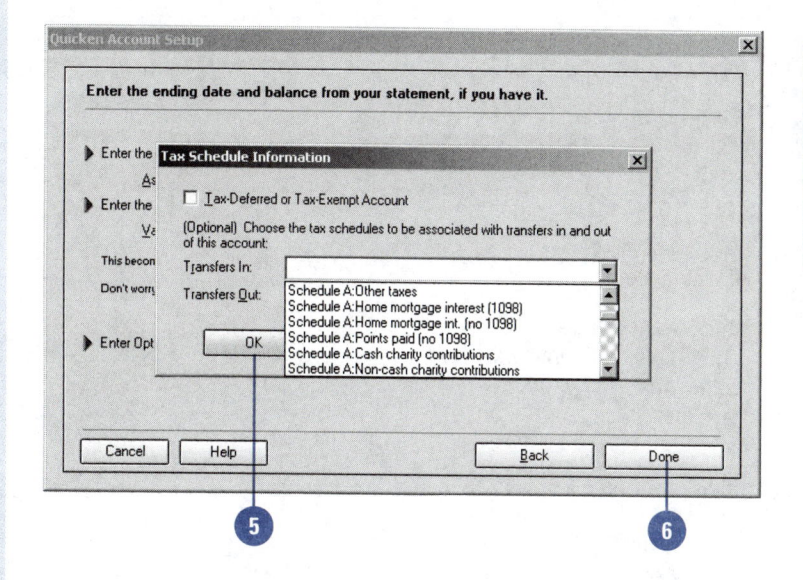

Setting Up Quicken **31**

Set Up Liability Accounts

1. Click Add Account next to Liability.

2. Type a name for the account and then click Next.

3. Type the date of the liability and the balance on the account.

4. If you want to select tax-related options, click Tax and make your selections.

5. Click Done.

6. If you are asked if you want to set up an amortized loan for the account, click Yes to proceed with setting up the loan or No to complete the liability.

7. Repeat steps 1–6 to add additional liabilities.

Did You Know?

An amortized loan is a loan that is associated with an asset. For example, if you have a car, it is considered an asset, and if you have a car loan, it is considered a liability.

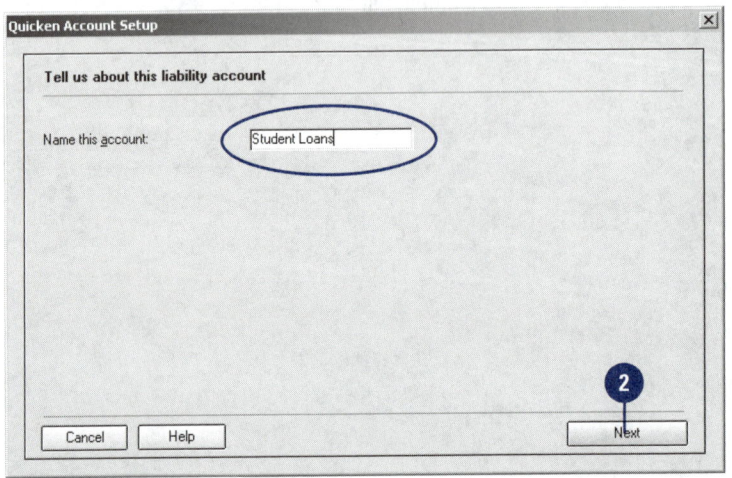

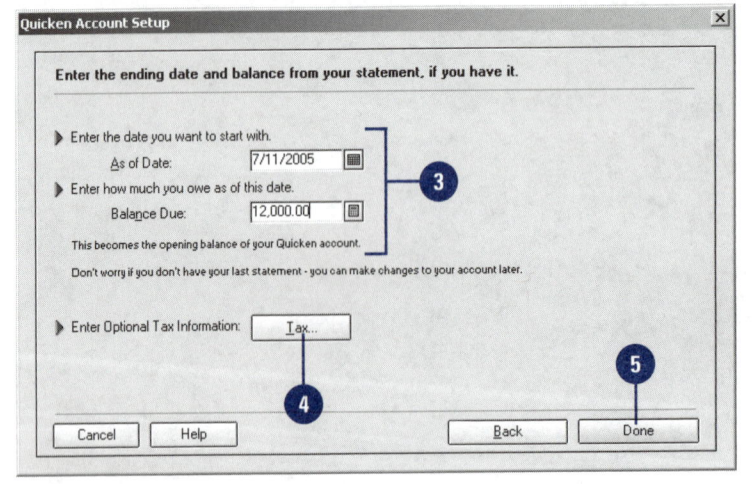

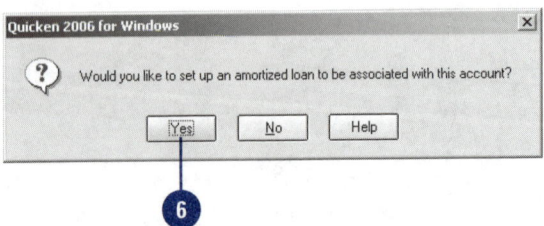

Setting Up Your Paychecks

To track your income, you should enter your paycheck(s) information for you and/or your spouse. Quicken uses this information to manage your income and expenses, track taxes you pay, and help you plan for the future. Before proceeding, you should grab your paycheck stubs to help enter the information.

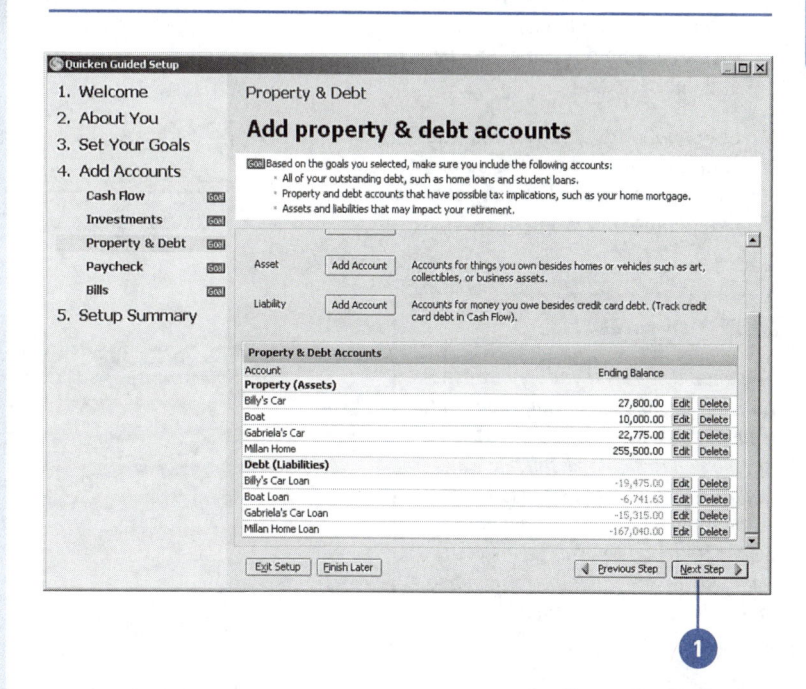

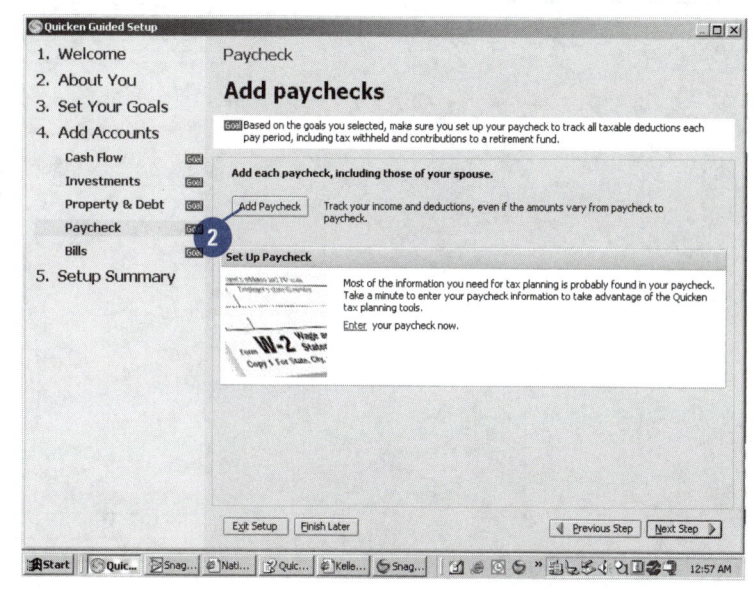

Set Up Your Paychecks

1. Click Next Step.
2. Click Add Paycheck.

Setting Up Quicken 33

③ Click Next.

④ Select whether this is your or your spouse's paycheck, type the name of your employer or source of income, type a unique identifier, if needed, for paychecks that are received from the same employer, and click Next.

⑤ Select whether you want to track your earnings, taxes, and so on or whether you want to track your net income only. Then click Next.

Did You Know?

You should set up scheduled transactions for paychecks or other recurring transactions. *Scheduled transactions enable you to repeat a specific transaction during a specified time frame, without entering it every time the transaction occurs. This saves you time and ensures that the transaction is entered into your account in a timely fashion.*

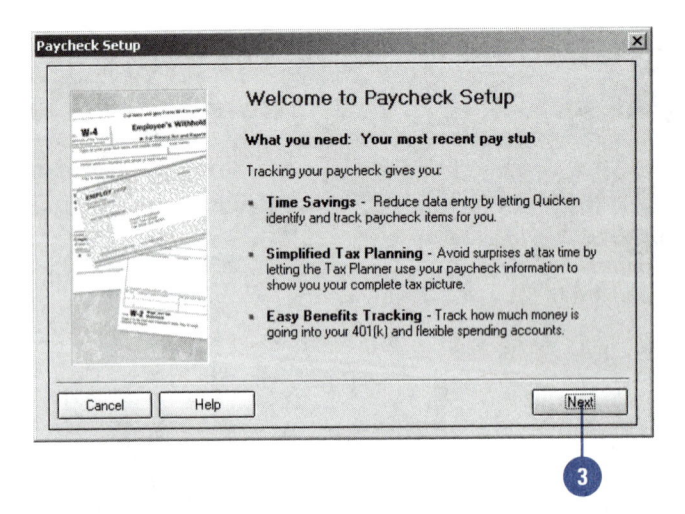

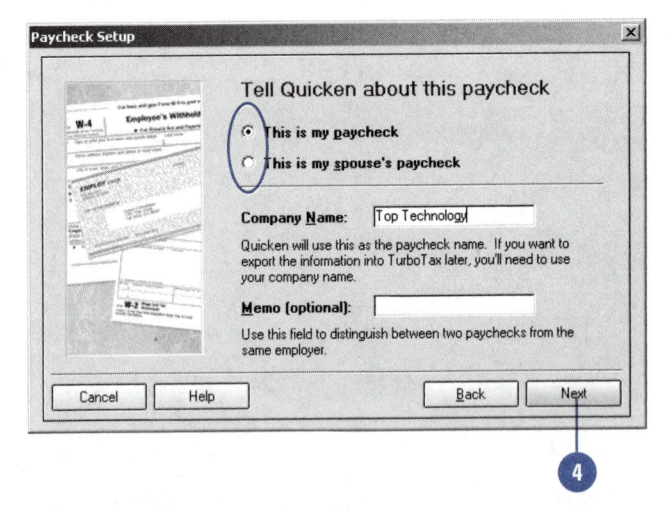

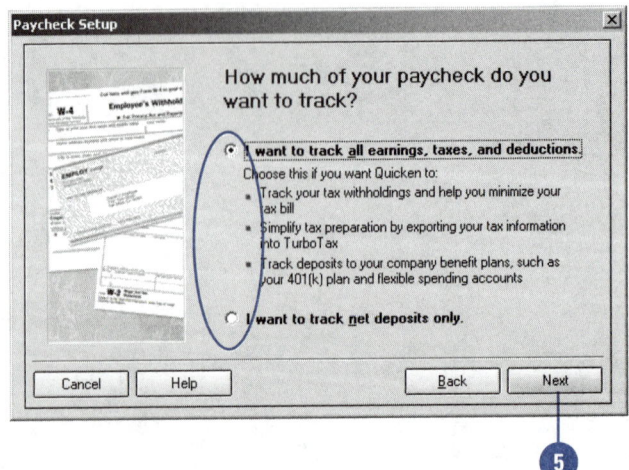

6. Select to which account the paycheck is deposited.

7. Click Scheduling to set up a recurring scheduled transaction for your paycheck deposits.

8. To add pre-tax deductions (for example, retirement contributions), click Add Pre-Tax Deduction.

9. Using 401(k) as an example, type the deduction information and click OK.

10. Click Add After-Tax Deduction to enter deductions that are taken from your paycheck after taxes.

11. In the Deposit Accounts section, verify the account used for your paycheck. To change it, click Add Deposit Account.

12. When you are finished setting up all your paycheck information, click Done.

13. If you are prompted to enter year-to-date information select whether you want to add this information and click OK.

14. If you opted to enter year-to-date totals in step 13, in the Year to Date column of the Taxes section, type the totals for each tax category.

15. Repeat steps 2–14 to add additional paychecks.

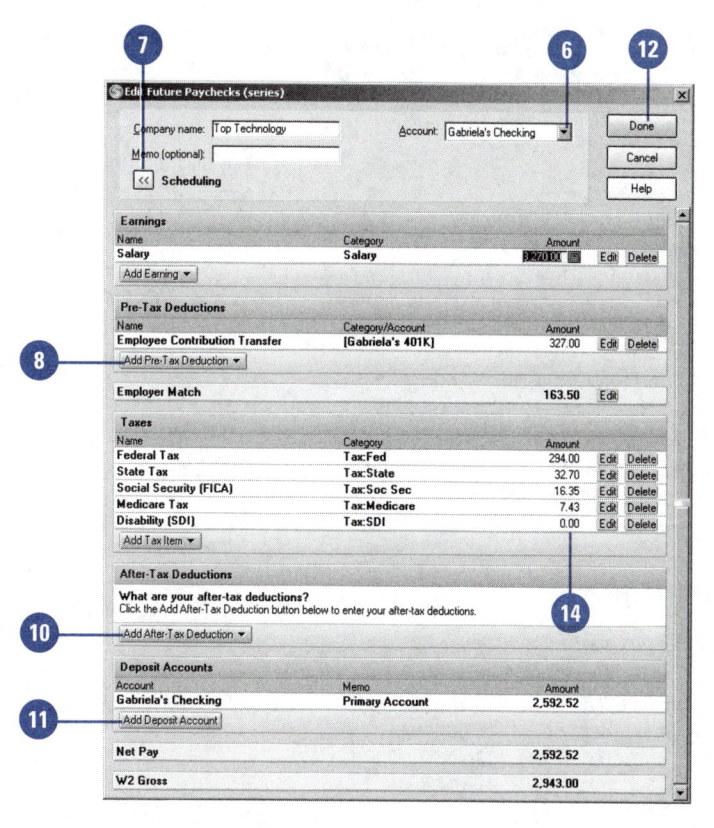

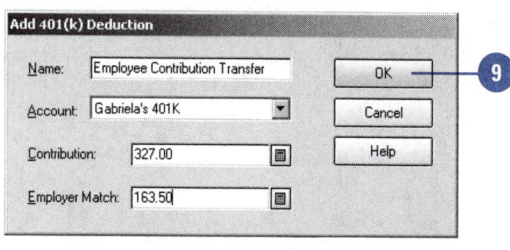

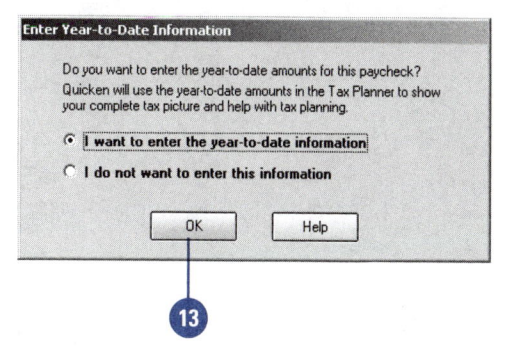

Setting Up Quicken **35**

Setting Up Your Bills

Now comes the fun part: adding all your bills. You need to pull out all your bill statements for your utilities, magazine and newspaper subscriptions, association dues, and any other bills you pay regularly. Next, we'll walk through setting up bills in Quicken Guided Setup. Don't worry if you don't have all the information you need to set up your bills. You will have plenty of opportunities to add them later.

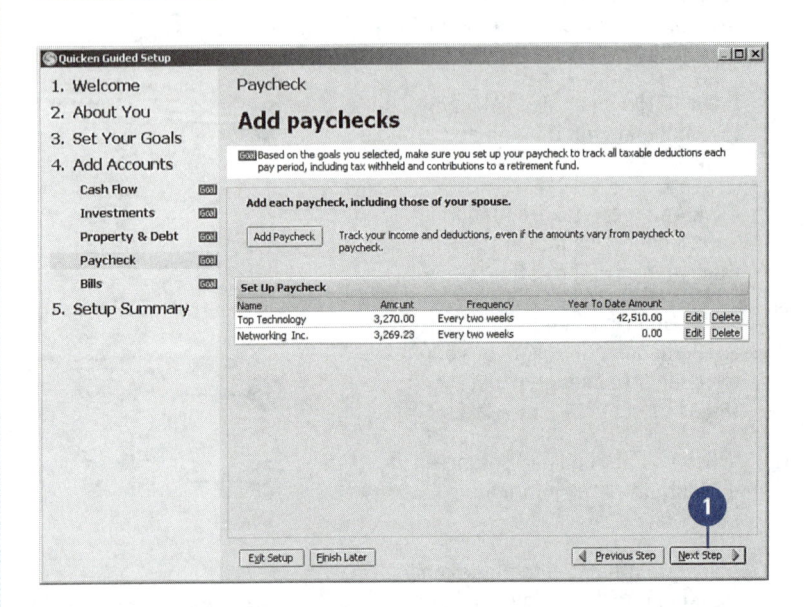

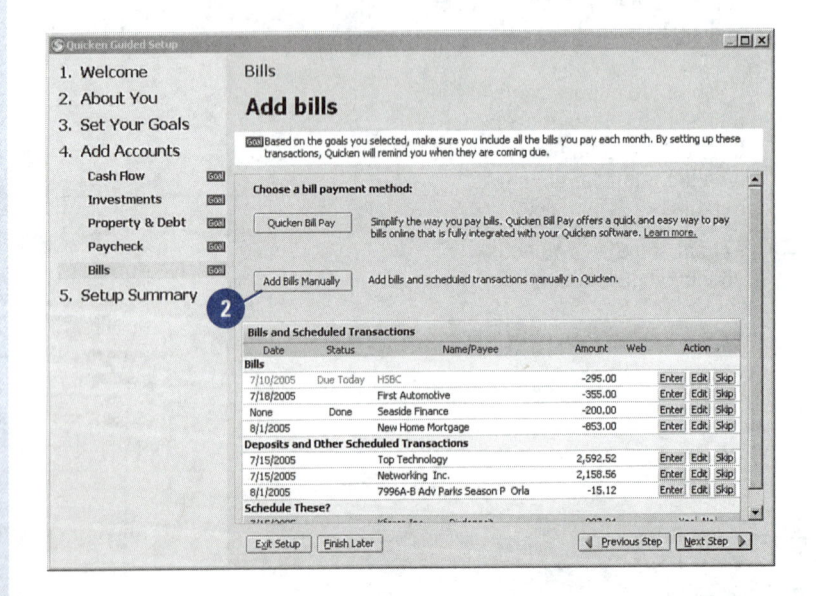

Set Up Your Bills

1. Click Next Step.

2. To enter your bill information, click Add Bills Manually. Some of your bills may already appear in the Set Up Bills Window. These are accounts you've added thus far.

> **Did You Know?**
>
> **You can pay your bills by using Quicken Bill Pay.** Quicken offers an online bill payment service that you can use to pay all your bills automatically. There is a fee associated with the service, but you may find the service worth the price. If you are interested in having all your bills in one place and paying them with a click of a button, or if you already use an online bill payment service and are looking for a new one, click Quicken Bill Pay to learn more. Be aware that in order for you to be able to pay your bills online, the company has to offer online access to your accounts.

36

③ Add a new bill to the list by clicking New.

④ Type the name of the company you pay.

⑤ Select the account from which payments are made for the bill.

⑥ Select a category that you want to use to track your payments. If you don't find the category you want to use, type the name you want to use to create a new category. A message appears, asking if you want to create a new category.

⑦ Click Yes.

⑧ Type the name and description of the new category, select the type of category, and select tax-related options. Then click OK.

⑨ Type the approximate amount you pay. You will have the opportunity to change the amount before the transaction is entered into your account register.

⑩ Select how frequently you pay this bill.

⑪ Type the date the bill is next due.

⑫ Repeat steps 3–11 for each bill you want to add, and when you are finished adding all your bills, click OK.

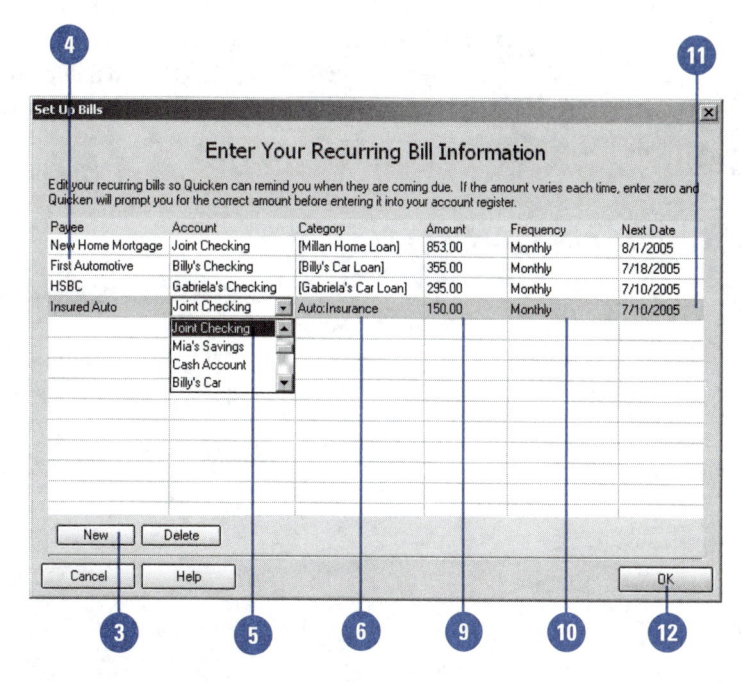

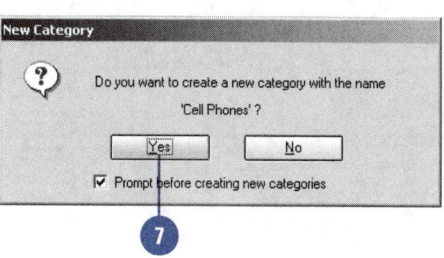

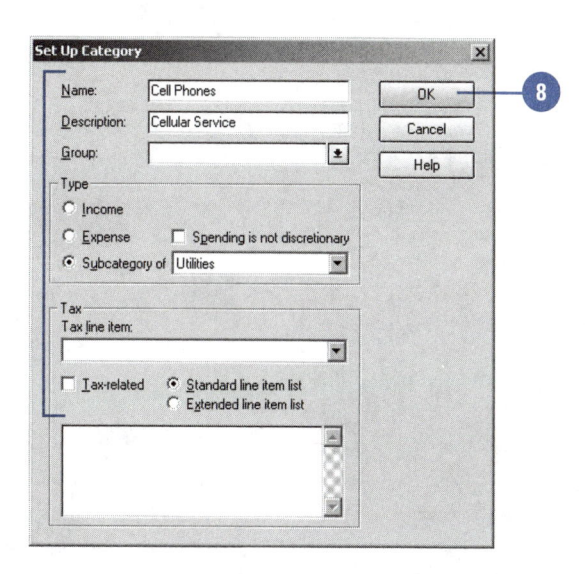

Setting Up Quicken **37**

Reviewing and Completing the Setup

Review and Complete the Setup

1 Click Next Step.

Now that you have entered all your account and financial information into Quicken Guided Setup, you have the opportunity to review it all, make changes, if necessary, and get started using Quicken.

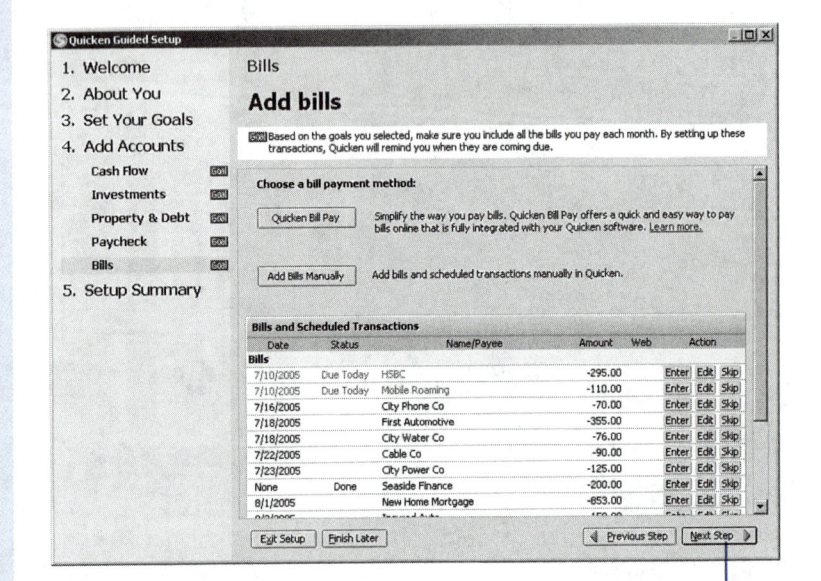

② Review all your information.

③ If you want to make changes to a specific account, paycheck, or bill, select the item and then click Edit. You can then make your changes.

④ To remove an account, a paycheck, or a bill, select the item and click Delete. A message appears, asking if you want to delete the item. Type Yes and click OK to remove it or click Cancel to keep it.

⑤ To change the credit limit for an account, click the amount and change the limit.

⑥ When you are finished reviewing and making changes, click Done.

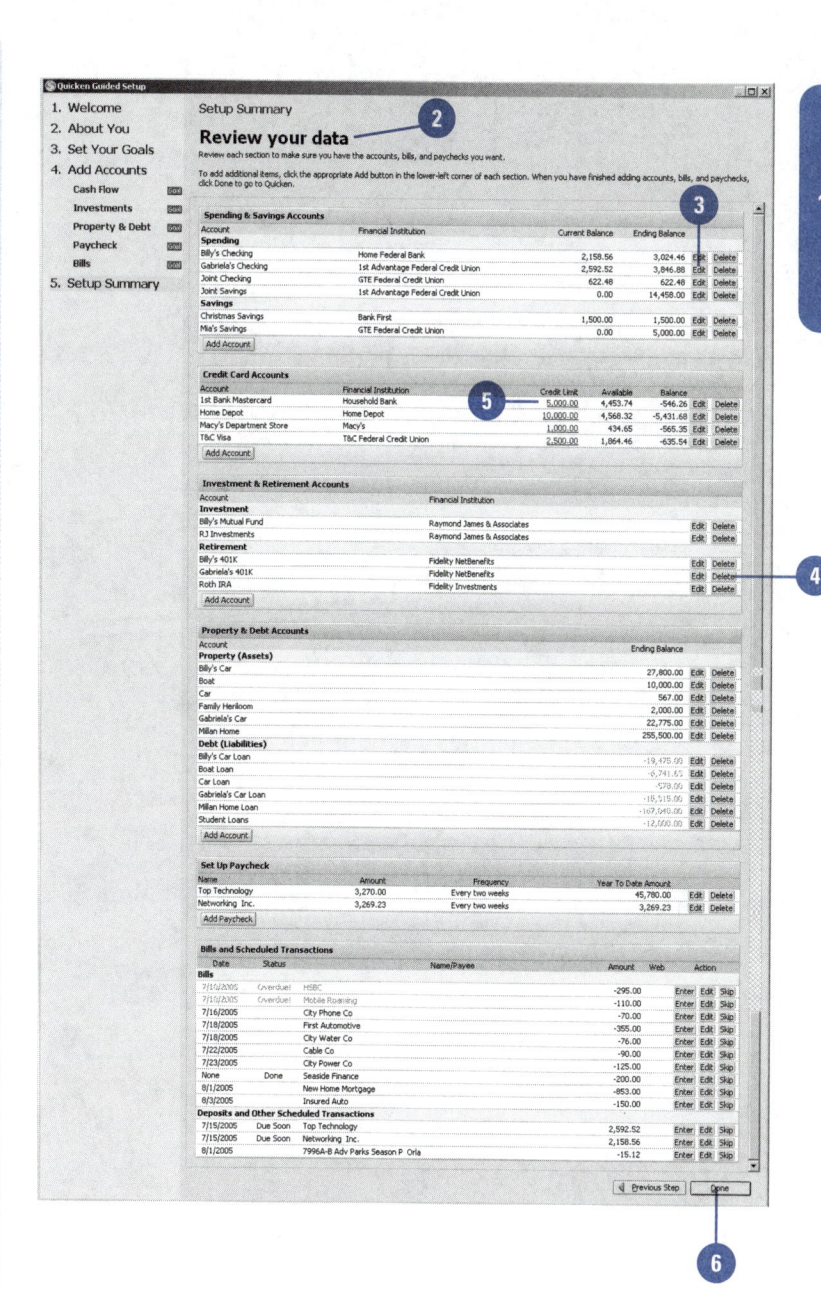

Setting Up Quicken **39**

7 Review your next steps, click a link to get more information, or click OK to start using Quicken.

> ### Did You Know?
>
> ***This is not your last chance to make changes to all your setup information.*** *You can later add, change, or delete information after you're in Quicken by going to the accounts, or you can click* ***Setup*** *on the toolbar and go back into Quicken Guided Setup.*

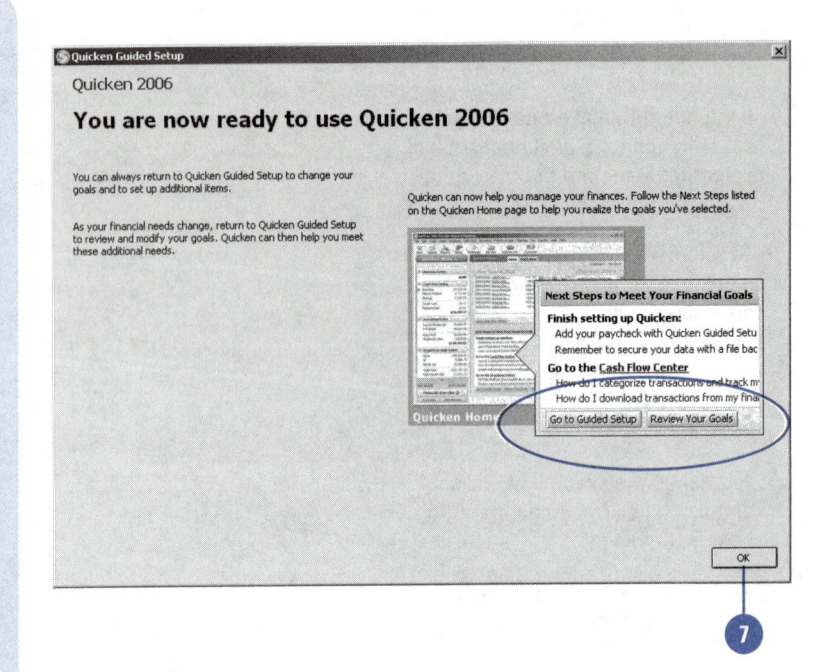

Learning Quicken Basics

Introduction

There are basic Quicken options and features that you should become familiar with to cut down on the amount of information you have to manually enter into Quicken and make using it more efficient. For example, some options allow you to tell Quicken how you want it to present some information, and you can import financial information from a previous version of Quicken or from other financial software. In addition, you can ensure that Quicken serves your needs quickly by customizing the toolbar or setting preferences so that you can use Quicken the way you want to use it and so you can easily find what you're looking for.

Other Quicken features allow you to take advantage of online access to your accounts. If you have an Internet connection and have accounts that provide online access to your statements and transactions, you can download the information right into Quicken. Downloading your account information ensures that the information is accurate, timely, and easier to maintain and manage, and it saves you a lot of time over manually entering it. In addition, a feature allows you to access your account information remotely by using Quicken.com.

What You'll Do

Customize the Toolbar

Create New Quicken Files

Back Up Files

Import and Export Files

Set Up Passwords

Set Quicken Preferences

Set Up Remote Access to Your Accounts

Set Up an Internet Connection

Customizing the Toolbar

The *toolbar* is your portal to quickly moving to specific areas of Quicken. To make accessing specific information even more convenient, you can customize the buttons on the toolbar to show only the buttons you want to use and the order in which you want them to appear. Handpicking and organizing the buttons on the toolbar ensures that the areas most important to you are only a click away.

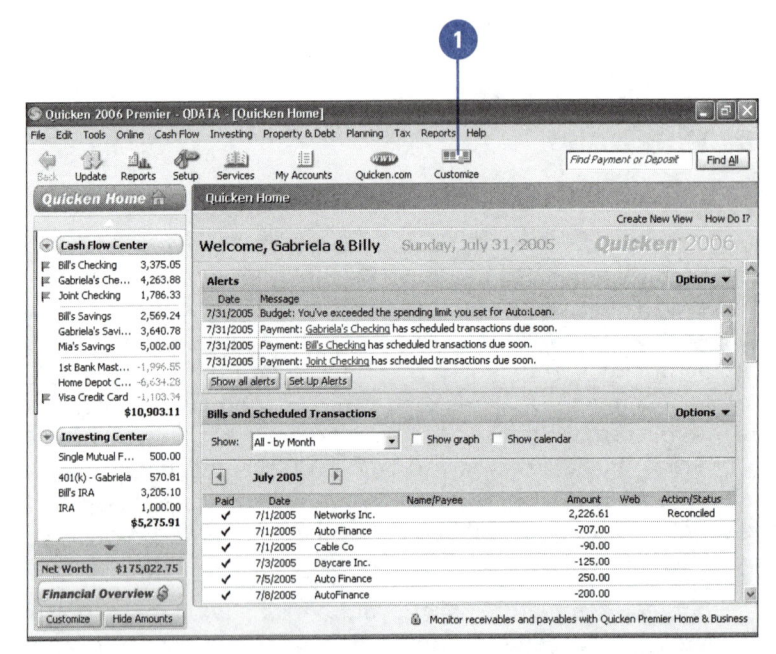

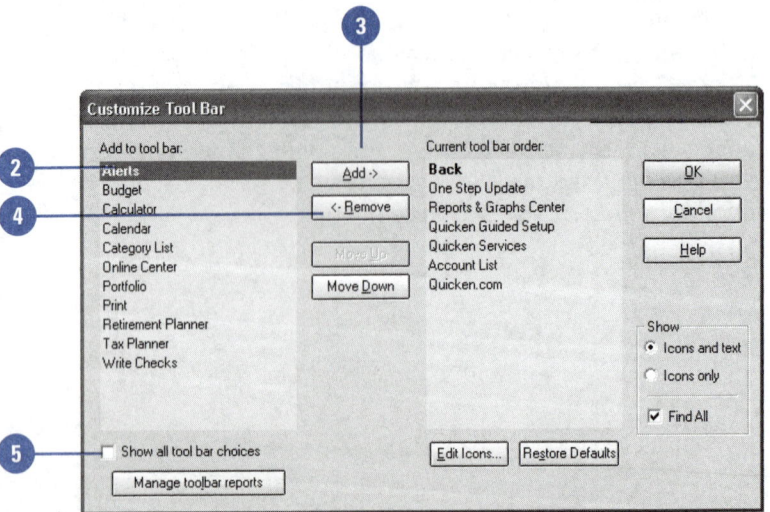

Add and Remove Buttons

1. On the toolbar, click Customize. The buttons that are currently on the toolbar are listed under the Current Toolbar Order column in the order in which they appear on the toolbar; those that are not on your toolbar are listed under the Add to Toolbar column.

2. To add a button to the toolbar, from the Add to Toolbar column, select a button title. You can add more than one button at a time by holding down the Ctrl key and clicking each title you want to add. The titles you select are boldfaced.

3. When you have selected all items you want to add to the toolbar, click Add.

4. To remove a button from the toolbar, from the Current Toolbar Order column, select the button title(s) and click Remove.

5. To view all available toolbar buttons, select Show All Toolbar Choices.

See Also

See page 65 for more information on the Home page.

Change the Order and Appearance of Buttons

1. To move a button to the left on the toolbar, select the button that you want to move and click Move Up. Each time you click Move Up, the button moves left one position. Click Move Up as many times as necessary to move it where you want it.

2. To move a button to the right on the toolbar, select the button you want to move and click Move Down. Click Move Down as many times as necessary to move it where you want it.

3. To view only the button icon (and not the text), select icons only.

Rename Buttons and Assign Shortcuts

1. To rename a button title, select the button title and click Edit Icons.

2. In the Label box, type the new name for the button, keeping in mind the amount of space on the toolbar for lengthy names.

3. If you want to assign a shortcut to the button, in the Shortcut box, type the shortcut you want to use. For example, if you type **A** for the Accounts List button, you can open the My Accounts window by pressing Alt+Shift+A.

4. Click OK.

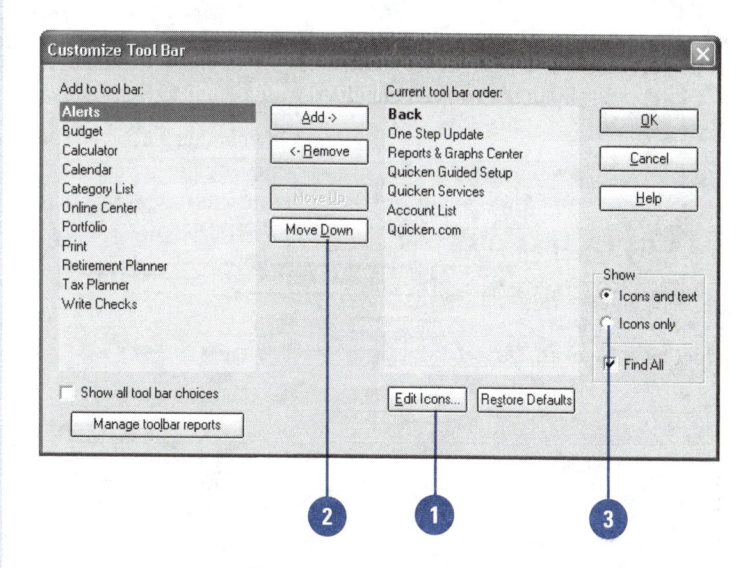

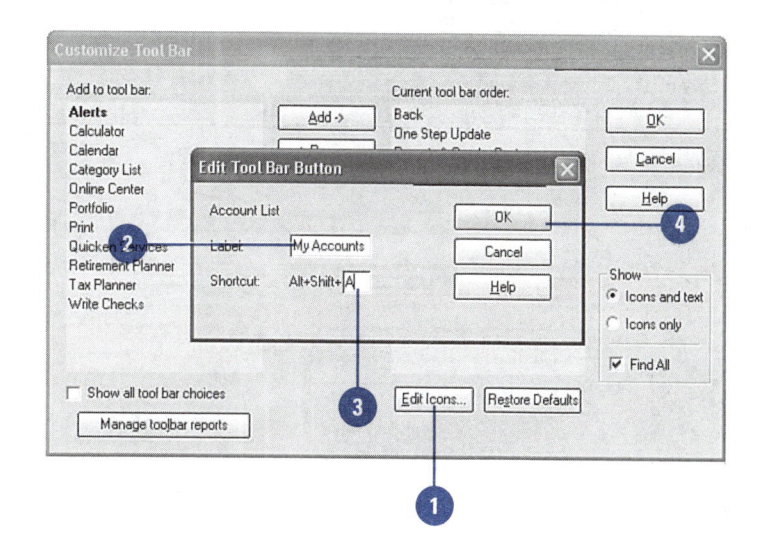

Did You Know?

Changing a button title does not change where the button takes you. For example, if you change the button titled Accounts to My Accounts, when you click that button on the toolbar, the window titled Account List always opens, no matter what you've titled the button.

Learning Quicken Basics **43**

Creating New Quicken Files

It is recommended that you create separate Quicken files if you intend to track expenses, assets, taxes, or other financial information for a business, for volunteer work, or for someone else. You can also keep separate Quicken files to keep your financial information separate from that of your spouse; however, it is not entirely necessary. If you share some of your bills and finances with your spouse but want to keep only certain accounts separate, you can hide the accounts you don't want included in joint financial areas, such as certain bills. We will talk more about hiding accounts in Chapter 3. For now, let's walk through creating a new Quicken file.

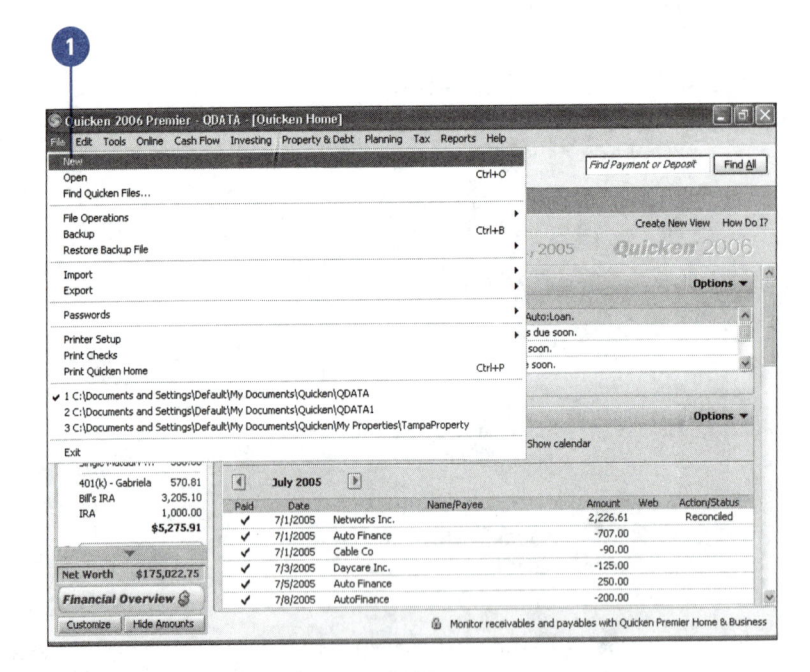

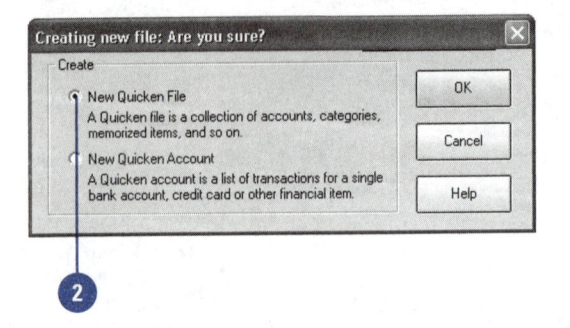

Create a New Quicken File

1. Click File, New.
2. Select New Quicken File.

Did You Know?

You can quickly open files you have recently worked with. To open a file that you recently worked on, you can click the File menu and select a filename from the bottom of the menu. Files are numbered in the order in which they were last opened.

③ To change where to save the file, click the Save In drop-down menu and select the new location.

④ To create a new folder, click the Create New Folder button and type the name of the new folder.

⑤ Click in the File Name text box and type the name of the new file. You do not have to type the **.qdf** extension. Quicken automatically adds it for you.

⑥ Click OK.

⑦ Set up your new file by using Quicken Guided Setup, just as you did when you set up your first Quicken file in Chapter 1, "Setting Up Quicken."

⑧ If you do not want to go through Quicken Guided Setup at this time, click Exit Setup. You can open the new file at another time to set it up.

Did You Know?

You can name and store Quicken files logically. *It's a good idea to keep your Quicken files in separate folders and name them logically (for example, Mom's Finances). This will help you identify and manage your Quicken files more efficiently.*

See Also

See "Using Quicken Guided Setup" on page 10 for more information on using Quicken Guided Setup.

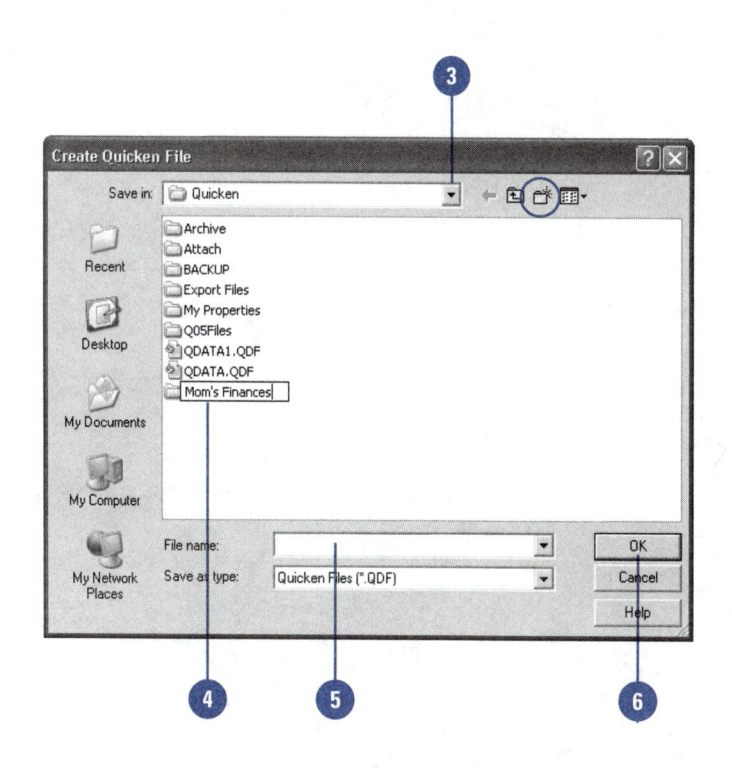

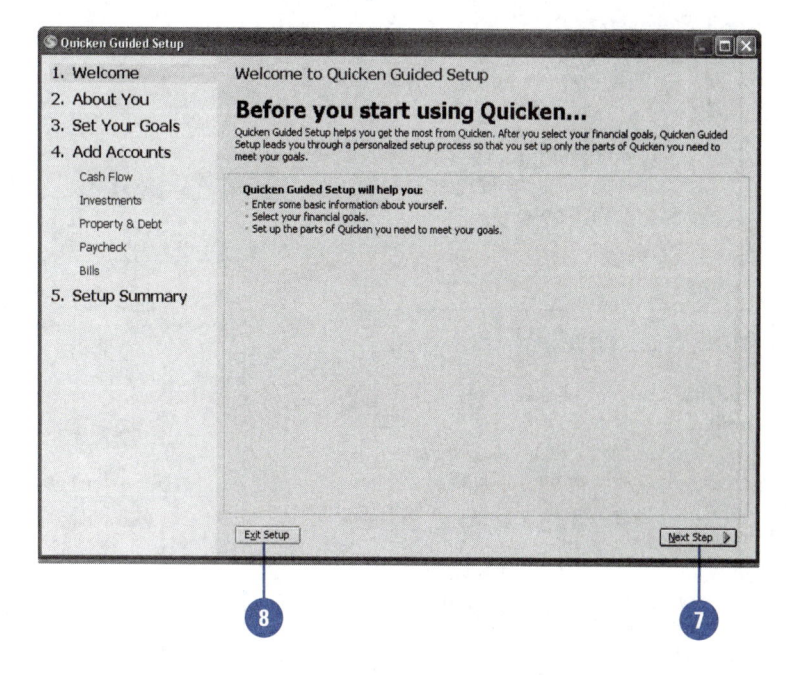

Learning Quicken Basics **45**

Backing Up Files

As you work in Quicken, adding accounts, transactions, securities, and so on, a lot of important and valuable information is being built. So, what happens if your file is accidentally deleted or becomes corrupt, or if your computer goes down? Creating a backup of your Quicken files ensures that you have another copy in case you need to recover some or all of your financial information.

Back Up a File

1. Click File, Backup.

2. If you want to back up the file you have open, don't change anything in the first section, with the exception of the Add Date to File Name option. Select this option to help distinguish between backup files.

3. In the second section, click Browse and then select the location where you want to save your backup file. Saving the file to a disk or CD is recommended because if you are not able to use your computer or the file is lost, you can recover your file from the disk or CD.

4. If you want to burn your file to a CD, select the Use Windows CD Writing Wizard option.

5. Click OK.

Did You Know?

You can store your backup files online. *As part of Quicken Services, you can elect to use the Quicken data center to store your backup files by selecting the Online option shown in the second section of the Quicken Backup dialog box. The data center uses two servers in two separate locations to ensure that your files are safe and retrievable. However, this service does come at a price. If you're interested in looking into this service, click the Learn More link.*

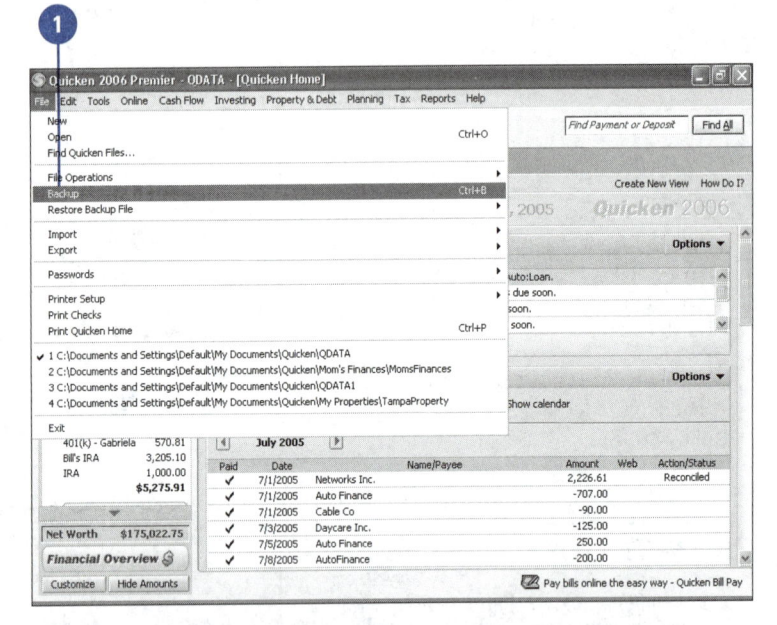

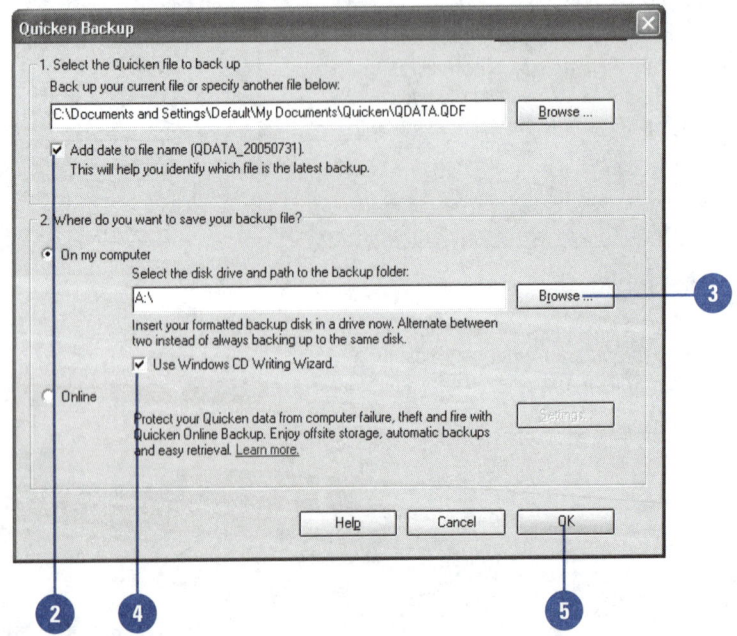

46

Restoring Backups

Let's play devil's advocate for a minute. Let's say that you've been working hard getting all your financial information into Quicken and regularly keeping it up-to-date. Then, your Quicken file becomes corrupt or you accidentally delete vital information from the file. What do you do? Well, if you created regular backups, you can restore the information by restoring the backup file. To restore the backup file, follow these steps:

1. Click File, Restore Backup File, Browse.

2. If you backed up to a CD or disk (as recommended), insert the CD or disk into your CD or disk drive.

3. From the Restore Quicken File dialog box, click Look In. Locate the CD or disk drive and select the file you backed up.

4. Click OK. A message appears, telling you that the backup was restored.

5. Click OK.

6. Click File, Open and open the file you just restored.

Importing and Exporting Files

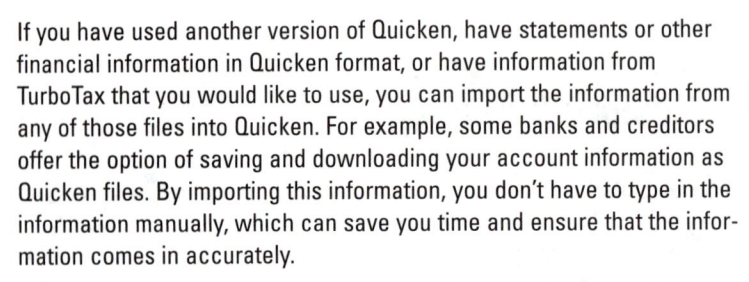

If you have used another version of Quicken, have statements or other financial information in Quicken format, or have information from TurboTax that you would like to use, you can import the information from any of those files into Quicken. For example, some banks and creditors offer the option of saving and downloading your account information as Quicken files. By importing this information, you don't have to type in the information manually, which can save you time and ensure that the information comes in accurately.

On the flip side, if you need to export any information from Quicken into a file to save or send to someone (for example, your accountant), you can do that as well.

Import Files

1. Click File, Import and select the file type that you want to import. (QIF is a Quicken file, Web Connect allows you to download transactions from your financial institute's Web site, and TurboTax is the tax file format used for that software.)

2. Click Browse and locate the file that you want to import and click OK.

3. From the drop-down menu Quicken account to import into, select the account you want to import the new information into.

4. From the Include in import section, select the information from the file that you want to import.

See Also

See "Reviewing, Adding, Editing, and Deleting Spending and Savings Accounts" on page 101 for more information on setting up online accounts.

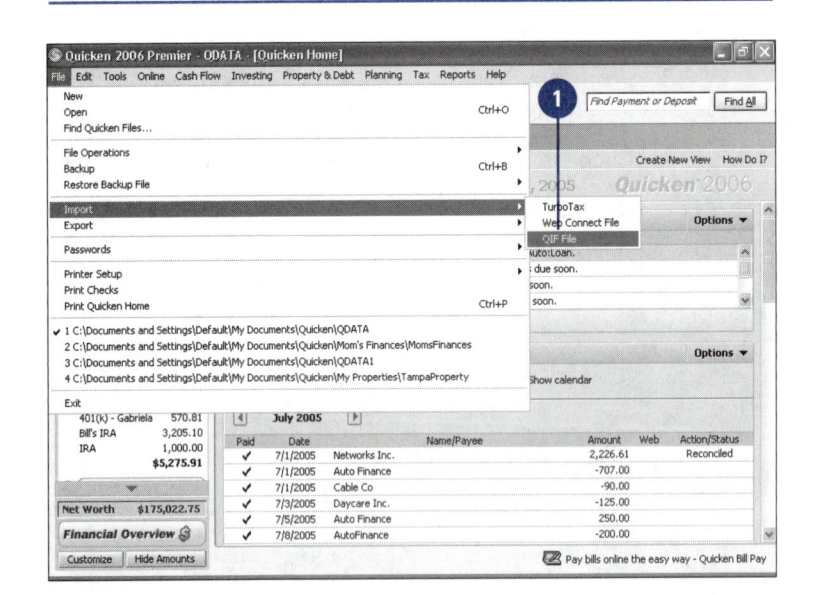

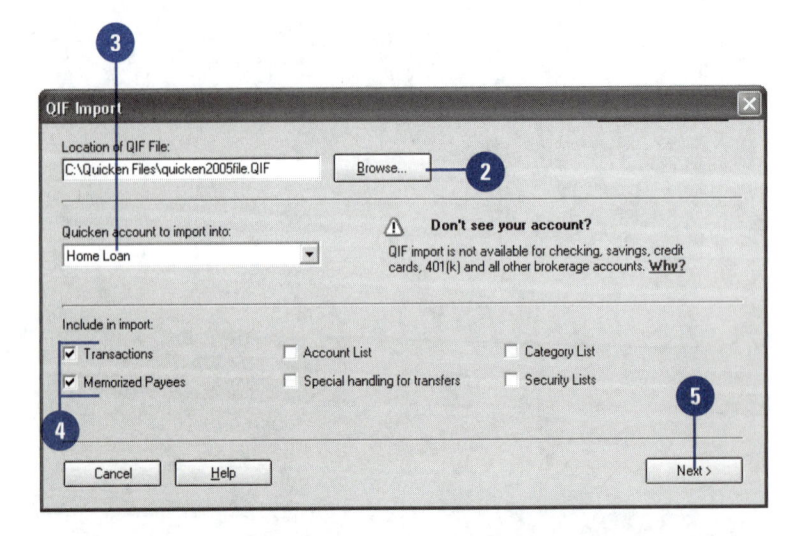

5 Click Next. If Quicken finds information that pertains to your Quicken file, a message appears, asking if you want to include it.

6 Click Yes to import the information or No to continue without importing the information.

7 Click Go to Register to enter the new transactions in the account register(s).

8 To accept all imported transactions, click Accept All. To accept one at time, select a transaction and click Accept for each transaction you want to accept.

9 To delete a transaction, right-click the transaction and select Delete Transaction. A message appears, asking if you want to delete the transaction; click Yes.

See Also

See "Adding, Editing, and Deleting Spending and Savings Account Transactions" on page 107 for more information on downloading transactions from your financial institute.

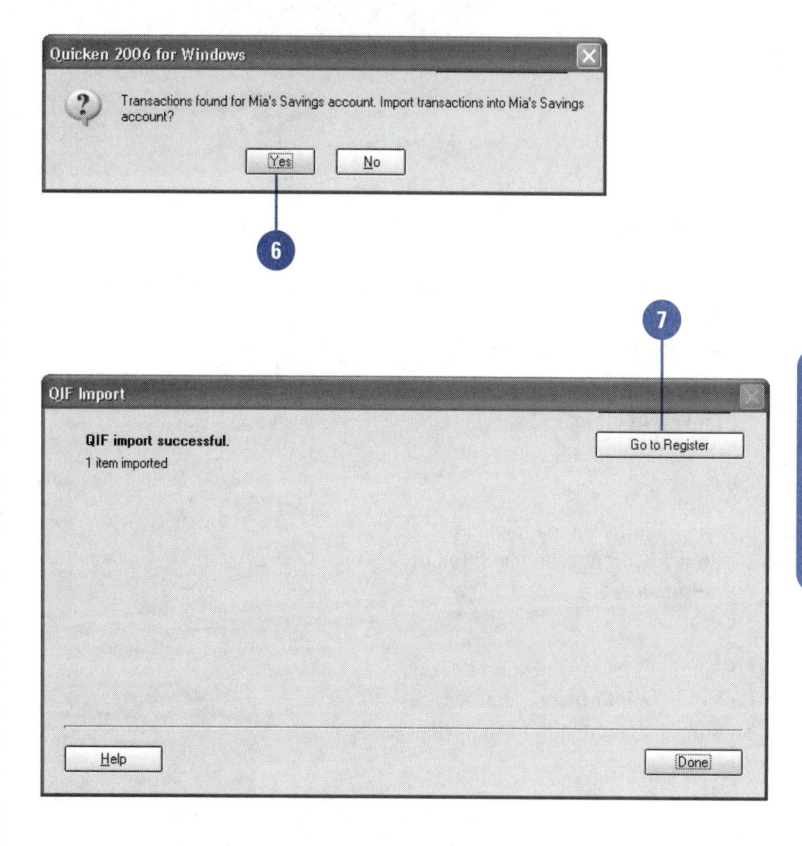

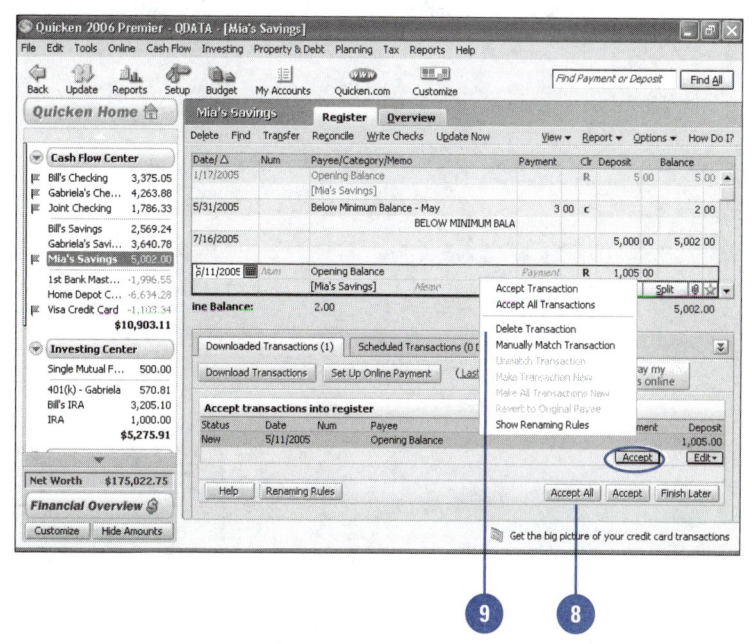

Learning Quicken Basics **49**

Export Files

1. Click File, Export, QIF File.
2. Click Browse.
3. Locate and select the location to which you want to save the Quicken file and then click OK.
4. From the drop-down menu Quicken Account to Export From, select the account you want to export.
5. From Include Transactions in Dates, select or type the dates of the transactions you want to export.
6. From the Include in Export section, select the information that you want to include in the exported file.
7. Click OK.

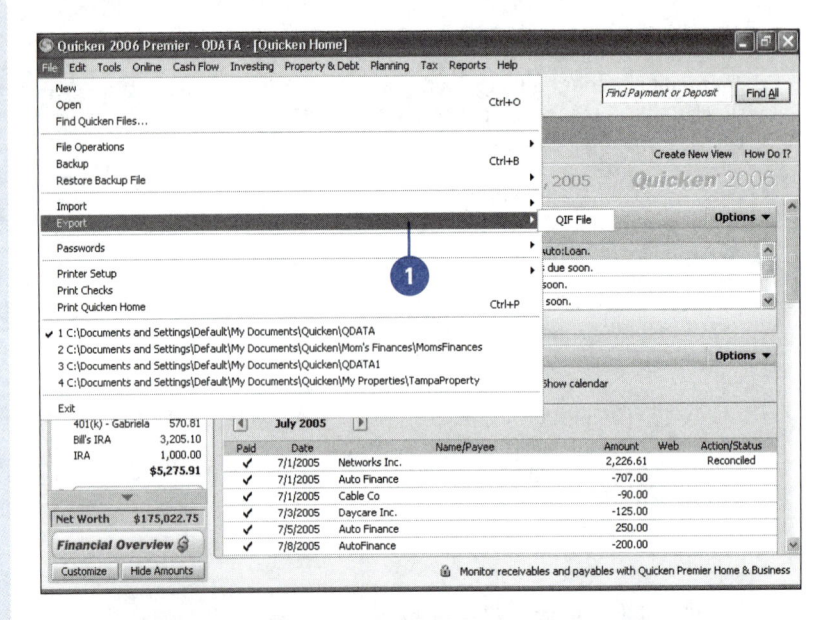

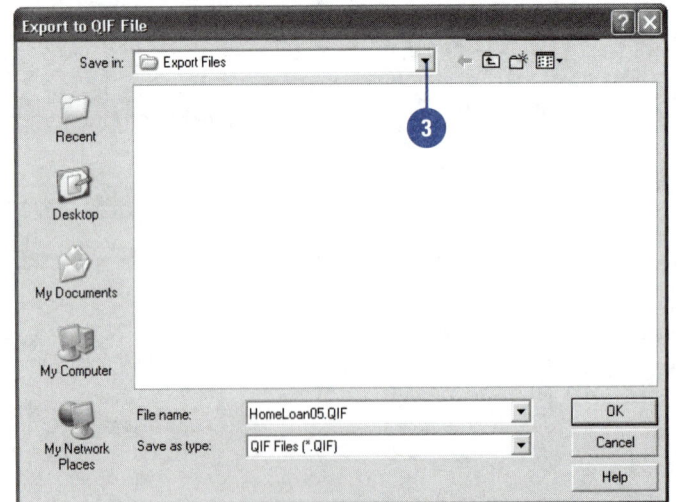

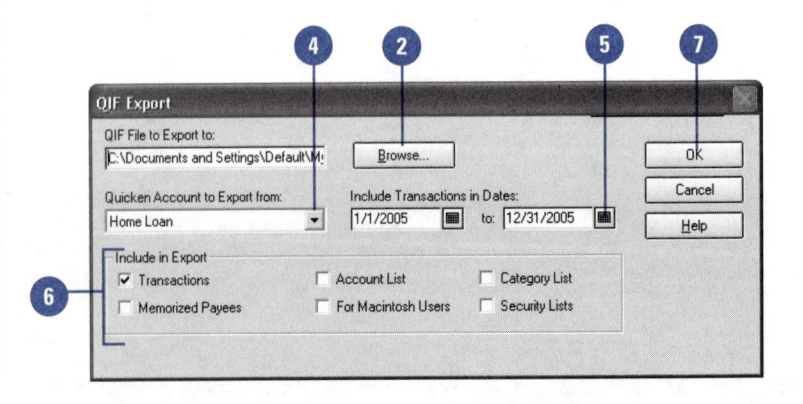

Password-Protecting Your Files

An easy way to provide a basic level of security for your financial information is to set up a password in Quicken. You can set up a password for every Quicken file you create, and you can also protect transactions that occur before a specific date. After you set up a password, you are prompted to enter it each time you open the Quicken file or the transaction(s) to which you assign the password. Make sure that you commit your passwords to memory or keep them in a safe place.

Assign a Password to a File

1. Open the Quicken file you want to password-protect and click File, Passwords, File.

2. In New Password, type your password. It is best to use at least six characters, including uppercase letters, and lowercase letters, and numbers.

3. In Confirm Password, type the password again.

4. Click OK.

Did You Know?

Passwords are case-sensitive. *When you type your password, you can use both uppercase and lowercase letters. When you are prompted to enter your password, you need to be sure to type it using the proper case. For example, if you decide your password is going to be MyPassword03, you need to type it exactly that way. For example, mypassword03 would not work.*

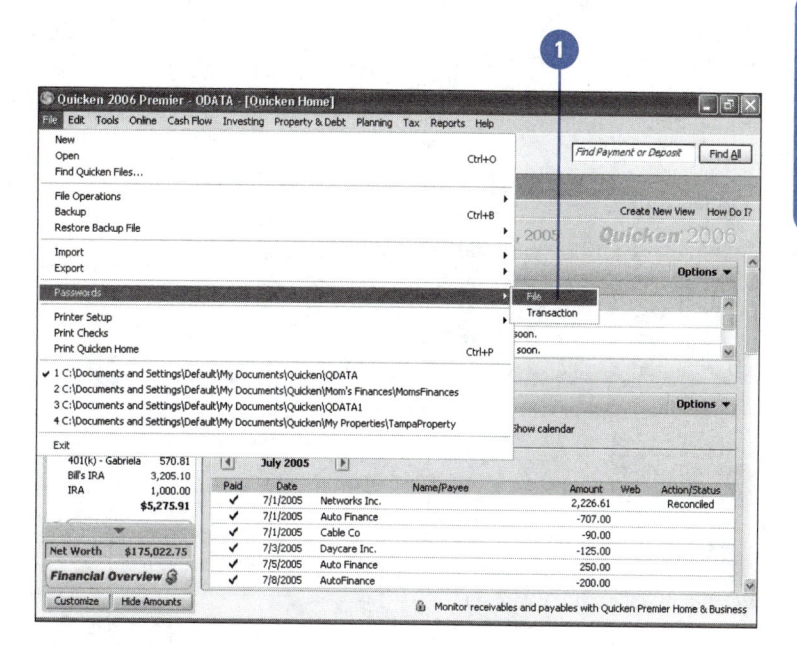

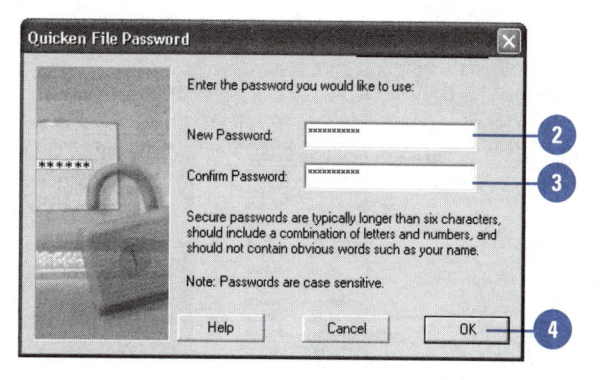

Did You Know?

You should change your passwords every three months. *It is good practice to change your password every three months or so. To change your password, click File, Passwords, File. Type the old password, type the new password, and confirm the new password by typing it again. Then click OK.*

Learning Quicken Basics **51**

Assign a Password to a Transaction

1. Click File, Passwords, and select either File or Transaction. The Change Transaction Password dialog box opens.

2. In Password, type your password. It is best to use at least six characters, including uppercase letters, lowercase letters, and numbers.

3. In Confirm Password, type the password again.

4. In Required for Dates Through, type or select from the calendar the date through which you want all transactions to be password-protected. You can set this date as far in the future as you want.

5. Click OK.

Did You Know?

You can remove a password. To remove a password completely for either a file or a transaction, click File, Passwords, and select either File or Transaction. The Change Transaction Password dialog box opens. In Old Password, type the existing password, leave both the New Password and Confirm Password text boxes blank, and click OK.

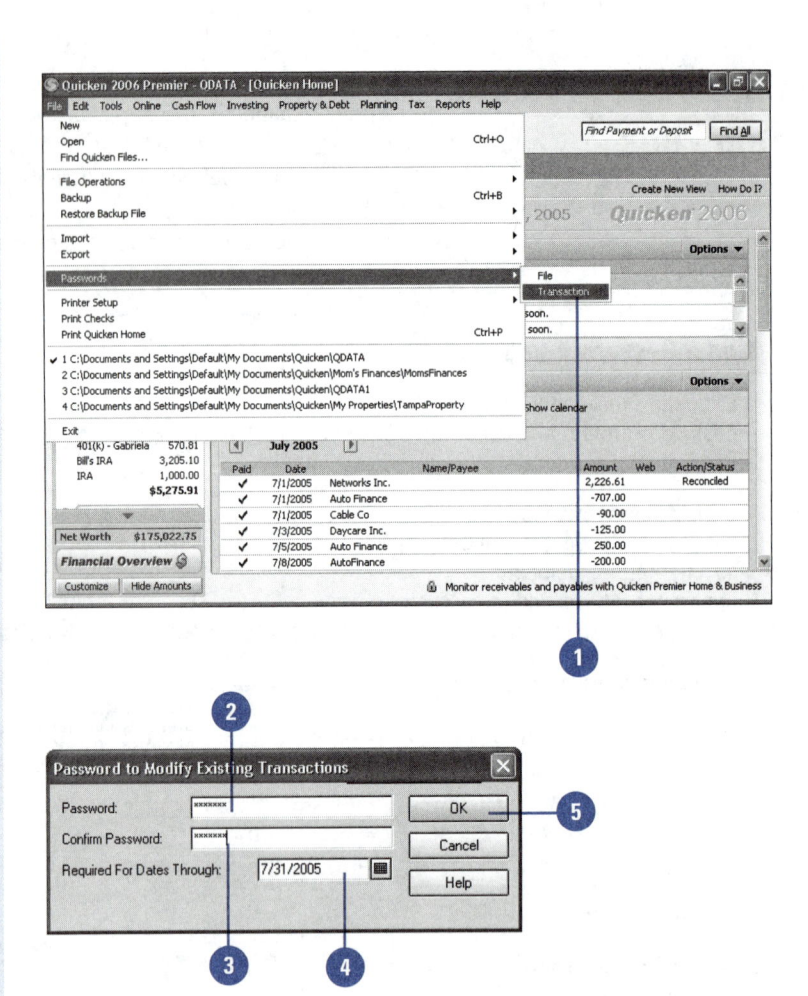

Setting Quicken Preferences

There are preferences or settings that you can change in Quicken to help control how you interact with Quicken and how you want it to work for you. For example, you can tell Quicken to track the fiscal year, instead of the calendar year, or you can tell it to track foreign currency. In addition, you can specify what information you want to see when you open Quicken and set other preferences. Some of the options available to you are a little advanced. So, if you are not sure whether you should change a setting, don't.

Set Quicken Preferences

1. Click Edit, Preferences, Quicken Program.

2. To change the page you see when you first open Quicken, from the On startup open to drop-down menu, select a center or an account.

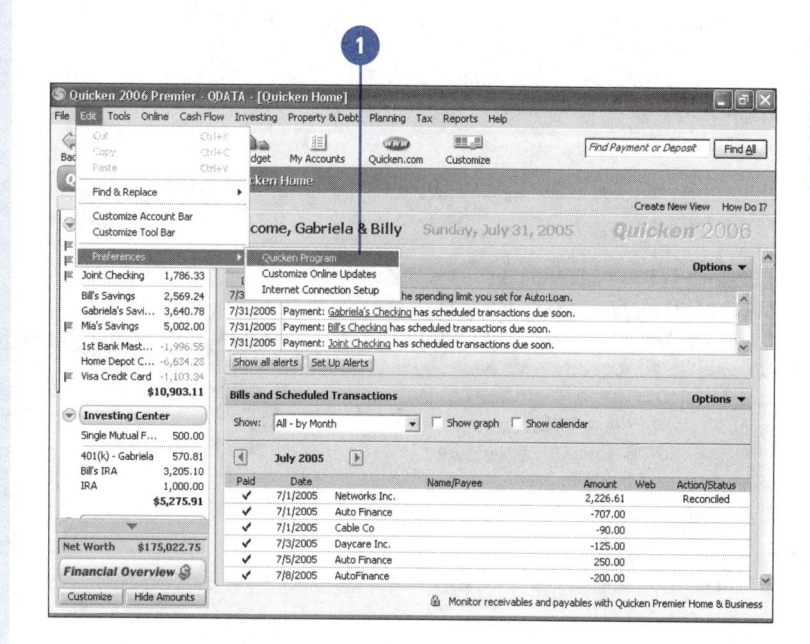

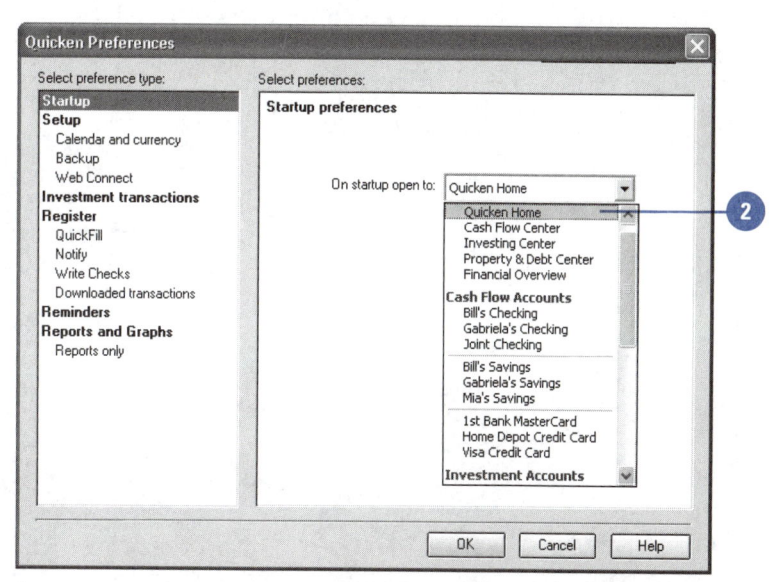

Learning Quicken Basics 53

③ From the Setup preferences type, you can change the location of the account bar (which contains the activity centers) or remove it. In addition, you can change keyboard commands and turn the sound on or off.

④ From the Calendar and currency preferences type, you can select the working calendar you want to use and indicate that you want to use and track other currencies besides the American dollar.

Did You Know?

You can track foreign currency in Quicken. If you elect to use foreign currency, Quicken assigns your preset currency to all your accounts and investments. In addition, it places a symbol next to the amounts in your registers, the Portfolio View window, and wherever else monetary amounts are listed.

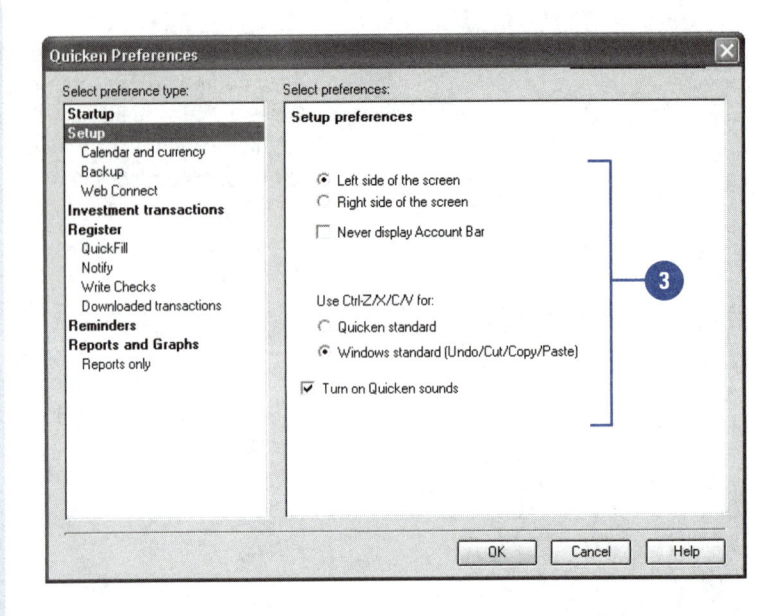

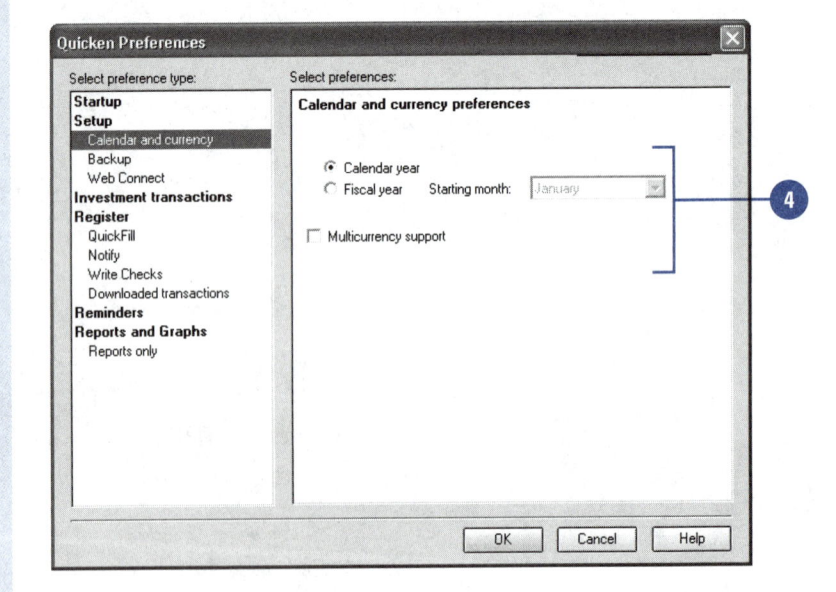

5 From the Backup preferences type, you can specify how many times you want to be reminded to back up your files, the maximum number of backups you want to create and whether you want to be warned before overwriting one.

6 From the Web Connect preferences type, you can tell Quicken to save in a separate file the information that is used to automatically update your online accounts in Quicken. This inhibits Quicken from automatically updating your online accounts. In addition, you can elect to keep the Web connection open after downloading and updating files.

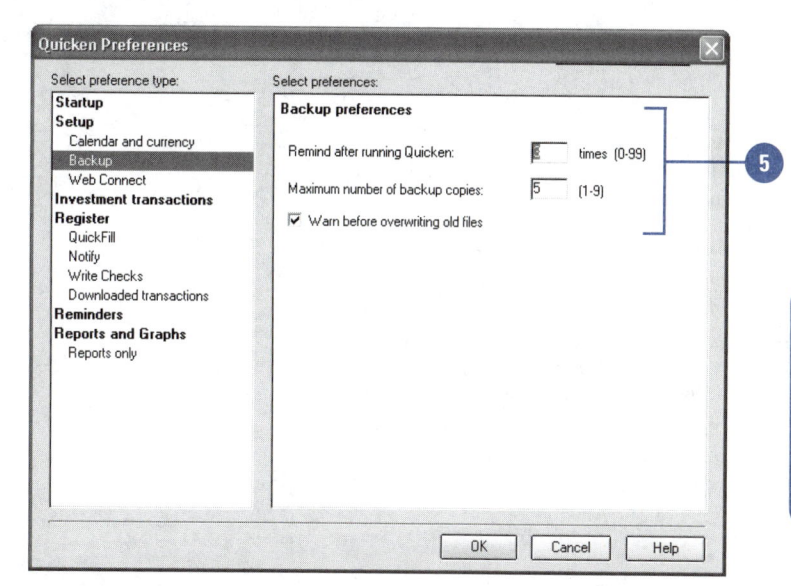

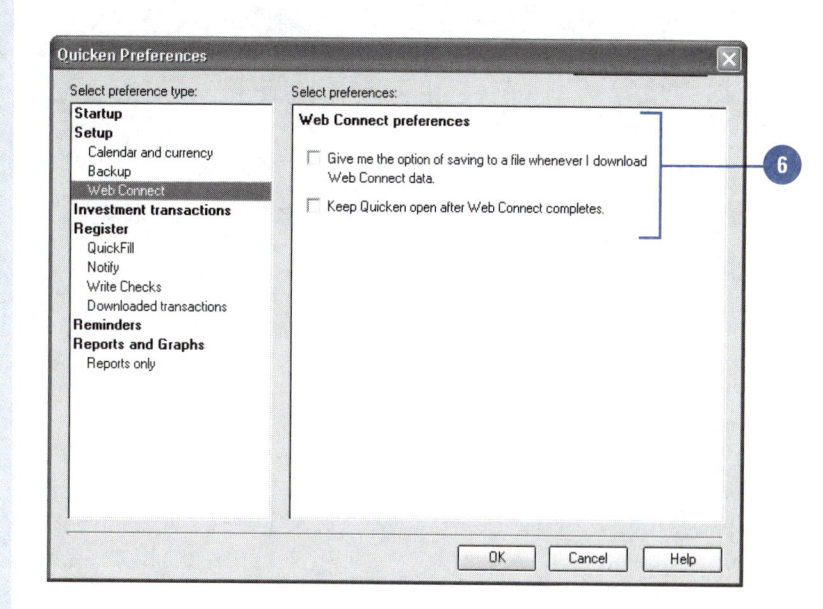

Learning Quicken Basics **55**

7 From the Investment transactions list preferences type, you can select one or two lines to display at a time and select how lists are sorted. In addition, you can select to view hidden transactions.

8 From the Register preferences type, you can specify how you want information to appear on your account registers, including the fonts and colors used. In addition, you can have payee names that have not been used in a while removed from your registers and filters saved after you shut down Quicken.

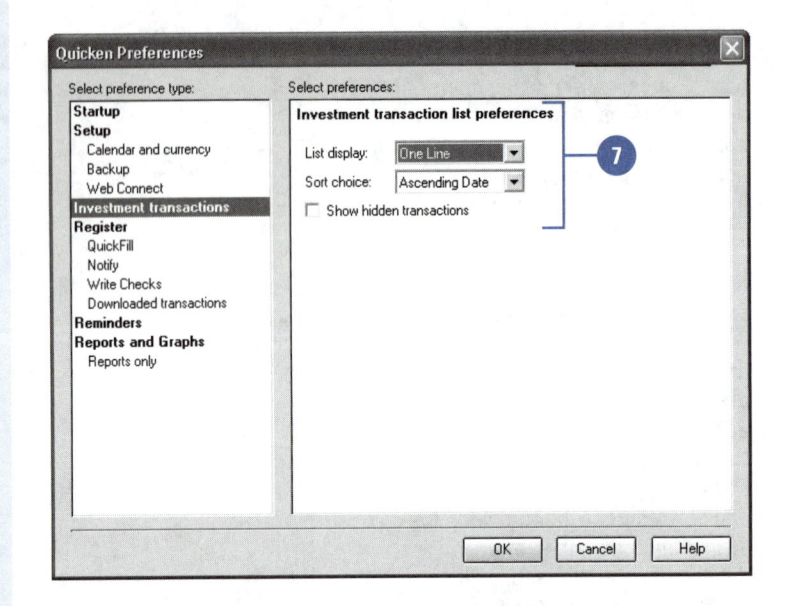

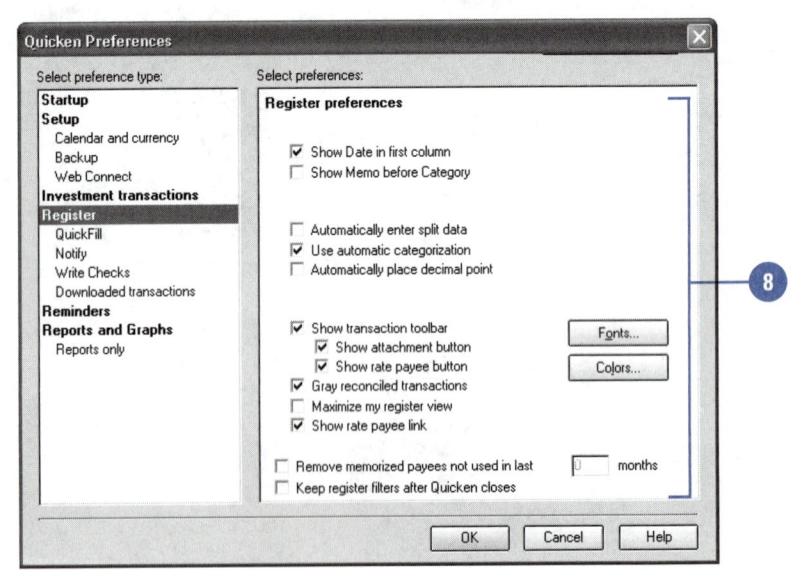

9 From the QuickFill preferences type, you can tell Quicken what you want it to do with the information you enter. In addition, you can specify whether you want it to automatically update list information.

10 From the Notify preferences type, you can select what you want Quicken to warn you about when working with your account information. It is recommended that you keep all options that are currently selected.

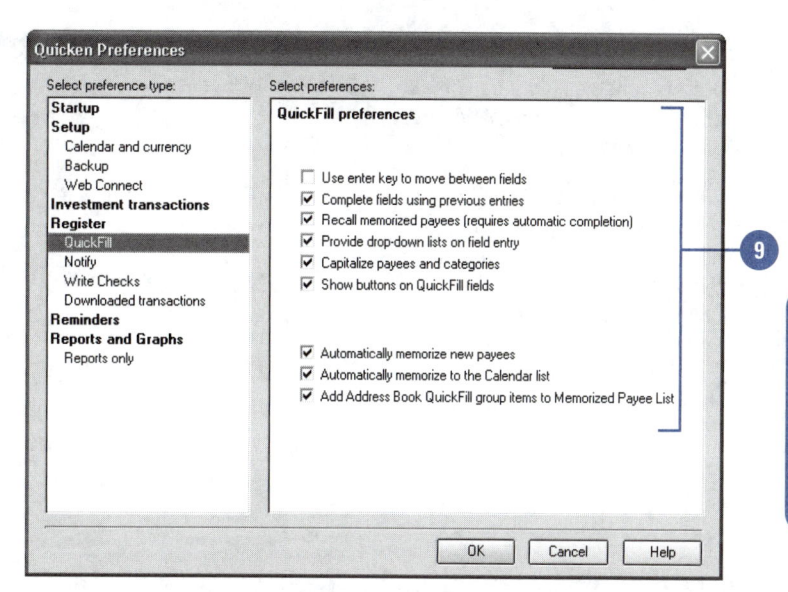

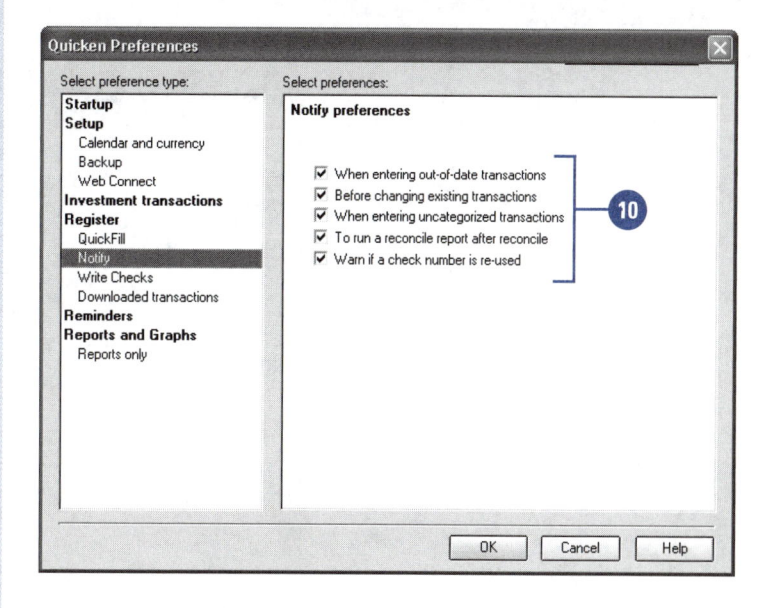

Learning Quicken Basics **57**

11 From the Write Checks preferences type, you can select check printing options, if you use online checks.

12 From the Download transactions preferences type, you can select how you want Quicken to handle the information that is downloaded.

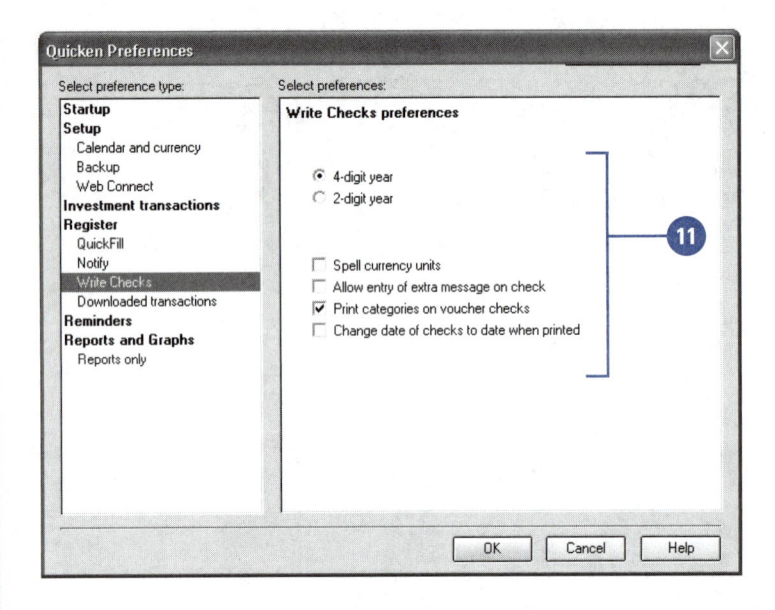

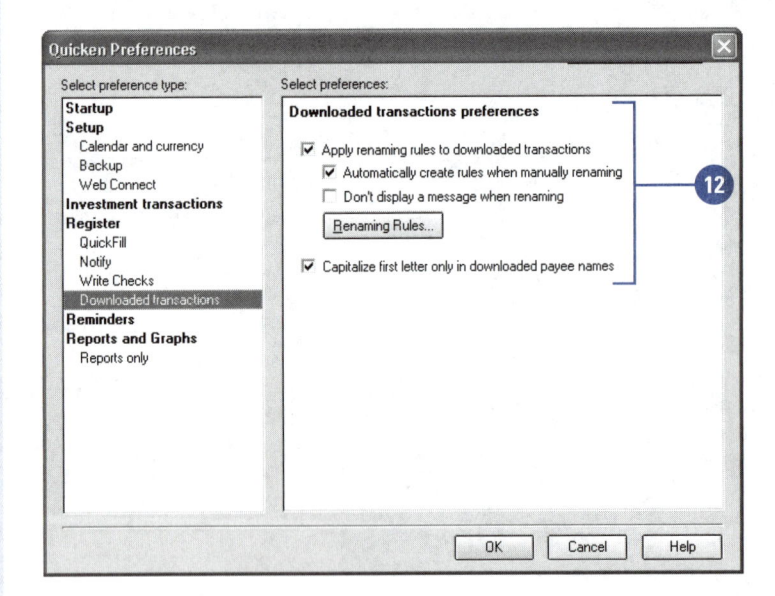

13 From the Reminders preferences type, select the timeframe during which you would like Quicken to remind you of upcoming scheduled transactions.

14 From the Reports and Graphs preferences type, set default date ranges and how you want to customize reports and graphs.

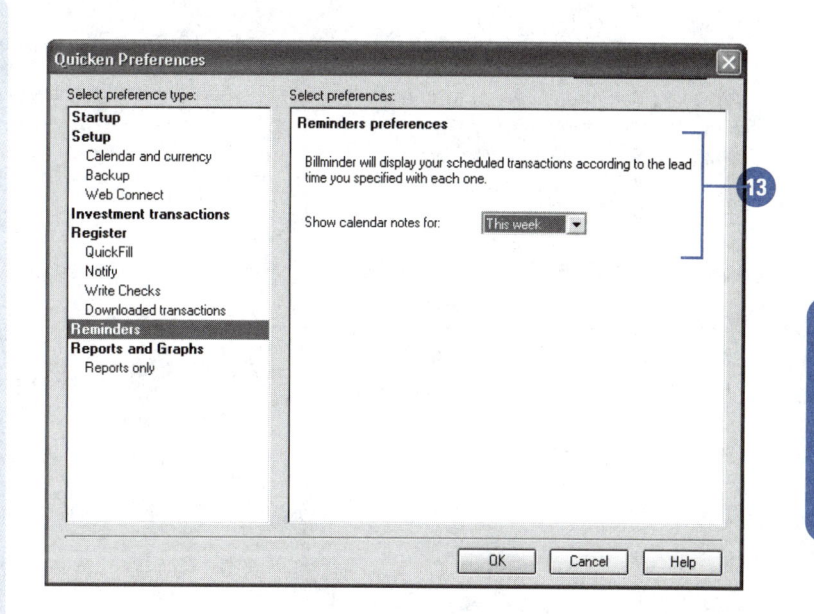

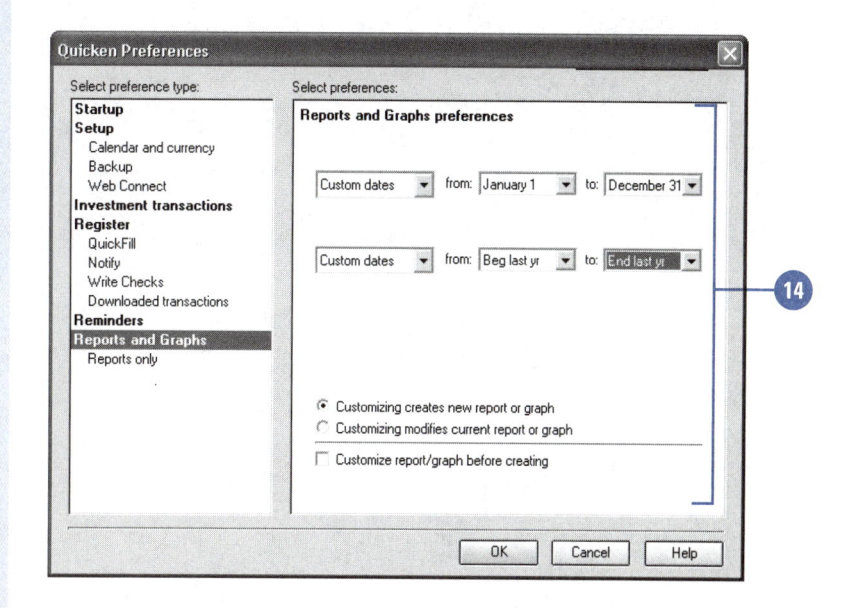

Learning Quicken Basics **59**

15 From the Reports only preferences type, you can choose the account and category information that you want to appear on reports, how to use color, QuickZoom options, and save reminders. In addition, you can set the decimal points you want to use in numerals.

16 When you are finished setting up your options, click OK to save all of the changes.

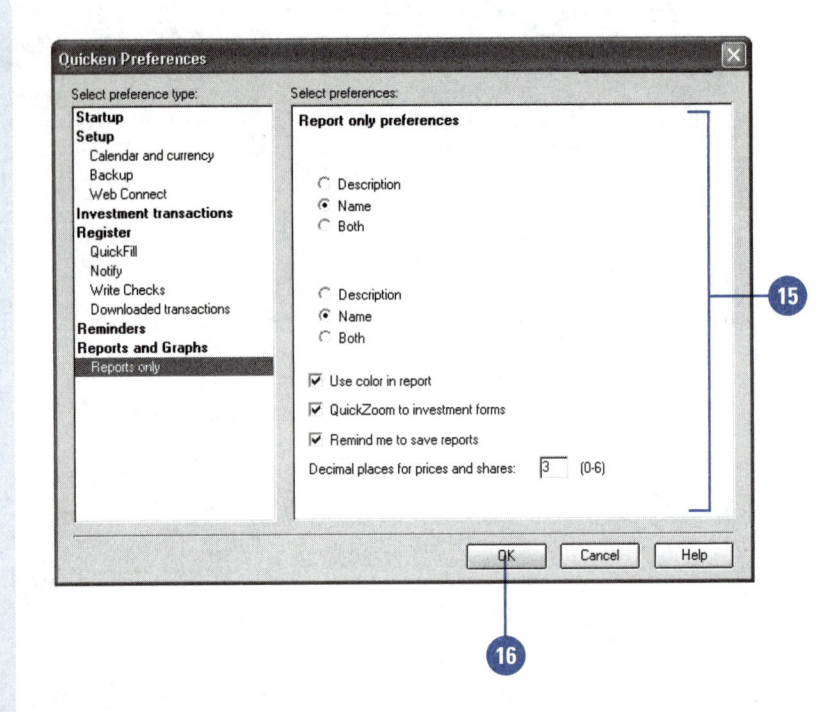

Setting Up Remote Access to Your Accounts

Quicken offers a feature that allows you to access account and portfolio information (that is available for online access in Quicken) from anywhere that you have an Internet connection. For example, if you are on vacation, traveling for your job, or just away from your computer, you can tell Quicken to send your account information to Quicken.com. From that website, you can access your accounts, get updated portfolio share information, and so on. It's a way to remotely manage your accounts and portfolio information.

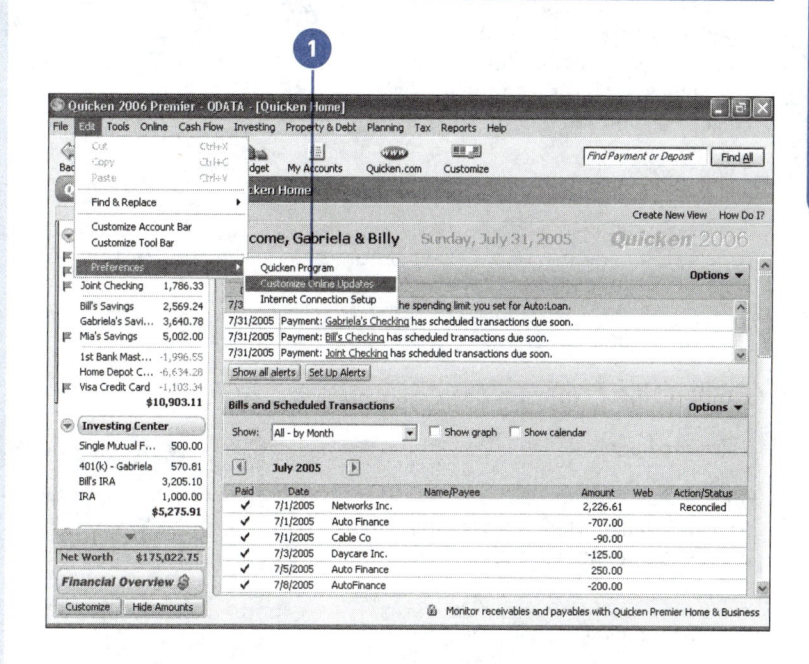

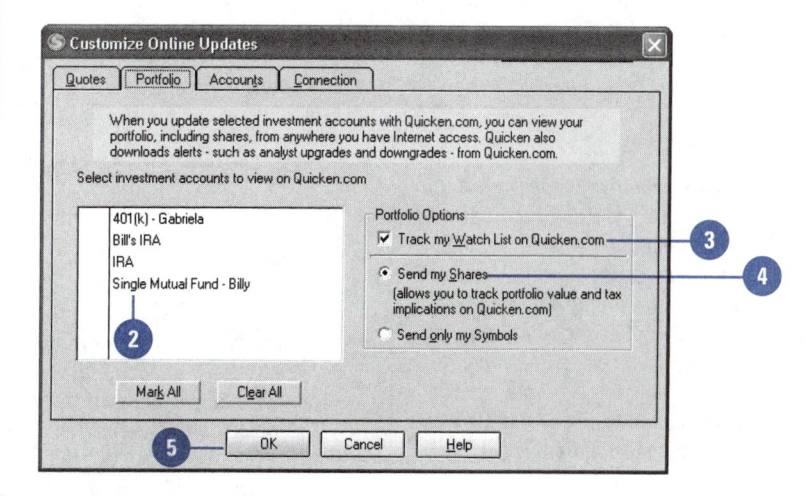

Set Up Portfolio Accounts for Internet Access

1. Click Edit, Preferences, Customize Online Updates.

2. Click the investment accounts that you want to access via the Internet. A check mark appears next to the accounts you select.

3. If you have investments on a watch list that you want to continue to track remotely, click the Track My Watch List on Quicken.com option.

4. To view share (value and tax) information on Quicken.com, select Send my Shares. Or, to only see the symbols, select Send only my Symbols.

5. Click OK to finish the setup or click the Accounts tab to set up or change remote access for your bank accounts.

Learning Quicken Basics **61**

Set Up Accounts for Internet Access

1. Click the Accounts tab.
2. Select the accounts that you want to access from Quicken.com.
3. If you already have accounts set up for remote access and you want to update the information on Quicken.com with the latest information from Quicken, select Resend all items to Quicken.com.
4. Click OK.

Set Connection Preferences

1. Click the Connection tab.
2. Select the preferences you want Quicken to use whenever you are connected to the Internet.
3. When you are finished making all changes to the Customize Online Updates window, click OK to save your changes.

Did You Know?

You can select the quotes you want to download. On the Quotes tab, you can select the quotes that you want to download to Quicken by clicking the security name. To add a new security, you click New Security. To change an existing one, you select the security name and click Edit Security. In addition, you can look up security symbols by clicking the Look Up Symbol button.

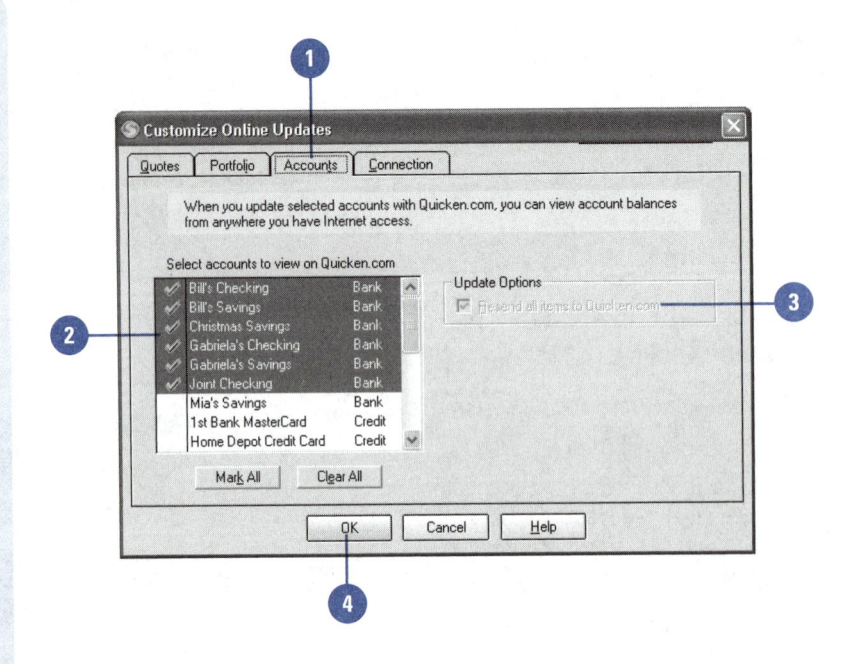

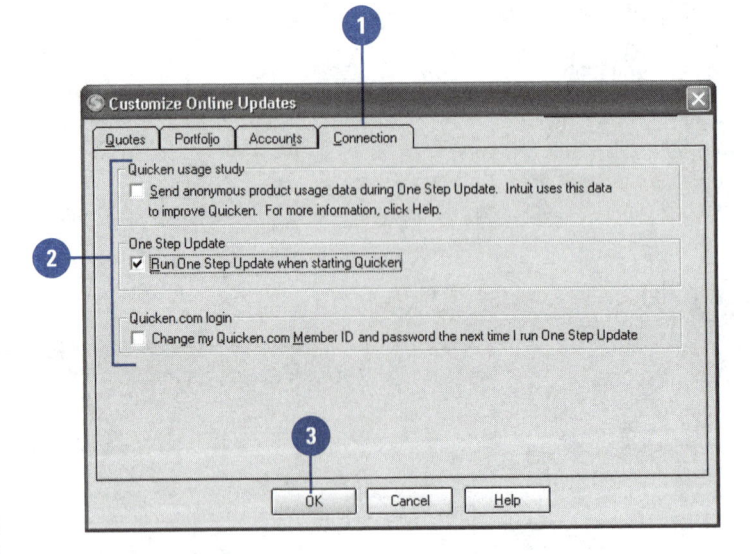

Did You Know?

You can select all or remove all selected accounts with one click. If you have a list of accounts and you want all of them to be accessible from the Internet, you can quickly select them all by clicking Mark All. To quickly remove all accounts that are currently selected (check marks appear next to the accounts that are selected for Internet access)—for example, when you are back home and don't need remote access any longer—click Clear All.

Setting Up Your Internet Connection

To use the online features in Quicken, such as downloading account information into Quicken or getting the latest stock quotes by using One Step Update, you must have an Internet connection. If you plan on using the online features, you can tell Quicken how you would like for it to connect to the Internet.

Set Up an Internet Connection

1. Click Edit, Preferences, Internet Connection Setup.

2. If you already have an Internet connection set up on your computer, select Use my computer's Internet settings to establish a connection when this application accesses the Internet.

3. Click Next.

Did You Know?

Selecting accounts for remote access allows you to view them on Quicken.com. If you select accounts for remote access on Quicken.com, you can review account balances from anywhere, as long as you have Internet access and a login ID and password for Quicken.com.

See Also

See "Setting Up Remote Access to Your Accounts" on page 61 for more information about setting up and accessing your accounts on Quicken.com.

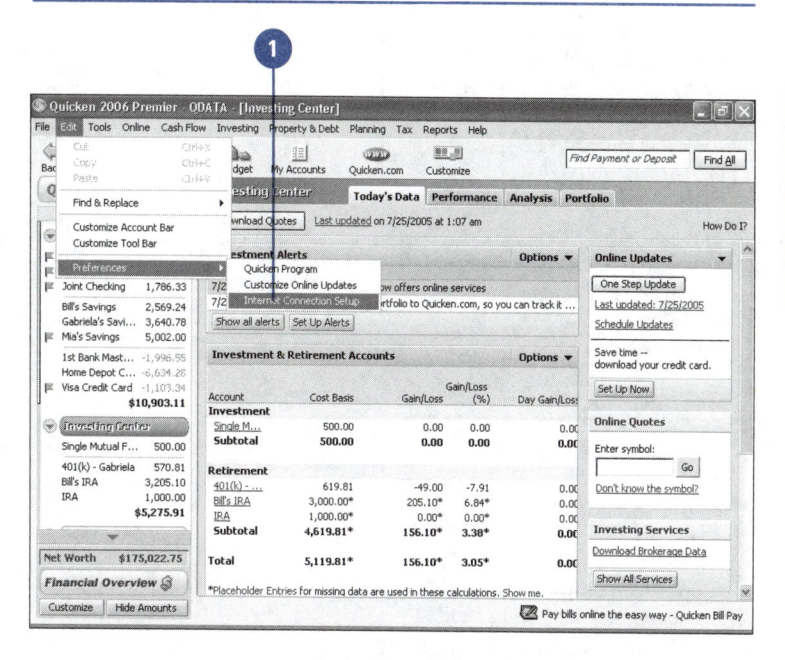

Learning Quicken Basics **63**

④ Review your connection information and click Done.

Did You Know?

You must register your copy of Quicken and have Internet service. *Before you can use Quicken's online features, you must register your copy of the software and have Internet service set up on your computer. In addition, your creditor or bank must offer online services in order to set up and use online accounts.*

Did You Know?

You can update Quicken.com automatically and you can change your ID or password. *You can automatically send updated account information to Quicken.com each time you open Quicken by selecting the Run One Step Update when starting Quicken option on the Connection tab. You can also set up an update reminder to notify you when your account balances have changed by selecting Remind Me to Run One Step Update When Exiting Quicken. In addition, you can have Quicken prompt you to change your Quicken.com ID or password on the Connection tab by selecting Change my Quicken.com Member ID and password the next time I run One Step Update.*

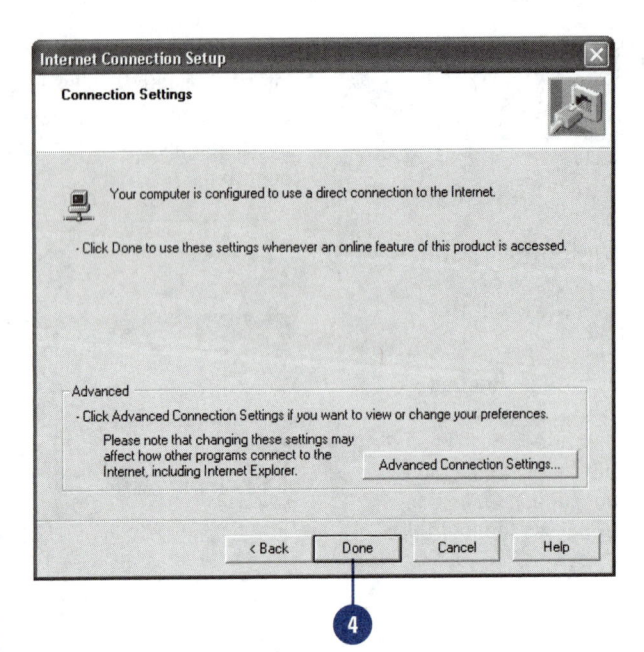

Using Quicken Home Page Features

Introduction

Whether you've been following along so far with installing and setting up Quicken or you've already been exploring other chapters and features in Quicken, this chapter brings it all home—to the Quicken Home page, that is. The Quicken Home page is a central location for all your account information, where you can access, organize, and update account information; view a big picture of your financial health and well-being; and explore your net worth. The account bar, which appears alongside the Home page, provides quick access to all your accounts and is divided into activity centers that group or categorize your accounts. You can use the centers to access each of your accounts. In this chapter, you will also learn how to use alerts to remind you of important actions or warnings concerning your accounts, how to record and manage your account transactions, how to automatically update account information using online updates, and some helpful tips and services. In addition, you'll be privy to some keyboard shortcuts that will have you tooling around Quicken like a pro in no time.

What You'll Do

Use the Account Bar and Activity Centers

Get the Big Picture

Select Accounts to Include in Your Net Worth

Use Alerts

Use Bills and Scheduled Transactions

Take the Next Steps with Your Financial Goals

Use Online Updates

Use Tips and Services

Create Links to Your Favorite Financial Websites

Using the Account Bar and Activity Centers

The account bar contains the activity centers and is located on the left side of the Home page (unless you changed the position to the right side in Chapter 2, "Learning Quicken Basics," when we covered setting Quicken preferences). The activity centers include the Cash Flow Center, which contains all your banking and credit card accounts; the Investing Center, which contains all your investment and retirement information; and the Property & Debt center, which contains account information for your property, assets, and liabilities. Each of these centers provides access to all your accounts, where you can review, change, or remove account information. The following task provides an overview of the activity centers and shows you how to quickly access your accounts and customize the account bar. We'll get into more of the specifics of using each activity center in Chapters 4, "Managing Your Spending and Savings Accounts," through 9, "Managing Your Property and Debt."

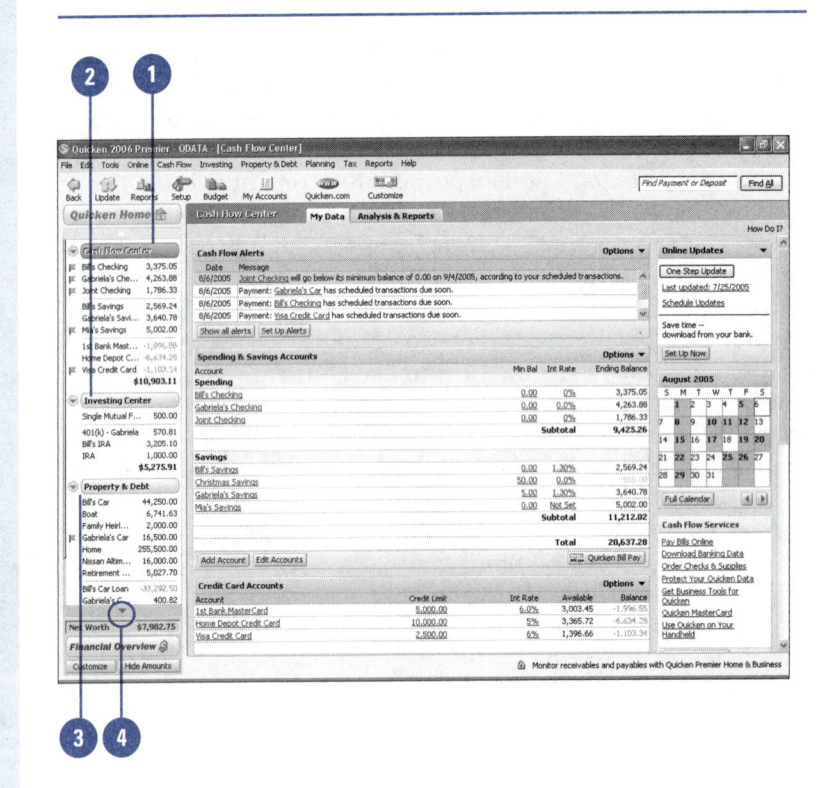

Use the Account Bar and Activity Centers

1. To access your bank and credit card account information, in the account bar, click Cash Flow Center. You can also click an account name to go directly to the register for that account.

2. To access your investments, securities, or retirement account(s), click Investing Center.

3. To view property and debt accounts, such as your home, car, property loans, and so on, click Property & Debt.

4. Click the arrows at the bottom or top of the activity center to scroll down or up. The arrows appear darker when there is information hiding and lighter when there is no information hiding.

See Also

See "Setting Quicken Preferences" on page 53 for more information on changing the position of the activity centers. See Chapters 4 through 9 for more information on using the different activity centers.

5 Right-click in any area of the account bar to view a menu of actions you can perform. For example, you can hide the account bar completely, move it, or choose to view more or less information about each account.

6 Your total net worth appears at the bottom of the account bar. To view a detailed breakdown of your net worth, click Financial Overview.

7 Hide account balances by clicking the Hide Amounts button.

8 Click Show Amt. to show account balances.

9 To change the accounts that appear and the order in which they appear on the account bar, click Customize.

Did You Know?

You can review special messages. If there is a red flag next to one of your accounts, you can hover your mouse pointer (point, but don't click) over the account name to view the special message. Balances that appear in red represent debt. Use the flags to help you manage your accounts. In the time it takes to take a quick glance at the activity bar, you'll know which accounts need your attention. This saves you time and the effort of going into each account to review them.

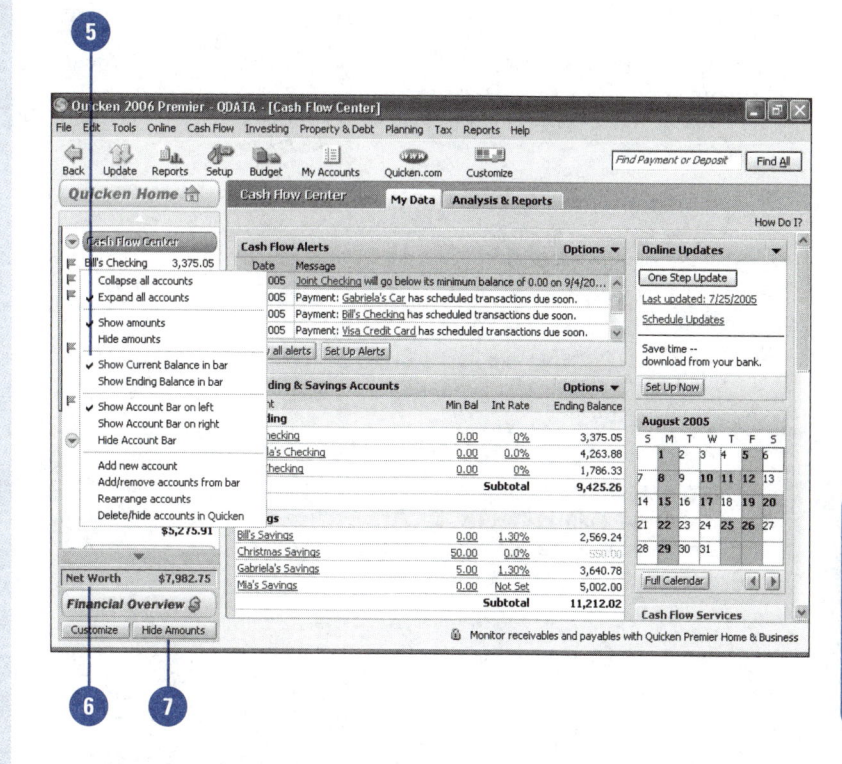

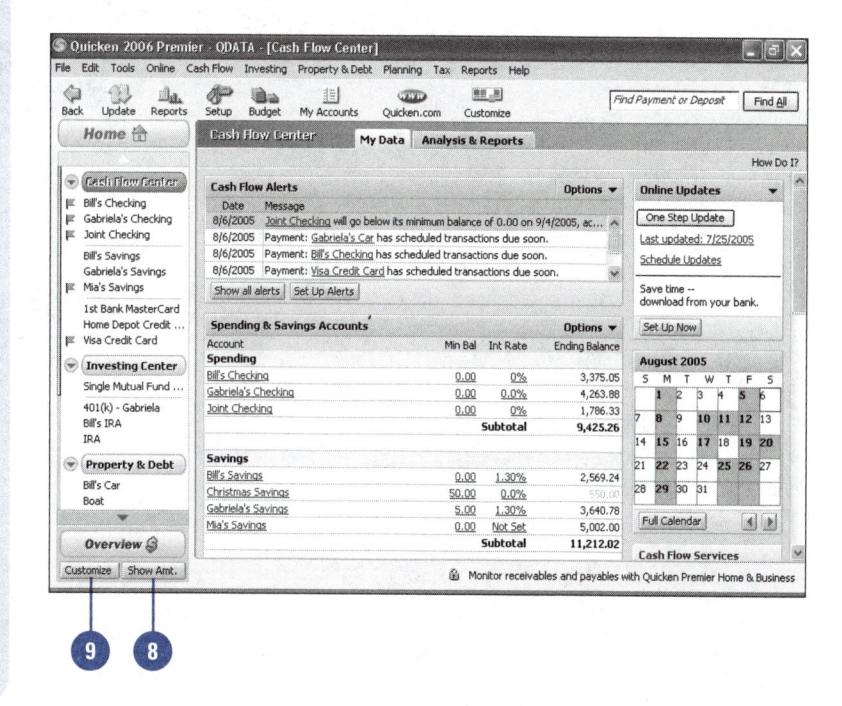

Using Quicken Home Page Features **67**

10. Click the boxes in the Remove from Bar column for the accounts you do not want to appear on the account bar or click a box that has a check mark to add an account to the account bar.

11. Accounts automatically appear in alphabetical order. To move an account up or down on the list, select the account and click Move Up to move it up the list or Move Down to move it down the list. Repeat the move until the account appears where you want it on the list.

12. To move an account to a different category (for example, to move a savings account to a spending account), select the account and click Change Group.

13. Select the new category for the account and click OK.

14. To return to the Quicken Home page, click Close.

Did You Know?

You can view a hidden account bar. To show a hidden account bar, click the double-arrow (>>) in the upper-left corner of the Quicken window.

See Also

For more information on the Financial Overview center, see "Getting the Big Picture" on page 69.

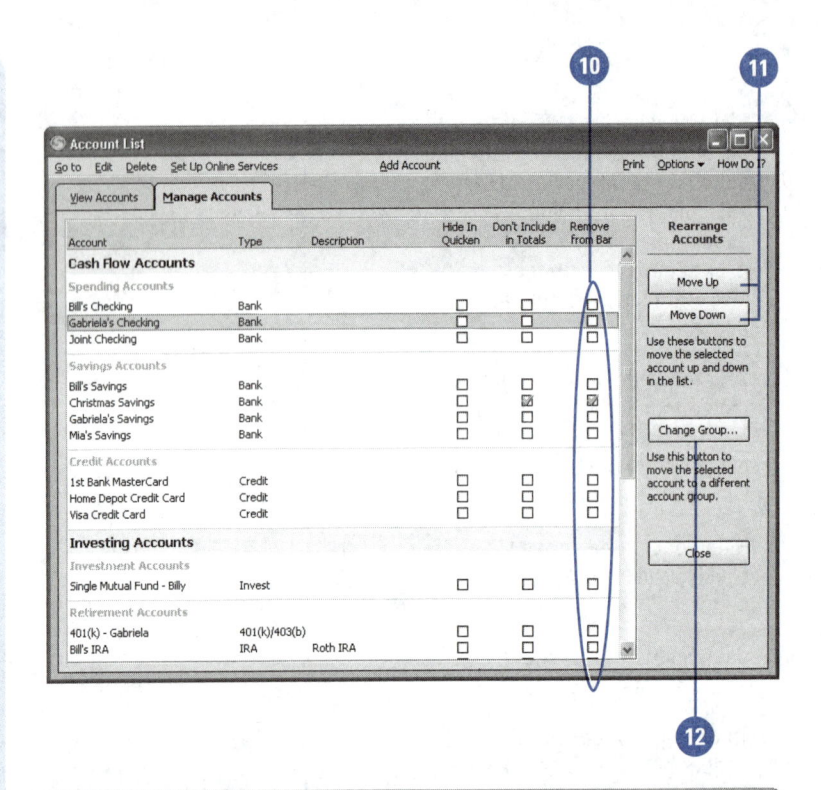

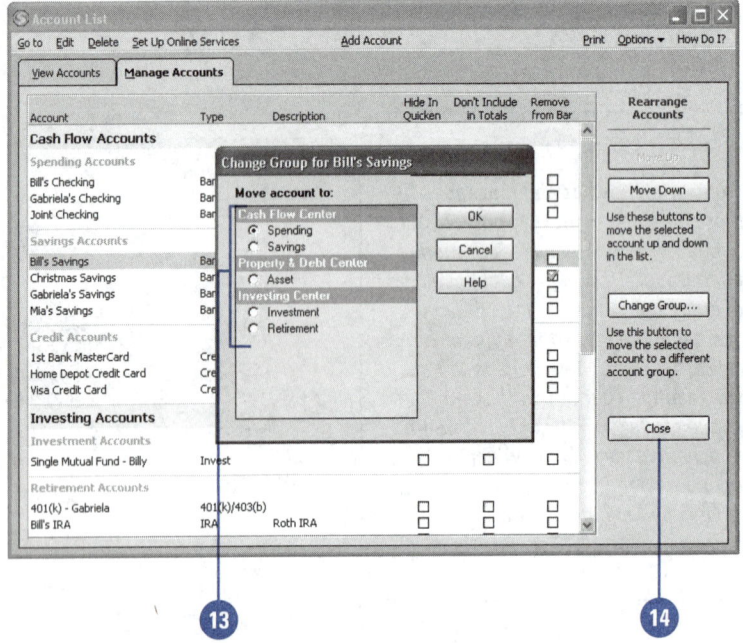

Getting the Big Picture

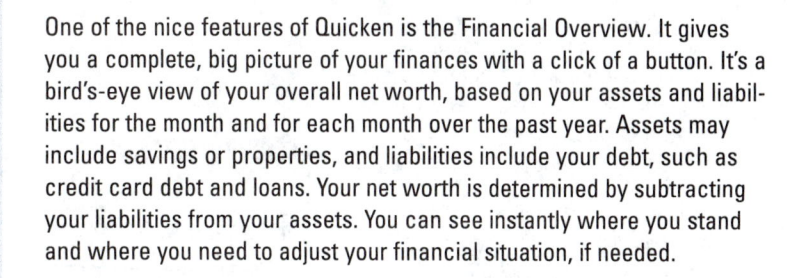

One of the nice features of Quicken is the Financial Overview. It gives you a complete, big picture of your finances with a click of a button. It's a bird's-eye view of your overall net worth, based on your assets and liabilities for the month and for each month over the past year. Assets may include savings or properties, and liabilities include your debt, such as credit card debt and loans. Your net worth is determined by subtracting your liabilities from your assets. You can see instantly where you stand and where you need to adjust your financial situation, if needed.

Get the Big Picture

1. In the activity bar, click Financial Overview.

2. If you're not already there, click the Net Worth tab to view a graph view of your assets, liabilities, and net worth over the past year.

3. To view your assets, liabilities, or net worth for a specific month, hover your mouse pointer (point, but don't click) over a bar on the graph. A figure pops up, showing you what your net worth was for that time period.

4. To see a full view of the graph, click Show Full Graph.

See Also

See Chapter 10, "Planning for the Future," for more detailed information on using the Planning Center and creating plans. See Chapter 11, "Managing Your Tax Information," for more information on using the Tax Center.

Did You Know?

You can get a clue with the color key. *There is a color key in the upper-right corner to help you determine which colors on the graph represent assets, liabilities, and net worth.*

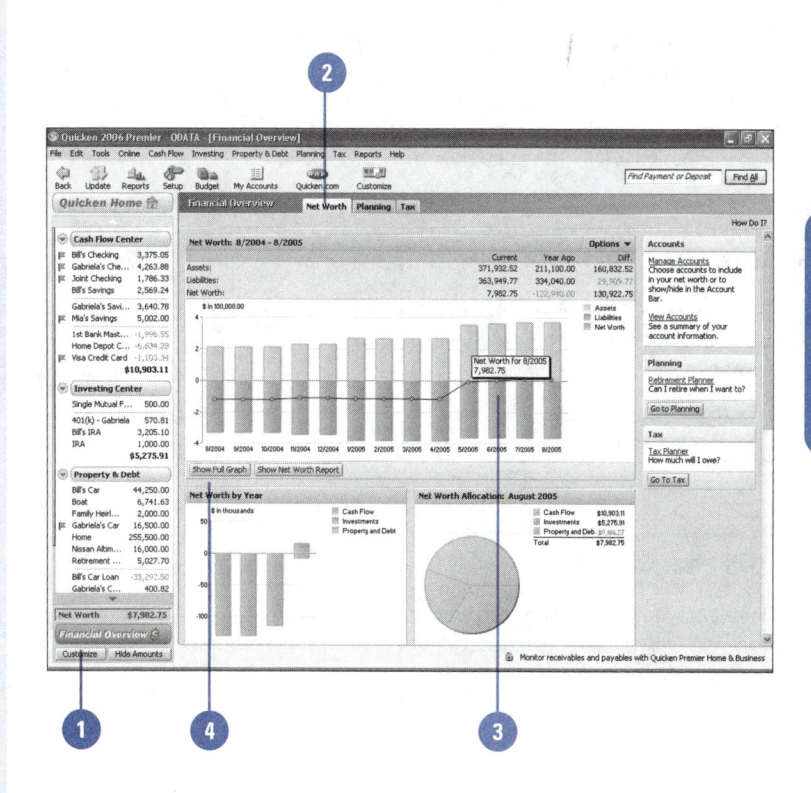

Using Quicken Home Page Features

5 In the Net Worth window, you can customize the graph by selecting a custom date from the Date range menu or a different interval of time from the Interval menu.

6 Click Show Report to see a detailed breakdown of your assets and liabilities, including their totals.

7 Click Hide Graph to view only the report showing the breakdown of your assets and liabilities. When you are finished reviewing the information, close the window.

See Also

See Chapter 12, "Working with Reports," for more information on viewing, customizing, saving, and printing reports.

Did You Know?

There are alternate ways of opening the graph and report. There are multiple ways to access the full graph net worth view or the net worth report. You can use the Options menu located in the upper-right corner to access the same information as by using the button in step 4 and the Show Report icon in step 6. Clicking the Show Net Worth Report button shown next to the Show Full Graph button in step 4 also opens the Net Worth report. In addition, you can right-click the graph to access the full graph net worth view and report.

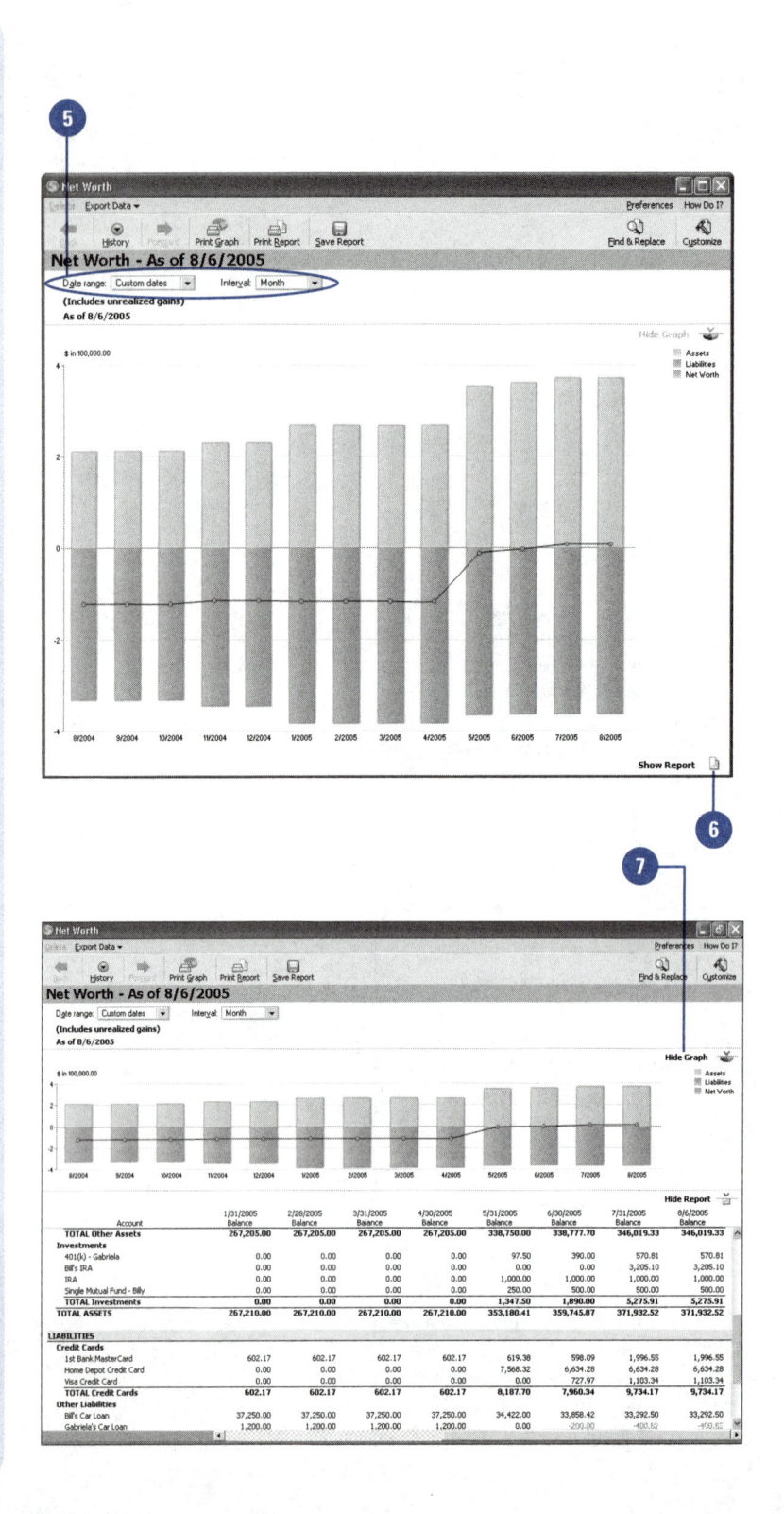

8. Click Show Net Worth Report to view the breakdown of your assets and liabilities (shown in step 7) without the graph.

9. Net Worth by Year shows your cash flow, investment, or property and debt net worth for a specific year or year-to-date. Hover your mouse over the bars to see the net worth for each type of activity.

10. Net Worth Allocation shows what percentage of your net worth comes from your cash flow, investment, or property. Hover your mouse over the pie chart to see how the net worth percentages break down.

11. Scroll down to view the Net Worth Summary. It provides net worth by year and year-to-date for each of your cash flow, investment, and property accounts. Figures that appear in red are negative net worth.

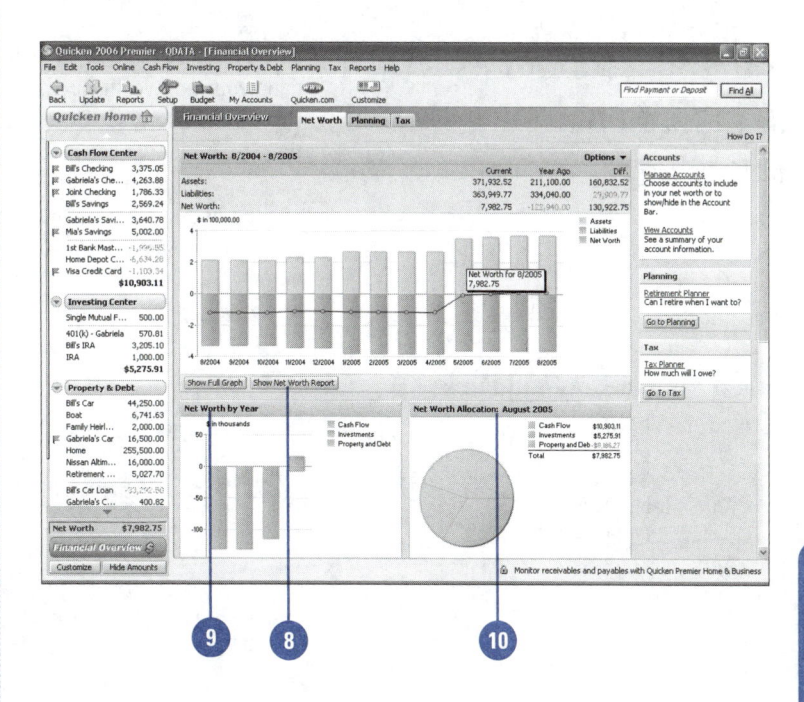

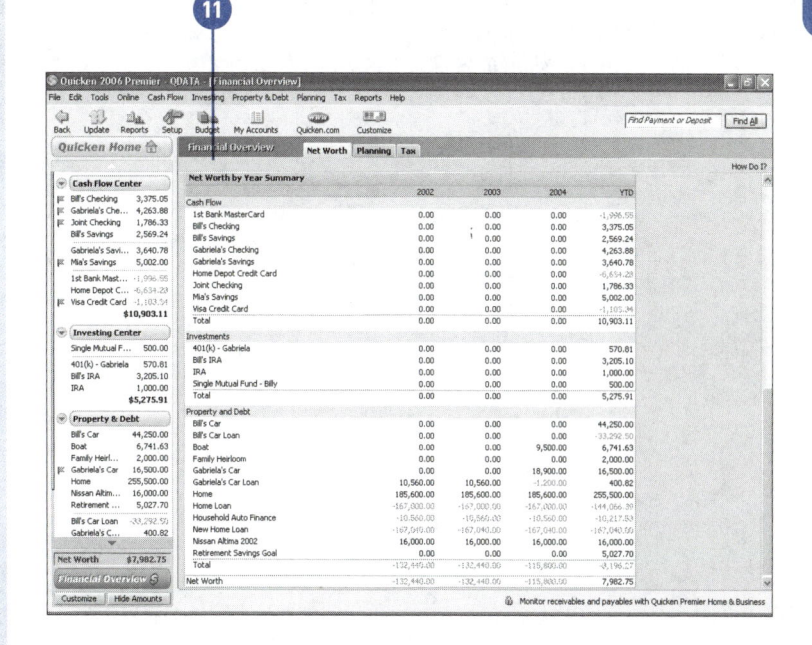

Using Quicken Home Page Features 71

Selecting Accounts to Include in Your Net Worth

By default, Quicken uses all the accounts that you have set up to determine your net worth. You can add and remove the accounts you want Quicken to use when determining your net worth. Removing an account that you don't want to use for your net worth does not remove it from Quicken. You are simply telling Quicken that you don't want Quicken to use the financials for that account when it calculates your net worth. By changing the accounts you want used for your net worth, you can make better financial decisions about your savings, investments, debt, and so on by seeing which accounts are working for you or against you.

Select Accounts to Include in Your Net Worth

1. In the Accounts section of the Net Worth tab in the Financial Overview, click the Manage Accounts link.

Did You Know?

There is an alternate way to navigate the Account List window. You can access the Account List window two other ways: by clicking My Accounts on the toolbar or by clicking Customize on the account bar.

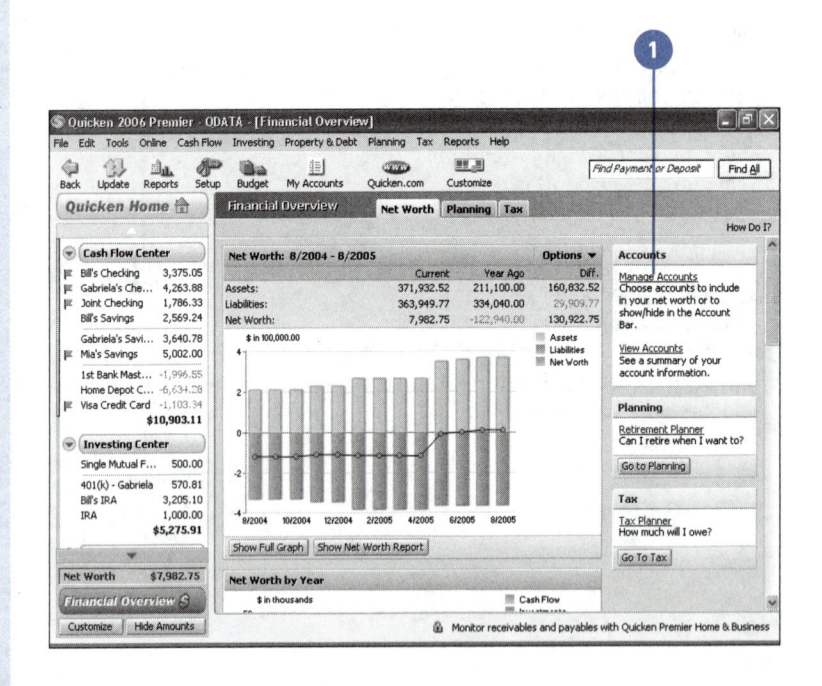

② Select the boxes in the Hide In Quicken column for each account you want to keep hidden from account lists and out of the totals for your net worth. Or, to include hidden accounts in the net worth, remove the check marks by clicking them.

③ Select the boxes in the Don't Include in Totals column for each account you want to exclude from the totals for your net worth. Or, to include totals for an account, remove the check mark by clicking it.

④ When you are finished selecting or removing accounts for your net worth totals, click Close.

> **Did You Know?**
>
> **You can hide accounts in Quicken.**
> Hiding an account doesn't mean you'll need to open up a Swiss bank account with an alias name in another country. When you want Quicken to track the balance of an account, but you don't want that balance used for net worth or considered for a debt reduction plan, you can hide it. For example, if you have a savings goal, you can continue to save the set amount each month; Quicken tracks how much you are saving, but the account and the amount are hidden until you reach your goal. Another situation where you should hide an account is when an account is closed or has a zero balance. Instead of deleting it, you should hide it so that Quicken can still use it for reporting and forecasting, but the account(s) won't clutter up your account lists.

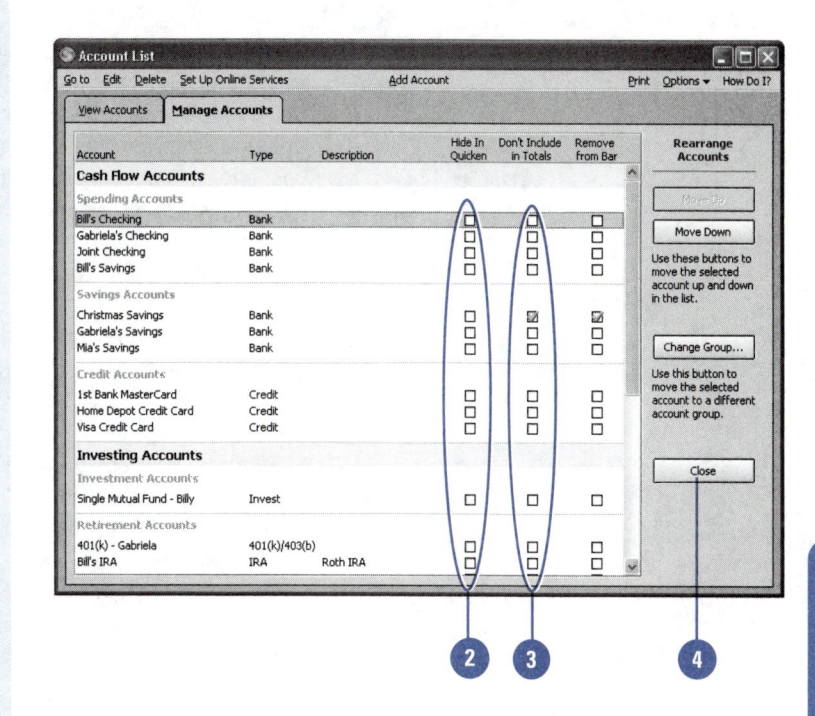

Using Quicken Home Page Features **73**

Using Alerts

The first section on the Quicken Home page is Alerts. Quicken uses alerts to remind you of any actions you need to take with your accounts (for example, paying a bill, transferring money to savings) and warnings (for example, when one of your balances is reaching its limit or when your checking account is getting too low). Alerts can save you money by notifying you before you are charged over-the-limit fees or non-sufficient funds (NSF) fees. Alerts can also make you money too (for example, by watching your securities).

You have full control of the alerts you use and how often you are reminded. Alerts for each center are listed at the top of the center. For example, alerts for the Cash Flow Center appear in the Cash Flow Alerts section at the top of that center. However, the Alerts section at the top of the Quicken Home page is home to all alert types for all centers. You can view, change, and delete all alerts from the Quicken Home page by using the Alerts Center. You can also access the Alerts Center to manage alerts from any of the centers. With taxes, interest charges, fees of all sorts, and other financial leaches sucking the life out of your hard-earned money, you should protect yourself, take control, and set those alerts.

Use Alerts

1. If you don't already have the Quicken Home page open, click Quicken Home.

2. To see a list of all alerts that are currently active, click Show all alerts.

Did You Know?

You can review and delete alerts. You can review all alerts by clicking the Show All tab. If you no longer need an alert, you can delete it by clicking the box next to the alert you want to remove and then clicking the Delete button at the bottom of the window. A message appears, asking if you want to delete the alert; click OK. Deleting an alert only removes one instance of the alert; it does not remove the alert altogether. If you no longer want to be reminded of an alert, you must disable it by performing step 9 in this task.

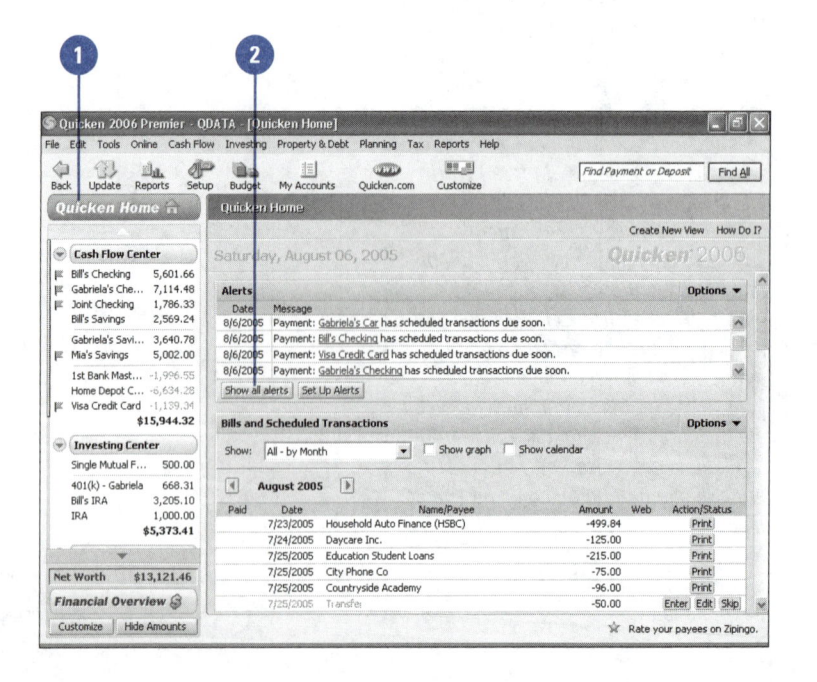

③ To take action on an alert, click the links within the Description column.

④ To make changes to alerts, click the Setup tab. You can also do this by clicking the Set Up Alerts button in the Alerts section of the Quicken Home page. Alerts are listed by type.

⑤ Click a plus sign to expand the list. A check mark means that the alert is active. A blank box means that the alert is not active.

⑥ To select an alert, click in the box next to its name.

⑦ To change alert details, click the alert name and change the alert to meet your needs. For example, for Credit Card Limits, click the amount under Remind Me At and type the amount at which you want Quicken to alert you that you are getting close to your credit limit.

⑧ From the Show me the alert as options, select the type of alert you want: a text message or a pop-up type of message.

⑨ From the Keep the alert in this list for drop-down menu, select how long you'd like Quicken to show you the alert.

⑩ To remove an alert altogether, clear the check box next to the alert name.

⑪ Review and change all alerts as needed and click OK when you are finished. The alerts you set up are now active. When you complete a task in an alert, it automatically goes away until it is triggered again.

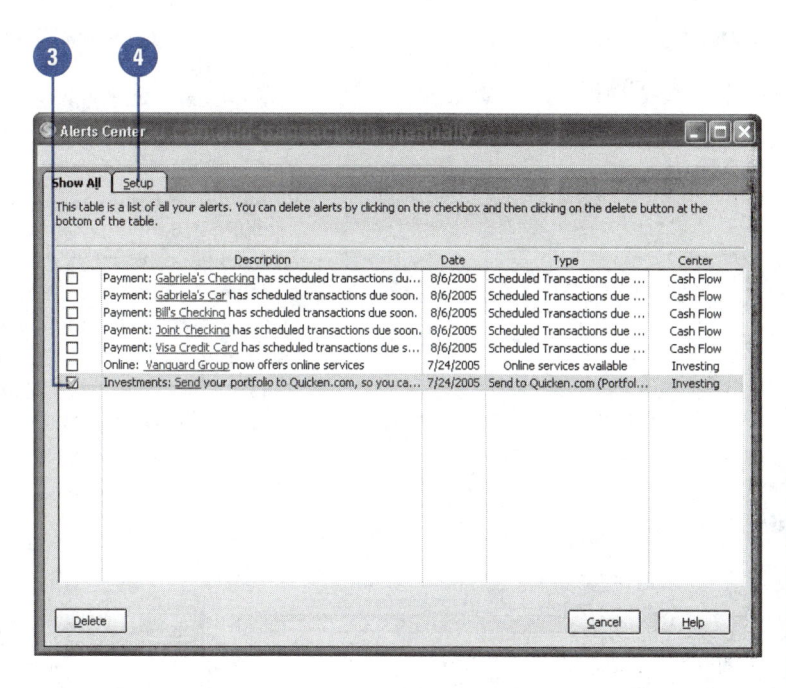

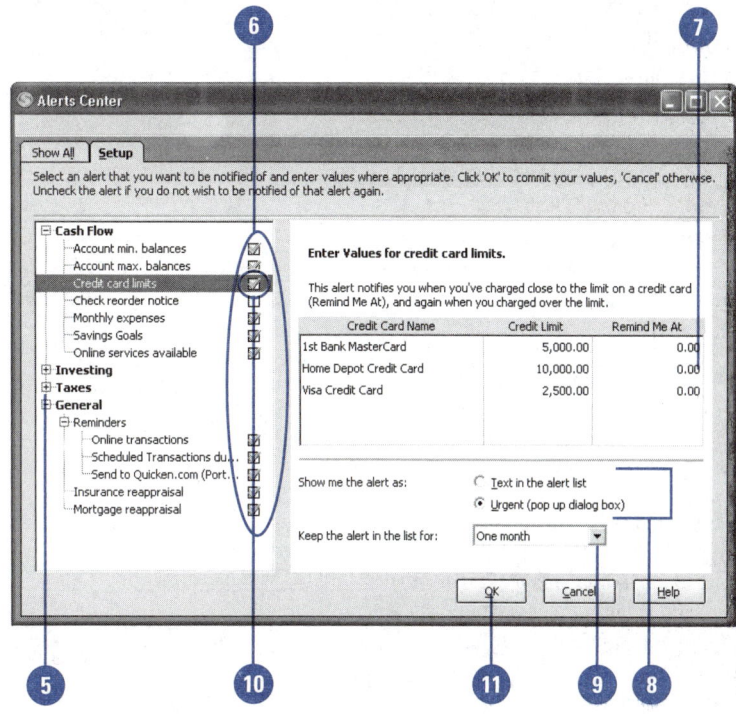

Using Quicken Home Page Features **75**

Using Bills and Scheduled Transactions

The area beneath the Alerts section on the Quicken Home page is Bills and Scheduled Transactions. All transactions for the current month and those that have not been completed from previous months are listed here. Transactions include paychecks, bills, mortgage payments, utilities, banking, and every other account transaction you have entered in Quicken. You can use Bills and Scheduled Transactions to enter the transactions in your register—for example, when you make a payment for a bill or when a paycheck has been deposited into your bank account. In addition, you can add new transactions, change information for a single transaction, make changes to all transactions for an account, or delete a transaction. There are also some tools you can use to review your account checks and balances over a specific period of time by using graphs, or you can use the calendars to see exactly where your transactions fall within a month. Bills and Scheduled Transactions provides an efficient and quick way of keeping up with your incoming and outgoing account transactions.

Record Transactions

1. If a Print button appears next to a transaction, it is because that transaction is paid using Quicken checks. Quicken checks are covered in more detail in Chapter 6, "Managing Your Bills."

2. Click Enter to log the transaction in your register. The transaction information opens in an edit window. The edit window differs, depending on the transaction type.

Did You Know?

Changes that you make when entering a transaction apply only to that transaction. When you register a transaction and make changes to the transaction information, the change applies only to the current transaction. The change does not apply to future transactions for the account. If you want to make changes that apply to all transactions for an account, you must edit the transaction.

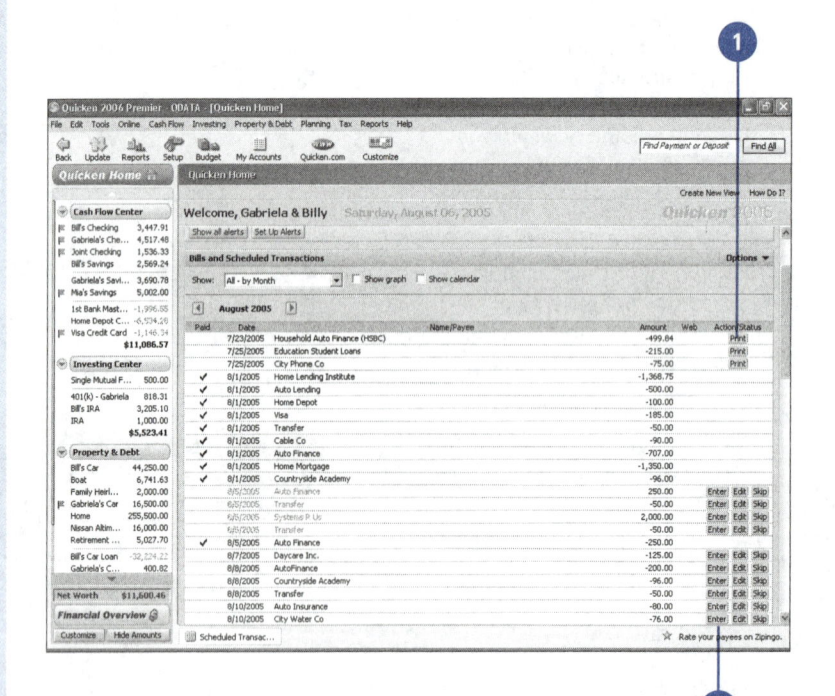

③ If needed, make changes to this transaction by clicking in any of the fields and typing over the existing information, or click the Edit buttons. Remove information by clicking the Delete buttons.

④ To add information to the current transaction, click one of the Add buttons. For example, in this instance we are updating a paycheck transaction by clicking Add Pre-Tax Deduction to add medical insurance information.

Did You Know?

The color of a transaction and the check mark next to it tell you what actions you need to take. When you select the All – by Month option from the Show menu, the check marks next to transactions mean those transactions have already been recorded in your register. If the transaction appears in red, it means that it is overdue. If the transaction appears in green, it means that the transaction is due on the current day, and if it appears in black, it is not due yet. Use Current – by Status to quickly see which transactions are overdue and which are coming up.

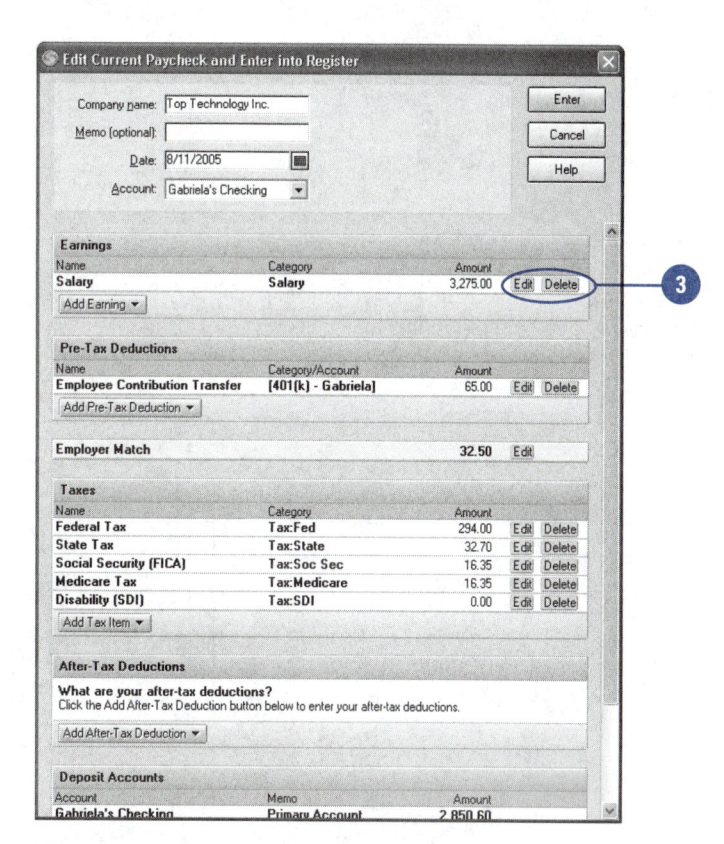

Using Quicken Home Page Features **77**

5. Change the name, if needed, select the category that you want to use to track this expense, type the amount, and click OK.

6. When you are finished making changes, or if you don't need to make any changes to the transaction, click Enter (as in this example). Or, if you are recording a payment, click Record Payment.

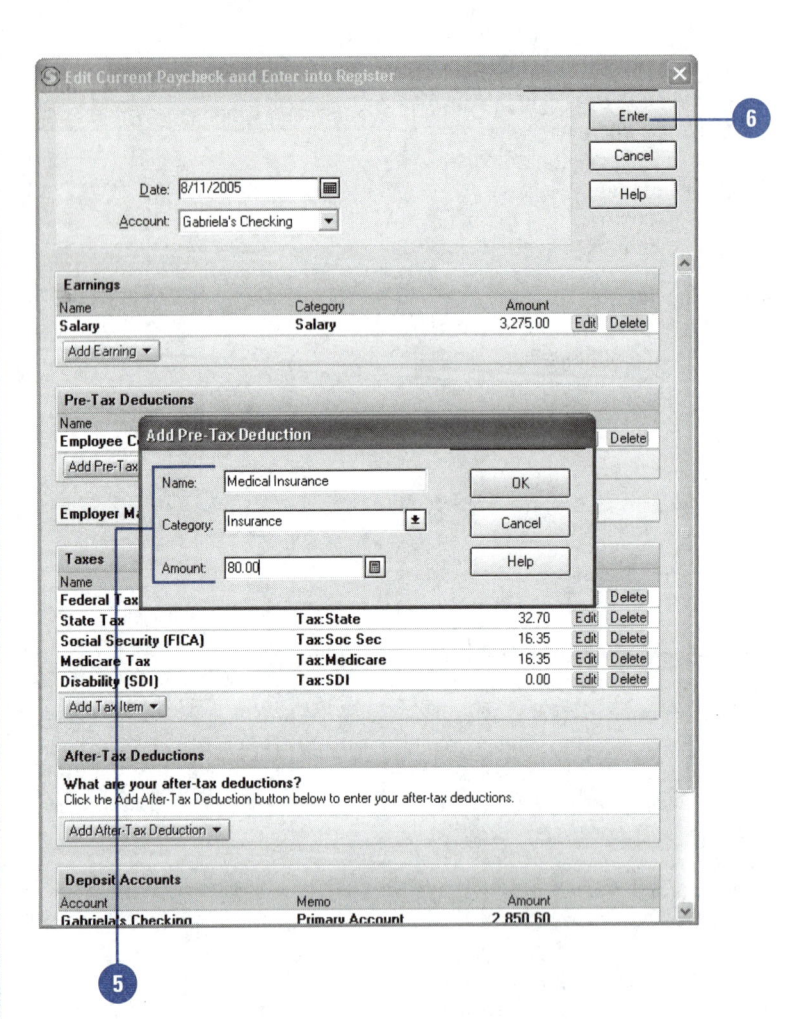

Edit Transactions

1. To edit all future instances of a transaction, select the transaction and click Edit.

2. Make any changes needed, keeping in mind that these changes will take effect for all future transactions for this account.

3. Click OK to save the changes.

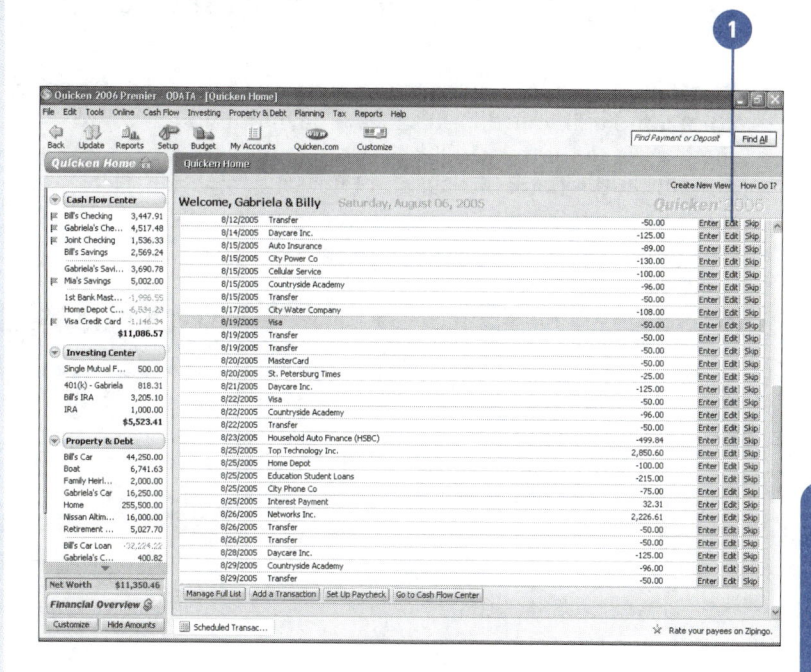

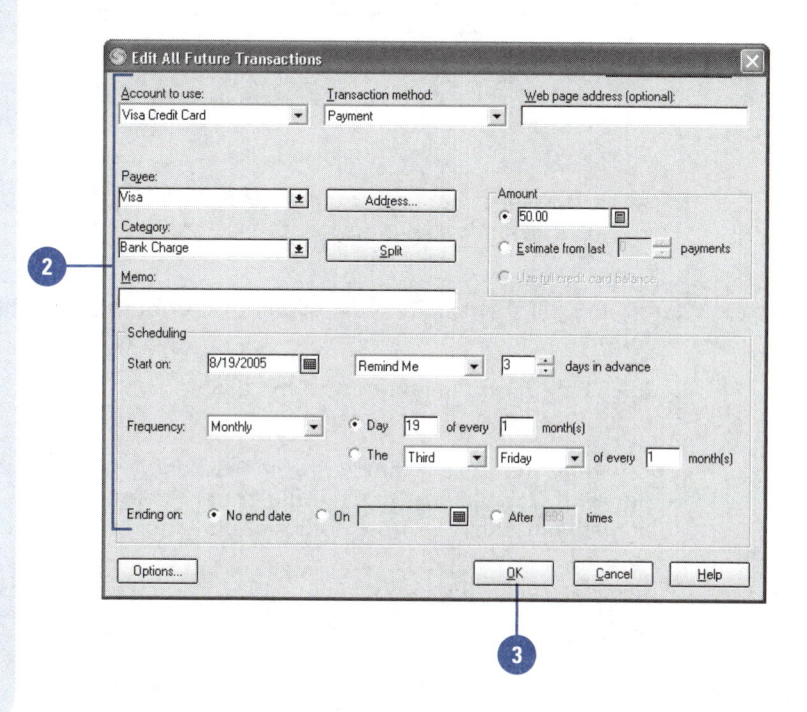

Using Quicken Home Page Features **79**

Tracking Transactions with Multiple Categories

If you want to track a transaction between different categories, you can add up to 30 categories. For example, if you want to track a payment you make to a credit card, for which part of the payment goes to the principal balance and part goes to satisfy interest, you could track this transaction under the Bank Charge and Interest categories. Here's how you track transactions with multiple categories:

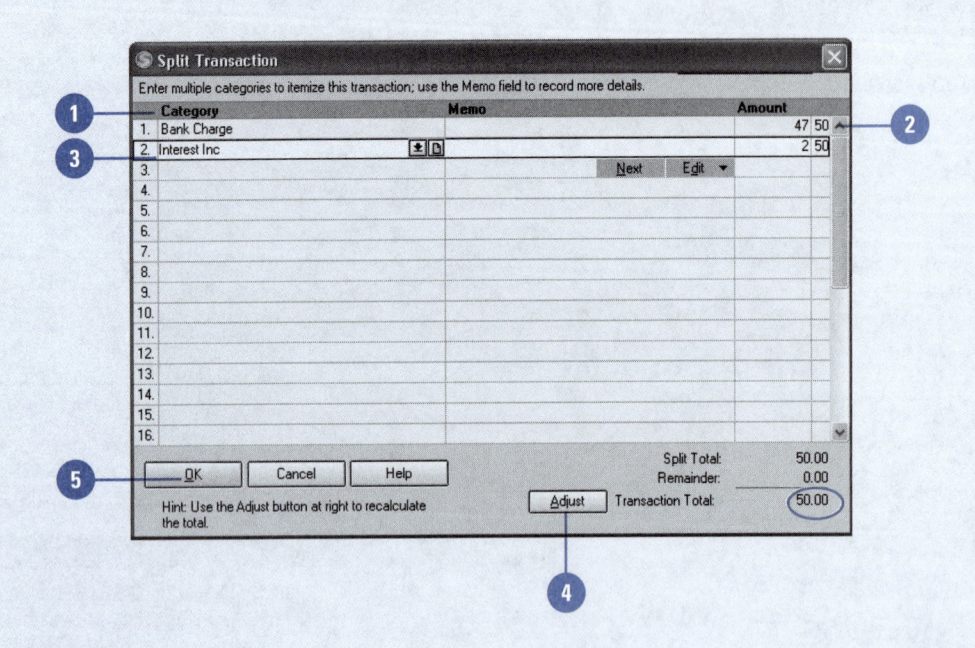

1. After you select the first category from the Category drop-down in either the Edit All Future Transactions window or the Create Scheduled Transaction window, click Split (not shown).

2. In the Split Transaction window, in the Amount box, type the amount you want to track for the first category.

3. Click the second line and from the drop-down menu, select the second category. Then type the amount for that category.

4. Create as many categories as you need and when you are finished, click Adjust. The figure in Transaction Total should equal the total amount of the transaction. If it does not, adjust your split amounts until the total equals the correct amount.

5. Click OK to complete the split.

Skip Transactions

1. To skip the current transaction—for example, if you don't intend to apply a transaction for the current time period (for example, for the current month)—click Skip.

2. Click Yes to skip the current transaction or No to cancel. If you click Yes, the transaction will show up in the Bills and Scheduled Transactions list the next time it is due.

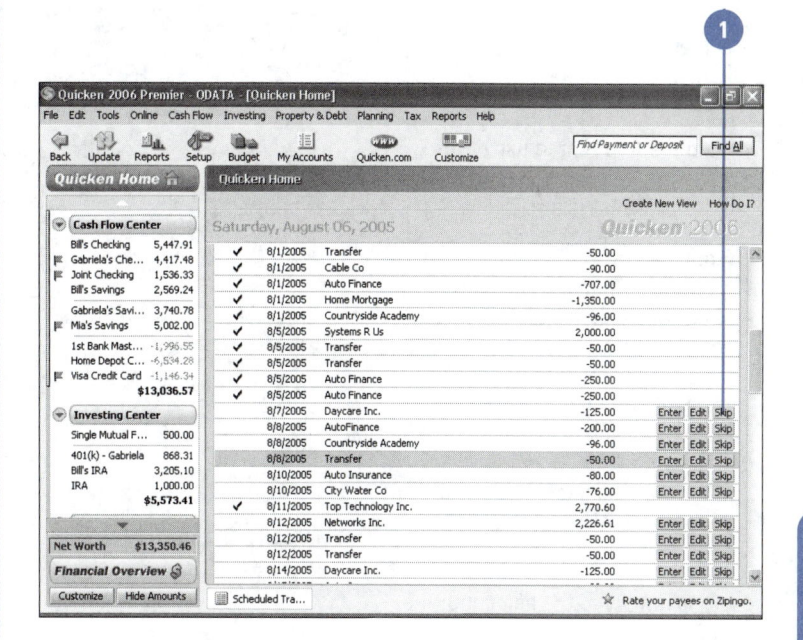

Using Quicken Home Page Features

Add a New Transaction

1. Click Add a Transaction.

2. From the Account to use drop-down menu, select the account that this transaction affects.

3. From the Transaction method drop-down menu, select the type of transaction. In Payee, type the name of the recipient (a person, a company, or for money transfers, the name of the account) to which the transaction is being made, if applicable. From Category drop-down menu, select the category you want tracked for this transaction.

4. In Amount, type the amount of the transaction. If you used split transactions, the amount will already be there, but will be grayed out so that you can't enter an amount.

5. In the Scheduling section, select or enter the begin, end, and frequency information for the transaction. If this is a one-time transaction, from the Frequency drop-down menu, select Only Once. You don't have to complete any of the other scheduling information.

6. Click OK.

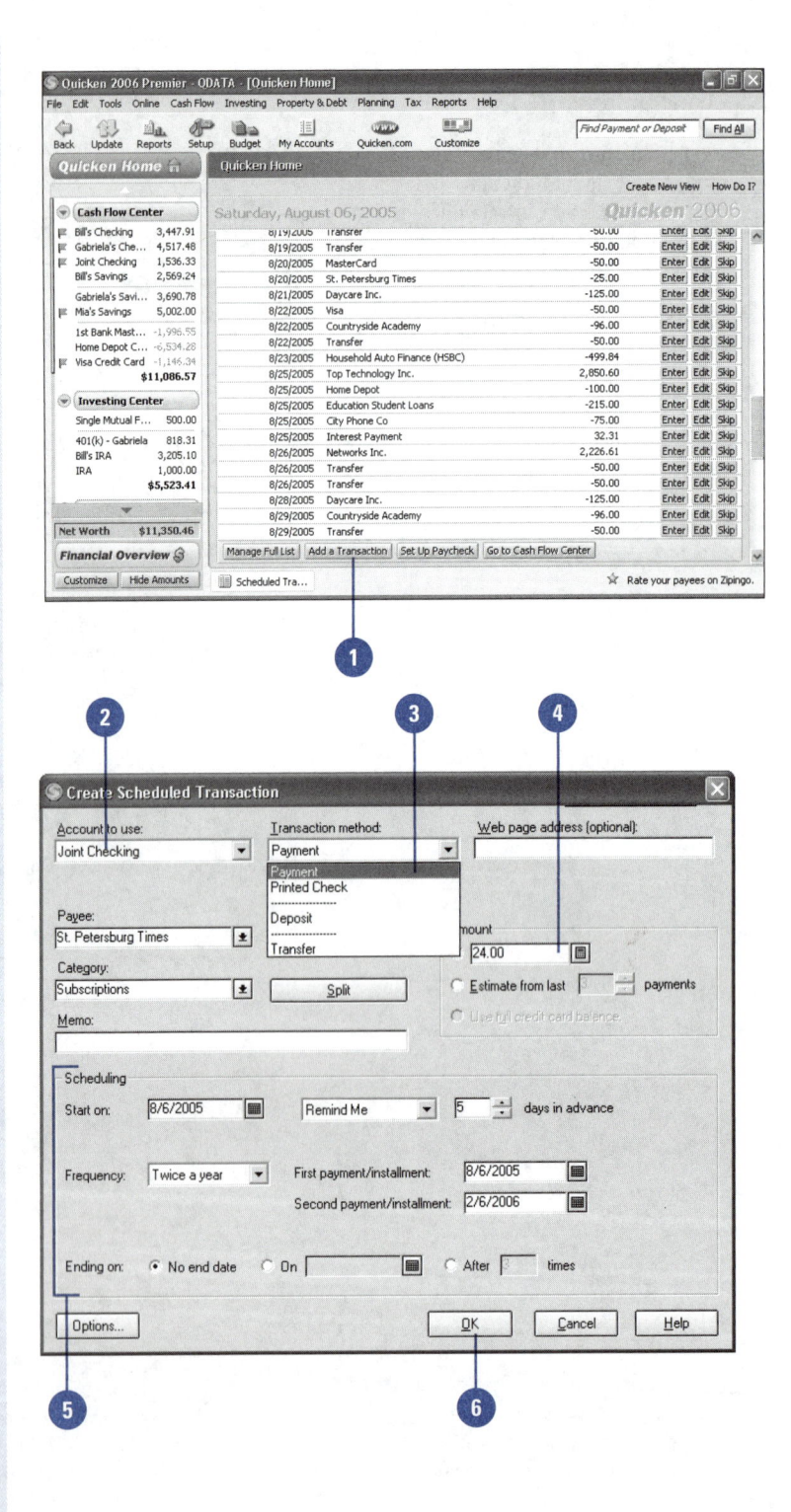

Create an Alternate View of the Transactions

1. To change the transactions you see, from the Show drop-down menu, select an option.

2. To move forward or backward a month, click the forward arrow (>) or the backward arrow (<).

Did You Know?

You can use the Options menu or the buttons to perform tasks. Many of the tasks covered in "Using Bills and Scheduled Transactions" are accessible from the Options menu and the buttons below the transaction list. A check mark next to an item on the Options menu indicates that the option is active.

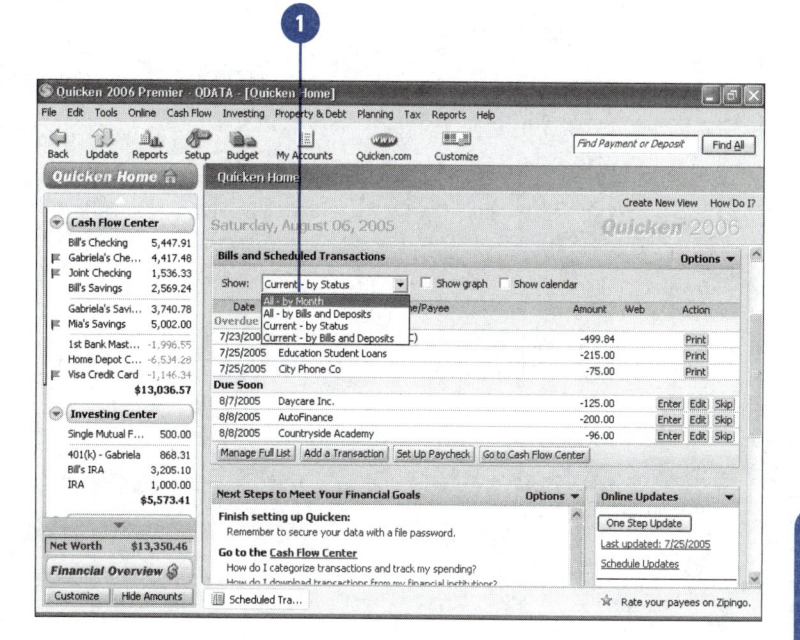

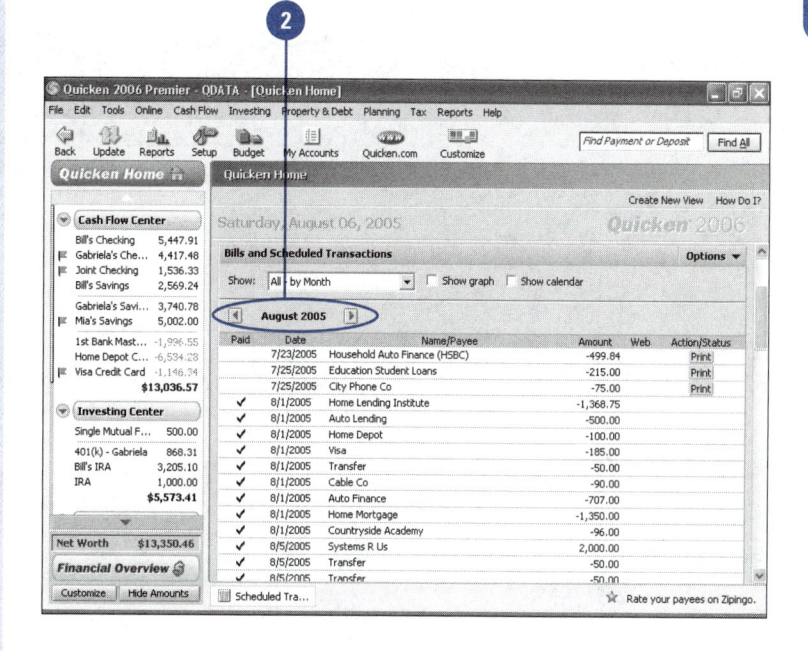

Using Quicken Home Page Features 83

③ To see a bar graph view of your finances, select Show graph. Hover your mouse over a bar on the graph to view your account for that time period.

④ To view calendars with the dates of all your transactions boldfaced, select Show calendar.

⑤ Click a day on the calendar to view the transactions for that month in detail. You can print this calendar to keep as a reminder or reference when paying your bills.

⑥ Double-click a day to view the transactions for that day. You can even perform actions from here, such as creating a new transaction and editing a transaction.

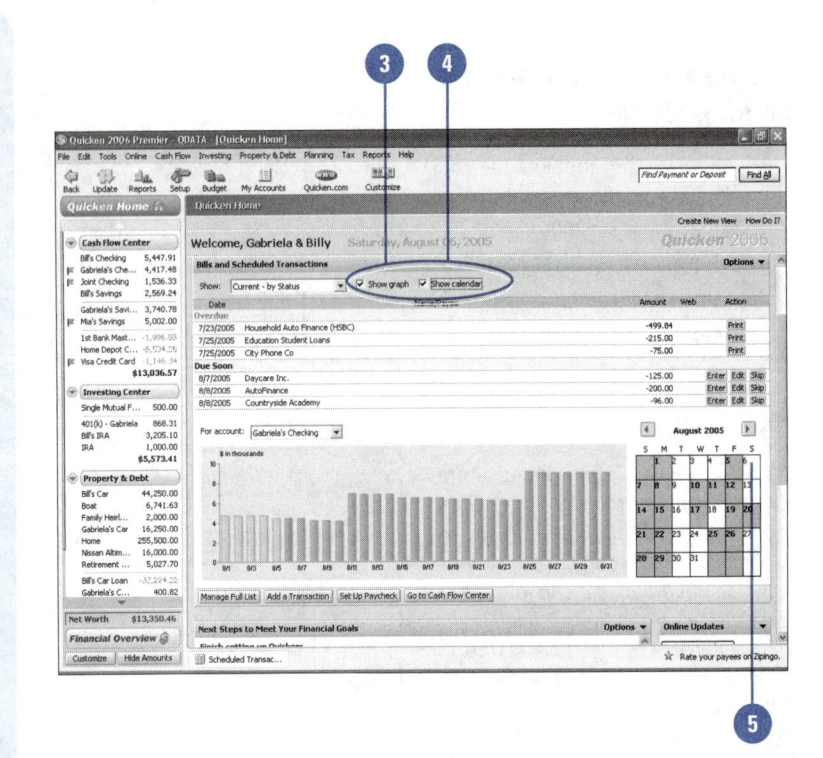

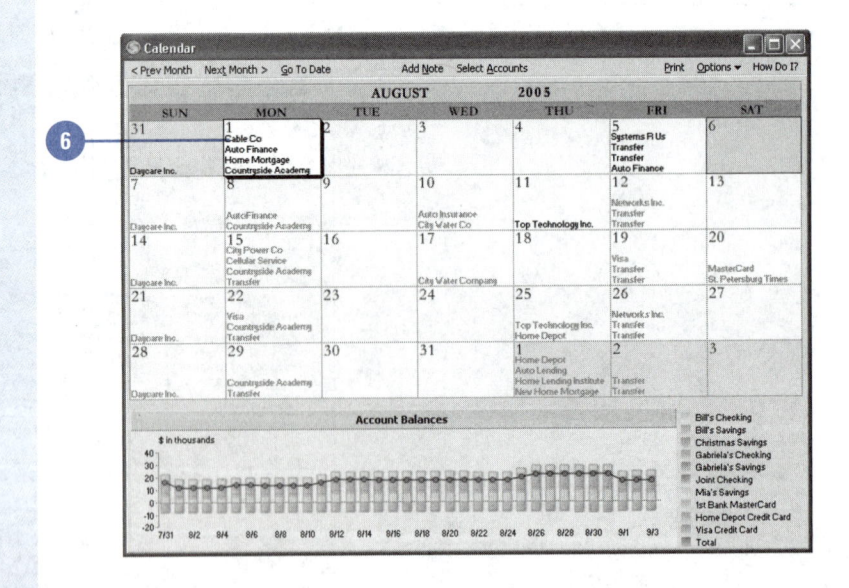

7. To view your total account balances for a specific day, hover your mouse over a day on the bar graph. The day is automatically highlighted on the calendar to show you the transactions for that day.

8. To add a note to a day on the calendar, right-click the day and select Note.

9. Type your note and click Save. The note shows up on the calendar as a small sticky note, which you can click to open and then view or delete it.

10. When you are finished using the calendar and ready to return to the Quicken Home page, close the calendar.

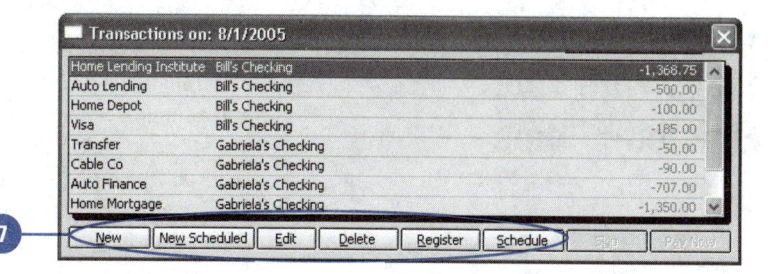

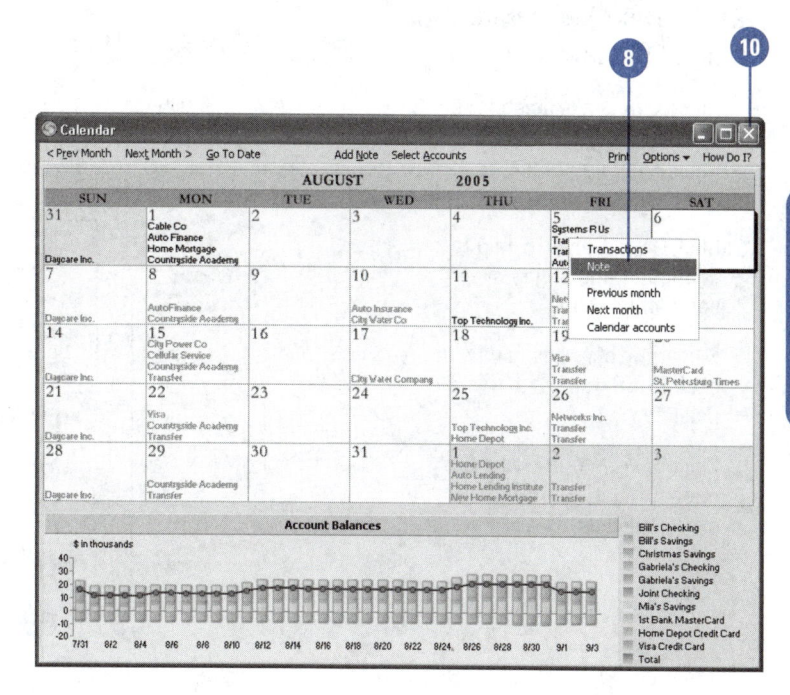

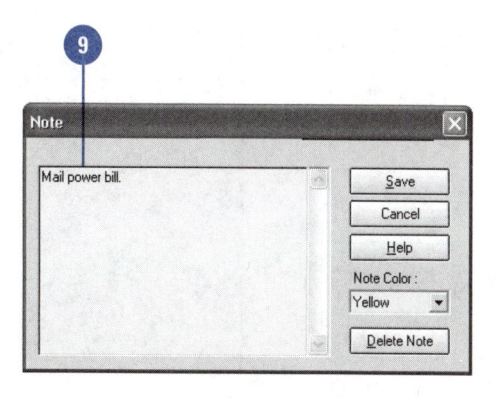

Using Quicken Home Page Features **85**

Taking the Next Steps with Your Financial Goals

We are almost finished reviewing the Quicken Home page. We've covered a lot of ground with the activity centers, the big picture, net worth, and transactions. You've spent some time setting up your financial goals and accounts, entering transactions, and setting up reminders to help you stay on track. So where do you go from here? The last section on the Quicken Home page is Next Steps to Meet Your Financial Goals. This section contains stepping-stones to areas in Quicken where you can adjust your financial goals and then proceed with managing your finances and meeting your financial goals.

Take the Next Steps with Your Financial Goals

1. Review the links listed for each activity center and click any of the links to go to an area of interest.

2. Click Go to Guided Setup to change or complete any of the setup information.

3. Make any changes needed and click Exit Setup when you are finished.

4. Click Review Your Goals to open the Set Your Goals section of the Quicken Guided Setup.

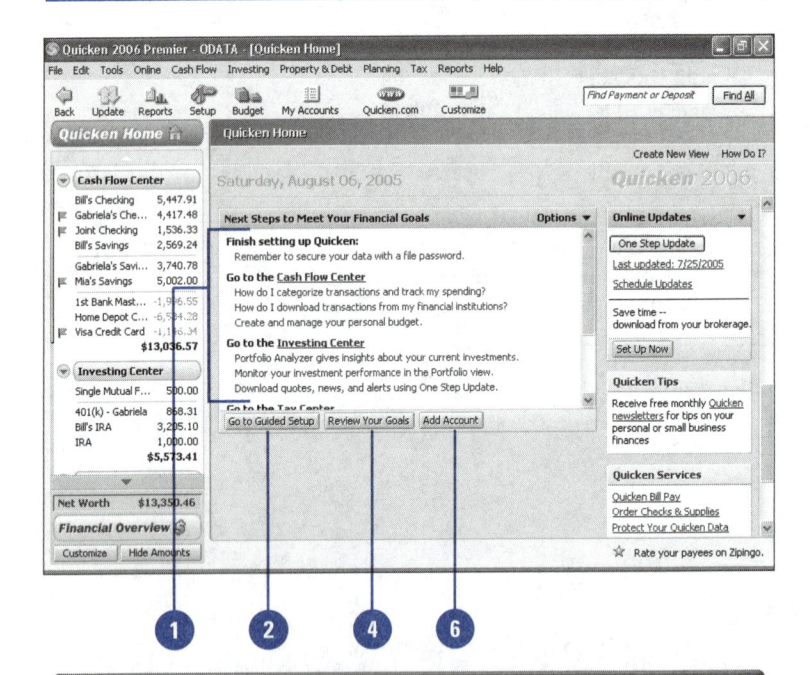

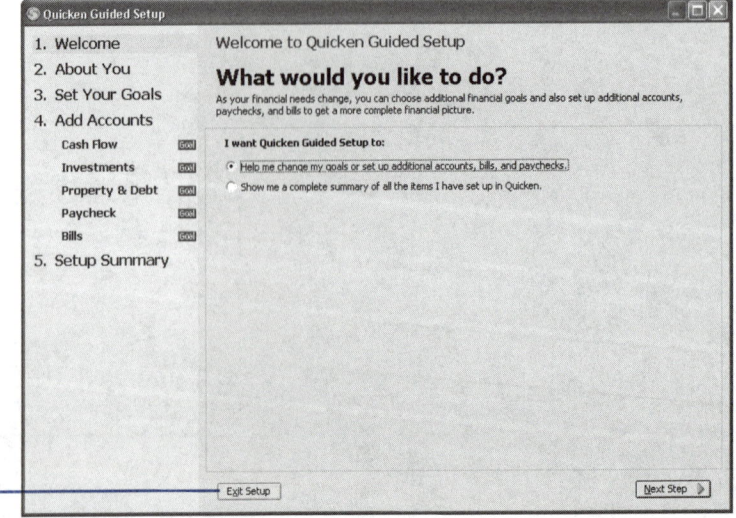

86

5. Remove or add goals as needed and click Exit Setup when you are finished.

6. Click Add Account to open the Quicken Account Setup window.

7. Enter information for a new account and click Next to continue through and complete the setup.

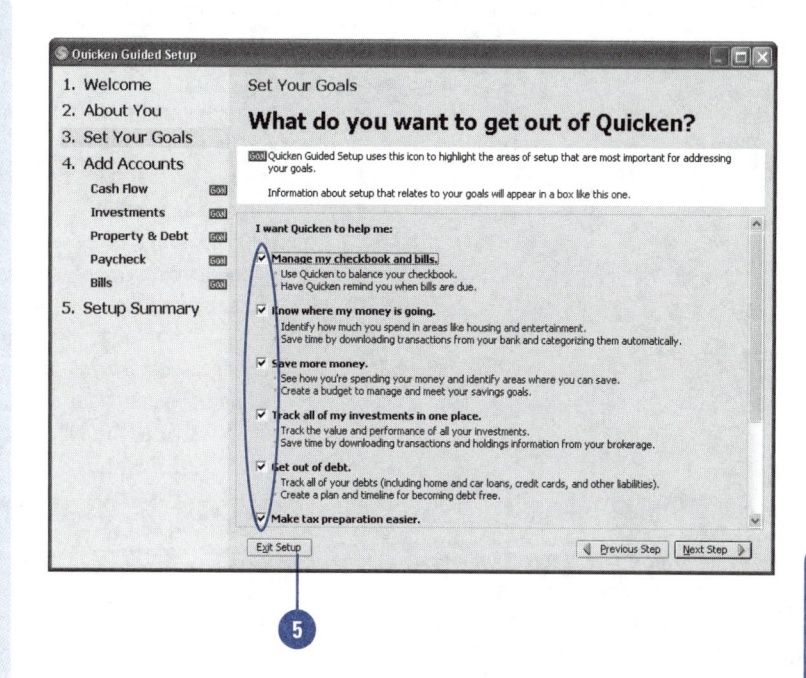

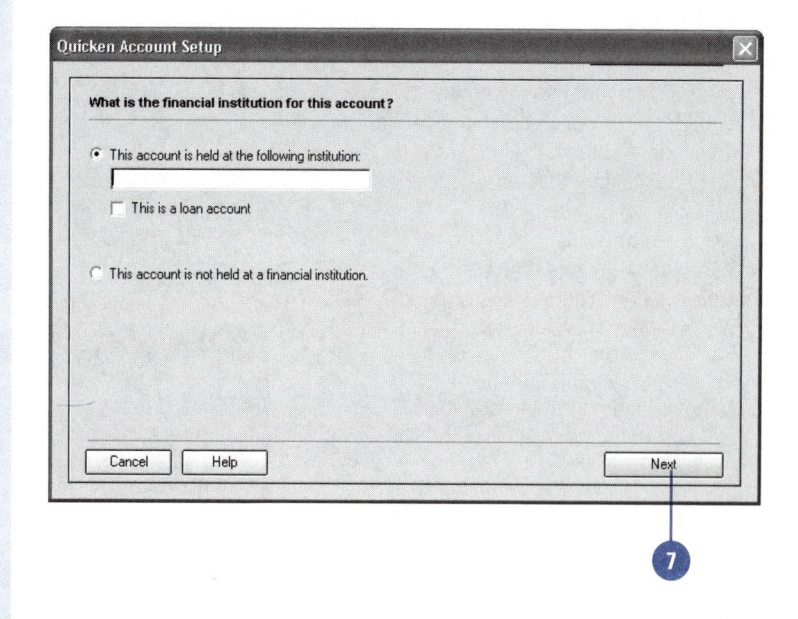

Using Quicken Home Page Features **87**

Using Online Updates

There are a few extras on the Quicken Home page that you can use to make your life easier when it comes to managing your financial goals and maintaining all your accounts. One of them is online updates, which you can use to tell Quicken which accounts you want to download cleared transactions or send online payments, when, and how often. You can also select account information that you want to upload to Quicken.com to access via the Internet. We already covered online accounts when we set up your accounts in Quicken Guided Setup. Only the accounts that you have set up for online access are listed for you to choose from. Remember that you have to have your copy of Quicken registered before you can use this feature. If your bank or creditor offers online access to your account information, you should have a login ID and password. You will need this information to set up online updates.

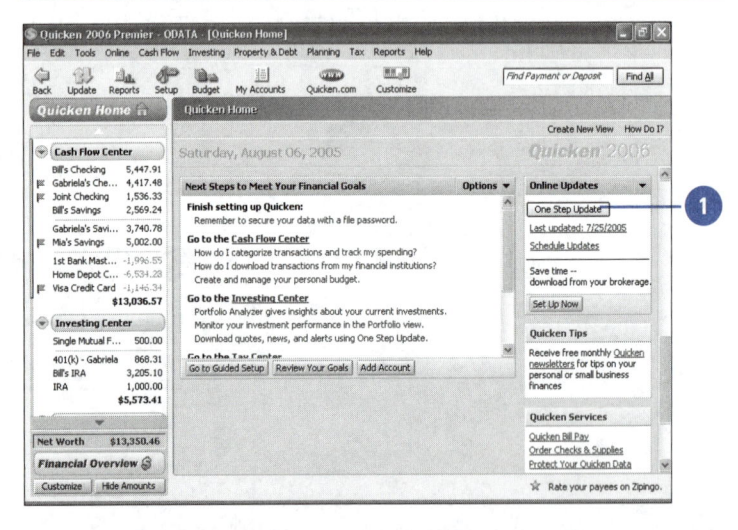

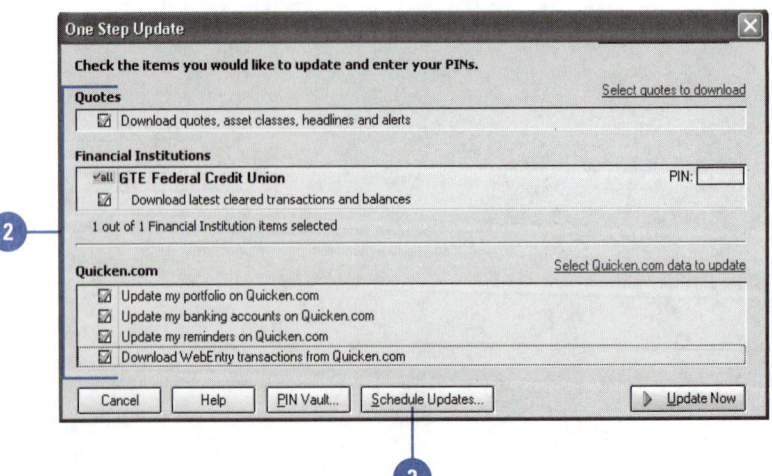

Use the Online Updates

1. Click One Step Setup. If you have not set up any of your accounts for online updates, you are prompted to complete the setup. Also, If you have not already registered Quicken, you are prompted to do so.

2. In Quotes select the download quotes check box to download investment quotes. In Financial institutes, select the accouns you want to download. In Quicken.com, select any information you want uploaded to Quicken.com. A green checkmark means an item is selected.

3. To select the information you want to download and/or update, click Schedule Updates.

See Also

See "Registering Quicken" on page 8 for more information on registering your copy of Quicken.

4 Select the information for which you want to schedule times to download.

5 Select the days on which you want the update to run and then from the At drop-down menu, select the time. Updates run within 15 minutes of the time you select.

6 Select when you would like to be prompted to enter your password.

7 To set up a PIN Vault password, click PIN Vault. A PIN Vault password is required in order to use scheduled updates.

8 Click Next.

Did You Know?

You can use online updates to always keep your accounts up-to-date. *You should take advantage of the online updates. Using online updates to download your account transactions and investment quotes and also send online payments enables you to always keep your accounts up-to-date with the latest information. When you download your transactions, Quicken automatically places the transactions on the Downloaded Transactions tabs in each of the appropriate account registers. From there, all you have to do is add the transactions to your register. This saves you time and ensures that your balances and transaction information are accurate, which saves you even more time and frustration when it's time to balance your accounts.*

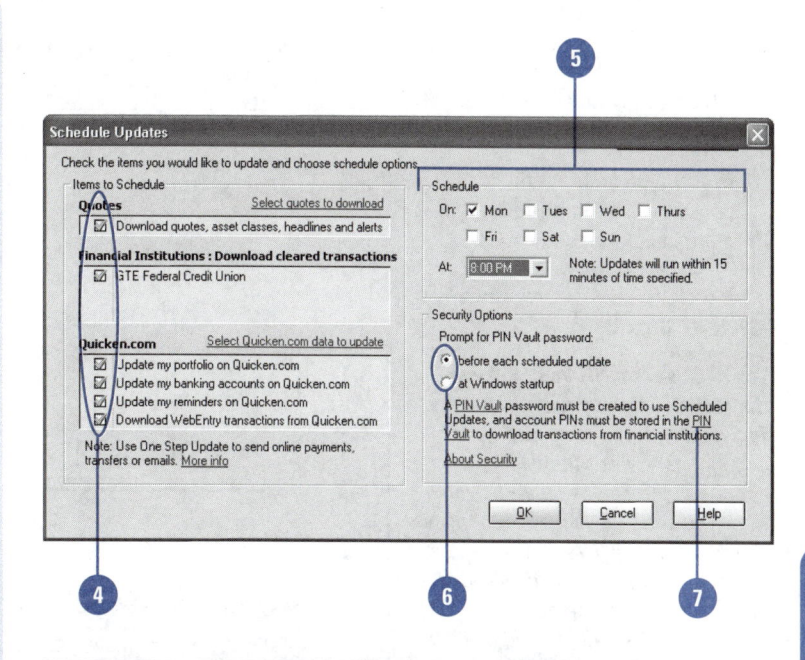

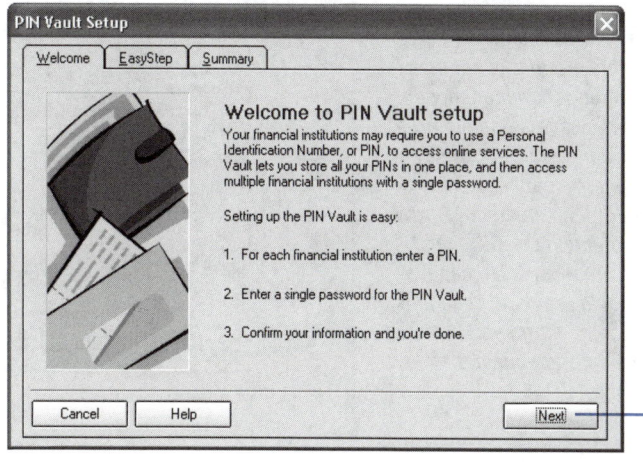

See Also

See "Setting Up Remote Access to Your Accounts" on page 61 for more information on using Quicken.com.

⑨ Select the financial institution for which you want to enter the account password and click Next.

⑩ In PIN type your account password and in Re-enter type it again, and then click Next.

Did You Know?

You can use the PIN Vault to keep track of all your account passwords. *To avoid having to remember your account passwords for all your online accounts, you can use the PIN Vault. After you enter all your account passwords into the PIN Vault, you can set up one password that allows you to access all your online accounts through Quicken. You should do your research, though, before doing this to ensure that your accounts are safe. You need to ensure that your financial institutions offer secure connections, ensure that you have a good Internet service provider that offers secure and private Internet access, secure your computer with a personal firewall and virus protection software, and password-protect your Quicken file. Also, you should regularly change your passwords as an extra security measure—and be sure to update them in the PIN Vault.*

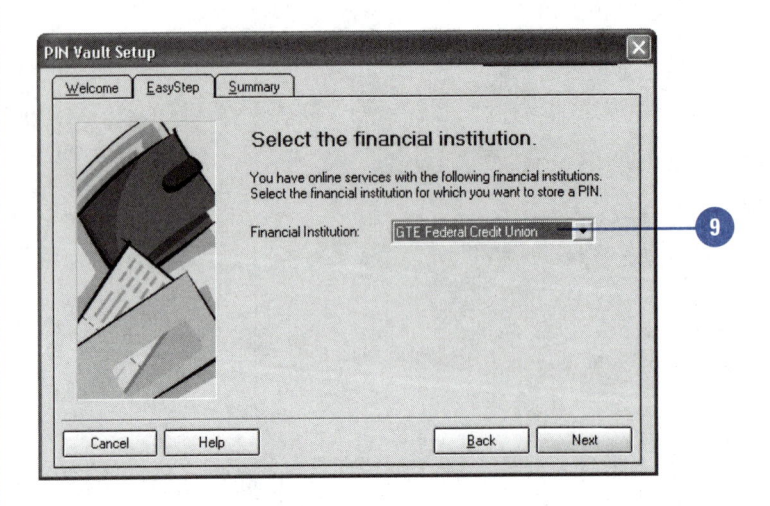

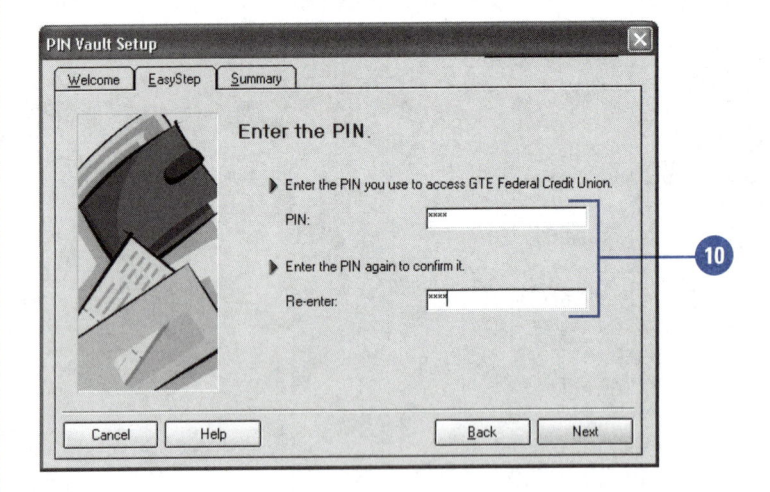

11 In Password, type your PIN vault password. In Re-enter, type it again, and then click Next.

12 Review the PIN information and click Done. If needed, you can change your password information by clicking Change PIN or delete a PIN by selecting it and clicking Delete PIN. In addition, you can print the list by clicking Print.

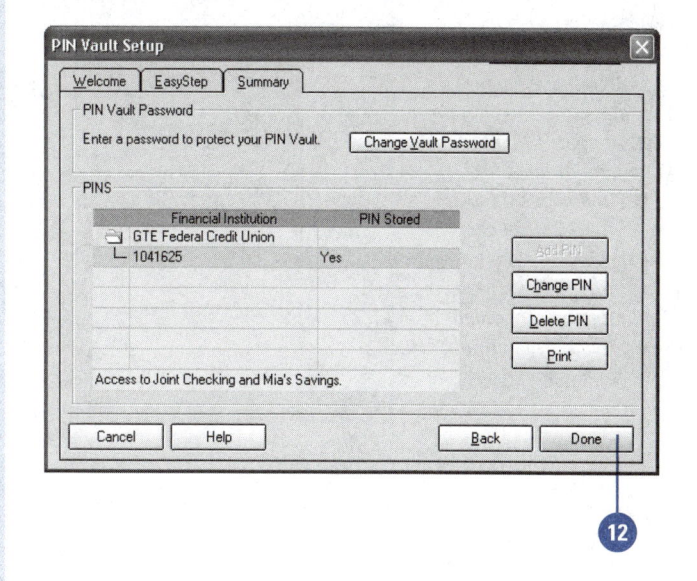

13 Click OK to complete the scheduled updates.

14 Click OK. At the scheduled time, Quicken displays the PIN dialog box, prompts you to type your PIN Vault password, and downloads/uploads the latest transactions. When the transmission is complete, a summary window opens, showing you the accounts that were successfully downloaded.

Did You Know?

Quicken cannot update accounts while it is open. *You cannot have Quicken open when it downloads account information. Instead, you are prompted to enter your PIN Vault password, and the information is downloaded at the designated time. You should see an icon in your Windows taskbar that lets you know it is downloading. If you are in Quicken at the time an update is scheduled to run, Quicken waits until you are out of the program to download the transactions and upload any online payments.*

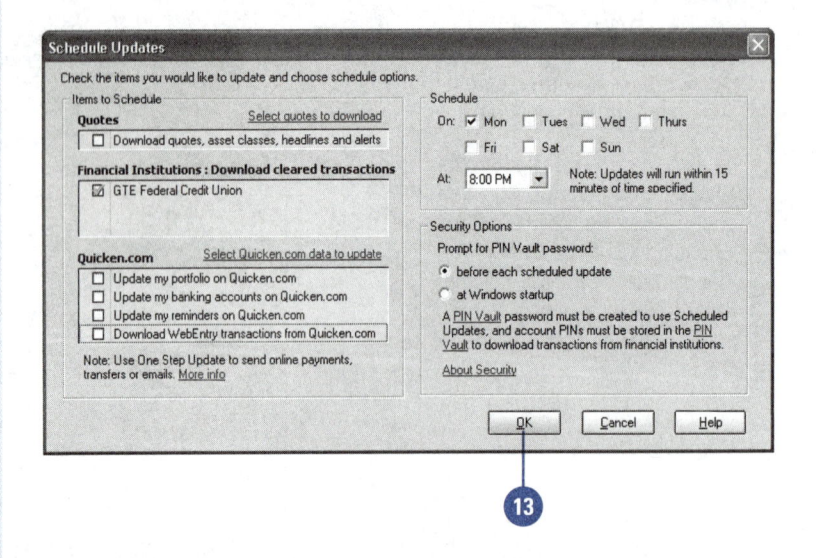

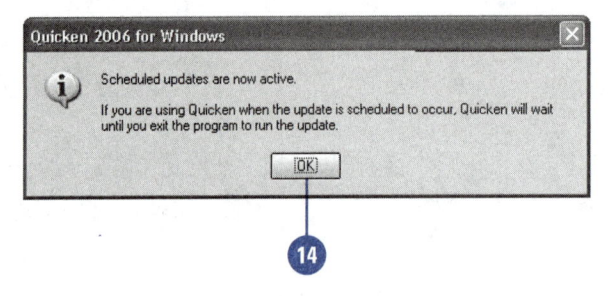

Using Tips and Services

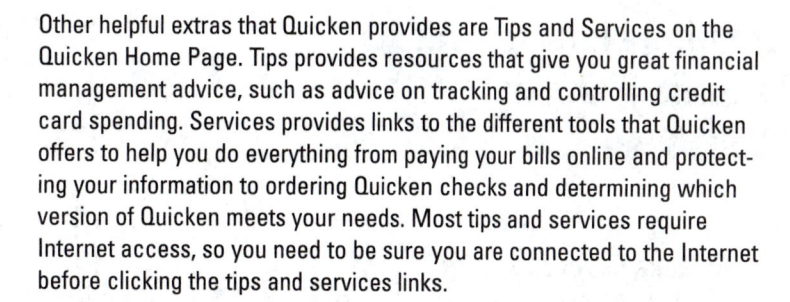

Other helpful extras that Quicken provides are Tips and Services on the Quicken Home Page. Tips provides resources that give you great financial management advice, such as advice on tracking and controlling credit card spending. Services provides links to the different tools that Quicken offers to help you do everything from paying your bills online and protecting your information to ordering Quicken checks and determining which version of Quicken meets your needs. Most tips and services require Internet access, so you need to be sure you are connected to the Internet before clicking the tips and services links.

Use Tips and Services

1. To subscribe to free newsletters with information on personal and business finances and taxes, click Quicken Newsletters.

2. Click any of the Quicken Services links to find out more about the service. For example, click Quicken Bill Pay to get information about Quicken's online bill payment service.

3. The remainder of the links work the same way:

    ◆ Clicking Order Checks & Supplies provides information on Quicken checks and other checking supplies.

    ◆ Clicking Protect Your Quicken Data provides information on PC backup and restoration services.

    ◆ Clicking Get Business Tools for Quicken provides information on Quicken Premier: Home & Business 2006.

    ◆ Clicking Quicken MasterCard provides information on Quicken's MasterCard and how to apply for it.

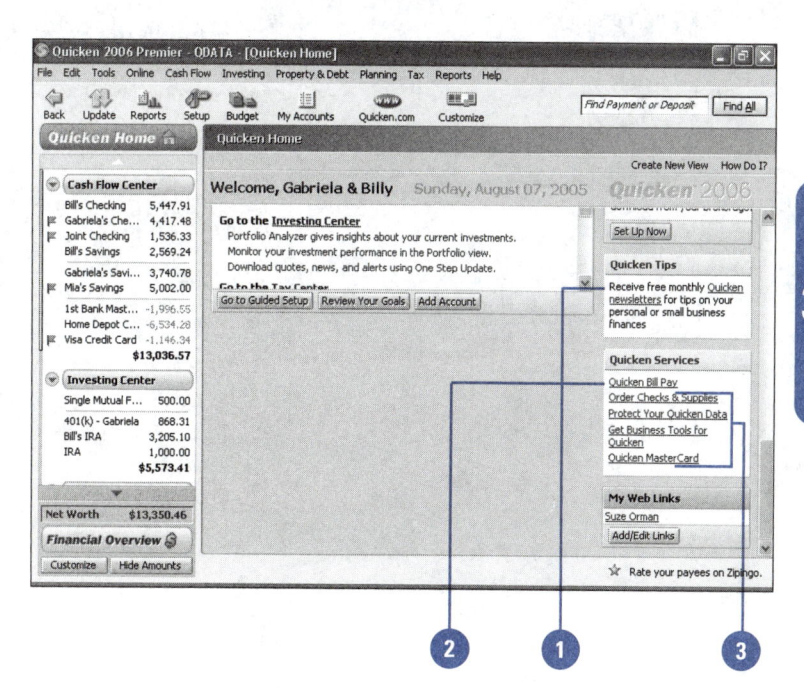

Using Quicken Home Page Features **93**

Creating Links to Your Favorite Financial Websites

One last little extra I want to point out is My Web Links. This is a tool that can be all your own making. If you frequent financial websites that you find useful, you can create links to those sites and keep them in My Web Links.

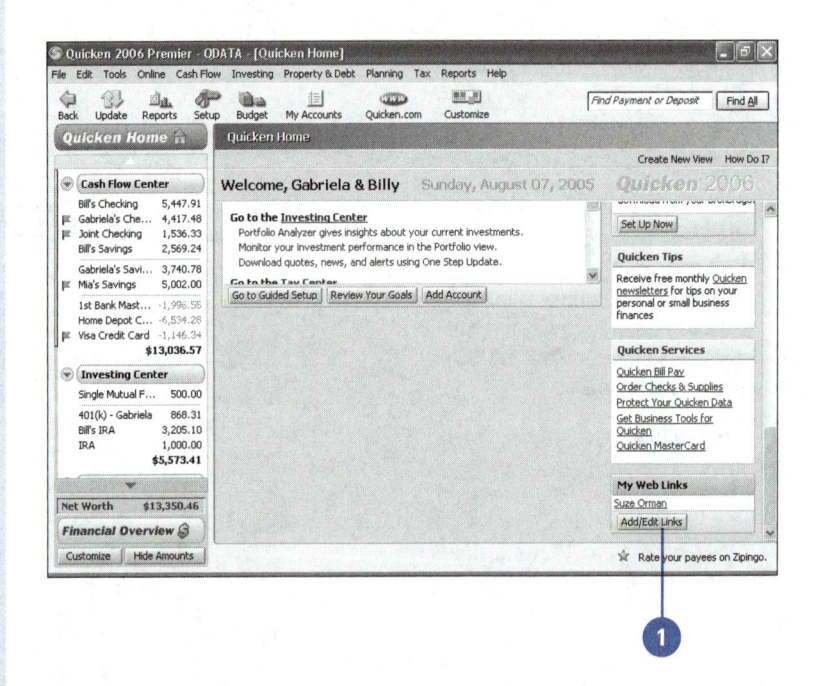

Create Links to Your Favorite Financial Websites

1. Click Add/Edit Links.
2. Click New.

3. In URL, type the Web address. Be sure to leave the http:// before the address (for example, http://www.suzeorman.com).

4. Click in Description and type a brief description of the site and then click OK.

5. Repeat steps 2–4 for each website you want to add.

6. To open the websites you added from the My Web Links section on the Quicken Home page, click a link.

7. Click Add/Edit Links to edit the existing sites or to add new ones.

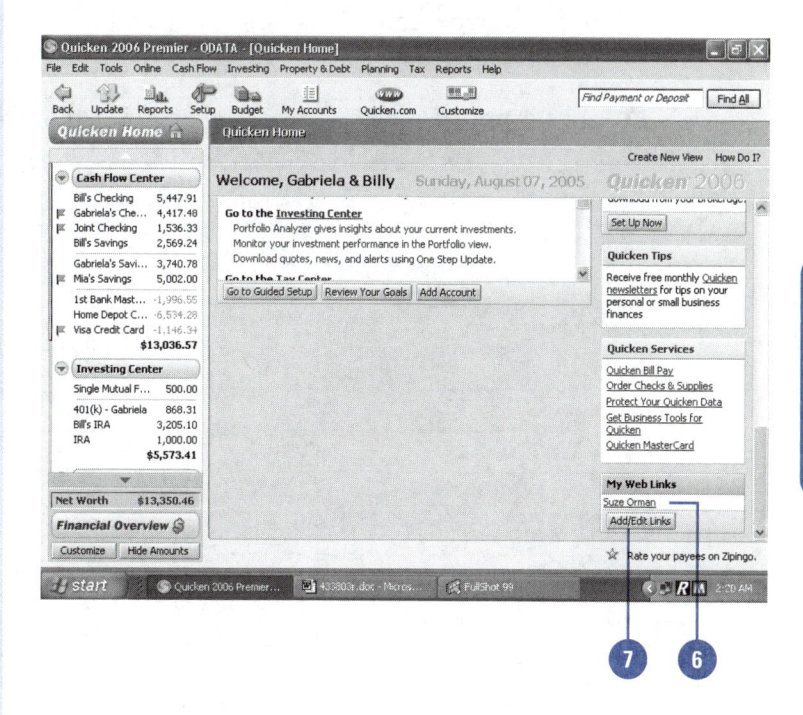

Keyboard Shortcuts

There are alternate ways you can move around in Quicken, other than using the menus or links found on Quicken windows. You can use certain keyboard key combinations, as shown in Table 3.1, to quickly get where you want to go. Keyboard commands are broken down into logical categories. Some shortcut commands require two (or more) keys. To use these shortcuts, you press the first key and then the second. For example, to open the Quicken Home page from anywhere in the program, you hold down the Alt key and then press the Home key.

Table 3.1 Quicken Keyboard Shortcuts

Command	Shortcut	Command	Shortcut
Quicken Features		***Check Features***	
Go to the Quicken Home page	Alt+Home	Cut a field in the register	Shift+Del
Go to the Register	Ctrl+R	Paste a field in the register	Shift+Ins
Write Checks	Ctrl+W	Delete a transaction or split line	Ctrl+D
Go to the calendar	Ctrl+K	Find a transaction	Ctrl+F
View loans	Ctrl+H	Go to a new transaction	Ctrl+N
Go to the Account List	Ctrl+A	Insert a transaction	Ctrl+I
Go to the Category List	Ctrl+C	Memorize a transaction	Ctrl+M
Go to the Class List	Ctrl+L	QuickFill, automatic recall name	Type payee
Go to the Scheduled Transaction List	Ctrl+J	QuickFill, automatic completion	Tab
Go to the Memorized Payee List	Ctrl+T	Record a transaction	Enter or Ctrl+Enter
Print	Ctrl+P	Open the Split Transaction window	Ctrl+S
Select an item in a list	Type the first letter of the item	Go to Transfer	Ctrl+X
Check Features		Void a transaction	Ctrl+V
Decrease date or check number	– (minus key)	***Investment Features***	
Increase date or check number	+ (plus key)	Go to Portfolio view	Ctrl+U
Copy data from the field above the currently selected field in the Split Transaction window	' (single quote key)	Decrease or increase a security price by $1/16$	– (minus key) or + (plus key)
Copy the payee name when the address field is selected in the Write Checks window	' (single quote key)	Select a security	Ctrl+Y
		Help	
Copy a field in the register	Ctrl+Ins	Open the Help contents	F1

Managing Your Spending and Savings Accounts

Introduction

The Spending & Savings Accounts section of the Cash Flow Center allows you to manage all your spending and savings account information. Spending and savings accounts include all your checking and savings accounts.

In the Cash Flow Alerts section, you can set up or change alerts for your spending and savings accounts. In the Spending & Savings Accounts section, you can view basic account information for each of your accounts, such as the beginning and ending balances; you can add new spending and savings accounts; and you can edit existing accounts.

You can also access the register for each of the accounts. In the account registers, you can add, edit, or delete transactions; add downloaded transactions to the register; set up scheduled transactions; search for transactions; transfer funds between accounts; and balance your account. In addition, you can view spending averages for transactions and reports for your spending and savings accounts.

What You'll Do

Set Up New or Edit Existing Cash Flow Alerts

Update Spending and Savings Account Balances

Review, Add, Edit, and Delete Spending and Savings Accounts

Add, Edit, and Delete Spending and Savings Account Transactions

Search for Spending and Savings Transactions

Transfer Funds Between Spending and Savings Accounts

Add Scheduled Spending and Savings Transactions to Your Register

Manage All Your Scheduled Transactions

View Spending and Savings Account Overviews

Balance Your Spending and Savings Accounts

Setting Up New or Editing Existing Cash Flow Alerts

Set Up New and Edit Existing Cash Flow Alerts

1. If you don't already have the Cash Flow Center open, on the account bar, click Cash Flow Center.

2. To take action on an alert, click the account link to open the register, where you can resolve the alert.

3. To view and manage all your alerts, click Show all alerts to open the Alerts Center window.

4. To create or edit Cash Flow alerts, click the Setup tab. You can also click the Set Up Alerts button in the Cash Flow Alerts section of the Cash Flow Center.

See Also

See "Using Alerts" on page 74 for more information on creating and changing alerts.

You can set up alerts in the Cash Flow Center to remind or warn you of actions you need to take for your bank, credit card, and bill accounts (for example, to notify you that your balance is close to your limit or that scheduled transactions are due).

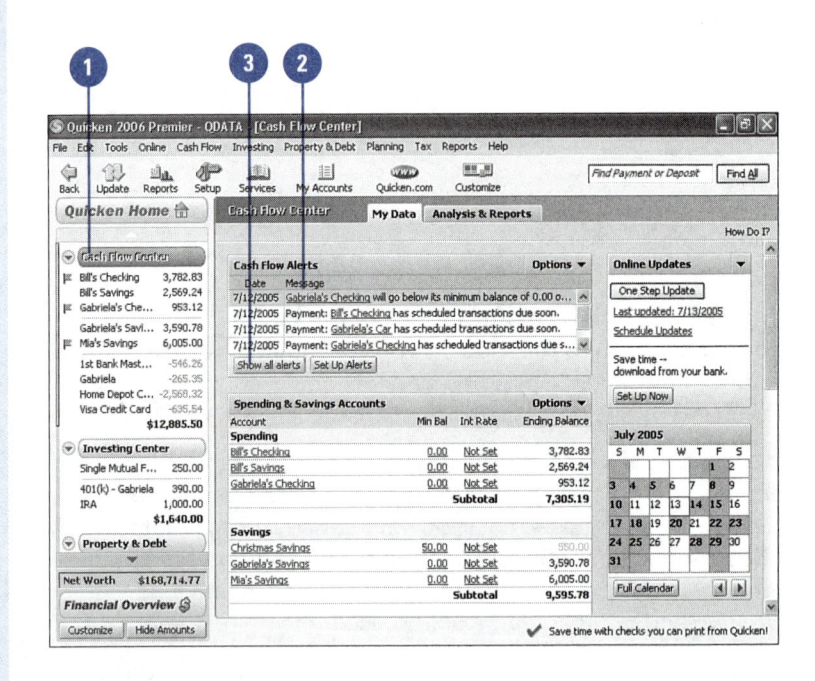

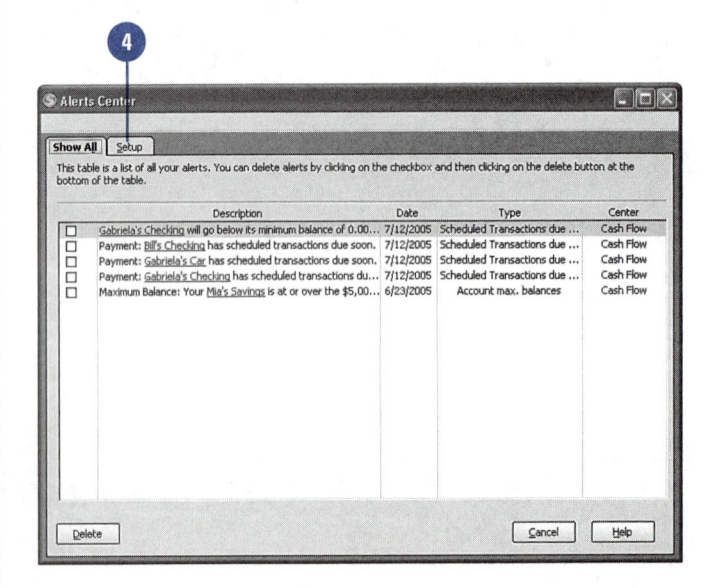

Updating Spending and Savings Account Balances

Before you start working with your spending and savings accounts, you should check to be sure that you are working with up-to-date balances and transactions. If you set up a spending or savings account for online access, you can use One Step Update to automatically update your account balance and transactions each time you open Quicken and connect to the Internet or each time you choose to update your balances. However, you can also update your balance manually, if needed. This task shows how you update your account balances by using One Step Update.

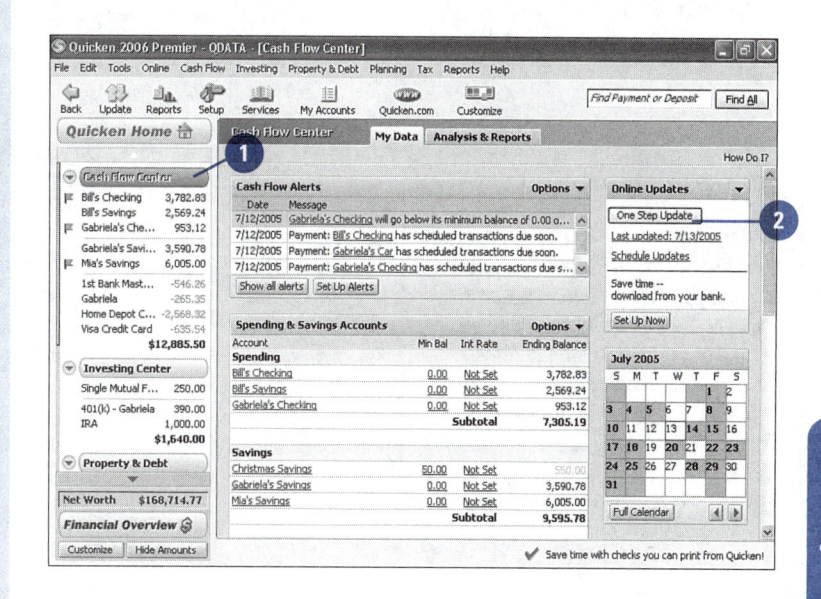

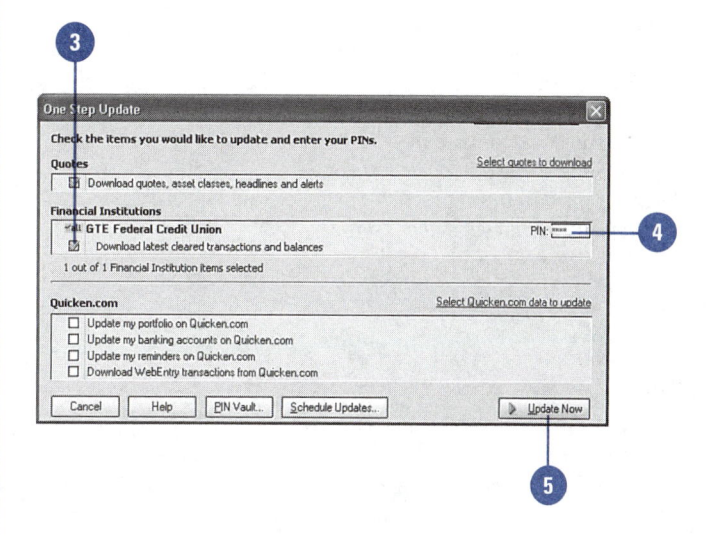

Update Spending and Savings Account Balances

1. If you don't already have the Cash Flow Center open, on the account bar, click Cash Flow Center.

2. Click One Step Update. If you set up a PIN vault password, you are prompted to enter your password before you can move to the next step.

3. Select the account(s) you want to update. A green check mark means the account is selected.

4. Type the password(s) for each account.

5. Click Update Now. The online Update Summary opens, unless you have previously opted for it not to open after downloads.

See Also

If you want to update your account manually, see "Balancing Your Spending and Savings Accounts" on page 120.

See "Using Online Updates" on page 88 for more information on updating accounts at Quicken.com, how to set up One Step Update, and how to schedule updates.

Managing Your Spending and Savings Accounts **99**

6. Notice that the download summary lists the accounts you are downloading, the number of transactions and balance for each account, and the dates and times you last downloaded.

7. If desired, go straight to your accounts from here by clicking Go to Portfolio (which you see only if you chose to download quotes) or Go to Register.

8. Click Done.

Did You Know?

You can turn off the online update summary. If you don't want to see a summary each time you download your account information—only if there are problems with the download—select the option Don't show this summary again unless there is an error.

See Also

See "Balancing Your Spending and Savings Accounts" on page 120 for information on updating your caccount manually. See "Using Online Updates" on page 88 for information on updating account Quicken.com, how to set up One Step Update, and how to schedule updates.

Reviewing, Adding, Editing, and Deleting Spending and Savings Accounts

The Spending & Savings Accounts section of the Cash Flow Center is divided between your expenditure accounts and your savings accounts. In this section, you can add new accounts and edit accounts by using the Account List window, where you can also access account registers, set up online access, and completely remove an account from Quicken by deleting it.

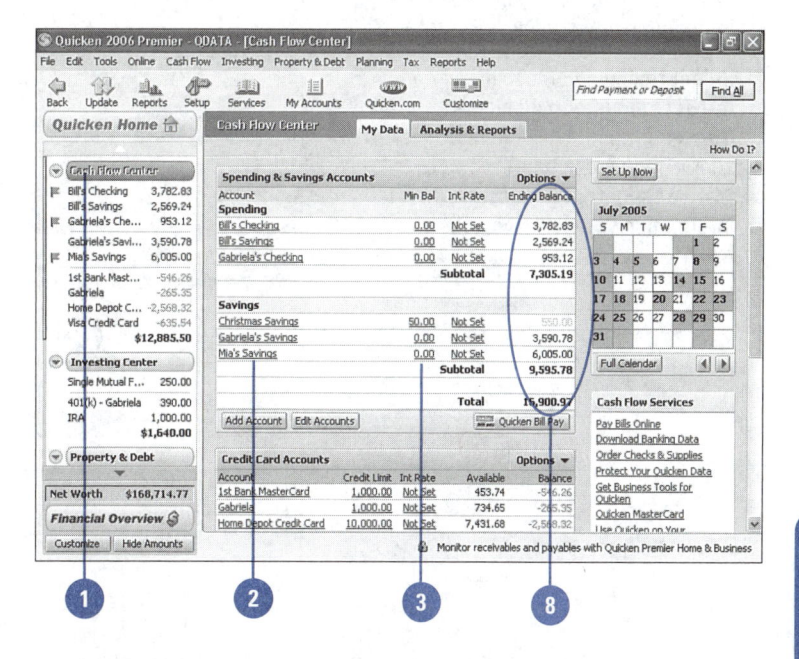

Review Spending and Savings Accounts

1. If you don't already have the Cash Flow Center open, on the account bar, click Cash Flow Center.

2. Click an account name to open the register for that account.

3. The minimum balance for each account is listed. If the account has a minimum balance and you have not set it, zeros appear. Click the zeros to open the Account Details window.

4. In Max Balance and Min Balance, type the maximum and minimum account balances allowed, if applicable.

5. If you have not entered the interest rate, in the Interest Rate box, type the interest rate. You can also click Not Set in the Spending & Savings Accounts section of the Cash Flow Center.

6. If the account is not in the correct section, from Account Location, select the appropriate section.

7. Enter any other account information, such as the account number or bank contact name and number, and click OK.

8. An ending balance is provided for each account, along with spending subtotals and savings subtotals, and a comprehensive total for all spending and savings accounts.

Managing Your Spending and Savings Accounts **101**

Add Spending or Savings Accounts

1. To add a new spending or savings account, click Add Account.

2. Type or select the name of the financial institution where this account is held and click Next.

3. Select Online if you can download the account information directly from your financial institution (as shown in this example) or select Manual to enter the account information yourself. Then click Next.

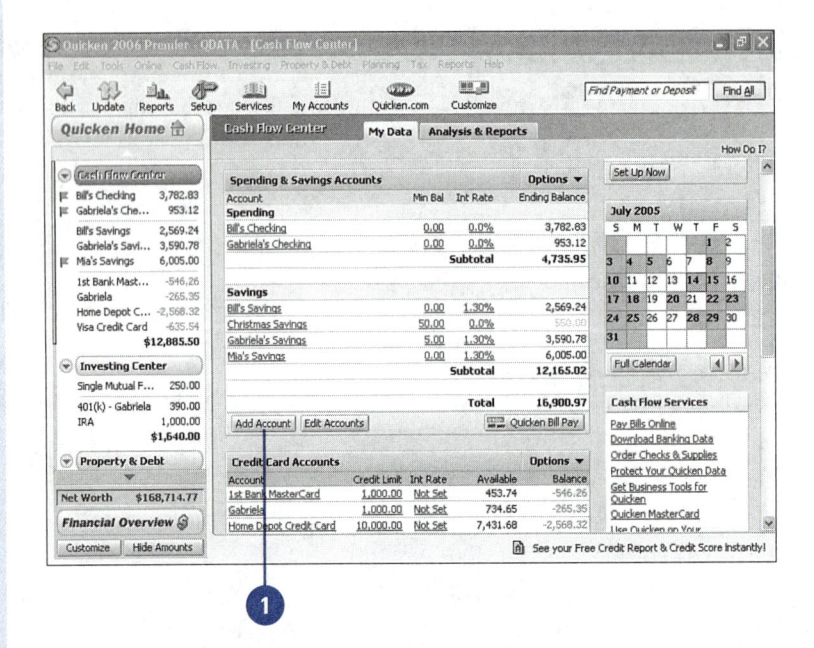

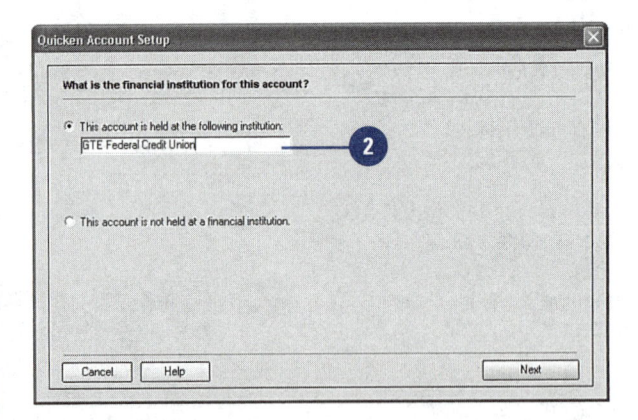

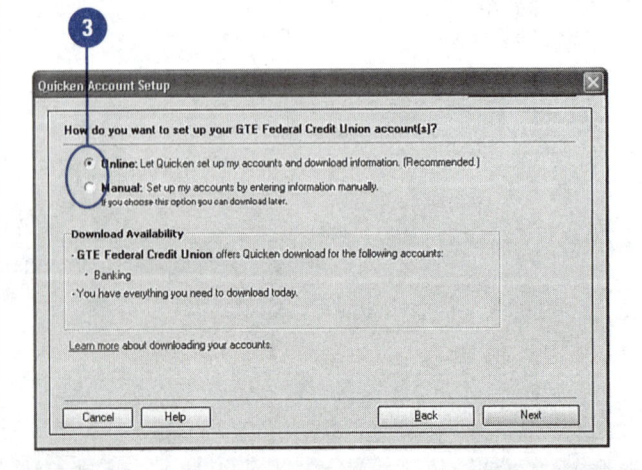

④ Make sure you are connected to the Internet, type your login ID (Customer ID) and password (PIN), and click Next. Quicken connects to your financial institution and locates your account(s).

⑤ Type the name of the new Quicken account and click OK.

⑥ Click Done.

⑦ On Online Update Summary, click Done.

⑧ Repeat steps 1–7 for each spending or savings account you want to add.

Did You Know?

You must have a login ID and password to download your bank account information. *In order to download your bank account information, you must already have a login ID and password. If you don't, you can click the Sign Up Now button to request the ID and password, or you can call your financial institution. If you don't have online access now, you can enter your bank information manually, and when you get your login ID and password, you can start downloading your account information from then on.*

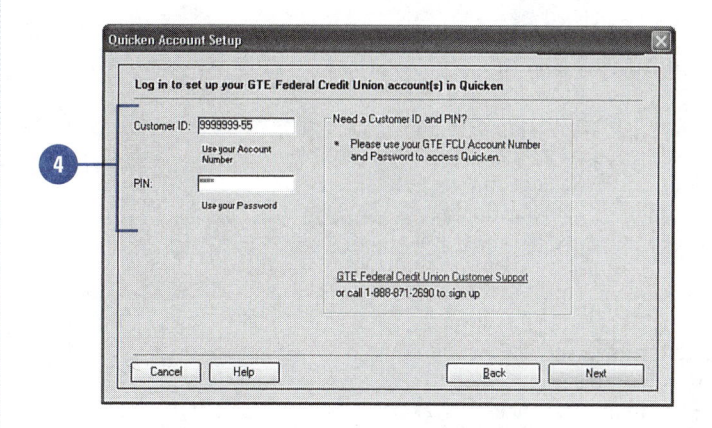

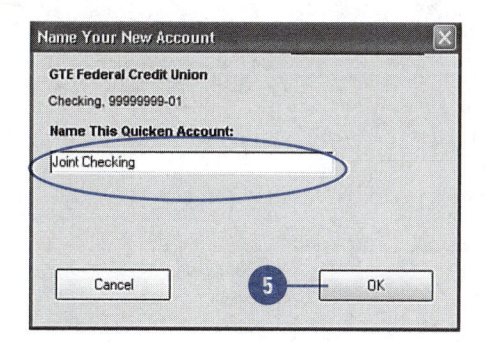

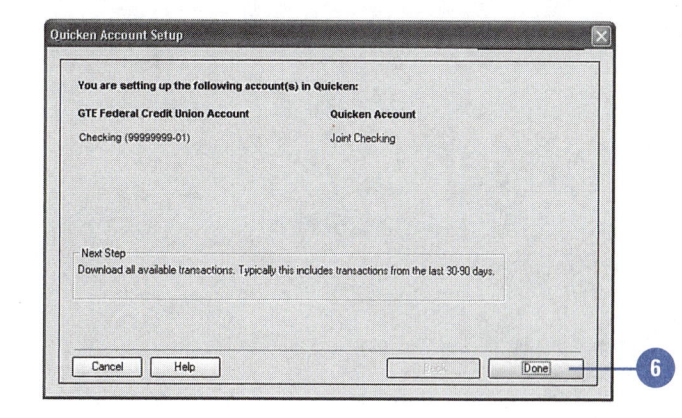

Managing Your Spending and Savings Accounts **103**

Edit Spending and Savings Accounts

1. To update account information, in the Spending & Savings Accounts section in the Cash Flow Center, click Edit Accounts.

2. To update an account, in the Spending Accounts or Savings Accounts sections of the Account List window, select the account you want to update and then click Edit.

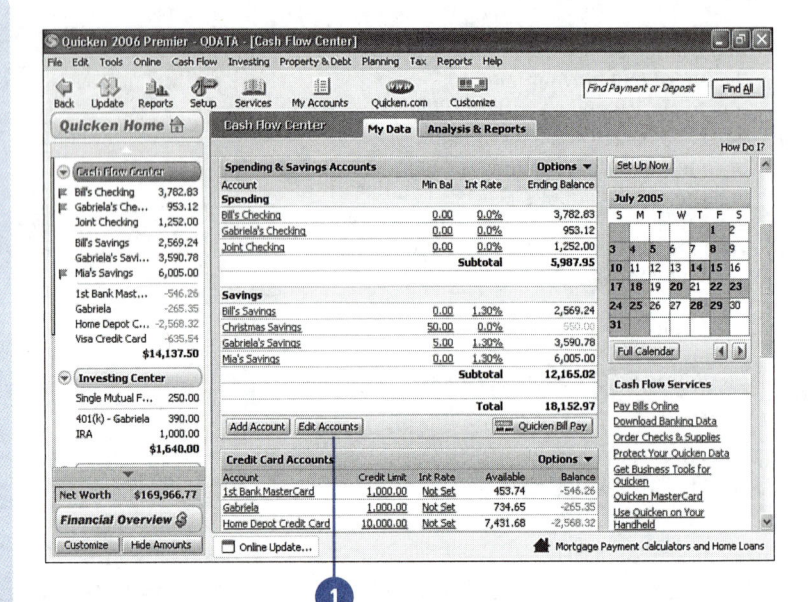

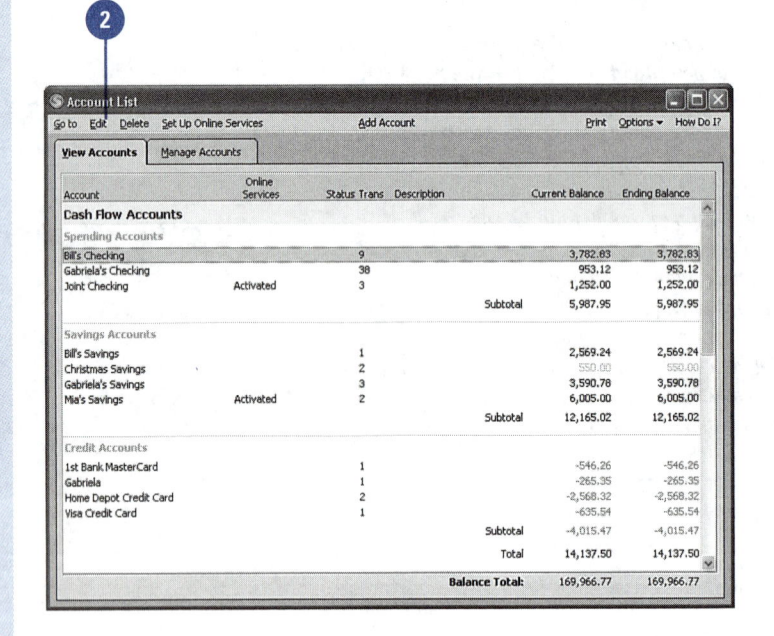

3. In the Account Details window, type, select, or change the account information.

4. To review or change the tax schedules associated with this account, click Tax Schedule Info.

5. Select the new tax schedules, if needed, and click OK.

6. When you are finished making changes, click OK.

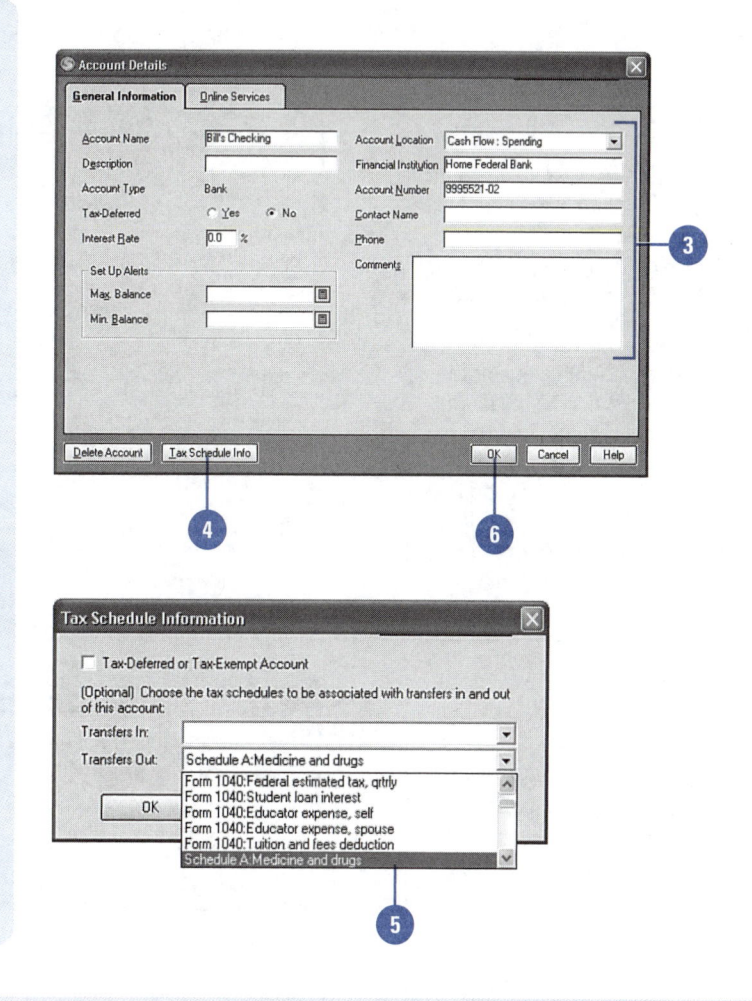

Performing Additional Functions in the Account List Window

You can use the menu bar to access other areas of Quicken, such as the following:

- You can open an account register by selecting the account and clicking Go to.
- You can set up an account for online access by selecting the account and clicking Set Up Online Services.
- You can add a new account by clicking Add Account.
- You can print the account list by clicking Print.
- You can select print options or change the list view by using the Options menu.
- You can click How Do I? to access Quicken's Help system.

Managing Your Spending and Savings Accounts **105**

Delete Spending and Savings Accounts

1. To completely remove an account from Quicken, in the Account List window, select the account and click Delete. A message appears, asking if you want to delete the account.

2. If you are sure that you want to delete the account, type **Yes** and click OK. If you do not want to delete the account, click Cancel. A message appears, telling you that the account has not been deleted. Click OK.

Did You Know?

You can delete accounts by using the Account Details window or the Account List window. You can delete an account by clicking the Delete Account button in the Account Details window or by using the Delete menu option in the Account List window. However, before you delete an account from Quicken, you need to be sure you don't need the account, even if it's closed, for reporting or historical tracking. Deleting an account is permanent, and the only way to restore it is if you have a backup of your Quicken file that you made before you deleted the account.

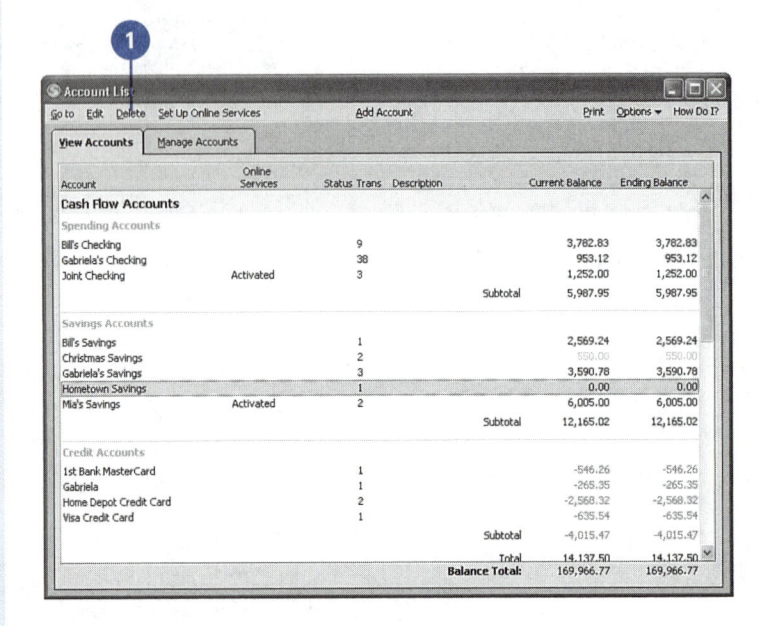

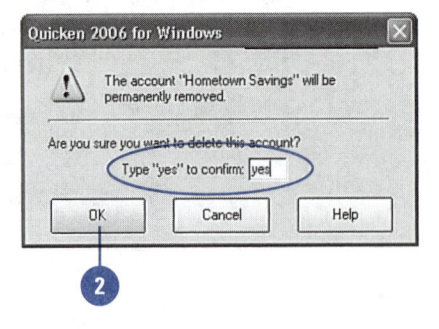

Did You Know?

You cannot delete accounts that have active transactions. If an account has active transactions, such as scheduled transactions, you must delete the transactions before you can remove the account. Remember: You need to think it through before you remove an account. The information can be used for historical reasons or for forecasting.

Adding, Editing, and Deleting Spending and Savings Account Transactions

Add Downloaded Spending and Savings Transactions to Your Register

1. On the account bar, click the spending or savings account to which you want to add downloaded transactions.

2. To download account transactions, connect to the Internet and in the Downloaded Transactions tab, click Download Transactions. If you have already downloaded the transactions, skip to step 5.

3. In the Online Update for This Account dialog box, select the account you want to download, type your PIN, and click Update Now.

4. If the Download Summary window opens, review the downloaded transactions and click Done.

5. To add all transactions to your register, click Accept All.

6. To add individual transactions to your register, click Accept next to each transaction. A message appears asking if you want to assign a category to each transaction.

If you set up any of your accounts for online access, each time you use One Step Update, your most recent account transactions download to the appropriate account in Quicken. You can then review and add the transactions to your register, edit transactions before you add them to your register, or delete them if they are duplicates. If you don't use the online updates, you can add transactions manually.

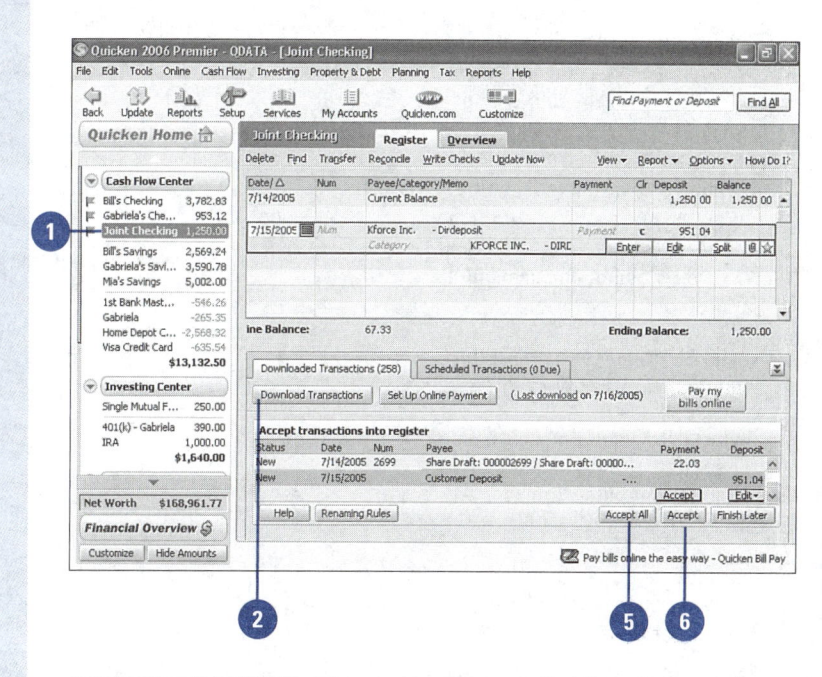

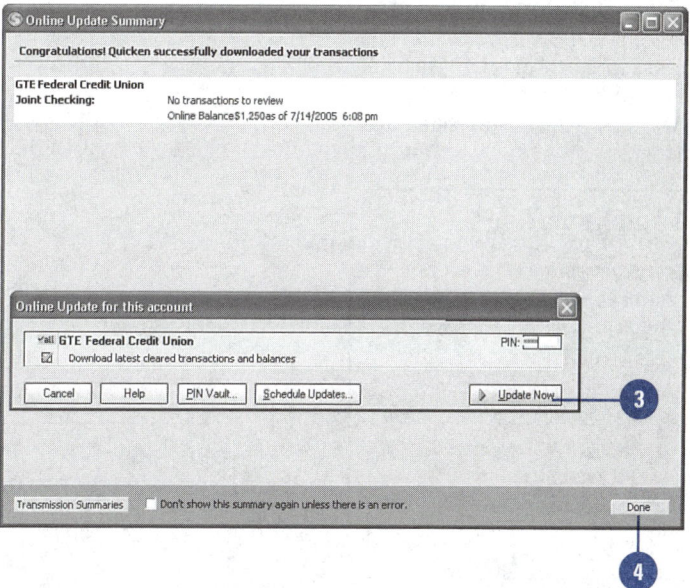

Managing Your Spending and Savings Accounts   **107**

7 Click Yes to assign a category or No to enter the transaction without assigning a category.

8 To assign a category, select the category you want to use or click Split to assign more than one category to a transaction.

9 To view spending totals and averages for the category, click the Report icon. You can change the time period for spending by clicking the down arrow and then selecting a different time period. You can also view payee spending totals and averages by clicking in the Payee column and clicking the Report icon.

10 To view a transaction report for spending, click Show Report.

11 Click Enter. The status of the transaction changes to Accepted on the Downloaded Transactions tab.

12 To remove a transaction, select the transaction, click Edit, and then select Delete.

13 To finish adding transactions at a later time, on the Dowloaded Transactions tab, click Finish Later. The transactions you added to your register no longer appear on the tab.

Did You Know?

Assigning categories can help you track your spending. By assigning categories to your transactions, you can see exactly where your money is going when you run transaction reports, as shown in step 10. Quicken tracks categories across all your accounts so you can see exactly how much you've spent in a specific category.

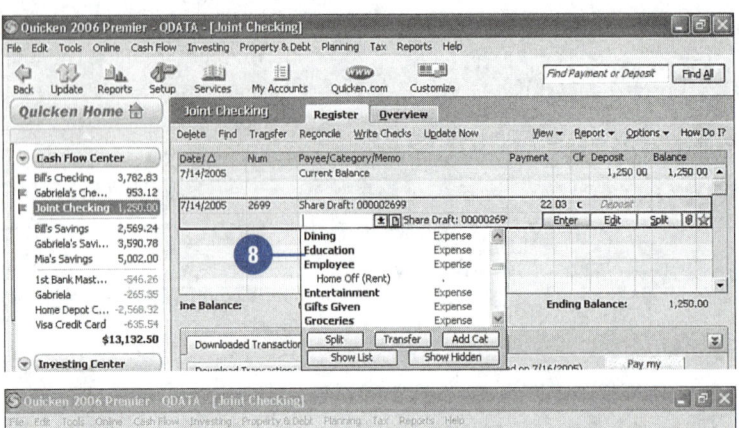

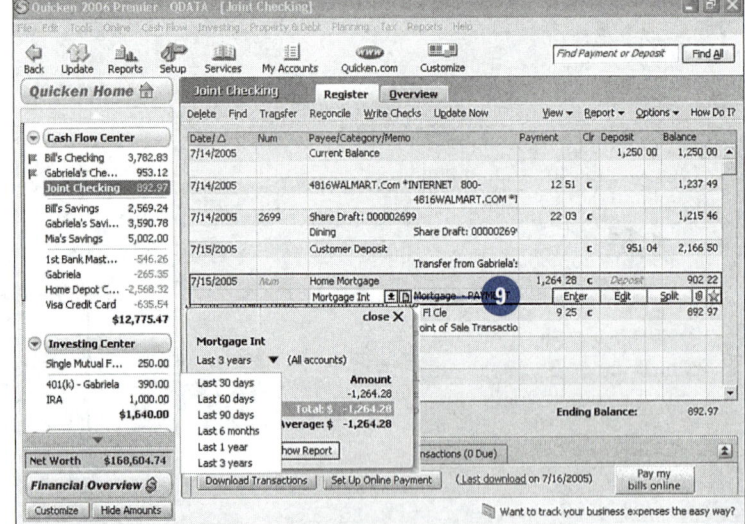

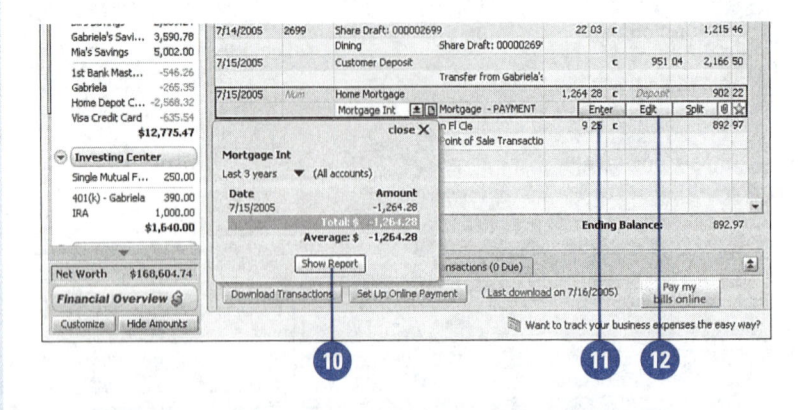

See Also

See "Tracking Transactions with Multiple Categories" on page 80 for information on assigning split categories to transactions.

Flag and Attach Documents to Transactions

1. To flag a transaction to follow up on later, select the transaction and click the paper clip button.

2. Click Add follow-up flag.

3. Type a note or message about the follow-up, select the color you want for the flag, and type a date when you want to be reminded of the follow-up. Then click OK.

4. To attach a document such as a receipt click the paper clip button and select the type of attachment.

5. Click Add Attachment.

6. Locate and select the document you want to attach and click Open. The attachment appears in the Transaction Attachments window.

7. Click Close Viewer. The Attachment button appears beneath the transaction date in the Date column.

8. To remove an attachment, double-click the Attachment button and in the Transaction Attachments window, click Delete Attachment. A message appears, asking if you want to delete the attachment.

9. Click Yes to remove the attachment or No to keep it. Then, close the viewer.

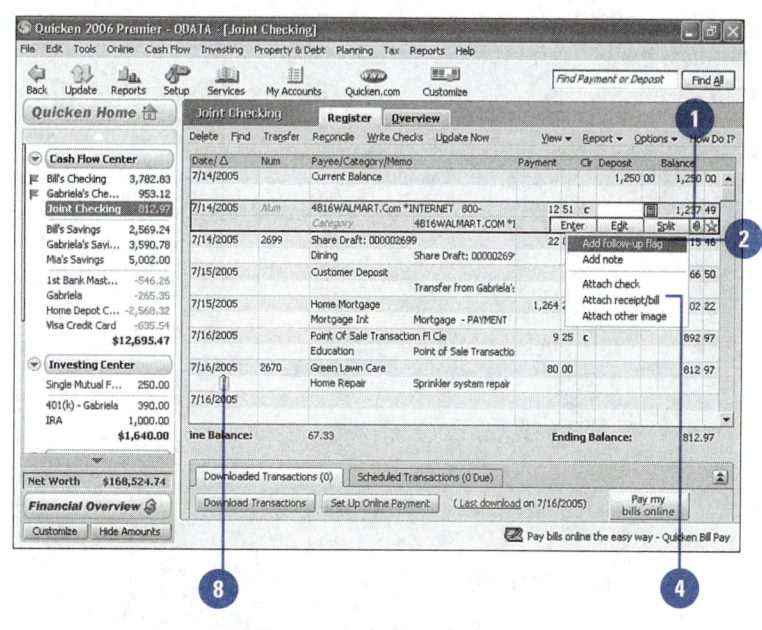

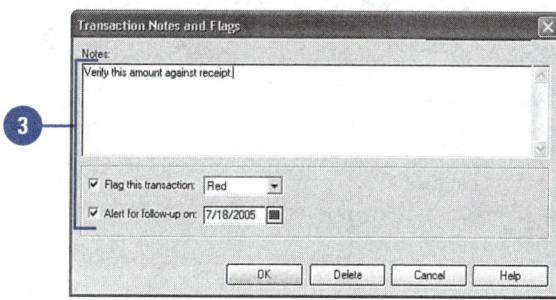

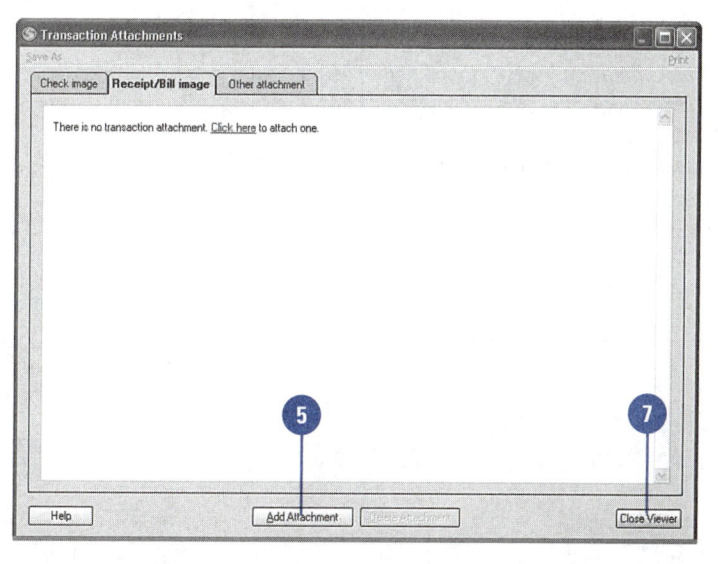

Managing Your Spending and Savings Accounts **109**

Manually Add Transactions to Your Register

1. If you don't already have the Cash Flow Center open, on the account bar, click the spending or savings account to which you want to add transactions.

2. To add a transaction, click in the Date column of an empty row and type the date of the transaction.

3. In the Num column, select the type of transaction.

4. Type in the Payee name.

5. Click Category and select a category to assign to the transaction.

Did You Know?

You can assign more than one category to a transaction. To track more than one category for a transaction, click Split. Then from the Split Transaction window, click a line, select a category, and type the amount for the category. Repeat this for each category you want to add. When you are finished adding the categories and amounts, click Adjust. The sum of the splits must equal the total amount of the transaction. If the sum of the categories does not equal the total amount of the transaction, adjust the category amounts. When the sum equals the total, click OK.

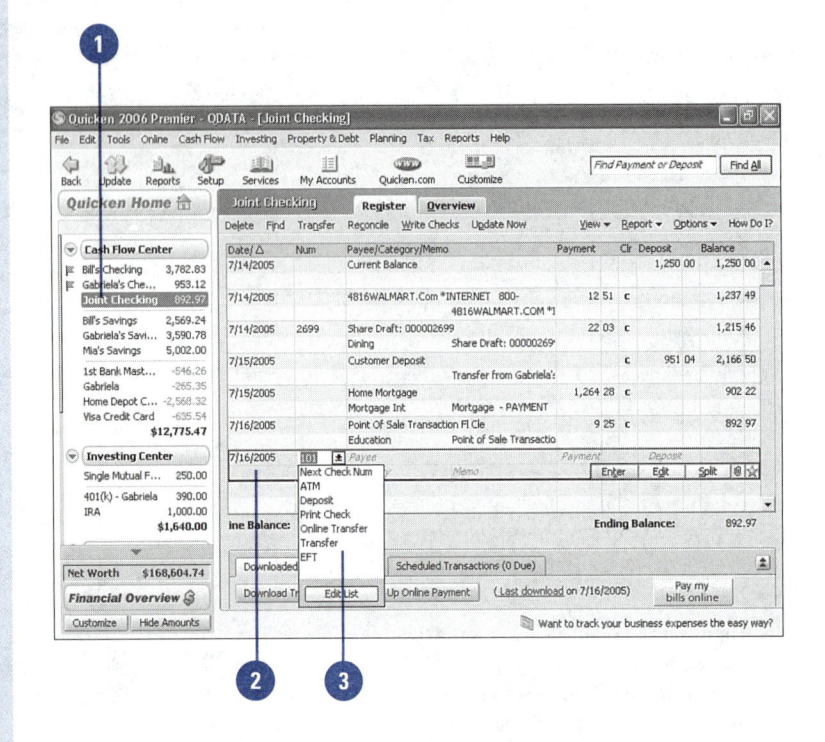

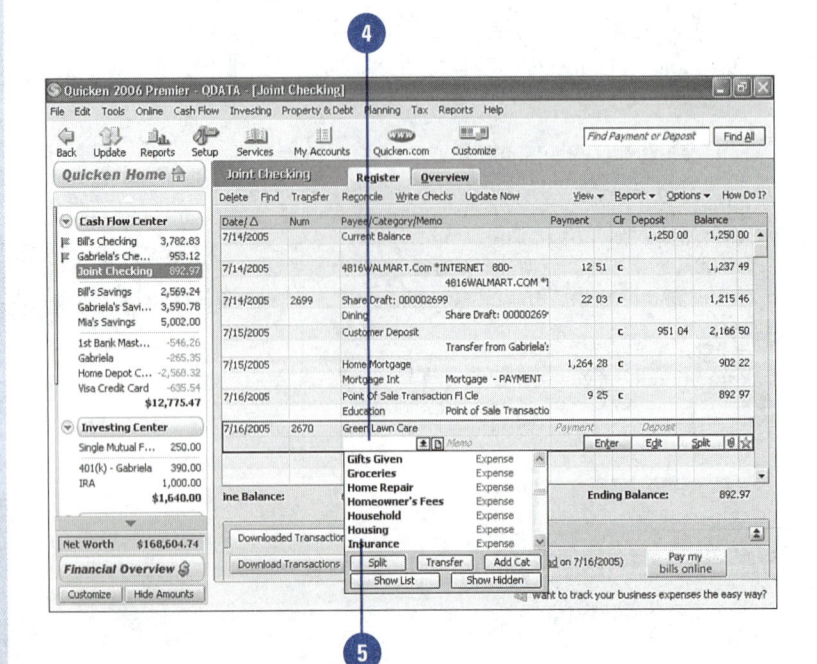

6. Click in Memo to type a note about the transaction.

7. Click in Payment or Deposit and type the amount of the transaction.

8. To flag this transaction to follow up on later, or to attach any documentation, such as an electronic copy of a receipt, click the paper clip button.

9. Click Enter.

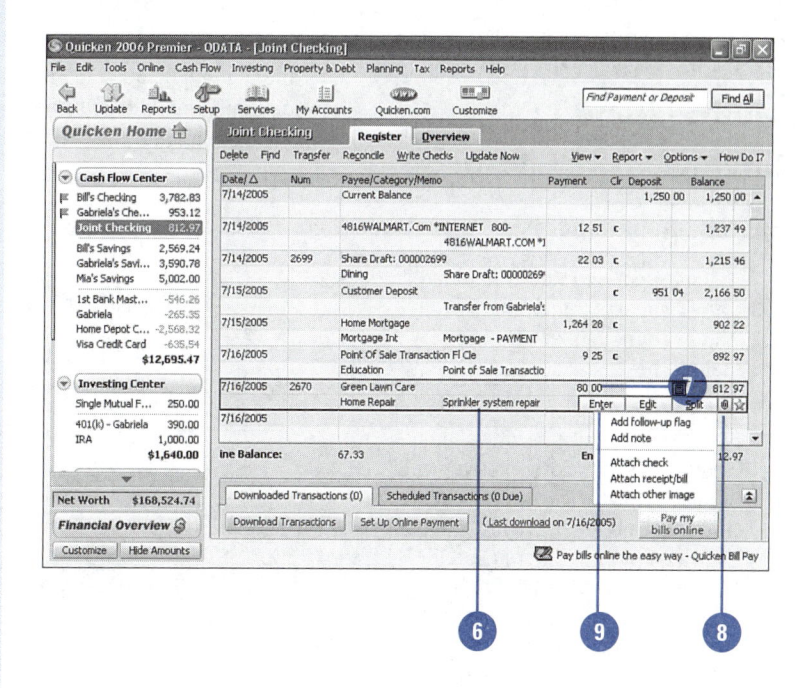

See Also

See "Flag and Attach Documents to Transactions" on page 109 for more information on flagging transactions for follow-up and attaching documents to transactions.

Edit and Delete Spending and Savings Transactions

1. Click in the area you want to change (for example, in the Payee column to change the name) and type over the existing text.

2. Click Enter to apply the change.

3. Follow steps 1 and 2 to change this information in any of the other fields, as needed.

4. To delete an entire transaction, select the transaction and click Delete. A message appears, asking if you want to delete the transaction.

5. Click Yes to delete the transaction or No to keep it.

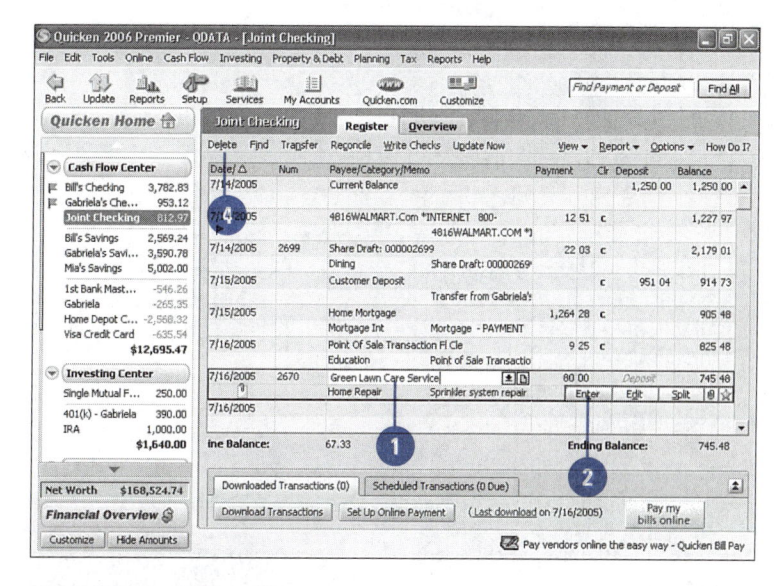

Managing Your Spending and Savings Accounts   111

Searching for Spending and Savings Transactions

As you've seen when downloading all your transactions, the list of transactions can be quite long. If you have to look for a specific transaction, locating it could take some time. This is where the Quicken Find tool comes in handy.

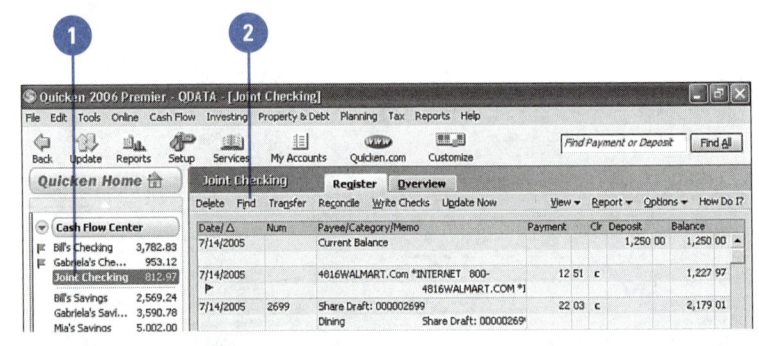

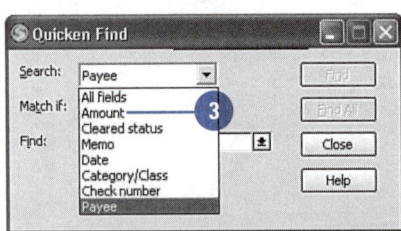

Search for Transactions

1. If you're not already there, open the Cash Flow Center and select the account you want to use to search for transactions.

2. Click Find.

3. From the Search drop-down menu, select the main keyword or the focus of your search. For example, if you want to find a transaction that cleared your account for $12.51, but you don't know the payee's name, select Amount.

4. From the Match if drop-down menu, select the criterion you want to use to narrow the search further.

5. Type the word or number you are searching for. For example, using the example here, you type **12.51**.

6. If you want Quicken to search backward from the current date, select Search Backwards.

7. Click Find to locate transactions in the current register or click Find All to locate transactions in all registers. Quicken locates and highlights the transactions that contain the search criteria you specified.

8. If you don't see what you are looking for, perform the search again, using different search criteria.

Did You Know?

The Match if and Find criteria work together to locate the transaction. What you select from the Match if drop-down menu corresponds with what you type in the Find box. For example, because you know that the amount cleared your account for $12.51, you can select Exact because you know that the transaction is for 12.51.

Did You Know?

Sorting transactions is another way of finding transactions. You can sort your transactions by clicking the column headings. For example, clicking the Payee/Category/Memo heading sorts the transactions list in alphabetical order by the payee name.

112

Transferring Funds Between Spending and Savings Accounts

Transferring funds between accounts means withdrawing money from one account and depositing it into another. When you transfer funds between accounts, Quicken automatically logs the transaction in the register from which the money is being removed and creates a parallel transaction in the register for the account to which the money is being deposited. Transferring funds between accounts only happens within Quicken, though; it does not affect the accounts at your bank or other financial institution. You can, however, use your financial institution's online features to transfer money between accounts at that institution, but the accounts must share the same login or customer ID. You should check with your financial institution before trying to do an online transfer. If you do use online accounts and transfer money between accounts and then download the transactions and enter them into your Quicken registers, you don't need to perform a separate transfer in Quicken. However, if you are not using the online features or are experimenting with moving your funds around, you can use the following task to step through a transfer.

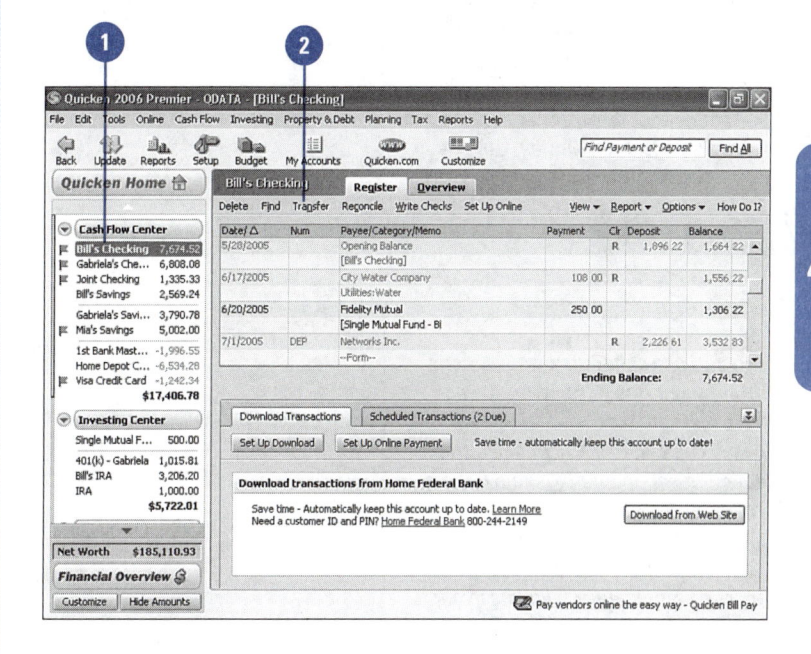

Transfer Funds Between Spending and Savings Accounts

1. If you're not already there, open the Cash Flow Center and select one of the spending or savings accounts you want to use to transfer funds. It does not matter which account you open first.

2. Click Transfer.

Managing Your Spending and Savings Accounts   **113**

③ Select the account from which you want to transfer the funds; the money will come out of this account.

④ Select the account to which the funds are going; the money will be deposited into this account.

⑤ Type the date that the transfer is to take place. You can future-date the transaction; however, the balances for each account are immediately adjusted.

⑥ Type the dollar amount of the transfer.

⑦ Type a description or reason for the transfer.

⑧ Click OK. The transfer shows up as TXFR in the account register from which the money is taken. In the register to which the money is deposited, the transaction shows up as Transfer Money. Quicken automatically adjusts the balances.

Did You Know?

You can use scheduled transactions for frequent transfers. *If you have a transfer that takes place on a regular basis, you can use a scheduled transaction to set up an automatic transfer. You can also set the dates and amounts of the transfer. When it comes time for the transfer to occur, Quicken automatically updates your scheduled transactions list. Refer to the task "Adding Scheduled Spending and Savings Transactions to Your Register," on the next page for more information.*

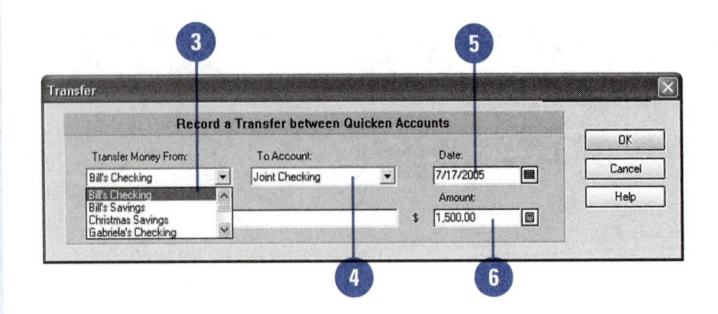

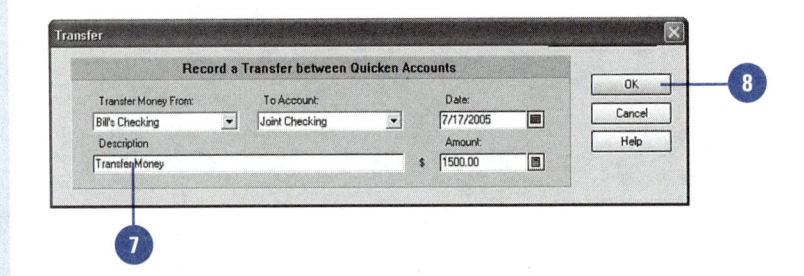

114

Adding Scheduled Spending and Savings Transactions to Your Register

When you set up your accounts and tell Quicken about any regularly scheduled transactions for your spending and savings accounts, Quicken creates a scheduled transaction list for you. The scheduled transactions for your spending and savings accounts appear on the Scheduled Transaction tab in each of your spending and savings account registers. They also appear on the Bills and Scheduled Transactions section in the Cash Flow Center and in the master list in the Scheduled Transaction List window. The Bills and Scheduled Transactions section of the Cash Flow Center is covered in Chapter 6, "Managing Your Bills," and the Scheduled Transaction List window is covered in Chapter 3, "Using Quicken Home Page Features."

In your spending and savings account registers, you can view the list, add transactions to your register, edit, and delete transactions. In addition, you can access the master list of all your scheduled transactions for all accounts in Quicken.

If you have online access to some of your accounts, you can download the transactions and enter them into your Quicken registers, you don't need to add scheduled transactions for your online accounts. However, if you do not have online access for some or all of your accounts, you can use the following task to step through the process. If you want to be reminded when your scheduled transactions are due, you can use the Cash Flow alerts.

Add Scheduled Spending and Savings Transactions to Your Register

1. If you're not already there, open the Cash Flow Center and select the spending or savings account to which you want to add scheduled transactions.

2. Click the Scheduled Transactions tab. The number in parentheses represents the number of transactions waiting to be added to your register.

3. To add a scheduled transaction to your register, click Enter.

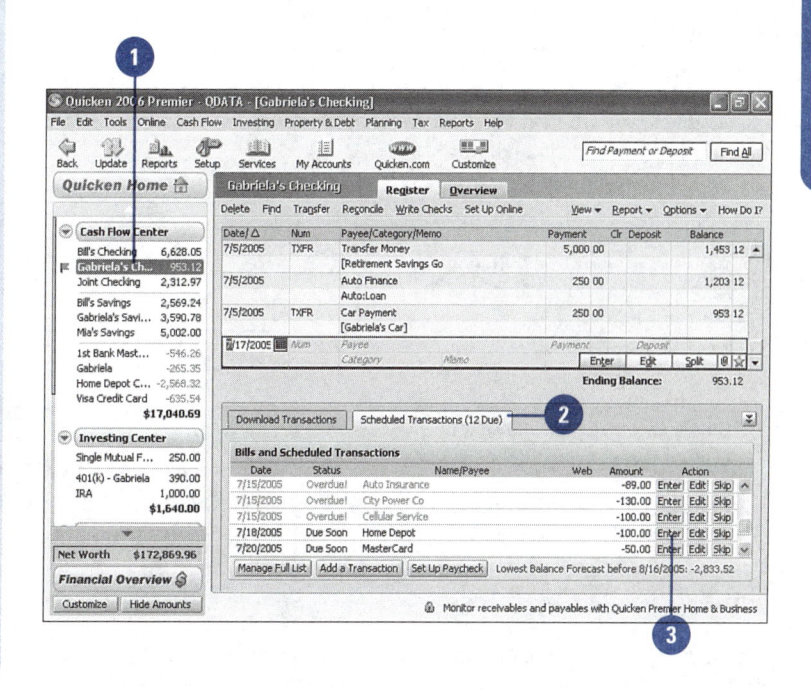

Managing Your Spending and Savings Accounts   115

④ Review the information to ensure that it is correct and make changes, if needed.

⑤ To add the transaction to your register, click Record Payment. Any changes that you make here do not apply to all future transactions—only to the current transaction.

⑥ Click Cancel to take no action on the transaction and return to the scheduled transaction list. The transaction remains in the scheduled transaction list until you are ready to record it or skip it.

⑦ Hover your mouse (point, don't click) over transaction name to see the average amount spent for that transaction.

⑧ Click Skip to remove the transaction from your scheduled transactions for this period but have it reappear the next time it is scheduled to show up.

⑨ To delete a transaction, click Manage Full List and use the Scheduled Transaction List window. Refer to the next task, "Managing Your Scheduled Transactions," for more information.

⑩ To add a new transaction, click Add a Transaction and complete the Create Scheduled Transaction window.

⑪ To add a new paycheck, click Set Up Paycheck and complete the Manage Paychecks window.

⑫ Review, edit, and enter each scheduled transaction until you are finished. Transactions you record are entered into your register, and your balance is adjusted accordingly.

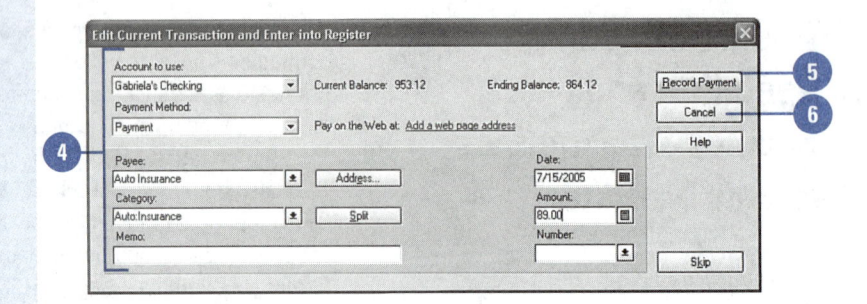

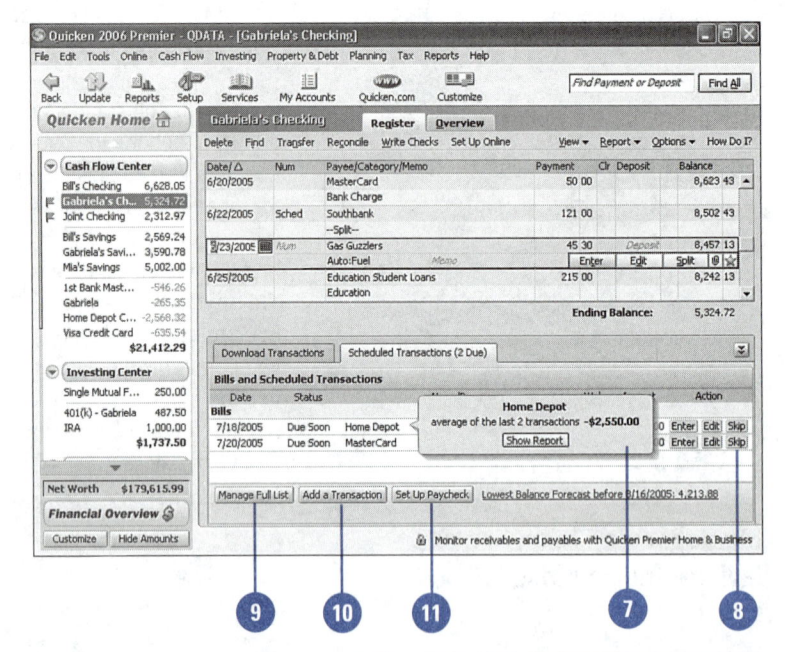

See Also

See "Using Bills and Scheduled Transactions" on page 76 for more information on adding and editing scheduled transactions.

Did You Know?

Unscheduled transactions appear under the Schedule These? section. If there are transactions that have not been scheduled, Quicken creates a temporary section on the Scheduled Transactions tab called Schedule These?. You click Yes to schedule a transaction or No to leave it unscheduled. This does not remove the transaction from your scheduled transactions. If there are no unscheduled transactions, you do not see this section.

A red flag means that there are scheduled transactions waiting. If there is a red flag next to an account in the account bar, there are scheduled transactions waiting to be entered in that account register.

Managing All Your Scheduled Transactions

To make changes to or delete scheduled transactions, you use the Scheduled Transactions List window. You can also create new scheduled transactions in this window. All your transactions are included in the Scheduled Transactions List window, not just for your spending and savings accounts. You can access the Scheduled Transactions List window from the Scheduled Transactions tab on any spending and savings account register, from any other account register, or from the Tools menu.

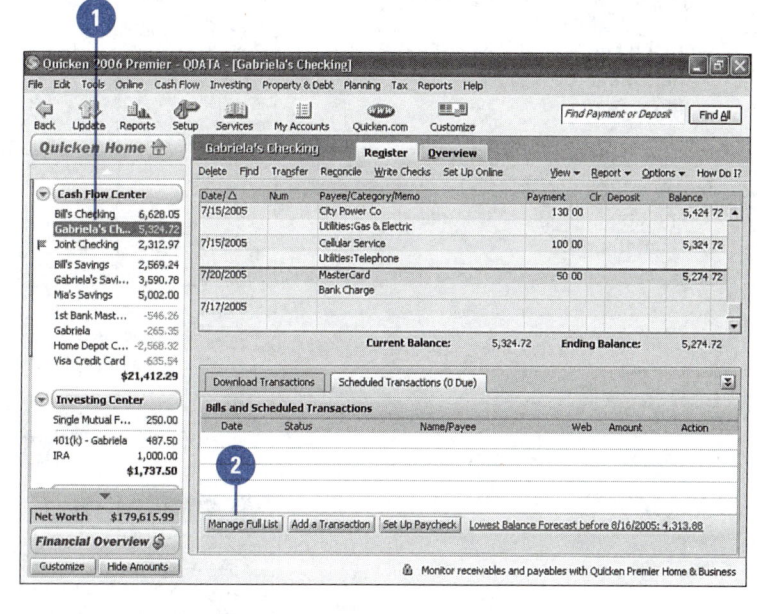

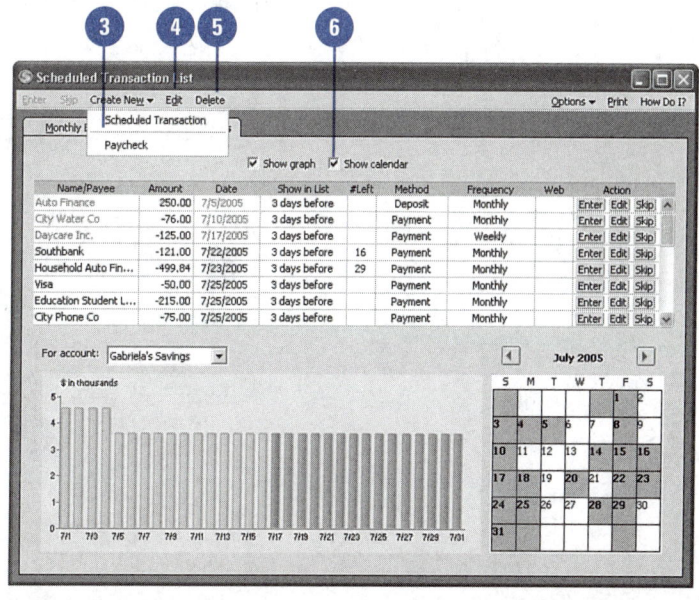

Manage Your Scheduled Transactions

1. If you're not already there, open the Cash Flow Center and select the spending or savings account for which you want to manage scheduled transactions.

2. From your Register tab, click the Scheduled Transactions tab and then click Manage Full List.

3. To add a new scheduled transaction or paycheck, click Create New and then select Scheduled Transaction or Paycheck.

4. To edit a transaction, select it and click Edit.

5. To delete a transaction—for example, if you no longer use the account for the transaction—select the transaction and click Delete.

6. To view the transaction calendar for the current month, select Show calendar. The days on which transactions are due are bolded.

See Also

See "Using Bills and Scheduled Transactions" on page 76 for more detailed information on adding, editing, and deleting scheduled transactions.

Managing Your Spending and Savings Accounts 117

7. To view the calendar in detail, click a day of the month.

8. You can print the calendar, go to a future or previous month, make a note for a specific day, or select only the accounts you want to see on the calendar.

9. To view a graph of daily transactions, select Show graph.

10. From the For account drop-down menu, select the account you want to view.

11. To view your estimated account balance for a specific day, hover (point, don't click) your mouse over a bar of the graph.

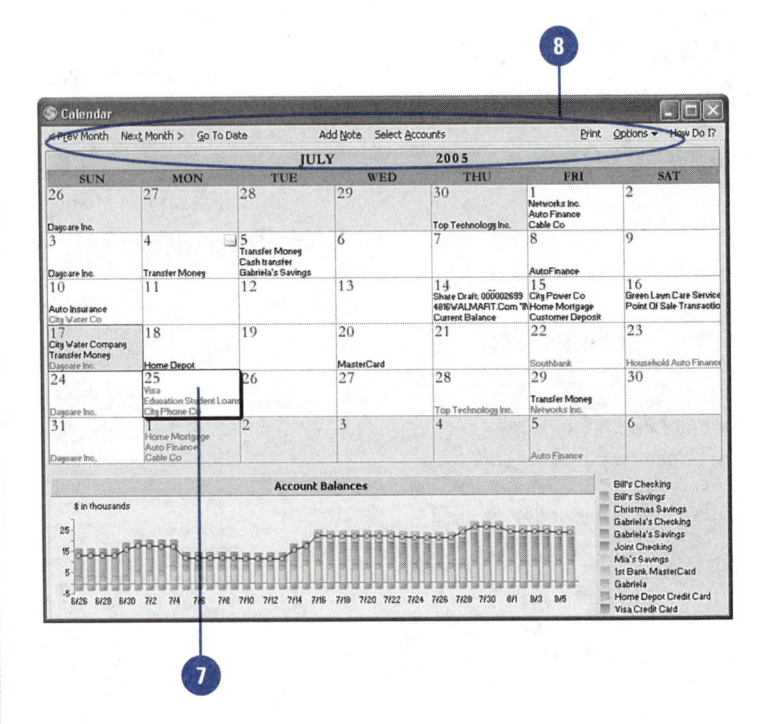

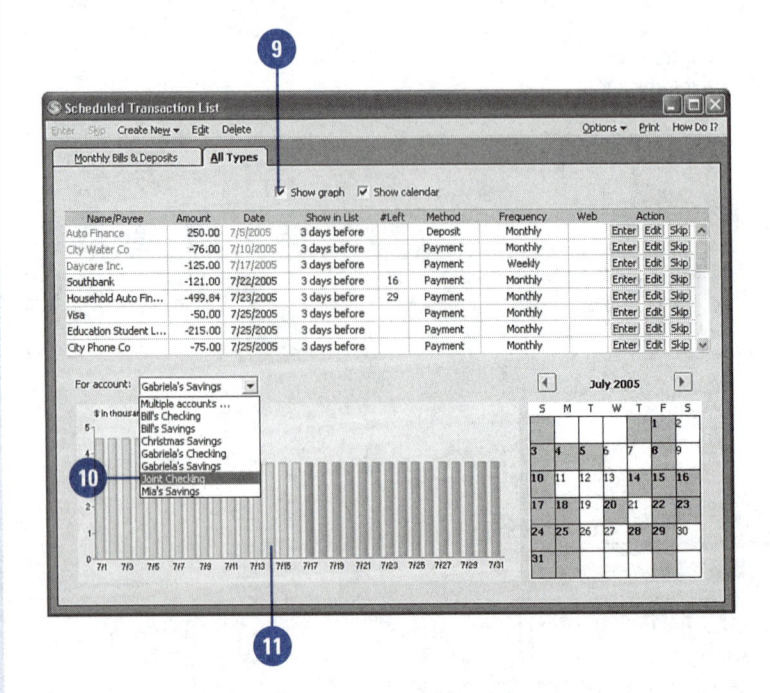

Viewing Spending and Savings Account Overviews

View Spending and Savings Account Overviews

① On the account bar, click the savings or spending account for which you want to view.

② Click the Overview tab.

③ In the Account Attributes section, you can view basic account information.

④ To make changes to the account, click Edit Account Details.

⑤ In the Account Status section, you can view balance and transaction information.

⑥ The number of checks to be printed and tax-related items are also provided.

⑦ The Account Balance section provides a bar chart of your account balance over the current month's time. Click Show Calendar to view the transactions due for each day of the month.

⑧ In the Account Attachments section, you can add new documents to the account by clicking Add and completing the Add Attachment window.

⑨ The Expenses section lists expenses that are related to the account. These expenses are provided for the year-to-date, month-to-date, and totals.

⑩ Click Show Expense Report to view the Expenses report.

An account overview is provided for each of your accounts when you open the account. The overviews include account attributes, such as the account name and description; the status, such as the balance and equity; a graph view of the equity; and any expenses associated with the account. In addition, you can edit account details and view reports for the account. The options on each overview vary by account type.

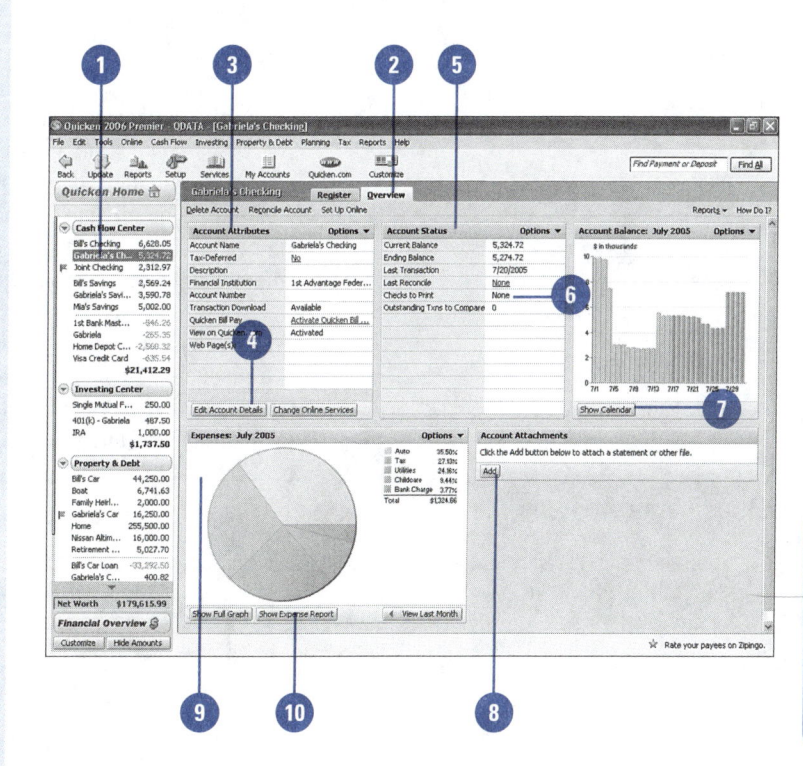

Managing Your Spending and Savings Accounts **119**

Balancing Your Spending and Savings Accounts

You should balance your spending and savings accounts in Quicken as often as you normally would by using your monthly statements. Balancing or reconciling spending and savings accounts in Quicken is very similar to balancing your accounts by using your paper register and monthly statement. However, if the account has online access, each time you download your transactions, Quicken automatically clears each transaction in your register and reconciles the account. Therefore, you don't have to compare your statement to the register in order to balance an online account.

If the account you are balancing does not have online access, you still need your monthly bank statement to compare against your Quicken register. If you find discrepancies, you can reconcile your balance by adding missing transactions, downloading the latest transactions, and so on to ensure that your ending balance matches that on your paper statement. You need to keep in mind that some transactions may not have cleared yet and therefore might not show up on your statement.

Before you begin to balance your accounts, you should make sure that all transactions (deposits, withdrawals, purchases, payments, interest, and so on) have been downloaded and recorded or entered in your account register, and you should have your statement ready.

Balance Your Account Manually

1. Open the Cash Flow Center and select the account you want to balance.

2. Compare the transactions on your statement to those that appear in your Quicken account register. When you find a match, click in the Clr column to tell Quicken that this transaction has cleared. A message appears, asking if you want to reconcile this account.

See Also

See "Edit Transactions" on page 79 for more information on adding new, editing existing, and deleting transactions.

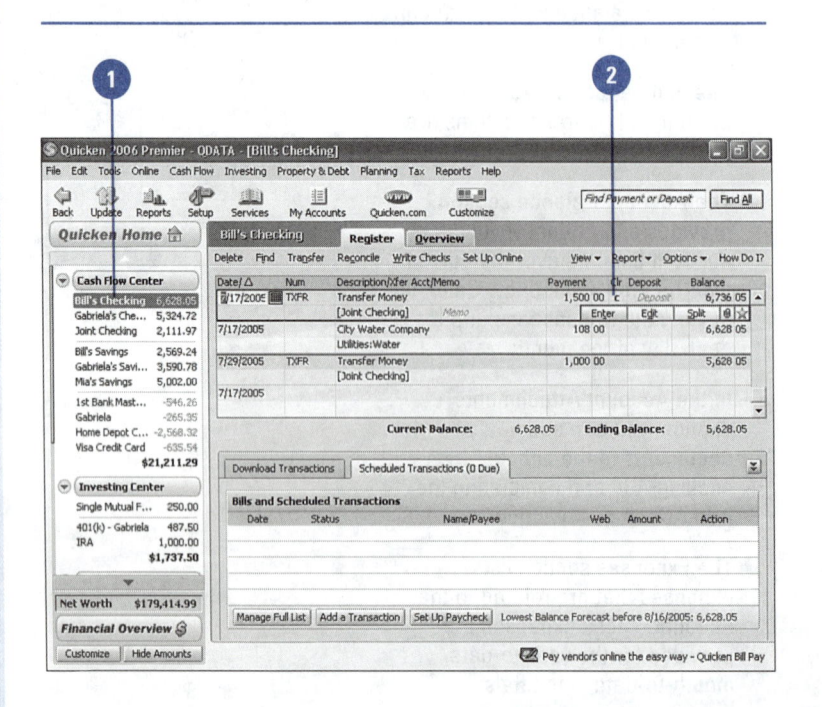

3. Click No. Quicken places a C in the Clr column to indicate that the transaction has cleared. Click Enter if you want to save a cleared transaction.

4. To add a missing transaction, click in the next empty transaction row and type the information. Then click Enter.

5. To edit a transaction, select the transaction, click Edit, make your changes, and click Enter.

6. Continue comparing transactions and clearing each transaction, as needed. When you are finished, compare your statement balance to your register. If there is a difference, determine the reason for the discrepancy (for example, maybe fees and interest were added).

7. When you are ready to enter the balance, click in the Clr column of an empty transaction.

8. When you are asked whether you want to reconcile the account, click Yes.

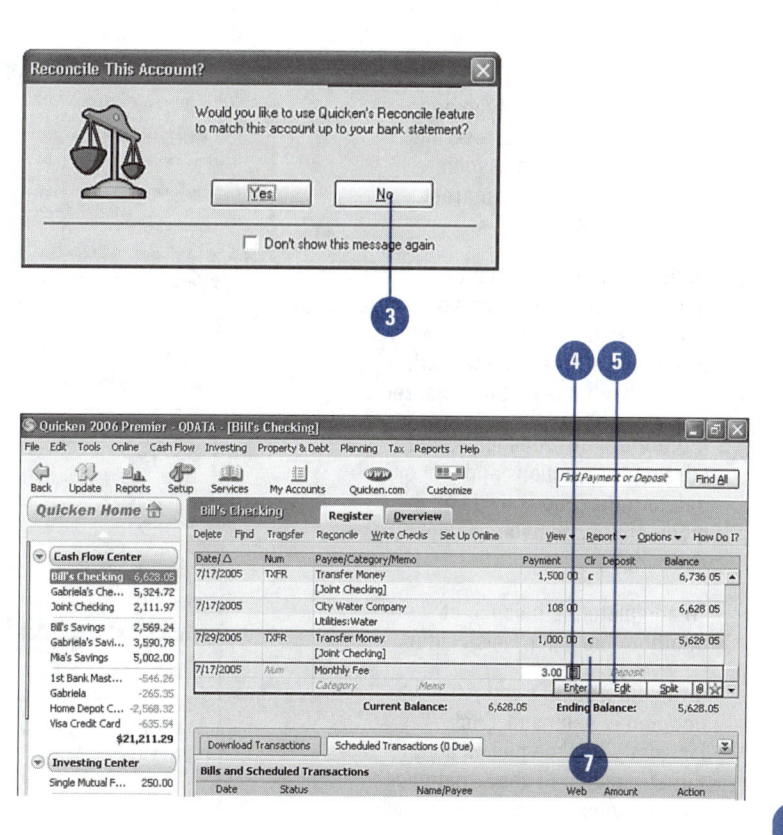

Did You Know?

You can reconcile when you want to change your balance or to skip clearing the transactions individually in your register. You can reconcile a spending and savings account when there is a discrepancy between your statement balance and your Quicken register balance. Reconciling the balance gives you the opportunity to synch up the two balances. When you reconcile your blance, the next time you balance your account, Quicken works from the reconcile balance. You can also check off your cleared transactions using the Statement Summary window by selecting Yes in step 3.

Managing Your Spending and Savings Accounts **121**

⑨ Type the ending balance and date from your statement, type any bank charges and interest, and select a category to associate with the charges and interest. Then click OK.

⑩ Notice that the Statement Summary window shows you which transactions have cleared by placing a green check mark next to each one that has cleared.

⑪ If there are discrepancies, add missing transactions and edit or delete transactions by using the menu options to balance your account.

⑫ To complete the balance at another time, click Finish Later.

⑬ If the difference is zero, the account is balanced. Click Finished. Quicken places an R in the Clr column to show that your transactions have been reconciled.

⑭ If the account balanced, the Reconciliation Complete dialog box opens, asking if you want to view a reconciliation report. Click Yes if you want to view the report; otherwise, click No.

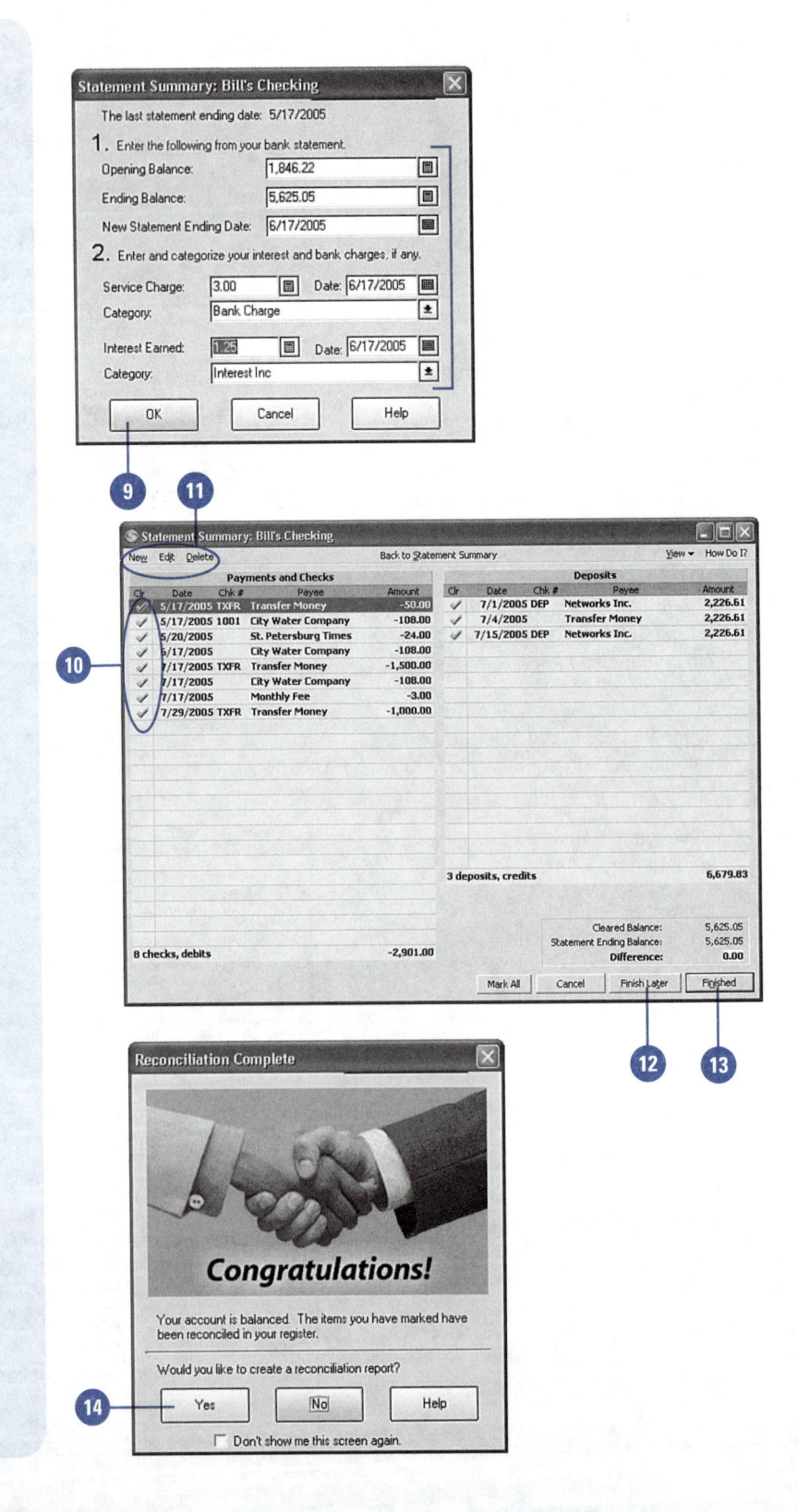

Balance Your Online Accounts

1. In the Cash Flow Center section of the account bar, select the account you want to balance and click Update Now to download the most recent transactions.

2. If you use the PIN Vault, you may be prompted to enter your PIN Vault password. If not, the Online Update window appears. Type your password (PIN) and click Update Now. Once the download is complete, the Online Update Summary window may appear (unless you have opted for it to only appear if there are errors). Click Done to close it.

3. Select Online Balance.

4. To let Quicken compare your transactions and reconcile your account, select Auto reconcile after compare to register and click OK.

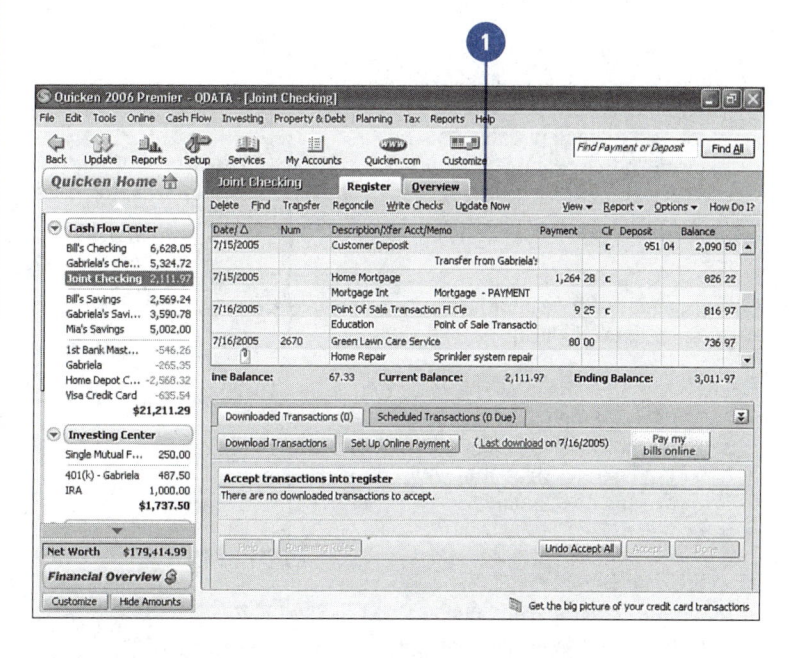

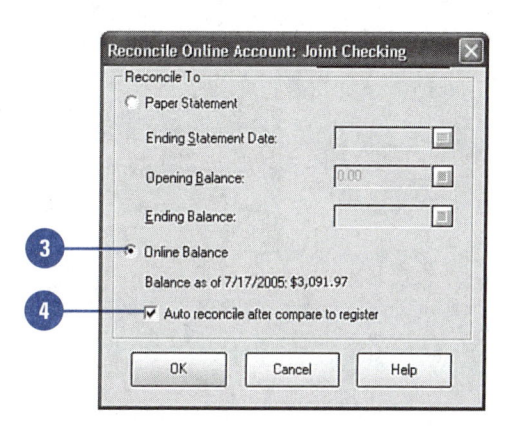

Managing Your Spending and Savings Accounts **123**

5 The Statement Summary window shows which transactions have cleared by placing a green check mark next to each one that has cleared. In this example, there is an $80 discrepancy; however, that is because a payment has not yet cleared.

6 To complete the balance at another time, click Finish Later.

7 If the difference is zero, the account is balanced. Click Finished. Quicken places an R in the Clr column to show that your transactions have been reconciled.

8 If the account balanced, the Reconciliation Complete dialog box opens and asks if you want to view a reconciliation report. Click Yes of you want to view the report; otherwise, click No.

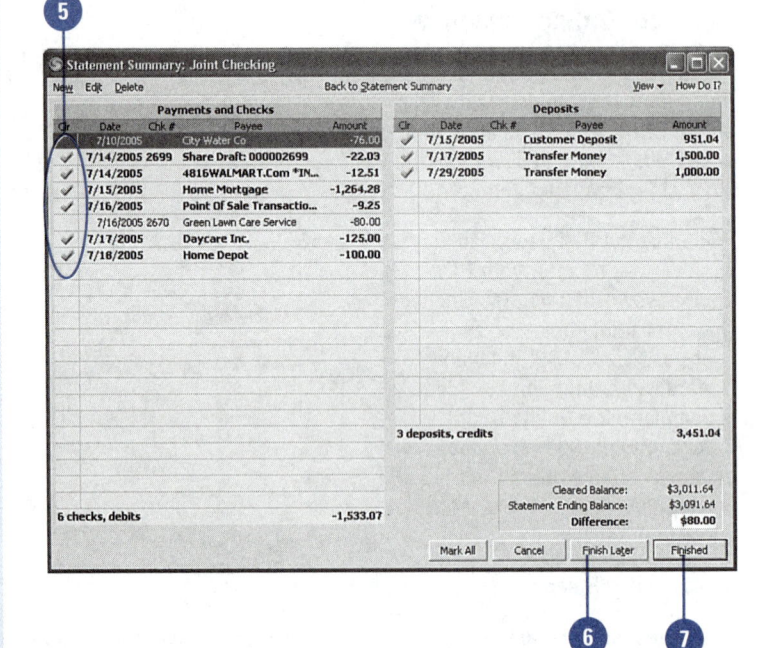

Managing Your Credit Card Accounts

Introduction

The Credit Card Accounts section of the Cash Flow Center allows you to manage all your credit card account information.

In the Cash Flows Alerts section, you can set up or change alerts for your credit cards. In the Credit Card Accounts section, you can view basic account information for each of your accounts, such as the beginning and ending balances; you can add new credit card accounts; and you can edit existing accounts.

You can also access the register for each of the accounts. In the account registers, you can add, edit, or delete transactions; add downloaded transactions to the register; set up scheduled transactions; search for transactions; and balance your account. In addition, you can view spending averages for transactions and reports for your credit card accounts.

What You'll Do

Set Up New and Edit Existing Cash Flow Alerts

Update Credit Card Account Balances and Transactions

Review, Add, Edit, and Delete Credit Card Accounts

Add, Edit, and Delete Credit Card Account Transactions

Search for Credit Card Transactions

Add Scheduled Credit Card Transactions to Your Register

Manage All Your Scheduled Transactions

View Credit Card Account Overviews

Balance Your Credit Card Accounts

Setting Up New and Editing Existing Cash Flow Alerts

Set Up New and Edit Existing Cash Flow Alerts

1. If you don't already have the Cash Flow Center open, on the account bar, click Cash Flow Center.

2. To take action on an alert, click the account link to open the register, where you can resolve the alert.

3. To create or edit credit card alerts, click Set Up Alerts.

4. To view all alerts in the Alerts Center window, click Show all alerts.

See Also

See "Using Alerts" on page 74 for more information on creating and changing alerts.

You can set up alerts in the Cash Flow Center to remind or warn you of actions you need to take for your bank, credit card, and bill accounts, for example, to notify you that your balance is close to your limit or that there are scheduled transactions that are due.

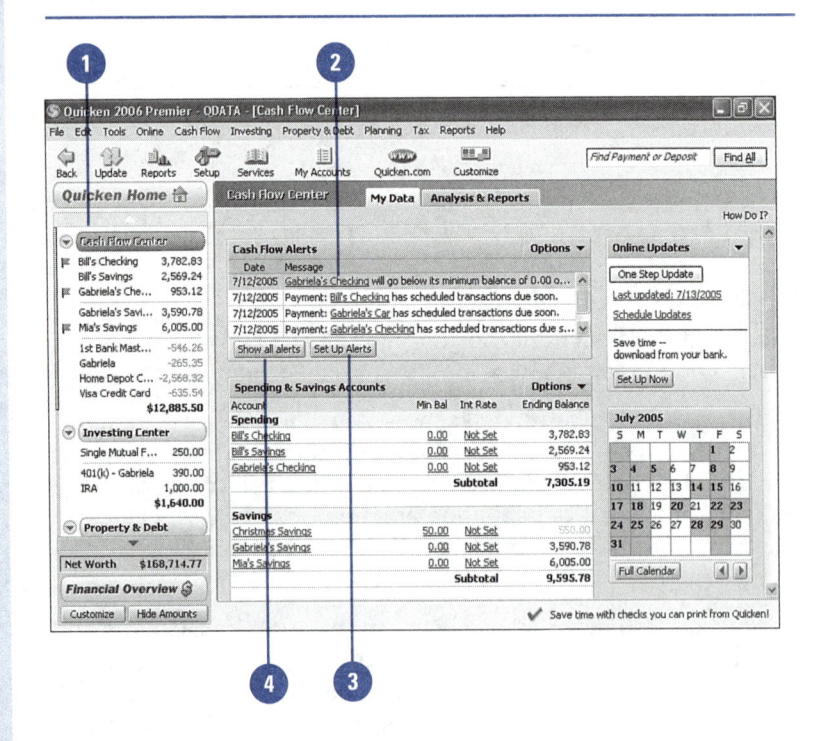

Updating Credit Card Account Balances and Transactions

Before you start working with your credit card accounts, you should check to ensure that you are working with up-to-date balances and transactions. If you set up any of your credit card accounts for online access, you can use One Step Update to automatically update your account balances and transactions. Each time you open Quicken and connect to the Internet, you are prompted to download your account transactions and update your balances. However, you can also update your balance manually, if needed. This task shows how you update your account balances by using One Step Update.

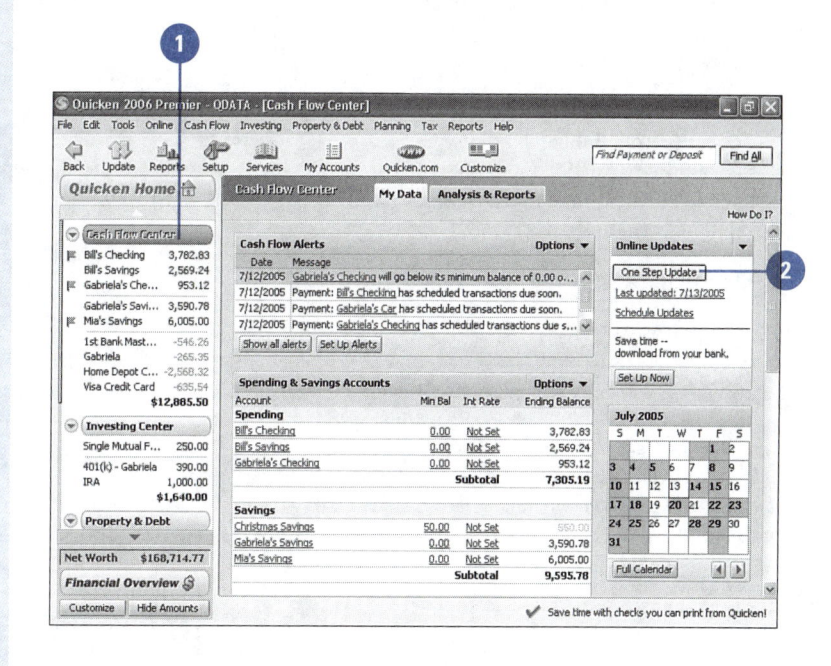

Update Credit Card Account Balances and Transactions

1. On the account bar, click Cash Flow Center.

2. Click One Step Update. If you set up a PIN vault password, you are promoted to enter your password before you can move to the next step.

See Also

If you want to update your account manually, see "Balancing Your Credit Card Accounts" on page 149.

Did You Know?

You can import your account statement if you cannot download transactions directly into Quicken. *If your financial institution does not offer download access from Quicken but does allow you to download your statements from its website, you can import the statements into your account register in Quicken. To do this, you log in to your account via the financial institution's website, download your statement either as a Web Connect or QFX file, and then import that file into Quicken. Refer to "Importing and Exporting Files" in Chapter 2, "Getting Started with Quicken" for more information on importing your statement.*

Managing Your Credit Card Accounts **127**

③ Select the account(s) you want to update. A green check mark means the account is selected.

④ Type the password(s) for each account.

⑤ Click Update Now. The Online Update Summary window opens, listing the accounts you are downloading, the number of transactions and balance for each account, and the dates and times you last downloaded.

⑥ If desired, go straight to your accounts from the summary by clicking Go to Portfolio (which you see only if you chose to download quotes) or Go to Register.

⑦ Click Done.

See Also

See "Using Online Updates" on page 88 for more information on updating accounts at Quicken.com, how to set up One Step Update, and how to schedule updates.

Did You Know?

You can turn off the online update summary. *If you don't want to see a summary each time you download your account information, but only if there are problems with the download, select the option Don't show this summary again unless there is an error.*

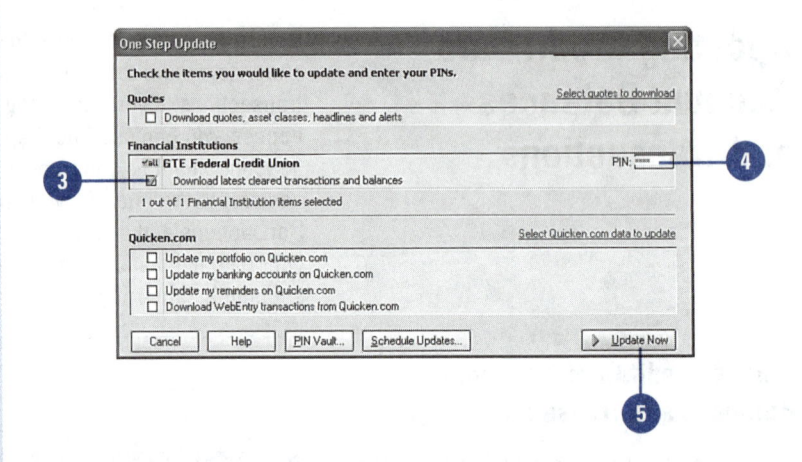

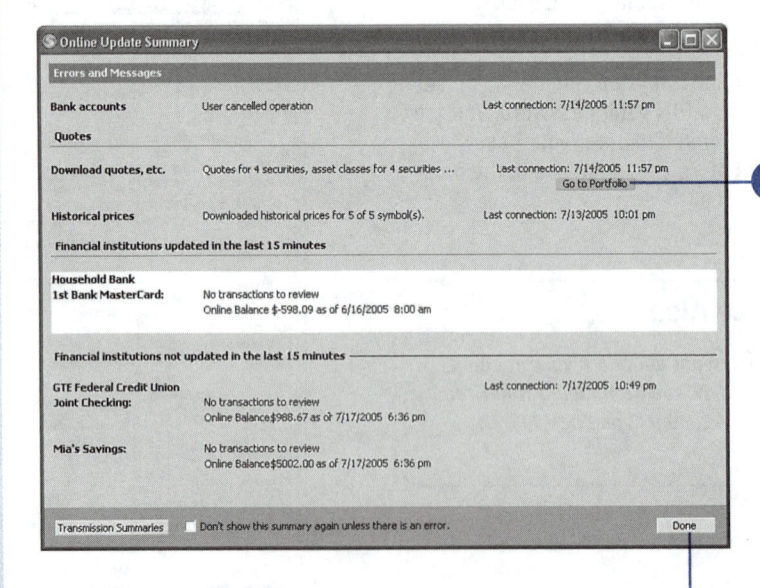

Reviewing, Adding, Editing, and Deleting Credit Card Accounts

The Credit Card Accounts section of the Cash Flow Center lists all your credit card accounts. In this section, you can add new accounts and edit accounts by using the Account List window, where you can also access account registers, set up online access, and completely remove an account from Quicken by deleting it.

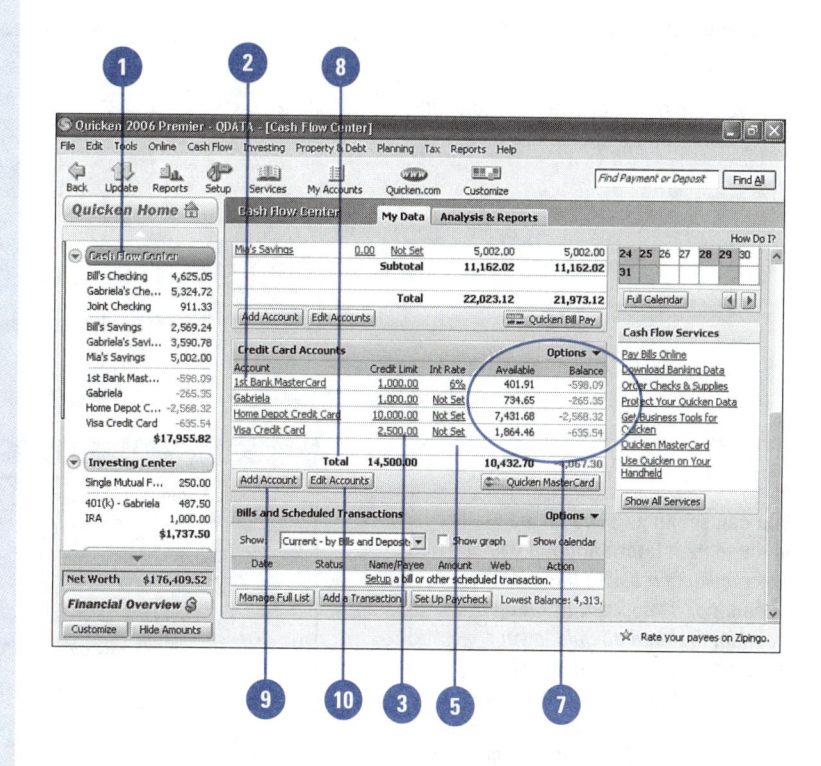

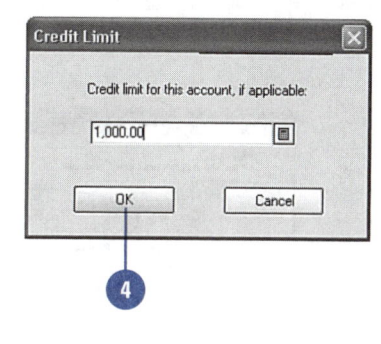

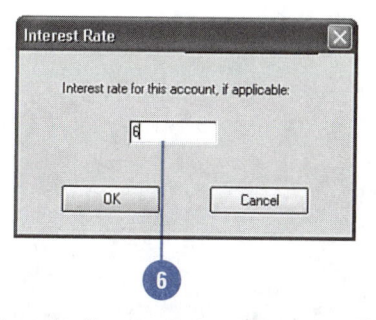

Review Credit Card Accounts

1. On the account bar, click the credit card account to which you want to add transactions.

2. To view an account register, click the account name.

3. The credit limit is listed for each account. If needed, click the dollar amount to open the Credit Limit window where you can change the dollar amount.

4. Type the credit limit dollar amount and click OK.

5. The interest rate is provided for each account. If you have not entered the interest rate, click Not Set. The Interest Rate window opens.

6. Type the interest rate and click OK.

7. Notice that the available credit amount and current balance are listed for each account.

8. Notice that totals are provided for your credit limit, available credit, and balance for all your credit cards.

9. Click Add Account to open the Quicken Account Setup window, where you can add a new credit card account.

10. Click Edit Accounts to open the Account List window, where you can edit all your credit card accounts and the other accounts you have in Quicken.

Managing Your Credit Card Accounts   **129**

Add Credit Card Accounts

1. To add a new credit card account, click Add Account.

2. Type or select the name of the financial institution where the credit card account is held and click Next.

3. Type the name of the new Quicken account and click Next.

Did You Know?

You can set up an account manually and update it later online. *If you don't have online access to this credit card account or if you want to set up the account first and download your account transactions later, click Manual in step 3 and follow the setup prompts. When the account is created, you can go into the account register or use the Account List window to set up online access for the account.*

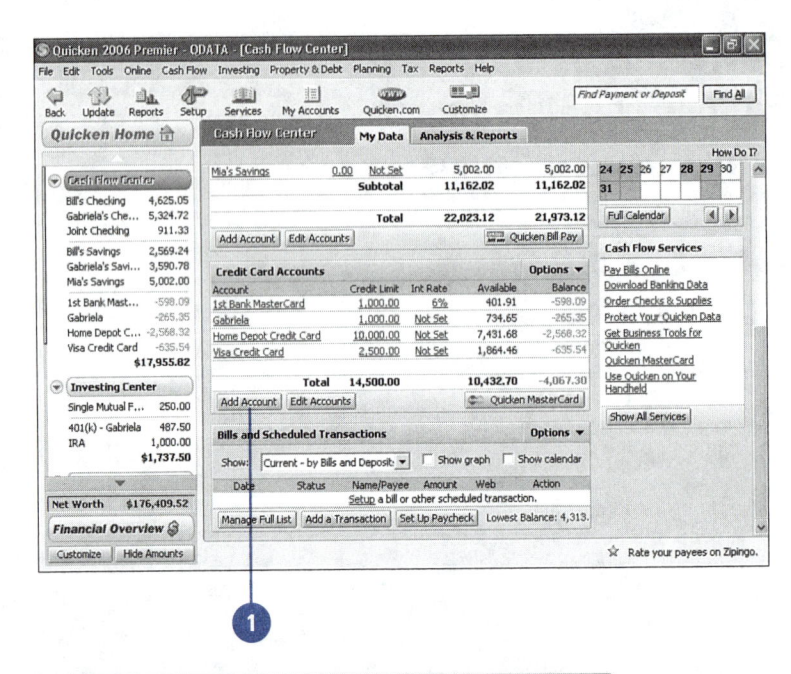

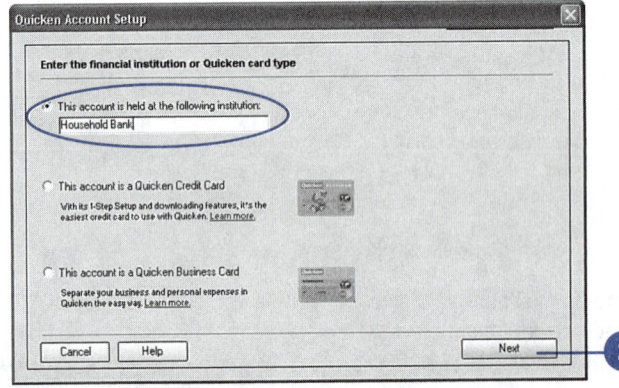

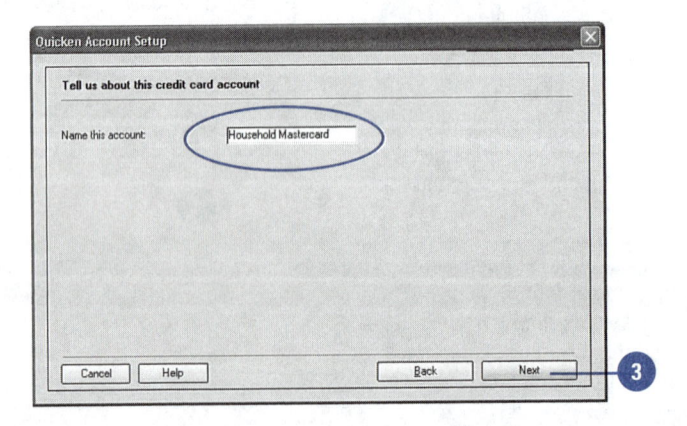

④ Select Online if you can download the account information directly from your financial institution. Select Manual to enter the account information yourself. Then click Next. This task uses the Online option.

⑤ If a message appears, asking if you have your login ID and password. Select Yes if you have access already, ensure that you are connected to the Internet, and click OK. Then follow the prompts to complete the download.

⑥ If you do not have a login ID and password yet, select No and then click OK to add the rest of the account information manually.

⑦ Type the statement ending date and ending balance and click Next.

⑧ Type your credit limit and click Done.

⑨ Repeat steps 1–8 for each credit card account you want to add.

Did You Know?

You must have a login ID and password to download your bank account information. *In order to download your credit card account information, you must already have a login ID and password. If you don't, you can click the Sign Up Now button to request the ID and password, or you can call your credit card company. If you don't have online access now, you can enter your credit card information manually, and when you get your login ID and password, you can start downloading your account information from then on.*

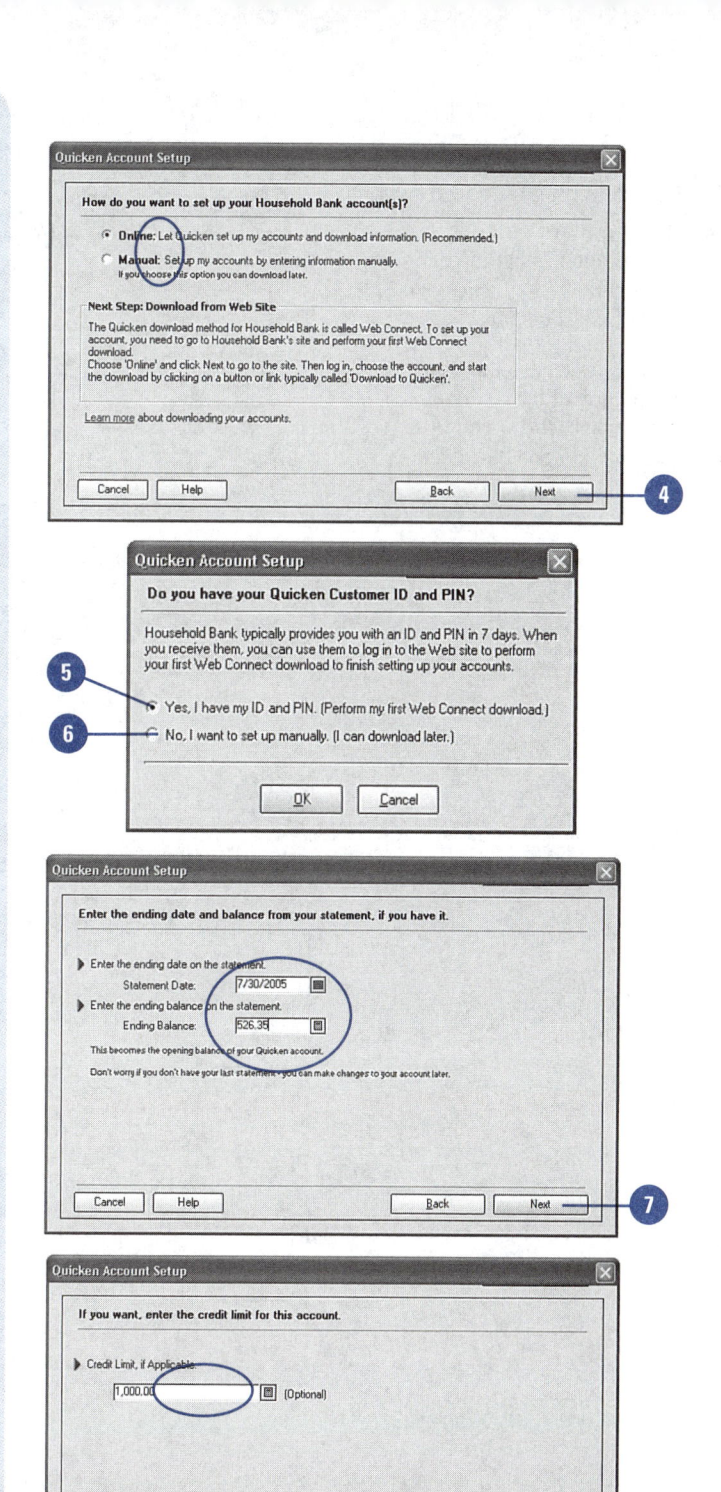

Managing Your Credit Card Accounts **131**

Edit Credit Card Accounts

1. To update credit card account information, in the Credit Card Accounts section of the Cash Flow Center, click Edit Accounts.

2. To update an account, in the Credit Accounts section of the Account List window, select the account you want to update and click Edit.

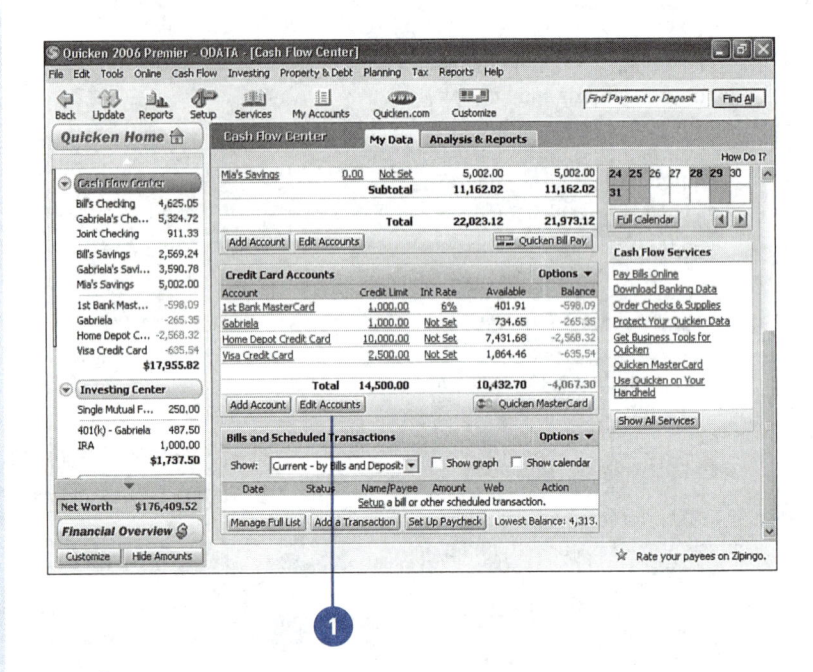

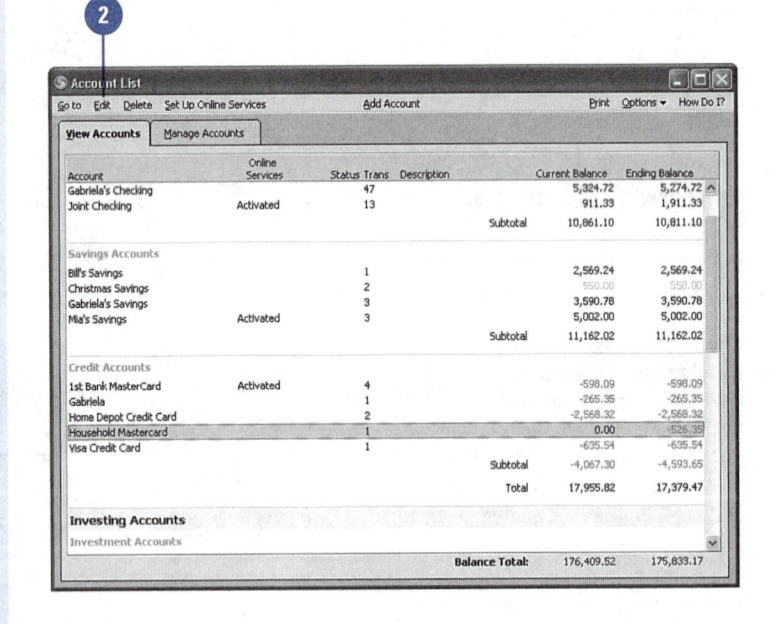

3 In the Account Details window, change the account information as needed.

4 To review or change the tax schedules associated with this account, click Tax Schedule Info.

5 Select new tax schedules, if needed, and click OK.

6 When you are finished making changes, click OK.

Did You Know?

Performing Additional Functions in the Account List Window

You can use the menu bar to access other areas of Quicken, such as the following:

- *You can open an account register by selecting the account and clicking Go to.*
- *You can set up an account for online access by selecting the account and clicking Set Up Online Services.*
- *You can add a new account by clicking Add Account.*
- *You can print the account list by clicking Print.*
- *You can select print options or change the list view by using the Options menu.*
- *You can click How Do I? to access Quicken's Help system.*

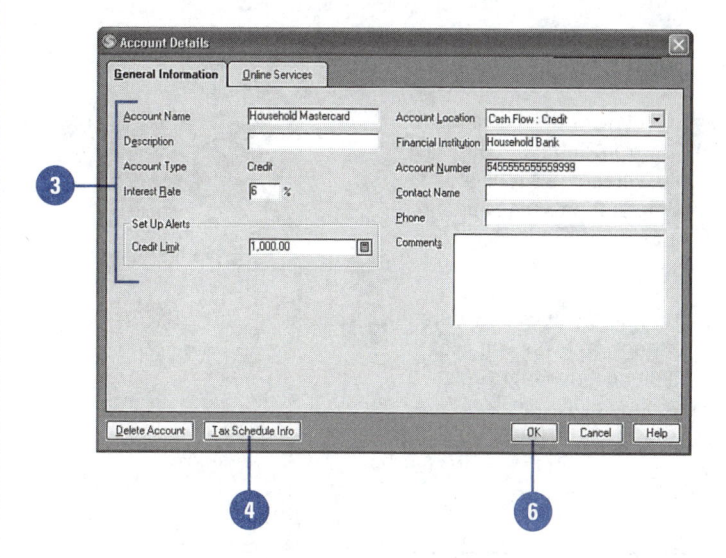

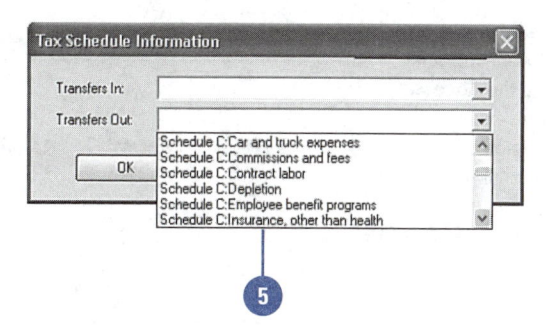

Managing Your Credit Card Accounts **133**

Delete Credit Card Accounts

1. To completely remove an account from Quicken, in the Account List window, select the account and click Delete. A message appears, asking if you want to delete the account.

2. If you are sure you want to delete the account, type Yes and click OK. If you do not want to delete the account, click Cancel. A message appears, telling you that the account has not been deleted. Click OK.

Did You Know?

You can delete accounts by using the Delete Account button on the Account Details Window. *You can delete an account by clicking the Delete button in the Account Details window or by using the Delete menu option in the Account List window. However, before you delete an account from Quicken, you need to be sure you don't need the account, even if it's closed, for reporting or historical tracking. Deleting an account is permanent, and the only way to restore it is if you have a backup of your Quicken file that you made before you deleted the account.*

Did You Know?

You cannot delete accounts that have active transactions. *If an account has active transactions, such as scheduled transactions, you must delete the transactions before you can remove the account. Remember: You need to think it through before you remove an account. The information can be used for historical reasons or for forecasting.*

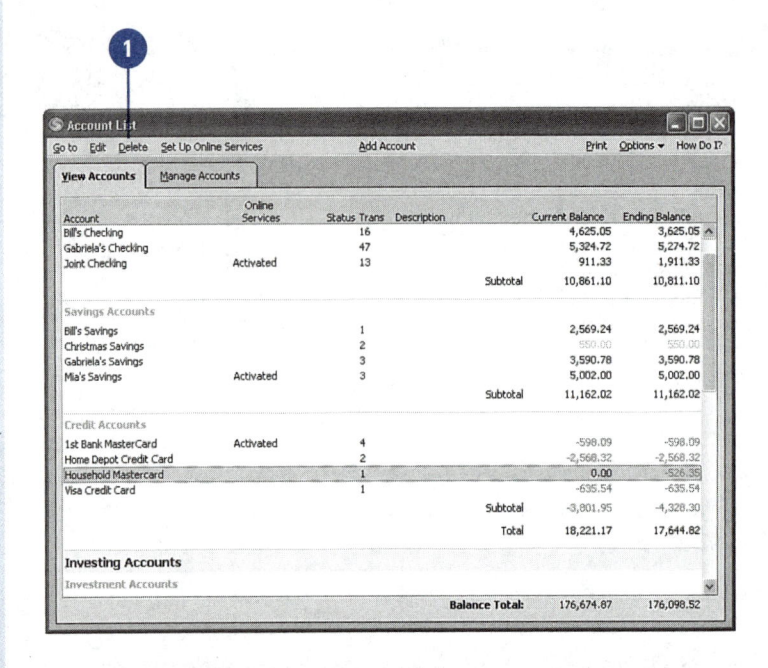

Adding, Editing, and Deleting Credit Card Account Transactions

If you set up any of your accounts for online access, each time you use One Step Update, your most recent account transactions download to the appropriate account in Quicken. You can then review and add the transactions to your register, edit transactions before you add them to your register, or delete them if they are duplicates. If you don't use the online updates, you can add transactions manually.

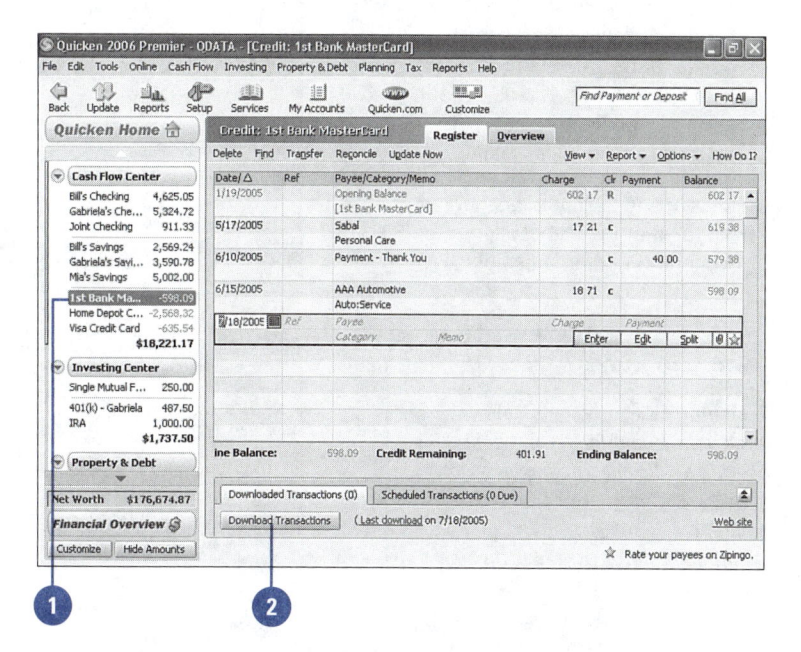

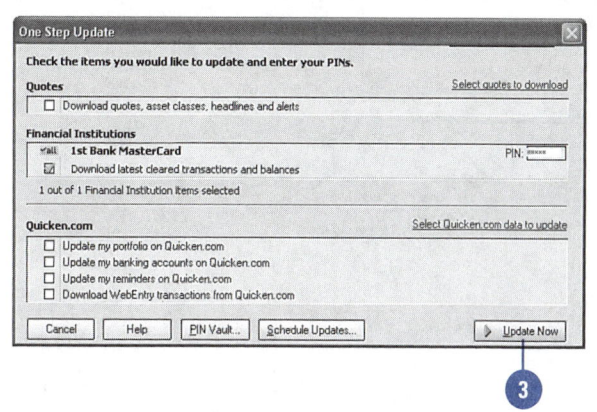

Add Downloaded Credit Card Transactions to Your Register

1. On the account bar, click the credit card account you want to download.

2. If you have not already downloaded account transactions, make sure you are connected to the Internet and in the Downloaded Transactions tab, click Download Transactions. If you have already downloaded the transactions, skip to step 5.

3. If the One Step Update Window opens, select the account to download transactions, type your PIN, and click Update Now. Otherwise, you may be prompted to log into your credit card website and download the latest transaction and/or statement.

Did You Know?

Firewalls may try to inhibit you from downloading transactions. *If you have security protection on your PC, such as a firewall or virus protection software, you may be prompted to allow access for the download.*

Managing Your Credit Card Accounts 135

④ If the Online Update Summary window opens, review the transactions that were downloaded and click Done.

⑤ To add all transactions to your register, click Accept All.

⑥ To add only individual transactions to your register, click each transaction you want to add and click Accept. A message appears, asking if you want to assign a category to each transaction.

⑦ Click Yes to assign a category or No to enter the transaction without assigning a category.

Did You Know?

Assigning categories can help you track your spending. *By assigning categories to all your transactions, you can see exactly where your money is going when you run transaction reports, as shown in step 9. Quicken tracks categories across all your accounts so that when you run a report, it can show you exactly how much you've spent in a specific category.*

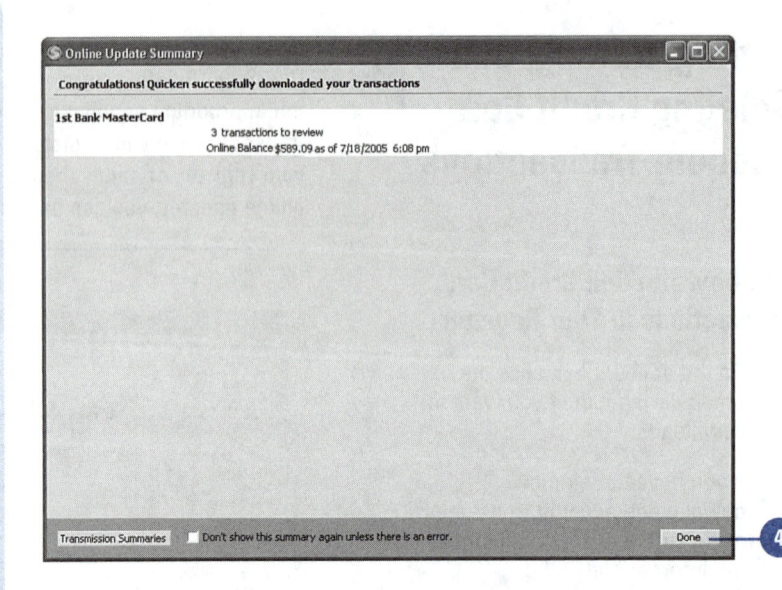

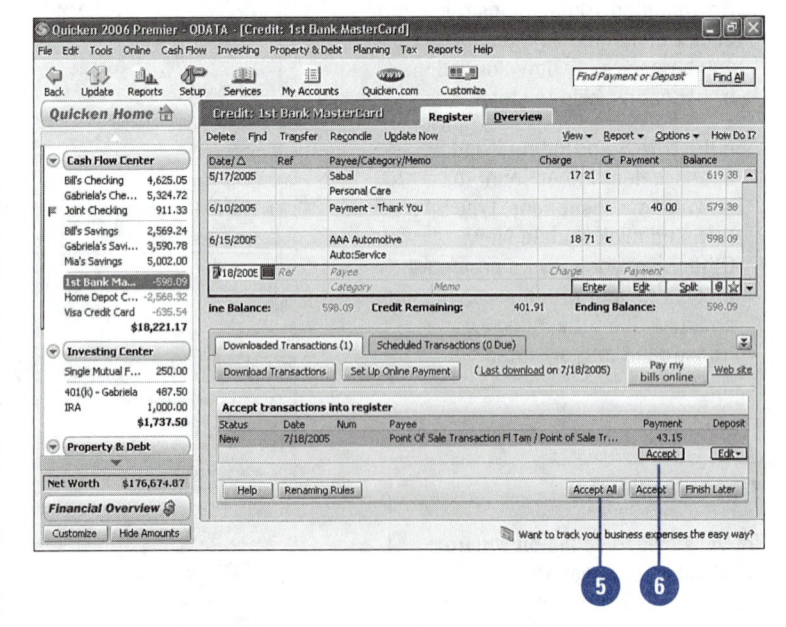

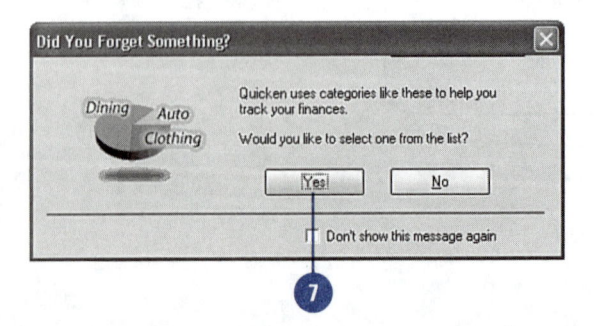

136

⑧ To assign a category, select the category you want to use or click Split to assign more than one category to a transaction.

⑨ To view spending totals and averages for the category, click the Report icon. If needed, click the down arrow to select a different time period.

⑩ To view a transaction report for spending, click Show Report.

⑪ Click Enter. The status of the transaction changes to Accepted on the Downloaded Transactions tab.

⑫ To remove a transaction, select the transaction, click Edit, and then select Delete.

⑬ If you want to add transactions later, click Finish Later. After you add all transactions to your register, the transactions no longer appear on the Downloaded Transactions tab.

Did You Know?

View payee spending reports. *You can also view payee spending totals and averages by clicking in the Payee column in a transaction row and clicking the Report icon.*

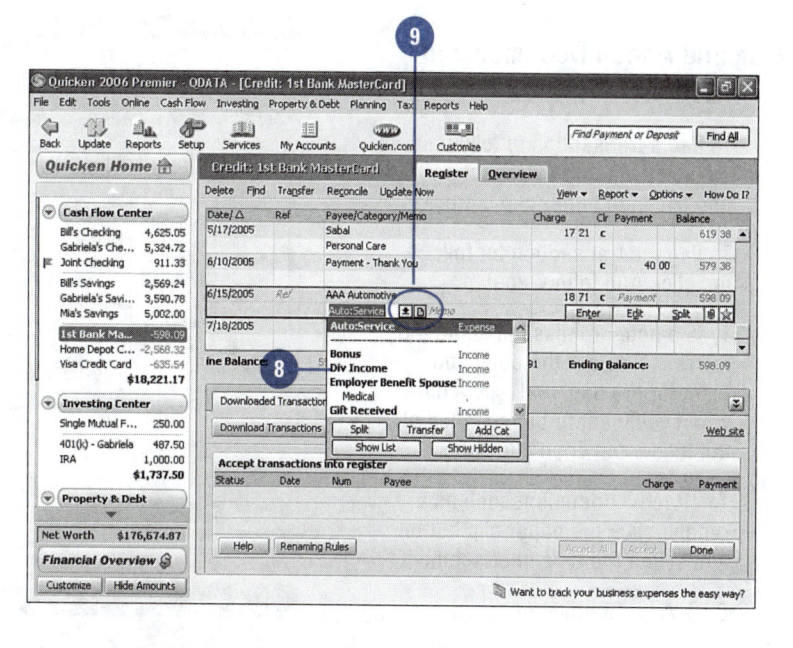

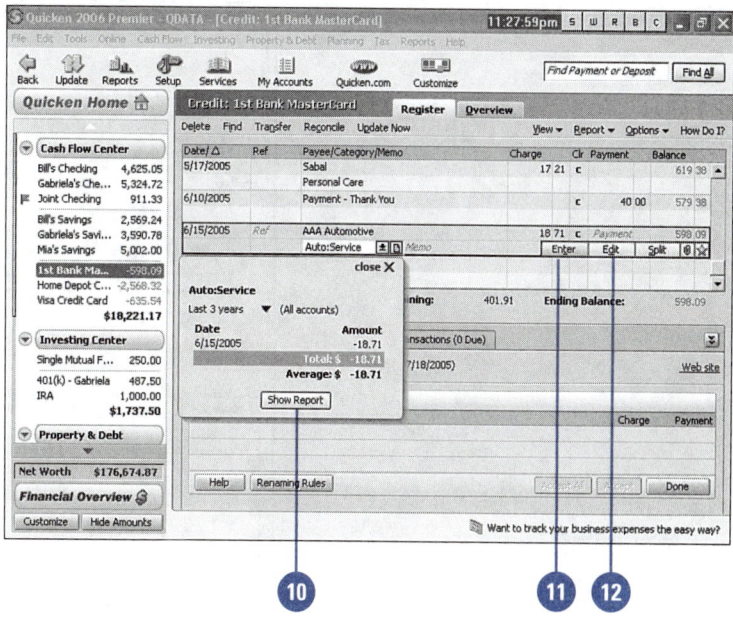

Managing Your Credit Card Accounts **137**

Flag and Attach Documents to Transactions

① To flag a transaction to follow up on later, select the transaction, and click the paper clip button.

② To flag the transaction for follow-up, click Add follow-up flag.

③ Type a note or message about the follow-up, select the color you want for the flag, and type a date when you want to be reminded of the follow-up. Then click OK.

④ To attach a document such as a receipt click the paper clip button and select the type of attachment.

⑤ Click Add Attachment.

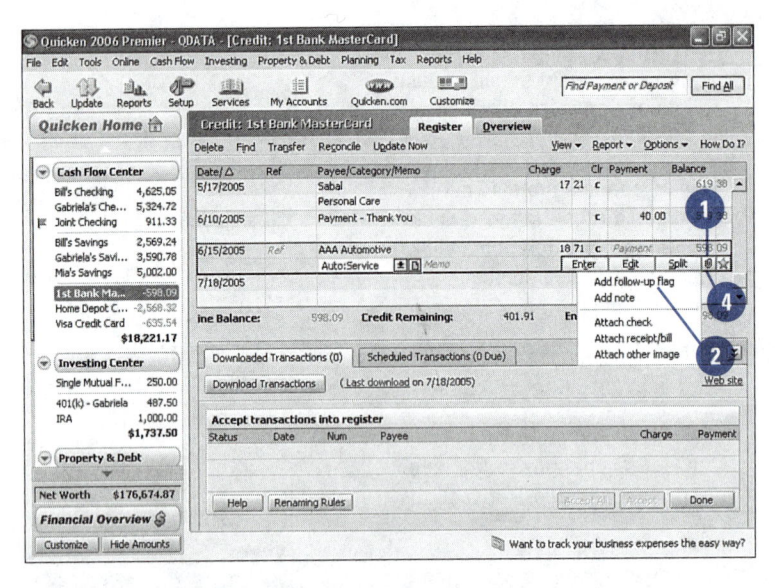

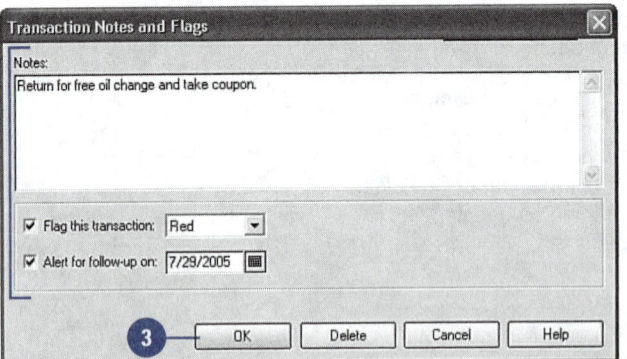

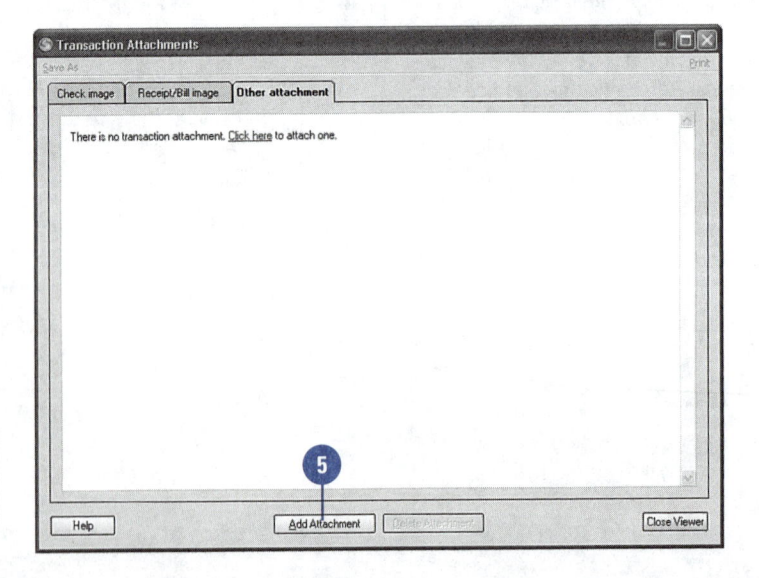

6. Locate and select the document you want to attach and click Open. The attachment appears in the Transaction Attachments window.

7. Click Close Viewer. The Attachment button appears next to the transaction.

8. If you want to remove an attachment, double-click the Attachment button and in the Transaction Attachments window, click Delete. A message appears, asking if you want to delete the attachment.

9. Click Yes and close the viewer.

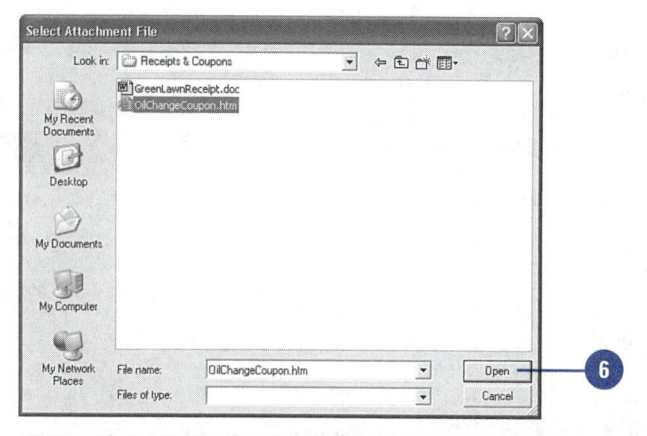

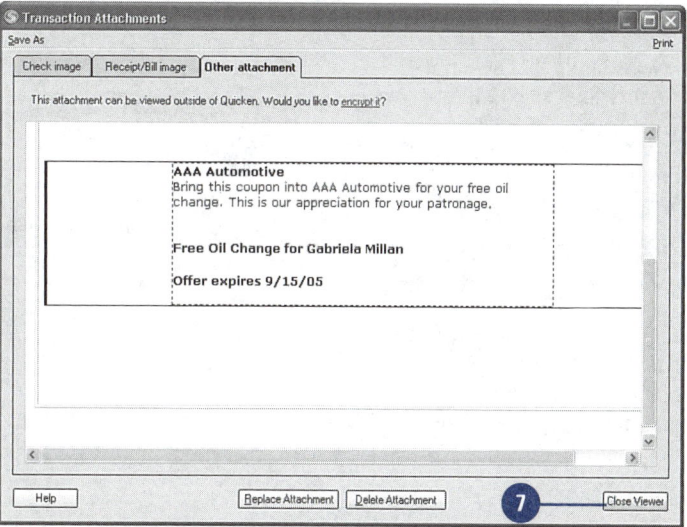

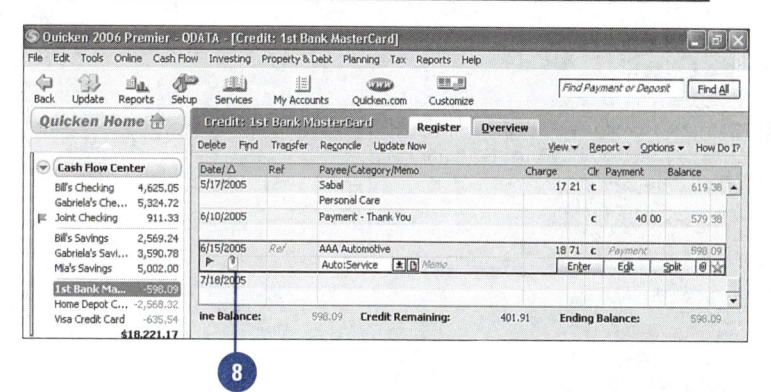

Managing Your Credit Card Accounts **139**

Manually Add Transactions to Your Register

1. If you don't already have the Cash Flow Center open, on the account bar, select the credit card account to which you want to add transactions.

2. To add a transaction, click in the Date column of an empty row and type the date of the transaction.

3. Click Payee and type the payee name.

4. Click Category and select a category to assign to the transaction.

5. Click in Memo to type a note about the transaction.

6. Click in Charge or Payment and type the amount of the transaction.

7. To flag this transaction to follow up on later, or to attach any documentation, such as an electronic copy of a receipt, click the paper clip button.

8. Click Enter.

See Also

See "Flag and Attach Documents to Transactions" on page 138 for more information on flagging transactions and attaching documents.

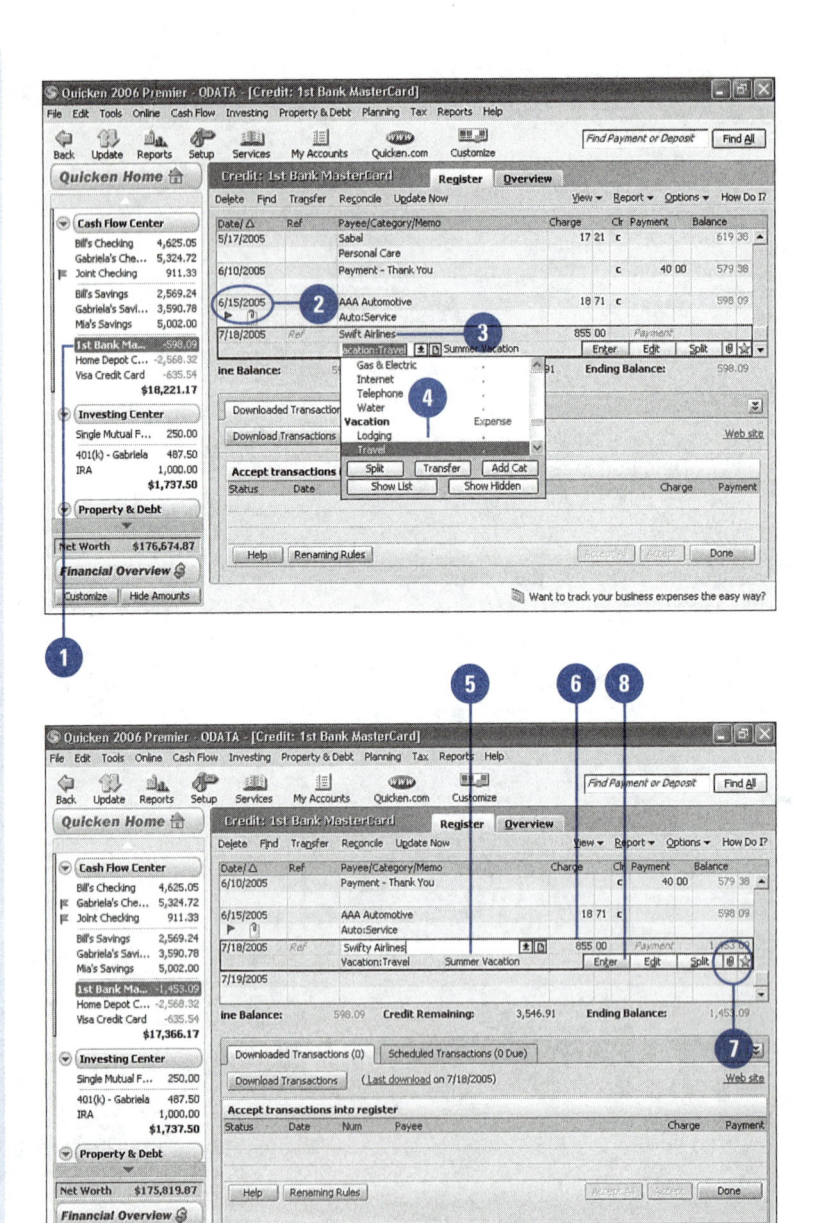

Did You Know?

You can assign multiple categories to a transaction. *To track multiple categories for a transaction, click Split (shown in step 4). From the Split Transaction window, click a line, select a category, and type the split amount. Repeat this procedure for each category you want to add. Ensure the sum equals the total transaction amount and click OK.*

Edit and Delete Credit Card Transactions

1. Click in the area you want to change (for example, in the Payee column to change the name) and type over the existing text.

2. Click Enter to apply the change.

3. Follow steps 1 and 2 to change the information in any of the other fields, as needed.

4. To delete an entire transaction, select the transaction and click Delete. A message appears, asking if you want to delete the transaction.

5. Click Yes to delete the transaction or No to keep it.

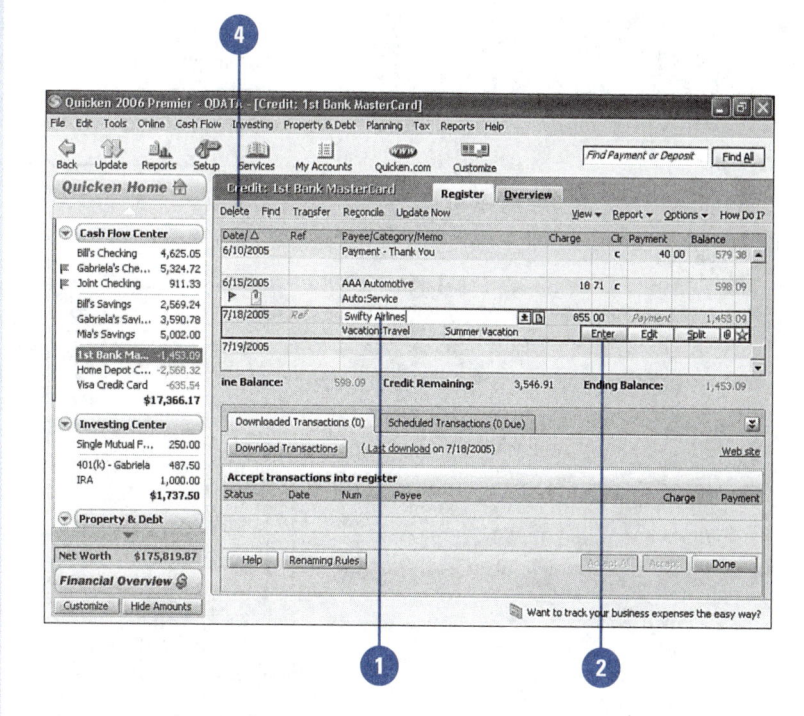

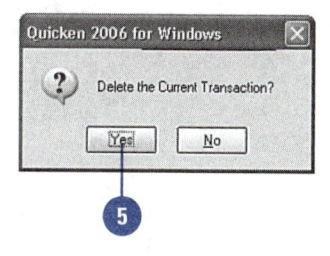

Managing Your Credit Card Accounts **141**

Searching for Credit Card Transactions

As you work with your accounts, your transaction lists grow. This makes finding a specific transaction you are looking for challenging. To help you locate the transaction you are looking for in the sea of transactions, use Quicken's Find tool.

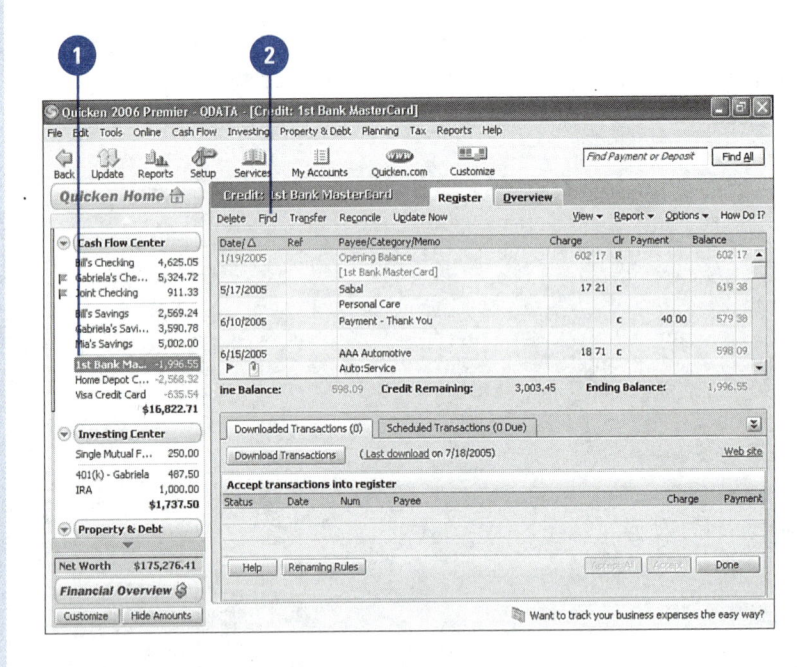

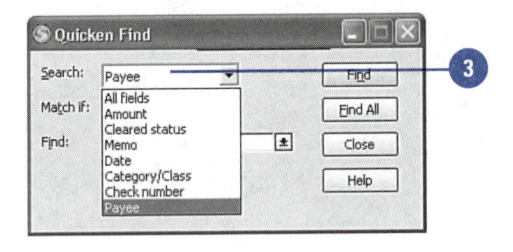

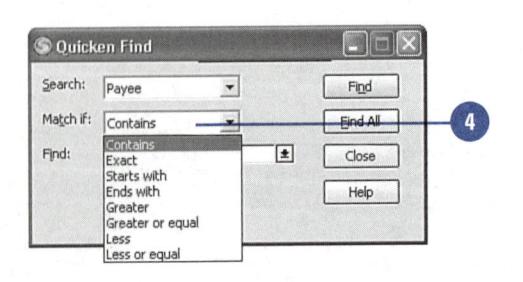

Search for Transactions

1. If you're not already there, open the Cash Flow Center and select the credit card account you want to use to search for transactions.

2. Click Find.

3. From the Search drop-down menu, select the main keyword or the focus of your search. For example, if you want to find the amount that cleared for a specific payee, select Payee.

4. From the Match if drop-down menu, select the criterion you want to use to narrow the search further.

Did You Know?

The Match If and Find criteria work together to locate the transaction. *What you select from the Match if drop-down menu corresponds with what you type in the Find box. For example, because you want to find a specific payee, you probably have the name or a partial name. Therefore, you can select Contains to ensure that Quicken looks for all transactions that contain the name you enter.*

142

5 Type the word or number you are searching for. For example, using the example here, you type **Auto**.

6 If you want Quicken to search backward from the current date, select Search Backwards.

7 Click Find to locate transactions in the current register or click Find All to locate transactions in all registers. Quicken locates and highlights the transactions that contain the search criteria you specified.

8 If you don't see what you are looking for, perform the search again, using different search criteria.

Did You Know?

Sorting transactions is another way of finding transactions. *You can sort your transactions by clicking the column headings. For example, clicking the Payee/Category/Memo heading sorts the transaction list in alphabetic order by the payee name.*

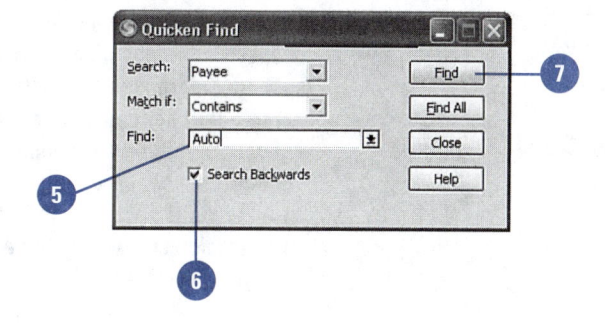

Adding Scheduled Credit Card Transactions to Your Register

When you set up your accounts and tell Quicken about any regularly scheduled transactions for your credit card accounts, Quicken creates a scheduled transaction list for you. The scheduled transactions for your credit card accounts appear on the Scheduled Transactions tab in each of your credit card account registers where you can view, add, edit, and delete transactions. Transactions also appear on the Bills and Scheduled Transactions section in the Cash Flow Center and on the Scheduled Transaction List window where you can also manage scheduled transaction for all your accounts.

If you have online access to some of your accounts, you can download the transactions and enter them into your Quicken registers. However, if you do not have online access for some or all of your accounts, you can use the following task to step through the process. To be reminded when your scheduled transactions are due, use the Cash Flow alerts.

Add Scheduled Credit Card Transactions to Your Register

1. If you're not already there, open the Cash Flow Center and select the credit card account to which you want to add scheduled transactions.

2. Click the Scheduled Transactions tab. The number in parentheses represents the number of transactions waiting to be added to your register.

3. To add a scheduled transaction to your register, click Enter.

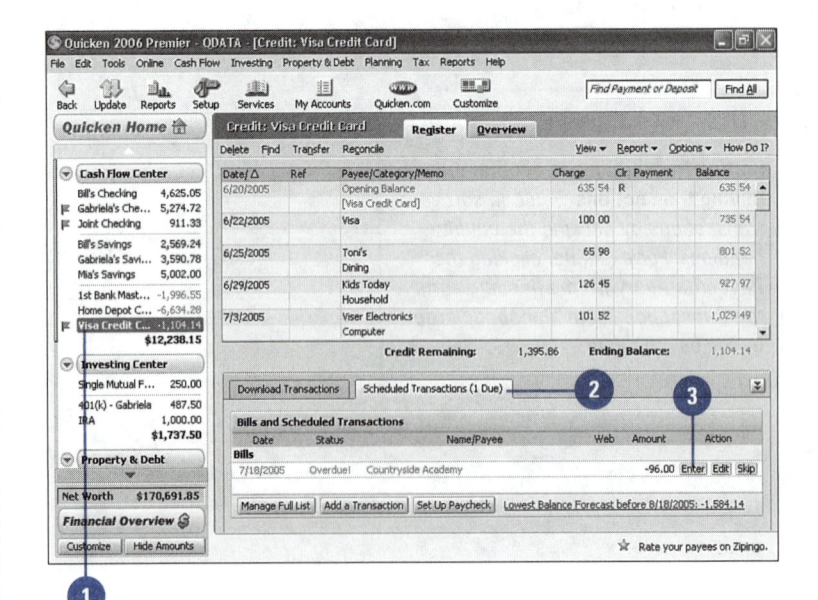

4. Review the information to ensure that it is correct and make changes, if needed.

5. To add the transaction to your register, click Record Payment. Any changes that you make here do not apply to all future transactions—only to the current transaction.

6. Click Cancel to take no action on the transaction and return to the scheduled transaction list. The transaction remains in the scheduled transaction list until you are ready to record it or skip it.

7. Click Skip to remove the transaction from your scheduled transactions for this period but have it reappear the next time it is scheduled to show up.

8. To delete a transaction, you use the Scheduled Transaction List window. Refer to the next task, "Manage Your Scheduled Transactions," for more information.

9. To add a new transaction, click Add a Transaction and complete the Create Scheduled Transaction window.

10. To add a new paycheck, click Set Up Paycheck and complete the Manage Paychecks window.

11. Review, edit, and enter each scheduled transaction until you are finished. Transactions you record are entered into your register, and your balance is adjusted accordingly.

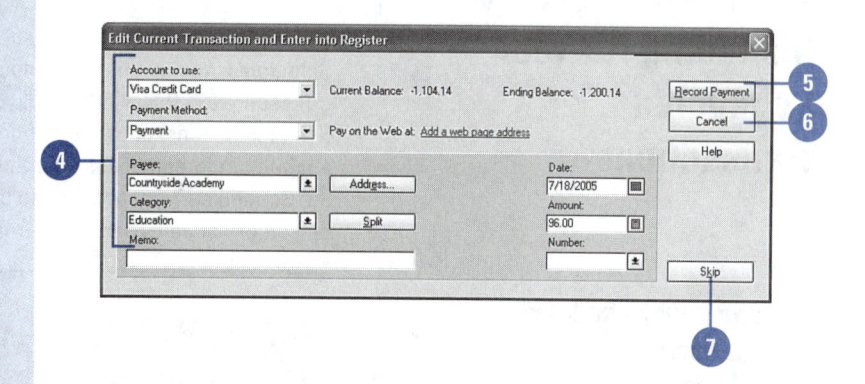

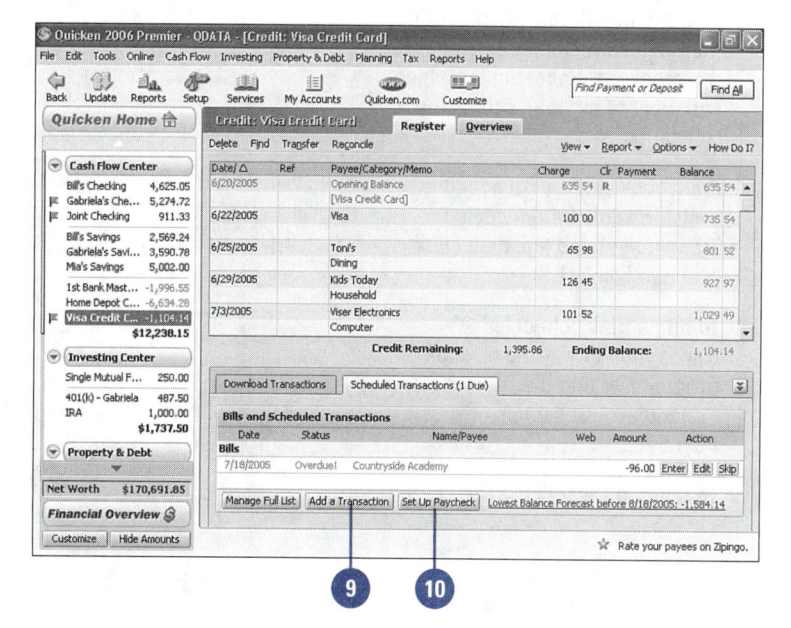

Did You Know?

A red flag means that there are scheduled or downloaded transactions waiting. *If there is a red flag next to an account in the account bar, there are scheduled or downloaded transactions waiting to be entered in that account register.*

See Also

See "Using Bills and Scheduled Transactions" on page 76 for more information on adding and editing scheduled transactions.

Managing Your Credit Card Accounts 145

Managing All Your Scheduled Transactions

To make changes to or delete scheduled transactions, you use the Scheduled Transaction List window. You can also create new scheduled transactions in this window. All your transactions are included in the Scheduled Transaction List window, not just for your credit card accounts. You can access the Scheduled Transaction List window from the Scheduled Transactions tab on the credit card account register, from any other account register, or from the Tools menu.

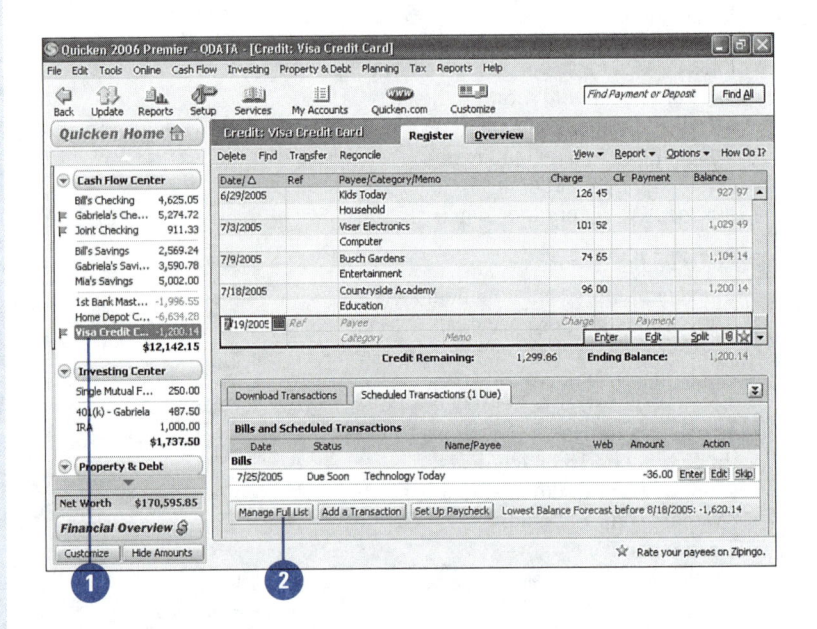

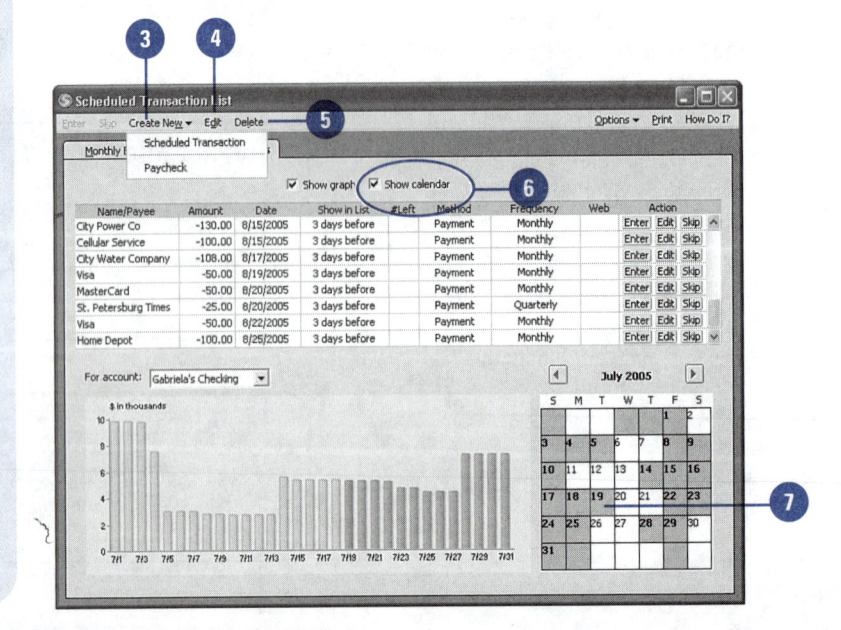

Manage Your Scheduled Transactions

1. If you're not already there, open the Cash Flow Center and select the credit card account for which you want to manage scheduled transactions.

2. From your credit card account register, click the Scheduled Transactions tab and then click Manage Full List.

3. To add a new scheduled transaction or paycheck, click Create New and then select either Scheduled Transaction or Paycheck.

4. To edit a transaction, select it and click Edit.

5. To delete a transaction—for example, if you no longer use the account for the transaction—select the transaction and click Delete.

6. To view the transaction calendar for the current month, select Show calendar. The days on which transactions are due are bolded.

7. To view the calendar in detail, click a day of the month.

8 You can print the calendar, go to a future or previous month, make a note for a specific day, or select only the accounts you want to see on the calendar.

9 To view a graph of daily transactions, select Show Graph.

10 From the For account drop-down menu, select the account you want to view.

11 To view your estimated balance for a specific day, hover (point, don't click) your mouse over a bar of the graph.

> **See Also**
>
> See "Using Bills and Scheduled Transactions" on page 76 for more detailed information on adding, editing, and deleting scheduled transactions.

> **See Also**
>
> See "Create an Alternate View of Transactions" on page 83 for more information on using the calendar.

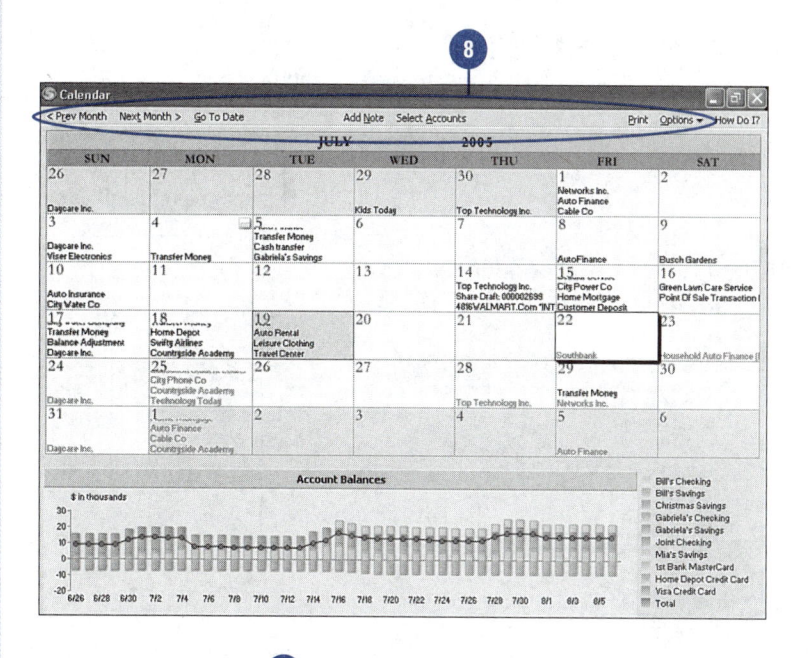

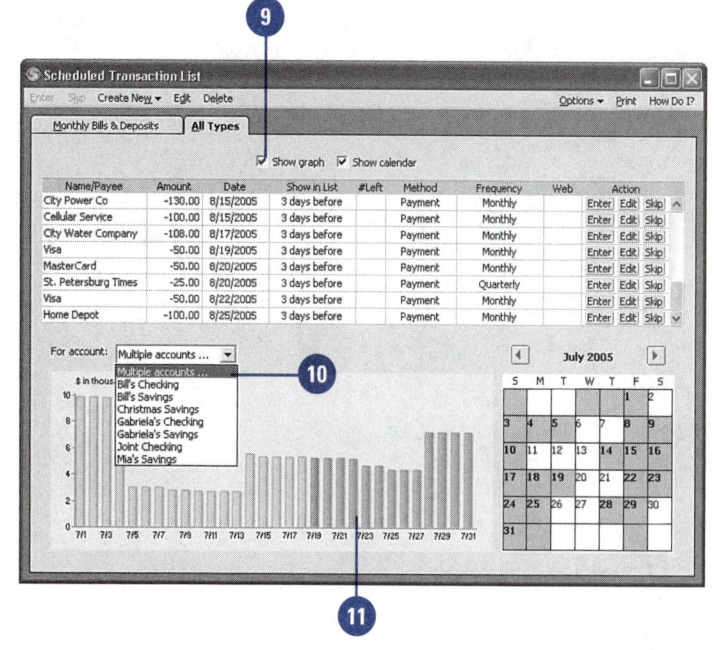

Managing Your Credit Card Accounts **147**

Viewing Credit Card Account Overviews

An account overview is provided for each of your accounts when you open the account. The overviews include account attributes, such as the account name and description; the status, such as the balance and equity; a graph view of the equity; and any expenses associated with the account. In addition, you can edit account details and view reports for the account. The options on each overview vary by account type.

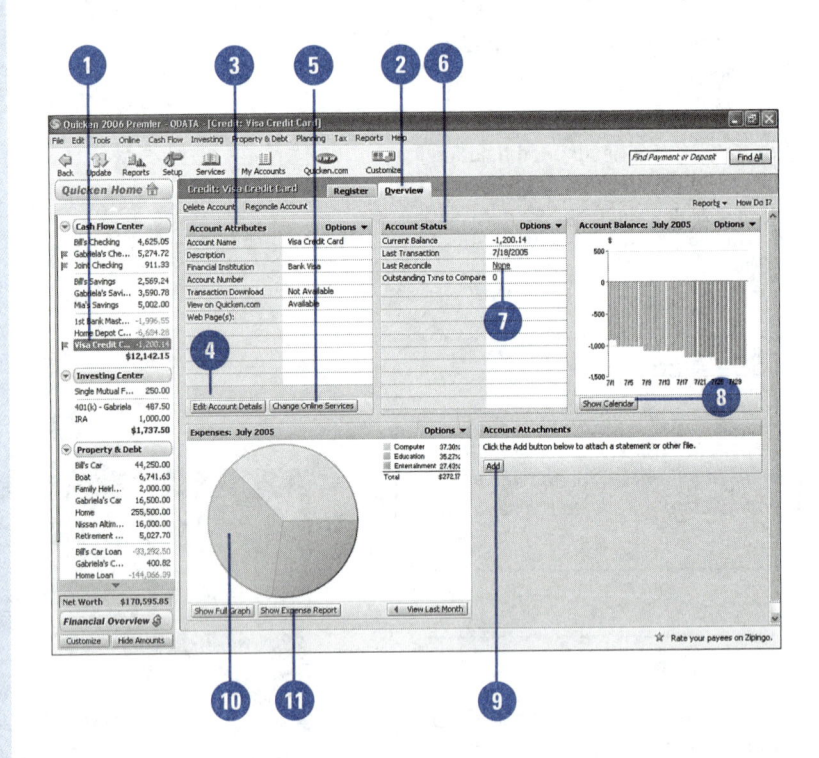

View Credit Card Account Overviews

1. On the Account bar, click the credit card account you want to view.

2. Click the Overview tab.

3. The Account Attributes section lists basic account information.

4. To make changes to the account, click Edit Account Details.

5. To set up online access, click Change Online Services.

6. In the Account Status section, you can view balance and transaction information.

7. You can balance the account by clicking the last reconcile date or click None if you have not balanced the account yet.

8. Click Show Calendar to view the account calendar.

9. You can add documents, such as online statements by clicking Add and completing the Add Attachment window.

10. The Expenses section lists any expenses that are related to the account. These expenses are provided for the year-to-date, month-to-date, and totals.

11. Click Show Expense Report to view the Expenses report.

148

Balancing Your Credit Card Accounts

You can balance or reconcile credit card accounts manually or by downloading your statements. If the account has online access, each time you download your transactions, Quicken automatically clears each transaction in your register and reconciles the account. Therefore, you don't have to compare your statement to the register in order to balance an online account.

If the account does not have online access, you can use your monthly bank statement to compare against your Quicken register. If you find discrepancies, you can reconcile your balance by adding missing transactions, updating transactions, and so on to ensure that your ending balance matches that on your paper statement. You need to keep in mind that some transactions may not have cleared yet and therefore might not show up on your statement.

Before you begin to balance your accounts, you should make sure that all transactions (deposits, withdrawals, purchases, payments, interest, and so on) have been downloaded and recorded or entered in your account register, and you should have your statement ready.

Balance Your Account Manually

1. In the Cash Flow Center section of the account bar, select the credit card account you want to balance.

2. Click in the Clr column of the first cleared transaction. A message appears, asking if you want to reconcile this account.

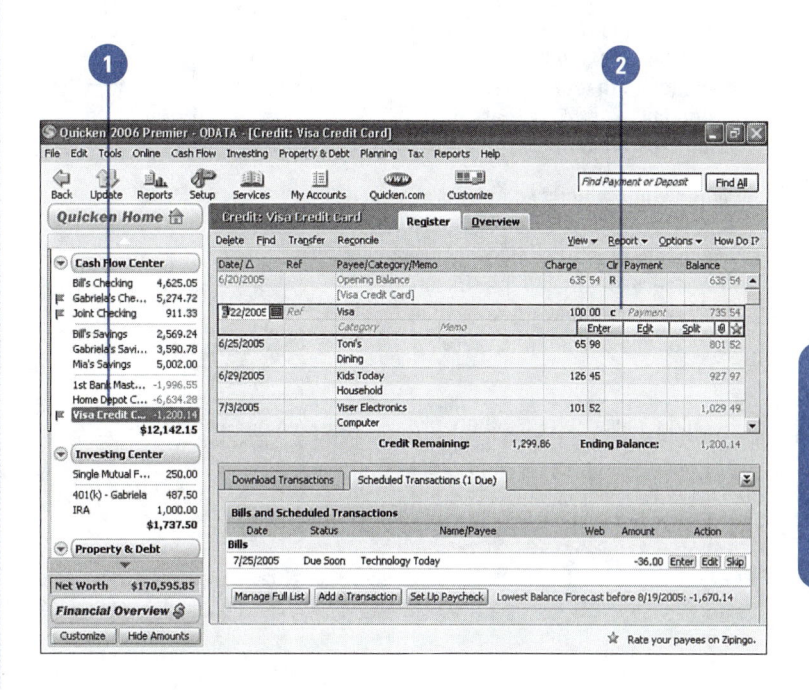

Managing Your Credit Card Accounts **149**

③ Click Yes. The Statement Summary dialog box opens.

④ Using your statement, type the total charges you made for the month and type the figure in the Charges, Cash Advances box.

⑤ Using your statement, type the total deposits for the month in the Payments, Credit box.

⑥ Type your ending balance and ending statement date.

⑦ Type any finance charges, the date of the finance charges, and then select a category to associate with the charges and interest.

⑧ Click OK. The Statement Summary window opens.

⑨ Using your statement, review the list of transactions and click in the Clr column next to each transaction that has cleared. A green check mark appears next to each cleared item.

⑩ When you are finished comparing and clearing transactions, look at the number next to Difference. If it is not zero, determine the reason for the discrepancy (for example, maybe fees and interest were added).

⑪ To add a missing transaction, click New.

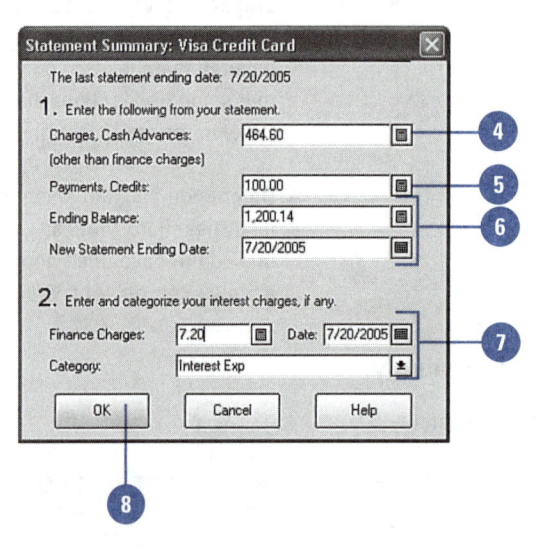

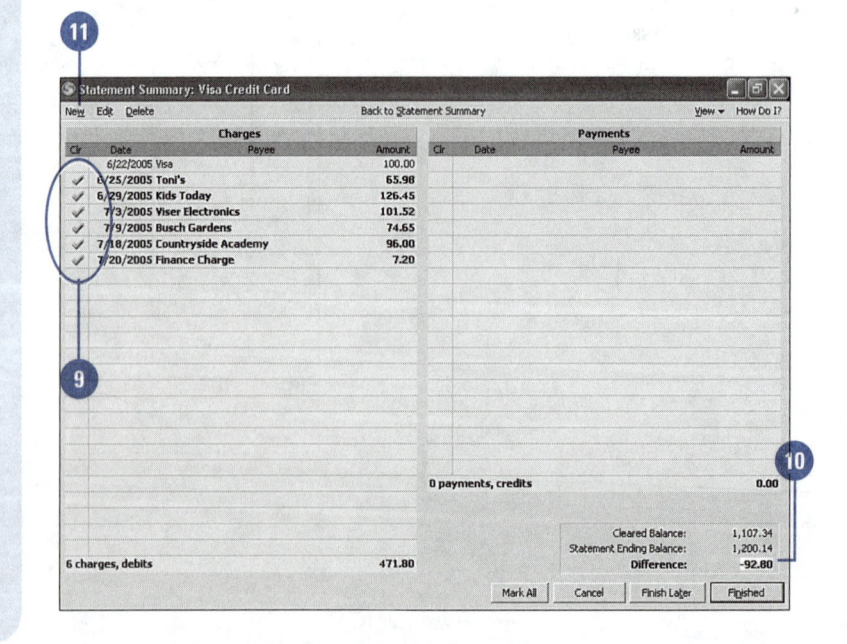

150

⑫ Type the information in your register, click Return to Reconcile to finish balancing your account.

⑬ To edit a transaction, select the transaction, click Edit, make your changes, and click Return to Reconcile.

⑭ To complete the balance at another time, click Finish Later.

⑮ When you finish balancing the account, click Finished. If the account is balanced, Quicken places an R in the Clr column of your register to show the transactions are reconciled. If the account does not balance, a message appears asking if you want to make a payment.

⑯ If you want to record a payment, select the payment method and click Yes; otherwise, click No.

Did You Know?

You can update figures in the Account Summary window. *If you need to go back to the Statement Summary dialog box shown in steps 4–8 and change any of the statement information, from the menu bar in the Statement Summary window shown in steps 13-15, click Back to Statement Summary. You can then make your changes and click OK. The figures adjust accordingly.*

See Also

See "Add Scheduled Credit Card Transactions to Your Register" on page 144 for more information on adding new, editing existing, and deleting transactions.

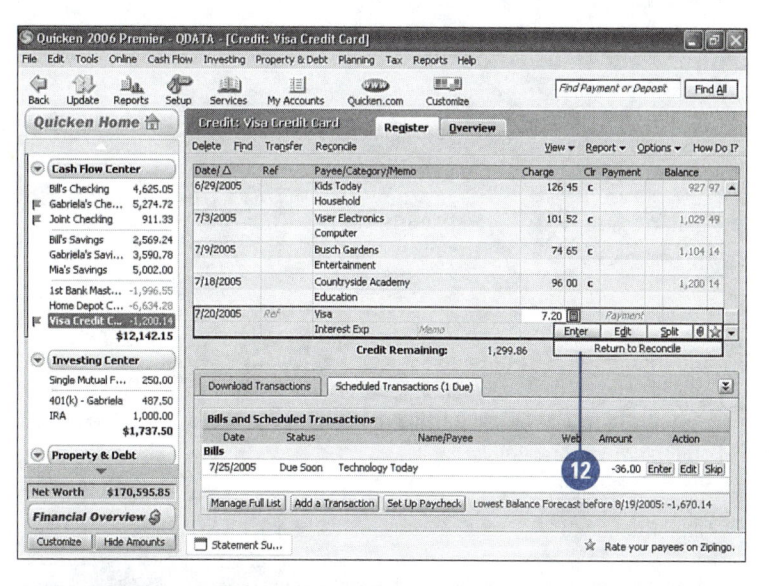

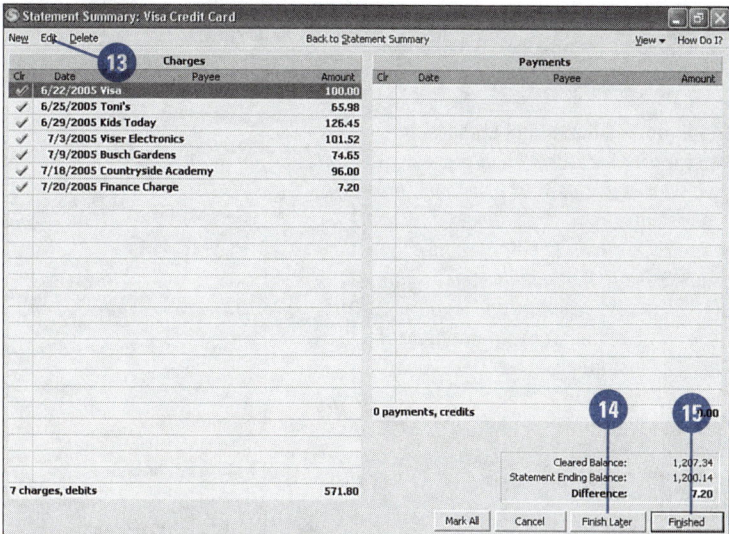

Managing Your Credit Card Accounts **151**

Balance Your Online Accounts

1. In the Cash Flow Center section of the account bar, select the credit card account you want to balance.

2. Click Update Now. If you use the PIN vault, you may be required to enter your PIN vault password.

3. Log in to your account and download the most recent transactions. If the Online Update Summary window appears, click Done to close it.

4. Click Reconcile.

Did You Know?

The login and download process differs for credit cards. *When you download your credit card transactions, the process may differ from what you see here. If your login and download process is not the same as this example, follow the prompts, and if you have trouble, contact your credit card financial institution.*

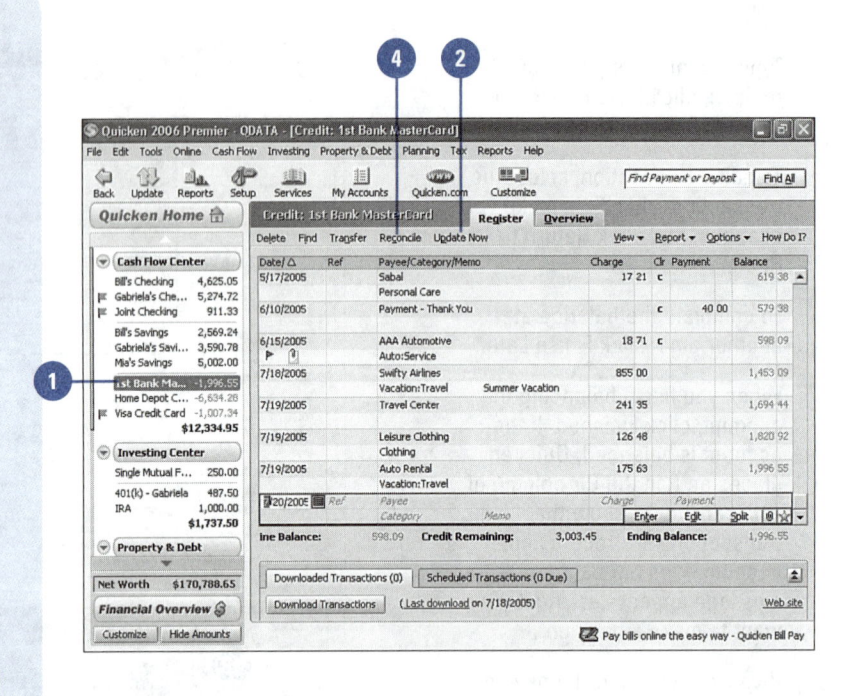

5 To let Quicken compare your transactions and reconcile your account, select Auto reconcile after compare to register and click OK. The Reconcile window opens.

6 Quicken places a green check mark next to each transaction that has cleared. In this example, even though there are transactions with no check marks, there is no discrepancy because these transactions have not yet cleared.

7 To add a missing transaction, click New.

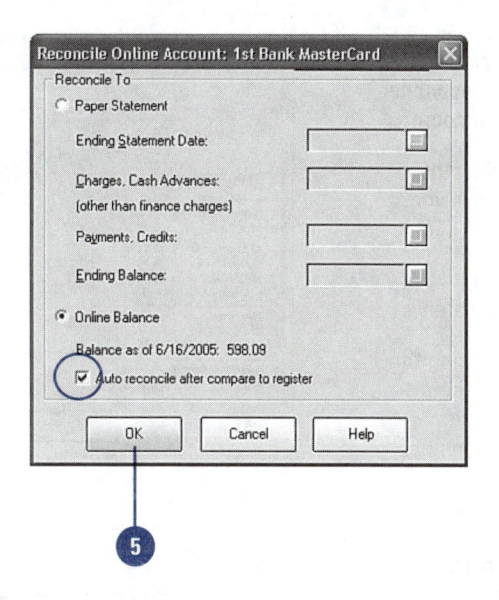

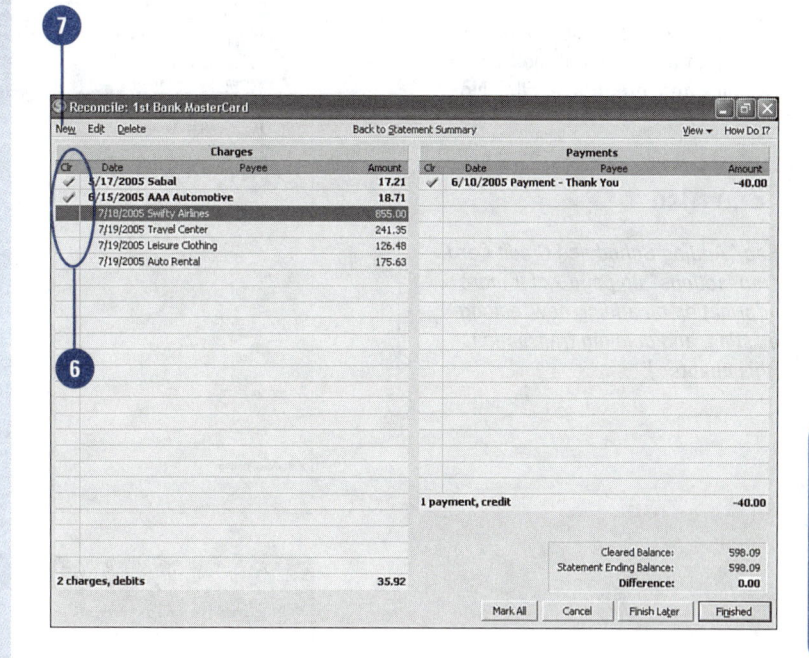

Managing Your Credit Card Accounts **153**

8. Update your register, click Enter, and then click Return to Reconcile to finish balancing your account.

9. To edit a transaction, select the transaction, click Edit, make your changes, and click Enter.

10. To complete the balance at another time, click Finish Later.

11. When you are finish balancing the account, click Finished. If the account is balanced, Quicken places an R in the Clr column of your register to show the transactions are reconciled. If the account does not balance, a message appears asking if you want to make a payment.

12. If you want to record a payment, select the payment method and click Yes; otherwise, click No.

See Also

See "Adding Scheduled Credit Card Transactions" on page xx for more information on adding new, editing existing, and deleting transactions. [this chapter]

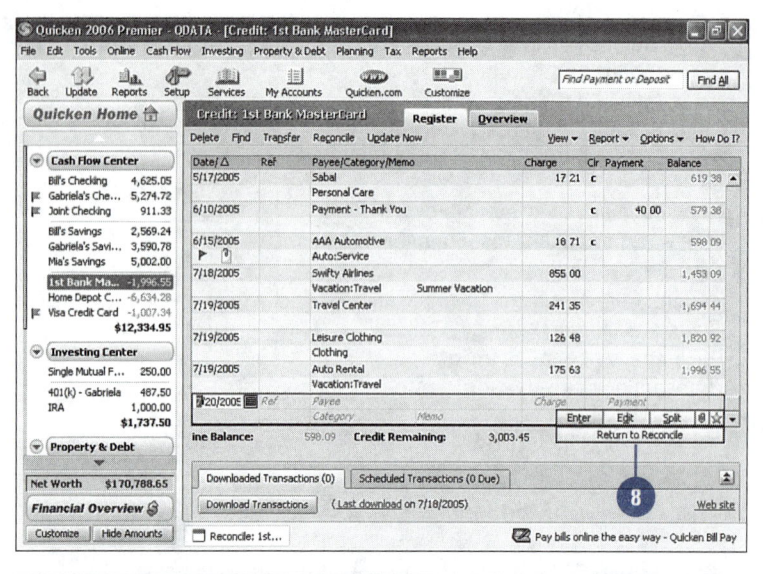

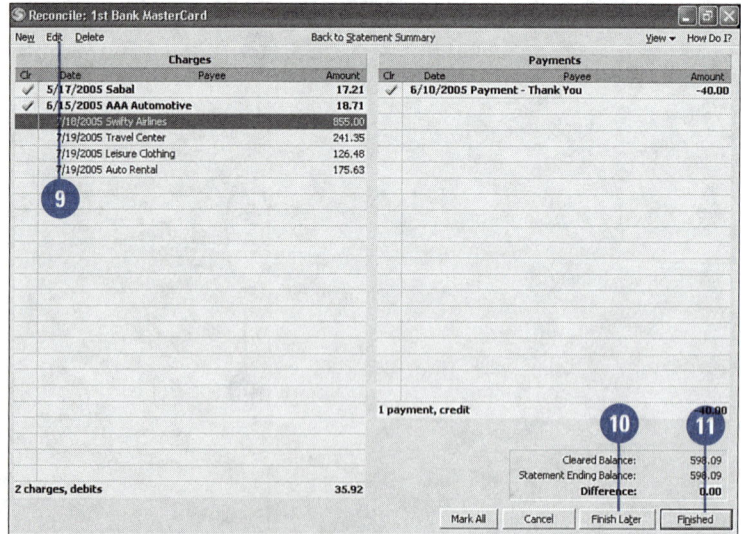

154

Managing Your Bills

Introduction

The Bills and Scheduled Transactions section of the Cash Flow Center allows you to view your bills that are due, enter them in your account registers, edit the transaction information, and choose to skip individual instances of transactions. In addition, you can add new transactions and paychecks. Using the Bills and Scheduled Transactions section to manage your bills and transactions is beneficial because all your bills and transactions are listed in one place. You don't have to open individual accounts to view the bills or scheduled transactions that are due for that account and then add, edit, or choose to skip them. The Bills and Scheduled Transactions section provides one-stop access to all your bills and account transactions that are due.

In addition to covering the Bills and Scheduled Transactions section, this chapter also covers reviewing and analyzing your income and expenses, running income and expense reports, setting up and paying your bills by using Quicken Bill Pay, and using and printing Quicken checks. This chapter is chock full of information to help you manage and take control of your bills and scheduled transactions.

What You'll Do

Set Up New and Edit Existing Bill and Scheduled Transaction Alerts

Review Your Bills and Scheduled Transactions

Add, Edit, and Skip Bills and Scheduled Transactions

Manage All Your Scheduled Transactions

Add New Scheduled Transactions

Add and Edit Paychecks

View and Analyze Income and Expenses

Use Quicken Bill Pay

Order and Print Quicken Checks

Setting Up New and Editing Existing Bill and Scheduled Transaction Alerts

Set Up New and Edit Existing Bill and Scheduled Transaction Alerts

1. If you don't already have the Cash Flow Center open, on the account bar, click Cash Flow Center.

2. To take action on an alert, click the link to open the account register to resolve the alert.

3. To view and manage all your alerts, click Show all alerts to open the Alerts Center window.

4. To create or edit cash flow alerts, click Setup. You can also click the Set Up Alerts button on the Cash Flow Alerts section of the Cash Flow Center.

See Also

See "Using Alerts" on page 74 for more information on creating and changing alerts.

You can set up alerts in the Cash Flow Center to remind or warn you of actions you need to take for your spending and savings accounts, credit cards, and bills (for example, to notify you that your bills are due). In addition, you can access alerts for all your other accounts, remove alerts, and change existing alerts.

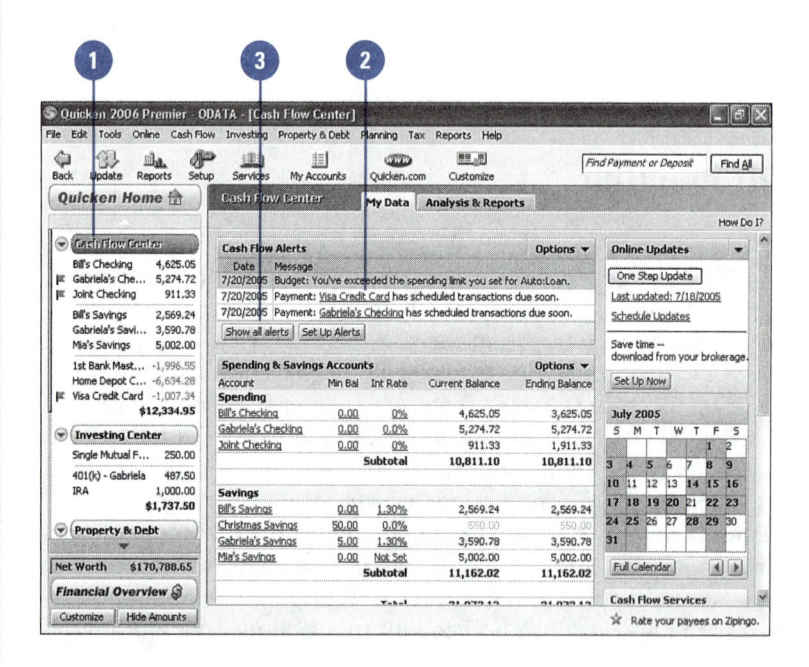

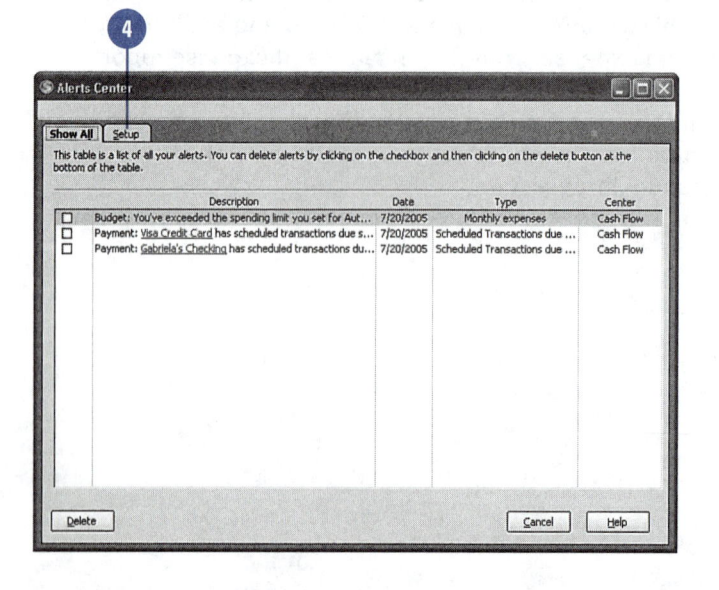

Reviewing Your Bills and Scheduled Transactions

The Bills and Scheduled Transactions section of the Cash Flow Center lists your bills and scheduled transactions that are due. Bills and scheduled transactions that are due also appear on the Bills and Scheduled Transactions section of the Quicken Home page.

Bills and transactions appear at the time that you specified when you set up the accounts. For example, if you indicated that you wanted to be reminded 3 days before a bill is due and it is due the 15th of every month, that bill will appear on the Bills and Scheduled Transactions list on the 12th of every month. You can view transactions, add them to account registers, or skip the current transactions. In addition, you can access the Scheduled Transaction List window, where you can set up and manage all your scheduled transactions and add new paychecks.

To help you avoid a financial bottleneck, your lowest account balance appears on the Bills and Scheduled Transactions section as well. In the Forecast Lowest Balance window, you can set preferences to track and display the lowest account balance for a specified future time frame or not at all. For example, if you want to see what your lowest account balance will be 30 days from the current day, you can tell Quicken to show that balance for you. The lowest account balance is a projection based on current bills, spending habits, account balances, and scheduled transaction trends.

Review Your Bills and Scheduled Transactions

1. If you don't already have the Cash Flow Center open, on the account bar, click Cash Flow Center and then scroll down to the Bills and Scheduled Transactions section. All bills, deposits, and other transactions that are due soon are listed.

2. Hover (point, don't click) your mouse over a transaction to see the average amount for the transaction. Click Show Report to view the Transaction report.

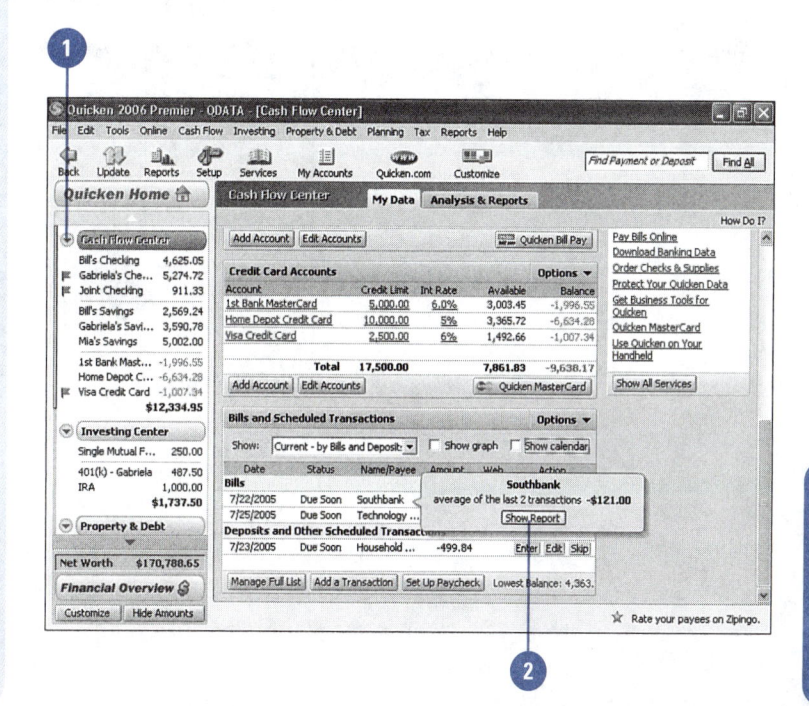

Managing Your Bills 157

③ You can sort the list by clicking the Show drop-down list and selecting a different sort.

④ To view a bar graph view of your account balance over a month's time, select Show graph. Hover your mouse over one of the bars to see your balance for that day.

⑤ To change the account used on the bar graph, from the For account drop-down menu, select an account.

⑥ To change the month, click the back arrow to move back a month or click the forward arrow to move ahead a month.

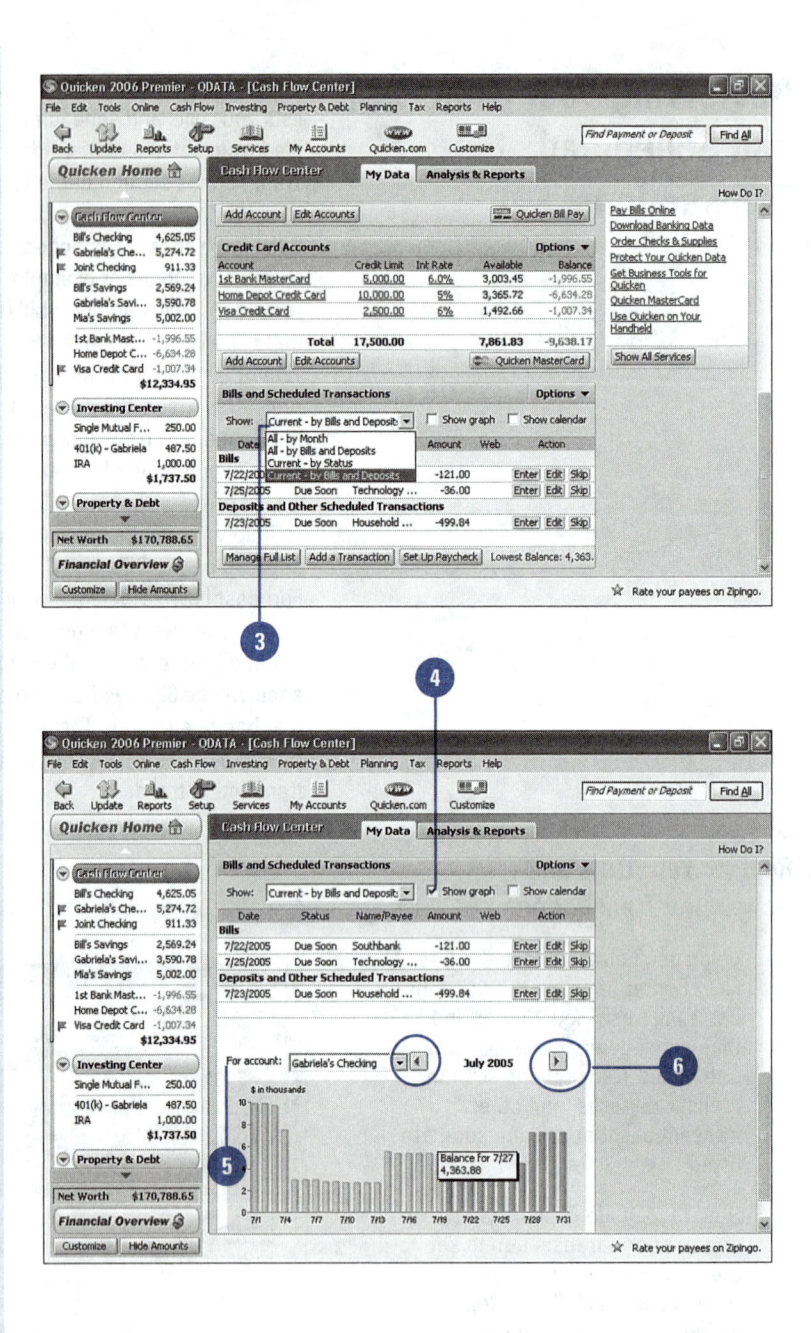

⑦ To view the calendar month with the dates highlighted for the bills and transactions that are due, select Show calendar.

⑧ The Bills section lists the date each of your bills are due, the status, the payee, and the amount of the payment. If the bill is accessible online, a link appears in the Web column.

⑨ The Deposits and Other Scheduled Transactions section lists regularly scheduled deposits and non-bill transactions, and it includes the same information as the Bills section.

⑩ You can click Enter to record a transaction in the account register, click Edit to change transaction information, or click Skip to skip the current instance of a transaction.

⑪ Lowest Balance provides the projected lowest balance for the time period that you specify. To set or remove it, click the Lowest Balance link.

⑫ From the Forecast Lowest Balance dialog box, select the time period you want Quicken to use when forecasting your balance and the time period or date, if applicable.

⑬ To remove the lowest balance, select Never display the lowest balance. Then click OK.

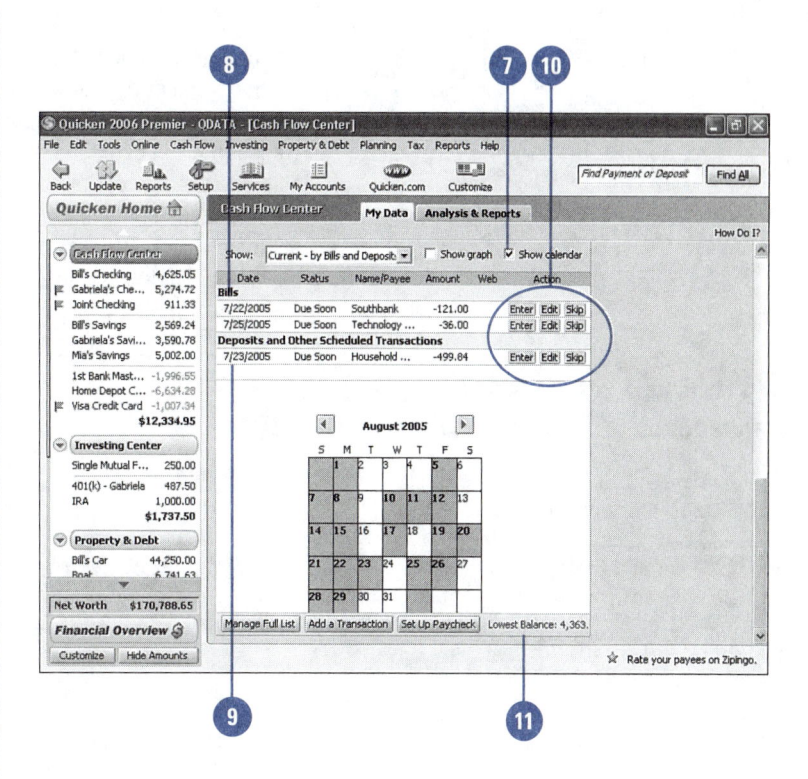

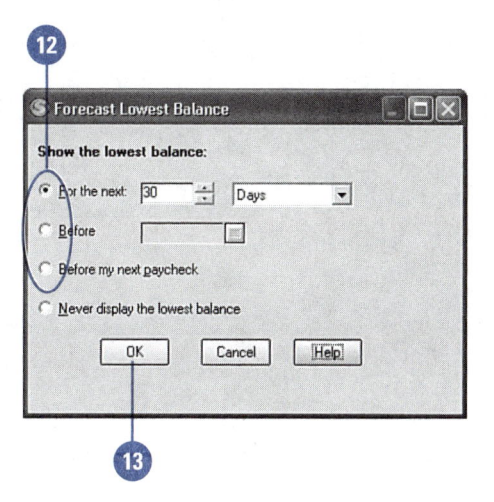

Managing Your Bills **159**

Adding, Editing, and Skipping Bills and Scheduled Transactions

As your bills and scheduled transactions become due, you can add them to your account registers, edit them, or skip an instance of a transaction. When you enter account transactions from the Bills and Scheduled Transactions section of the Cash Flow Center, they are automatically added to the appropriate account register. If you download transactions, the transactions appear on the Downloaded Transactions tab in the account register. You can then add the transactions to your register. You designate when bills and scheduled transactions show up on the list when you set up the account.

Add Bills and Scheduled Transactions to Your Register

1. If you don't already have the Cash Flow Center open, on the account bar, click Cash Flow Center and then scroll down to the Bills and Scheduled Transactions section.

2. To record a transaction in the account register, click Enter.

3. Review the transaction information to ensure that it is correct. Make changes, if needed, and click Record Payment. Any changes you make apply only to the current transaction, not to all future transactions.

4. Click Cancel to take no action on the transaction and return to the Bills and Scheduled Transactions list. The transaction remains on the list until you are ready to record it.

5. Click Skip if you want to remove the transaction from your scheduled transactions for this period but have it reappear the next time it is due.

6. Repeat steps 1–5 for each bill or transaction you want to add to your account registers.

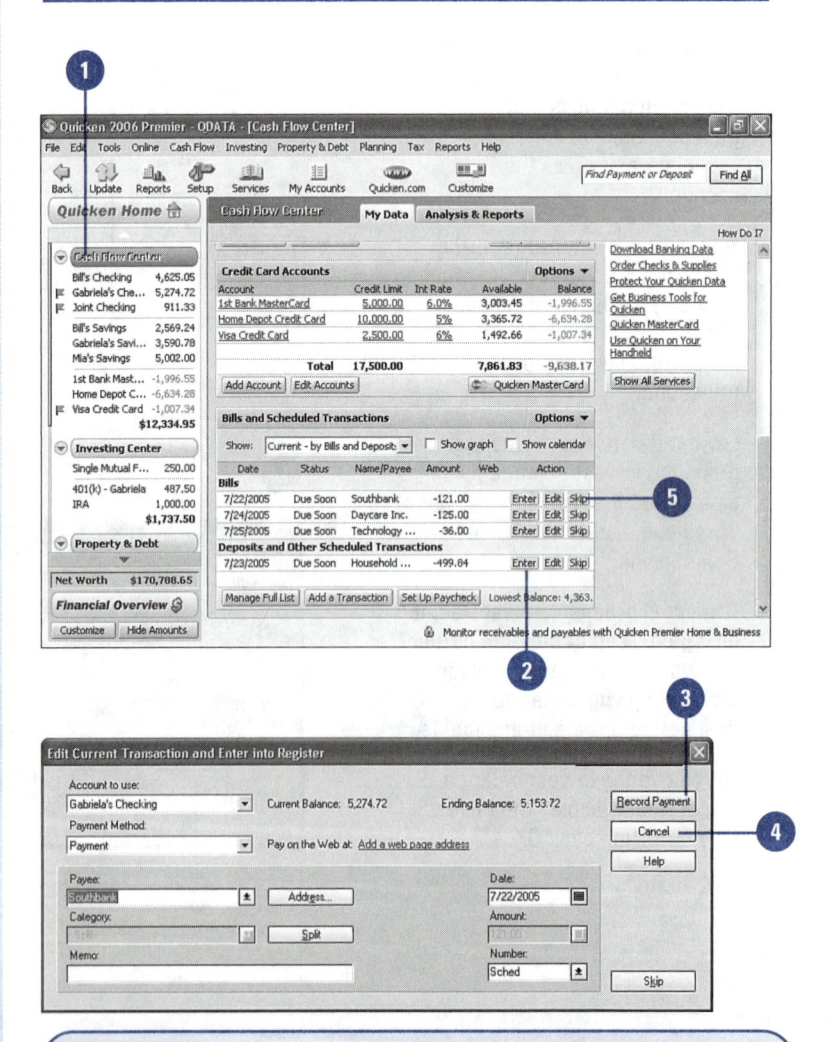

See Also

See the next task, "Edit Future Instances of a Transaction" on page 161 for information on making permanent changes to transactions.

Edit Future Instances of a Transaction

1. To edit all future instances of a transaction, click Edit.
2. Make any changes needed.
3. To disregard any changes you made, click Cancel. The transaction remains as is in the Bills and Scheduled Transactions section.
4. To save changes you made, click OK.

Did You Know?

To delete a transaction, you use the Scheduled Transaction List window. Refer to the task "Managing All Your Scheduled Transactions," on the next page, for more information.

See Also

See "Using Bills and Scheduled Transactions" on page 76 for more information on adding and editing scheduled transactions.

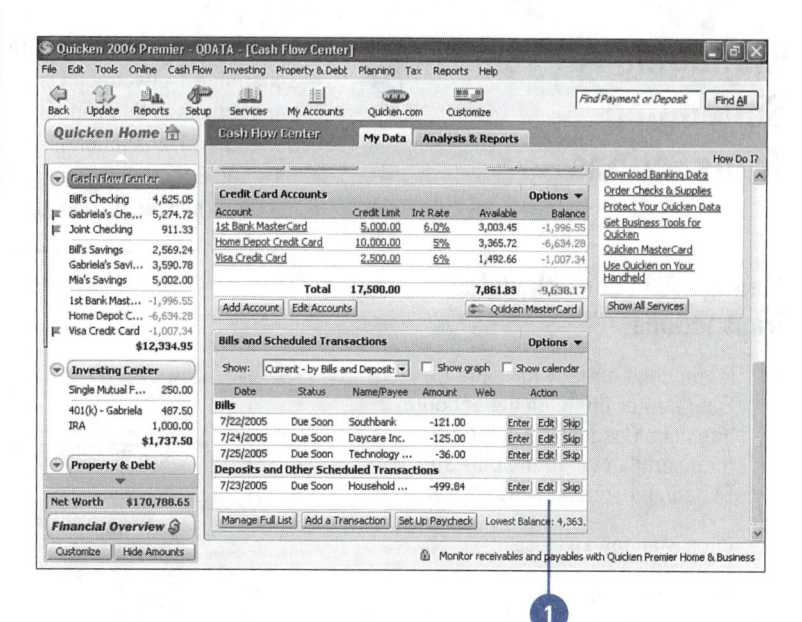

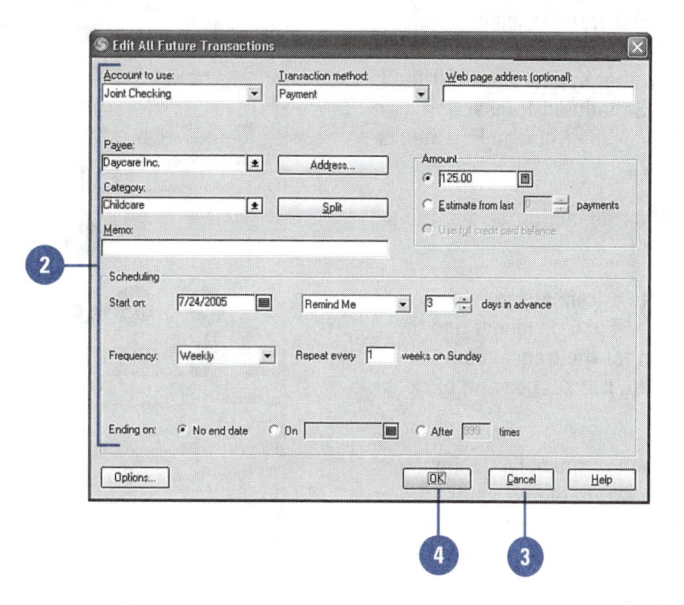

Managing Your Bills **161**

Managing All Your Scheduled Transactions

To make changes to or delete scheduled transactions, you use the Scheduled Transaction List window. You can also create new scheduled transactions in this window. All your transactions are included in the Scheduled Transaction List window. You can access this window from the Bills and Scheduled Transactions section of the Cash Flow Center, from any account register, or from the Tools menu.

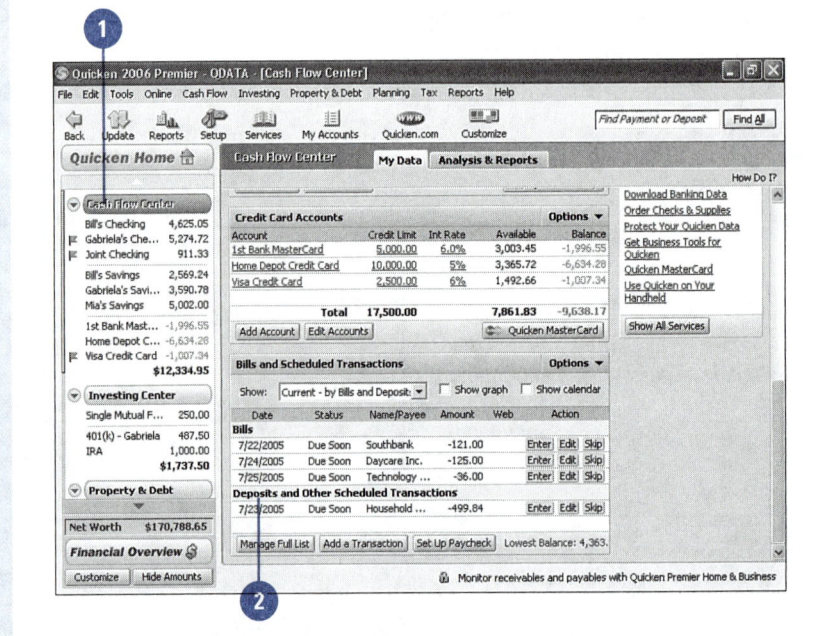

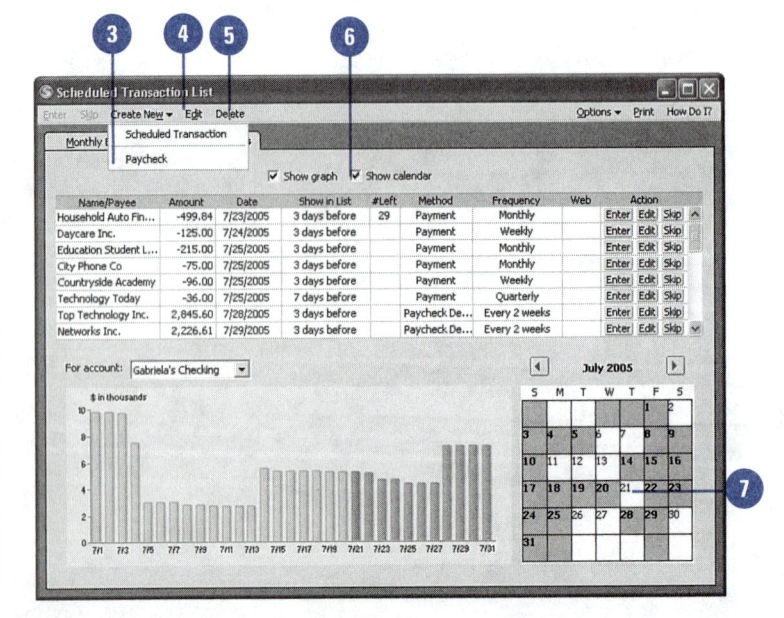

Manage All Your Scheduled Transactions

1. If you don't already have the Cash Flow Center open, on the account bar, click Cash Flow Center and then scroll down to the Bills and Scheduled Transactions section.

2. Click Manage Full List.

3. To add a new scheduled transaction or paycheck, click Create New and select either Scheduled Transaction or Paycheck, and then complete the window that appears—either the Create Scheduled Transaction window or the Manage Paychecks window.

4. To edit a transaction, select it and click Edit.

5. To delete a transaction—for example, if you no longer use the account for the transaction—select the transaction and click Delete.

6. To view the transaction calendar for the current month, select Show calendar. The days on which transactions are due are bolded.

7. To view the calendar in detail, click a day of the month.

8. If desired, print the calendar, go to a future or previous month, make a note for a specific day, or select only the accounts you want to see on the calendar.

9. To view a graph of daily transactions, select Show graph and from the For account drop-down menu, select the account you want to view.

10. To view your estimated balance for a specific day, hover (point, don't click) your mouse over a bar of the graph.

> **See Also**
>
> *See "Using Bills and Scheduled Transactions" on page 76 for more detailed information on adding, editing, and deleting scheduled transactions.*

> **See Also**
>
> *See "Create an Alternate View of Transactions" on page 83 for more information on using the monthly calendars.*

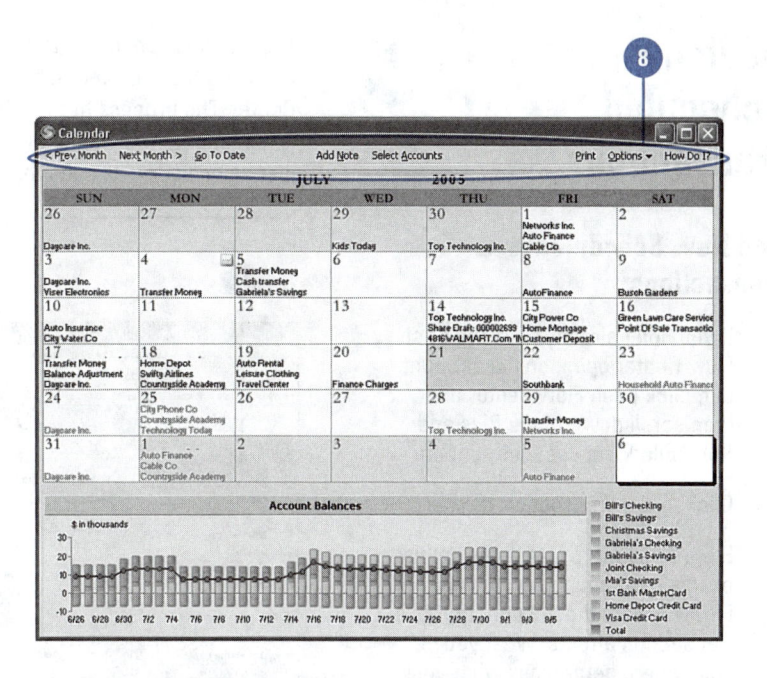

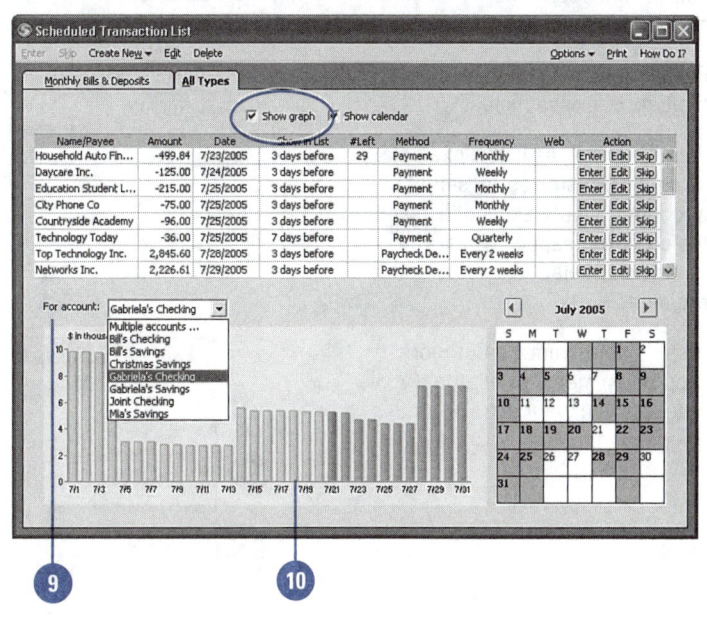

Managing Your Bills **163**

Adding New Scheduled Transactions

You can add scheduled transactions from several places in Quicken, including the Bills and Scheduled Transactions section of the Cash Flow Center. The process here is the same as in other areas of Quicken. This is just another convenient way to enter new transactions while you are managing your bills and other transactions.

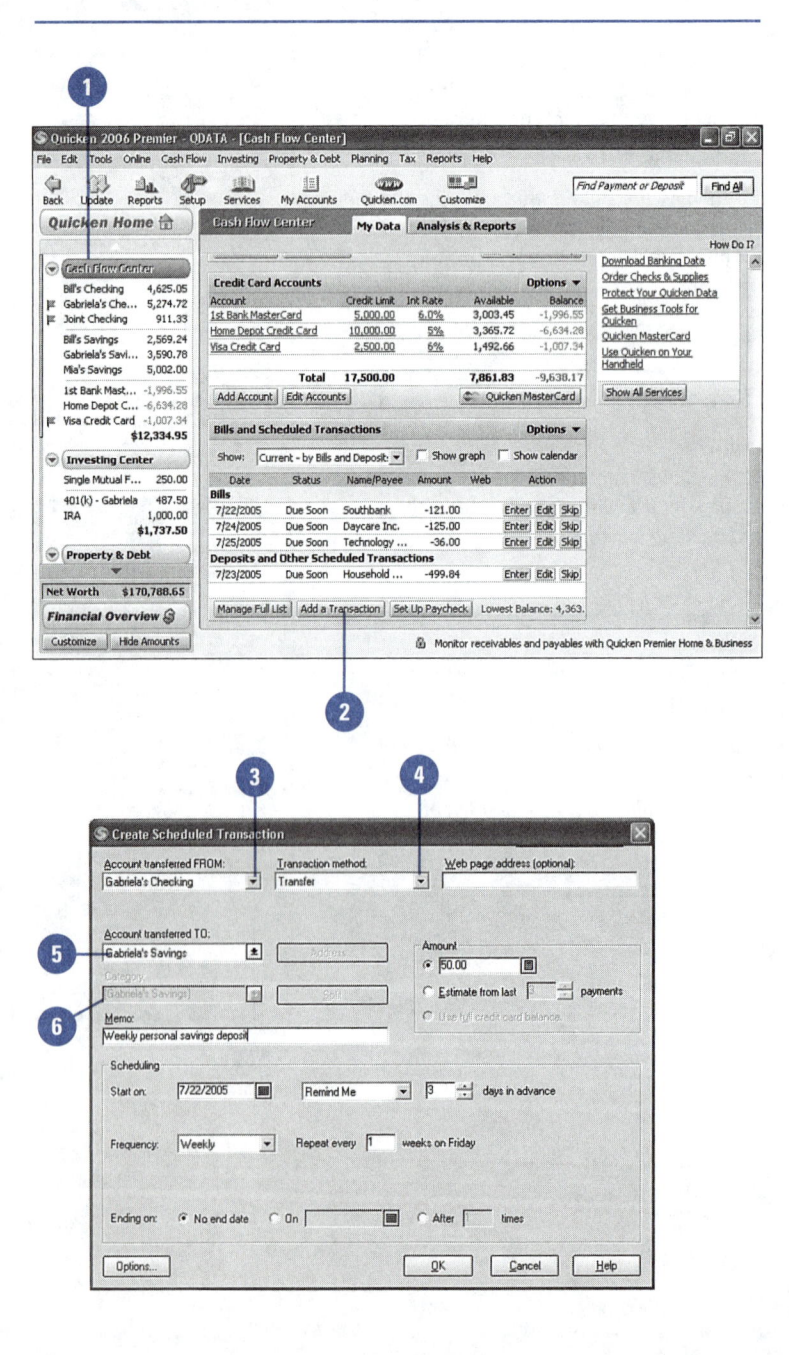

Add New Scheduled Transactions

1. If you don't already have the Cash Flow Center open, on the account bar, click Cash Flow Center and then scroll down to the Bills and Scheduled Transactions section.

2. Click Add a Transaction.

3. From Account to Use or, as in this example, Account transferred FROM, select the account that this transaction affects. What you select here determines what your options are on this window.

4. From Transaction method, select the type of transaction.

5. From Payee or, as in this example, Account Transferred To, select an account from the account list. For the other transaction types, you can type or select the name of the recipient.

6. If applicable, from the Category drop-down menu, select the category you want to track for this transaction.

164

7 In Amount, type the amount of the transaction.

8 Click in Memo to type a note about the transaction.

9 Type or select the due date and reminder information.

10 Select how frequently the transaction takes place. If this is a one-time transaction, select Only Once, and you don't have to complete any of the other scheduling information.

11 Select No end date if the transaction is continuous or type a date when the transaction will end.

12 Click OK. The transaction is added to the appropriate account and will appear in the Bills and Scheduled Transactions list and on the Quicken Home page when it is due.

Did You Know?

You can add the payee address from the Create Scheduled Transaction window. *If you are adding payment, printed check, or deposit transactions, you can add the payee address and contact information by clicking the Address button. If you use Quicken checks, you can also have this information printed on the checks. In addition, if you have the Premier Home and Business version of Quicken, you can use the address for printing mailing labels, envelopes, and business forms.*

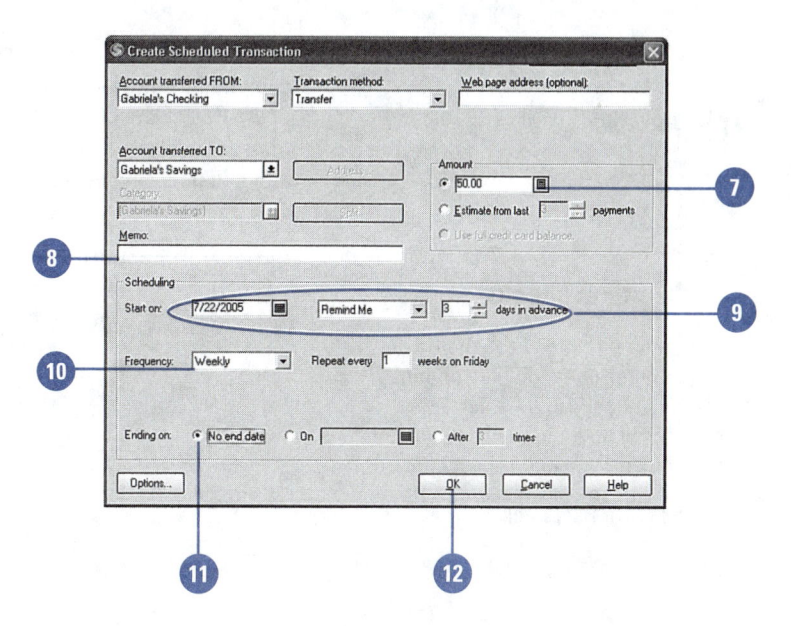

Did You Know?

You can assign more than one category to a transaction. *To track more than one category for a transaction, click Split. Then from the Split Transaction window, click a line, select a category, and type the amount for the category. Repeat this for each category you want to add. When you are finished adding the categories and amounts, click Adjust. The sum of the splits must equal the total amount of the transaction. If the sum of the categories does not equal the total amount of the transaction, adjust the category amounts. When the sum equals the total, click OK.*

Did You Know?

Some information is automatically updated. *If you used a split transaction, the amount is already updated but is grayed out so that you can't change it. In step 5, if you selected a payee you've used previously, the amount that you used previously is automatically entered, but you can change it.*

Managing Your Bills **165**

Adding and Editing Paychecks

As with scheduled transactions, there are several places from which you can add new paychecks, and the Bills and Scheduled Transactions section of the Cash Flow Center is one of those places. Also, as with scheduled transactions, as you manage and work with your bills and transactions, you can add new paychecks, edit existing paycheck information, and add one-time payments.

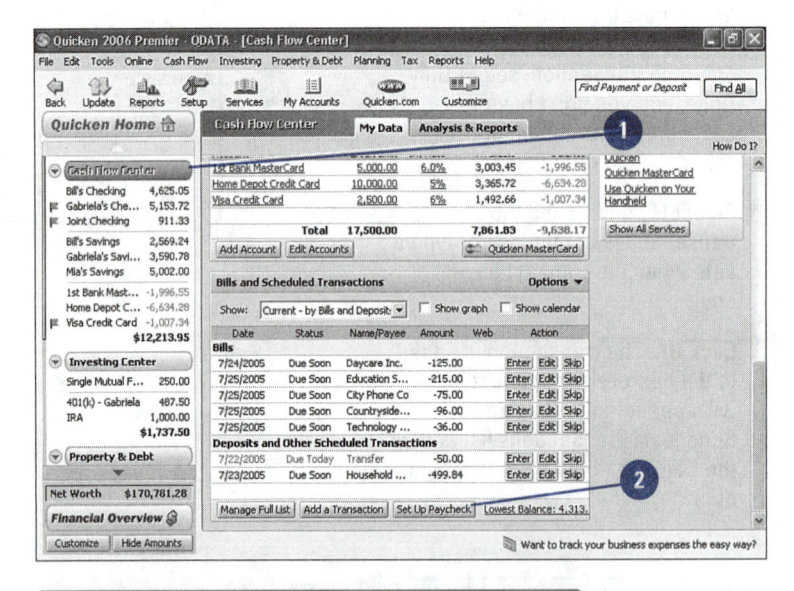

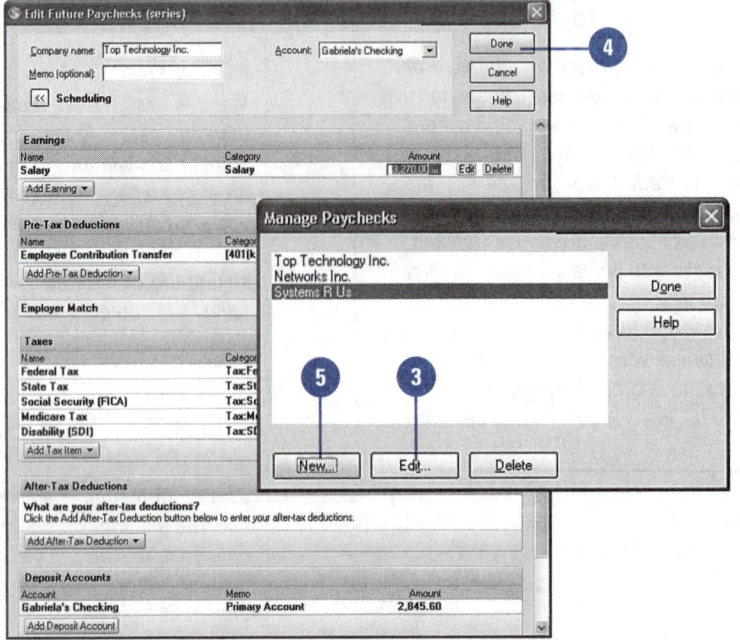

Add and Edit Paychecks

1. If you don't already have the Cash Flow Center open, on the account bar, click Cash Flow Center and then scroll down to the Bills and Scheduled Transactions section.

2. Click Set Up Paycheck.

3. To edit an existing paycheck, select it and click Edit.

4. Change any of the information and then click Done.

5. To add a new paycheck, click New.

6. Click Next.

7. Complete the setup information and click Next to proceed through the setup.

See Also

See "Setting Up Your Paychecks" on page 33 for more detailed information on completing paycheck information.

8. Enter the new paycheck information and then click Done.

9. Select whether you want to enter year-to-date information for the new paycheck and click OK. If this is a one-time payment, you don't need to enter this information. If this is a regularly paid paycheck, you can enter the information to use for tax purposes.

10. Click Done on manage Paychecks dialog box.

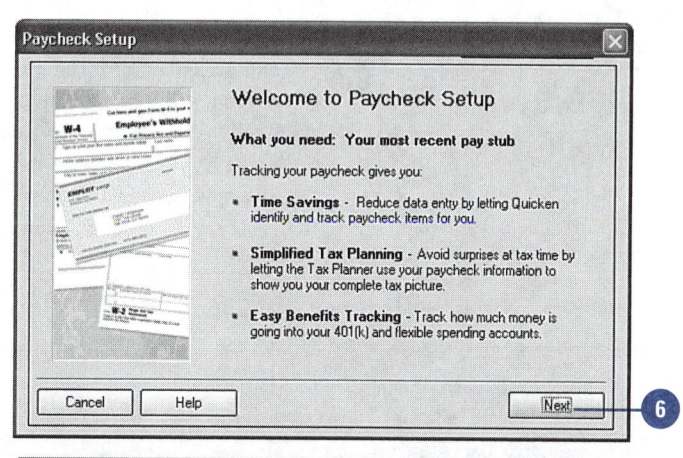

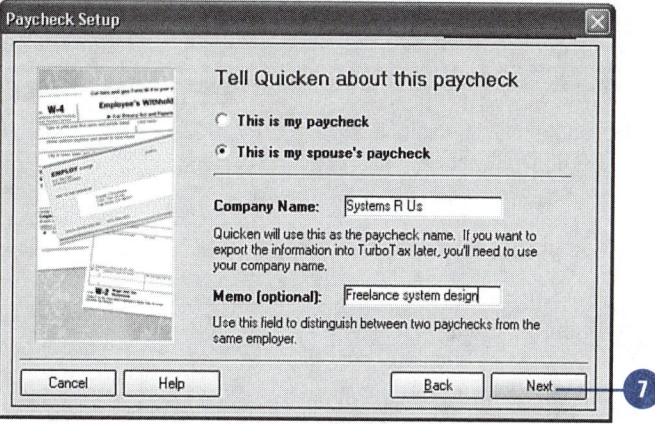

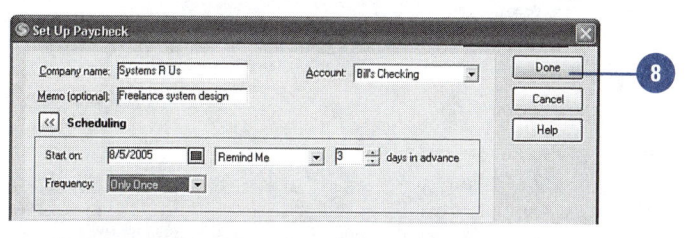

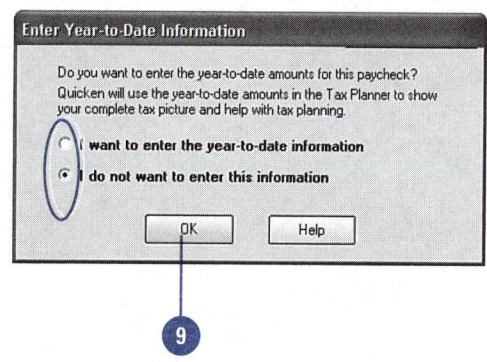

Managing Your Bills **167**

Viewing and Analyzing Income and Expenses

The Analysis & Reports tab of the Cash Flow Center provides monthly expense pie charts, income and expense comparisons, and budget information, if you have a budget. This information allows you to take a bird's-eye look at your financial situation and assess where all your money is going and exactly how much you have coming in on a monthly basis or over any time frame you choose. In addition, you can run reports to further review your income, expenses, and budget.

View and Analyze Income and Expenses

1. If you don't already have the Cash Flow Center open, on the account bar, click Cash Flow Center and then click the Analysis & Reports tab.

2. The Expenses section provides a pie chart view of all your expenses for the current month. Hover your mouse over a slice of the pie to view the percentage and dollar amount for that category.

3. The color key shows the expense categories, the percentages for each category, the color the category represents, and your total expenses. Hover your mouse over a category to view the amount of the expenses the slice represents.

4. Click Show Full Graph to view the Expenses report as a pie chart or click Show Expense Report to view the Expenses report by category.

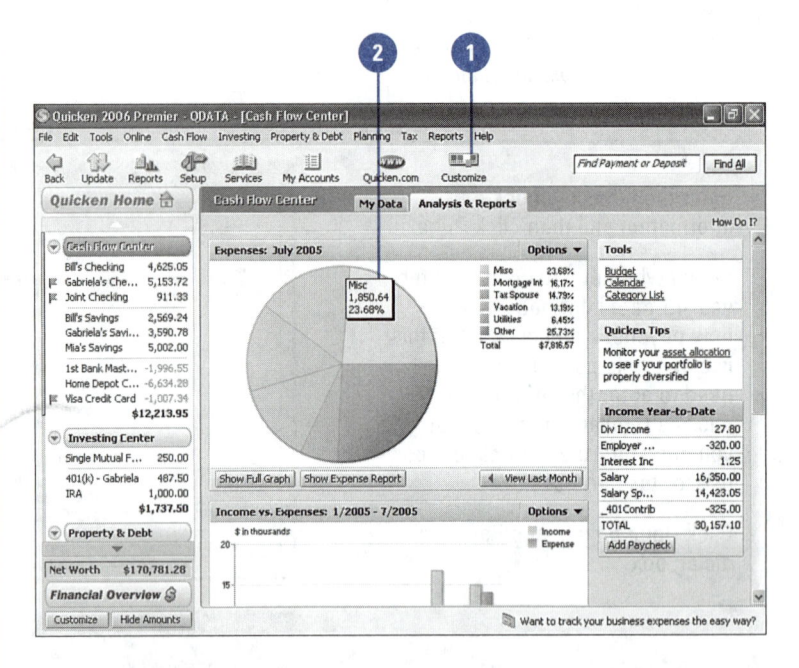

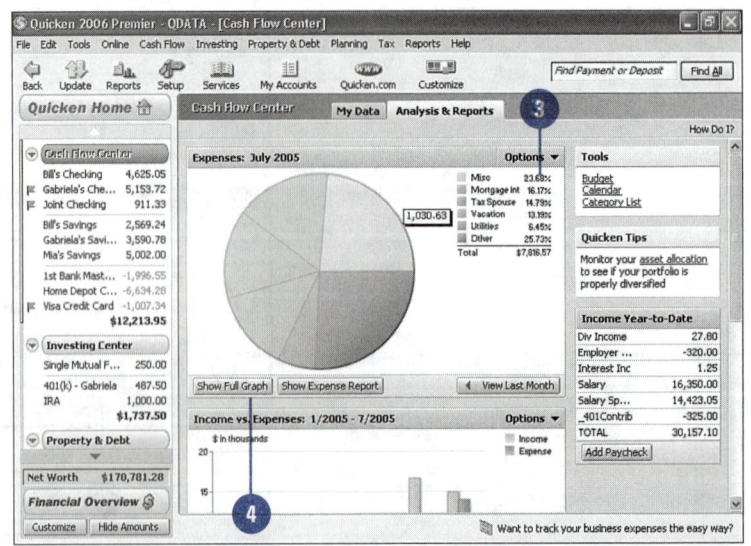

5 From the Income vs. Expenses section, you can view a bar graph of your total income and expenses over several months' time. Hover your mouse over a bar to view the total income or expenses for that month.

6 The color key shows the color the expenses and income represent. Hover your mouse over either Income or Expense to view your total income or total expense for the time period shown.

7 Click Show Full Graph to view the bar graph view of the Income vs. Expenses report or click Show Income/Expense Report to view the Expenses report by income and expenses categories.

8 The Budget section provides budget categories and budgeted amounts, what you actually spent for each category, and the difference between what you budgeted and what you spent.

9 Click Show Budget to review your budget or click Show Monthly Budget Report to view the Budget report for the current month.

10 Click View Current Month to view budget information for the current calendar month.

See Also

See "Getting Out of Debt" on page 326 for more detailed information on creating and managing a budget.

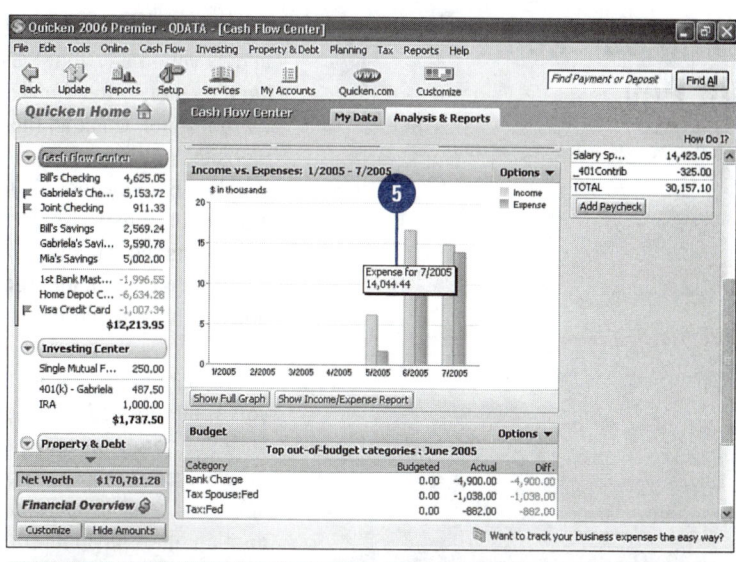

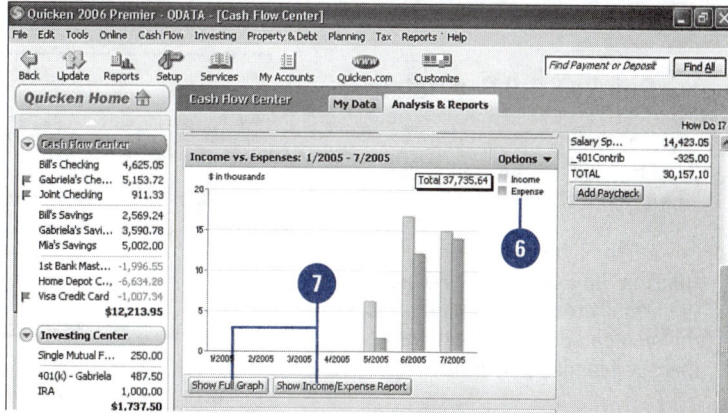

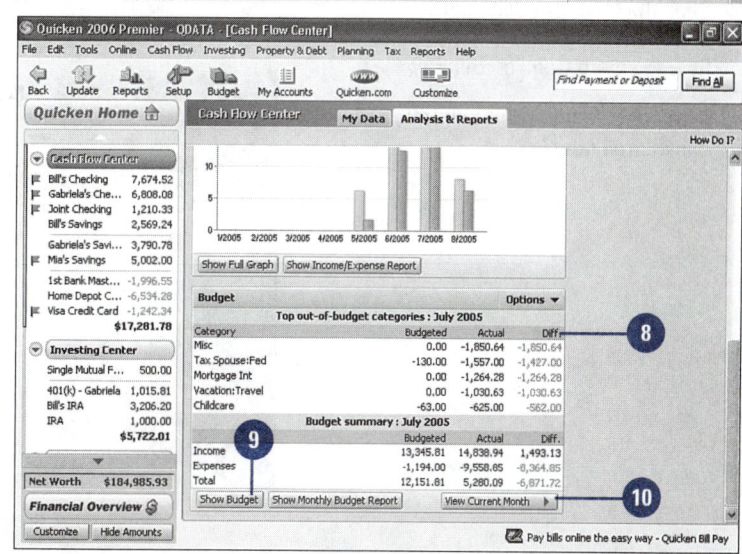

Managing Your Bills **169**

Using Quicken Bill Pay

Quicken offers a bill payment tool called Quicken Bill Pay. Quicken Bill Pay allows you to pay your bills and carry out non-bill transactions, such as sending money to a family member or a babysitter, from your Quicken software through Quicken Bill Pay. You can also pay bills through the Bill Pay website. Your accounts don't have to offer online services for you to use Quicken Bill Pay, though. If the payee or financial institution can receive electronic transfers, the money is electronically taken out of your account and deposited into the payee's account. However, for payees or financial institutions that cannot receive electronic transfers, Quicken prints a check and sends it the old-fashioned way, via U.S. mail.

There is, of course, a fee to use Quicken Bill Pay and some limitations. If you are interested in using Quicken Bill Pay, check out the details to be sure this service is for you. To enroll, you must complete an application and provide your personal information. When you are approved, you can start setting up your payee and bill information and start paying bills and conducting other payment transactions. You receive your login information by email.

Review Quicken Bill Pay Details

1. From the Online menu, select Quicken Bill Pay and then click Learn About Quicken Bill Pay.

2. Review the information about the Quicken Bill Pay service. Be sure to carefully read all information so that you can determine whether this service meets your needs.

3. Click the tabs for additional information and instructions on how to set up Quicken Bill Pay.

4. If you decide you want to enroll, click Enroll now.

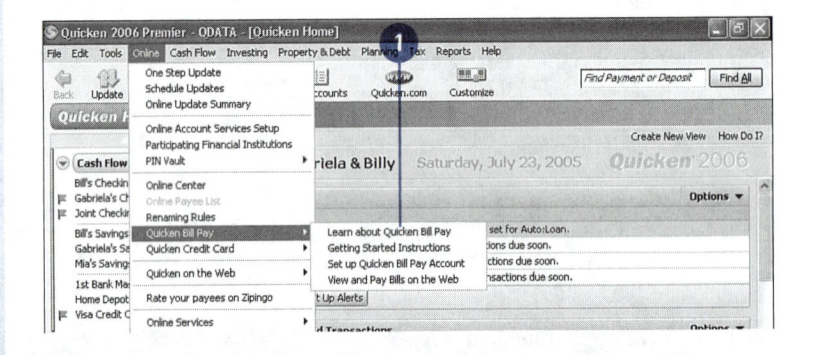

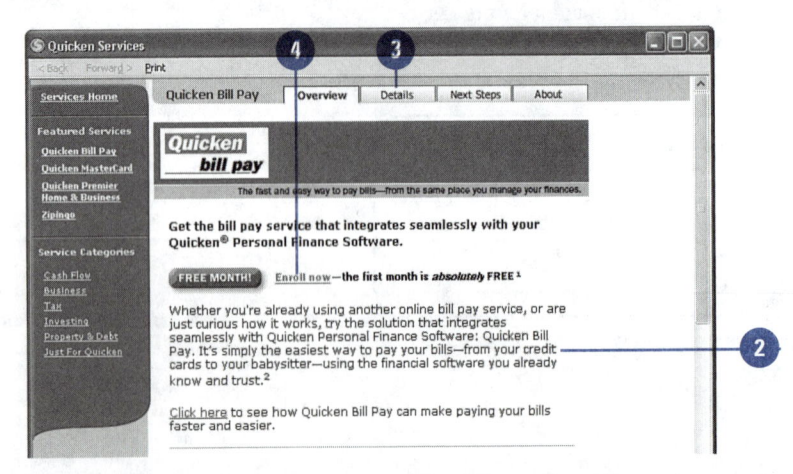

Enroll in Quicken Bill Pay

1. Review the Quicken Bill Pay introduction information, click any of the links to get more information, and then scroll down to complete the application. Required fields are bolded.

2. Type your personal and demographic information.

3. Type the login and password you want to use, select a secret question, and type the answer to the secret question. The secret question is used to identify you when you inquire on your account.

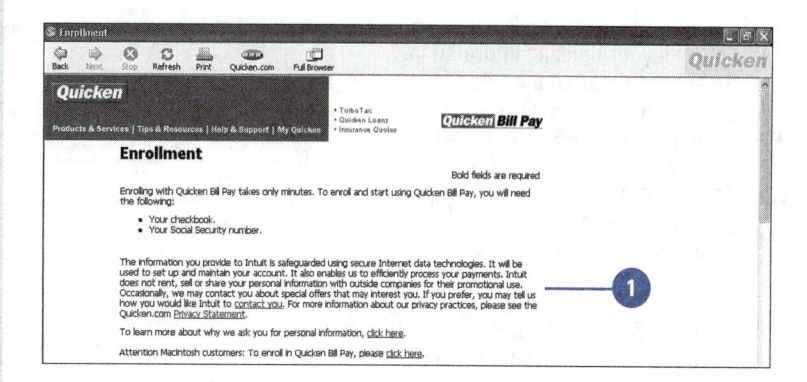

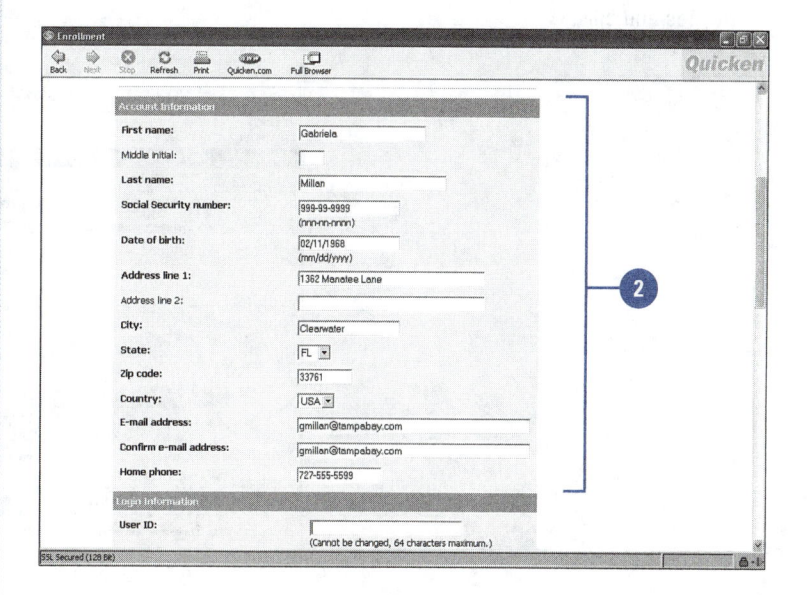

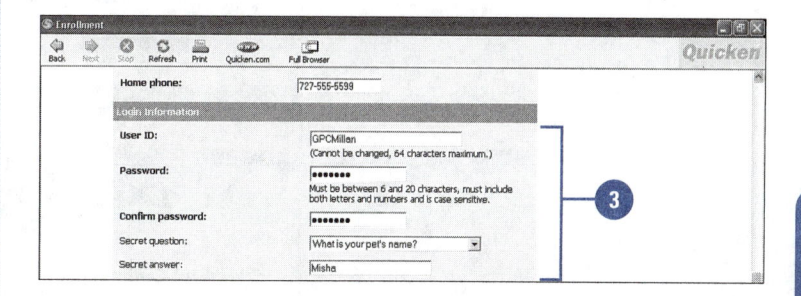

Managing Your Bills **171**

4. Enter all your banking information. Be sure to enter your entire account number, including any leading or trailing zeros.

5. Select the type of email messages you can receive, text or HTML, and then select the version of Quicken you use.

6. Read the privacy statement, select the check box next to it, and click Sign me up.

7. Click the here link to set up your payees and bills.

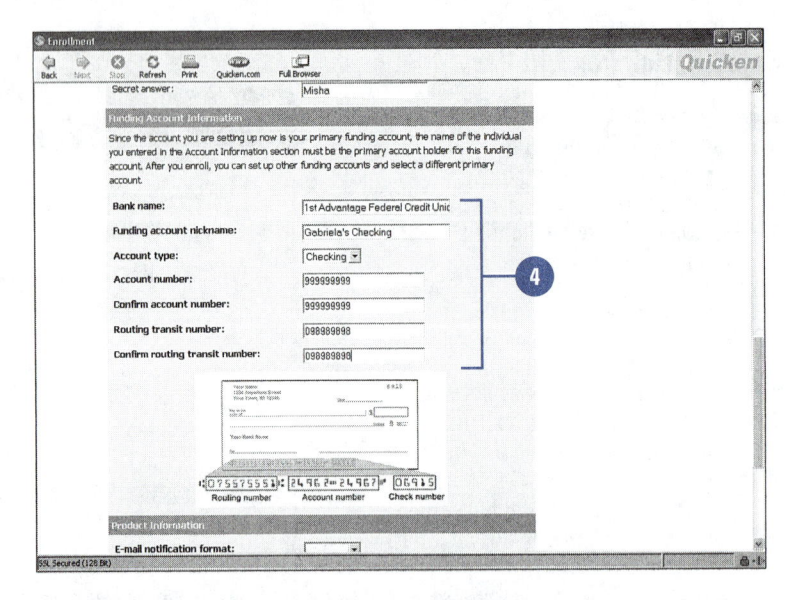

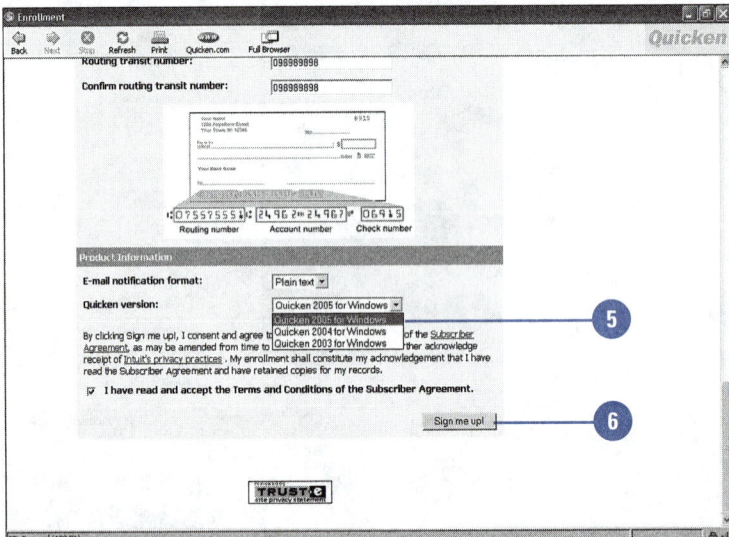

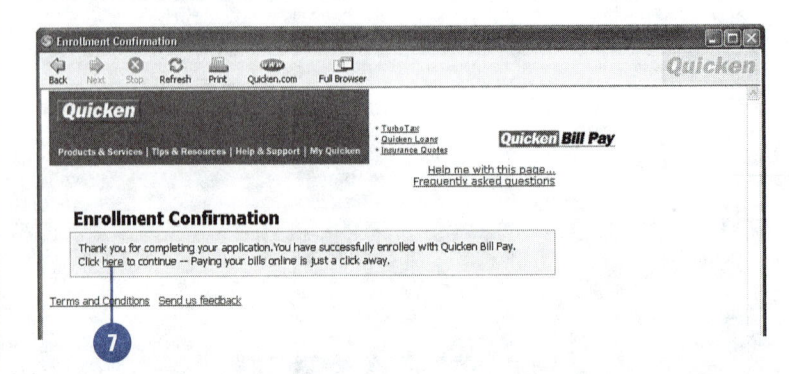

Set Up Your Payees

1. To set up your payees, from the Quicken Bill Pay web page, click Payee Setup.

2. Click Add new payee.

3. Type the payee name or, to view and select a payee from Quicken's list, click View our payee list.

4. Type the account number, the payment zip code, and the nickname or alternate name and then select the payee category.

5. Click Continue.

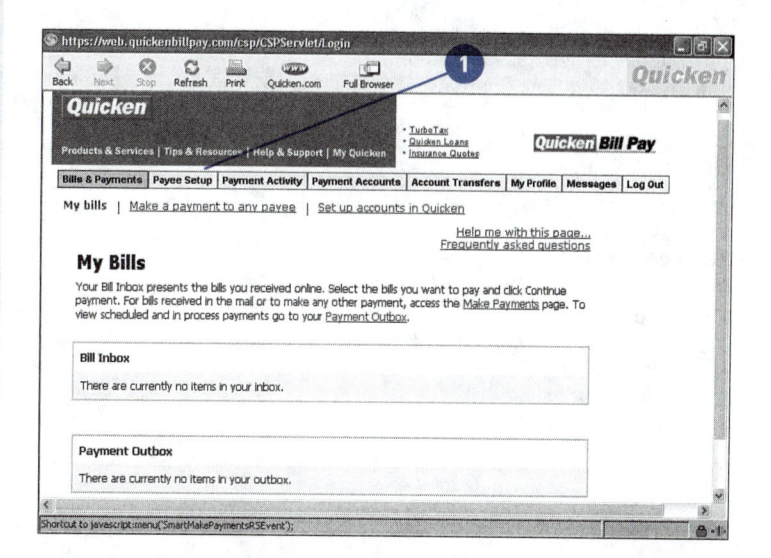

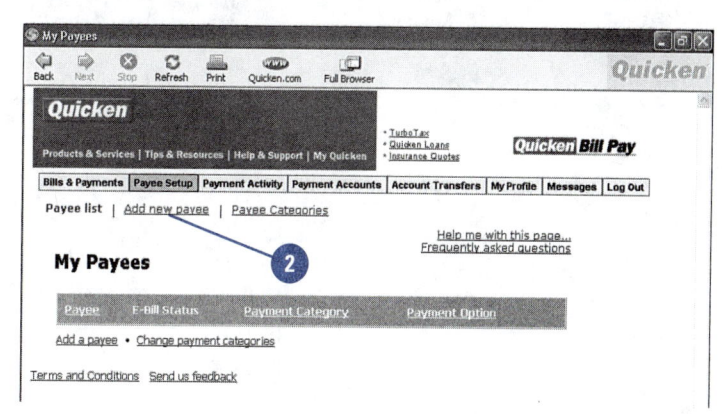

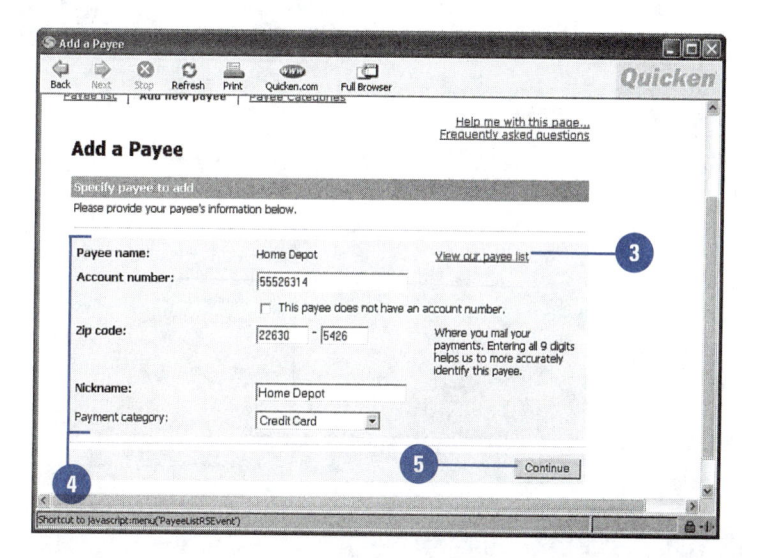

Managing Your Bills **173**

6. Type the payee address and phone number and then click Continue.

7. Type your login and password, select the billing cycle, and click Continue. When the payee information is confirmed, a message appears, letting you know that the payee was added successfully.

8. Add additional options or add more payees, if desired, by repeating steps 1–7.

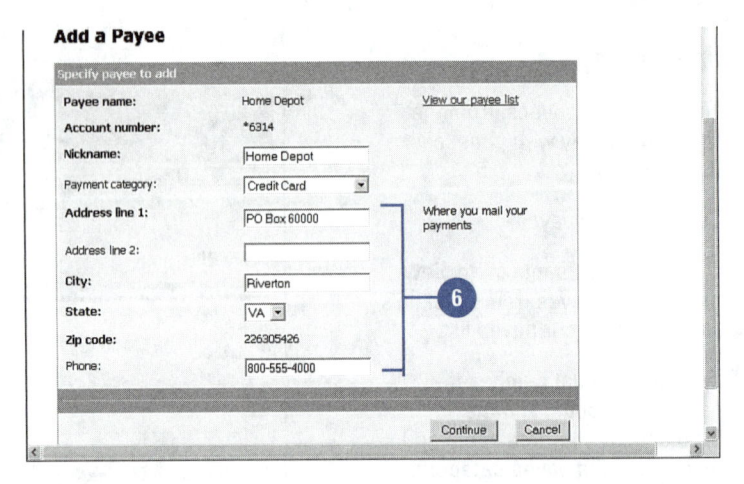

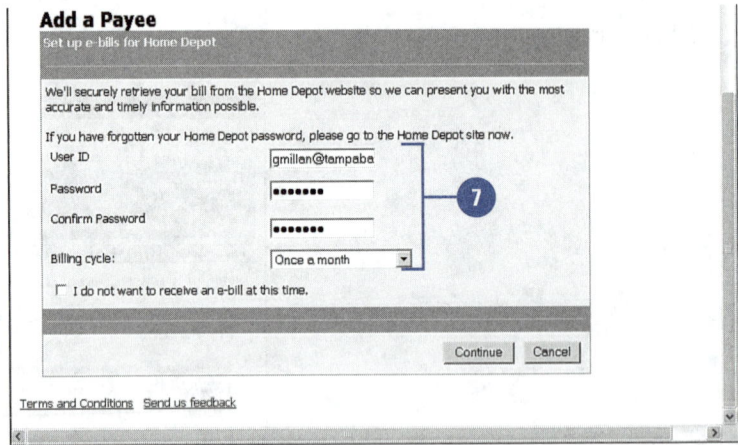

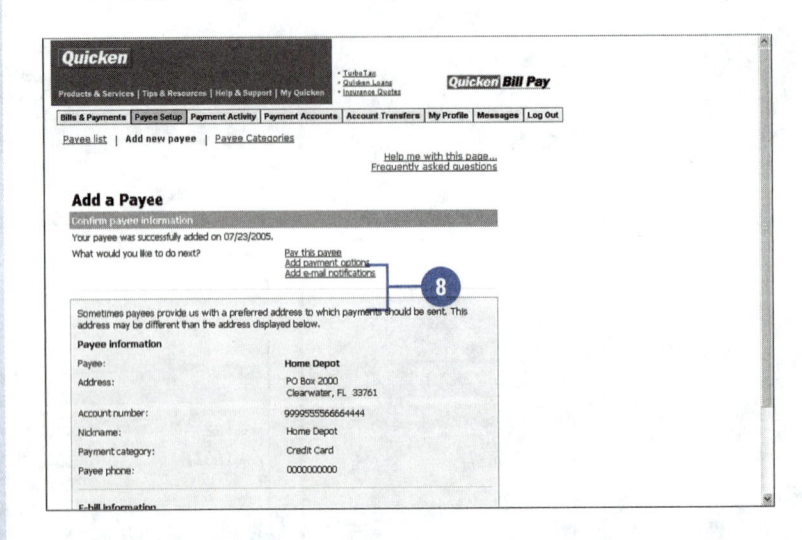

Pay Your Bills by Using Bill Pay

1. To pay a bill by using one of the payees you set up in Bill Pay, click Bills & Payments.

2. To make non-e-bill payments, click Make Payments.

3. Type the amounts that you want to pay for each of your bills and the dates you want the bills paid.

4. Click Make payments.

5. To review the bills scheduled for payment, click Payment Outbox. The My Bills page opens.

6. Click Payment detail to review payment information.

7. Click Edit to make changes to the payment.

8. Click Stop to cancel the payment.

9. Click Notes to add a note for the payment. If you don't have any changes, the payment(s) will be sent out in time to reach the payee by the designated time.

Did You Know?

The Bill Inbox section contains a list of your e-bills. When you first set up Quicken Bill Pay, the Bill Inbox on the My Bills page is empty. However, as you begin using Quicken Bill Pay, your e-bills show up in the Bill Inbox section. You can then select them and initiate payment from the inbox.

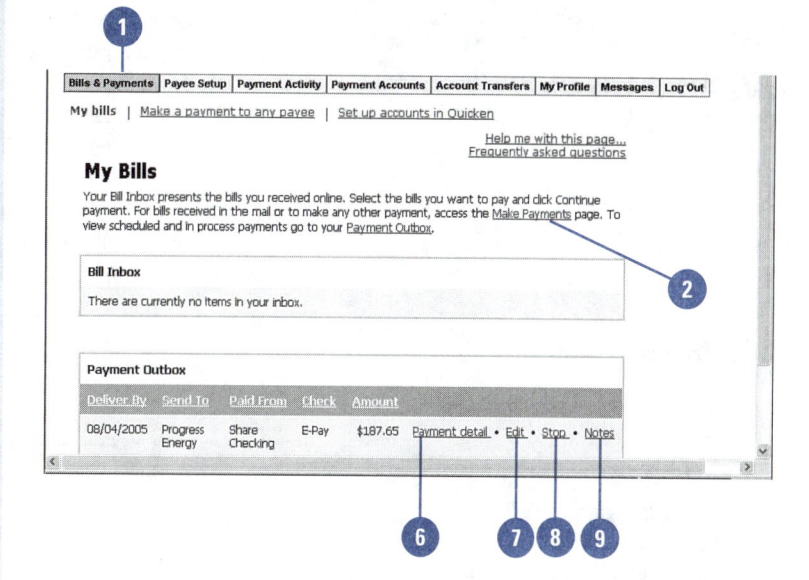

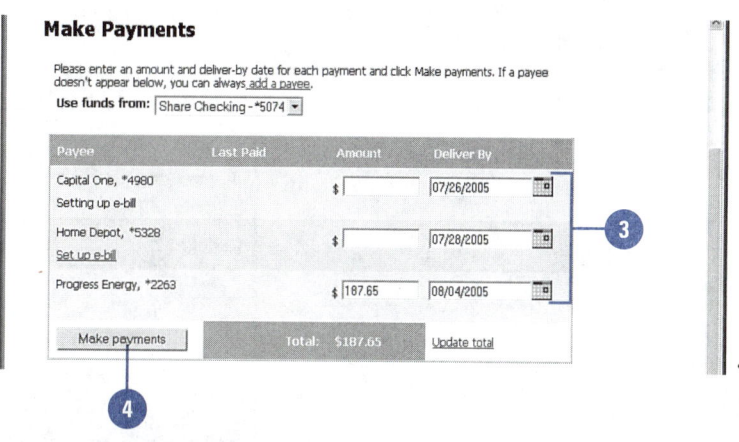

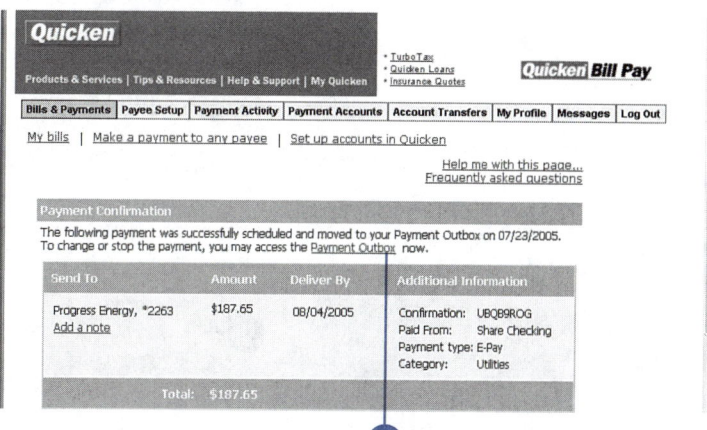

Managing Your Bills **175**

Ordering and Printing Quicken Checks

If you pay some of your bills by writing checks, Quicken offers the convenience of printing checks directly from Quicken so that you don't have to hand-write your checks. Currently, checks start at $57.99 for 250 checks. You can order checks, in addition to envelopes, labels, deposit slips, and more, through Quicken. When you receive the checks, you can enter the transactions you want printed on checks and then print the checks through Quicken on your printer. You can use the payee information that's already in Quicken, or you can add it if you don't have the payee set up, to print your checks.

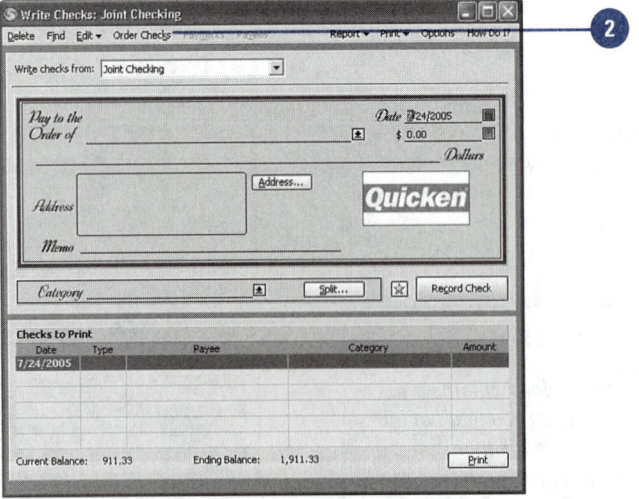

Order Quicken Checks

1. From the Cash Flow menu, select Write Checks.

2. Ensure that you are connected to the Internet and click Order Checks. The Intuit Checks, Forms & Supplies web page opens.

3. Select the type of checks you want to order.

176

④ Review the information about your printer type check options and then scroll down to select your check options.

⑤ Select your printer type, the number of sheets of checks, and the quantity of checks. Then click Continue

⑥ Proceed through the check ordering process by completing all the steps.

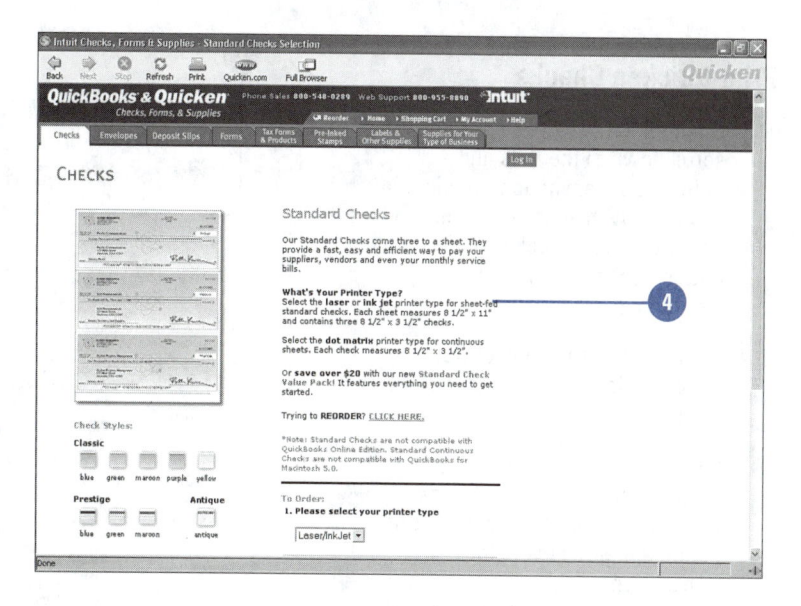

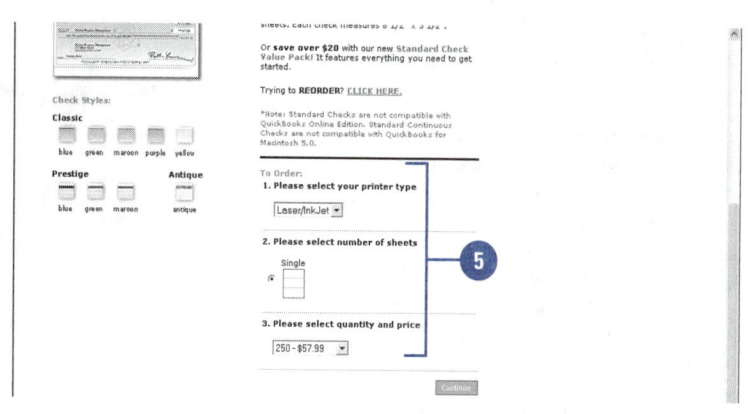

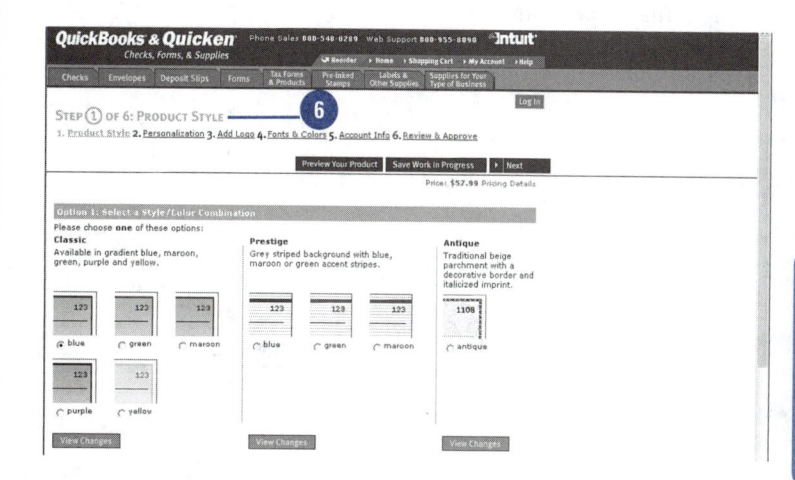

Managing Your Bills **177**

Print Quicken Checks

1. Open the Cash Flow Center and scroll down to the Bills and Scheduled Transactions section. If you already have transactions set up for Quicken checks, a Print button appears next to the transaction.

2. To set up transactions for Quicken checks, click Enter next to the transaction.

3. From the Payment Method drop-down menu, select Print Check and click Record Payment. A Print button appears next to the transaction.

4. Repeat steps 2–3 for each transaction that requires a printed check.

5. To print checks, click the Print button next to the transaction or click the Cash Flow menu and select Write Checks.

6. Select the payment account. All checks waiting to be printed for that account appear under Checks to Print.

7. Select the check you want to print. The check information automatically fills in for you if the payee's information is already saved.

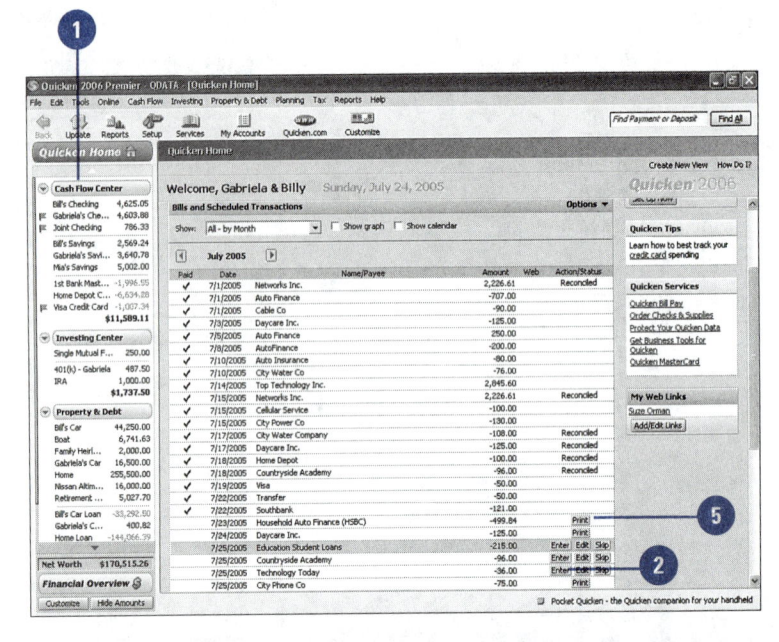

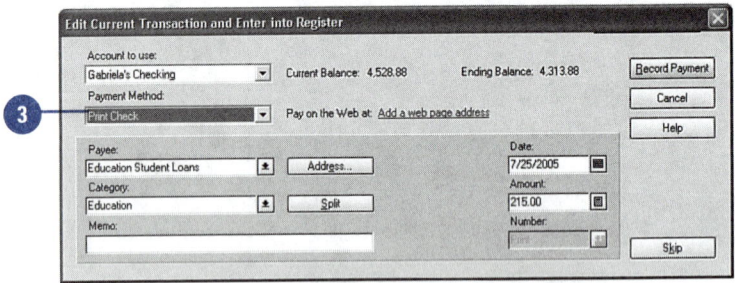

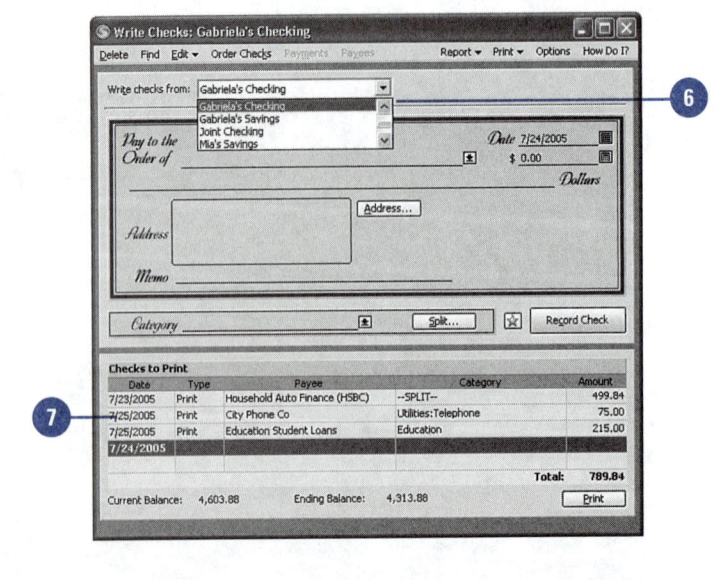

⑧ If the payee's information does not automatically fill in, the payee most likely does not have address information saved. Click Address to update or add the payee address information.

⑨ Enter the payee information or change it if it needs to be updated. Be sure to select QuickFill List to ensure this payee's information is available throughout Quicken. Then click OK.

⑩ If you made changes to an existing payee address, a message appears, letting you know that changing the information will also affect other transactions that use this payee. Click OK to accept the changes.

⑪ Make any additional changes (for example, the amount or the category) and click Record Check. A message appears, asking if the transaction is for the date indicated.

Did You Know?

You can change your payment method. *When you set up your accounts and scheduled transactions, you specified how you would make your payments or which printing method you would use for your payment transactions. There are four payment methods: Payment, Deposit, Print Check, and Online Payment. The payment method you selected when you set up the account is what automatically appears for the account transactions. You can change the payment method when you enter the transaction into your account register to change only that one transaction, or you can edit the transaction to change all future payments to another method.*

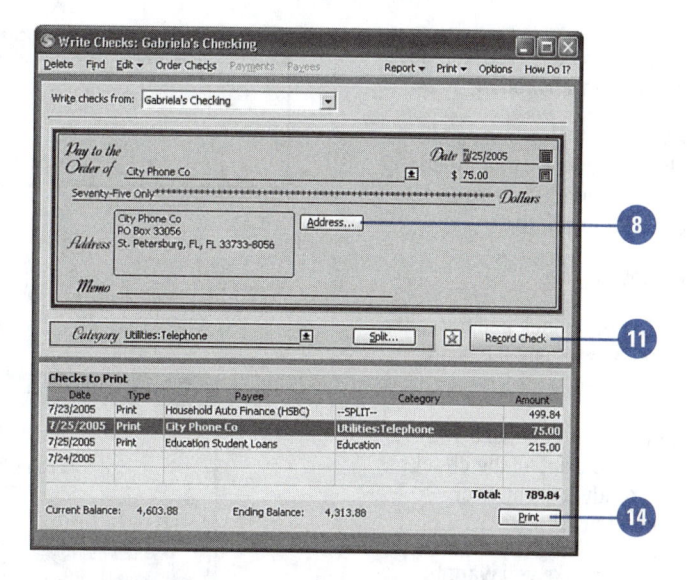

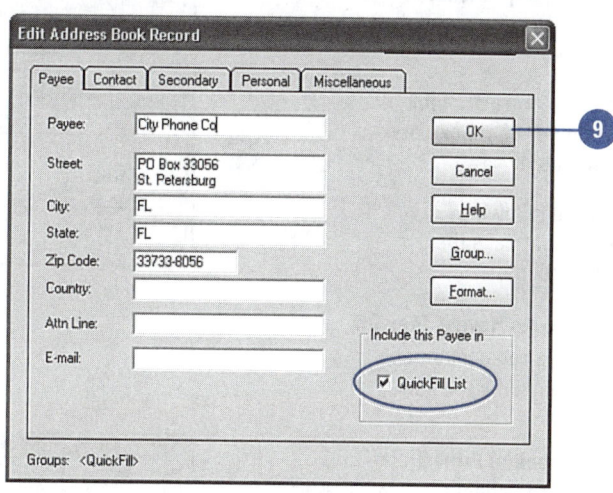

Managing Your Bills **179**

12. Click Yes. If you click No, you have to update the transaction.

13. Repeat steps 1–12 to set up all checks you want to print for each of your accounts. Then insert the checks in your printer.

14. Click Print.

15. Verify that the check number is the one you want to use. If it is not, change it.

16. Select the print options. If you don't want to print all the checks that are ready to print, click Selected checks.

17. Select the checks you want to print and click Done to close the window.

18. Ensure that the correct check style and number of checks per page are selected.

19. Click OK. If the following messages appear, take the appropriate actions:

    - **Do the Checks Have a Tear-Off Strip?**—It is recommended that you leave the tear-off strip on.

    - **Did the Check(s) Print OK?**—Click OK if the checks printed correctly. If the checks did not print correctly, type the number of the first check that printed incorrectly and click OK. Then determine what the problem is (for example, the checks jammed or the printer is out of checks). If the check information did not print correctly (for example, it is not aligned correctly), adjust the alignment.

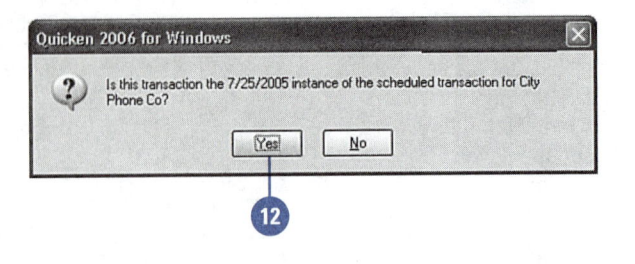

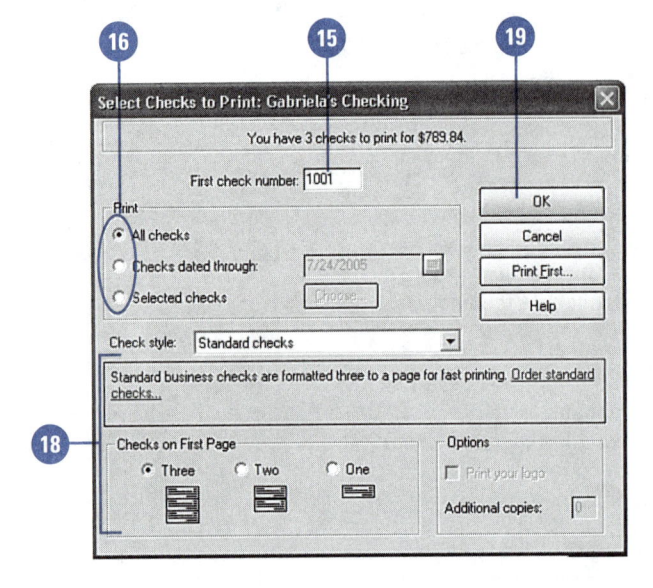

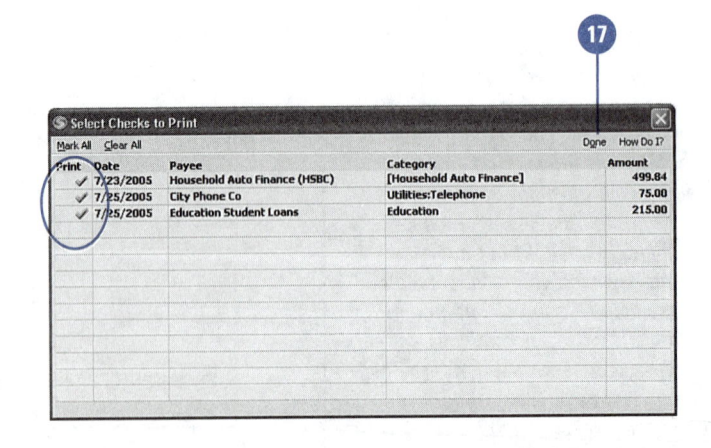

180

Managing Your Investments and Retirement Information

Introduction

The Investing Center contains all your investment and retirement account information and is where you can manage your accounts and portfolio, analyze investment performance, and run reports to further analyze your investments and securities. You can also download the latest quotes for your investments and securities, as well as historical quotes, to analyze how an investment or a security has performed over time.

Your account register for each of your investment and retirement accounts is accessible from the Today's Data tab in Investing Center. In the account register, you can add, edit, or delete transactions; update the register with transactions that have been downloaded; review, add, or edit scheduled transactions; and balance your account. In addition, you can set up alerts and watch lists to track investments and security performance for the investments and securities you own as well as those you are considering.

What You'll Do

Set Up New and Edit Existing Investment Alerts

Update Investment and Security Quotes and Transactions

Review, Add, Edit, and Delete Investment Accounts

Track Investment Performances

Review Investment and Retirement Account Summaries

Add, Edit, and Delete Investment and Retirement Transactions

Add, Edit, and Delete Scheduled Investment and Retirement Transactions

Manage All Your Scheduled Transactions

Review Investment and Retirement Performance

Balance Your Investment and Retirement Accounts

Setting Up New and Editing Existing Investment Alerts

Investment alerts are a bit different from the other alerts in Quicken. Yes, the purpose is the same (to remind you of predetermined activities). However, with investments, you can set up watch lists and use them in conjunction with your alerts—for example, to sell or buy shares or for simple tasks, such as to download the latest quotes for your investments. A watch list contains investments whose performance you are monitoring. (Watch lists are covered in more detail later in this chapter.) Creating or editing investment alerts works the same as with other alerts.

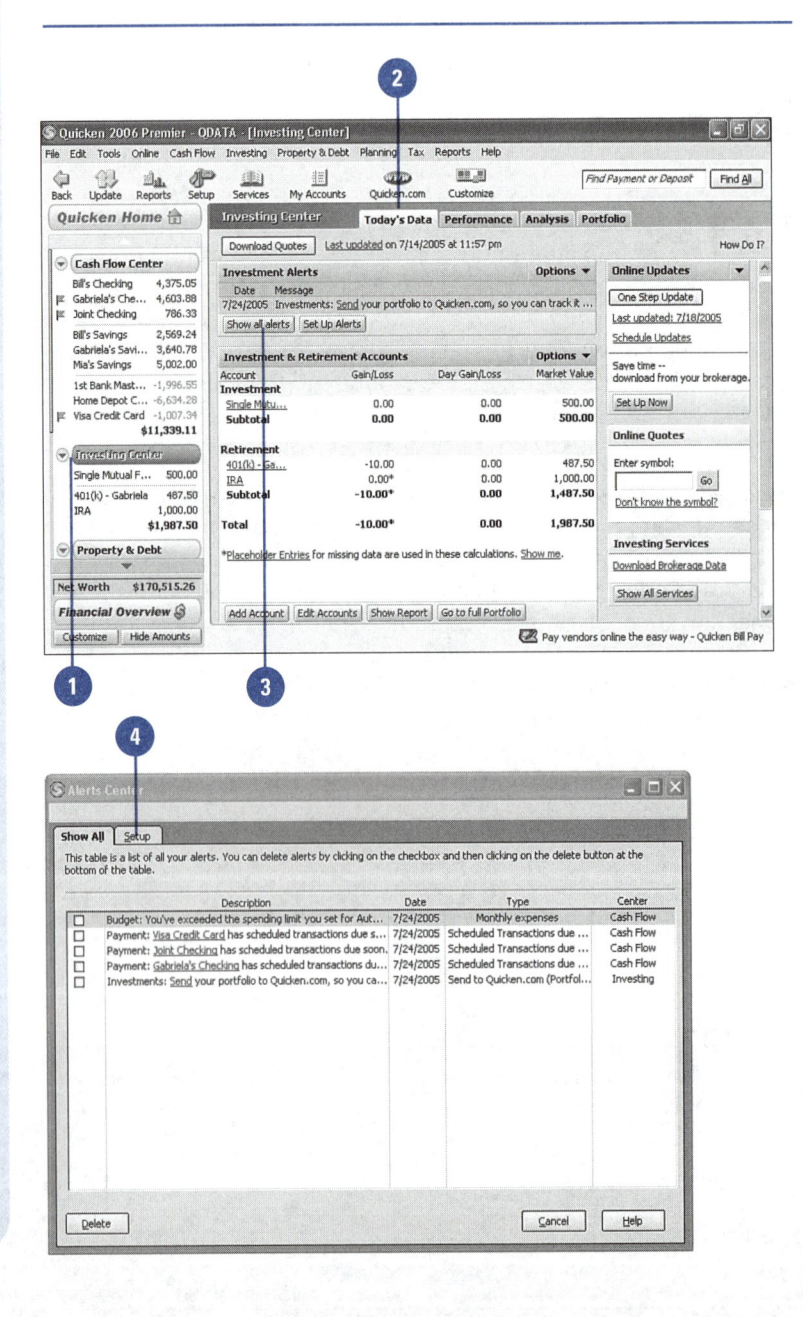

Set Up New and Edit Existing Investment Alerts

1. In the activity bar, click Investing Center.

2. Click the Today's Data tab.

3. To view and manage all your alerts, click Show all alerts to open the Alerts Center window.

4. To create or edit investment alerts, click Setup. Or you can click Set Up Alerts on the Today's Data tab in the Investing Center.

See Also

See "Using Alerts" on page 74 for more information on creating or changing alerts.

Updating Investment and Security Quotes and Transactions

Before you start working with your investment and retirement accounts, you should update the quotes to ensure that you are working with up-to-date security information and transactions. If you set up this account for online access, you can use One Step Update to automatically update your account balance and transactions each time you open Quicken and connect to the Internet or each time you choose to update your balances. You can also update the balance manually, if needed. This task shows you how to update your quotes in the Investing Center.

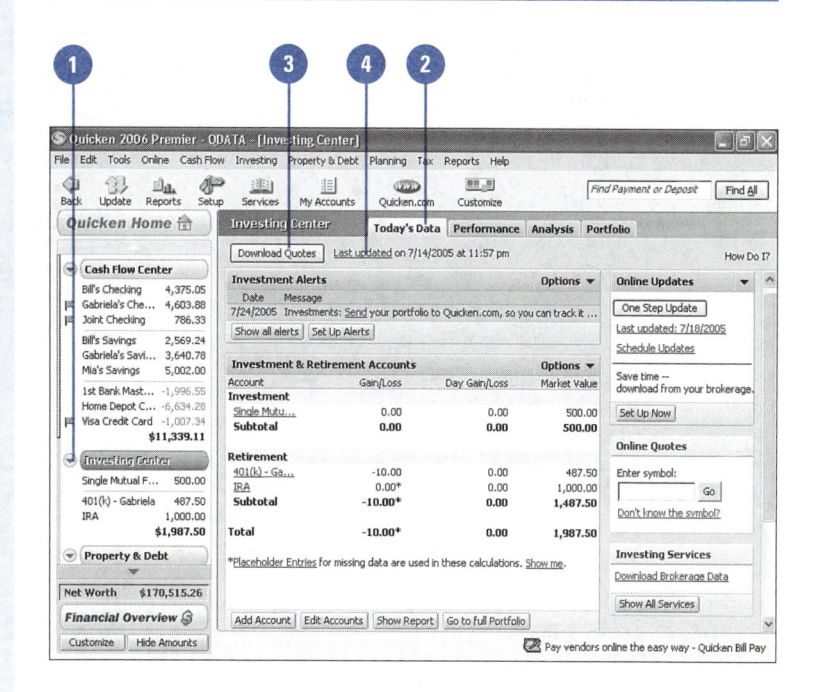

Update Investment and Security Quotes and Transactions

1. If you don't already have the Investing Center open, in the activity bar, click Investing Center.
2. Click the Today's Data tab.
3. Make sure you are connected to the Internet and then click Download Quotes. Quicken downloads the latest quotes and updates your portfolio with the latest quote information.
4. The date you last updated the quotes appears next to the Download Quotes button and in the Online Updates section of the Today's Data tab.

See Also

See "Using Online Updates" on page 88 for more information on updating accounts at Quicken.com, how to set up One Step Update, and how to schedule updates.

Did You Know?

Your online investment accounts are downloaded when you use One Step Update. *If you have online access to any of your investment accounts and have set up such an account to download your transactions when you use One Step Update, those transactions download each time you use One Step Update. Downloaded transactions appear on the Download Transactions tab in the account register.*

Managing Your Investments and Retirement Information **183**

Reviewing, Adding, Editing, and Deleting Investment Accounts

The investment and retirement accounts listed in the Investing Center are those that you set up when you set up all your accounts in Quicken. As you work with your investment and retirement accounts over time, you will most likely need to add new accounts, update existing accounts, and remove accounts.

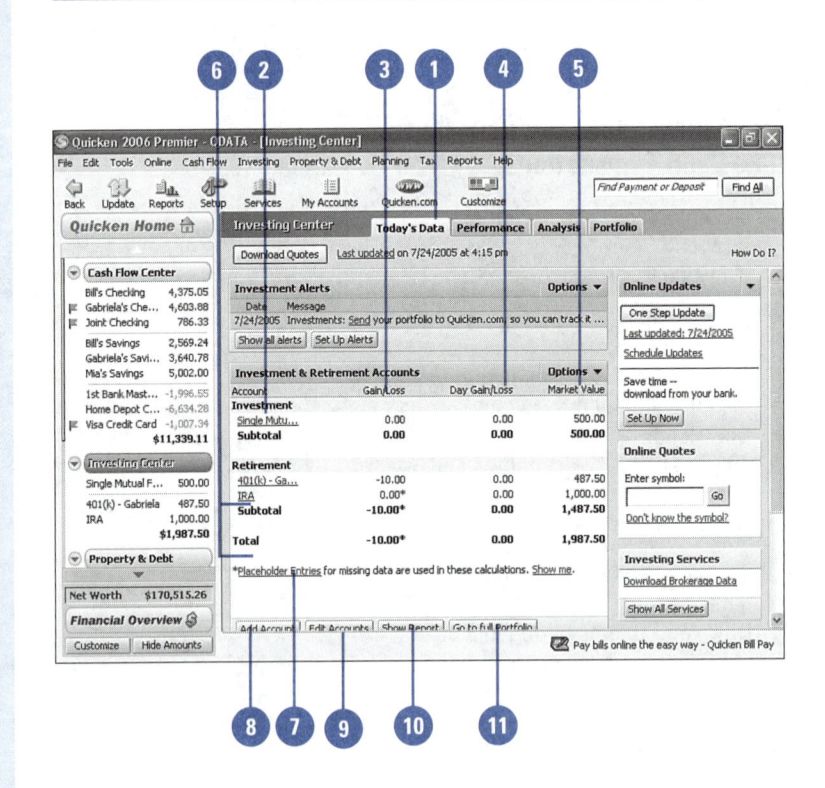

Review Investment Accounts

1. Open the Investing Center and click the Today's Data tab.

2. Your existing investment and retirement accounts are listed in the Investment & Retirement Accounts section. Click an account name to open that account's register.

3. The Gain/Loss column provides the total amount you have lost or gained for each security listed.

4. The Day Gain/Loss column provides the daily loss or gain amount for each security listed.

5. The Market Value column lists how much a security is worth.

6. A subtotal for your investments and for retirement accounts are provided, as is a combined total for both account types.

7. Click the Placeholder Entries link to complete account information, if needed.

8. Click Add Account to open the Quicken Account Setup dialog if you need to add new investment or retirement accounts.

9. Click Edit Accounts to make changes to any of your accounts.

10. Click Show Report to open the Portfolio Value report to review how your portfolio is doing.

11. Click Go to Full Portfolio to see a list of all your securities.

Add Investment or Retirement Accounts

1. To add a new investment or retirement account, click Add Account.

2. Type or select the name of the financial institution where the investment or retirement account is held and then click Next.

3. Select Online to download the account information directly from your financial institution. Select Manual (as shown in this example) if you don't have online access yet or to enter the account information yourself. Then click Next.

Did You Know?

You can set up an account to have online access. If you have online access to an account, select Online in step 3 and follow the setup prompts. When the account is created, you can get automatic updates each time you use One Step Update or download from the Investing Center. Then the account pretty much takes care of itself.

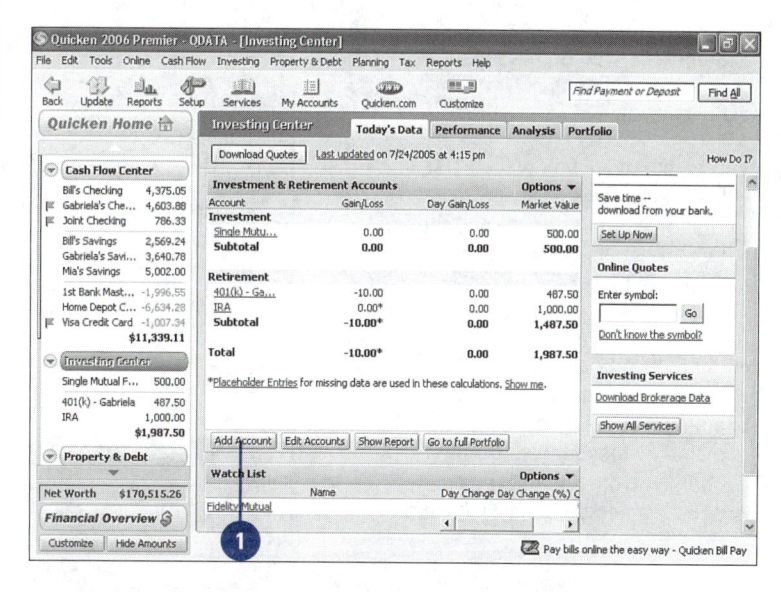

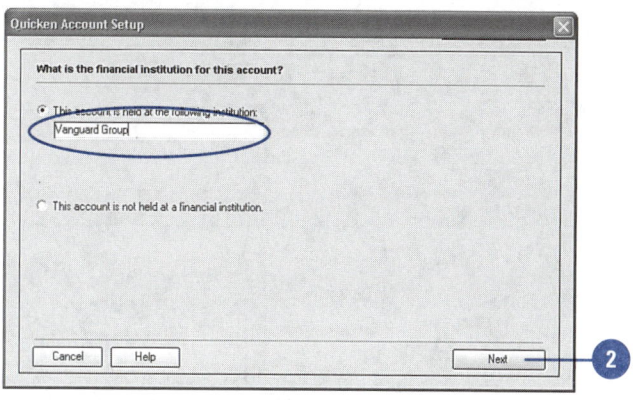

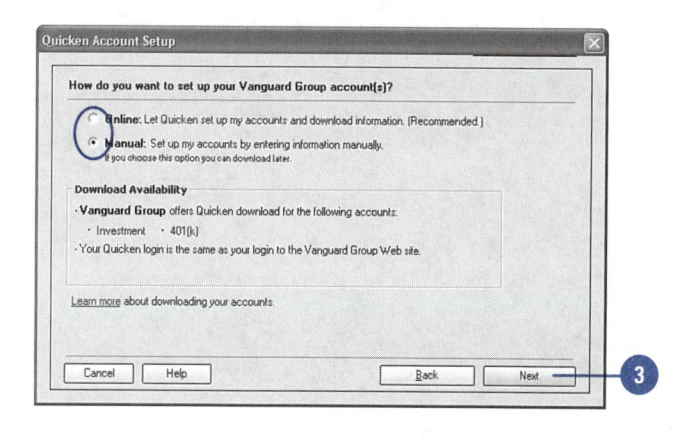

Managing Your Investments and Retirement Information **185**

4 Select the type of investment you are adding and click Next. This example shows a Roth IRA.

5 Type the name you want to use in Quicken for this account, select who owns the account, and the type of account, if applicable. Then click Next.

6 Type the statement end date or the date your account information was posted on the investment company's website, if you have online access to this account. Then type the amount you used to open the account and click Next.

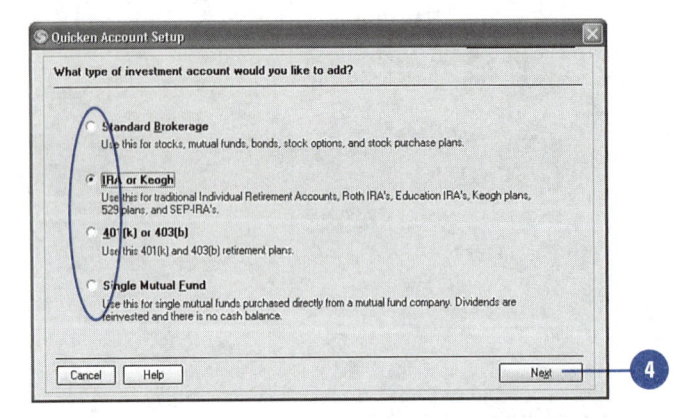

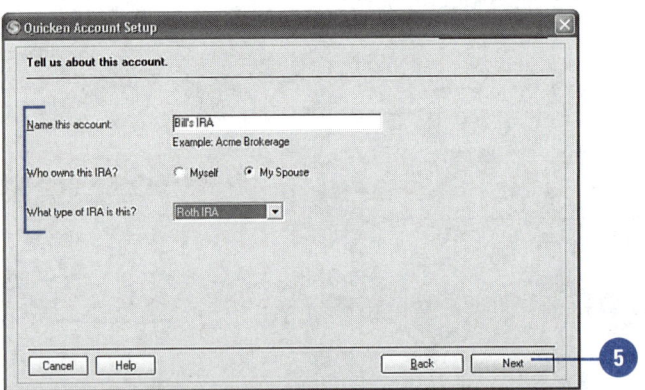

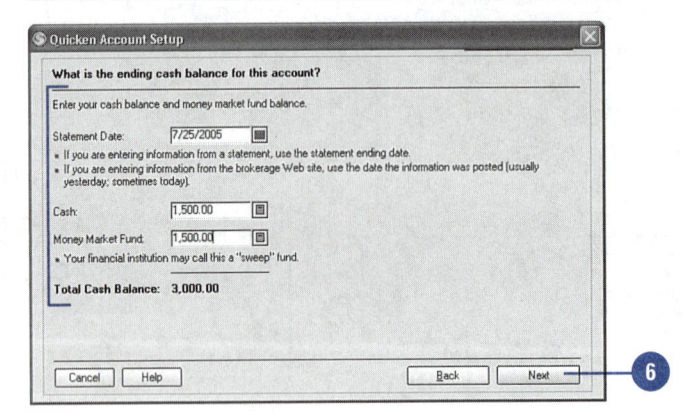

7. Type the ticker symbols and security names. If you don't know the ticker symbol, click Ticker Symbol Lookup to locate it and then copy and paste the symbol in the Ticker box. Then click Next.

8. If you have online access to the account, Quicken provides a list of the accounts it found. If you don't have online access (as shown here), click Add Manually to add the account.

9. Type the number of shares for each security type and click Next. Quicken provides a summary of the account information you just entered.

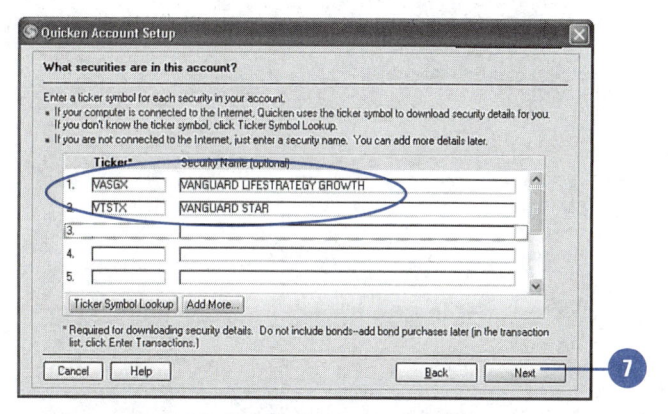

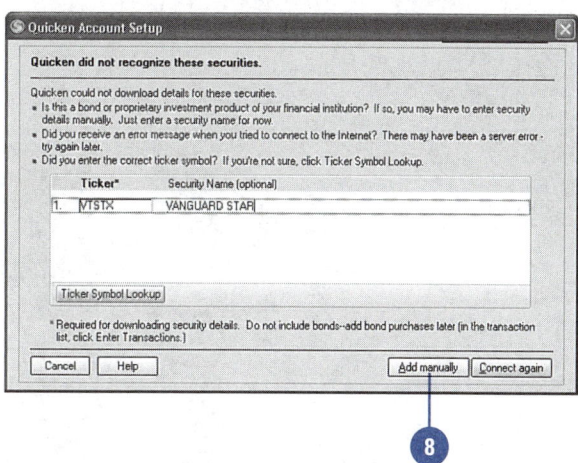

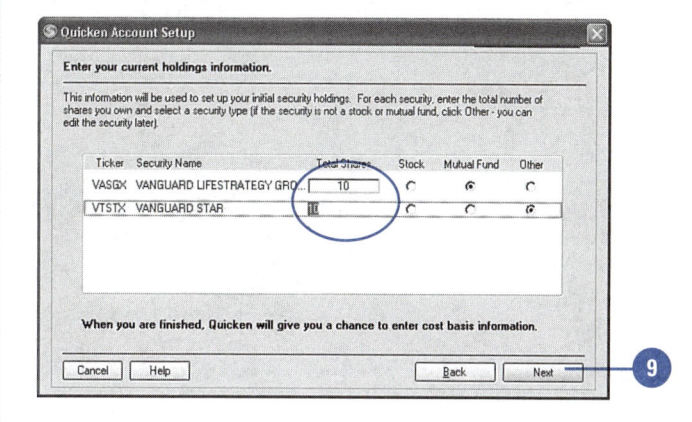

Managing Your Investments and Retirement Information **187**

10 Click Back to change any of the information or click Done if you are finished.

11 Repeat steps 1–10 for each investment or retirement account that you want to add.

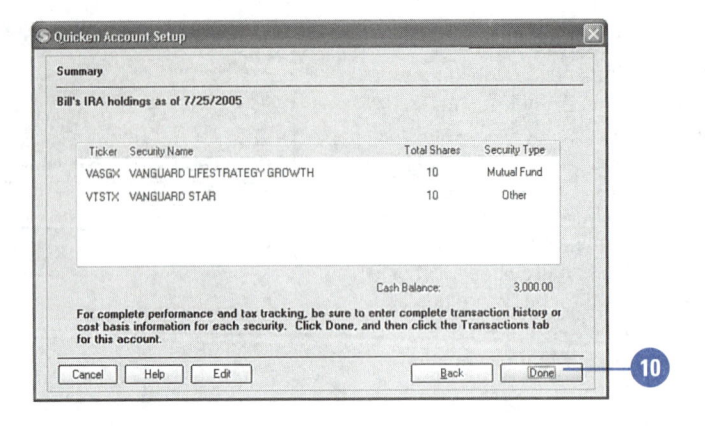

Edit Investment and Retirement Accounts

1 Go back to the Investment & Retirement Accounts section of the Today's Data tab in the Investing Center and click Edit Accounts.

2 In the Investing Accounts section of the Account List window, select the account you want to update and then click Edit.

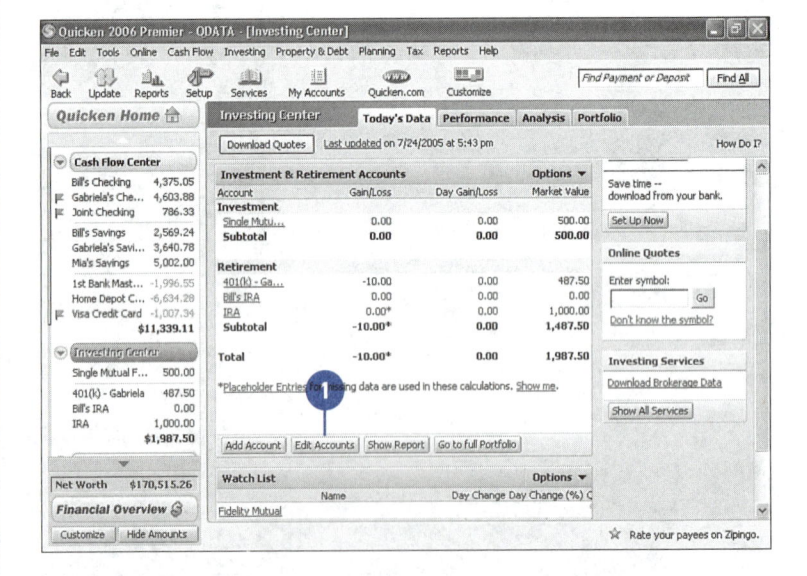

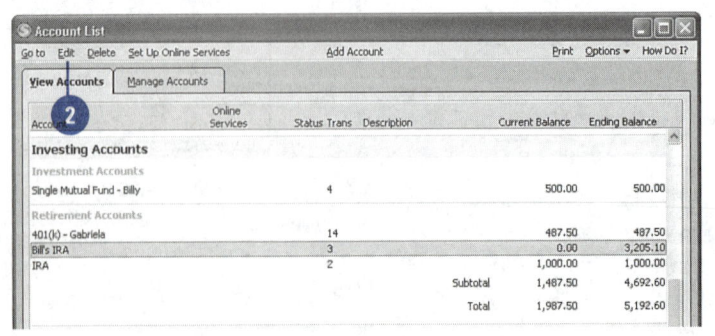

3. In the Account Details window, type, select, or change the account information.

4. To review or change the tax schedules associated with this account (Quicken usually assigns a schedule automatically), click Tax Schedule Info.

5. Select new tax schedules, if needed, and click OK.

6. To add fees for account transactions (for example, for early withdrawal), click Transaction Fees.

7. Type fixed fees for each transaction under the left column or percentages in the right column and then click OK.

8. When you are finished making changes, click OK.

9. Repeat steps 1–8 to edit other accounts.

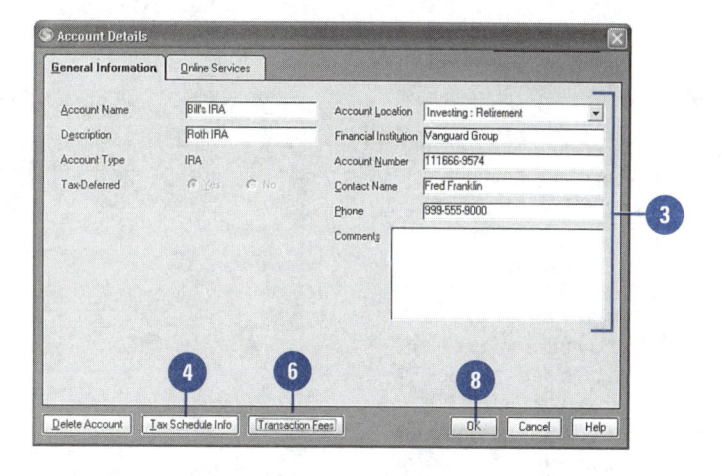

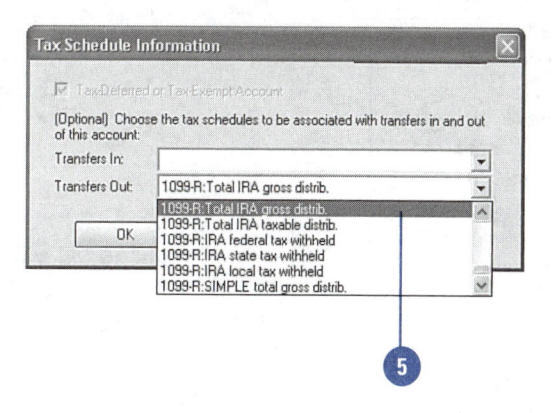

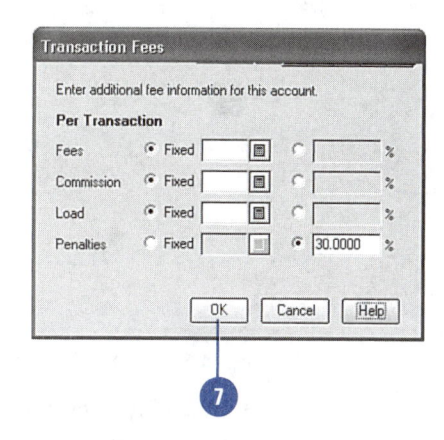

Managing Your Investments and Retirement Information **189**

Delete Investment or Retirement Accounts

1. To completely remove an account from Quicken, in the Account List window, select the account and click Delete. A message appears, asking if you want to delete the account.

2. If you are sure you want to delete the account, type Yes and click OK. If you do not want to delete the account, click Cancel. A message appears, telling you that the account has not been deleted. Click OK.

Did You Know?

You can delete accounts by using the Account Details window or the Account List window. *You can delete an account by clicking the Delete Account button in the Account Details window or by using the Delete menu option in the Account List window. However, before you delete an account from Quicken, you need to be sure you don't need the account, even if it's closed, for reporting or historical tracking. Deleting an account is permanent, and the only way to restore it is if you have a backup of your Quicken file that you made before you deleted the account.*

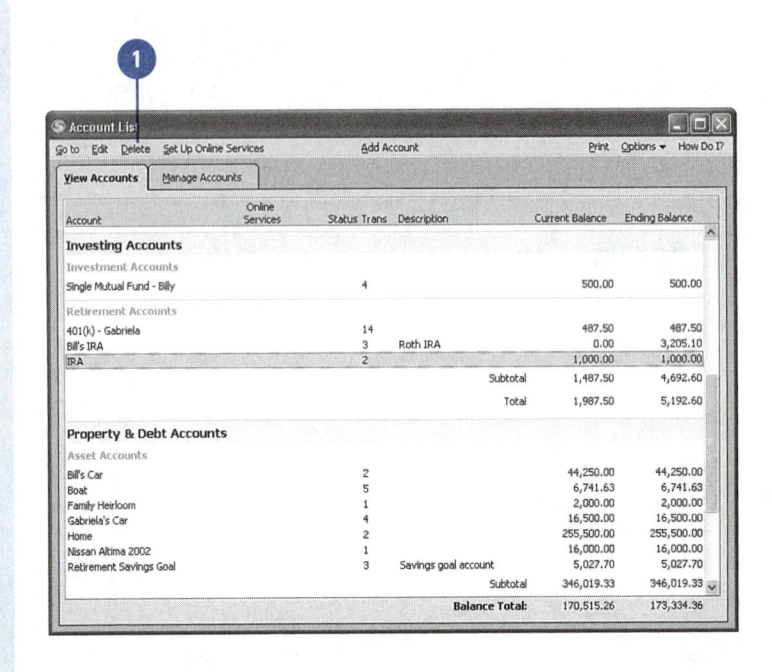

Did You Know?

You cannot delete accounts that have active transactions. *If an account has active transactions, such as, scheduled transactions, you must delete the transactions before you can remove the account. Remember: You need to think it through before you remove an account. The information can be used for historical reasons or for forecasting.*

Tracking Investment Performances

To help you keep an eye on your investments or to keep an eye on investments you are considering, you can set up a watch list. A watch list provides easy access to investments of interest. Securities on your watch list appear in the Watch List section on the Today's Data tab in the Investing Center. You can add, edit, and delete securities from here.

Track Investment Performance

1. If you are not already there, open the Today's Data tab in the Investing Center and scroll down to the Watch List section.

2. To add a security to your watch list, be sure that you are connected to the Internet and then click Add a security.

3. Type the ticker symbol and name of the security. If you don't know the ticker symbol, click Look Up to locate, copy, and then paste it in the Ticker Symbol box.

4. Then click Next. Quicken downloads the information for the security.

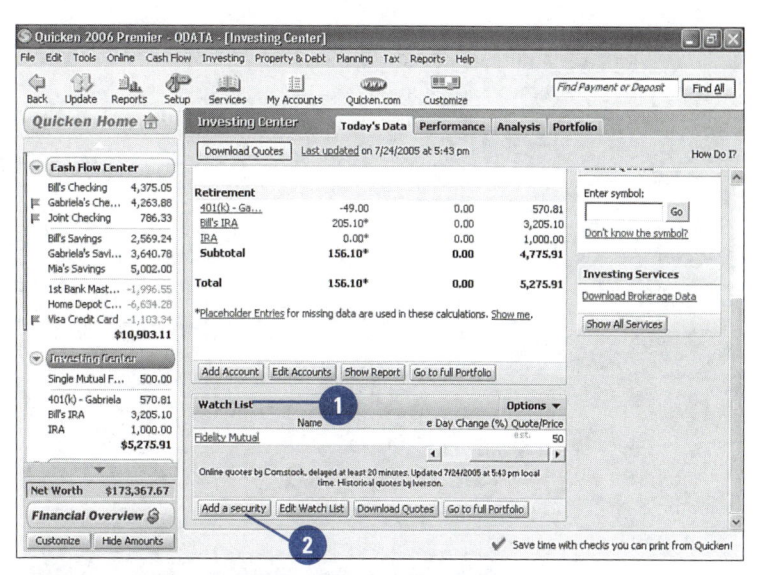

Managing Your Investments and Retirement Information **191**

5. To add another security, select Yes and repeat steps 1–3, or select No if you are finished. Then click Done.

6. To edit existing securities, select the security and click Edit Watch List.

7. To add existing securities to your watch list, select their boxes under the Watch column. A green check mark means the security is already on your watch list.

8. To remove securities from your watch list, clear the boxes next to the ones you want to remove.

9. To delete securities from your watch list, select the securities and click Delete.

10. To add new securities to your watch list, click New and complete the Add Security to Quicken setup process.

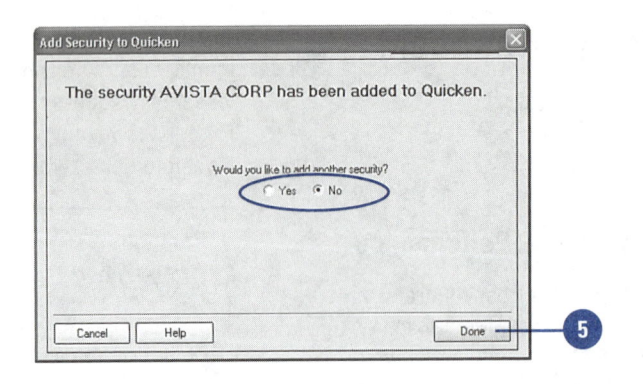

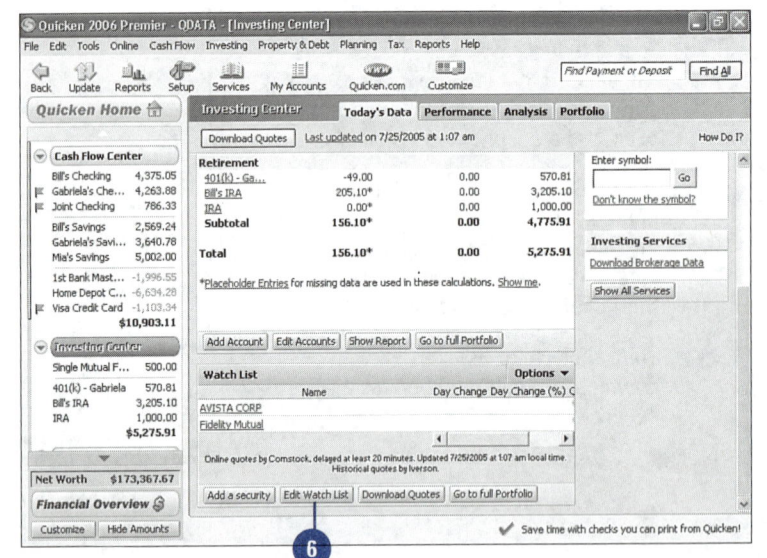

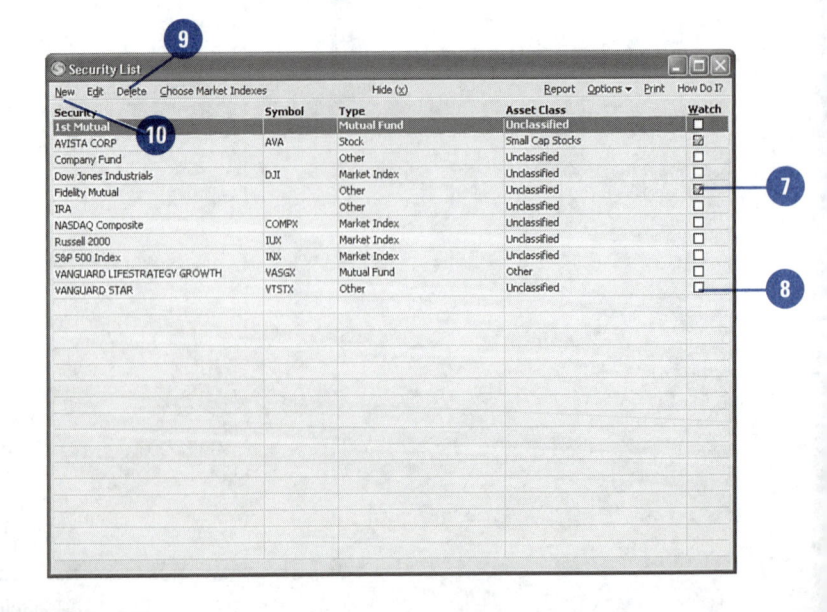

192

Reviewing Investment and Retirement Account Summaries

For each of your investment and retirement accounts, Quicken provides a summary for you to review and assess your account performance, security balances and values, account details, and activities. In addition, you can view reports to further analyze your account performance and attach documents, such as statements, to the account.

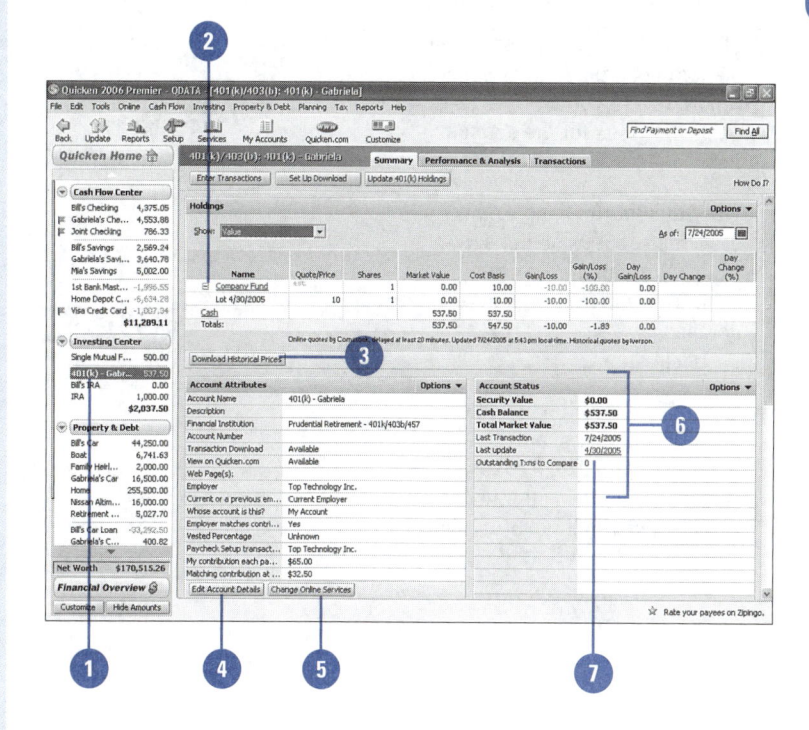

Review Investment and Retirement Account Summaries

1. In the activity bar, click the account you want to review. In this example, we review a 401(k) account.

2. The Holdings section lists all your securities for the account, including the quote, shares, and so on. Click a security to open the Security Detail View window for more information.

3. Click Download Historical Prices to open the Get Historical Prices window, where you can select the year and securities that you want to download and view.

4. In the Account Attributes section, you can view your account details. Click Edit Account Details to update account information.

5. Click Change Online Services to update online access information, if it's available.

6. The Account Status section lists account status information, such as your account value, balance, market value, and so on.

7. To update Statement Information, click the Last update date link.

Managing Your Investments and Retirement Information **193**

8. In the Investing Activity section, view activity and capital gains and losses for each quarter, quarter-to-date, and year-to-date.

9. Click Show Full Report to view and assess the activity for an investment.

10. Click Capital Gains Report if you want to open the Capital Gains report, where you can view any gains or losses for the account, if applicable.

11. The Account Holdings section provides security, share, and total value information. Click the security name to take a more detailed look at a security, as shown in step 2.

12. In the Account Attachments section, add documents to the account, if you like, by clicking Add and completing the Add Attachment window.

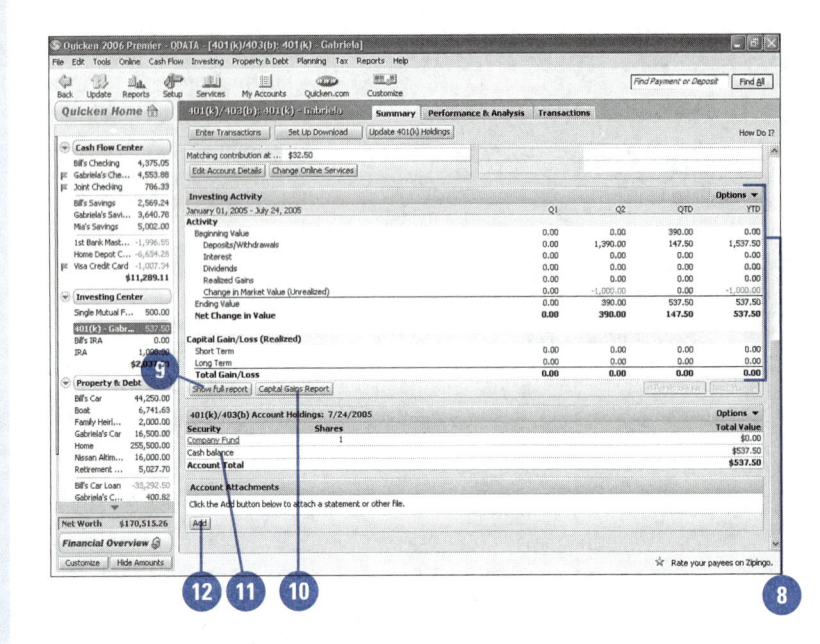

Performing Additional Functions in the Account List Window

You can use the menu bar to access other areas of Quicken, such as the following:

- You can open an account register by selecting the account and clicking Go to.
- You can set up an account for online access by selecting the account and clicking Set Up Online Services.
- You can add a new account by clicking Add Account.
- You can print the account list by clicking Print.
- You can select print options or change the list view by using the Options menu.
- You can click How Do I? to access Quicken's Help system.

194

Adding, Editing, and Deleting Investment and Retirement Transactions

All transactions for each of your investment and retirement accounts are listed in the account register. If you set up your accounts to update using One Step Update, the transactions download and appear automatically on the Downloads tab. You can then review and add the transactions to your register. If you don't use the online updates, you can manually add transactions in the register. In addition, you can edit or delete existing transaction information.

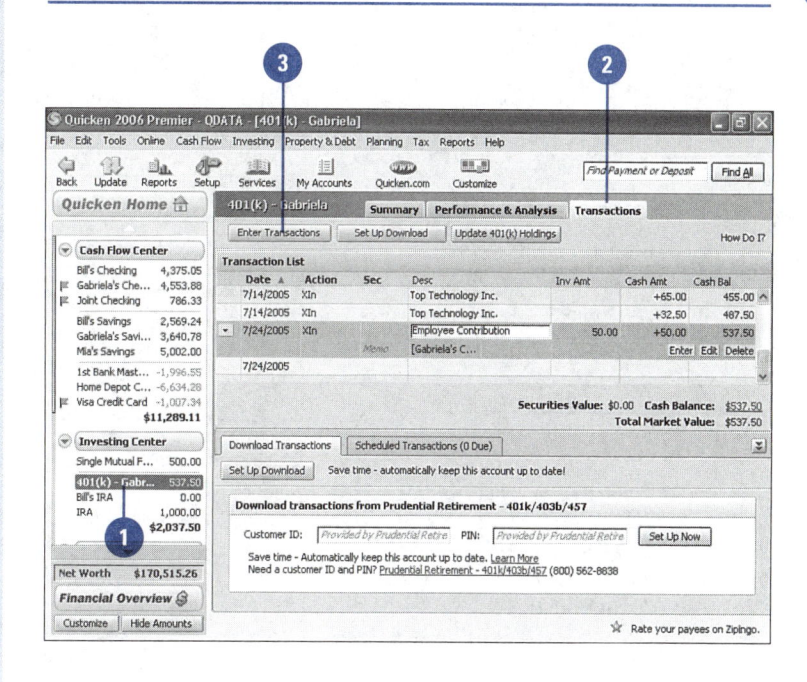

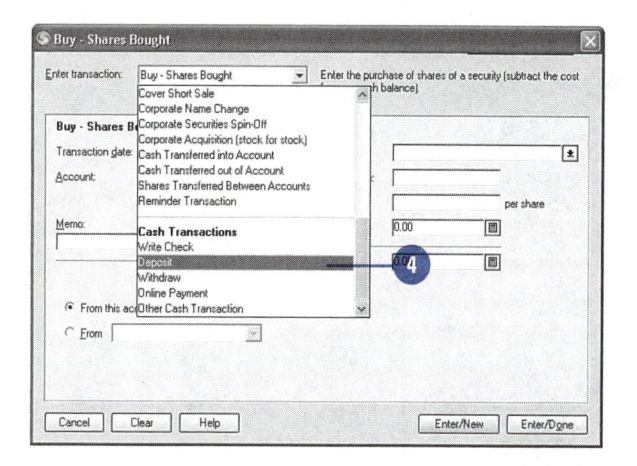

Manually Add Investment Transactions

1. In the activity bar, click the account you want to open.

2. Click the Transactions tab.

3. To manually add a transaction, click Enter Transactions.

4. Select the type of transaction. The information you enter from here on will vary, depending on the type of transaction you select.

Managing Your Investments and Retirement Information **195**

5. Type or select the transaction information. In this example, type the date the transaction takes place, the account from which the transfer is taking place, and the amount being transferred into the 401(k).

6. If you want to, type a memo or note about the transaction.

7. To enter an explanation for the new transaction, click in Description and type it.

8. Click Enter/Done.

9. In this example, Quicken wants to know if the contribution to the 401(k) is an employee contribution. Click Yes if it is or No if it is not.

See Also

See "Add Downloaded Spending and Savings Transactions to Your Register" on page 170 for information on adding transactions to your register in the Downloaded Transactions tab.

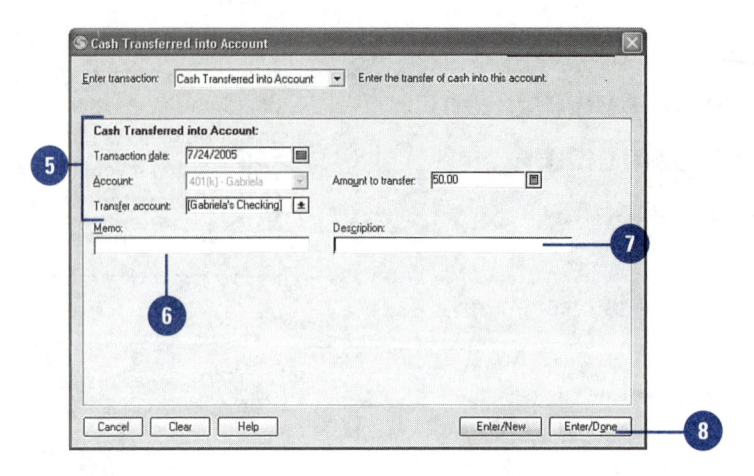

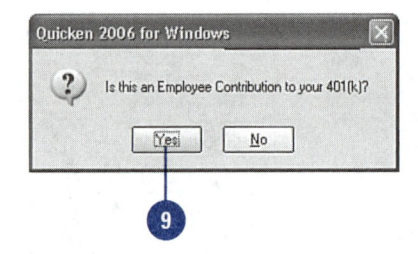

Edit and Delete Investment and Retirement Transactions

1. In the account register, click the area you want to change; for example, click in the Desc box to change the description.

2. Click Enter to update the transaction.

3. Click any of the other transaction fields to change the information, as needed.

4. To delete an entire transaction, select the transaction and click Delete. A message appears, asking if you want to delete the transaction.

5. Click Yes to delete it or No to keep it.

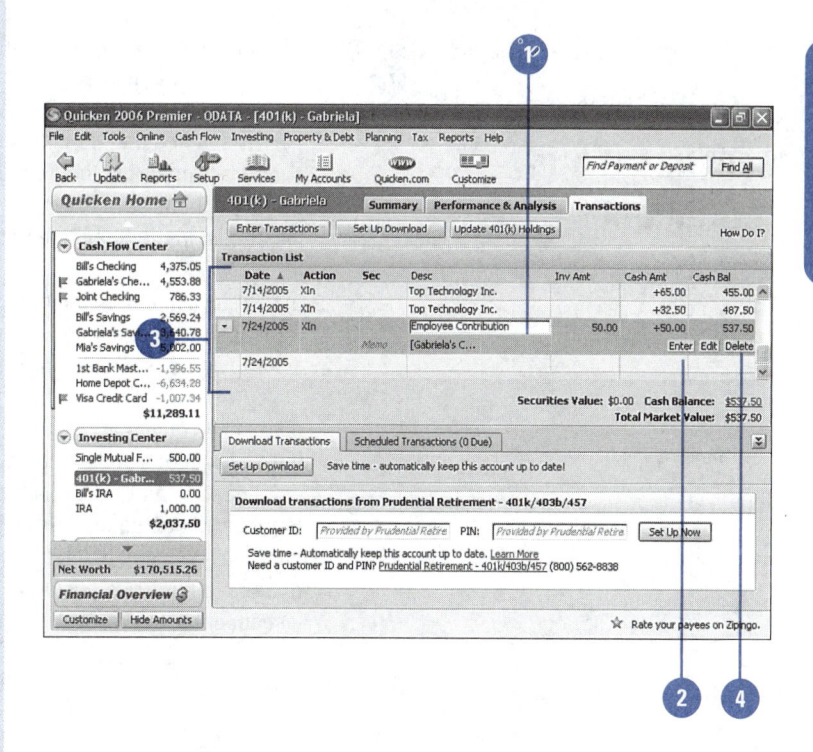

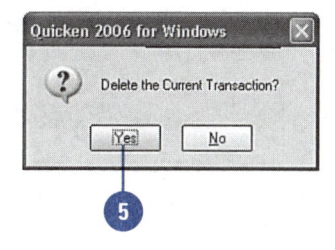

Managing Your Investments and Retirement Information **197**

Adding, Editing, and Deleting Scheduled Investment and Retirement Transactions

As with your other accounts in Quicken, when you set up your investment and retirement accounts and told Quicken about any regularly scheduled transactions, Quicken created a scheduled transaction list for you. The scheduled transactions for your investment and retirement accounts appear on the Scheduled Transactions tab in each of your investment and retirement account registers. They also appear on the master list in the Scheduled Transaction List window.

In your investment account registers, you can view, add, edit, or delete transactions. In addition, you can access the master list of all your scheduled transactions for all accounts in Quicken.

If you have online access to some of your accounts, you can download the transactions and add them to your Quicken registers, and then you don't need to add scheduled transactions for your online accounts. However, if you do not have online access for some or all of your accounts, you can use this task to step through the process. If you want to be reminded when your scheduled transactions are due, you can use investment alerts.

Add, Edit, and Delete Scheduled Investment and Retirement Transactions

1. In the activity bar, click the account for which you want to add scheduled transactions.

2. Click the Transactions tab.

3. Click the Scheduled Transactions tab. The number in parentheses represents the number of transactions waiting to be added to your register.

4. To add a new transaction, click Add a Transaction.

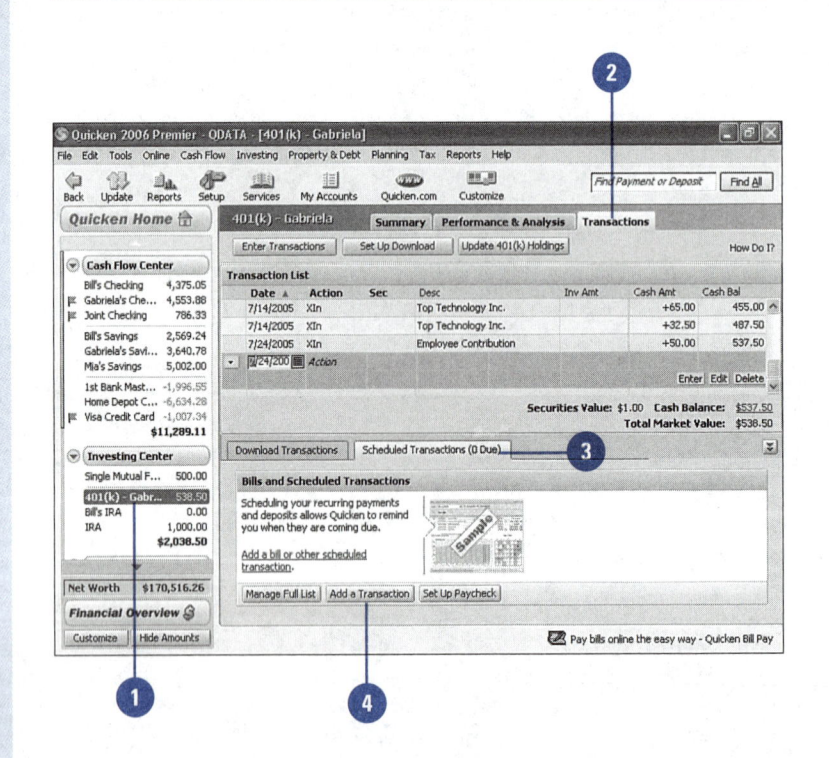

198

5. Complete the Create Scheduled Transaction window and click OK.

6. To add a scheduled transaction to your register, click Enter.

7. Review the information to ensure that it is correct, make changes, if needed, and add it to your register by clicking Enter/Done or Record Payment. Any changes that you make apply only to the current transaction, not to all future transactions.

8. Click Cancel to take no action on the transaction and return to the scheduled transaction list. The transaction remains in the scheduled transaction list until you are ready to record it or skip it.

9. Click Skip to remove the transaction from your scheduled transactions for this period but have it reappear the next time it is scheduled to show up.

10. To delete a transaction, use the Scheduled Transaction List window. Refer to the next task "Managing Your Scheduled Transactions," for more information.

11. To add a new paycheck, click Set Up Paycheck and complete the Manage Paychecks window.

12. Review, edit, and enter each scheduled transaction until you are finished. Your balance is adjusted accordingly.

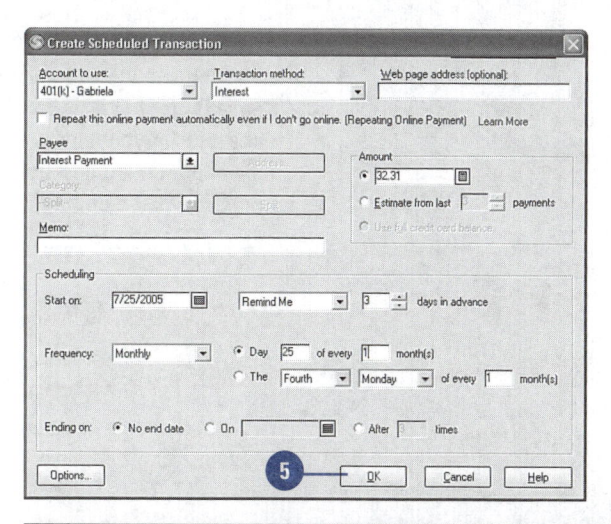

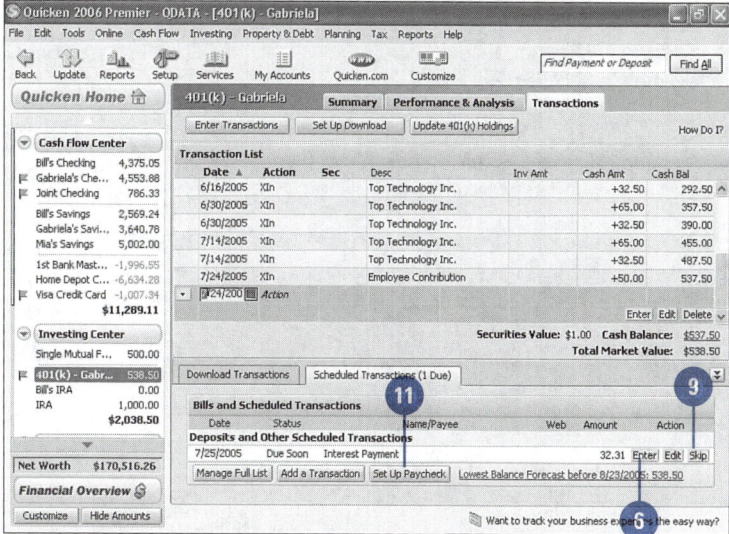

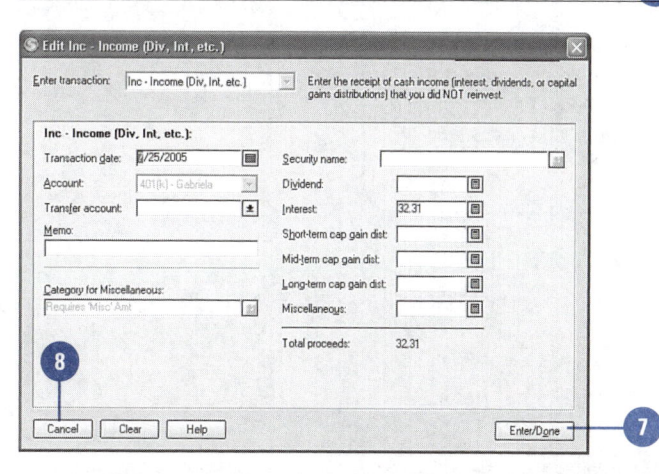

Managing Your Investments and Retirement Information **199**

Managing All Your Scheduled Transactions

When you want to review or make changes to your scheduled transactions, you can view them all in one place by using the Scheduled Transactions List window. All your transactions are included here—not just those for your investment and retirement accounts. You can access the Scheduled Transactions List window from the Scheduled Transactions tab on the register of any account or from the Tools menu.

Manage Your Scheduled Transactions

1. If you're not already there, open the investment account for which you want to manage scheduled transactions by selecting the account from the account book.

2. From an account register, click the Scheduled Transactions tab and then click Manage Full List.

3. Enter, edit, skip, or delete transactions, as desired, just as you have done in previous tasks.

4. To view the transaction calendar for the current month, select Show calendar. The days on which transactions are due are bolded.

5. To view the calendar in detail, click a day of the month.

See Also

See "Using Bills and Scheduled Transactions" on page 76 for more detailed information on adding, editing, skipping, and deleting scheduled transactions.

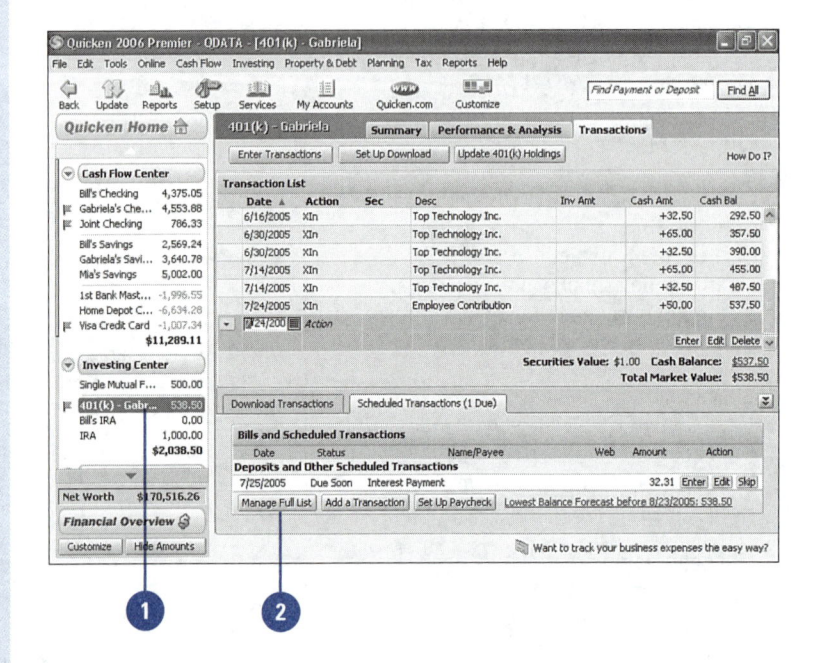

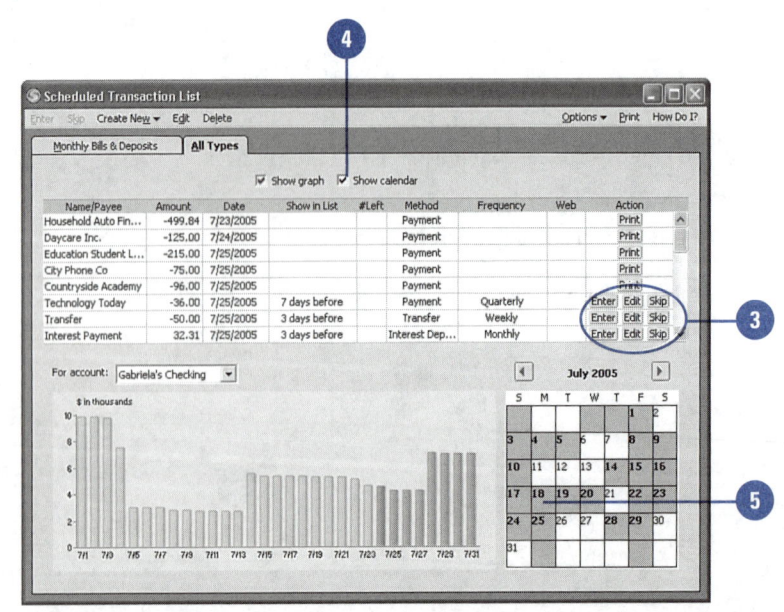

6. If desired, print the calendar, go to a future or previous month, make a note for a specific day, or select only the accounts you want to see on the calendar.

7. To view a graph of daily transactions, select Show graph and from the For account drop-down menu, select the account you want to view.

8. To view your estimated balance for a specific day, hover (point, don't click) your mouse over a bar of the graph.

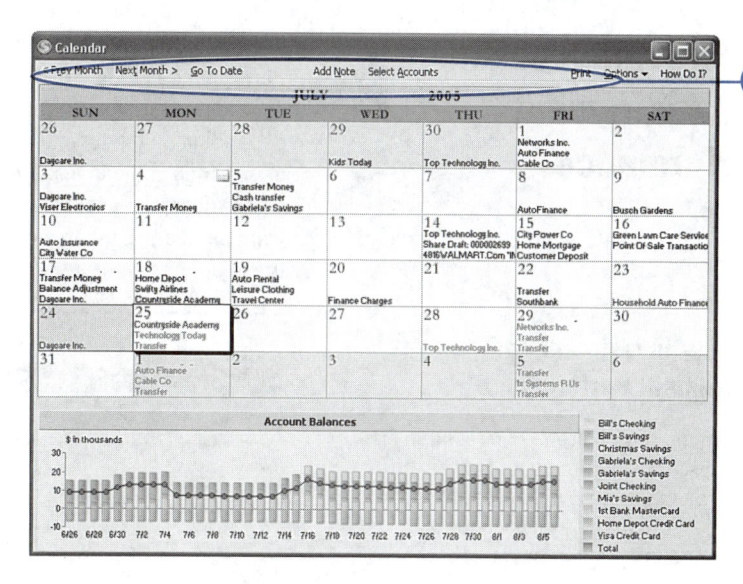

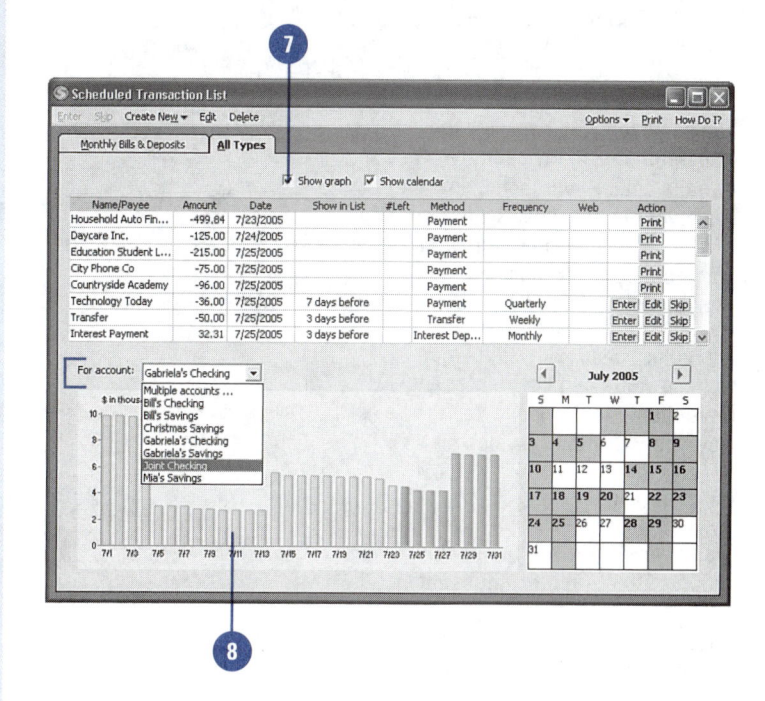

Managing Your Investments and Retirement Information **201**

Reviewing Investment and Retirement Performance

In each investment and retirement account, an Analysis and Performance tab is provided, with graphs and pie charts showing the account's overall performance. The information on this tab varies, depending on the type of investment or retirement account. Typically, the information you can expect to find includes the account value and a cost comparison, the asset allocation, and the security allocation. In addition, you can use this tab to view reports and different performance views; these options also vary by account type.

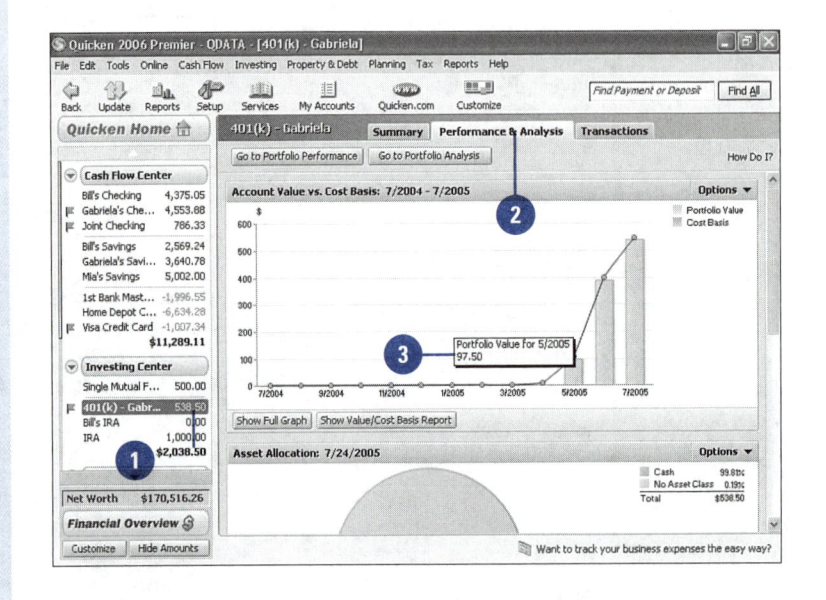

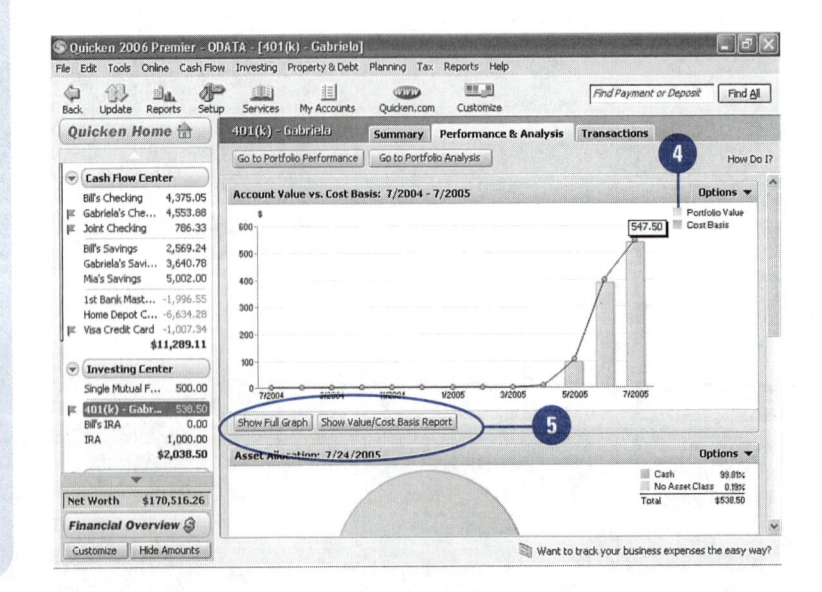

Review Investment and Retirement Performance

1. If you're not already there, open the investment account for which you want to view investment performance by clicking the account in the account bar.

2. Click the Performance & Analysis tab.

3. In the Account Value vs. Cost Basis section, you can view the value and cost of the security over a year's time. Hover (point, don't click) your mouse over the bar to view the value of the security for that month or over the point at the top of the bar to view the cost.

4. The color key provides the color that the value and cost represent. Hover your mouse over a key to view the totals for the value or cost.

5. Click Show Full Graph to view the graph view of the Account Value vs. Cost Basis report by account or click Show Value/Cost Basis Report to view the Account Value vs. Cost Basis report by security.

6. The Asset Allocation section provides a pie chart view of how your assets are allocated for the current day and is broken into slices that represent the allocation type.

7. Hover your mouse over a slice of the pie to view the percentage and dollar amount for that allocation.

8. The color key provides the color that each allocation type represents. Hover your mouse over a key to view the totals and percentages.

9. Click Show Full Graph to view the Asset Allocation report or click Show Allocation Guide to view or make changes to the Asset Allocation Guide.

10. The Allocation by Security section provides a pie chart view of your asset securities that is broken into slices that represent each security.

11. Hover your mouse over a slice of the pie or the color key to view the percentage and dollar amount for that security.

12. Click Show Full Graph to view the Allocation by Security report.

See Also

See "Getting Some Help with Asset Allocation" on page 215 for more information about the Asset Allocation Guide.

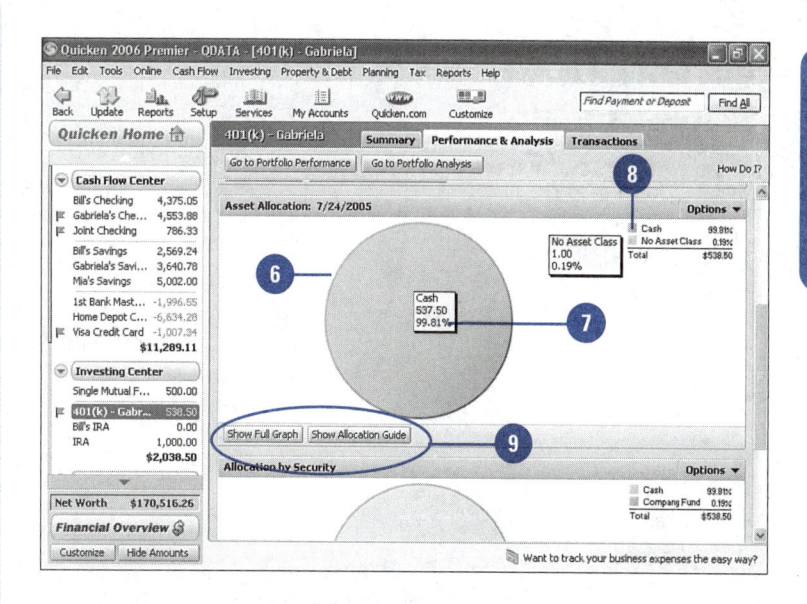

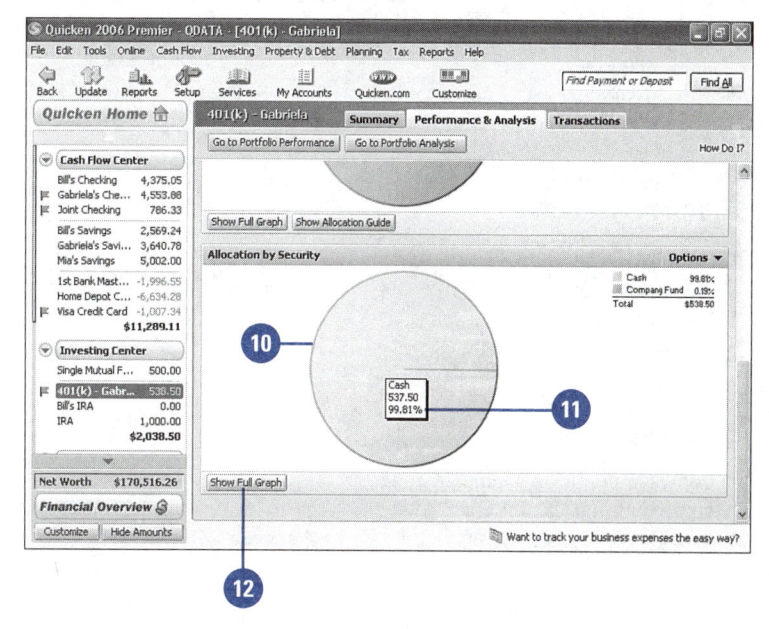

Did You Know?

You can analyze investments further by using the portfolio. *To assess and further analyze your investment and retirement accounts, you can click the Go to Portfolio Performance button at the top of the Performance & Analysis tab to open the Performance tab on your portfolio. You can click the Go to Portfolio Analysis button to open the Analysis tab in your portfolio.*

Managing Your Investments and Retirement Information **203**

Balancing Your Investment and Retirement Accounts

Balancing or reconciling your investment and retirement accounts works a bit differently from balancing your other accounts in Quicken. As with your other accounts, if you download your statements and your transactions are automatically updated, reconciling is a little easier than if you manually update all your transactions and balances. Either way, you still need to compare your paper statement to the transactions listed in Quicken. You then tell Quicken whether each transaction has cleared and move on to the next transaction. Of course, if you find discrepancies, you can reconcile your balance, add missing transactions, and so on to ensure that your ending balance matches that on your paper statement. You reconcile the same way you do for checking and savings accounts, except with investment and retirement accounts, you reconcile both cash and share balances. However, because mutual fund accounts have no cash balance, you balance the share balance only.

It's important that you take into consideration that some transactions may not have cleared yet and therefore might not show up on your statement. Before you begin, you should make sure that all transactions (deposits, withdrawals, purchases, payments, interest, and so on) have been downloaded and recorded or entered in your account register, and you should have your statement ready.

Balance Your Investment and Retirement Accounts

1. If you're not already there, open the investment or retirement account you want to balance by clicking the account in the account bar.

2. Click the Transactions tab.

3. Compare the transactions on your statement to those that appear in your Quicken account register. When you find a match, click in the column next to the date and select C.

4. Click Enter to update the transaction. Quicken places a C in the column to indicate that the transaction has cleared.

5. To add a missing transaction, click in the next empty transaction row and type the information. Then click Enter.

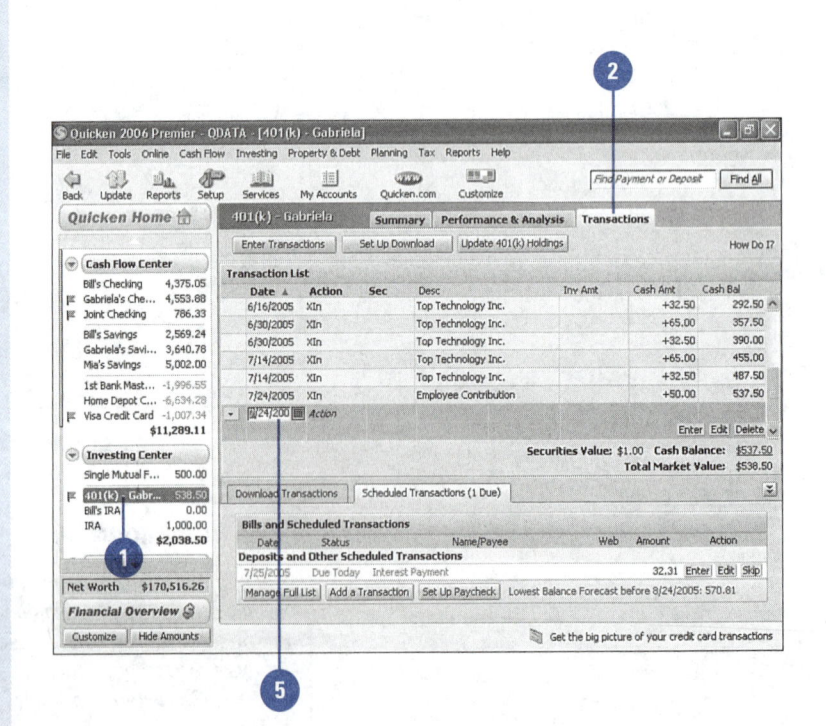

6. To edit a transaction, select the transaction, and click Edit.

7. Make your changes and click Enter/Done.

8. Continue comparing transactions and clearing each transaction as needed. Then compare your balance on the statement to the balance in your register. If there is a difference, determine the reason for the discrepancy (for example, fees and interest were added).

See Also

See "Adding, Editing, and Deleting Investment and Retirement Transactions" on page 195 for more information on adding new, editing existing, and deleting transactions.

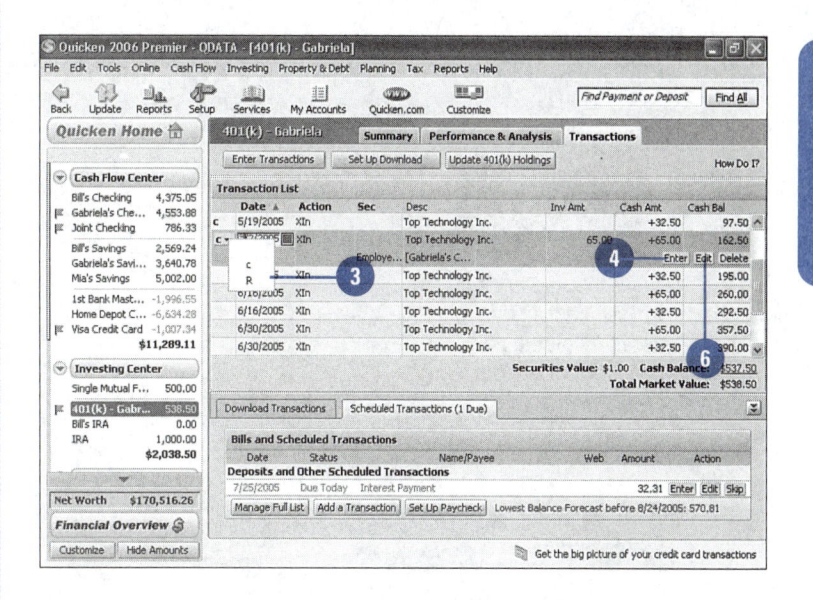

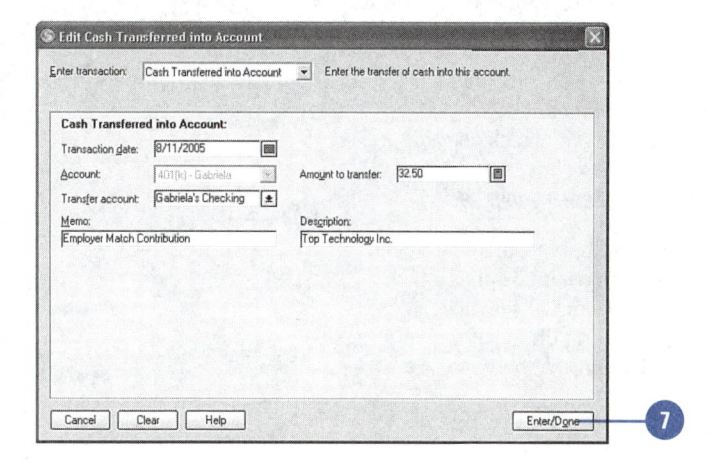

Managing Your Investments and Retirement Information **205**

9. To reconcile the account, select Investing, Investing Activities, Reconcile an Account.

10. Type the starting and ending balances from your statement and the statement end date. Click OK.

11. The Statement Summary window shows you which transactions have cleared by placing a green check mark next to each one that has cleared.

12. If there are discrepancies, you can add missing transactions and edit or delete transactions by using the menu options to balance your account.

13. To complete the balance at another time, click Finish Later.

14. If the difference is zero, the account is balanced. Click Finished. Quicken places an R in the C column to show that your balance has been reconciled.

15. If the register balanced, the reconciliation window opens, asking if you want to view a reconciliation report. Click Yes to view the report; otherwise, click No.

See Also

See "Balance Your Online Accounts" on page 123 for information on balancing online accounts.

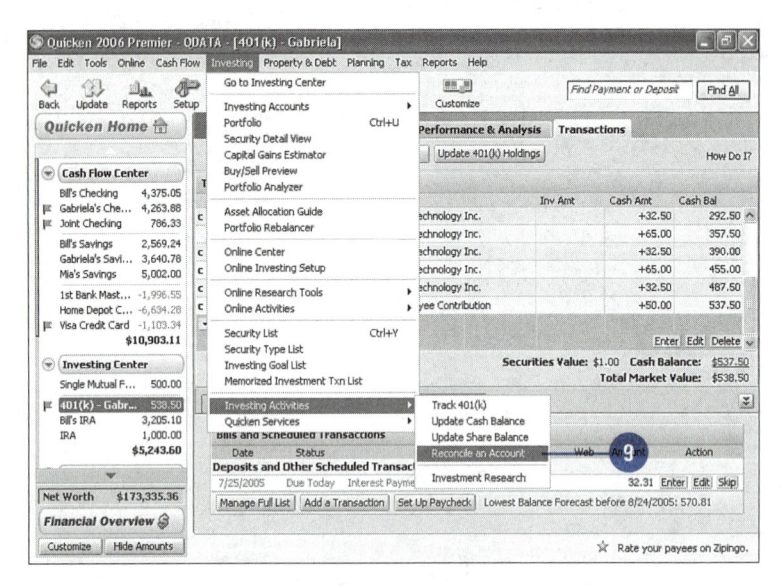

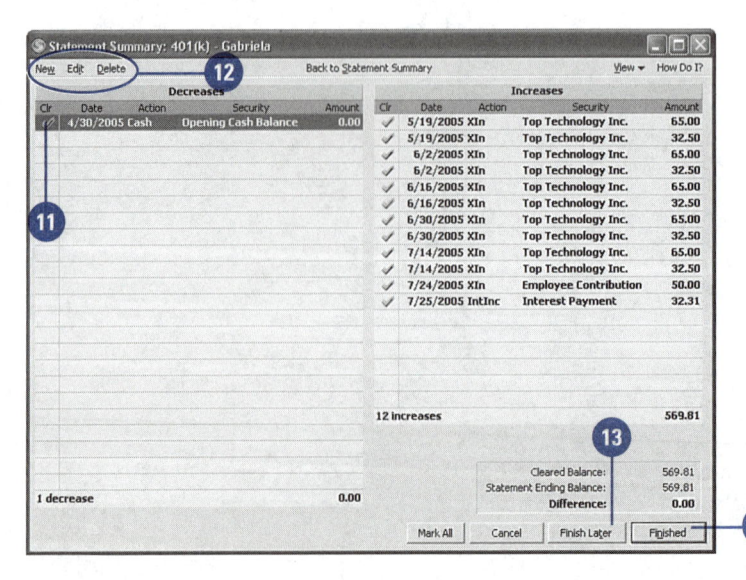

Analyzing Your Asset Allocations and Portfolio

Introduction

Now that you have all or most of your asset information in Quicken, such as stocks, bonds, and mutual funds, you can now take a step back to review and compare how your assets are doing. It's a good idea to review and analyze how your assets are allocated and get a big-picture view of your portfolio from time to time. The whole reason you have assets is to make money, right? Quicken provides some features that can give you that big picture in a matter of minutes and provide some good advice on where you might want to consider making some changes.

This chapter reviews the tools you can use to analyze your assets, see how you currently have your assets allocated, determine what your capital gain potential is with your existing investments, and analyze your portfolio to see if you have well-balanced investments. All these tools help you determine whether you need to adjust where you are putting your money and how you can get the most out of your assets and investments.

What You'll Do

Review and Analyze Your Asset Allocations

Get Some Help with Asset Allocation

Estimate Capital Gains

View Your Entire Portfolio

Analyze Your Portfolio

Determine Whether You Need to Rebalance Your Portfolio

Reviewing and Analyzing Your Asset Allocations

The Analysis tab in the Investing Center provides pie charts that show you how your assets are spread out among your investments. When you set up your investments in Quicken, you most likely indicated how much you were allocating to each investment. When you do this, Quicken logs which asset classes or groups (for example, bonds) your investments belong to. Using the Analysis tab, you can analyze where your money is by viewing just your investment allocations, just your retirement allocations, all accounts, or individual accounts. In addition, pie charts show you how your accounts are allocated and how your securities, such as cash, are allocated. By viewing your asset allocations from all angles, you can see exactly which assets are growing and how fast they are growing, which assets aren't growing, and where you may need to make adjustments.

Review and Analyze Your Asset Allocations

1. In the account bar, click Investing Center.

2. Click the Analysis tab.

3. The Actual pie chart shows your assets as they are allocated today, and the Target pie chart shows your assets as they should be. Hover your mouse over a slice to see the amount and percentage allocated.

4. Beneath the actual pie is the total amount of your assets.

5. The table beneath the pie charts provides a comparison of your actual and target percentages and serves as a color key to the slices in the pie chart.

6. To change your target percentages to see how your totals change, click Change target allocations. If you haven't set up your asset allocation targets yet, the Set Target link appears instead of the Change Target link.

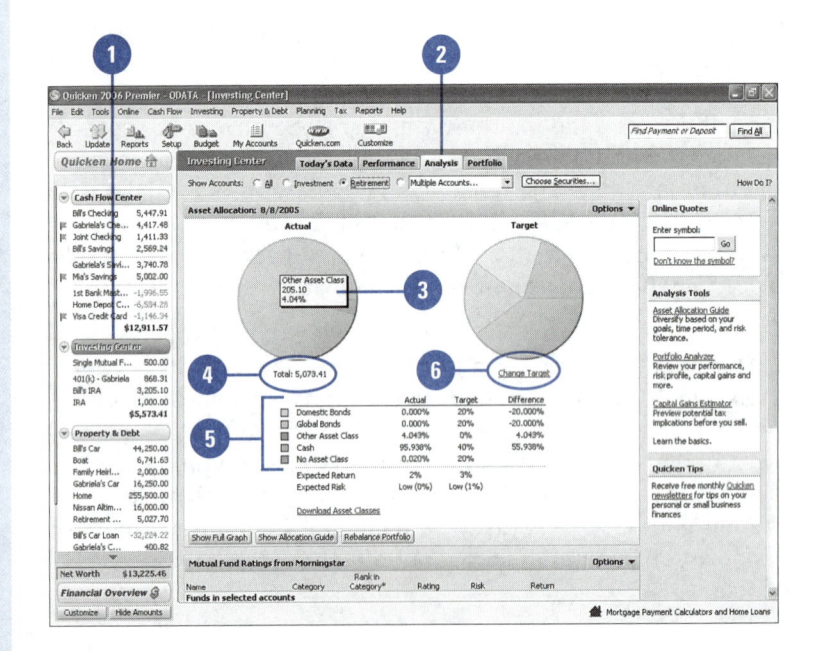

208

7 Click in the Percentage column for the asset class you want to change and type the new percentage. Remember, your asset percentages must total 100%.

8 Click OK.

Did You Know?

Changing your target percentages does not actually change your investments. *By changing your target asset allocation percentages, you are not actually changing how your assets are allocated. This feature allows you see what the potential is, should you change your allocations. Be sure to check with an advisor before making changes to your investments.*

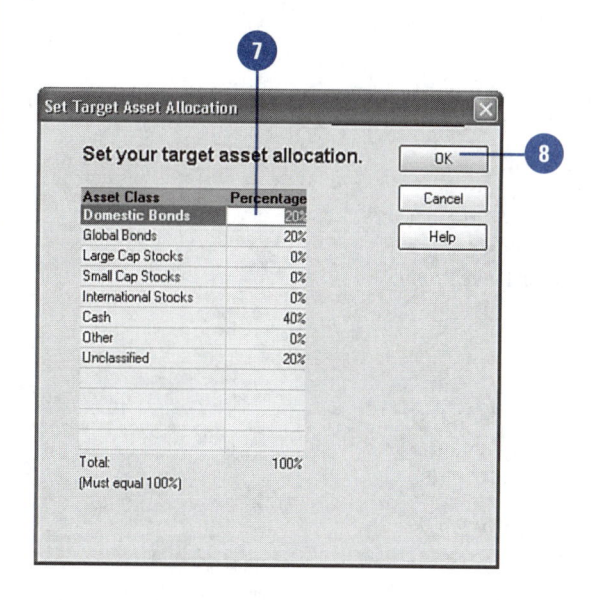

Set Target Asset Allocation

Set your target asset allocation.

Asset Class	Percentage
Domestic Bonds	20%
Global Bonds	20%
Large Cap Stocks	0%
Small Cap Stocks	0%
International Stocks	0%
Cash	40%
Other	0%
Unclassified	20%

Total: 100%
(Must equal 100%)

OK | Cancel | Help

Analyzing Your Asset Allocations and Portfolio

Select the Accounts and Securities You Want to View

1. To change the accounts you are viewing, from Show Accounts, select All to view both retirement and investment accounts, select Investment to view just investment accounts, or Retirement to view only those accounts.

2. Click the drop-down menu and select an account you want to view or select Multiple Accounts to choose a variety of accounts.

3. Select the accounts you want to view and click OK.

4. To select specific securities to view, click Choose Securities.

5. Select or clear the securities that you want to view and click OK.

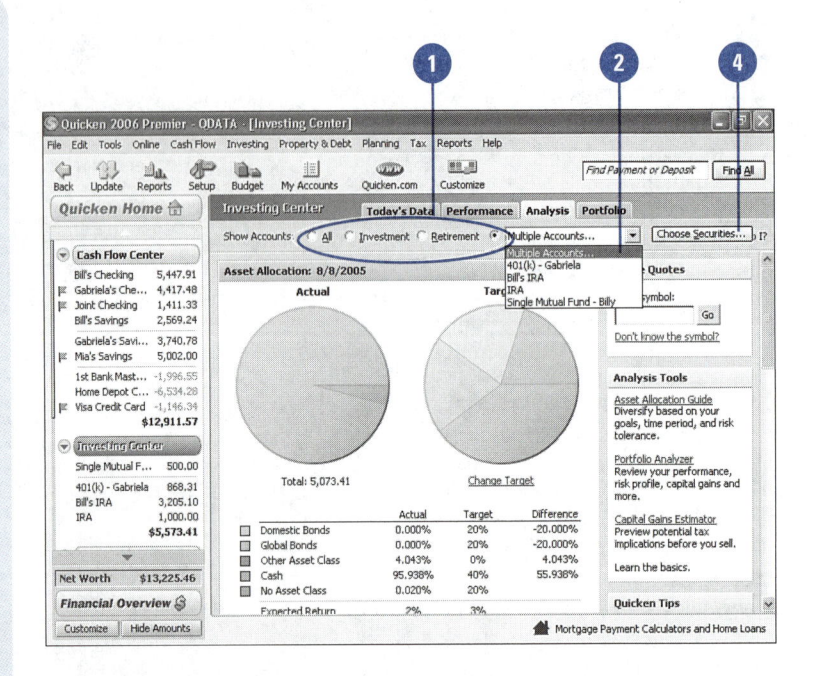

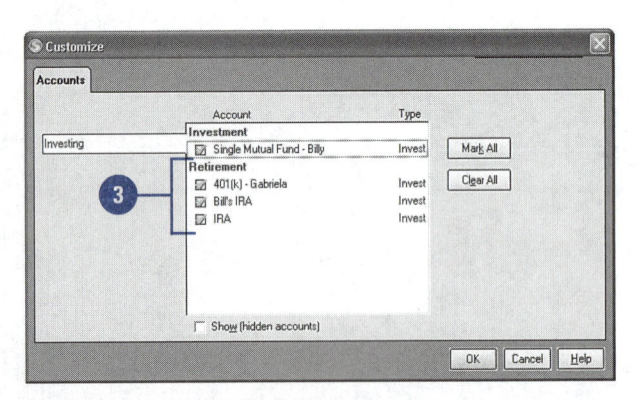

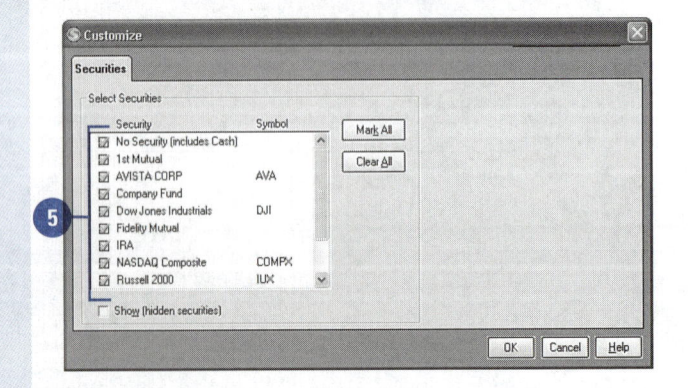

View the Asset Allocation Report

1. To view the pie chart and a detailed report for the accounts and securities currently reflected on the Actual pie chart, click Show Full Graph.

2. To view a detailed breakdown by security, click Show Report.

See Also

See "Customizing Reports" on page 368 for more information on changing the information in the pie chart and printing it. See "Saving and Viewing Saved Reports" on page 375 to learn how to save a pie chart.

3. To print just the pie chart, click Print Graph.

4. To print just the report, click Print Report.

5. To remove the pie chart, click Hide Graph.

6. To remove the report, click Hide Report.

7. Close the report when you are finished.

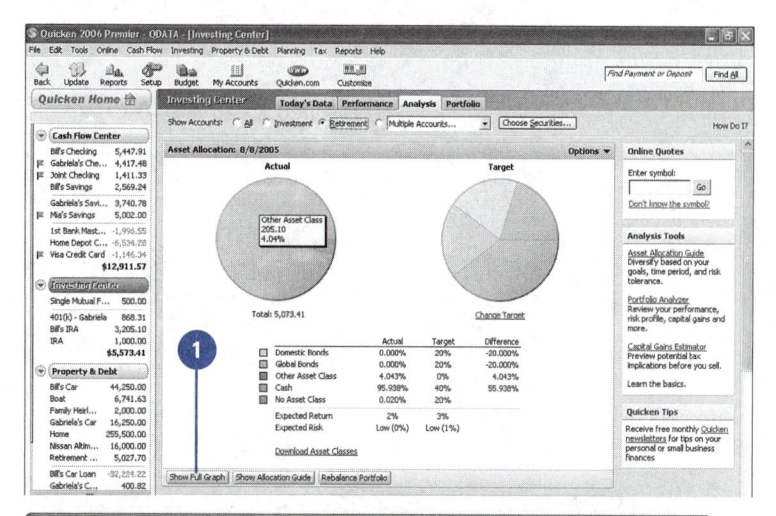

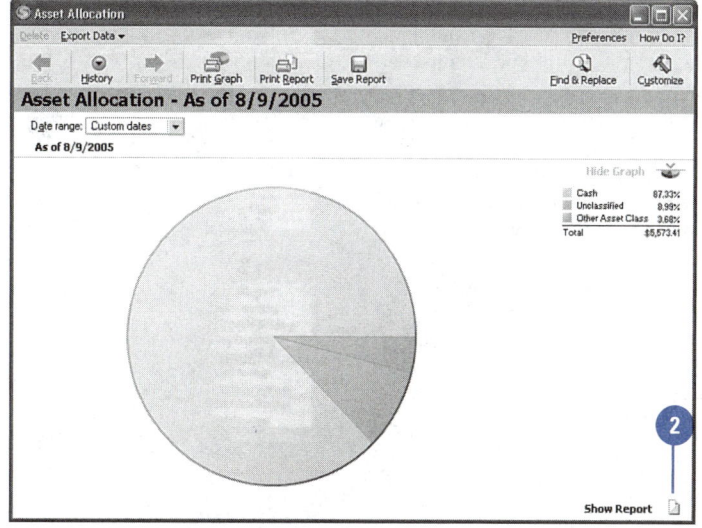

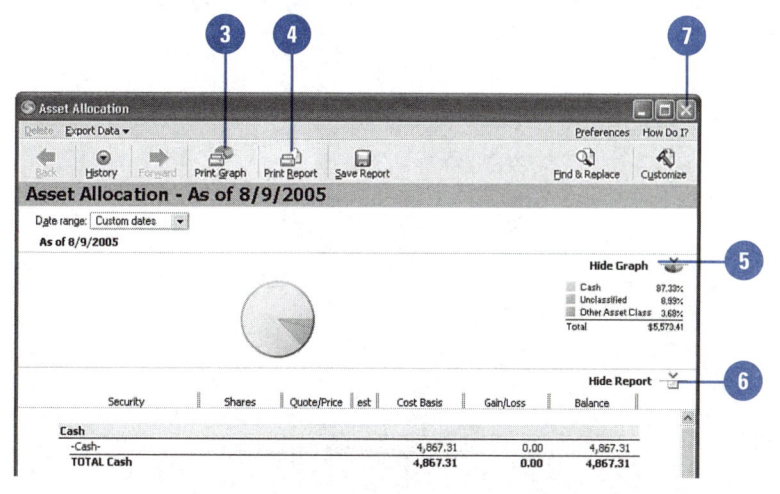

Analyzing Your Asset Allocations and Portfolio **211**

Review and Compare Mutual Funds

1. If you have mutual funds, the Mutual Fund Ratings from Morningstar section lists the funds that are included in the accounts that are currently selected from Show Accounts and those in your watch list, if you have one.

2. The Category column shows you the types of funds associated with the accounts.

3. The Rank In Category column shows you the ranking of the fund, based on performance among all mutual funds in the Morningstar mutual fund category. Ranking ranges from 1 (best) to 100 (worst).

4. The Rating column provides the current rating for the fund, based on Morningstar's five-star range.

5. To add a new fund, click Add a mutual fund and complete the Add Security to Quicken dialog box.

6. Complete the Add Security to Quicken dialog box and click Next to proceed with the lookup.

7. To compare the category, rank, rating, risk, and potential return for each fund, click Show Full Comparison.

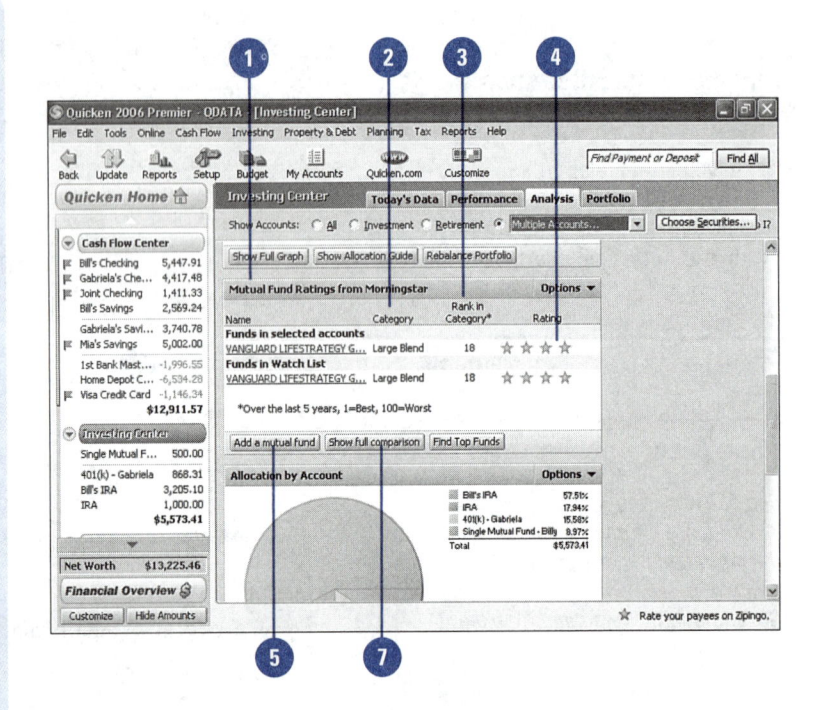

212

8. Review the ratings information and close the window when you are finished.

9. To research everything you would ever want to know about mutual funds, click Find Top Funds to open the Yahoo! Finance web page.

See Also

See "Tracking Investment Performances" on page 191 for more information on setting up and using watch lists.

Did You Know?

Morningstar is a mutual fund rating service. As one of the leading mutual fund rating services, Morningstar rates mutual funds using stars, five being the top rating. Ratings are based on two areas—risk assessment and load adjusted performance (return)—and three time periods—3, 5, and 10 years. However, a fund must have at least a 3-year track record before Morningstars rates it. When a rating is calculated, the result determines how risky the fund is, compared to the average funds in the same class or type of fund.

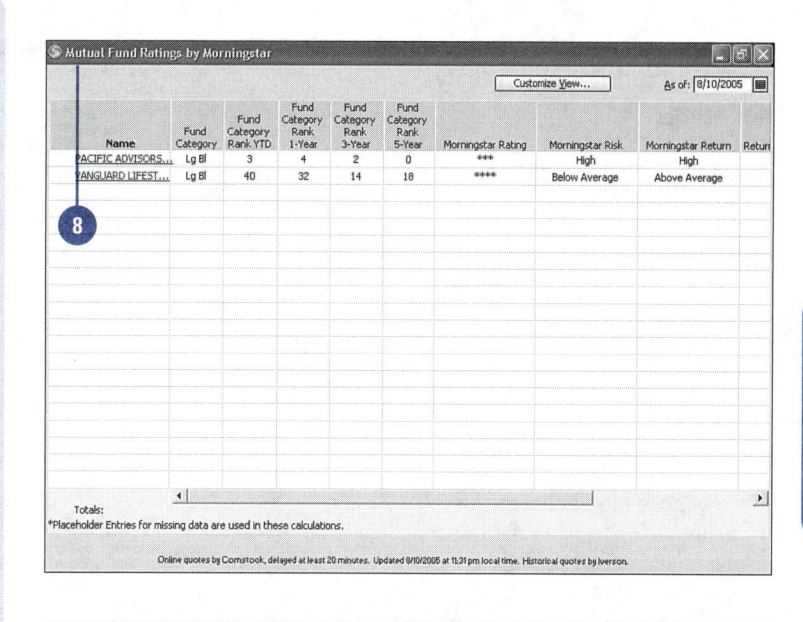

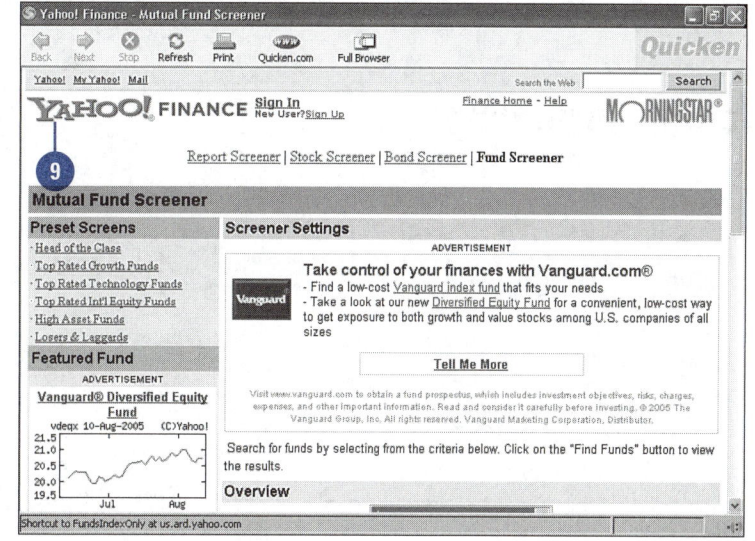

Analyzing Your Asset Allocations and Portfolio 213

Review Account and Security Allocations

1. From the Analysis tab, scroll down to the Allocation by Account section. Then click Show Full Graph to see the pie chart in detail and to access reporting features.

2. Allocation by Security shows how your securities are allocated. Click Show Full Graph to see the pie chart in detail and to access reporting features.

3. To change the date range for either pie chart, click the Options menu and select Customize this graph for either section.

4. Select a new date range and click OK.

Getting Some Help

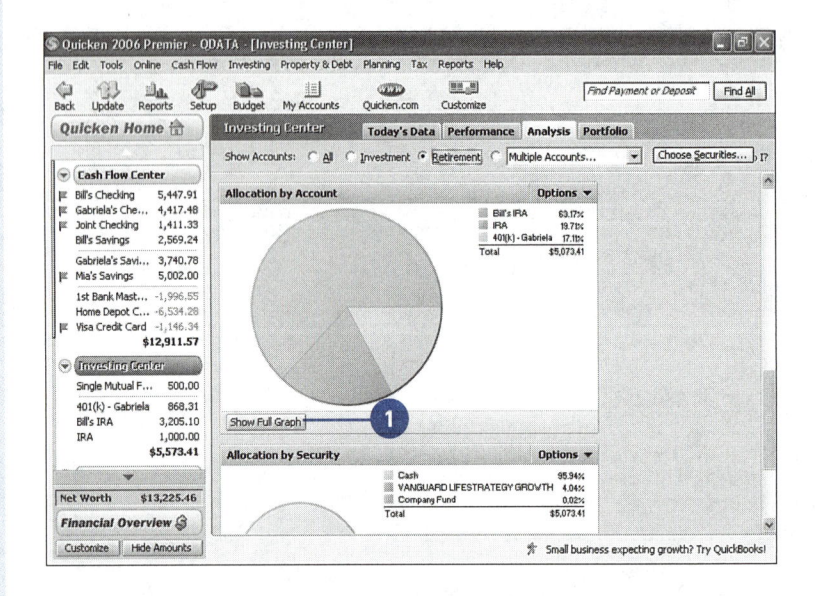

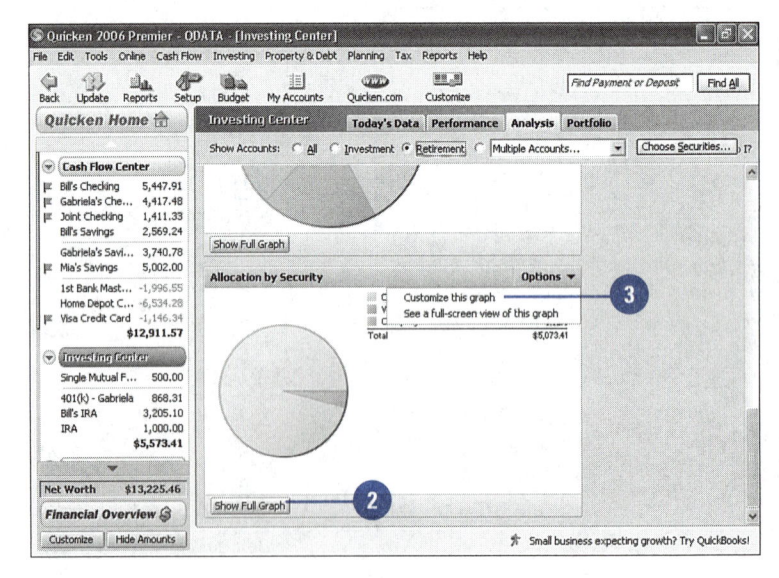

with Asset Allocation

Asset allocation is very important, and sometimes the slightest change can make a big difference. There are principles that you can use as guidelines when determining and evaluating how you want to allocate your assets or make changes to them. So, how about a little advice from a reputable source to help you out? Don't worry, there's no insider-trading going on here, just Quicken's Asset Allocation Guide, which has some great tips. This guide has some very helpful information about assets and asset classes, how to go about allocating your assets, what an ideal portfolio looks like, monitoring your assets, and rebalancing your portfolio. In addition, this guide should be able to answer some of your questions about risks, how to reach your goals, finding a reputable financial advisor, and much more. Maybe Martha Stewart should have checked here first.

Get Help with Asset Allocation

1 If you're not already there, open the Analysis tab in the Investing Center and click Show Allocation Guide. Or you can click the Asset Allocation Guide link in the Analysis Tools box.

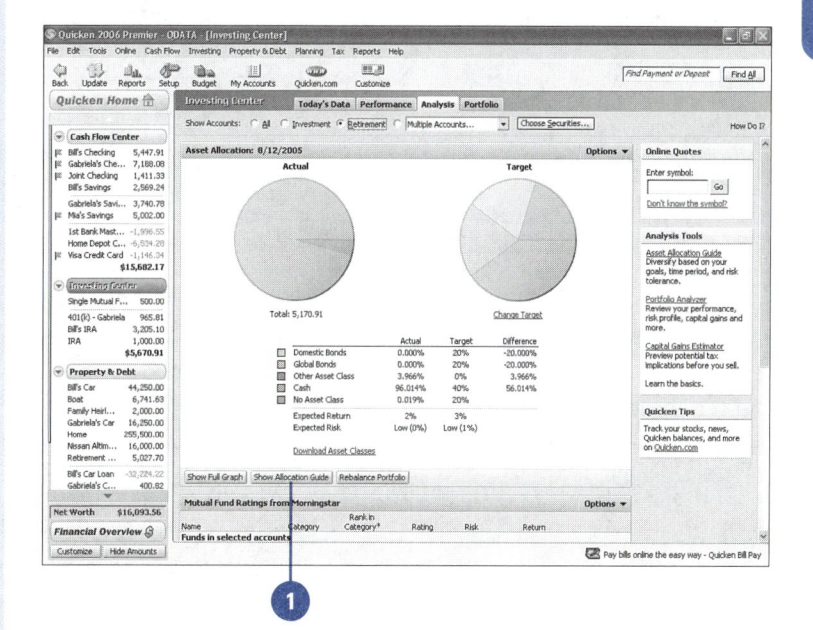

Analyzing Your Asset Allocations and Portfolio   **215**

② The guide starts with some basic information about assets and a pie chart view of your current asset allocations. For more information about asset classes, click What are asset classes and why should I use them?

③ To proceed to the next window, click Next: How do I update asset classes? You can also use the menu on the left to move through the guide.

④ Review the information about updating asset classes and common questions. If you want to download the latest classes, click Go online and update classes. Be sure you are connected to the Internet before proceeding.

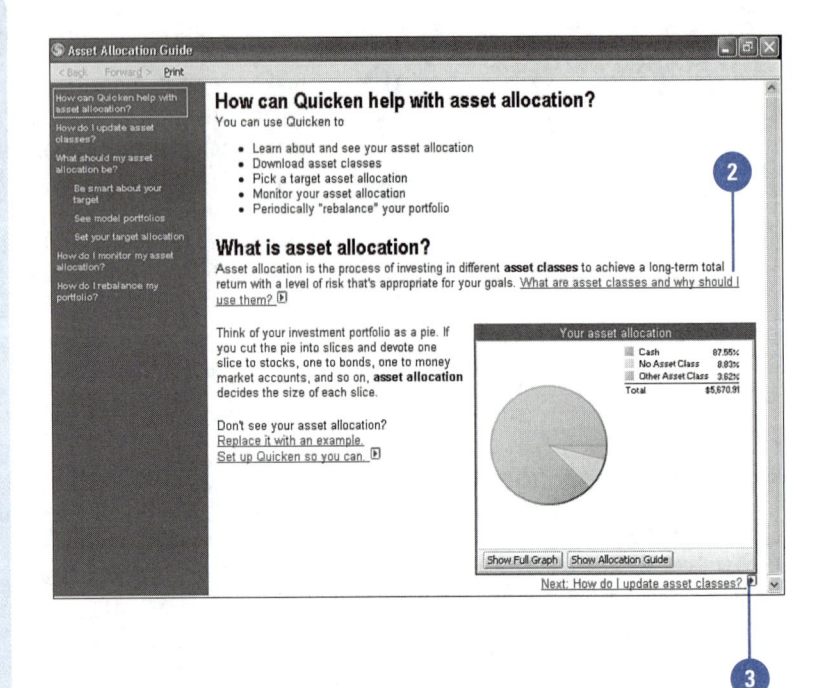

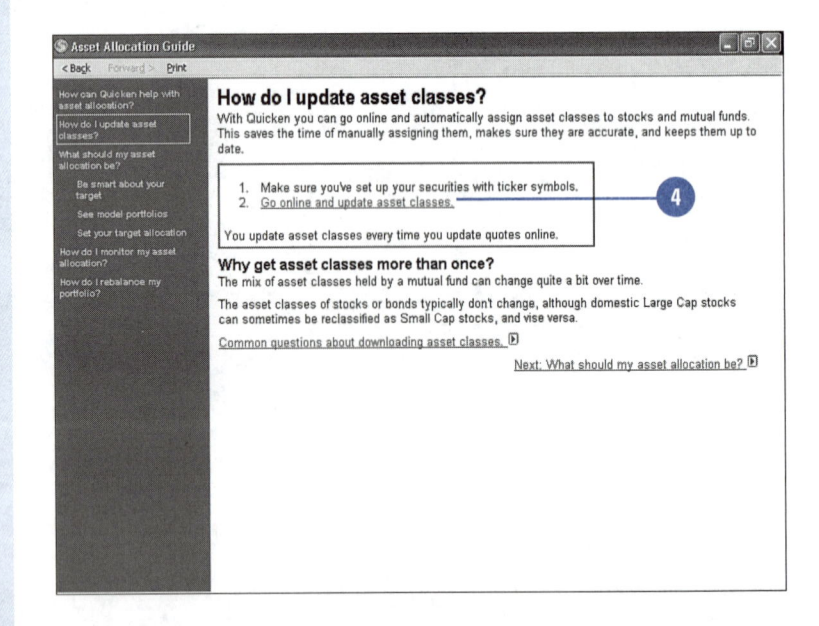

5. Select the securities for which you want asset class information and click Update Now to download the information.

6. Explore the links to get more information on a subject or to set up or change information about your allocations, such as your target allocation.

7. Continue to review all the asset allocation information and click the Next link to move to each new window.

8. When you get to the last window (titled What is Rebalancing?) review the steps you need to take to rebalance your portfolio and click the links to get additional information.

9. When you are finished, close the window.

See Also

See "Determining Whether You Need to Rebalance Your Portfolio" on page 233 for more information on rebalancing your portfolio.

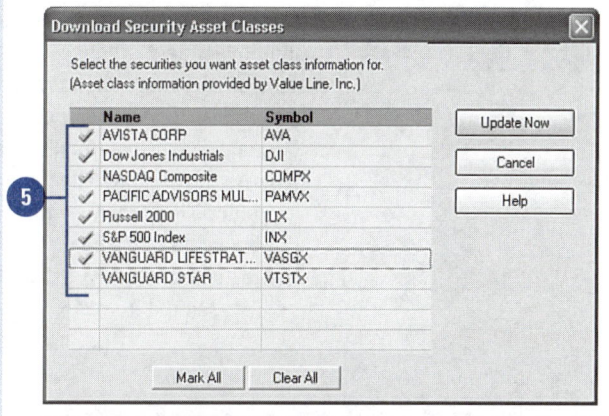

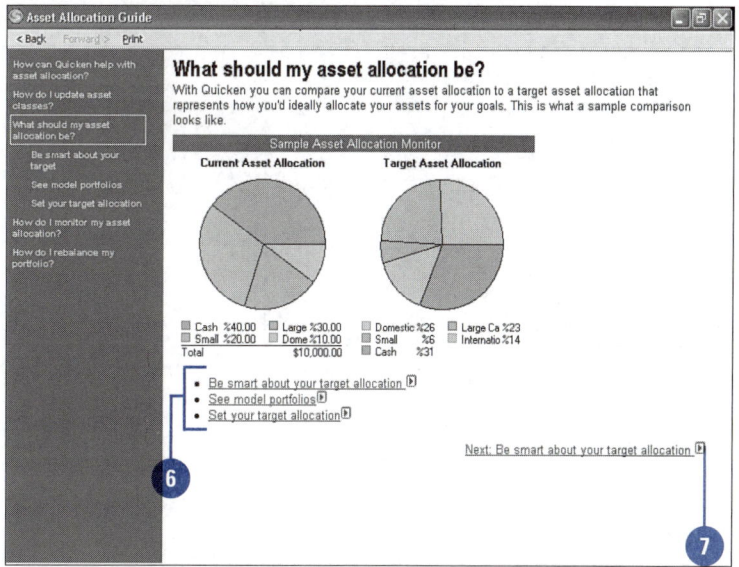

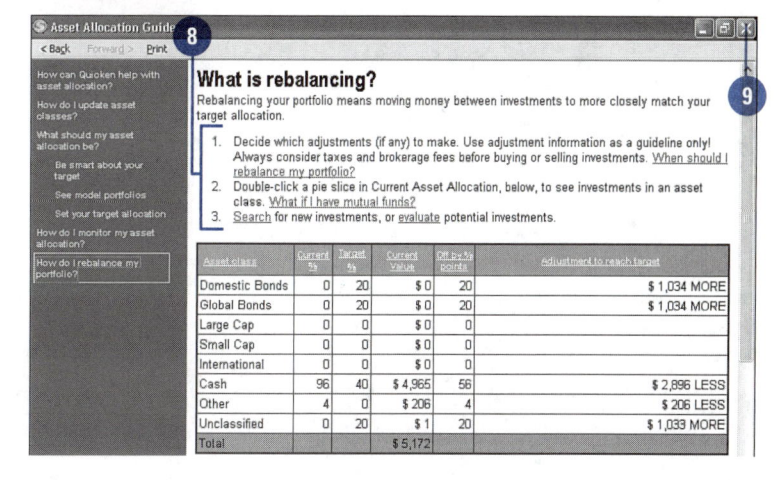

Analyzing Your Asset Allocations and Portfolio 217

Estimating Capital Gains

If you sell an investment and the selling price exceeds the purchase price, that investment produces a profit for you. This is known as *capital gain*. Quicken provides a feature to help you determine what your capital gain potential is, using your existing investments. This feature is called the Capital Gains Estimator. Estimating your capital gains helps you determine whether it would be advantageous to sell an investment and what tax liability you could encounter. You can access the Capital Gains Estimator from the Investment and Tax menus, from the Analysis tab in the Investing Center, or from the Portfolio Analyzer. For the purposes of this task, you will be accessing it from the Analysis tab.

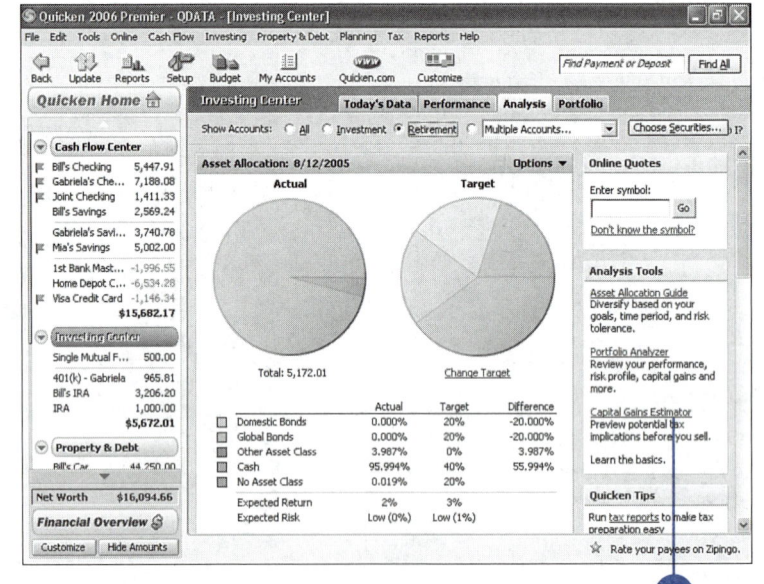

Estimate Capital Gains

1. If you're not already there, open the Analysis tab in the Investing Center and click Capital Gains Estimator.

See Also

See Chapter 11, "Managing Your Tax Information," for information on determining tax liabilities and setting up your tax information using the Tax Planner.

② Review the Welcome window and click Let's get started to proceed.

③ Select a scenario and click Next. You can set up as many as three scenarios to compare and contrast situations. But you have to create the scenarios one at a time.

Did You Know?

You can use the menu to move through the Capital Gains Estimator. If you already know your way around this feature or you prefer to navigate it by using the menu, click the menu options on the left side of the window to move through or go to a specific place in the Capital Gains Estimator. If you have saved scenarios you are working with, click a scenario under the Scenarios section to go directly to it.

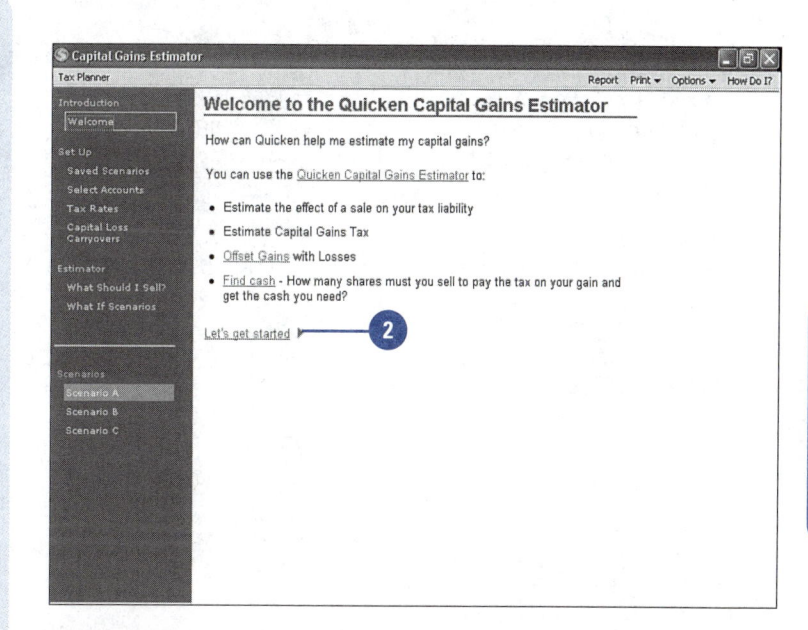

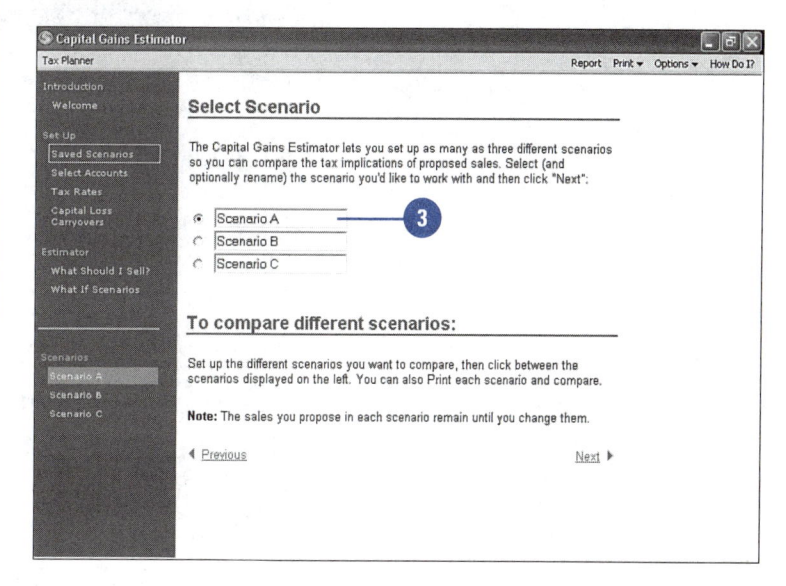

Analyzing Your Asset Allocations and Portfolio **219**

4. Select the investments you want to include by clicking in the column next to the investment name. A green check mark means the investment is selected.

5. Your estimated taxes are determined using the information you have entered into Quicken about your investments and tax information. If you have not already set up your tax information, click the Tax Planner link to do so now.

6. In the Federal Tax Rates section, if you're sure of your federal tax rate, select it from the list. Otherwise, use the rate that Quicken has selected for you.

7. In the State Tax Rates section, type your state tax rate. If you are unsure of what it is, click How do I find my state tax rate? to get information on how to determine the rate.

8. Click Next.

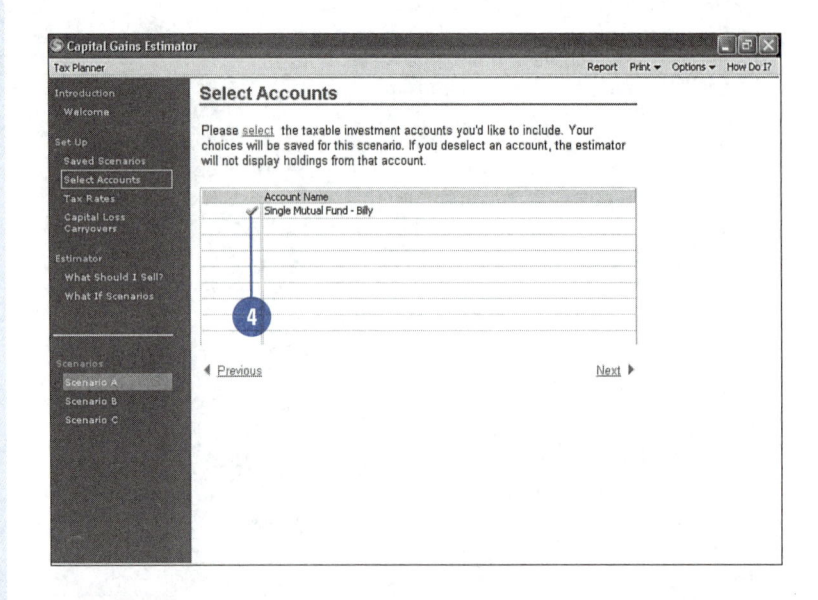

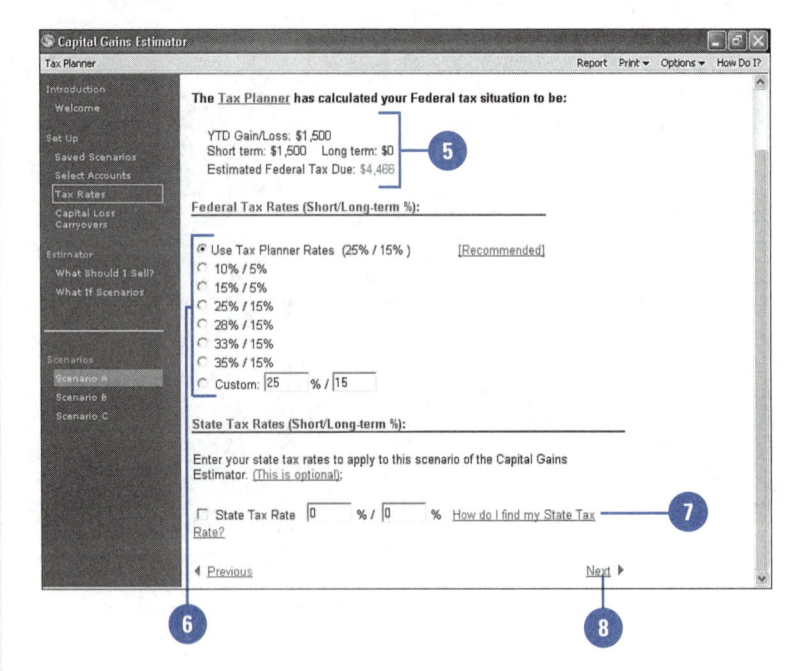

9. Select Use Tax Planner Values to use losses from previous years. The figures are automatically updated. Or, select Enter Different Values to type the figures yourself. Then click Next.

10. Type the amount you would like to make on the sale. This does not have to be an exact figure. You can change it if it ends up not meeting your goal.

11. Select a goal.

12. Click Search. Quicken searches your investments and locates securities that you can sell to meet your goal.

Did You Know?

There are limits for the losses you can claim. You can claim up to $3,000 (or $1,500 if you are married and file separately) above any capital gains.

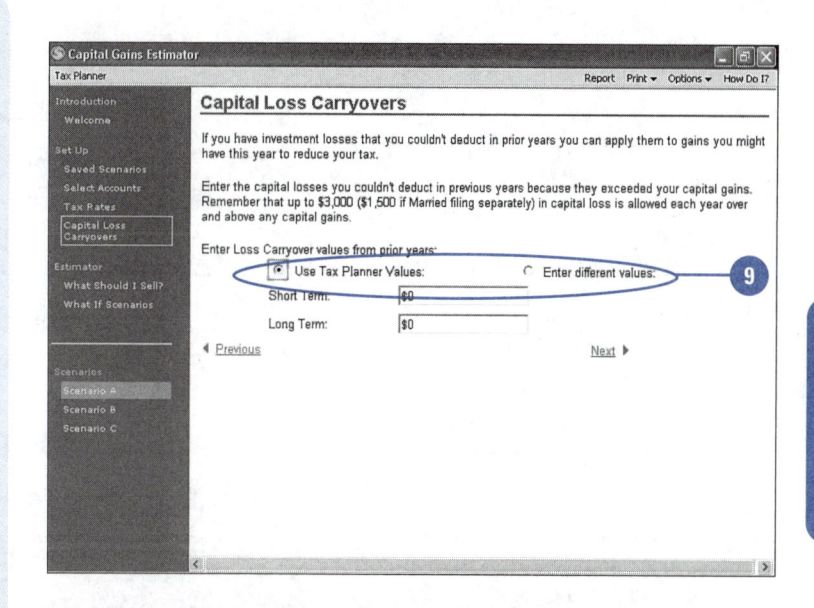

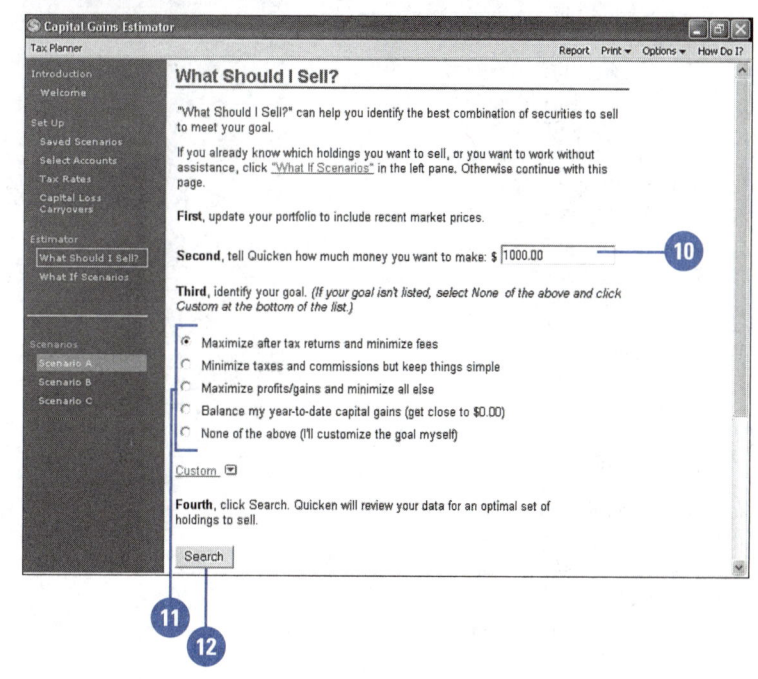

Analyzing Your Asset Allocations and Portfolio 221

13 Click View Results.

14 Select the security or lot that you are thinking of selling. The number of shares and selling price automatically update in the Proposed Sales table, based on the security or lot you select.

15 Click in Shares to Sell or Sale Price to change the figures, if needed.

16 Notice that any losses or gains are listed in the Taxable Gains from Proposed Sales table.

17 Notice that the potential total gross sales and total estimated taxes or refund due are calculated and provided toward the bottom of the window.

18 You can go back through this scenario and make changes or set up another scenario to compare to this one by repeating steps 1–17, However, be sure to select the next scenario (for example, Scenario B) in step 3.

19 When you are finished, close the window.

Did You Know?

You can compare taxes before and after sales. *To see what your taxes would be before and after you sell an investment, click the links under Detailed Calculations at the bottom of the window.*

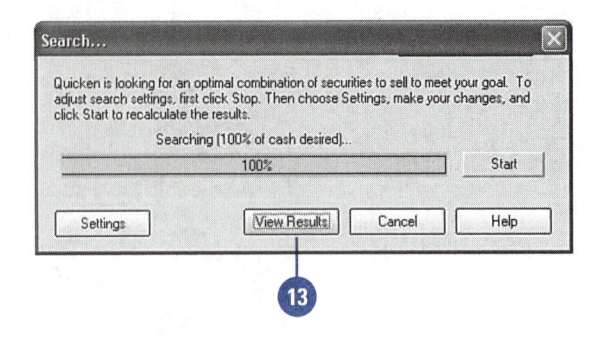

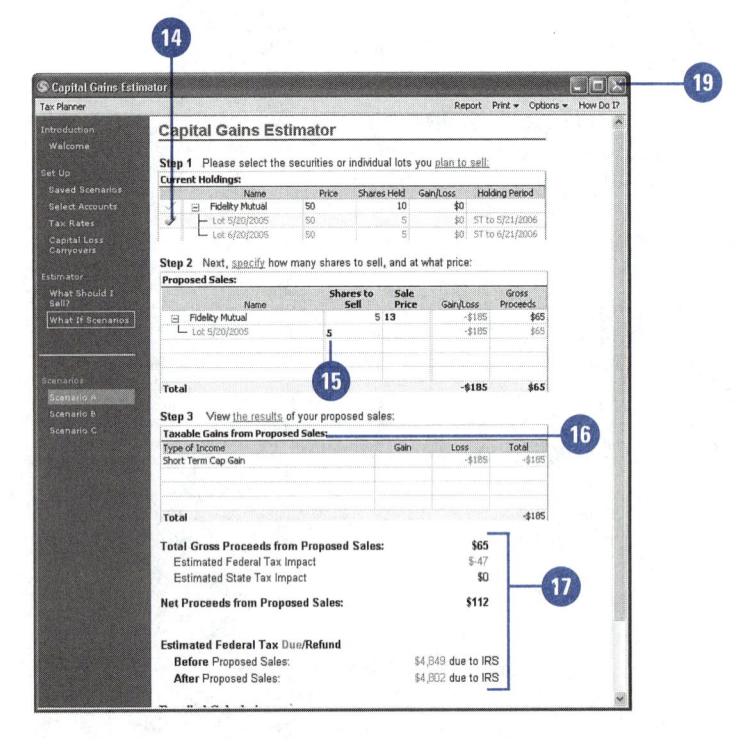

Viewing Your Entire Portfolio

Your portfolio consists of all your asset information (retirement accounts, stocks, bonds, and so on). All your assets are listed in Quicken in detail so that you can review or take action on every type of asset you own. Your securities or assets are listed by name. For each security, you can see a host of information. For example, the default view provides the quote or price, the number of shares, the market value dollar amount, the total cost of all shares, the loss or gain dollar amounts, the loss or gain percentages, the losses or gains per day, and the daily value of each, in dollar amounts and percentages. In addition, you can download the latest or historical quotes for your securities, change the view to see your securities from different angles, and customize the information you see. Basically, you can slice and dice your portfolio any way you want.

Review Your Portfolio

1. If you're not already in the Investing Center, open it and click the Portfolio tab.

2. Review the list of your securities. You can open and close the folders by clicking them. The portfolio view differs, depending on what is selected from the Show menu. This example uses the Quotes view.

3. The Watch List folder contains any securities that you have set up for your watch list.

4. If you use One Step Update, the latest quotes may already update automatically. If not, you can update quotes by clicking Download Quotes. Quicken connects to the Internet and downloads the quotes.

5. To view prices for previous dates click Download Historical Prices.

See Also

See "Tracking Investment Performance" on page 191 to learn how to set up or edit watch lists.

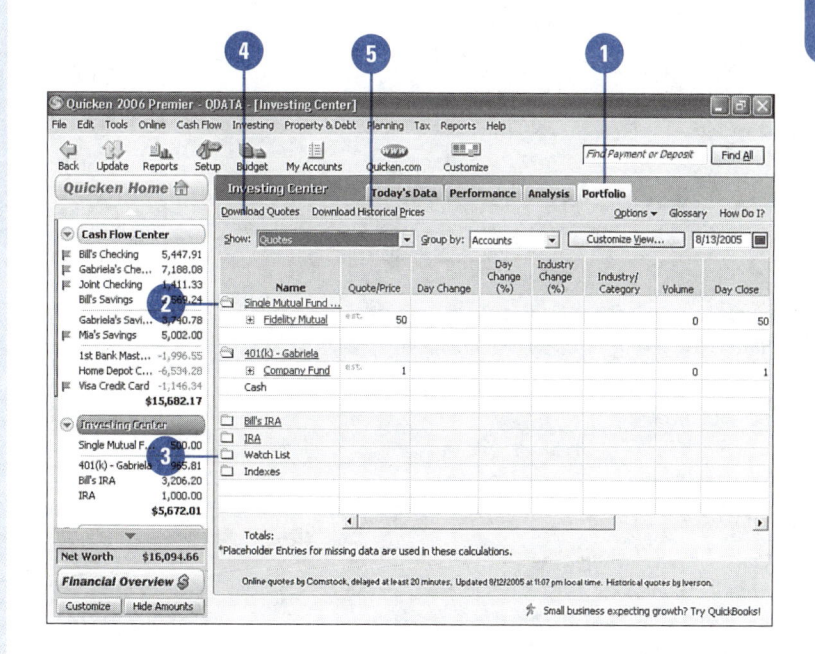

Did You Know?

You can use the glossary for column definitions. *To read detailed descriptions about each column in the portfolio, from the menu bar at the top of the Portfolio tab, click Glossary.*

Analyzing Your Asset Allocations and Portfolio

6. Select the time frames (they range from the previous month to the past five years) and click Update Now. Quicken connects to the Internet and downloads the historical quotes.

7. To change the view, from the Show drop-down menu, select a different view.

8. To change how the listing is grouped, click Group by and select another option.

9. To view figures for a different date, click in the box next to the calendar icon and type the date you want to see or click the calendar icon and select the date.

See Also

See "Setting Up Your Internet Connection" on page 63 for more information about One Step Update.

Did You Know?

There are some things to consider when downloading quotes. If you are downloading a lot of historical prices, it may take a while to download, depending on your Internet connection speed. Keep this in mind when you are selecting the securities you want to download. Consider breaking up how much you are downloading into manageable chunks appropriate for your connection speed (for example, a few at a time for a dial-up connection). If you have cable or DSL, downloading large amounts of information may not be a problem.

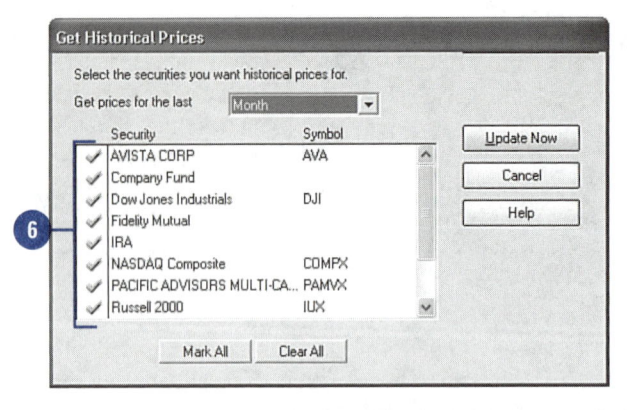

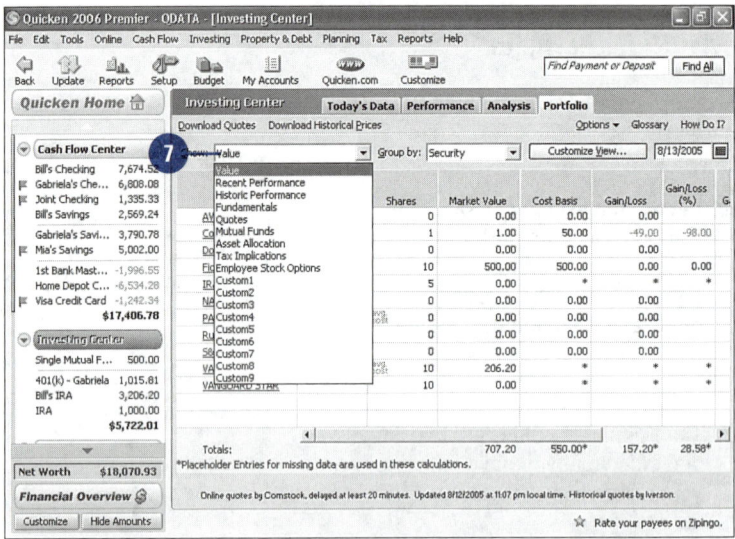

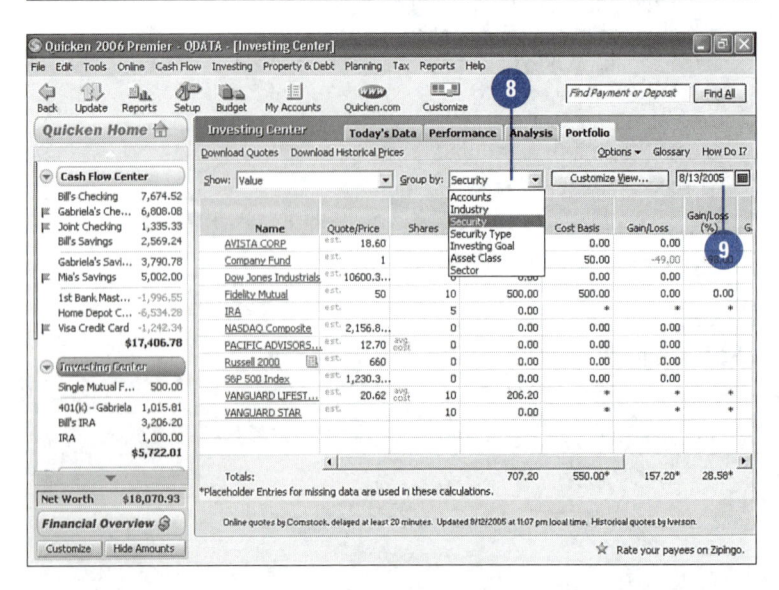

View Security Details

1. To view security details, hover your mouse over the name of the security. A pop-up menu appears, giving you options you can select to see more information about that security.

2. To go to the account summary, view performance and analysis information, or access the account register, click the account name or click Edit.

3. To evaluate stocks or mutual funds on Quicken.com, click Evaluate. You are required to log in to Quicken.com, provide the ticker symbol, and select an Evaluator tool.

4. To see how a security has been doing in the market, click Scorecard. This feature requires Internet access to Quicken.com.

5. To view more detailed information about a security, click the security name.

6. To change the security name, symbol, type, or asset class, click Edit Security Details.

Did You Know?

Pop-up menu options with lightning symbols require online access. *If you see a lightning bolt symbol when you hover your mouse over a pop-up menu option, you are required to log in to Quicken.com to use these features, and you therefore need your Quicken.com login and password.*

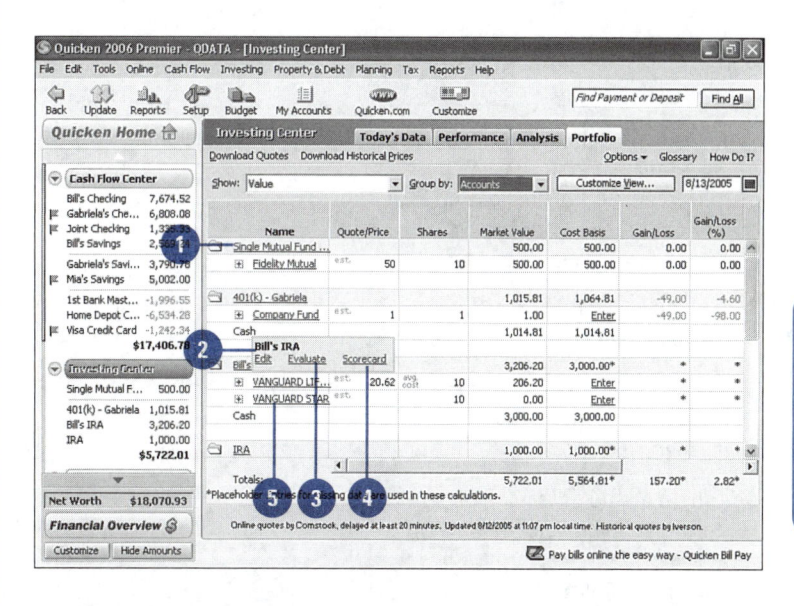

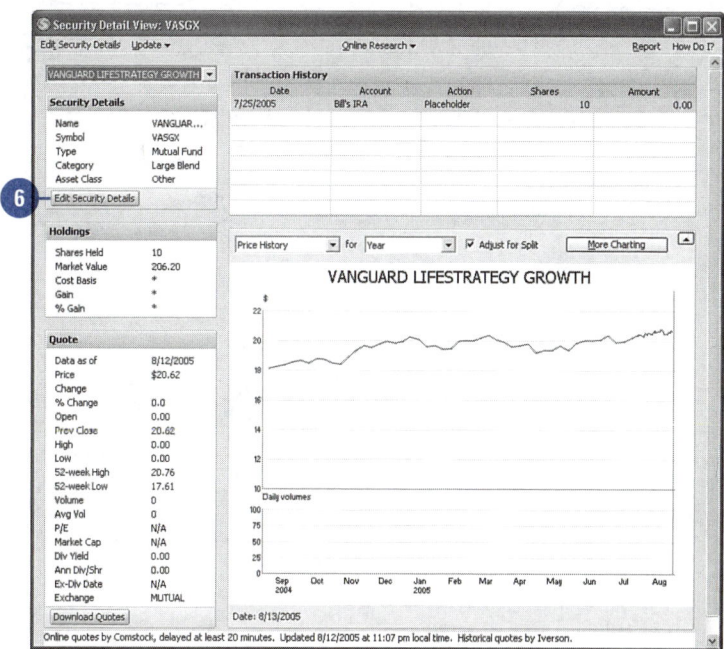

Analyzing Your Asset Allocations and Portfolio **225**

7. Make the changes and click OK when you are finished.

8. To view or change transaction information, double-click a transaction. If transactions need to be entered, the Enter Missing Transactions window opens.

9. Add the missing transaction(s) by clicking Enter Missing Transaction.

10. You can also edit or delete the transaction. When you are finished, click Done.

11. If there are no missing transactions, the Edit window opens, where you can view or change the transaction information. Click Enter/Done when you are finished.

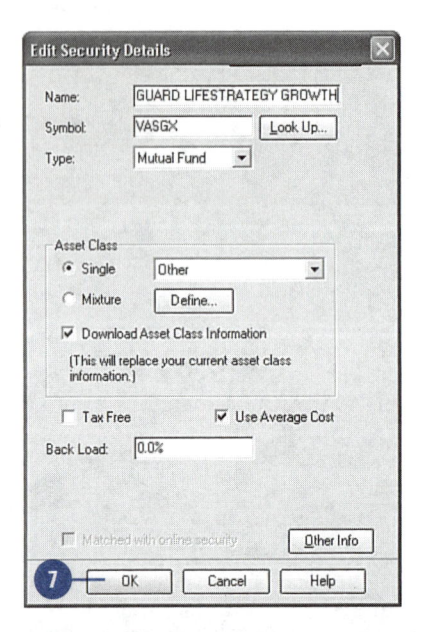

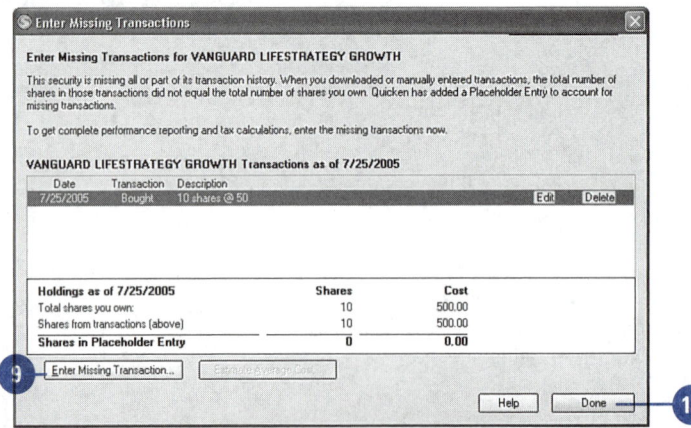

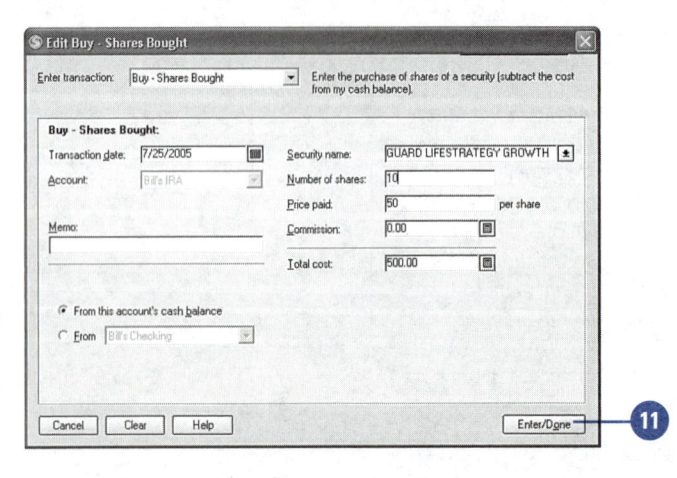

12 The line chart (which appears using the Price History view) provides the volume for the security over the course of a specific time period. Click a date and then click the vertical bar to move it across the lines to see what the price and volume were for that period.

13 Use the drop-down menus to change the view and time period.

14 Click More Charting to explore additional types of charts you can view.

15 Close the window when you are finished working with the security.

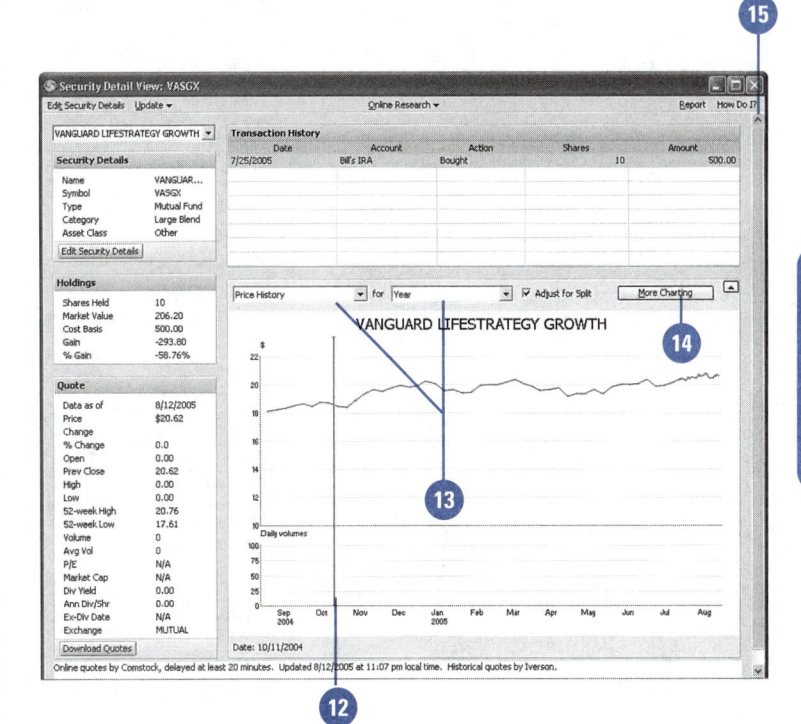

Analyzing Your Asset Allocations and Portfolio   **227**

Customize or Create a New Portfolio View

1 Click Customize View to either customize the current view or create a new view.

2 If you want to customize the current view, do not change the name. If you want to create a new view, click in Name and type a new name for the view.

3 To add a column or columns that you want to see, from Available Columns, select the column name(s) and click Add.

4 To remove a column or columns, from Displayed Columns, select the column name(s) and click Remove.

5 To see the symbols associated with each account on the Portfolio tab instead of the account names, select Show symbols in name column.

6 To select or remove the accounts and securities you see, click an account or a security. A green check mark means it is selected, and no check mark means it is not selected.

7 To change the order of accounts and securities, select an account or security and click Move Up to move it up the list or click Move Down to move it down the list. Repeat this step until the list appears the way you want.

8 Click Mark All to select all accounts or securities or click Clear All to remove all accounts or securities from the view.

9 Click OK to save your new or customized view. If you create a new view, the name will appear in the Show menu.

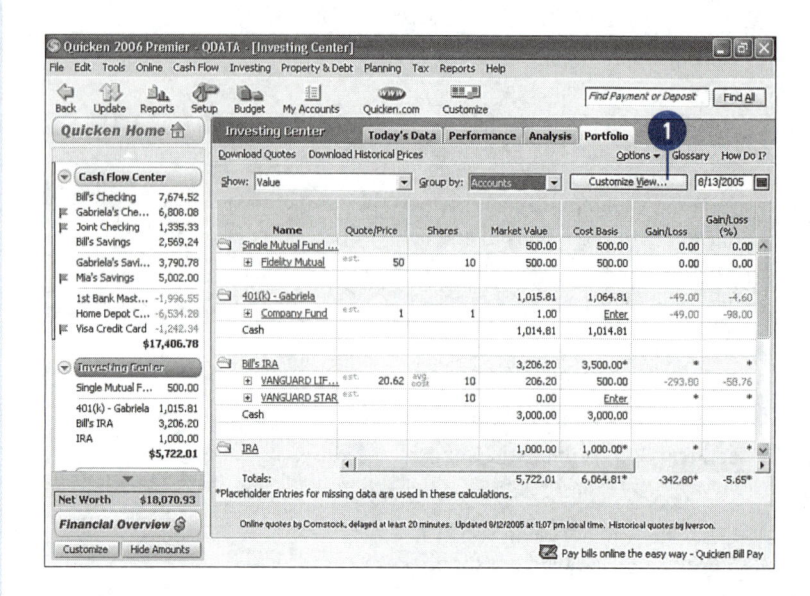

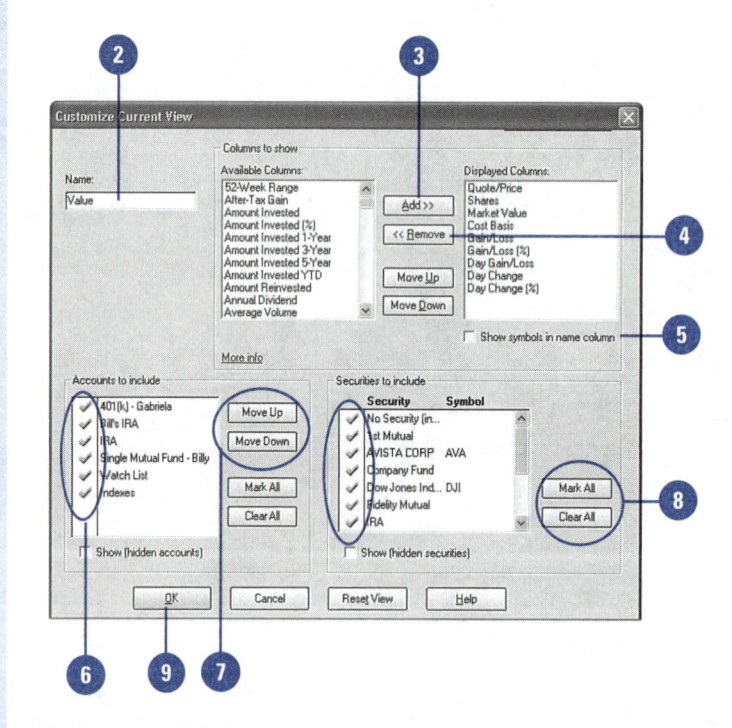

Analyzing Your Portfolio

Financial advisors recommend that you review and evaluate your portfolio at least once per year, or when your financial goals or circumstances change. Fortunately, Quicken offers an easy and painless way of analyzing your portfolio: by using a tool called the Portfolio Analyzer. This feature analyzes the performance of your investments, holdings, asset allocations, risk factors, and possible tax liabilities. This information can help you with any decisions you need to make about your investments and financial planning.

Analyze Your Portfolio

1. Click the Investing menu and select Portfolio Analyzer.

2. Click the menu options on the left side of the window or scroll down to view each section.

3. The Performance section provides a bar chart that shows the rate of return, in percentages, over a five-year period.

4. To see which securities did the best and which did the worst, select a timeframe from the Time Period menu.

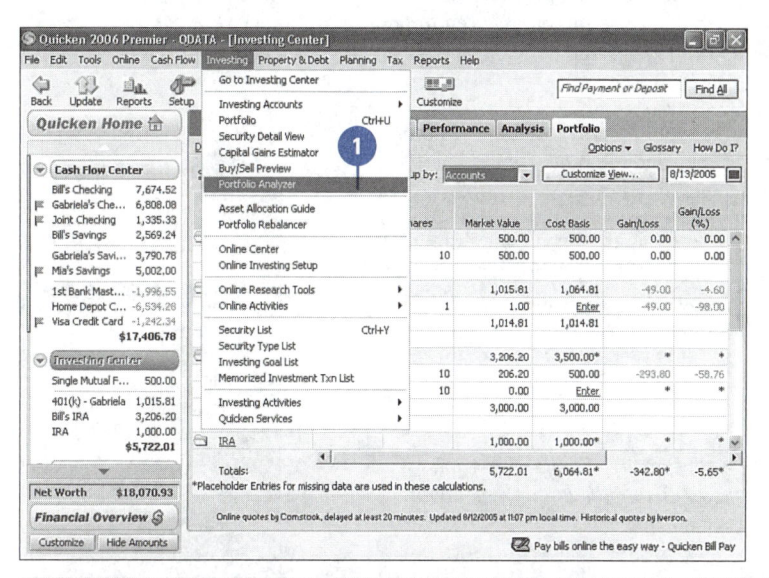

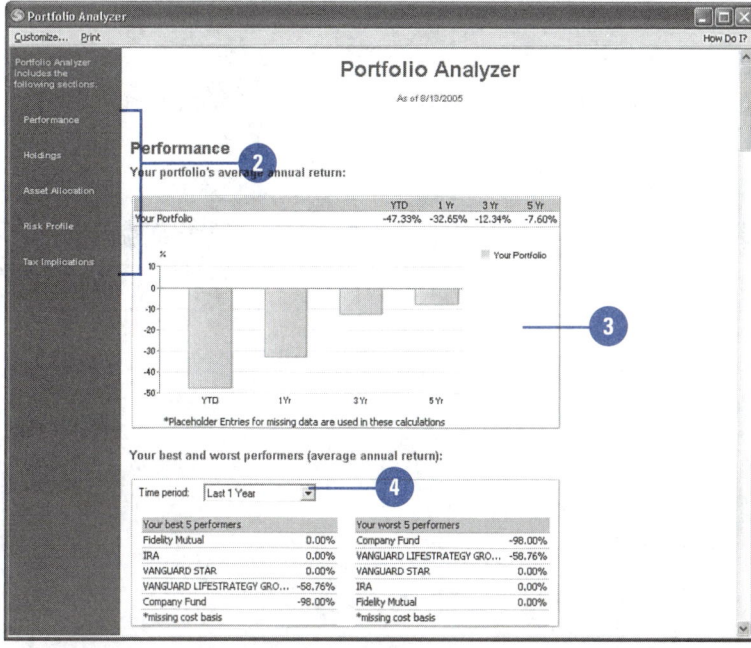

Analyzing Your Asset Allocations and Portfolio **229**

5. See the What to Look for in Performance and Actions for Performance sections for advice on what to look for in your securities and what you can do to get the best return.

6. The Holdings section provides pie charts of your accounts, how much they are currently worth in the market, and what percentage of the pie each is.

7. Review what your largest securities are, what their values are, and what percentage of the pie they are.

8. Hover your mouse over a piece of either of the pies to see the value. You also get advice for your holdings.

> **See Also**
>
> *See "Estimating Capital Gains" on page 218 for more information about capital gains.*

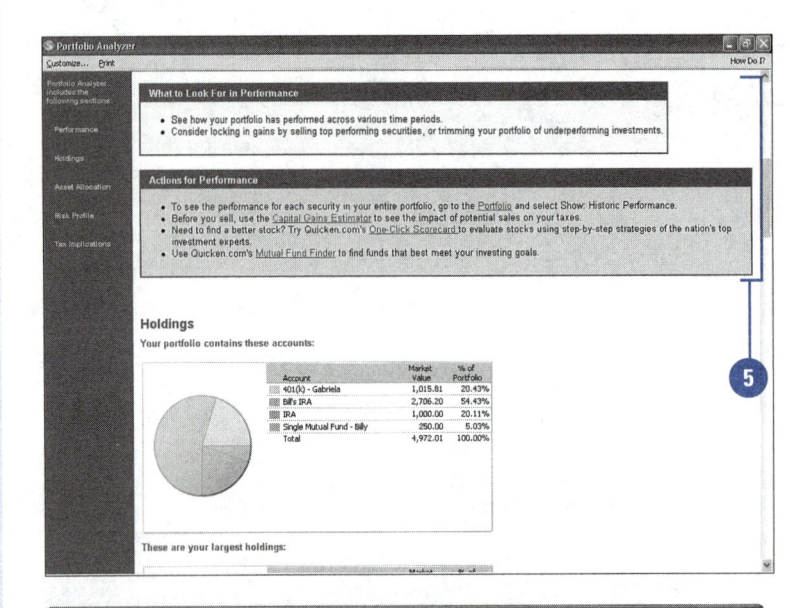

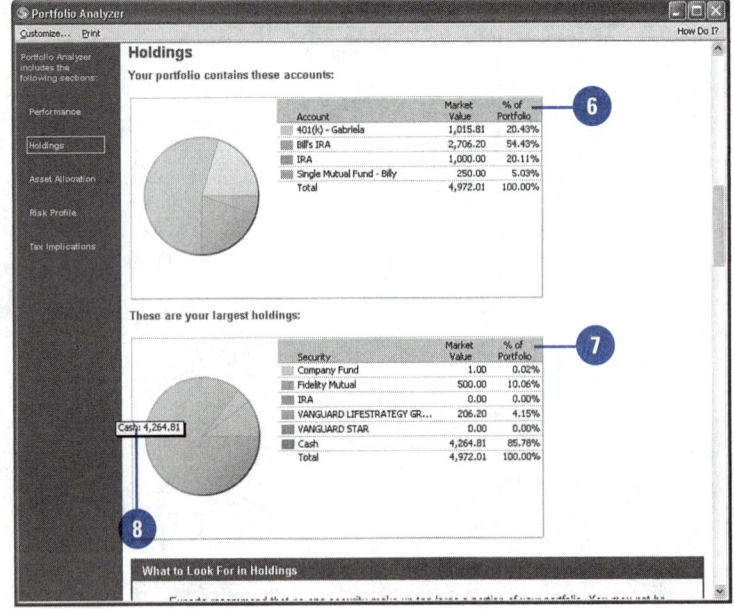

⑨ The Asset Allocation section provides two pie charts, one for your assets as they are allocated today (Actual) and one for your target assets (Target).

⑩ Hover your mouse over a section of the pie chart to see the amount and allocation percentage.

⑪ The table shows the comparison of your actual and target asset allocations. In addition, you get advice for your asset allocations.

⑫ The Risk Profile section provides a visual of what your projected risk and rate of return are, compared to the risk and rate of return for some standard assets.

⑬ Look at the guidelines for determining risk and rate of return.

Did You Know?

There are links you can use to get more information. *Within the What to Look For and Actions boxes for each area of the Portfolio Analyzer, there are links to other areas of Quicken and to the Quicken.com website that can help you further your knowledge about investments and learn how to get the best returns. Some of these topics—such as the Asset Allocation Guide, Portfolio, Capital Gains Estimator, and Tax Planner—are covered in other areas of this book. Other links to Quicken.com—such as the One-Click Scoreboard and the Mutual Funds Finder—are not covered here but are definitely worth checking out on your own. You need your member ID and password to access the information on the Quicken.com site.*

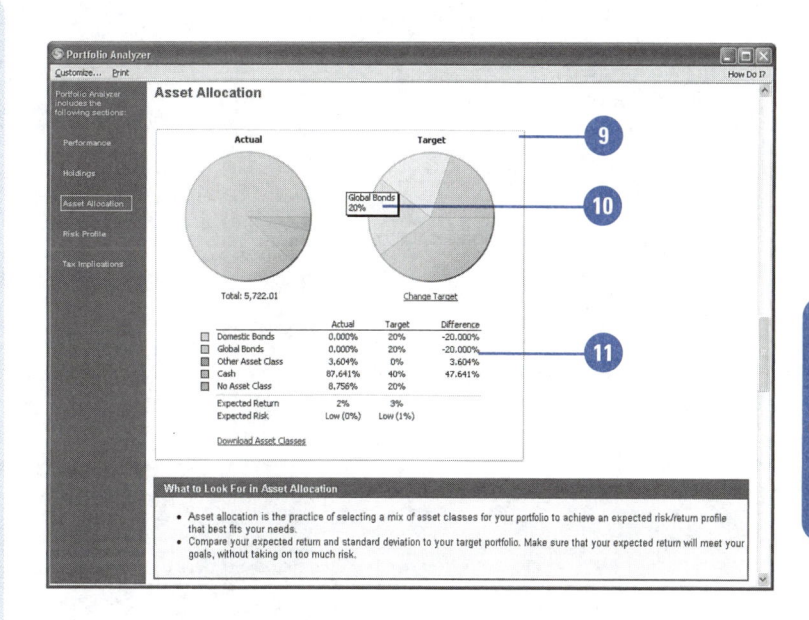

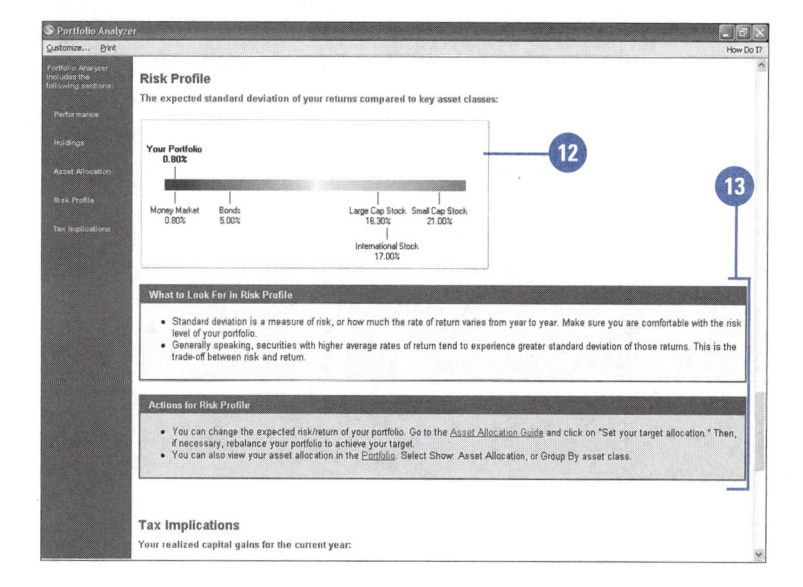

Analyzing Your Asset Allocations and Portfolio **231**

⑭ The Tax Implications section provides information on your possible capital gains, and possible taxes you might need to pay for each of your holdings.

⑮ Review the additional information about tax implications and what you can do to improve your tax situation.

⑯ When you are finished, close the Portfolio Analyzer.

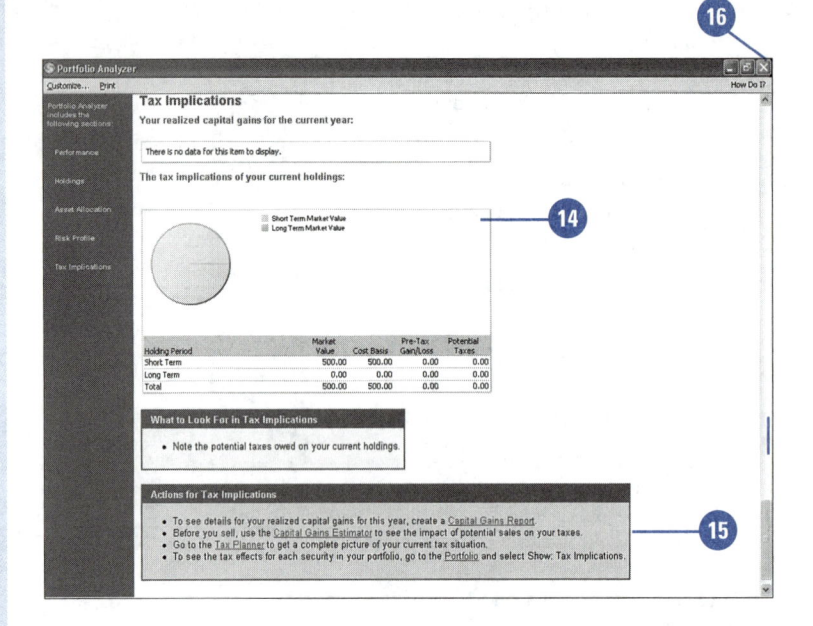

Determining Whether You Need to Rebalance Your Portfolio

If you haven't already analyzed your portfolio by using the Portfolio Analyzer, I suggest you go back to the previous task and do that before proceeding with this task. The Portfolio Analyzer should show you exactly which assets are working in your favor and which ones aren't. Now that you are armed with this information, what should you do with it? Fortunately, Quicken offers yet another helpful tool that you can use to determine when and if you should rebalance your portfolio, research and evaluate new investments, and determine what adjustments you should make to meet your target. This tool is called the Portfolio Rebalancer. You may not be familiar with what *rebalancing* means; simply stated, it means moving your money where it benefits you most. Moving your money might mean selling stocks, buying stocks, changing your asset allocations, and so on. By rebalancing your portfolio, you reduce risk and improve the chances for good returns, which in turn helps get you closer to meeting your financial goals. However, you should do your research and get some advice from a trusted source before you start moving your money around.

Determine Whether You Need to Rebalance Your Portfolio

1. Click the Investing menu and select Portfolio Rebalancer.

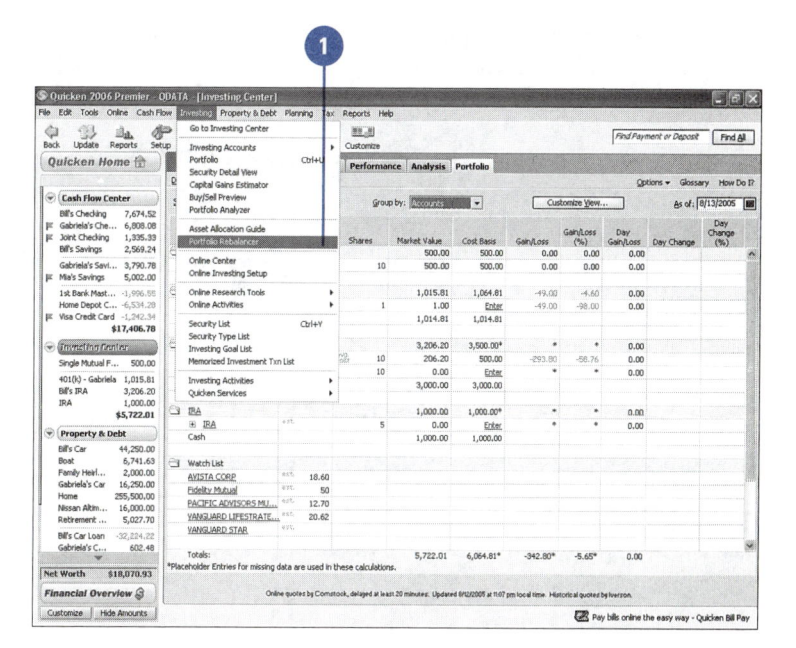

Analyzing Your Asset Allocations and Portfolio **233**

② Click When should I rebalance my portfolio? to review some key points to consider when evaluating rebalancing your portfolio.

③ If you have mutual funds, click What if I have mutual funds? for key points about rebalancing mutual funds.

④ If you are considering looking into new investments, click Search to research stocks, mutual funds, and bonds.

⑤ Click a link to get more information about that subject. Some sites (for example, the Stock Screener) may require that you complete information about the subject.

⑥ To evaluate an existing stock or mutual fund, click Evaluate.

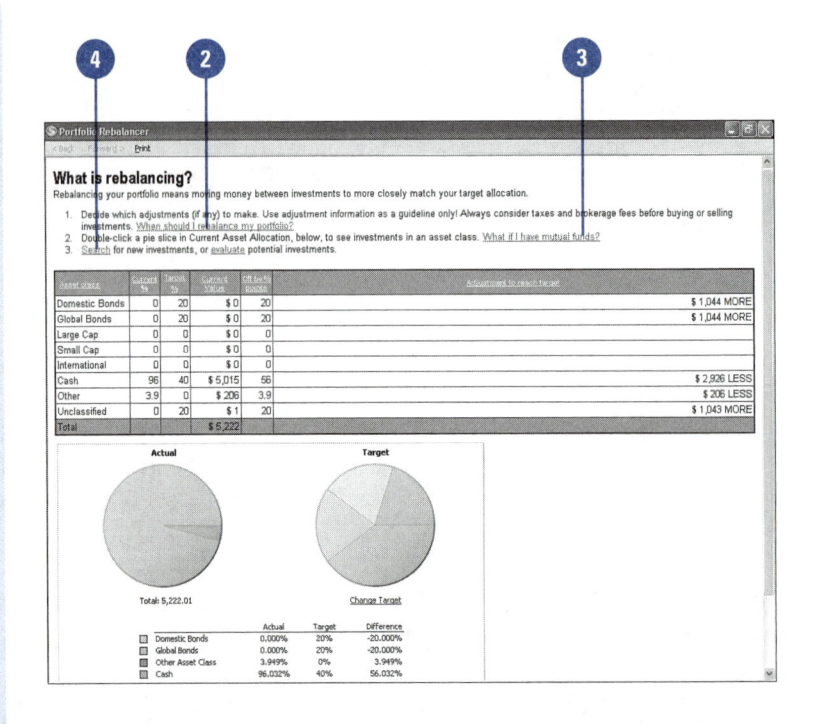

⑦ For either the stock or mutual fund, type the ticker symbol, select the type of information you want to see, and click Go Online to Evaluate Stock(s) or Fund(s).

⑧ The table lists all your assets by asset class, the current and target percentages, the value for each, and how far off you are from your target.

⑨ The dollar amount you are over or under is also provided.

⑩ Click a heading to view a column description.

⑪ Double-click a pie chart to get a more detailed view of that asset.

⑫ To set your target allocation percentages, click Set Target if you haven't set it or click Change Target to change it. If you have not set your target, the Asset Allocation Guide opens, where you can set the target.

Did You Know?

You can locate the ticker symbol through Quicken. *If you are uncertain of the stock or mutual fund ticker symbol, click the look up a ticker symbol link. You need Internet access to view this information. Select the type of symbol you are looking for, type the full or partial name of the stock or mutual fund, and click Search. The search results are listed by name and then by ticker symbol. There are also links to the One-Click Scorecard and the Evaluator, which you need a Quicken member ID and password to view.*

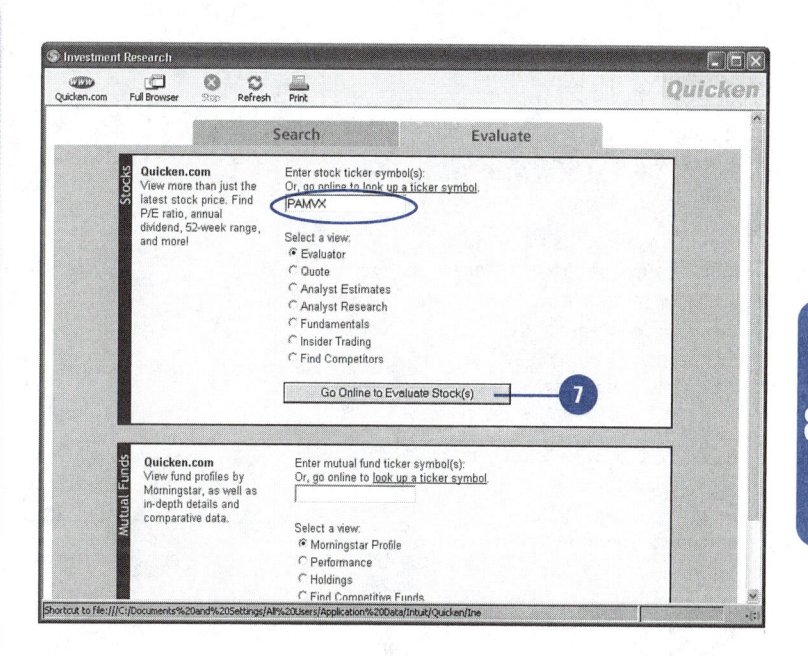

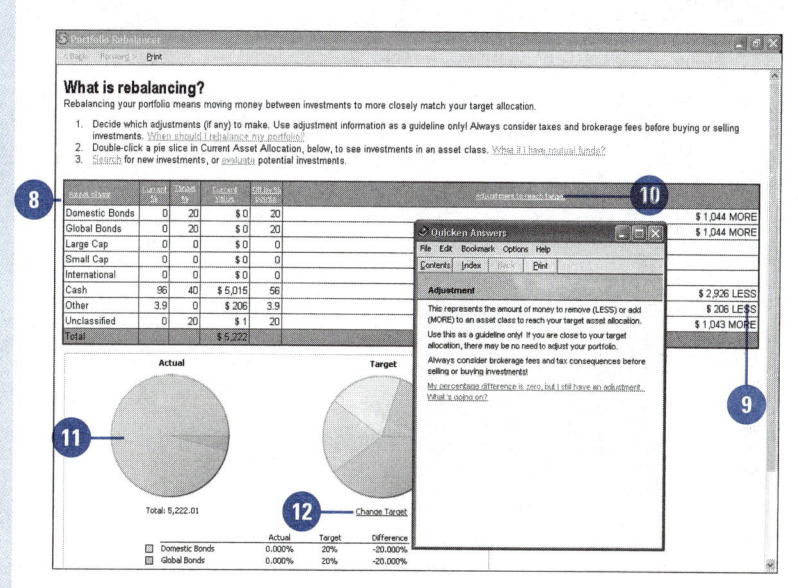

Analyzing Your Asset Allocations and Portfolio **235**

13 If you are changing your target, the Set Target Asset Allocation dialog box opens. Change your percentages, if desired. Then click OK.

14 Review your adjustments to see where you need to make changes in order to meet your target, and repeat any of these steps to research your assets or investment considerations further.

> **See Also**
>
> *See "Getting Some Help with Asset Allocation" on page 215 for more information about the Asset Allocation Guide and setting target allocation percentages.*

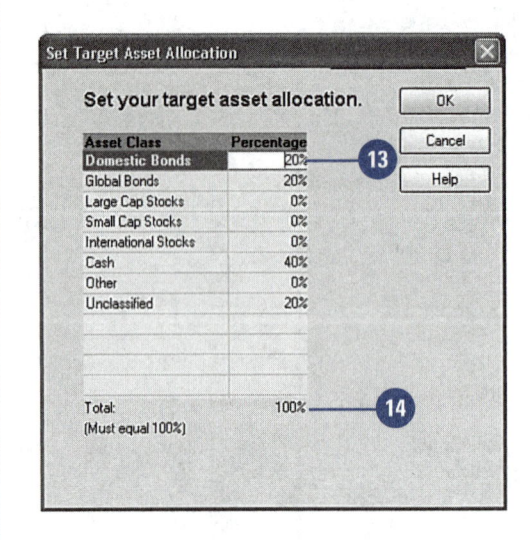

Set Target Asset Allocation

Set your target asset allocation.

Asset Class	Percentage
Domestic Bonds	20%
Global Bonds	20%
Large Cap Stocks	0%
Small Cap Stocks	0%
International Stocks	0%
Cash	40%
Other	0%
Unclassified	20%

Total: 100%
(Must equal 100%)

Managing Your Property and Debt

Introduction

The Property & Debt Center contains account information for your property and other assets, such as your home and car, and your liabilities or debt, such as your mortgage and car loans. You can access the account register for each of your property and debt accounts in the Property & Debt Accounts section of the Property & Debt Center. In the account register, you can add, edit, or delete transactions; update the roster with transactions that have been downloaded; review, add, and edit scheduled transactions; search for specific transactions; transfer funds between accounts; and balance your register. In addition, you can set up alerts and access reports.

The Property & Debt Center allows you to add new loans and manage your existing loans, and you can use it to view your automobile-related expenses and automobile expense reports. In addition, you can record and track your home inventory, insurance policies, claims, and other important records.

What You'll Do

Set Up New and Edit Existing Property and Debt Alerts

Review, Add, Edit, and Delete Property and Debt Accounts

Update Property and Debt Account Balances

Add, Edit, and Delete Property and Debt Transactions

Search for Property and Debt Transactions

Transfer Funds Between Property and Debt Accounts

View, Add, Edit, and Delete Scheduled Property and Debt Transactions

Manage All Your Scheduled Transactions

View Property and Debt Account Overviews

Balance Your Property and Debt Accounts

Review and Add Loans

View Auto Expenses

Keep Track of Your Home Inventory

Keep Track of Your Emergency Records

Setting Up New and Editing Existing Property and Debt Alerts

Set Up New and Edit Existing Property and Debt Alerts

1. If you don't already have the Property & Debt Center open, on the account bar, click Property & Debt Center.

2. To view all alerts, if not all of them are showing, click Show All Alerts.

3. To create or edit property or debt alerts, click Set Up Alerts.

See Also

See "Using Alerts" on page 74 for more information on creating or changing alerts.

As with the other centers in Quicken, with the Property & Debt Center, you can set up alerts to remind or warn you of actions you need to take for your property or debt accounts (for example, to notify you that your insurance is getting ready to expire or that your mortgage loan rate is changing). Creating and editing property and debt alerts works the same here as in the other centers.

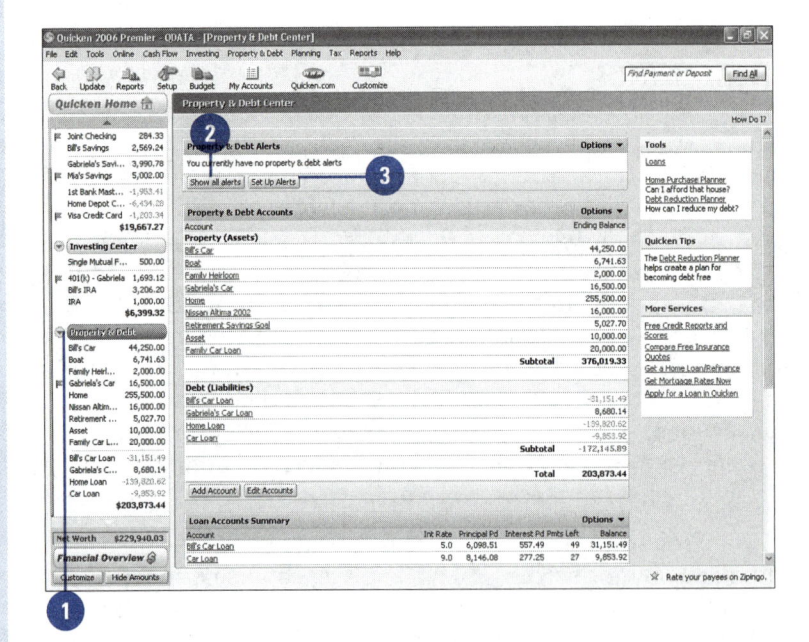

Reviewing, Adding, Editing, and Deleting Property and Debt Accounts

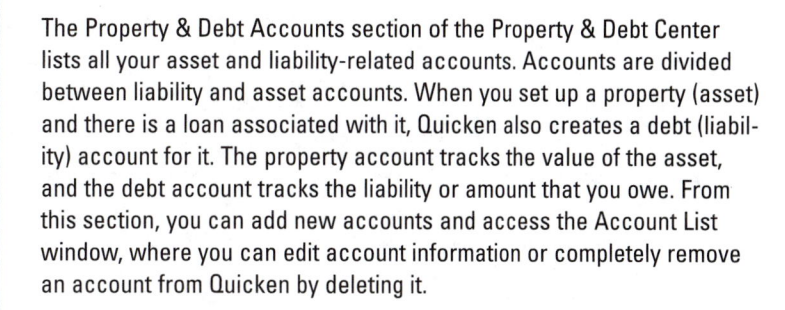

The Property & Debt Accounts section of the Property & Debt Center lists all your asset and liability-related accounts. Accounts are divided between liability and asset accounts. When you set up a property (asset) and there is a loan associated with it, Quicken also creates a debt (liability) account for it. The property account tracks the value of the asset, and the debt account tracks the liability or amount that you owe. From this section, you can add new accounts and access the Account List window, where you can edit account information or completely remove an account from Quicken by deleting it.

Review Property and Debt Accounts

1. The ending balance for each property or debt account is provided. Click an account name to go to the register for that account.

2. Note that the subtotal is provided for your assets and your liabilities. The subtotal is the sum of all your assets or the sum of all your liabilities.

3. Note that the total is determined by subtracting your liabilities from your assets.

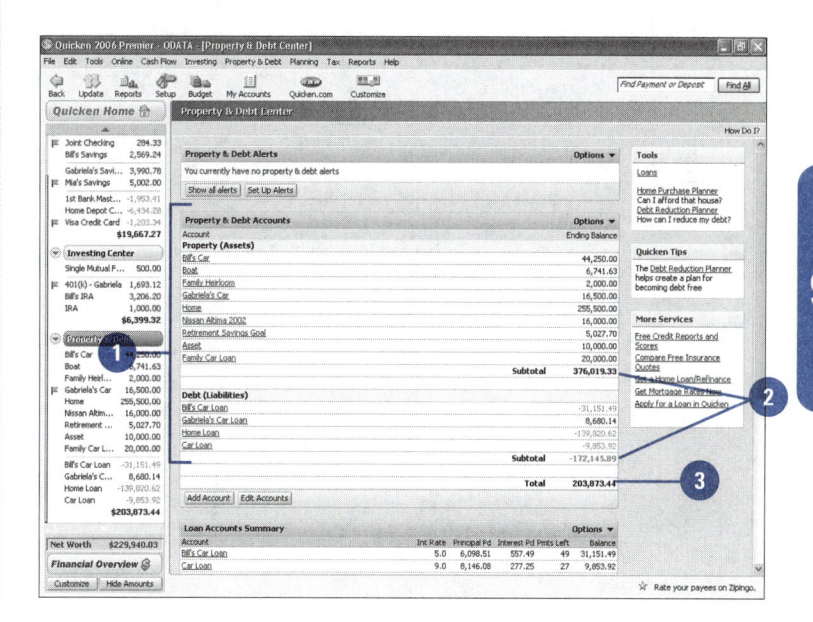

Managing Your Property and Debt 239

Add Property and Debt Accounts

1. To add a new property or debt account, click Add Account.

2. Select the type of property or debt account you want to add and click Next. The setup options you see depend on which type you select. For the purposes of this example, add an asset.

3. Click in Name this account and type a descriptive name for the new account. Then click Next.

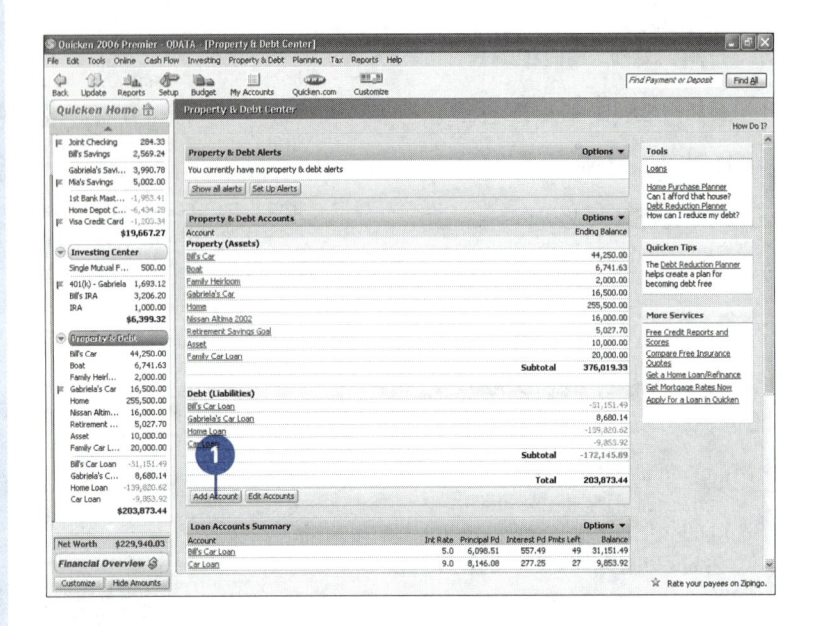

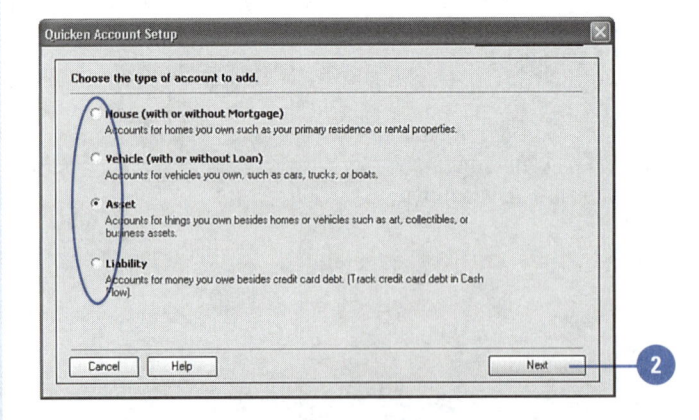

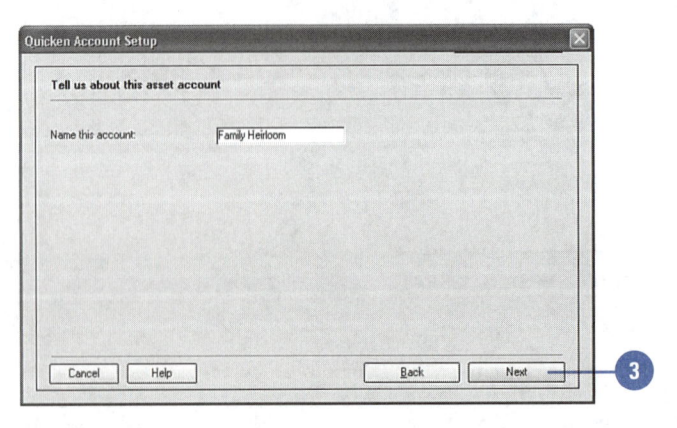

240

④ Type the date you want to begin tracking the account and the approximate value of the asset. You can edit this account later and update the amount when you have an exact value.

⑤ If the asset or liability you are adding is eligible to be tax deferred or if you want to specify the tax schedule associated with incoming and outgoing funds for the account, click Tax.

⑥ If the account you are adding is a 401(k), 403(b), IRA, SEP-IRA, or Keogh, select Tax-Deferred or Tax-Exempt Account.

⑦ If incoming or outgoing funds can be associated with a specific tax schedule, select the schedule from the Transfers In and Transfers Out drop-down menus and then click OK.

⑧ Click Done. The account register for the new account opens, and in it you can add, edit, and delete account transactions, and you can perform other procedures.

See Also

See "Adding, Editing, and Deleting Property and Debt Transactions" on page 245 for more information on creating new, updating, or deleting account transactions.

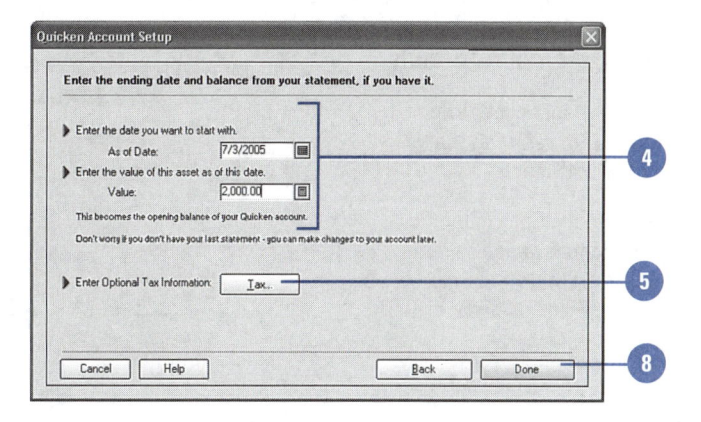

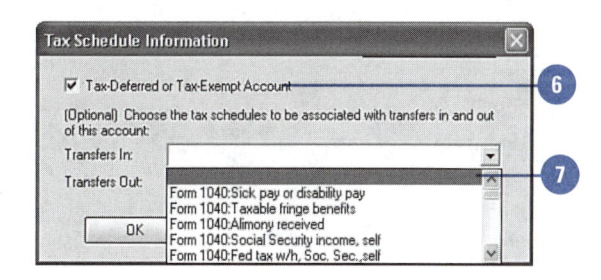

Did You Know?

It is beneficial to track tax-deferred accounts and tax schedules for accounts. *You should make sure to tell Quicken if an account can be tax deferred or is tax exempt, and you should also tell Quicken about the tax schedules used for incoming and outgoing account funds. Quicken uses this information for tax reports, when estimating your taxes (for example, in the Tax Planner), and when you export tax-related information to TurboTax.*

Managing Your Property and Debt **241**

Edit Property and Debt Accounts

1. On the account bar, click Property & Debt Center to return to the Property & Debt Center.

2. To update account information or delete an account altogether, in the Property & Debt Accounts section, click Edit Accounts.

3. To update an account, scroll down to the Property & Debt Accounts section of the Account List window, select the account you want to update, and click Edit.

4. Type, select, or change the Account Details information.

5. To review or change the tax schedules associated with this account, click Tax Schedule Info, select new tax schedules, if needed, and click OK.

6. When you are finished making changes, click OK.

> **See Also**
>
> See "Add Property and Debt Accounts" on page 240 for more information on adding or changing tax schedules.

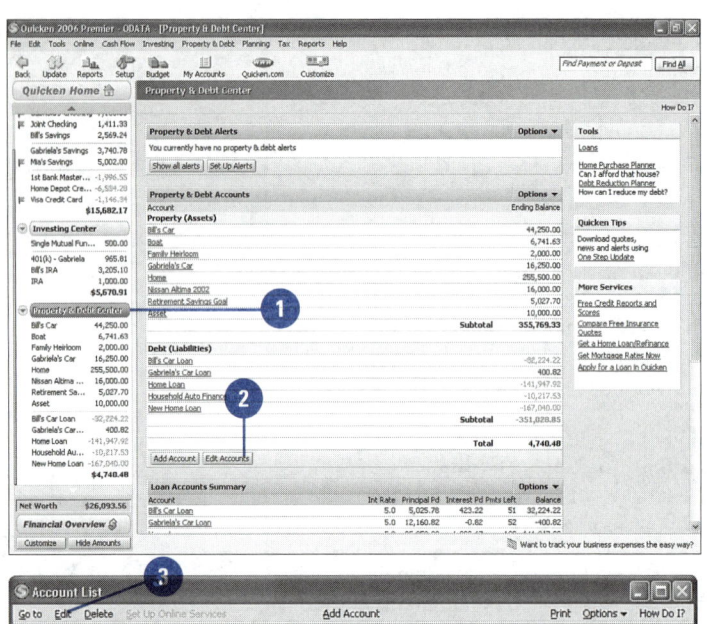

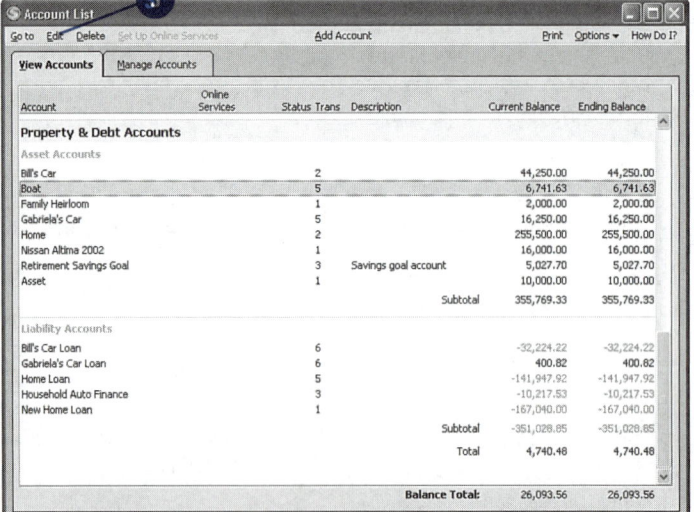

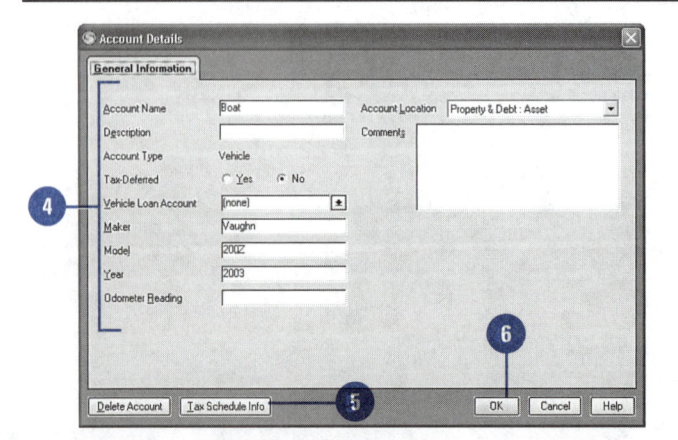

Delete Property and Debt Accounts

1. To completely remove an account from Quicken, select the account and click Delete. A message appears, asking if you want to delete the account.

2. If you are sure you want to delete the account, type Yes and click OK. If you do not want to delete the account, click Cancel. A message appears, telling you that the account has not been deleted.

3. Click OK.

Did You Know?

You can delete accounts by using the Account Details window or the Account List window. You can delete an account by clicking the Delete Account button in the Account Details window or by using the Delete menu option in the Account List window. However, before you delete an account from Quicken, you need to be sure you don't need the account, even if it's closed, for reporting or historical tracking. Deleting an account is permanent, and the only way to restore it is if you have a backup of your Quicken file that you made before you deleted the account.

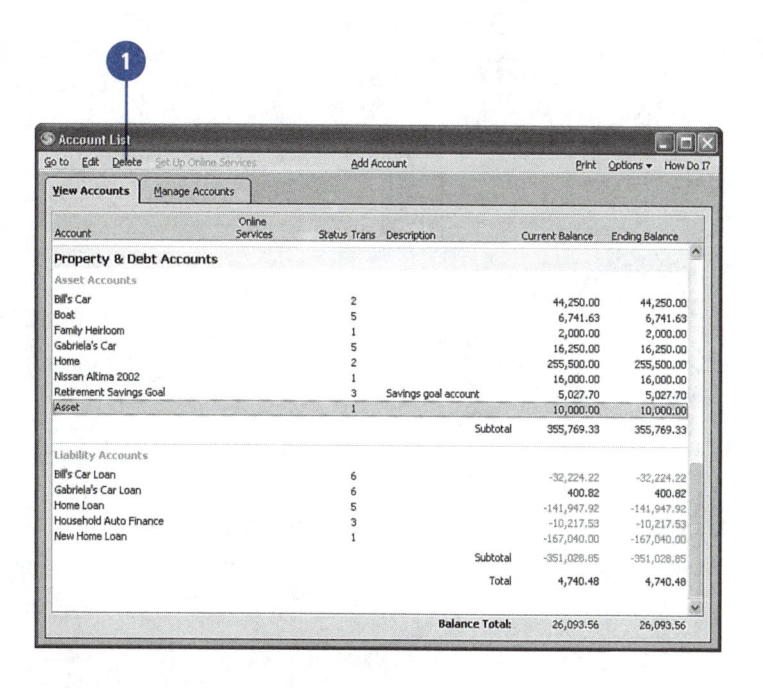

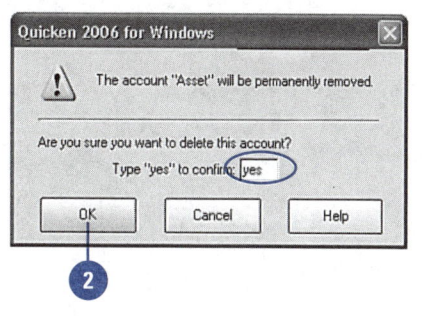

Managing Your Property and Debt **243**

Updating Property and Debt Account Balances

Before you start working in your register, you should check to make sure you are working with an accurate balance. If you set up an account for online access, you can use One Step Update to automatically update the account balance and transactions. However, you can also update the balance manually, if needed.

Update Property and Debt Account Balances Manually

1. If you don't already have the Property & Debt Center open, on the account bar, click Property & Debt Center.

2. Click the account you want to open.

3. Click Update Balance.

4. In the Update Balance to box, type the balance or click the calculator icon to enter it.

5. In the Adjustment Date box, type the date the balance is going into effect.

6. From the Category for Adjustment drop-down menu, select the reason for the new balance.

7. Click OK. The balance is entered in your account register, and your account balance is adjusted accordingly.

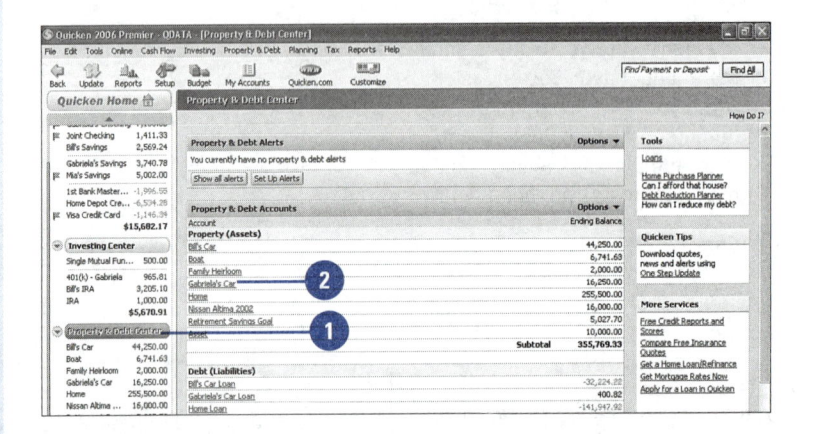

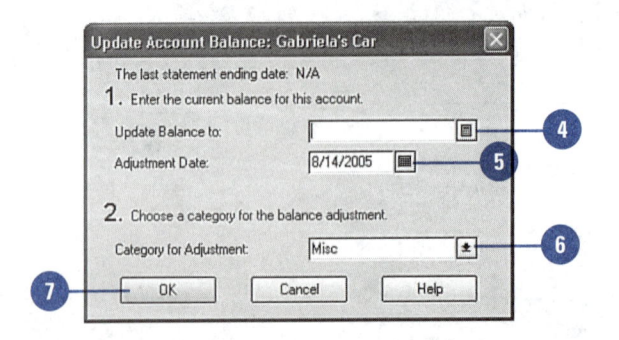

244

Adding, Editing, and Deleting Property and Debt Transactions

You can add transactions to your property and debt accounts manually, and if you set up your accounts to use One Step Update, the transactions download and appear in the Download Transactions tab. You can then review and add the transactions to your register. However, most property and debt accounts do not offer the capability of downloading transactions. Therefore, this task shows you how to manually add transactions to your register. In addition, you can edit or delete existing transaction information. For information on adding downloaded transactions, refer to "Add Downloaded Credit Card Transactions to Your Register" in Chapter 5, "Managing Your Credit Card Accounts."

Add Property and Debt Transactions Manually

1. If you don't already have the Property & Debt Center open, on the account bar, click Property & Debt Center.

2. Click an account you want to open.

3. To manually add a transaction, click in the date column of an empty row and type the date of the transaction.

4. Type the payee name.

5. Click Category and select a category from the drop-down menu to assign to the transaction.

6. To divide the transaction among different categories, click Split.

7. Click in Category and type or select the category you want to use to split the transaction. Then type the amount for each category you add and click Adjust to ensure the total equals the total transaction amount. Then, click OK.

8. Click Decrease to type a debit amount or in Increase to type a credit amount. The total amount here must equal the sum of the amounts you entered for the splits.

9. Click Enter.

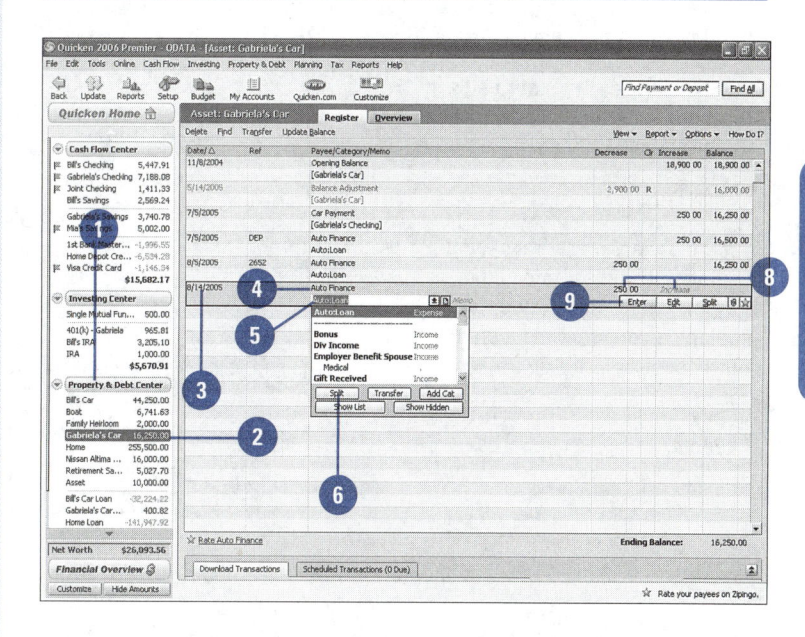

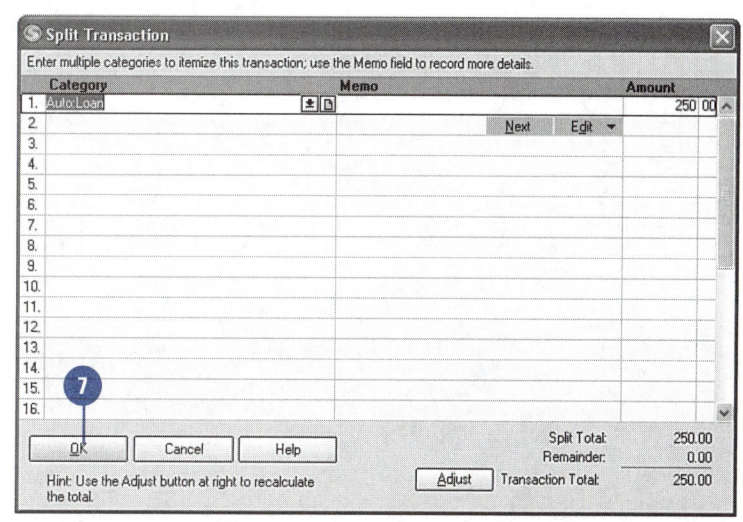

Managing Your Property and Debt **245**

Edit and Delete Property and Debt Transactions

1. If you don't already have the account open for which you want to edit or remove transactions, from the account bar, select the account.

2. Click the area you want to change (for example, click in Decrease or Increase to change the amount) and type the new amount.

3. Click in any of the other fields in the transaction to change the information, as needed.

4. Click Enter.

5. To delete an entire transaction, select the transaction and click Delete. A message appears, asking if you want to delete the transaction.

6. Click Yes to delete it or No to keep it.

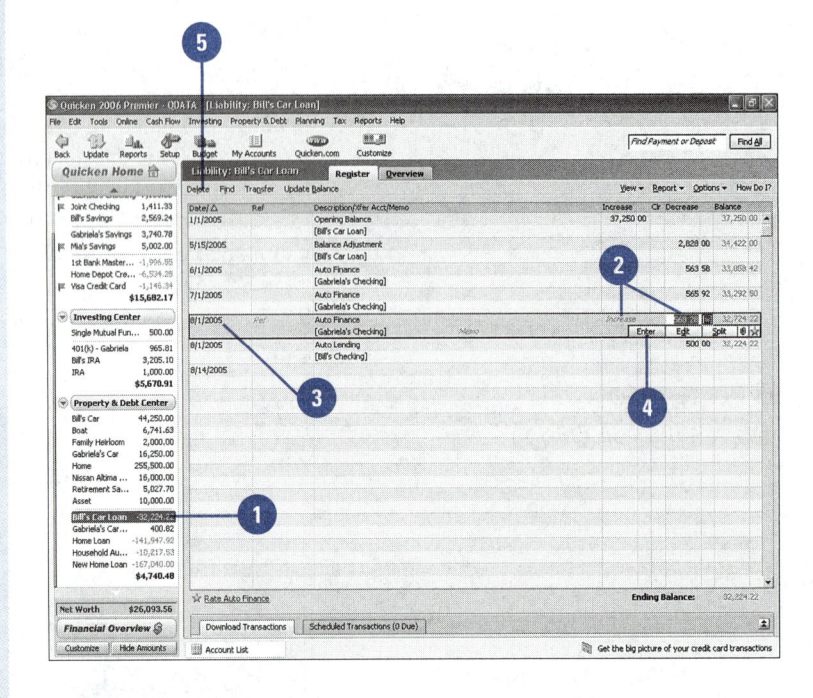

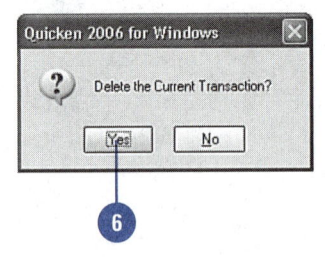

Searching for Property and Debt Transactions

As you use Quicken, your transactions grow in number. The more transactions you have, the harder it can be to find what you're looking for (for example, if you need to update a specific transaction). If you have hundreds of transactions, it could be like trying to find a needle in a haystack. Luckily, Quicken has a search tool, which you may have already used in the other center registers. You can also use it in the Property & Debt Center.

Search for Property & Debt Transactions

1. From the account bar, select the account you want to use to search for transactions.

2. Click Find.

3. From the Search drop-down menu, select the focus of your search. For example, if you want to find a transaction that cleared for 15.12, but you don't know the payee's name, select Amount.

4. From the Match if drop-down menu, select the criterion you want to use to narrow the search further.

5. Click in Find and type the word or number you are searching for. Using the example here, you would type **15.12**.

6. To search backward from the current date, select Search Backwards.

7. Click Find to locate transactions in the current register or click Find All to locate transactions in all registers.

8. To perform another search, repeat steps 3–7.

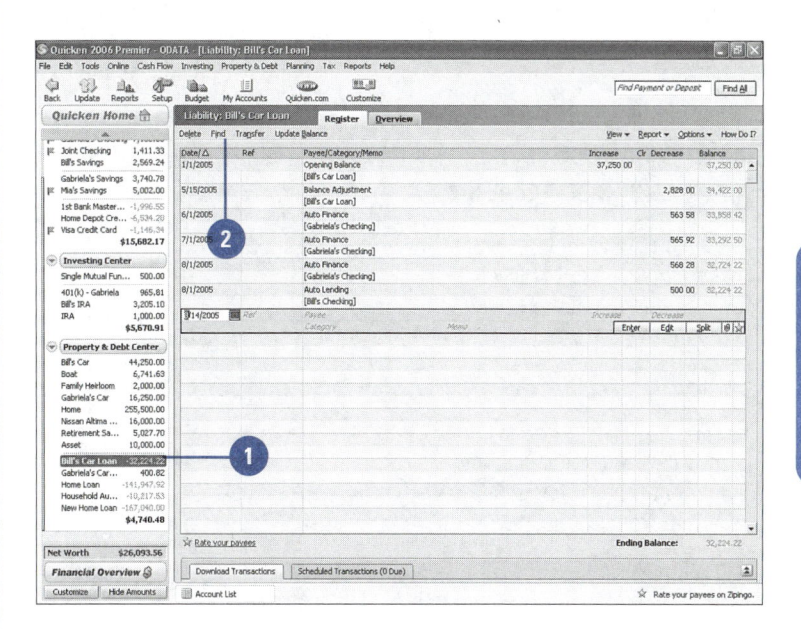

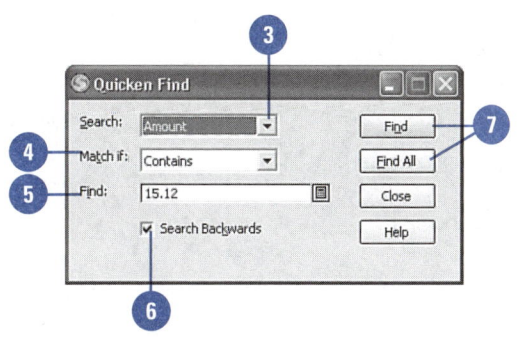

Did You Know?

Sorting transactions is another way of finding transactions. You can sort your transactions by clicking the column headings. For example, clicking the Payee/Category/Memo heading sorts the transaction list in alphabetical order by the payee name. The current sort for the transaction list is indicated by an arrow that appears next to the column title.

Managing Your Property and Debt **247**

Transferring Funds Between Property and Debt Accounts

Another function that is common among all centers is transferring funds. You can record a transfer from one account to another. Quicken automatically logs a transaction in your register and logs a parallel transaction in the register for the other account. Transferring funds between accounts happens only within Quicken, though; it does not affect the accounts at your bank. You can, however, use your financial institution's online features to transfer money between accounts at that institution, but the accounts must share the same login or customer ID. Check with your financial institution before attempting an online transfer. This task steps through how to transfer money between accounts and how to log a transfer that has already taken place in Quicken.

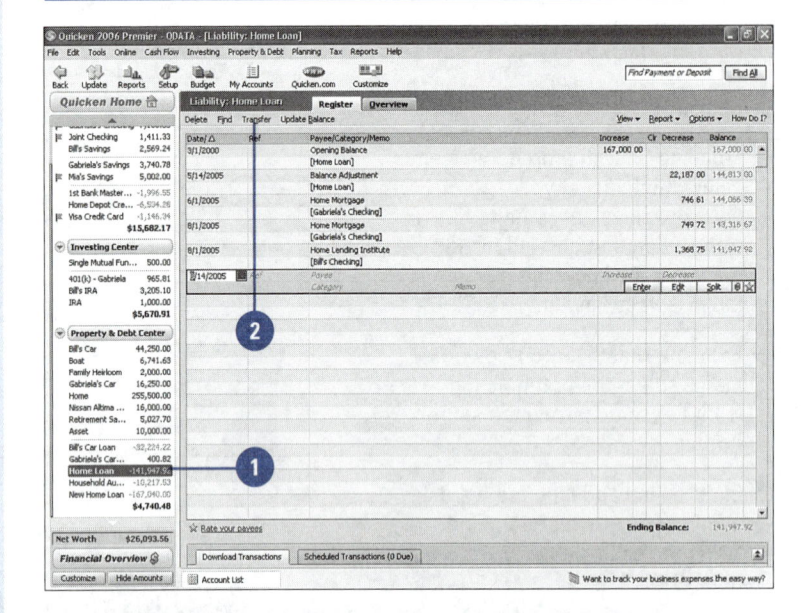

Transfer Funds Between Property and Debt Accounts

1. From the account bar, select the account you want to use to transfer funds. It does matter which account you open first.

2. Click Transfer.

3. From the Transfer Money From drop-down menu, select the account from which the fund will be removed.

4. From the To Account drop-down menu, select the account to which the funds will be deposited.

5. In the Date box, type the date the transfer is to take place. You can future-date the transaction; however, the balances for each account are immediately adjusted.

6. In the Amount box, type the dollar amount of the transfer.

7. In the Description box, type a description or reason for the transfer.

8. Click OK. A TXFR transaction appears in the account register from which funds were removed and as Transfer money in the register to which the funds were deposited. Quicken adjusts the balances accordingly.

Did You Know?

You can use scheduled transactions for frequent transfers. *If you have a transfer that takes place on a regular basis, you can use a scheduled transaction to set up an automatic transfer. You can also set the dates and amounts of the transfer. When it is time for the transfer to occur, Quicken automatically updates your scheduled transaction list. Refer to the new task for more information.*

Viewing, Adding, Editing, and Deleting Scheduled Property and Debt Transactions

The scheduled transactions that need to be added to your register appear on the Scheduled Transactions tab in your property and debt account registers. You can view the list, add the transactions you want to include in your register, edit them, or delete them from the tab. In addition, you can access the master list of all your scheduled transactions for all accounts in Quicken.

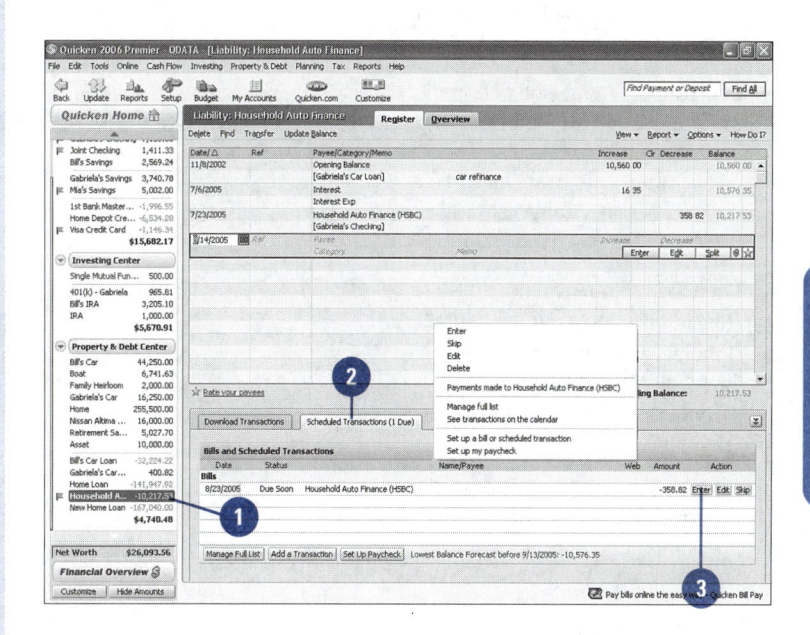

View, Add, Edit, and Delete Scheduled Property and Debt Transactions

1. From the account bar, select the Property & Debt account your want to use.

2. Click the Scheduled Transactions tab. The number in parentheses represents the number of transactions waiting to be added to your register.

3. To review, edit, or add a scheduled transaction to your register, select the transaction and click Enter.

Did You Know?

Unscheduled transactions are listed in a separate section. If there are transactions that have not been scheduled, they appear under the Schedule These? Section on the Scheduled Transactions tab. Click Yes to schedule a transaction or No to leave it unscheduled. This does not remove it from your scheduled transactions.

See Also

See "Using Bills and Scheduled Transactions" on page 76 for more information on adding and editing scheduled transactions.

Managing Your Property and Debt **249**

4. Review the information to ensure that it is correct and make changes, if needed.

5. To add the transaction to your register, click Record Payment. Any changes that you make here do not apply to all future transactions—only to the current transaction.

6. Click Cancel to take no action on the transaction and return to the scheduled transaction list. The transaction remains in the scheduled transaction list until you are ready to record it or skip it.

7. Click Skip to remove the transaction from your scheduled transaction for this period. It reappears the next time it is scheduled to show up.

8. If you are positive that you want to remove a transaction, right-click the transaction and from the pop-up menu that appears, select Delete.

9. To add a new transaction, click Add a Transaction and complete the Create Scheduled Transaction window.

10. Review, edit, and enter each scheduled transaction until you are finished. Transactions you record are entered into your register, and your balance is adjusted accordingly.

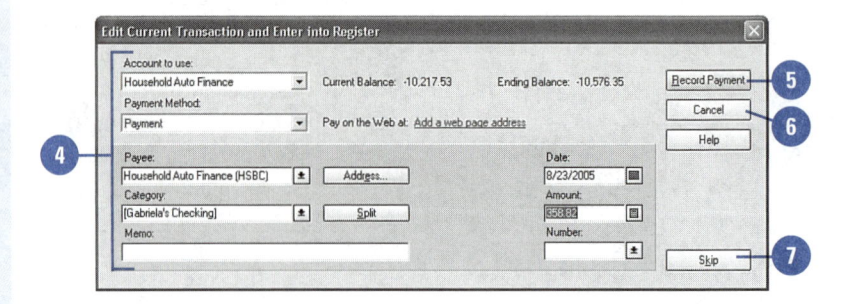

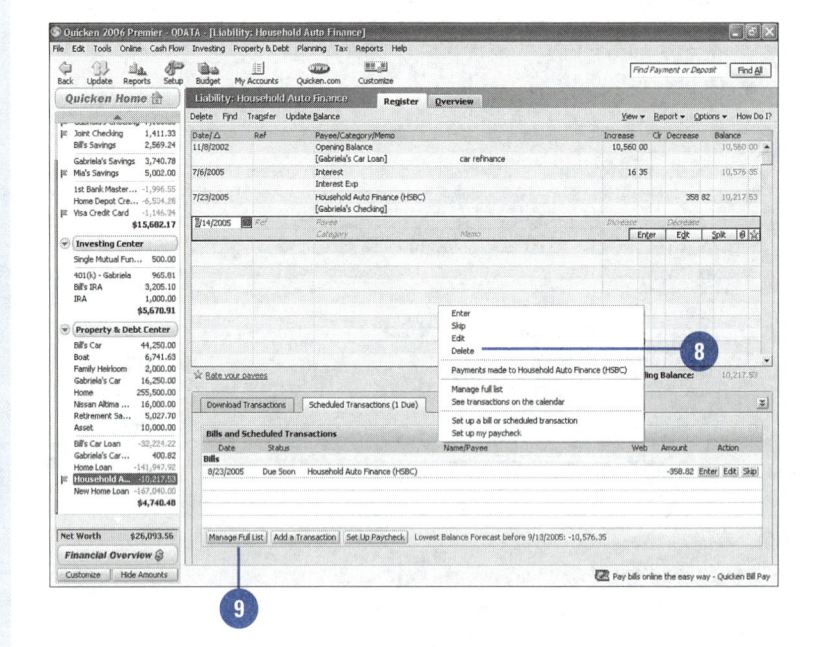

250

Managing All Your Scheduled Transactions

When you want to review or make changes to your scheduled transactions, you can view them all in one place by using the Scheduled Transactions List window. All your transactions are included here—not just those for your property and debt accounts. You can access the Scheduled Transactions List from the Scheduled Transactions tab on the register of any account or from the Tools menu.

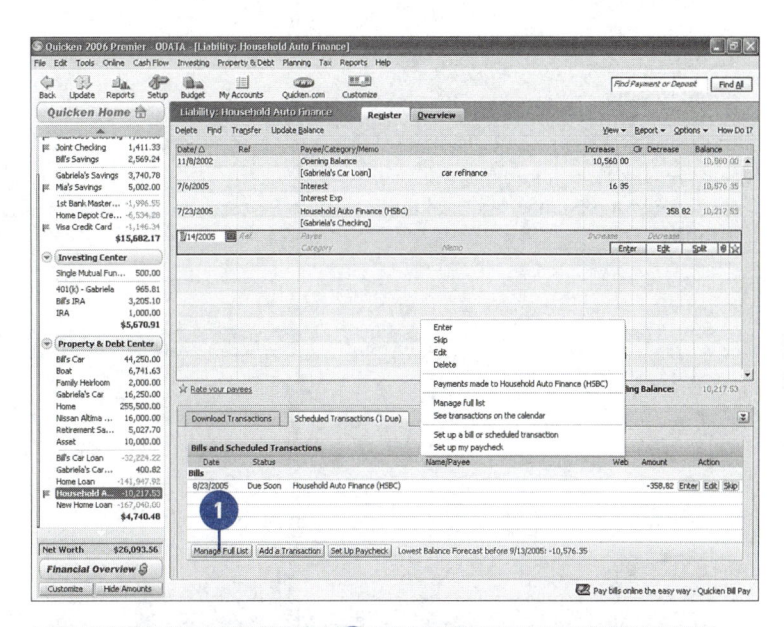

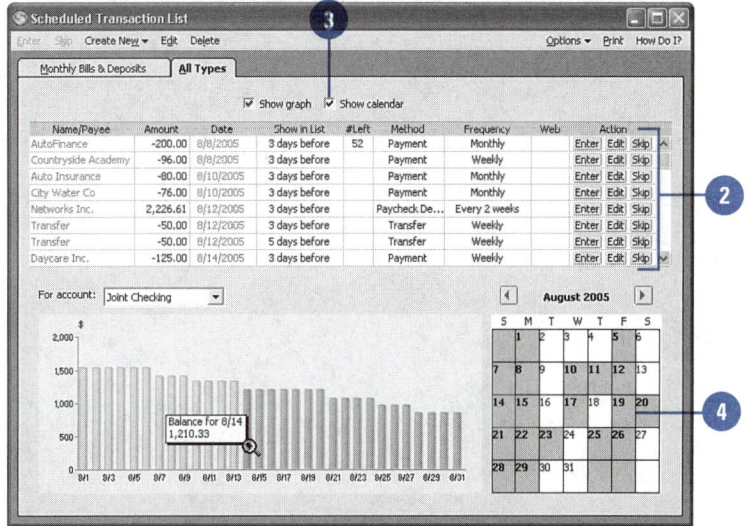

Manage Your Scheduled Transactions

1. From a Property & Debt account register, click the Scheduled Transaction tab then click Manage Full List.

2. Enter, edit, skip, or delete transactions as shown in previous tasks.

3. To view the transaction calendar for the current month, select Show calendar. The days on which transactions are due are bolded on the calendar.

4. To view the calendar in detail, click a day of the month.

See Also

See "Using Bills and Scheduled Transactions" on page 76 for more detailed information on adding, editing, skipping, and deleting scheduled transactions, and using the calendar.

Managing Your Property and Debt 251

5. You can print the calendar, go to a future or previous month, make a note for a specific day, or select only the accounts you want to see on the calendar.

6. To view a graph of daily transactions, select Show graph.

7. From the For account drop-down menu, select the account you want to view.

8. To view your estimated balance for a specific day, hover (point, don't click) your mouse over a bar of the graph.

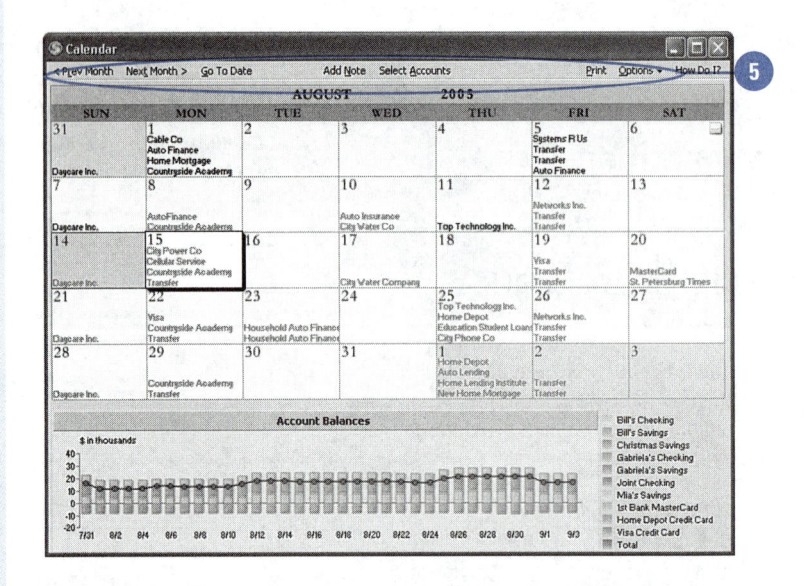

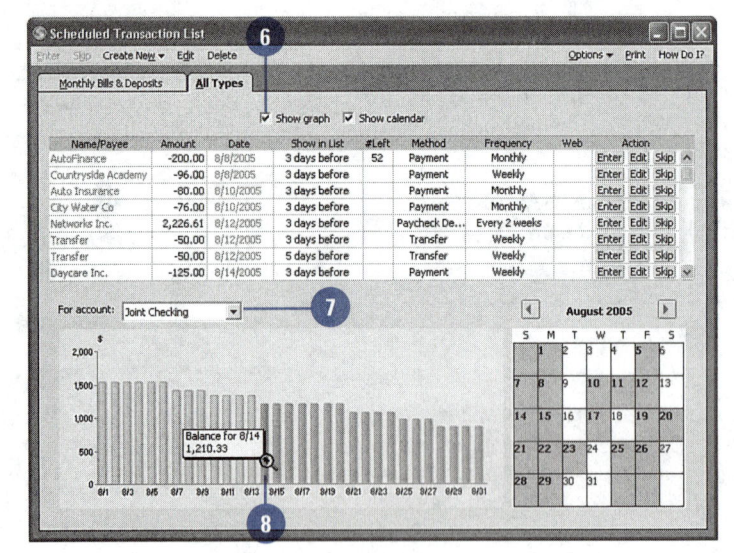

Viewing Property and Debt Account Overviews

An account overview is provided for each of your accounts when you open the account. The overviews include account attributes, such as the account name and description; the status, such as the balance and equity; a graph view of the equity; and any expenses associated with the account. In addition, you can edit account details and view reports for the account. The options on each overview vary by account type.

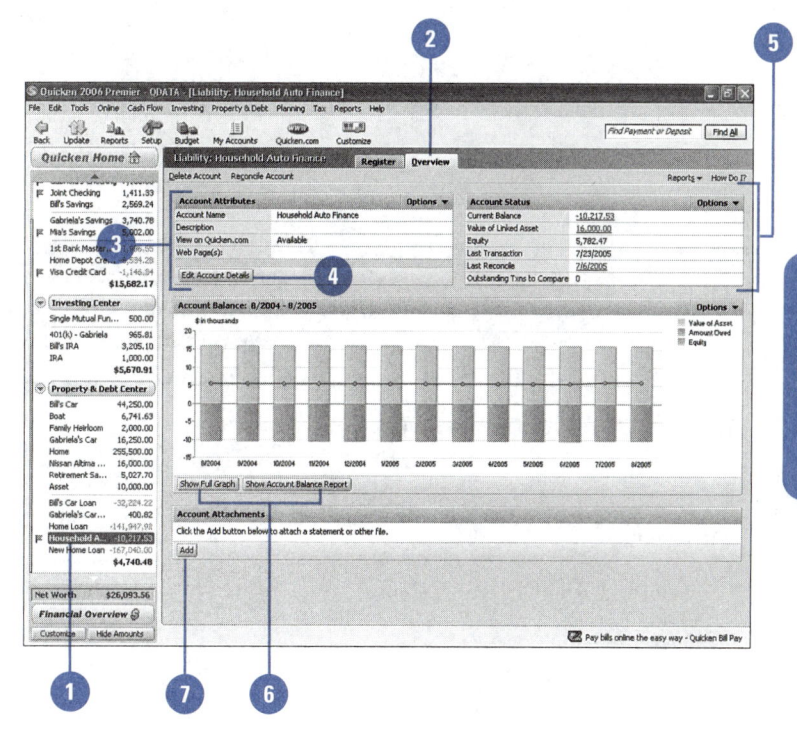

View Property and Debt Account Overviews

1. On the account bar, click Property & Debt Center and select the account for which you want to view an overview.

2. Click the Overview tab.

3. In the Account Attributes section, you can view basic account information, such as the name and description, and so on. If there are websites linked to the account, click the links to access the sites.

4. To make changes to the account, click Edit Account Details.

5. Note that in the Account Status section, you can click your balance to update it, click the value to access the account register, or click the reconciliation date to balance the account.

6. Note that in the Account Balance section, you can view a bar graph view of your equity over a year's time. Click Show Full Graph to view a larger view of the graph. Click Show Account Balance Report to view the Account Balance report for the current time period.

7. Note that in the Account Attachments section, you can add new documents to the account by clicking Add and completing the Add Attachment window.

Managing Your Property and Debt 253

Balancing Your Property and Debt Accounts

As with your other accounts, you should balance your property and debt accounts by using your monthly statements. Balancing or reconciling property and debt accounts doesn't work quite like it does for other accounts, such as your checking account(s). With a checking account, the Reconcile option opens a window you can use to reconcile all your transactions. With property and debt accounts, unless you use the online features to download and reconcile your accounts, you must compare transactions on your paper statement to those in Quicken. You then tell Quicken that a transaction has cleared and reconciled and then move on to the next transaction. Of course, if you find discrepancies, you can reconcile your balance, add missing transactions, and so on to ensure that your ending balance matches the ending balance on your paper statement. Keep in mind that some transactions may not have cleared yet and therefore might not show up on your statement.

Before you begin to balance your accounts, you need to make sure that all transactions (deposits, withdrawals, purchases, payments, interest, and so on) have been recorded or entered in your account register, and you should have your statement ready.

Balance Your Account Manually

1. On the account bar, select the property or debt account you want to balance.

2. Compare transactions on your statement with those on your Quicken account register. To clear a transaction, click in the Clr column. A message appears, asking if you want to reconcile this account.

3. Click No. Quicken places a C in the Clr column to indicate that the transaction has cleared.

4. Click Enter to save the cleared transaction.

5. To add a missing transaction, click the next empty transaction row and type the information. Then click Enter.

6. To edit a transaction, select the transaction, click Edit, make your changes, and click Enter.

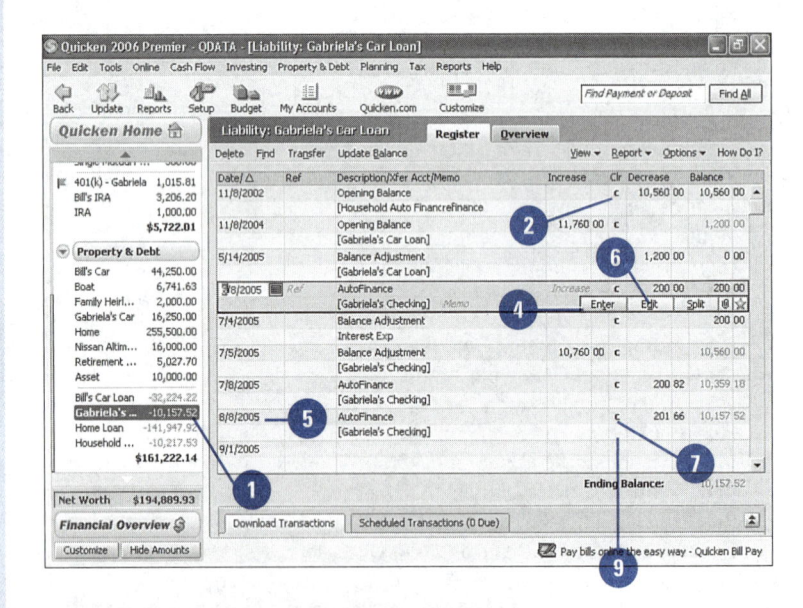

254

7 Continue comparing transactions and clearing each transaction, as needed. As you clear transactions, you can also reconcile them by double-clicking the C in the Clr column. The message asking if you want to reconcile the account appears.

8 Click No. Quicken places an R in the Clr column.

9 When you are finished clearing and reconciling transactions, if your statement and register balances match, you are finished. If the balances do not match and you've added all missing transactions, you can reconcile the balance by clicking in the Clr column of an empty row.

10 When you are asked whether you want to reconcile the account, click Yes.

11 Click in the Update Balance to box and type the balance from your statement.

12 Click in the Adjustment Date box and type the date of the balance from your statement.

13 From the Category for Adjustment drop-down menu, select a category to associate with the new balance. Then click OK. Quicken places an entry in your register, with an R in the Clr column to show that your balance has been reconciled, and it adds a transaction for the difference.

See Also

See "Adding, Editing, and Deleting Property and Debt Transactions" on page 245 for more information on adding, editing, or deleting transactions.

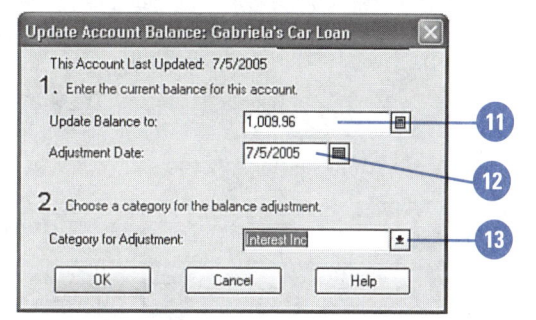

Did You Know?

You can use the pop-up menus as an alternative way of clearing and reconciling transactions. Instead of double-clicking in the Clr column, you can right-click in the Clr column, select Reconcile, and then select either Clear or Reconcile. To remove the C or R from a cleared or reconciled transaction, select Not Reconciled from the Reconcile option on the pop-up menu.

Did You Know?

You should reconcile when you want to update your balance. The only time you should reconcile a property or debt account balance is when there are discrepancies between the balance on your statement and the balance in your Quicken register. Reconciling the balance gives you the opportunity to sync up the two balances. When you reconcile your balance, the next time you balance your account, Quicken works from the reconciled balance.

Did You Know?

You should not change reconciled transaction amounts. After you clear and reconcile account transactions, you should not change the amounts for those transactions. If you change the amounts, the next time you balance your account, matching up your account and statement balances will be difficult and confusing.

Managing Your Property and Debt

Reviewing and Adding Loans

The Loan Accounts Summary section of the Property & Debt Center lists all your loans for your property and debt accounts. It provides balances, interest rates, principal paid, and loan totals. Using this section, you can access your loan accounts, add new loans, edit existing loans, and register payments.

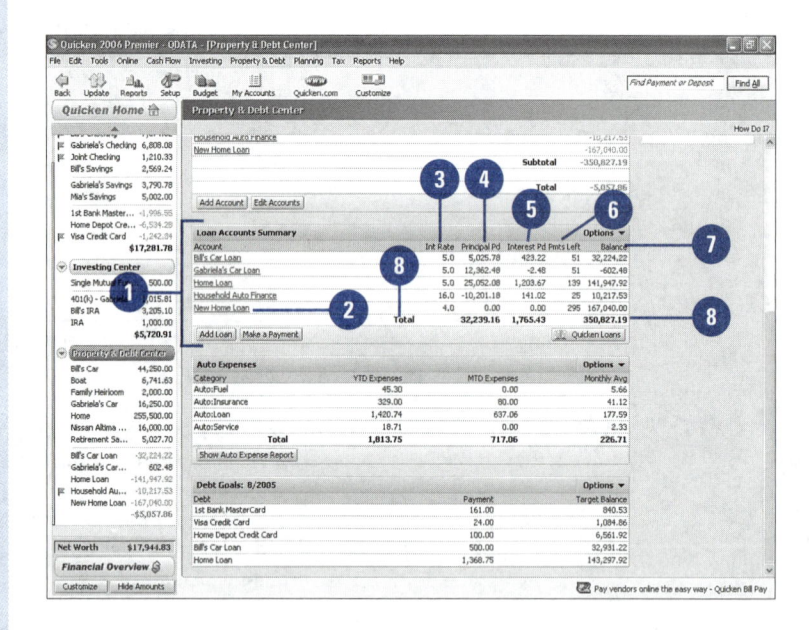

Review Loan Accounts

1. On the account bar, click Property & Debt Center and scroll down to the Loan Accounts Summary section.

2. Each loan account you enter in Quicken is listed here. Click a link to open the account register for a loan.

3. In the Int Rate column, review the interest rate for each of your loans.

4. In the Principal Pd column, review the amount of principal you've paid thus far for each loan.

5. In the Interest Pd column, review the amount you've paid in interest for each of your loans.

6. In the Pmts Left column, review the number of payments you have left to make for each of your loans.

7. In the Balance column, review the individual loan balances.

8. The Total row provides the sum of the principal paid, interest paid, and the balance for all your loans.

256

Add a Loan

1. To add a new loan, from the Loan Accounts Summary section of the Property & Debt Center, click Add Loan.

2. Click Next.

3. Select the type of loan you have and click Next. This example uses the Borrow Money option.

See Also

See "Review Loan Accounts" on page 256, for information on how to open the Property & Debt Center and access the Loan Accounts Summary section.

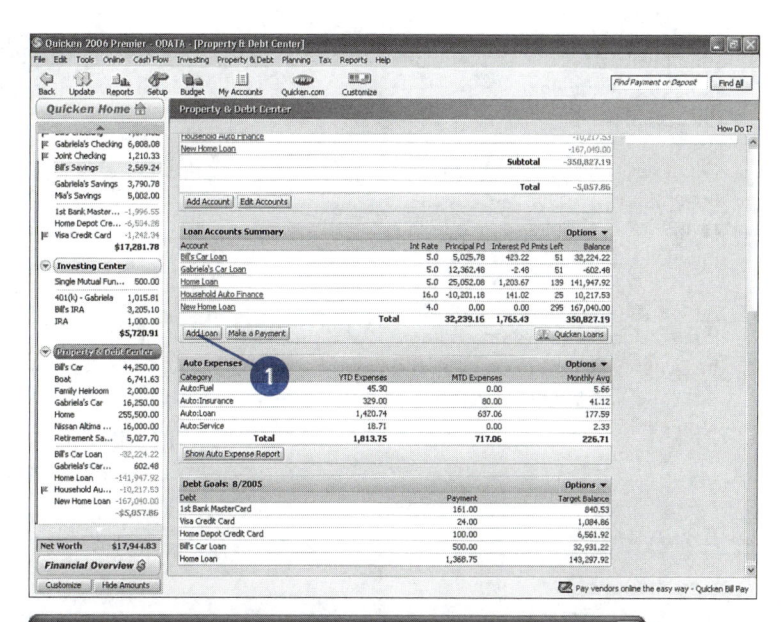

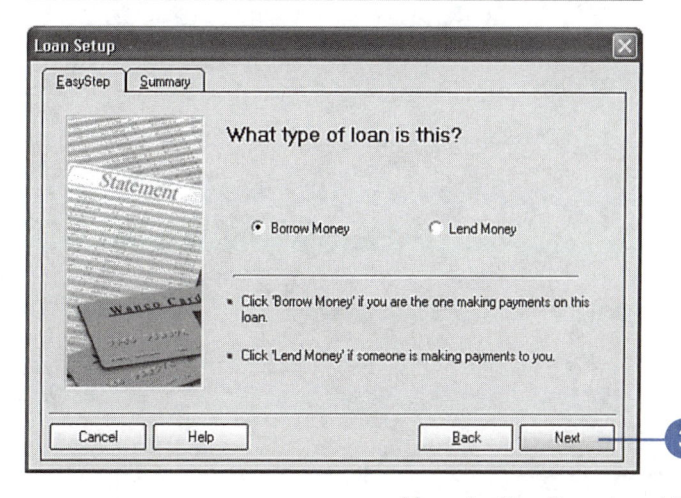

Managing Your Property and Debt **257**

4. Select New Account and type the name of the new loan account. Then click Next.

5. Select Yes (as shown in this example) if you have already made payments on the loan or No if you haven't. Then click Next.

6. In the Opening Date box, type the date the loan was created, and in the Original Balance box, type the amount of the beginning balance. Then click Next.

Did You Know?

If you are not sure of the beginning balance, enter an estimate in the Original Balance box. If needed, you can change the estimated amount later by editing the loan information. Refer to "Edit Loans and Payments" on page 267 for information on editing loans.

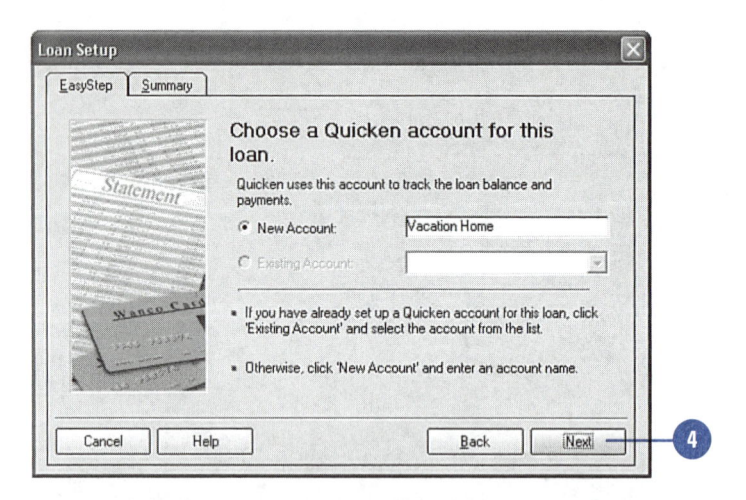

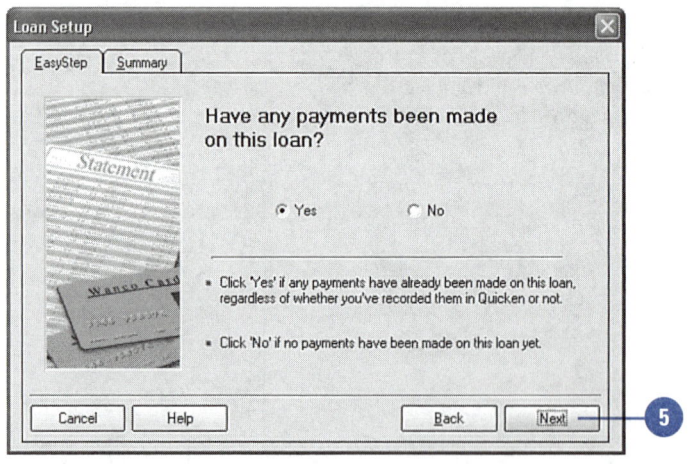

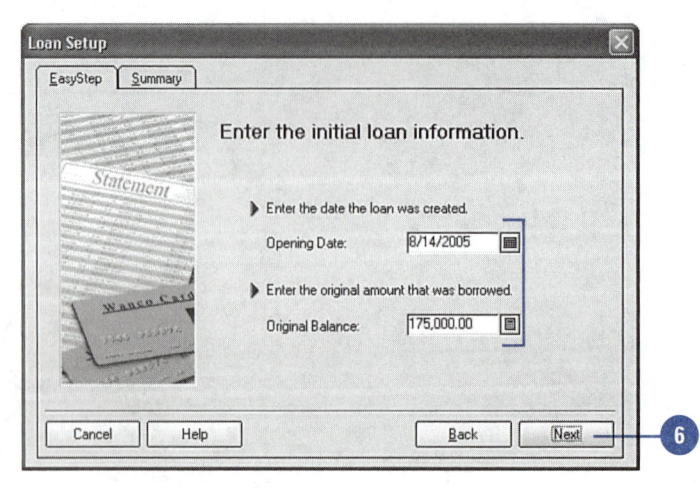

7. Select Yes if you will have a balloon payment at the end of your loan or No if you won't. Then click Next.

8. In the Original Length box, type the length of the loan, select the time period, and click Next.

9. Select Standard Period and select the frequency of payments or select Other Period and type the number of times per year you make the payments. Then click Next.

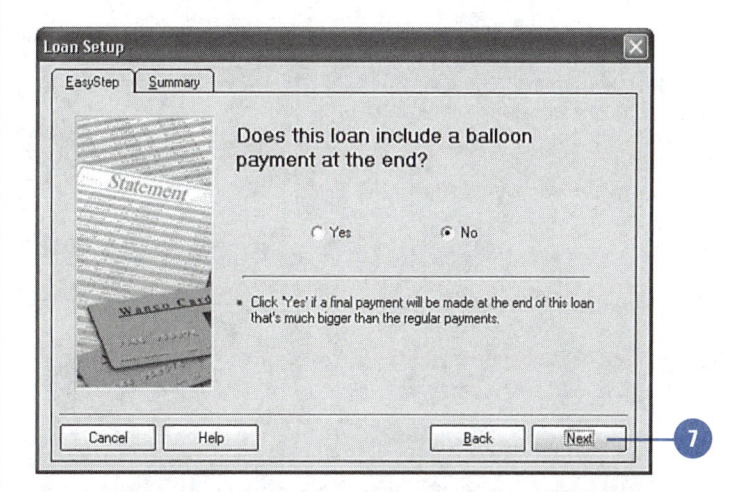

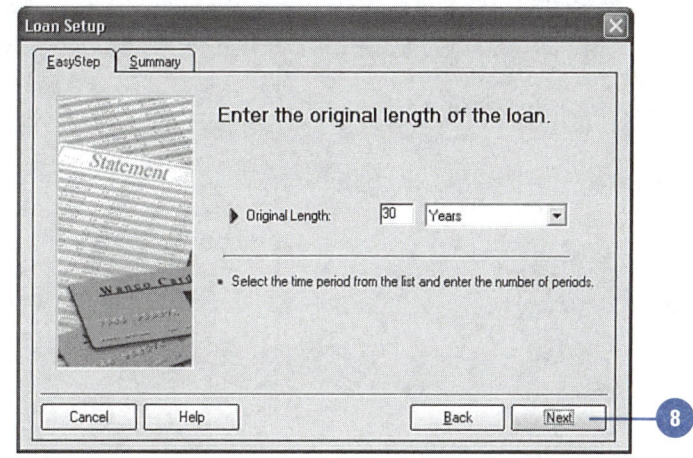

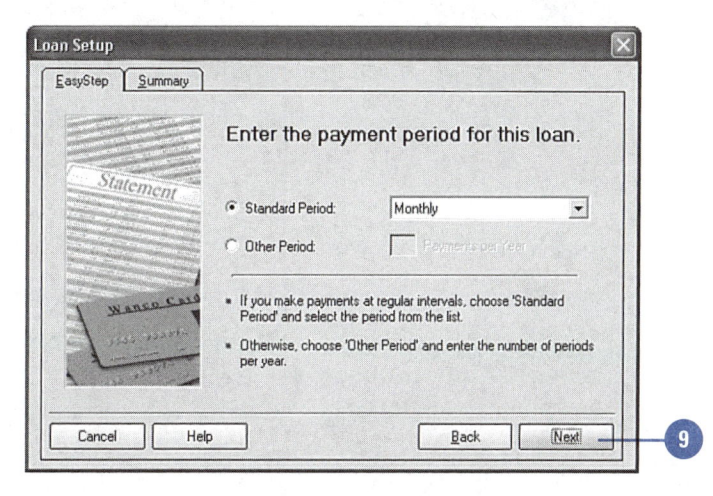

Managing Your Property and Debt **259**

10. From the Compounding Period drop-down menu, select how often the loan interest is calculated and click Next.

11. Select Yes if you know your balance or No if you don't. Then click Next.

12. If you selected Yes in step 11, in the Current Balance Date box, type the date of the balance and in the Current Balance Amount, type the balance. Then click Next.

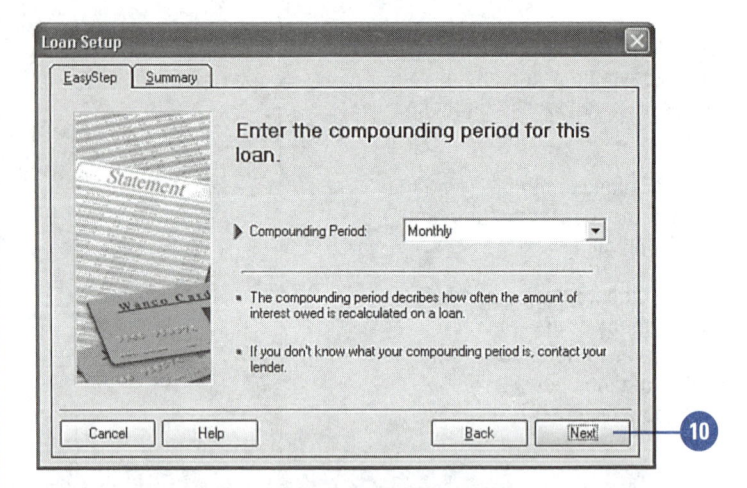

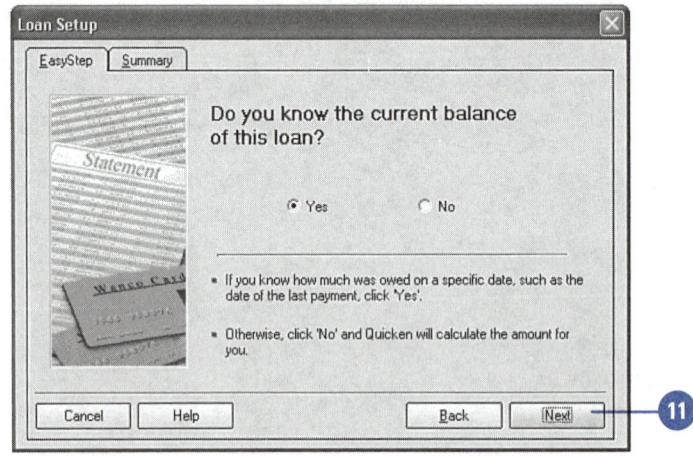

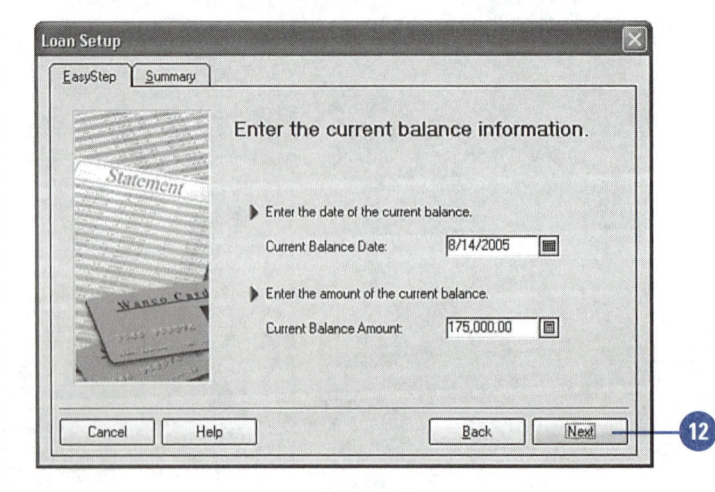

13 In the Date of Next Payment box, type the date your next loan payment is due and click Next.

14 Select Yes if you know the amount of your next loan payment or No if you don't. Then click Next.

15 If you selected Yes in step 14, in the Payment Amount box, type the your loan payment amount and click Next.

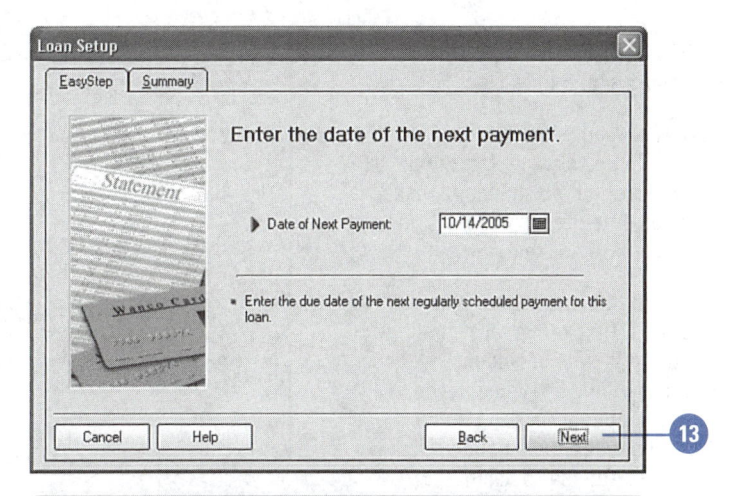

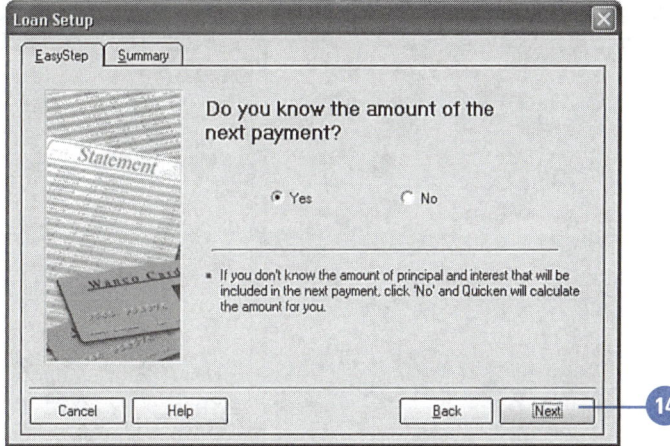

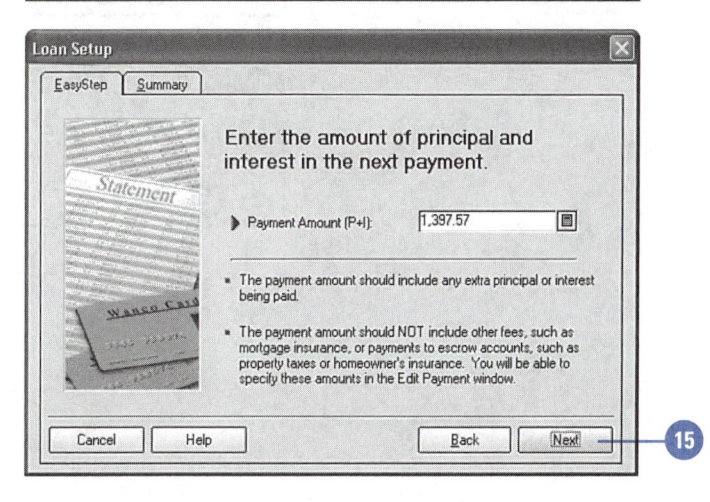

Managing Your Property and Debt **261**

16. In the Interest Rate box, type the interest rate and click Next.

17. Review all your summary information by clicking Next until you've finished the summary, make changes if needed, and click Done when you are finished.

18. Based on the information you entered, if Quicken determines that the principal balance is different from what you entered, a message appears, asking if you want to change the balance. Click Yes to use Quicken's balance or No to use the balance you provided.

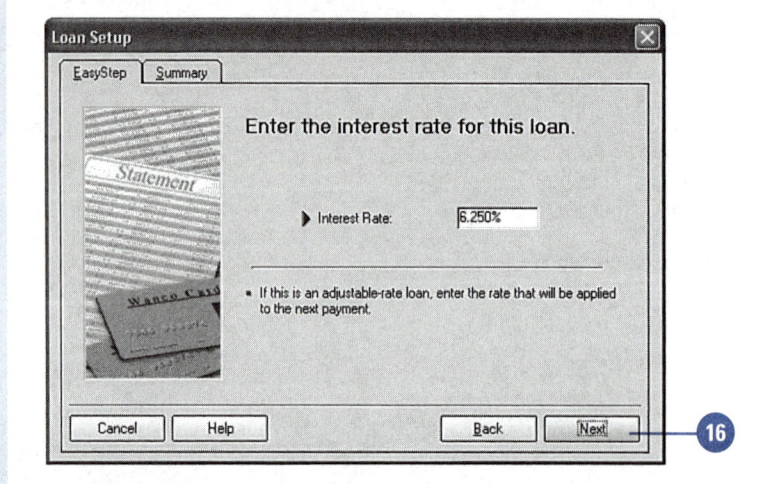

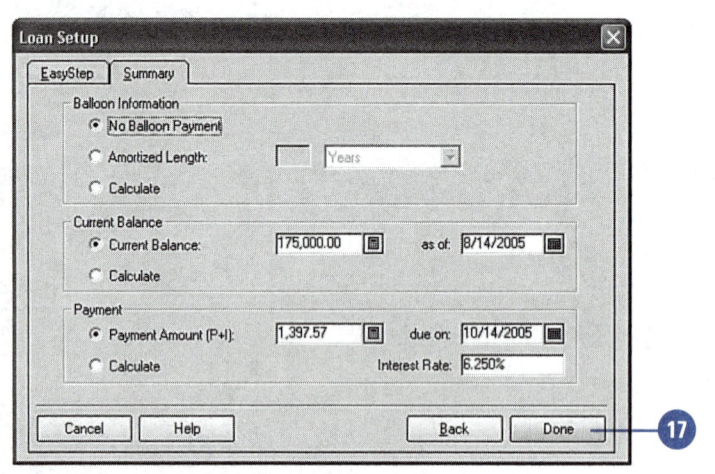

Set Up Your Loan Payments

1. When you are finished setting up your loan, you are automatically prompted to set up your loan payment. Review and change, if needed, the information in the Payment section.

2. From the Type drop-down menu, select how you want to make your payments and then click Payment Method to specify the payment details.

3. From the Payment Type section of the Select Payment Method dialog box, select the payment type.

4. From the Register Entry drop-down menu in the For Scheduled Transactions section, select how you want the transaction entered in your register.

5. From the Account to Pay from drop-down menu, select the account from which payments are made.

6. In the Days in Advance, type the number of days in advance that you want the payment transaction to be entered in your register. Then click OK.

7. In Payee, type the name of your lender.

8. In Memo, type any additional information you want to log for this loan.

9. The Next Payment Date and Category for Interest information is completed for you, based on the information you entered about the loan. Change it, if needed, and then click OK.

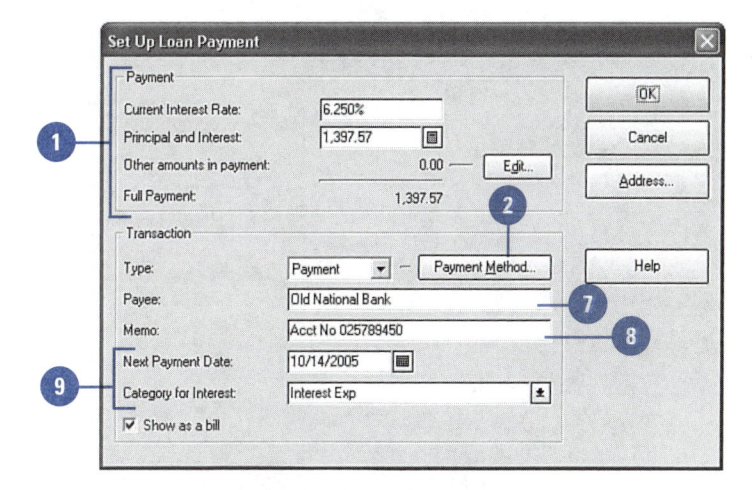

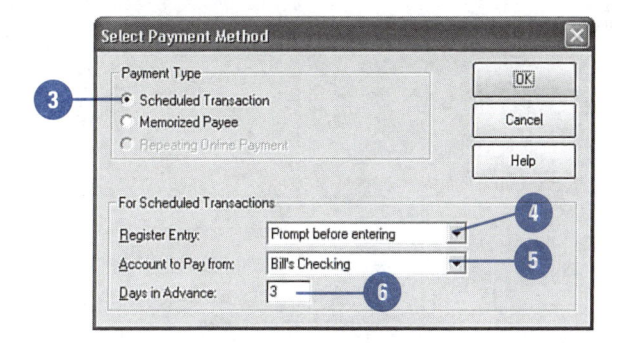

Did You Know?

Add new loans to your Bills and Scheduled Transactions list. *To have the new loan appear on your Bills and Scheduled Transactions list, select the Show as bill option on the bottom of the Set Up Loan Payment dialog box.*

Managing Your Property and Debt **263**

Create an Asset Account for a Loan

1. When you are finished setting up loan payments, if a message appears, asking if you would like to create an asset for a loan, click Yes so that you can track the value of the property.

2. In Name this account, type a name for the asset and click Next.

3. In As of Date, type the date the you would like to start tracking the asset. This doesn't have to be the same date that you acquired the object for which you have the loan.

4. In Value, type the value of the object. If you don't know it, estimate it now, and you can change it later.

5. If the asset is eligible to be tax deferred or if you want to specify the tax schedule associated with incoming and outgoing funds for the account, click Tax and select the associated tax schedules.

6. Click Done. When you create the loan and asset accounts, they are added to your property and debt accounts, and you can manage them just as you do your other accounts.

See Also

See "Viewing, Adding, Editing, and Deleting Scheduled Property and Debt Transactions" on page 249 for more detailed information on making changes to loan account transactions. See "Add Property and Debt Accounts" for more information on adding tax schedules.

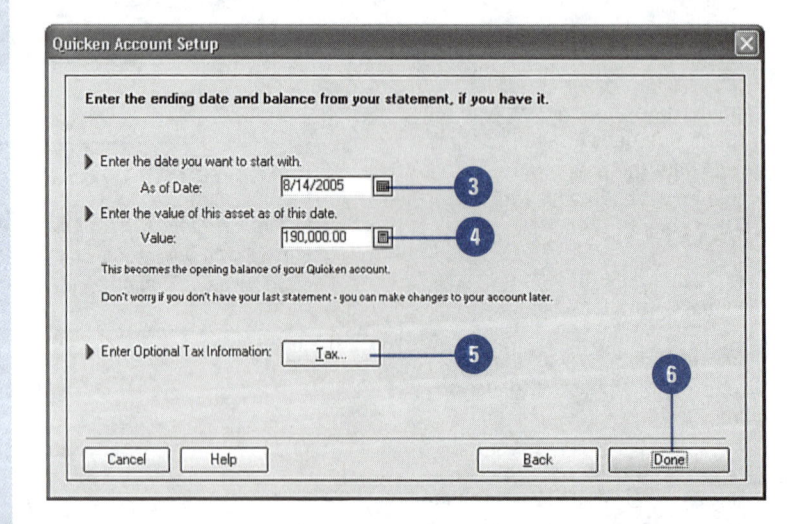

Tracking a Refinanced Loan

If you are refinancing a loan, such as your mortgage, you should create the refinanced loan as a new loan and then in the register of the new loan, use the Split Transaction window to enter the payoff amount and fees for the old loan. This enables Quicken to track the payoff of the old loan and manage the new loan. Here's how you do it:

1. In the Loan Accounts Summary section of the Property & Debt Center, click Add Loan.

2. Click Next and set up the new loan, as shown in the task "Add a Loan," earlier in this chapter.

3. In the Debt (Liabilities) section of the Loan Accounts Summary section, click the link for the new loan to open its register.

4. Select the Opening Balance transaction and click Split under the Balance column.

5. In the Split Transaction window, click in the first row of the Category column and select Transfer to/from + the name of the old loan, for example, Transfer to/from Home Bank Mortgage.

6. Click Amount, type the payoff amount for the old loan, and click Next.

7. In the second row of the Category column, select the Interest Exp category or whichever category you selected to track the interest you paid for the old loan. In Amount, type the amount of mortgage interest you paid when you closed on the old loan and click Next.

8. In the third row of the Category column, select the Bank Charge category or whatever category you use for refinance fees and in Amount, type the amount you paid for the refinance fee. Then click Next.

9. If you are to get cash back from equity, in the fourth row of the Category column, select Transfer to/from + the name of the account to which the money is being sent (for example, your savings account).

10. In Amount, type the amount of equity and click Next.

11. Click Adjust. Quicken recalculates the total for you.

12. Click OK to close the Split Transaction window.

13. In the account register, click Enter to save your changes. The balance of your old loan should now have a zero balance.

Record Loan Payments

1. To record a loan payment, in the Loan Accounts Summary section of the Property & Debt Center, click Make a Payment.

2. Click the Choose Loan menu, select the loan you want to use, and then click Make Payment.

3. If this is a regularly scheduled payment, click Regular. If this is an additional payment, click Extra.

4. Verify that the loan information is correct. If you selected to make a regular payment, the amount is already filled in for you. If you selected to make an extra payment, the amount is empty so that you can type the amount you want to pay.

5. Click OK.

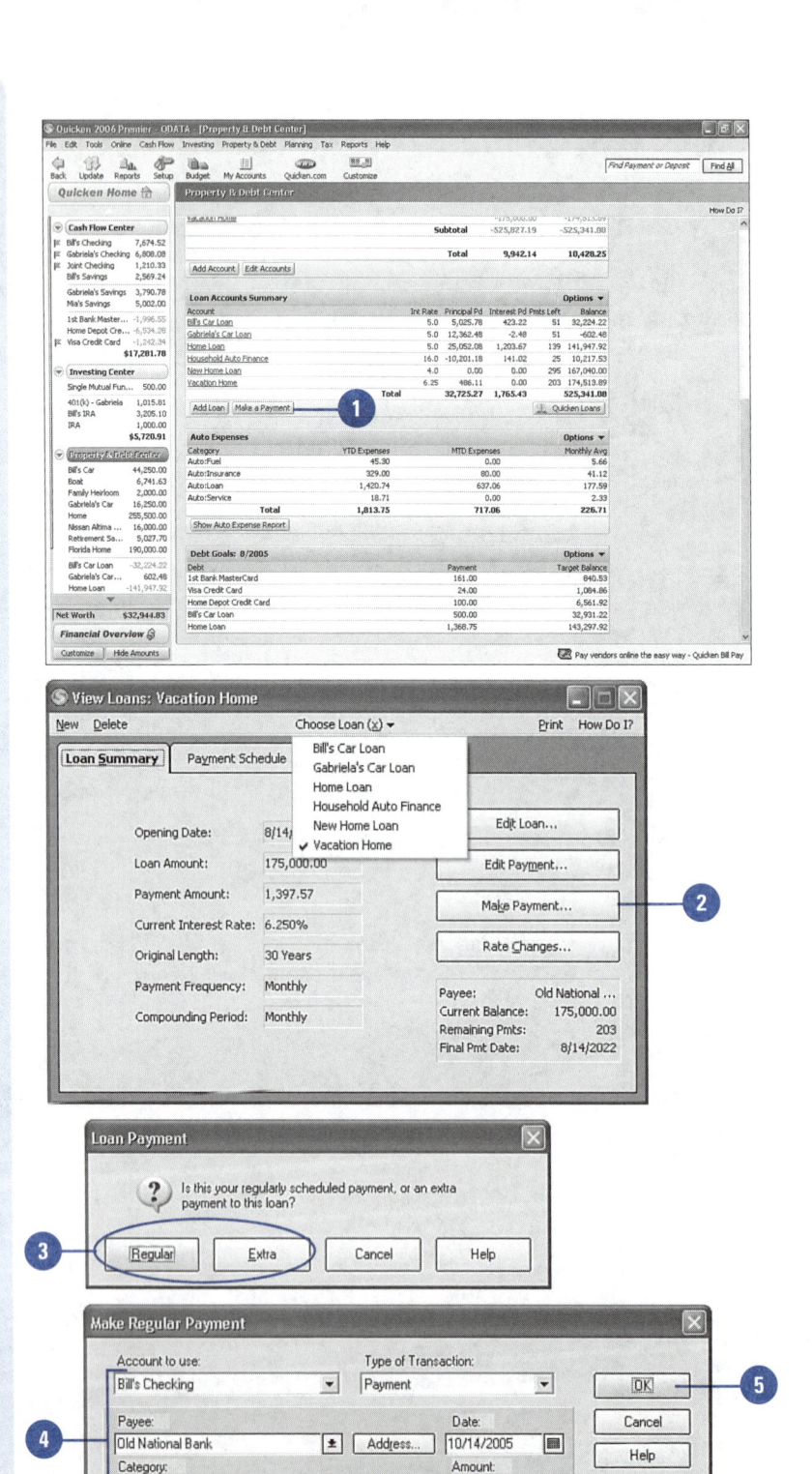

Edit Loans and Payments

1. To edit a loan, from the Choose Loan menu on the View Loans dialog box, select the loan you want to edit and then click Edit Loan.

2. Make any necessary changes to the Loan Information and Payment Period sections and click Next.

3. Review and make any changes to the Balloon Information, Current Balance, and Payment sections and then click Done.

4. To edit loan payments, from the Choose Loan menu, select the loan you want to edit and then click Edit Payment.

See Also

See "Record Loan Payments" on page 266 for information on accessing the View Loans dialog box.

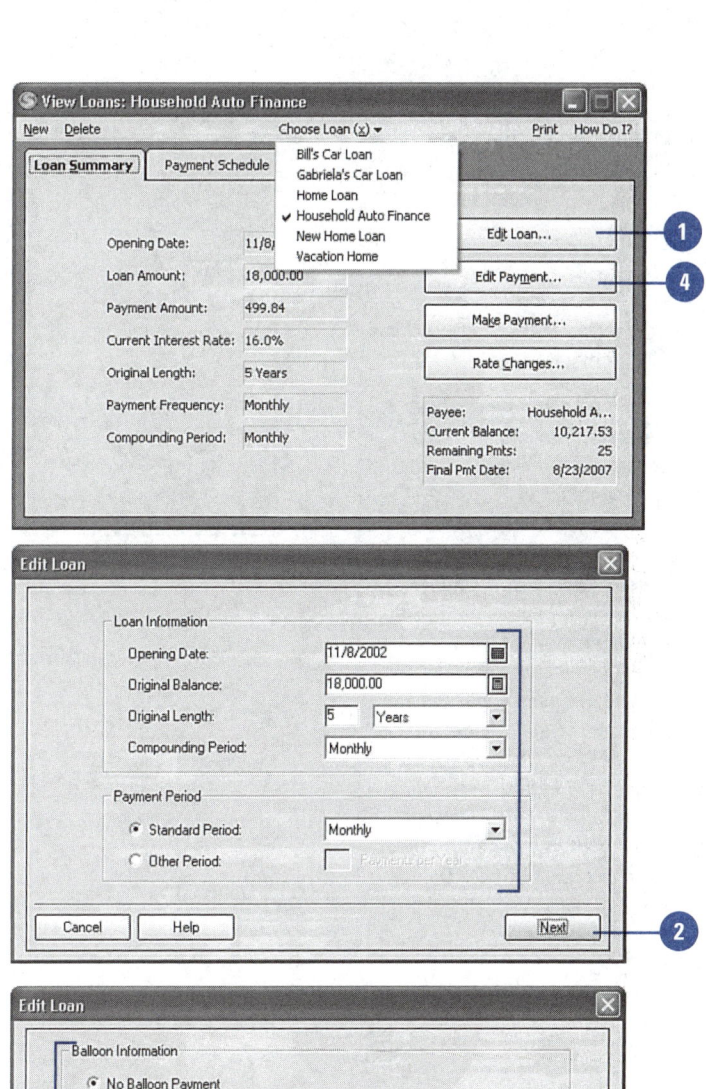

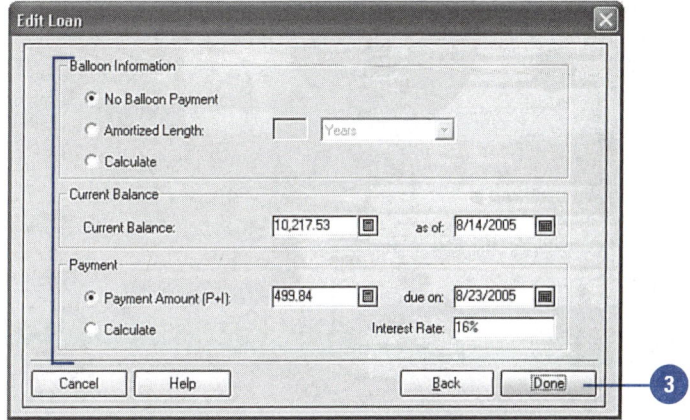

Managing Your Property and Debt **267**

5 Make any necessary changes, click Address to update your lender's address, click Pay Now to make a payment, and then click OK.

Did You Know?

You can use the Loan Rate Changes window to track rate changes. *You can track rate changes and estimated payment amounts for your variable-rate loans by using the Loan Rate Changes window. You can add new rate changes, change existing ones, or delete old ones. To open the Loan Rate Changes window, in the View Loans window, select the loan to which the rate changes apply and then click Rate Changes. To create a new rate, click New and type the date the rate change is to take effect, the new rate, and your regular payment amount. To edit or delete a rate, select the rate and click Edit or click Delete to remove it.*

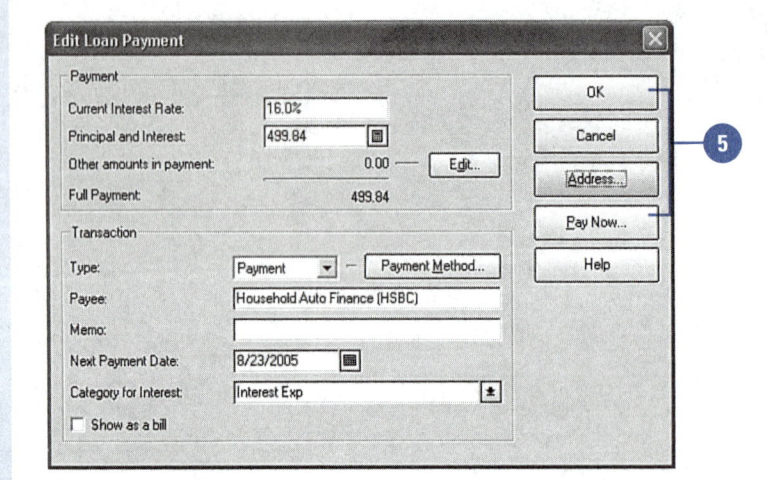

Viewing Auto Expenses

The Auto Expenses section of the Property & Debt Center lists your automobile-related expense totals for the year-to-date and month-to-date, monthly averages, and totals by category. When you enter transactions into your registers and select one of the automobile-related categories, such as fuel or insurance, Quicken tracks this information in the Auto Expenses section. You can use this information later for tax deductions, budgeting, or insurance purposes. In addition, you can run the Auto Expenses report, which lists all your auto expenses in detail for a specific period of time.

View Auto Expenses

1. In the YTD Expenses column, review the year-to-date auto expenses listed for each auto expense category.

2. In the MTD Expenses column, review the month-to-date auto expenses listed for each auto expense category.

3. In the Monthly Avg column, review the monthly average to determine how much you spend on average per month for each auto expense category.

4. In the Total row, review the totals to determine the sum of all auto expense categories for year-to-date, month-to-date, and the monthly average.

5. To view, print, or save the Auto Expenses report, click Show Auto Expense Report.

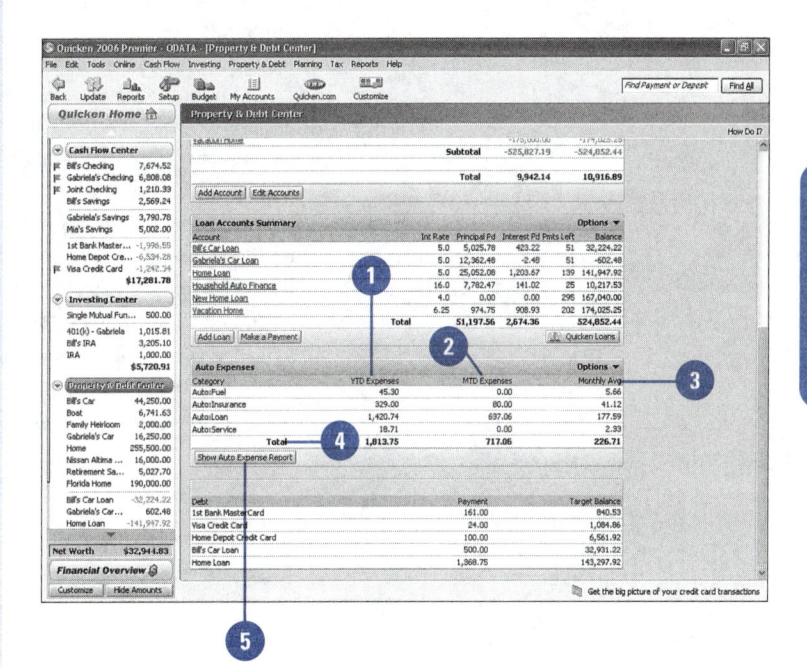

Managing Your Property and Debt **269**

Keeping Track of Your Home Inventory

I must admit that taking and keeping inventory of my belongings is not one of my favorite things to do. It's right up there with doing taxes, as far as I'm concerned. However, after enduring an action-packed hurricane season in 2004 and again in 2005 (it's ironic that as I write this, Hurricane Dennis, a category 4 hurricane, is making his way into the Gulf of Mexico), it behooves anyone living in Hurricane Alley to take inventory of his or her belongings. No matter where you live, though, accidents and disasters can happen.

Because luck favors the prepared, everyone should take inventory of their homes, and the Quicken Home Inventory tool makes keeping track of your belongings easy and painless. The Quicken Home Inventory tool steps you through a process of logging your belongings, room-by-room, and it even tracks the contents of your safety deposit box, and any other place you might have important belongings and papers. In addition, you can log claims that you've filed and details of your insurance policies.

When you have this information in Quicken, if ever you need to file a claim due to loss of any of your belongings, all the information is at your fingertips. However, I highly recommend that you run an inventory report that contains all your items after you are finished and keep it with your insurance and other emergency papers. You may not have access to your computer in some emergency situations.

Record Inventory Items

1. From the Property & Debt menu, select Quicken Home Inventory. If you have never used the Quicken Home Inventory before, the Welcome dialog box appears.

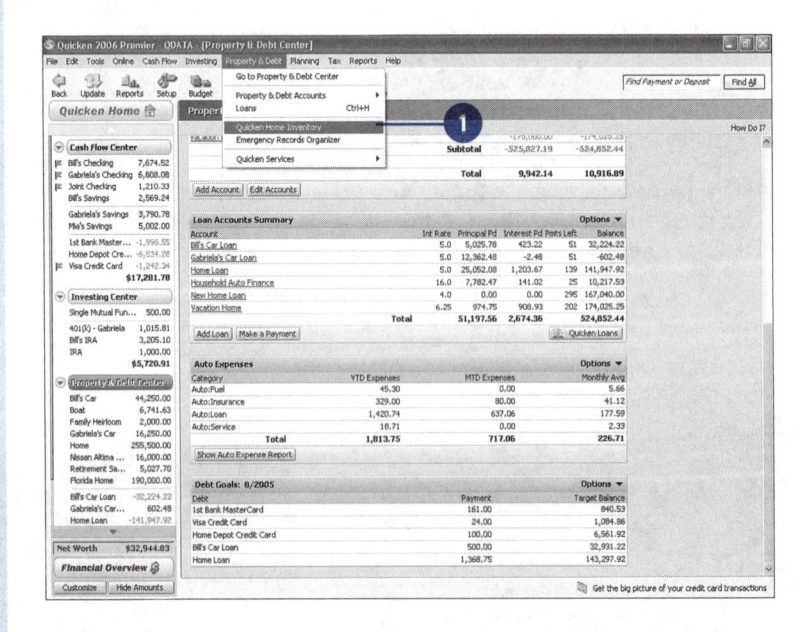

2 Review the information and click Continue.

3 From the View By Location drop-down menu, select the room or area where you want to start the inventory.

4 From the Item Category drop-down menu, select the category of items you want to view.

5 To add items to the inventory log, click in the first row and from Suggested Items for section, select the name of the item and then click Add Selected Item.

6 When you select on item from the Suggested Items for list, the estimated replacement cost and resale value are already filled in for you. If needed, change these amounts.

7 To add items to the current room that are not listed on any of the category lists, in the Item Description column, type the name of the item. Then select the category and type the replacement and value costs.

8 To delete an inventory item, select it and click Delete.

9 To copy an item to a new line to use some of the same information for another inventory item, click Copy.

10 Continue entering all the items for each room, and when you are finished, to enter detailed information about each inventory item, select the first item and click the Detail View button.

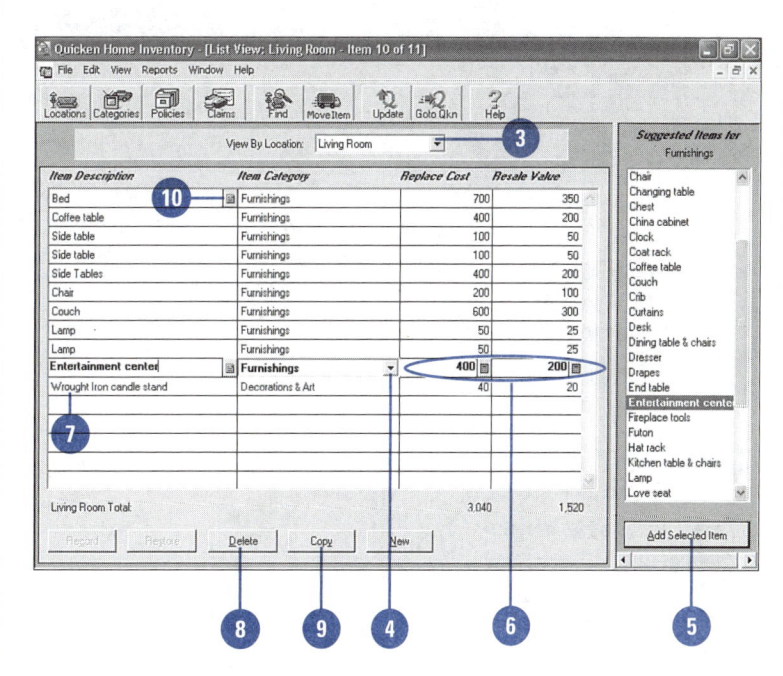

Did You Know?

You can create categories to meet your needs. If the categories, policies, or claims Quicken offers do not meet your needs, you can create new ones, edit existing ones, or delete the ones you don't need. To change categories, on the button bar, click Categories. Then you can click New to create a new category, type the name, and click OK. To change the name of a category, select the category, click Edit, change the name, and click OK. To remove a category, select it and click Delete.

Enter Detailed Inventory Information

1. Complete all the information about the item. If you are unsure of some of the information, leave it blank for now. You can update it later.

2. To select the receipts and records you have for the inventory item, click Receipts & Records.

3. Select all receipts and paperwork you have for the inventory item, and in Location of Records, type where you keep the paperwork. Then click OK.

4. If the resale value of the item changes, click Resale Value History.

5. Click New.

6. Type the new value and click OK.

7. To edit an existing value, select it, click Edit, change the value, and click OK. To close the Resale Value History dialog box, click Close.

Did You Know?

You can use the calendar or calculator buttons to insert dates and amounts. *You can use the calendar button to select the purchase date. You can use the calculator button to calculate and select amounts for the Original Price, Replace Cost, and Resale Value fields.*

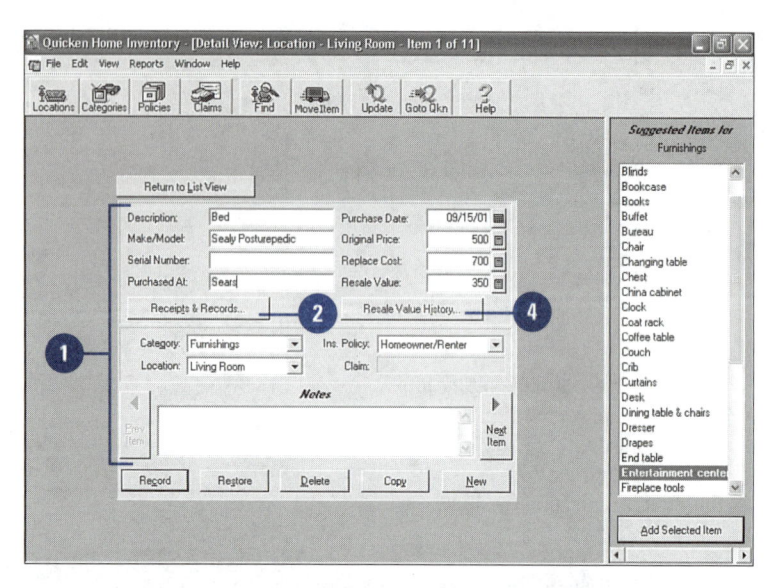

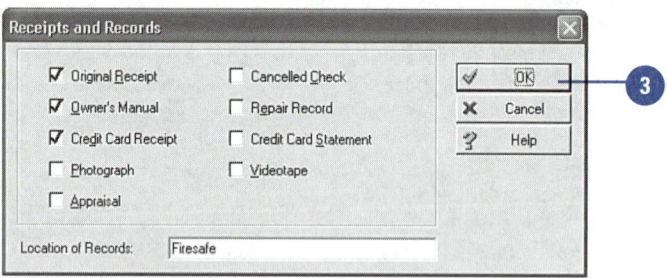

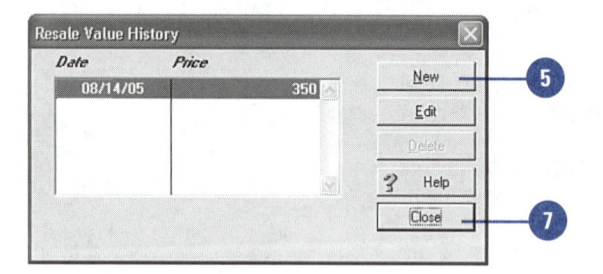

⑧ Click the Ins/Policy drop-down menu and select the policy under which the inventory item is covered. If the item is not covered, select Unassigned.

⑨ If you have any special concerns, comments, or notes about the inventory item, click Notes and type the necessary information.

⑩ Click Record to save the changes.

⑪ Click Next Item to enter information about the next inventory item.

⑫ Complete each item in the inventory, and when you are finished, click Return to List View. When you are finished, Quicken saves all your inventory items in a **QHI.IDB** file, which you can back up for safekeeping.

Did You Know?

You can search for inventory items. *When you have all your items in the Home Inventory tool and need to find a specific item, it could be time-consuming to scroll through all the items. Using the Find Item window is a much quicker way of finding what you are looking for. To search for an item, on the toolbar in the Quicken Home Inventory window, click Find. In the Search For box, type the name of the item you want to find (for example,* **chair***). You should keep Item Description and Item Notes selected to have a better chance of finding the item. You can then click Find All. The items found are listed in the List of Found Inventory Items window. You can select an item and click View to go to that item.*

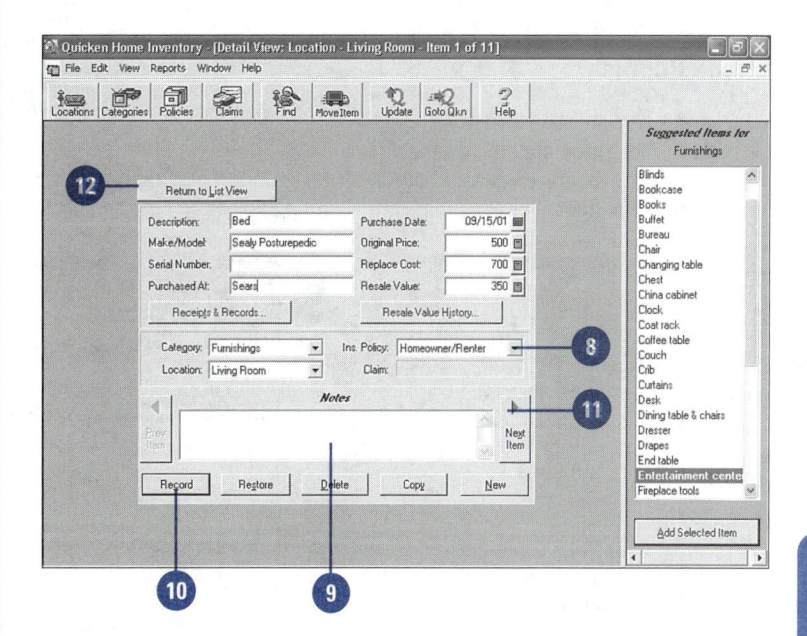

Managing Your Property and Debt **273**

Manage Policies

1. To add a new policy, change an existing one, or delete one, on the toolbar in the Quicken Home Inventory window, click Policies.

2. To create a new policy, click New.

3. Complete all the policy information.

4. To add information about the claims adjuster, click Claims.

5. Enter the information.

6. Click OK.

7. To make changes to a policy, select it, and click Edit.

8. Make your changes and click OK.

9. To delete a policy, select it and click Delete. A message appears, telling you that any items currently assigned to this policy will be reassigned to the Unassigned policy.

10. Click OK to accept this or Cancel to keep the policy.

11. When you are finished making changes to policies, click Close.

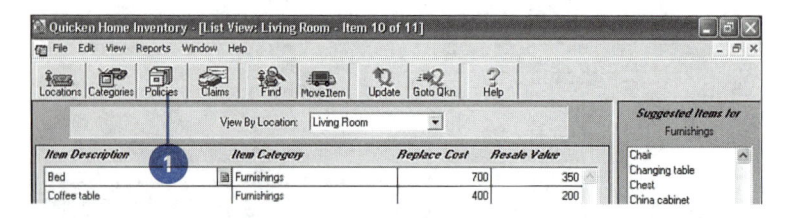

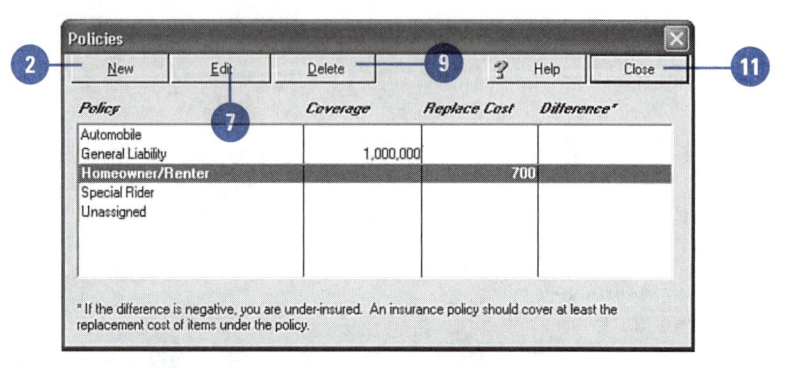

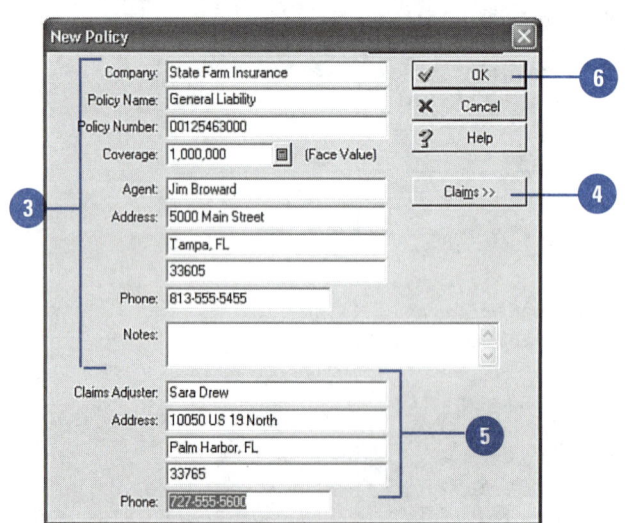

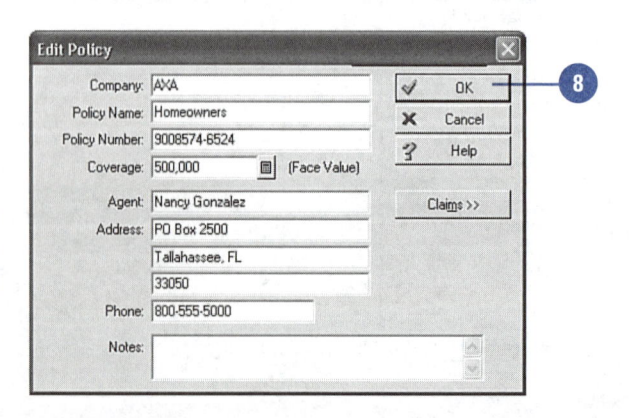

274

Manage Claims

1. To add a new claim, change an existing one, or delete one, on the toolbar in the Quicken Home Inventory window, click Claims.

2. To create a new claim, click New.

3. Review the claim instructions and click OK.

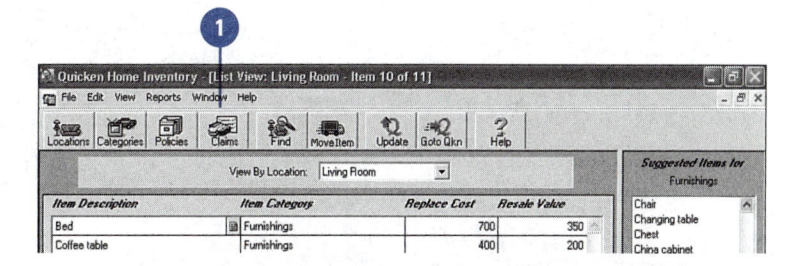

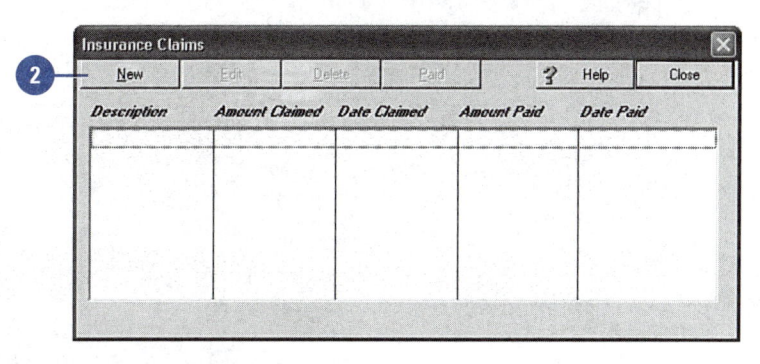

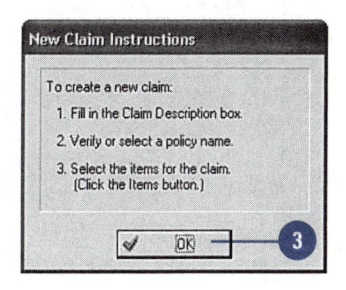

Managing Your Property and Debt **275**

4. Complete the claim information.

5. To add the item(s) for which the claim is being made, click Items.

6. Select the item(s) you want to include, and click OK.

7. To change the repair or replacement costs, select the item and click Adjust Cost.

8. Select whether the cost is for replacement or repair, type the amount, and click OK.

9. To add more detail about the claim, click in Notes and type a description.

10. Click OK to save the claim. A message appears, asking if you want to create a report for the claim.

11. Click Yes to create the report. You can print the report to keep in your records or to send to your insurance company.

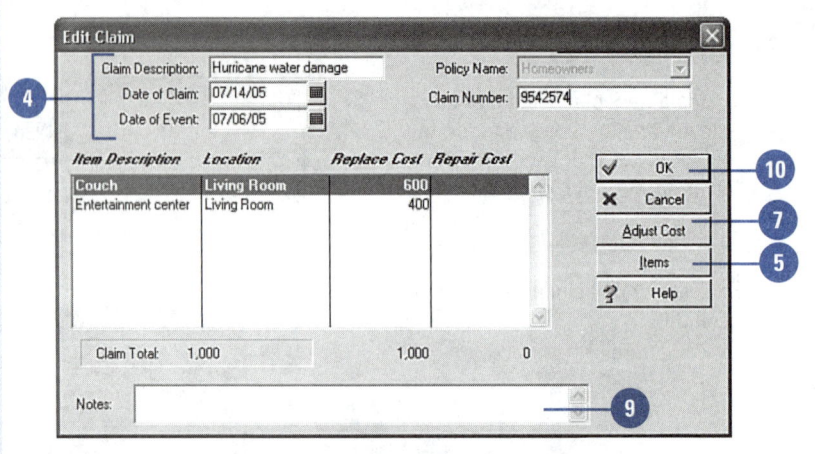

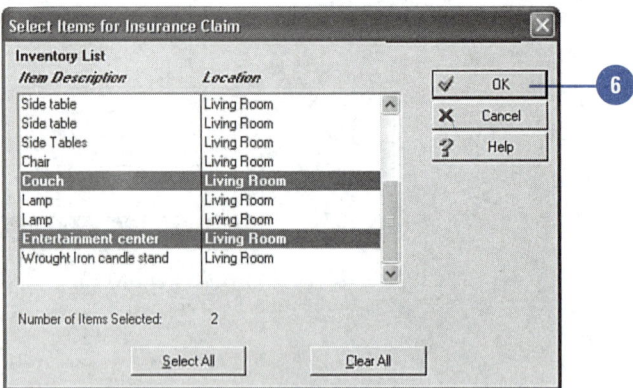

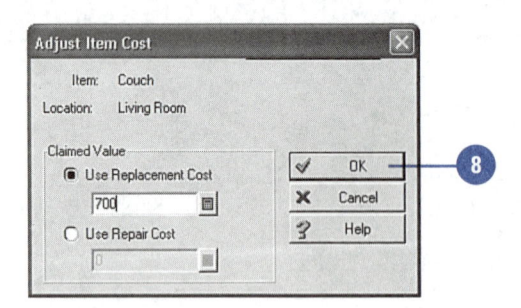

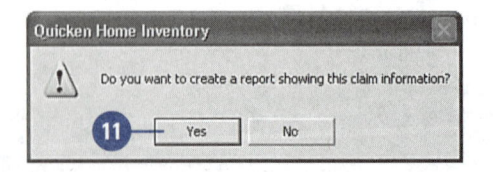

⑫ To edit a claim, select it, click Edit, make your changes, and click OK.

⑬ To remove a claim, select it and click Delete. A message appears, asking if you want to remove the claim.

⑭ Click OK to delete the claim or Cancel to keep the claim.

⑮ When a claim is paid, select the claim and click Paid.

⑯ Type the date the claim was paid and the amount you received and then click OK. A message appears, asking if you want to create a report for the claim.

⑰ Click Yes to create the report or No if you do not want to create it.

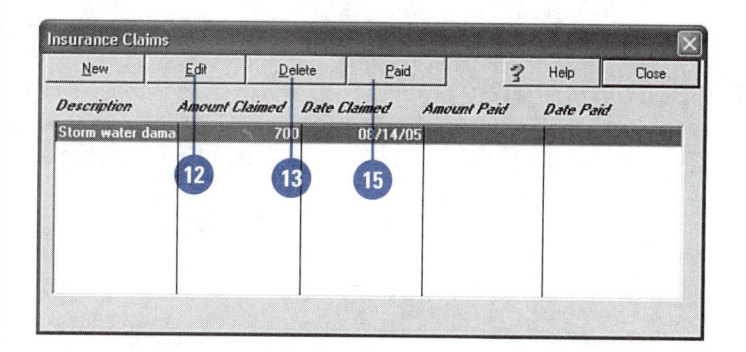

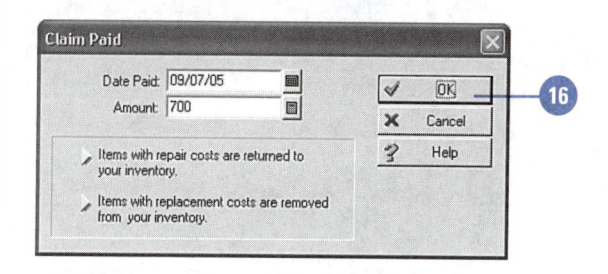

Viewing Home Inventory Reports

You can run reports in Quicken to get specific information about your inventory. For example, you can get a summary of the value of your items, a detailed report about every item, including specifics about each item, and reports about insurance and claims. These reports come in handy for insurance and claims purposes, and it is a good idea to keep such reports in a safe place, with your emergency papers. To view Quicken Home Inventory reports, from the Reports menu, select the report you want to view.

Managing Your Property and Debt

Keeping Track of Your Emergency Records

Whether you're organizationally challenged or meticulously organized and like to keep all your ducks in a row, you'll love the organizer tool I am getting ready to tell you about. The Emergency Records Organizer tool allows you to create emergency contact, medical, and hospital records for yourself and all your family members. In addition, with it you can create records for your finances, legal matters, and insurance. Creating and keeping these records up-to-date ensures that you have all your most important information in one place for you or anyone else to access whenever it's needed. In addition, you can run reports for specific records, and you can print and share them with anyone who needs the information.

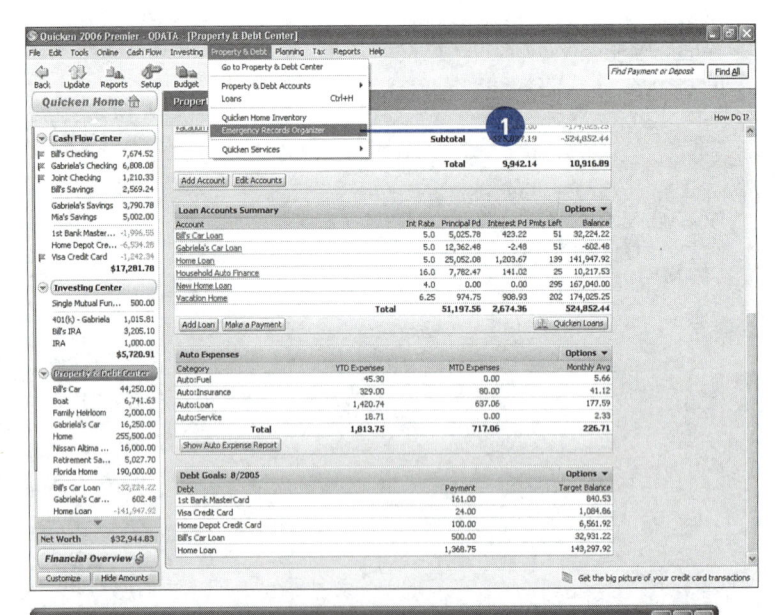

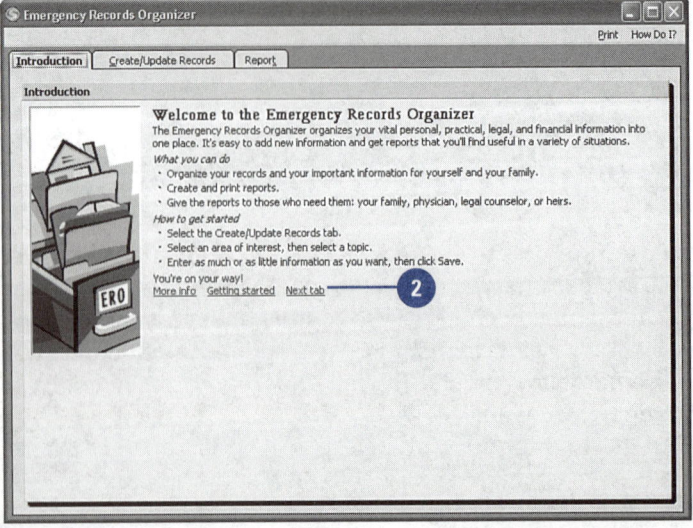

Keep Track of Your Emergency Records

1. From the Property & Debt menu, select Emergency Records Organizer.

2. Review the Introduction window and click the Next tab link.

3. The first record defaults to your contact information under the Adult's Emergency Info area. Review your information, make any necessary changes, and click Save. A green check mark next to a topic means it is saved.

4. To create a new contact record (for example, for each of your emergency contacts), click New Record. Then complete all the information and click Save. Repeat this step to create records for any other emergency contacts.

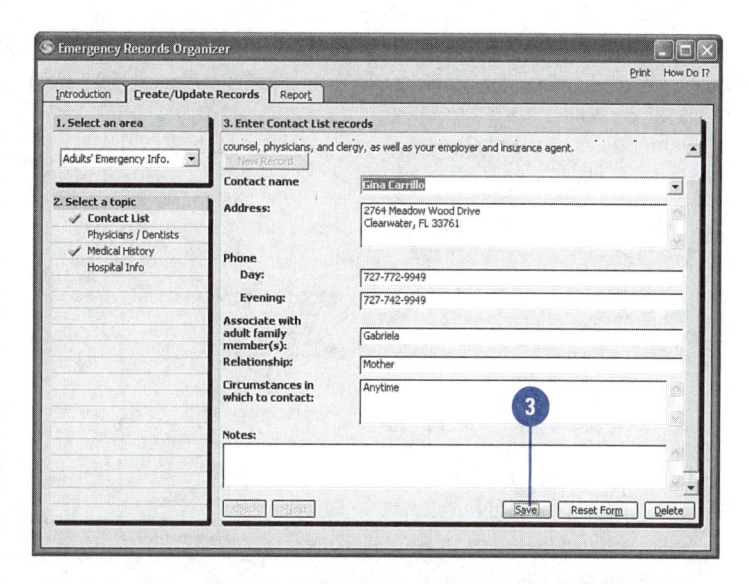

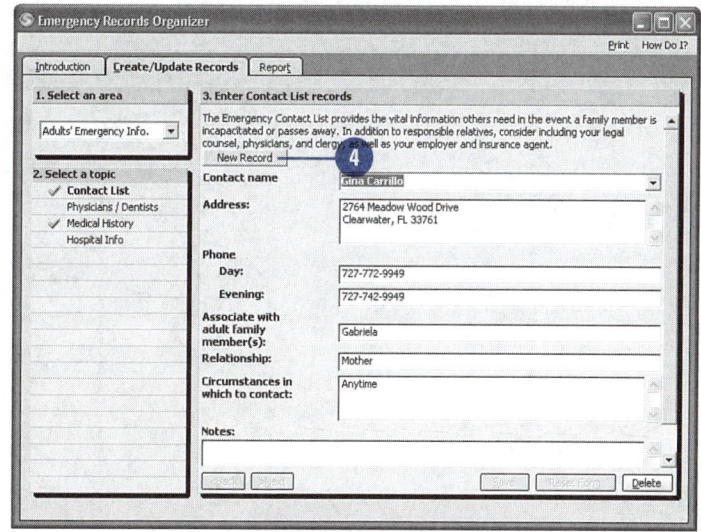

Managing Your Property and Debt **279**

5 To create records for your doctors and dentists, click Physicians/Dentists, complete the information for each doctor or dentist record, and click Save.

6 Click New Record to create a record for each of your doctors and dentists. The New Record button is visible after you save the record.

7 To create your medical record, click Medical History. Complete all the medical information and click Save. Then click New Record to create a medical record for each of your family members.

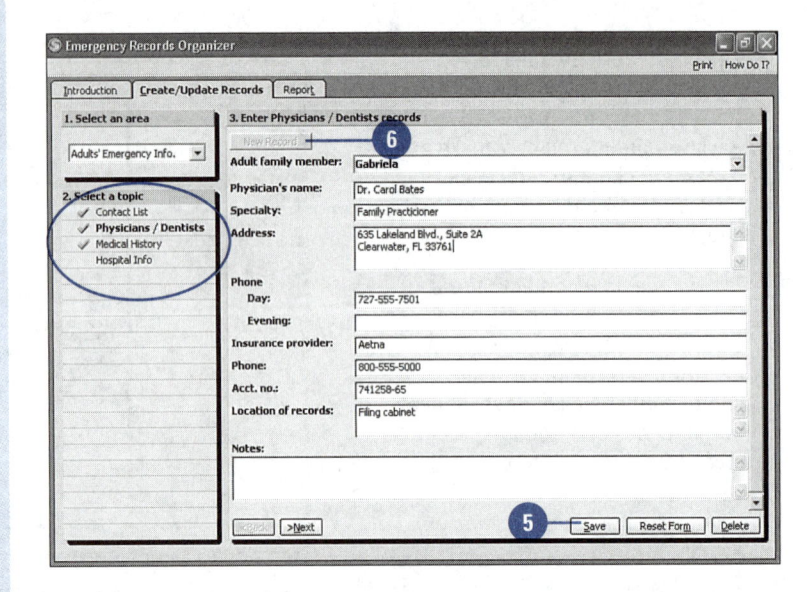

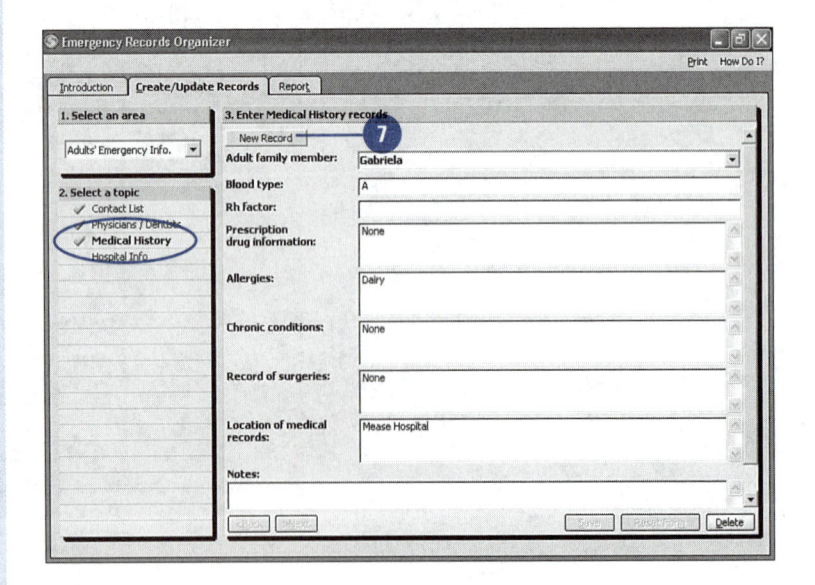

8. To create a record with all your hospital information, click Hospital Info.

9. Complete all the information about your hospital and click Save. You might want to include directions in the Notes column in case someone else has to take you to the hospital and doesn't know how to get there.

10. When you are finished entering all the records for each adult in your family, from the Select an area drop-down menu, select the next area for which you would like to create records.

11. Click a topic to create the record, complete the information as you did for the previous records, and click Save.

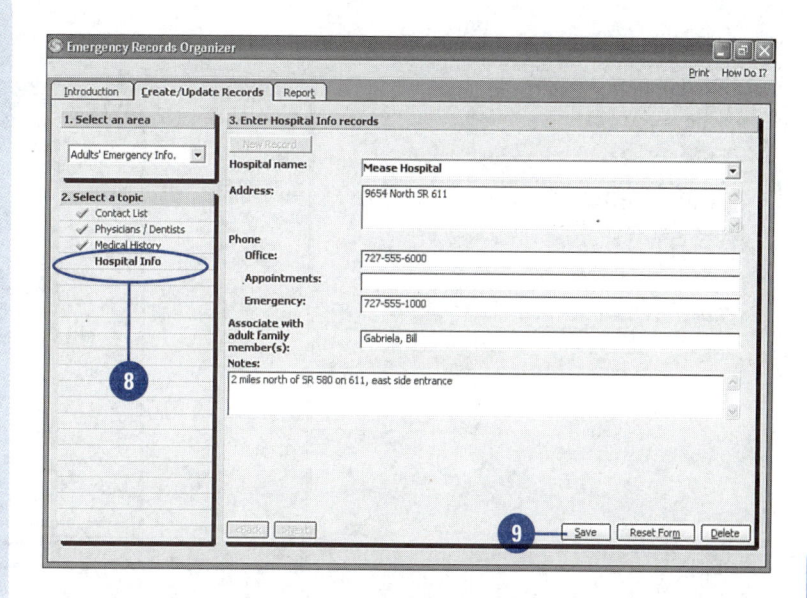

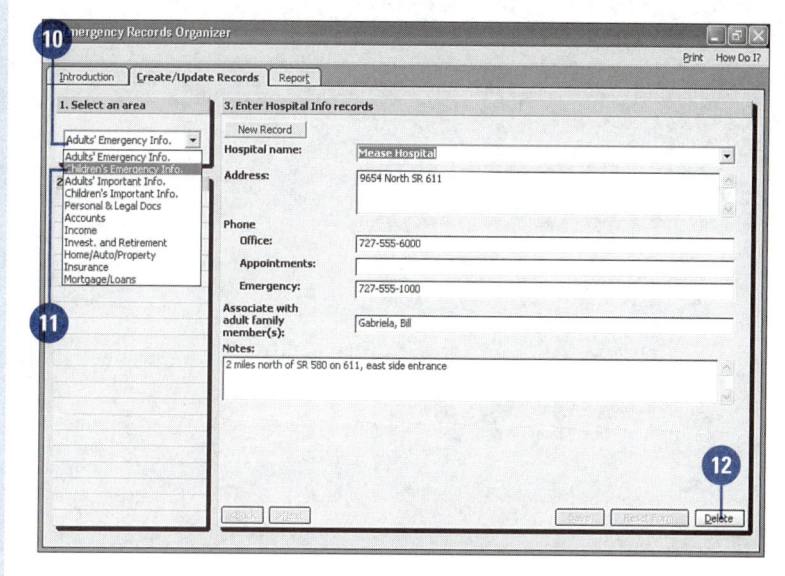

Managing Your Property and Debt   281

12 To remove a record, open it and click Delete. A message appears asking if you want to delete the record.

13 Click OK to delete the record or Cancel to keep it.

14 Repeat steps 3-13 to create all the records you want to create.

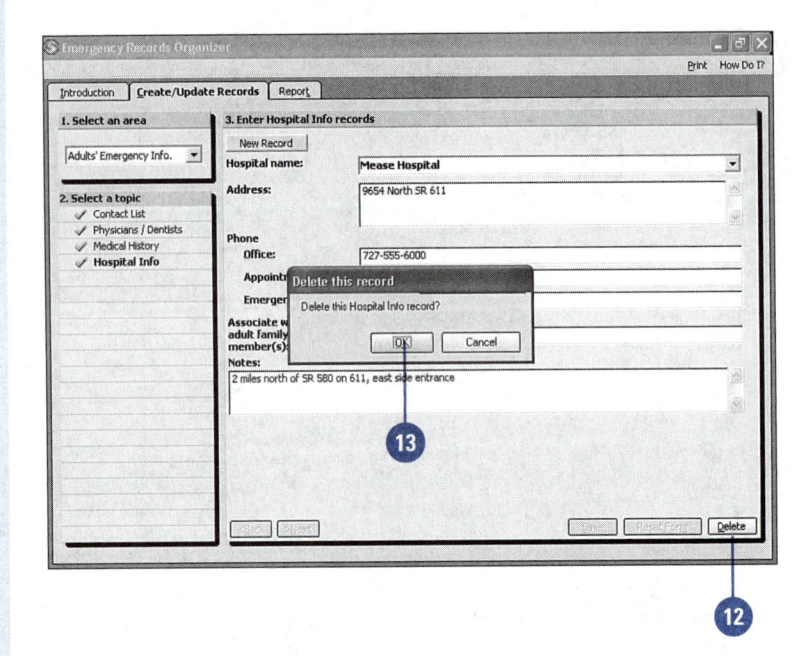

Planning for the Future

Introduction

Quicken provides planners for just about everything, with the exception of honey-do planners and how-to-get-a-spouse planners (those enhancements are coming in a future release, I think). But, for everything financial, Quicken has made it pretty easy to plan for most of life's financial events, including college, retirement, debt, budgeting, and more.

If planning is something you don't care to spend too much time on, the planners are for you. Quicken makes it easy to set up and manage plans and budgets because you have already done most of the work; all the account, investment, banking, and other financial information you have entered in Quicken is utilized by the planners. My favorite plan to set up is the budget. It literally takes all of about half of a minute to set up because Quicken has an automatic budget feature that scans all your account information, including transactions that have been entered in the past, and creates a budget for you. You can then adjust the budget to meet your needs, and that's it. Nothing is set in stone, though. All plans and budgets are flexible, in that you can change them, remove them, and create new ones to compare. You are in full control.

Quicken also has planners that can help you plan for buying a home and making special purchases, such as doing home remodeling, taking a dream vacation, or planning for a wedding. In addition, Quicken provides special calculators that allow you to get preliminary estimates for events such as retirement, college, or refinancing your home.

What You'll Do

Set Up New and Edit Existing Planning Alerts

Set Up and Change Your Planner Assumptions

Plan for Retirement

Plan for College

Plan to Purchase a Home

Get Out of Debt

Plan for a Special Purchase

Set Up a Budget

Review and Edit Your Plans

Setting Up New and Editing Existing Planning Alerts

Planning alerts work just like the other alerts in Quicken, except instead of setting alerts for balances and due dates, you can set alerts for bigger things, such as your retirement plan or budget. Creating and editing investment alerts works the same as creating and editing alerts in the other centers.

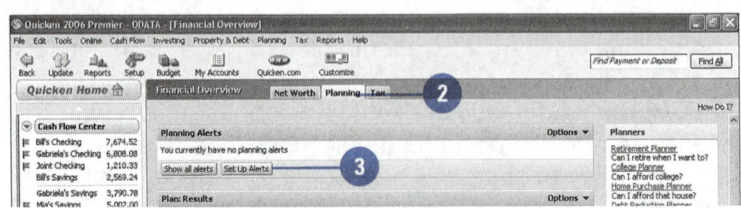

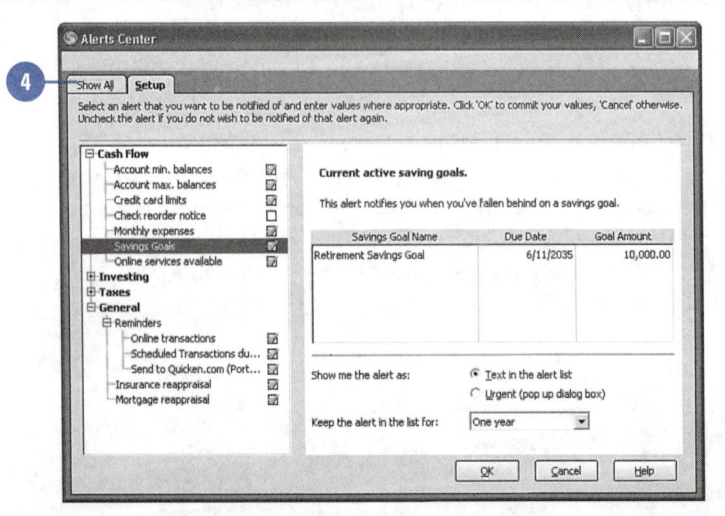

Set Up New and Edit Existing Planning Alerts

1. From the Planning menu, select Go to Planning Center.

2. Click the Planning tab.

3. To create or edit planning alerts, click Set up alerts.

4. To view and manage all your alerts, select the Show All tab. You can also click the Show All Alerts button on the Planning tab to open the Alerts Center.

See Also

See "Using Alerts" on page 74 for more information on creating or changing alerts.

Setting Up and Changing Your Planner Assumptions

Quicken gathers certain information about you and your finances to help you set up the different planners. For example, your age, income, and expenses are used to determine how much you need to save in order to retire. You can set up, change, and review your assumptions at any time. You should review your assumptions on a regular basis (for example, every six months or whenever your financial situation changes) so that Quicken can make adjustments, as needed, to ensure that your goals and plans are as accurate as possible.

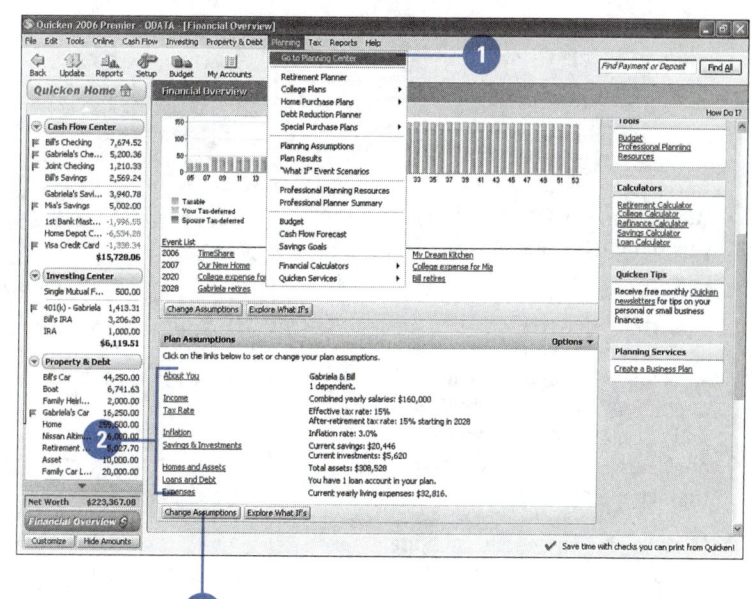

Review Planner Assumptions

1. If you don't already have the Planning tab open, from Planning menu, select Go to Planning Center and then click the Planning tab.

2. Scroll down to the Plan Assumptions section to review any information that's already listed. Click any of the links to view or change the information.

3. To set up or change all assumptions, click Change Assumptions.

Planning for the Future 285

Review and Change Your Personal Information

1. In the About you section of the Planning assumptions window, review your age, retirement, and dependent information. To change any of this information, click Edit.

2. Change any of the information about yourself or your spouse.

3. To add new dependent information, click New.

4. Enter the new dependent's information and click OK.

5. To change dependent's information, select the dependent you want to update and click Edit.

6. Make the required changes and click OK.

7. To delete a dependent, select the dependent you want to remove and click Delete. A message appears, asking if you want to remove the dependent.

8. Click Yes to remove the dependent or No to keep the dependent.

9. When you are finished making changes, click Done.

Did You Know?

You can exclude specific information from your plan. *If you don't want certain information (for example, dependents or a specific salary) to be used when calculating your plan, you can select Exclude from plan. If you later decide you want that information included, you can go back and clear Exclude from plan. This option appears throughout the planner.*

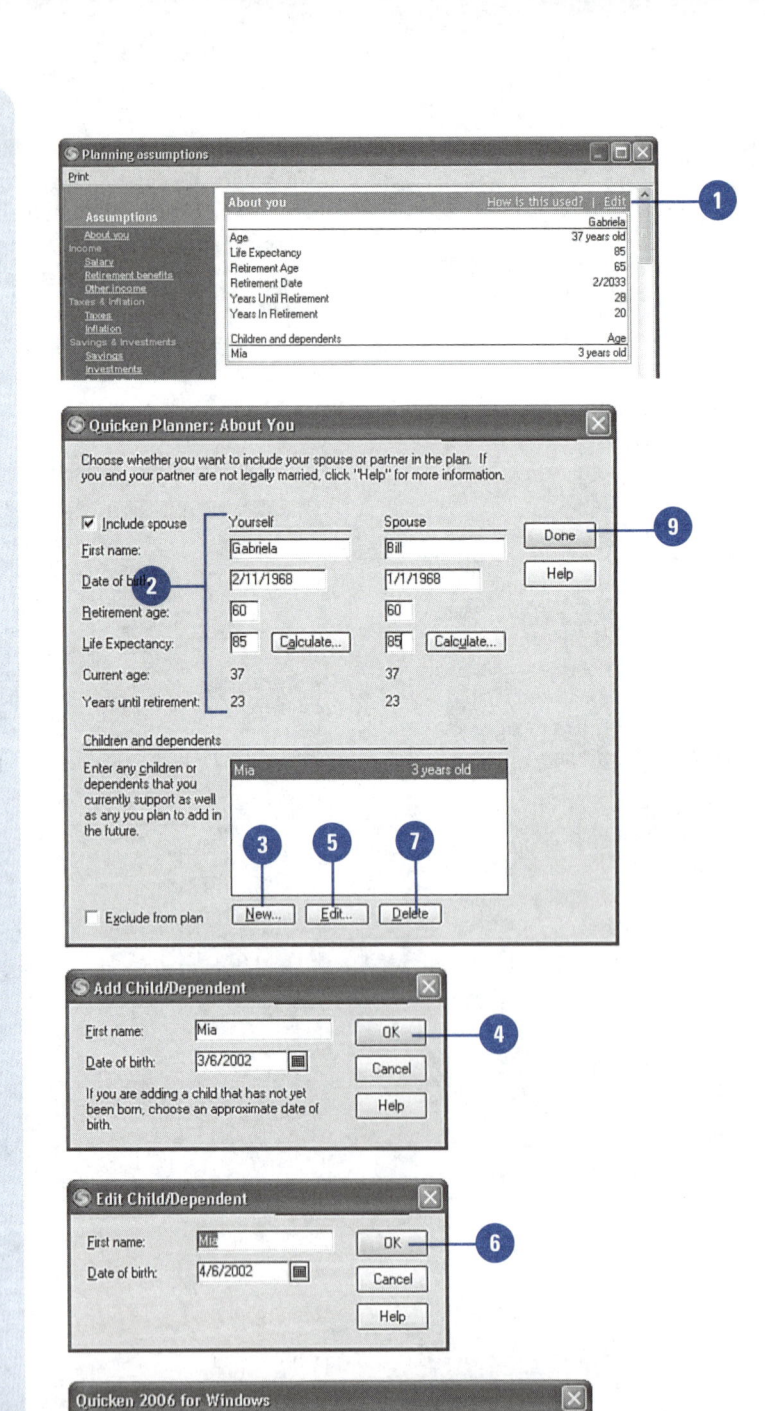

Review and Change Your Salary Information

1. Scroll down to the Salary section of the Planning assumptions window and review your salary information. To change any of the information, click Edit.

2. To make changes to a specific salary, select the salary and click Edit.

3. Make the changes and click OK.

4. To add a new salary, click New.

5. Select to whom the salary belongs.

6. Type the source of the salary and enter the yearly salary amount.

7. Leave the inflation amount as is. Quicken updates the inflation rates on a regular basis when you update your accounts and download quotes.

8. Select salary beginning and ending dates.

9. Select the employment status, and whether Social Security is taken from the salary.

10. Click OK.

11. When you are finished with the salaries, click Done.

Did You Know?

Adding and editing salaries does not change your paychecks in Quicken. *The salary information you enter in the Planning Assumptions window does not affect the paychecks already set up in Quicken. This information is used solely to make projections for your retirement income.*

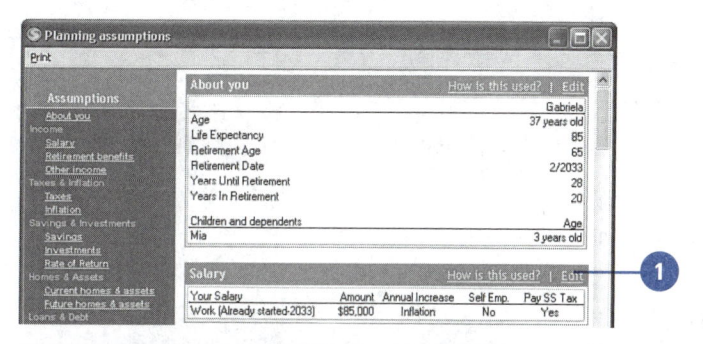

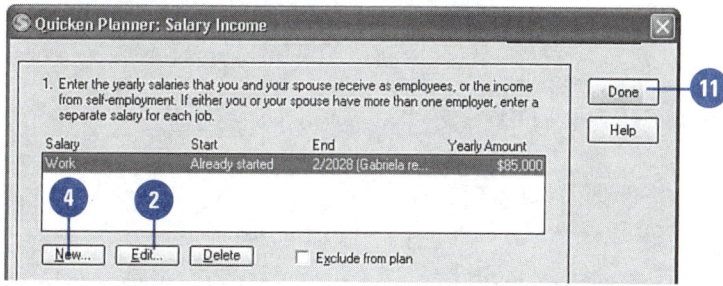

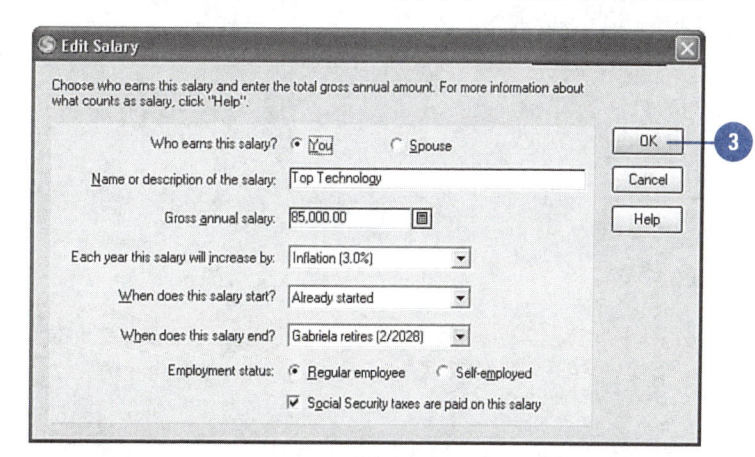

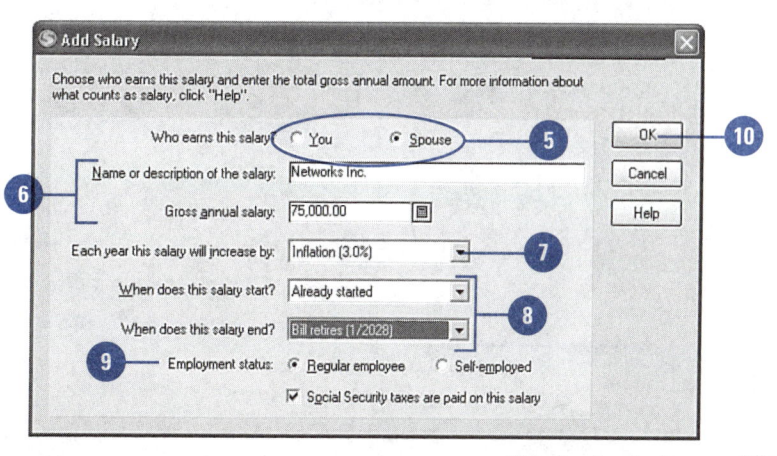

Planning for the Future **287**

Review and Change Retirement Information

1. Scroll down to the Retirement benefits section of the Planning assumptions window and review your retirement information. To make changes, click Edit.

2. Type the age at which you and your spouse (if applicable) would like to retire and the amount of Social Security you will be receiving per year. If you are not sure of the amount, click Estimate.

3. Complete your estimated Social Security benefits information and click OK.

4. To reduce the amount of Social Security you could recieve, select Yes and enter the reduction percentage. Otherwise, click No for Quicken to estimate your Social Security.

Did You Know?

You can exclude pensions to view the impact on your overall plan results. *You can exclude a pension from your plan by selecting the Exclude from plan check box on the bottom of the Quicken Planner; Retirement Benefits Window so that Quicken does not add the income from that pension into your overall plan. You can use this to view the impact to your retirement plan and then make adjustments to your plan, if needed. Excluding the pension does not remove it. You can return to the Retirement Benefits section of the Planning Assumptions window to add it back into the plan totals by clearing the check box.*

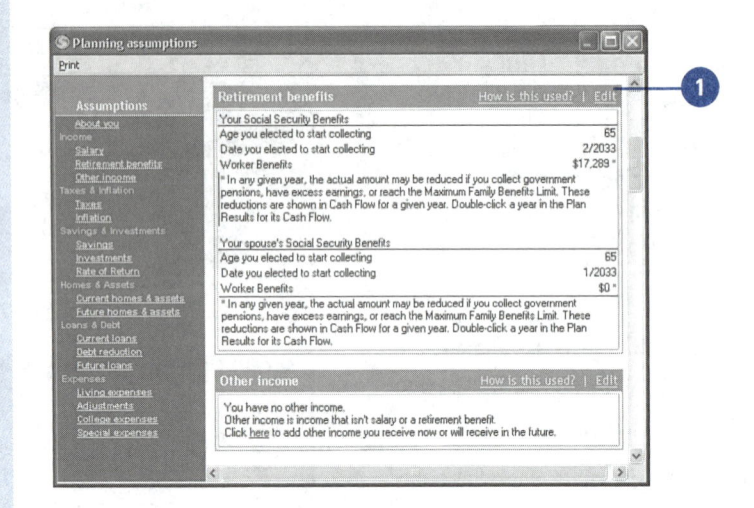

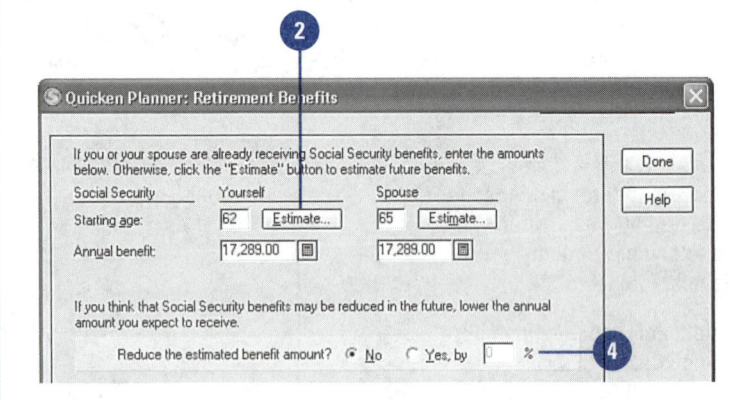

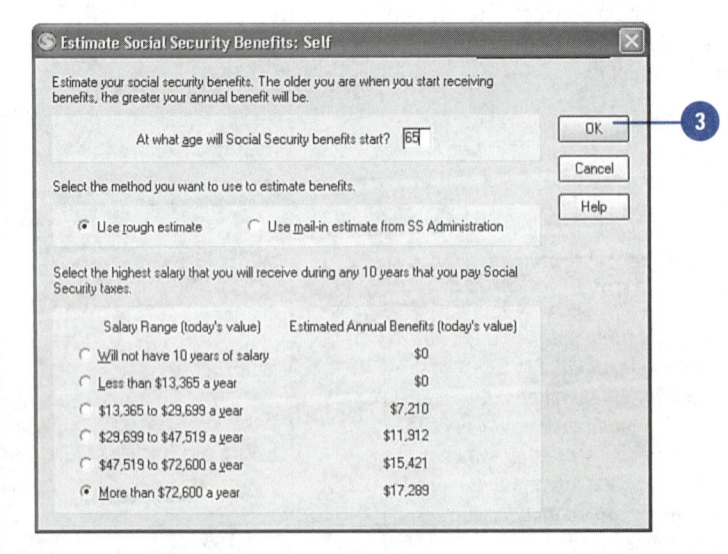

5. If you and/or your spouse have a pension, click New.

6. Complete the pension information. Be sure to use the standard inflation rate and click OK.

7. To change pension information, select it and click Edit.

8. To remove a pension, select it and click Delete.

9. When you are finished setting up and changing retirement information, click Done.

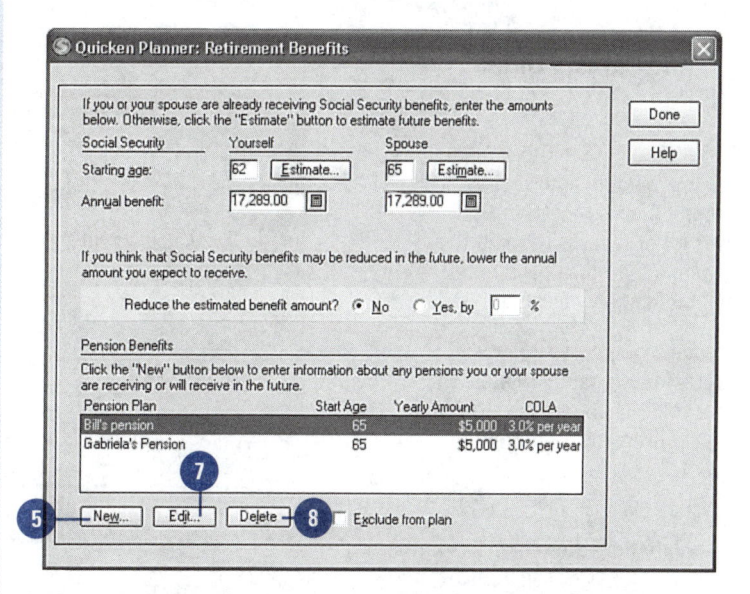

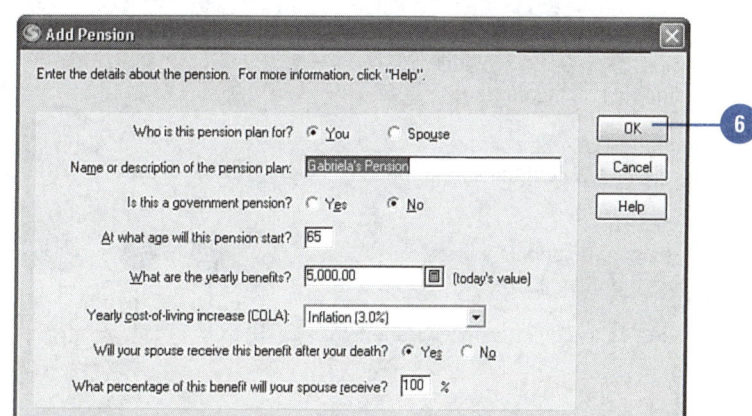

Planning for the Future **289**

Review and Change Other Income

1. Scroll down to the Other Income section of the Planning assumptions window and review your other types of income (for example, one-time payments). To make changes, click Edit.

2. If you have income that is not retirement or salary related but that you will be receiving through your retirement, click New to add it.

3. Select the type of income and then complete the information for that income type. When you are finished, click OK.

4. Repeat steps 2 and 3 to add additional income sources.

5. To change income source information, select the source and click Edit.

6. To remove an income source, select it and click Delete.

7. When you are finished, click Done.

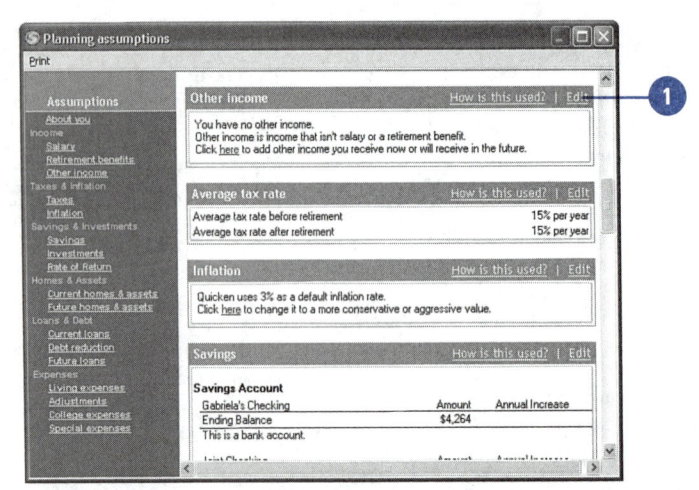

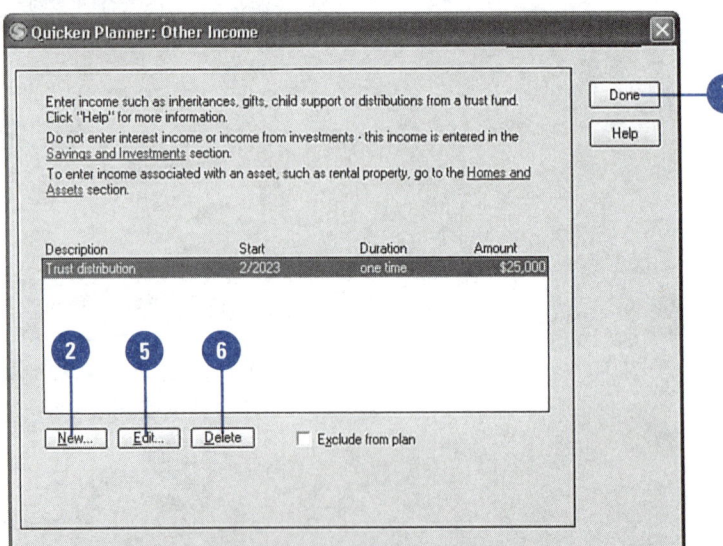

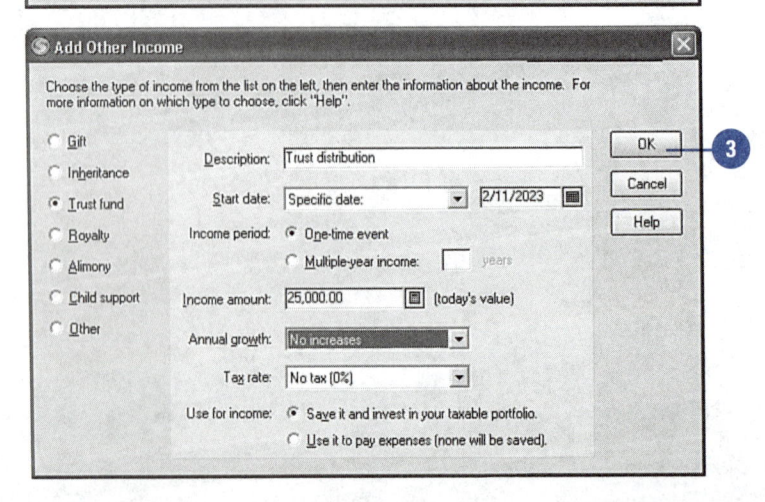

Review and Change Tax and Inflation Rates

1. Scroll down to the Average tax rate and Inflation sections of the Planning assumptions window and review your tax and inflation information.

2. To make changes to the average tax rate, in the Average Tax Rate section, click Edit.

3. To change your tax rate information, select Demographic average to use an average rate based on where you live or select Tax returns to enter the tax information from your last tax return.

4. Select or change the state you live in and select the range for your total household income.

5. If you know the adjusted rates you want to use, type the percentage rates.

6. When you are finished, click Done.

7. To change the inflation rate, from the Inflation section of the Planning assumptions window, click Edit.

8. To change the inflation rate, type the adjusted percentage rate and click Done.

Did You Know?

It is recommended that you use the standard tax and inflation rates
However, to see how changing either the standard tax and/or inflation rates might affect your plans, you can experiment with different rates in the Average tax rate and Inflation sections.

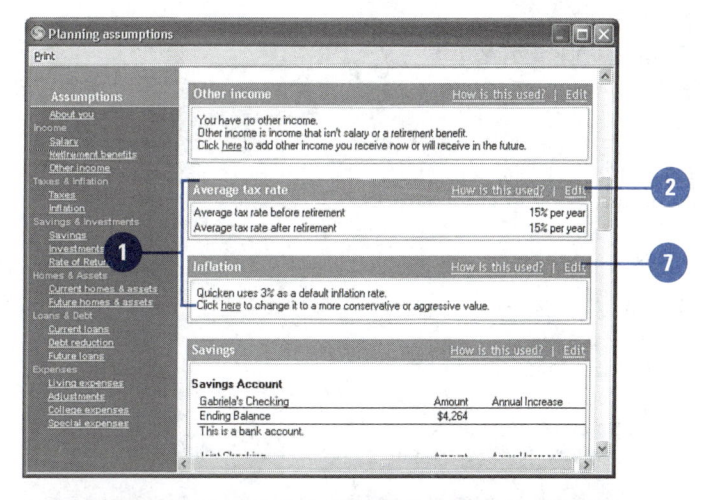

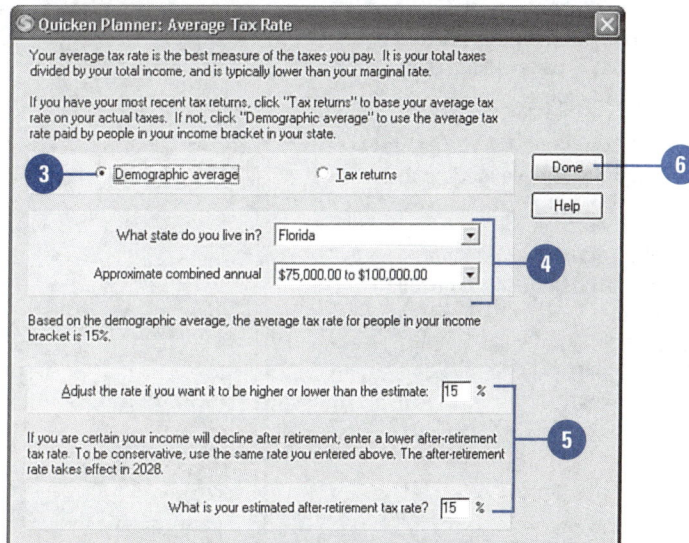

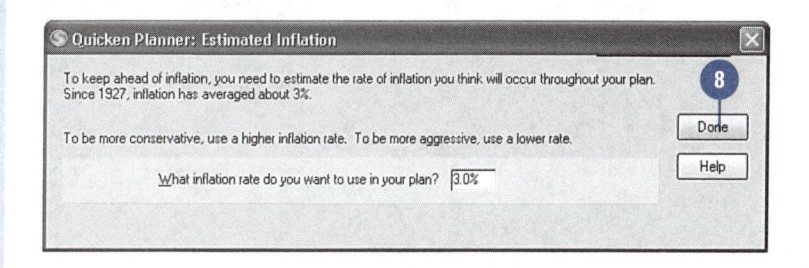

Planning for the Future **291**

Review and Change Savings Information

1. Scroll down to the Savings section of the Planning assumptions window and review your savings account information. To make changes, click Edit.

2. To exclude an account from this plan, select the account and select Exclude from plan. To view excluded accounts, select Show excluded accounts or clear it to see the accounts that are used in the plan.

3. To change the category for which an account is used, select the account and click Details.

4. From the Account will be used for drop-down menu, selelct the new category and click OK.

5. To enter regular contributions to a savings account (Quicken uses these contributions to figure your future retirement, debt, and savings goals), select the account and click New.

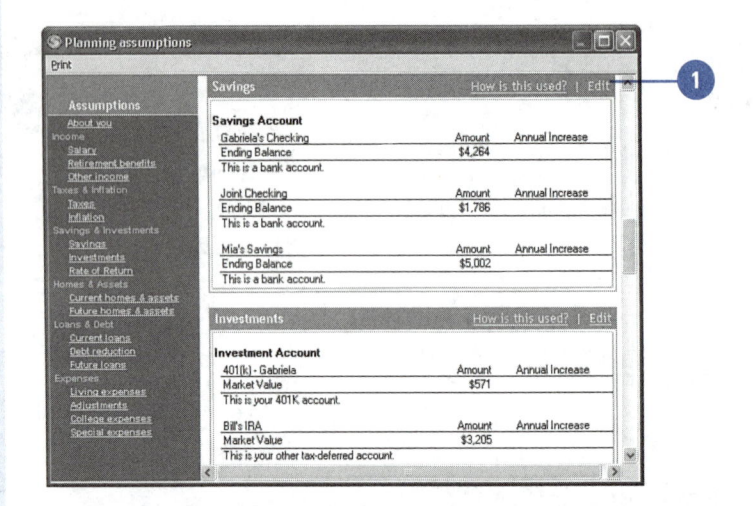

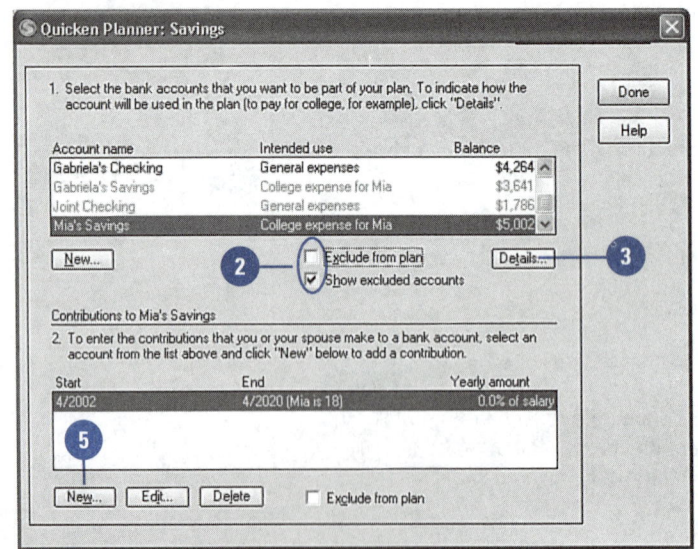

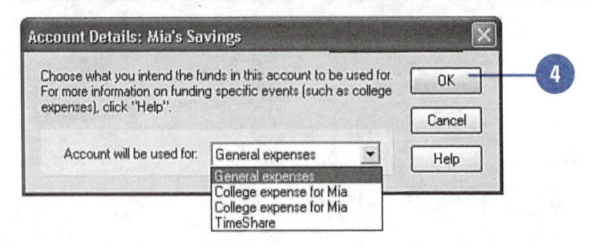

6 Select how contributions will be made to this account (using a percentage of a specific source of income or an inflation percentage). Your options after this step depend on which option you choose. Then click Next.

7 Type the contribution amount.

8 Select when the contributions are to begin or enter a specific date, if applicable.

9 If this is a one-time contribution, select One-time contribution; otherwise, enter an end date.

10 Click Done.

11 When you are finished making changes to your savings accounts, click Done.

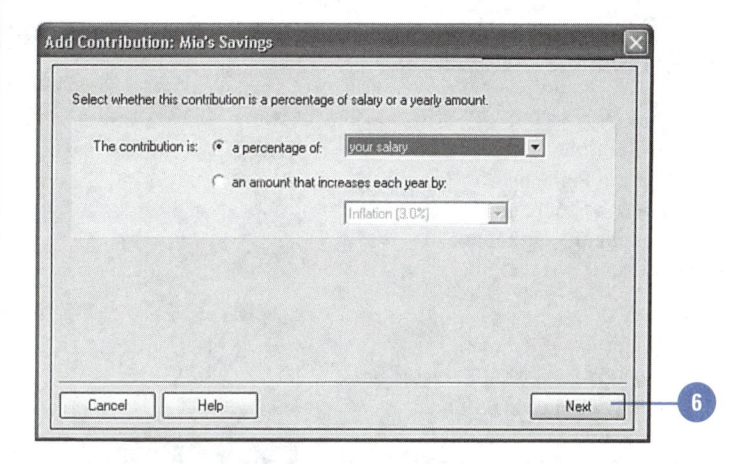

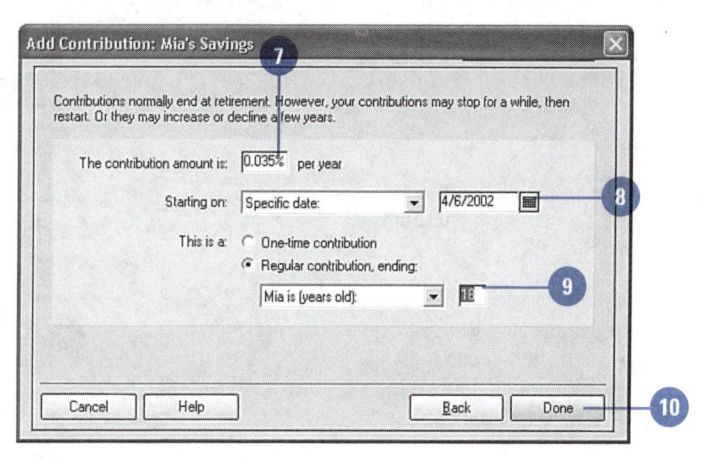

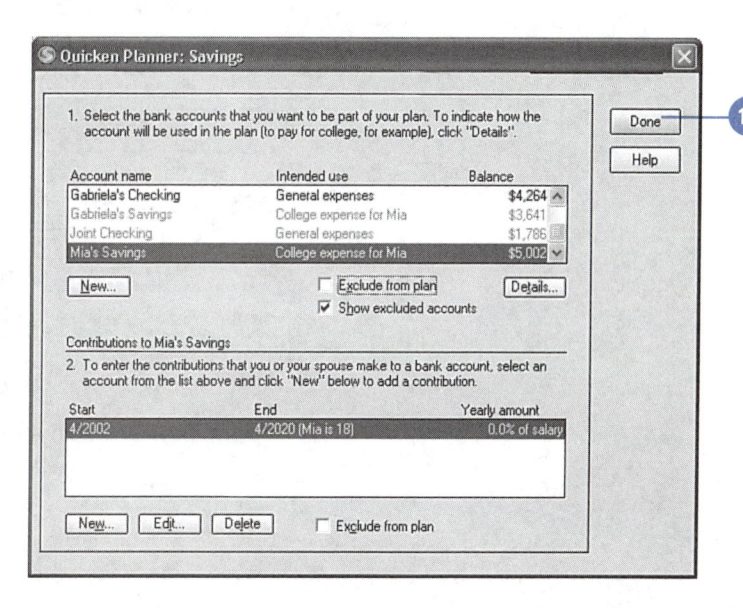

Planning for the Future **293**

Review and Change Investments Information

1. Scroll down to the Investments section of the Planning assumptions window and review your investment information. To make changes, click Edit.

2. To exclude an account from this plan, select the account and select Exclude from plan. To view excluded accounts, select Show excluded accounts or clear it to just see the accounts that are used in the plan.

3. To change the intended use for an account, select the account and click Details.

4. From the Account will be used for drop-down menu, select another option and click OK.

5. To enter regular contributions to an investment account (Quicken uses these contributions to figure your future retirement, debt, and savings goals), select the account and click New.

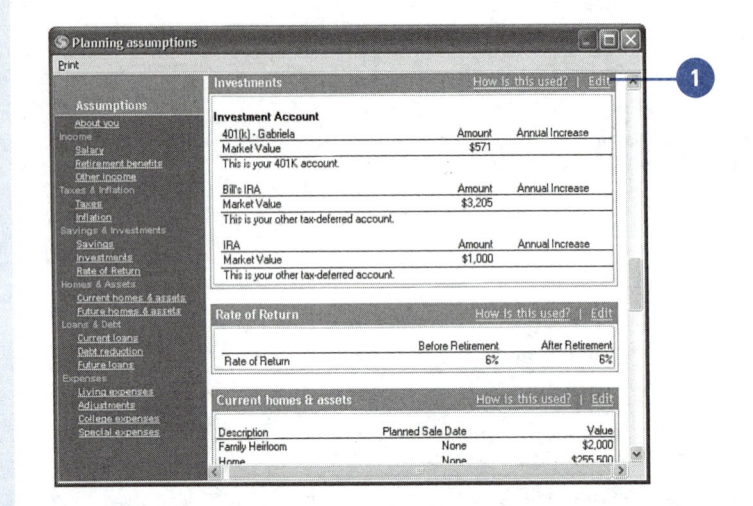

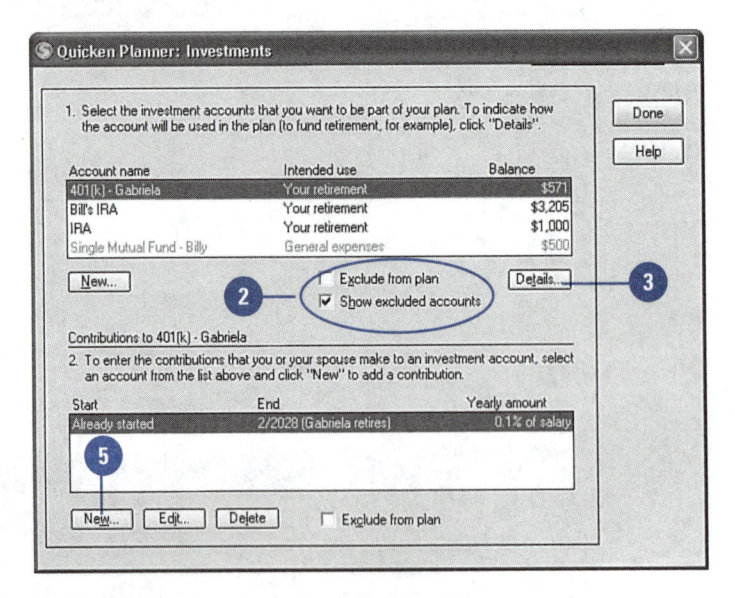

6. Select how contributions will be made to this account (using a percentage of a specific source of income or an inflation percentage). Your options after this step depend on which option you choose. Then click Next.

7. Type the contribution amount, enter start and end dates, and click Next.

8. Enter the employer contribution information and click Done.

9. When you are finished making changes to your investment accounts, click Done.

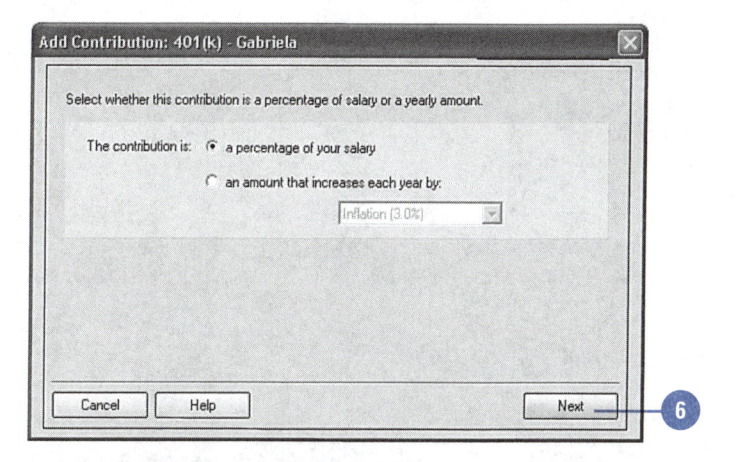

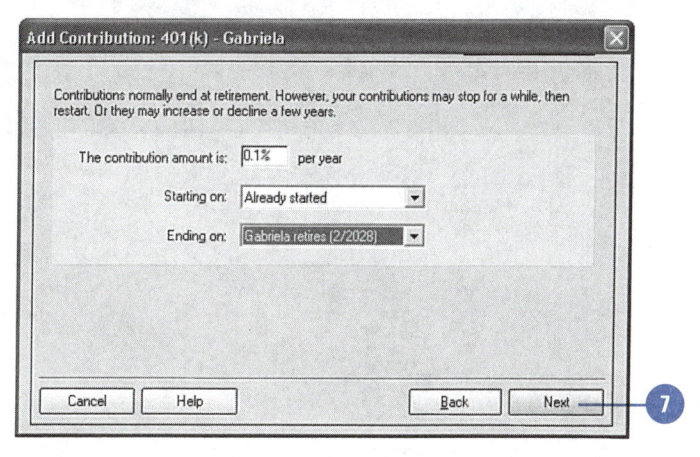

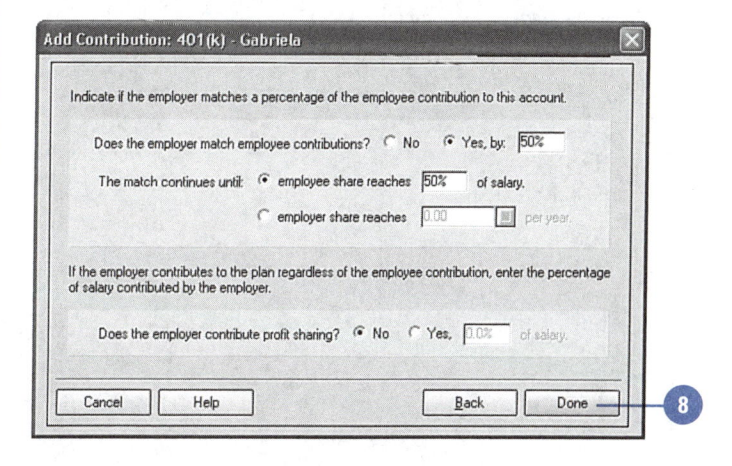

Review and Change Rate of Return Information

1. Scroll down to the Rate of Return section of the Planning assumptions window and review your return rates for before and after retirement. To make changes, click Edit.

2. Type the rates of return you expect to receive for your investments and savings accounts. If you and your spouse expect different rates, select Use Separate rates of return for taxable and tax-deferred accounts and enter the rates for each of you.

3. To err on the side of caution, keep 100% for the taxable return. This ensures that you plan adequately for taxes on your returns.

4. Click Done.

Did You Know?

Quicken uses the rate of return to help determine how much money you need in order to retire. The rate of return you enter is used to determine whether you will have the money you need to cover your expenses when you retire. The higher the rate, the more risk you should take with your investments.

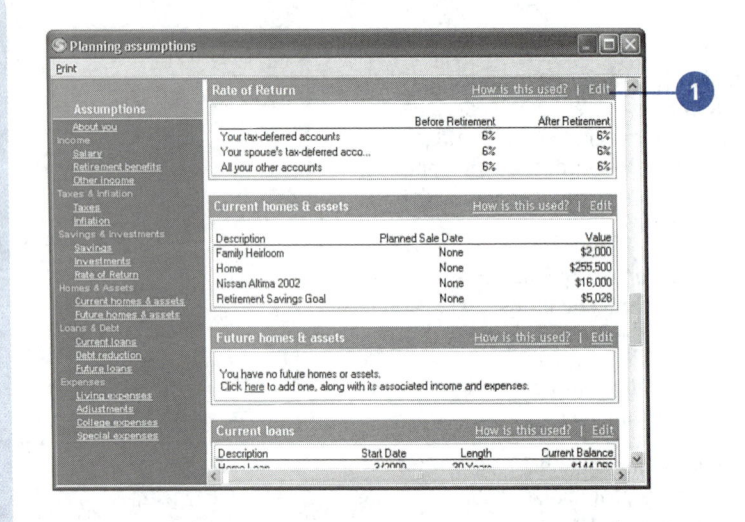

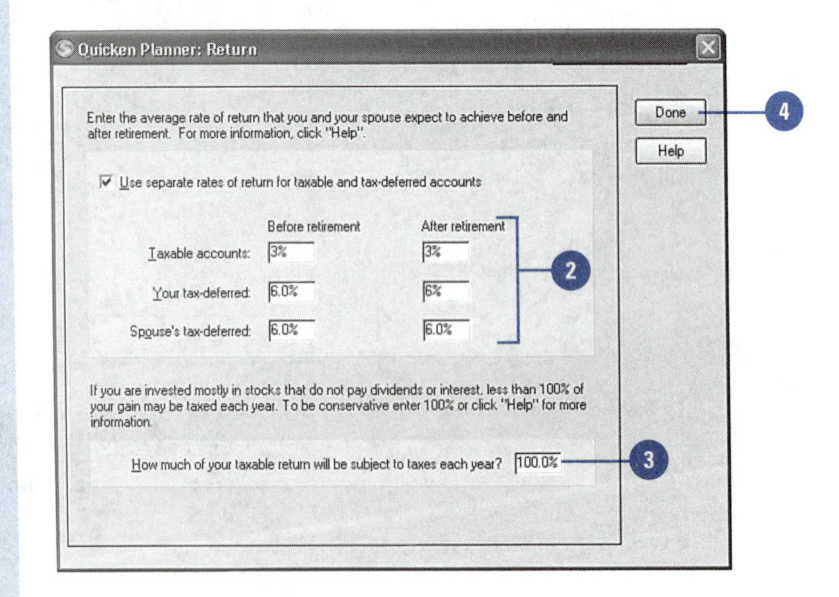

Review and Change Current and Future Asset and Property Information

1. Scroll down to the Current homes & assets section of the Planning assumptions window and review your assets information. To make changes, click Edit.

2. If you are planning to sell any of your property or assets, select the asset or property and click Sale Info. The option you select determines the options you see in the Asset Account Sale Information dialog box. This example uses a home.

3. Change any of the purchase or inflation information, if needed, and click Next.

4. If the property is your primary residence, select This house is or will be my primary residence and then select whether you intend to sell the property.

5. If you intend to sell the property, select approximately when you will sell it or enter an approximate date. Click Next.

Did You Know?

You should use the Future Homes & Assets section to set up homes or assets you are thinking of purchasing. To see how a new home or asset would affect your plan, in the Future home & assets section, you can click Edit and set up a new home or asset. When you see the results, you can remove the asset or save it to use in your plan.

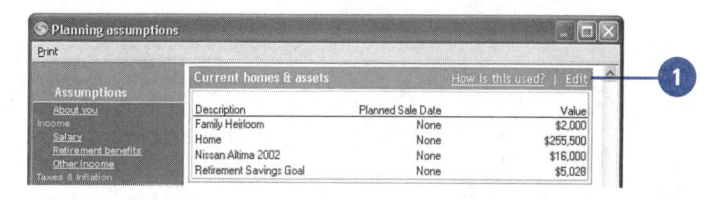

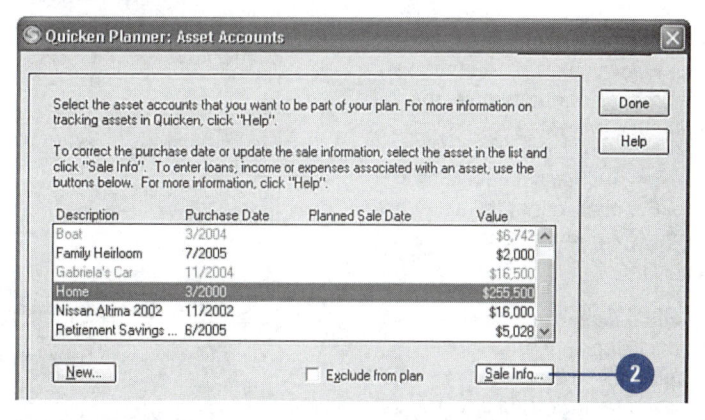

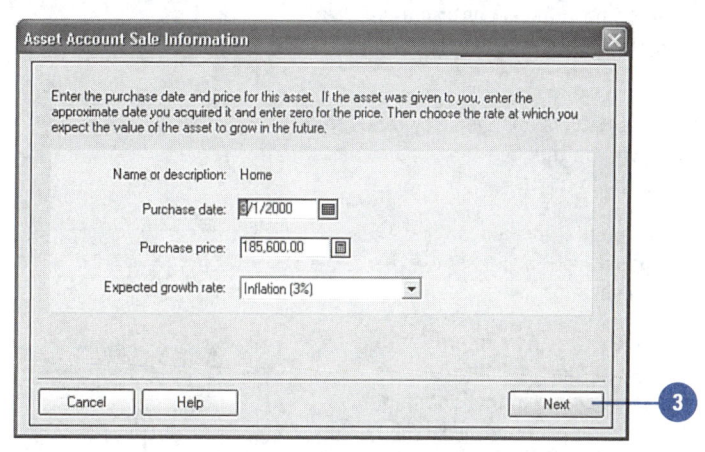

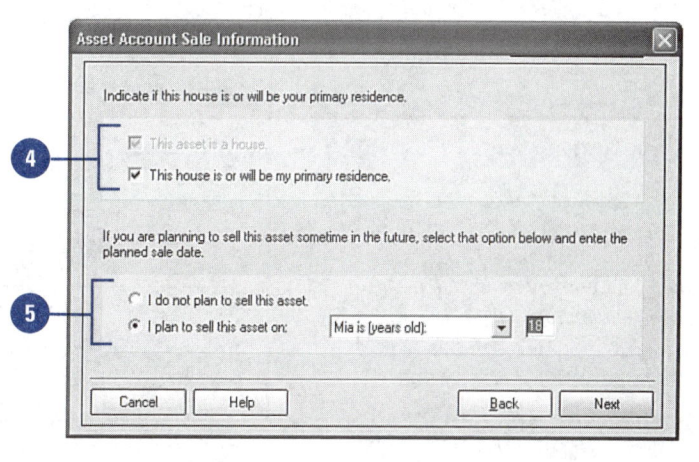

Planning for the Future **297**

6 Type an approximate total amount for home improvements between now and when you plan to sell and the expected sales fee. Use the defaults for both the tax rate and exemption, and click Next.

7 Select whether you intend to use the money you make from the sale to purchase another home and then click Done.

8 To exclude an asset or property from the plan, select the asset or property and then select Exclude from plan.

9 To add a loan, expenses (for example, upkeep for a rental property), or income (for example, rent you receive from a rental property) for an asset or property, select the asset and click Loan, Expenses, or Income.

10 To add a new asset, click New and complete the Quicken Account Setup dialog box.

11 When you are finished making changes to your assets and properties, click Done.

12 To add property as a future purchase, from the Future homes & assets section of the Planning assumptions window, click Edit and then click New. Follow the prompts to add the new property.

Did You Know?

Holding on to your property for at least two years pays off. You can exempt up to approximately $250,000 if you keep your primary residence for at least two years before selling it.

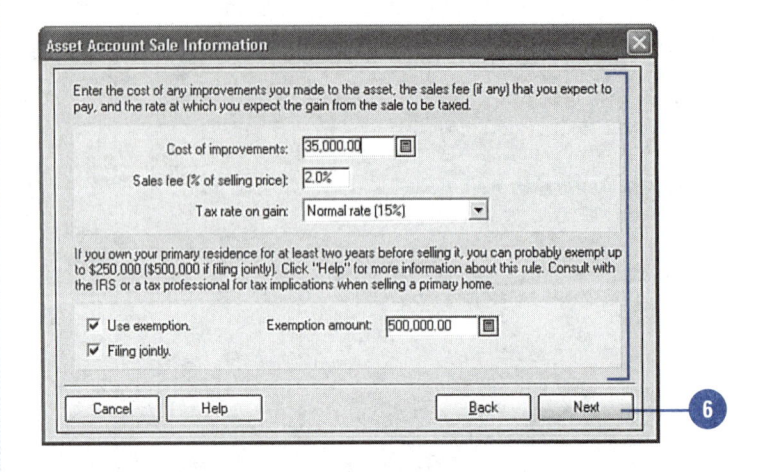

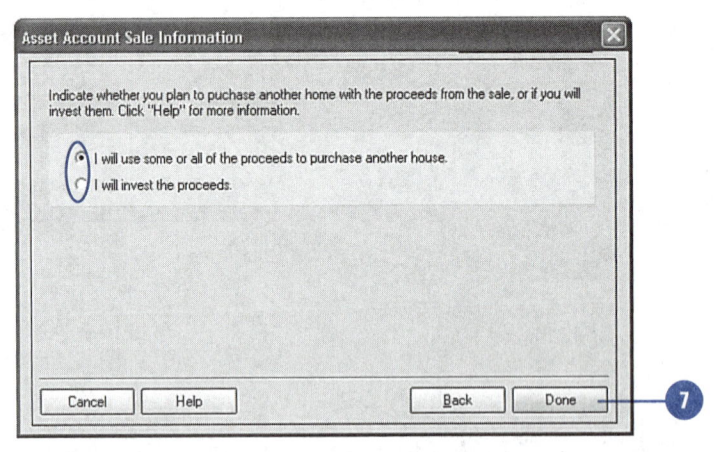

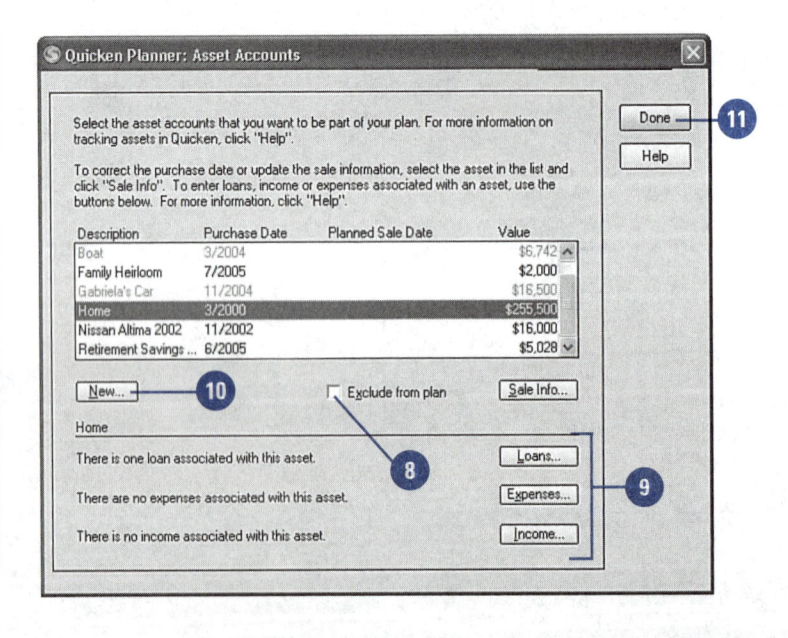

298

Review and Change Current and Future Loan and Debt Information

1. Scroll down to the Current loans section of the Planning assumptions window and review your loan information. To make changes, click Edit.

2. To review loan details, select the loan. The loan details appear at the bottom of the Loan Accounts window.

3. To exclude a loan from the plan, select the loan and then select Exclude from plan.

4. To adjust payoff information, select the loan and click Payoff.

5. Select whether there will be a balloon payment for early payoff and click OK.

6. To add a new loan, click New and complete the Loan Setup dialog box.

7. Click Done when you are finished reviewing and making changes to your loan accounts.

8. To add potential future loans that are not related to any property or asset, from the Future loans section of the Planning assumptions window, click Edit and then click New. Follow the prompts to add the new loan.

See Also

See "Getting Out of Debt" on page 326 for information on using the Debt Reduction section of the Planning assumptions window.

Planning for the Future 299

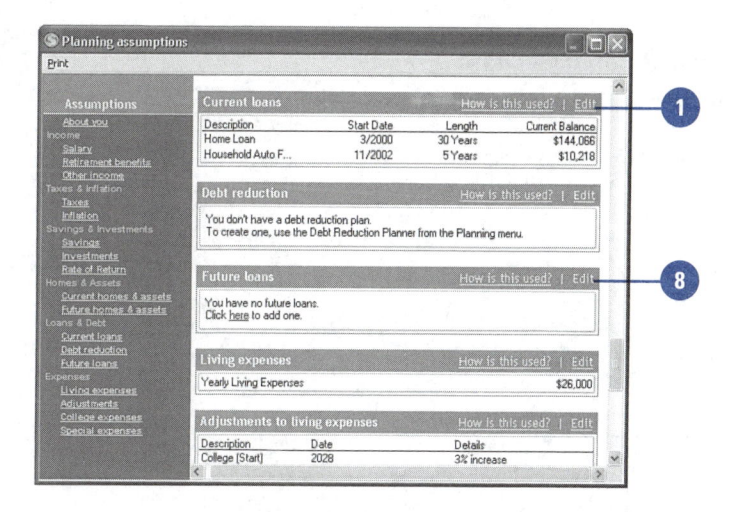

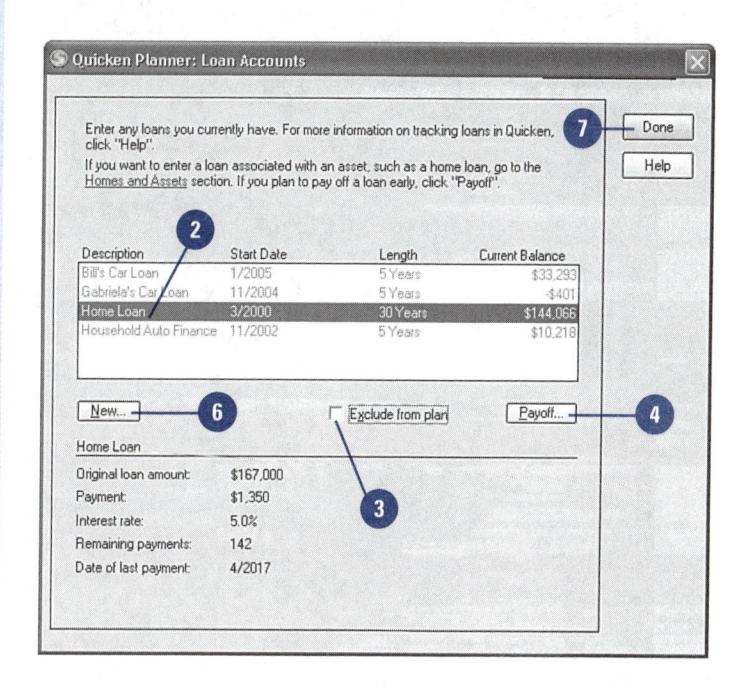

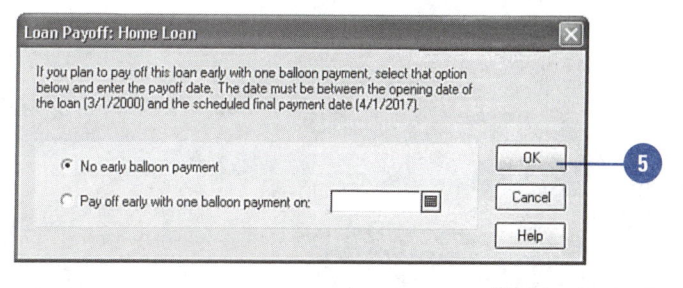

Review and Change Living Expenses Information

1. Scroll down to the Living expenses section of the Planning assumptions window and review your yearly living expense information. To make changes, click Edit.

2. To use an estimate that Quicken has predetermined (based on your current bills and expenses), select Rough estimate and change the yearly living expenses amount.

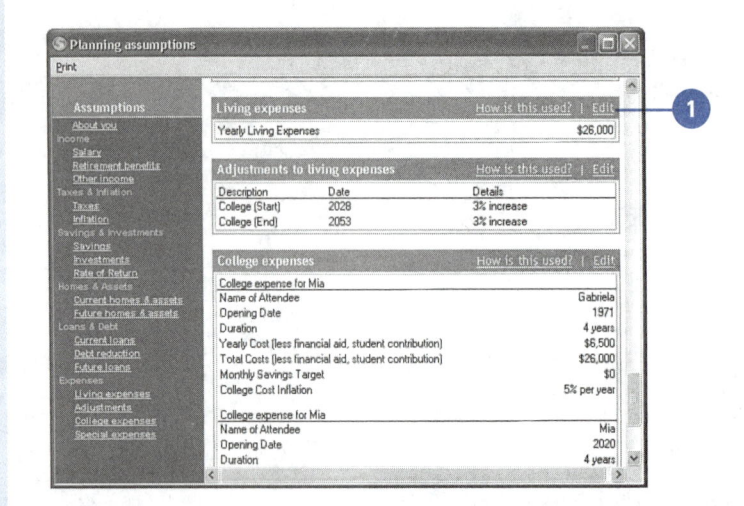

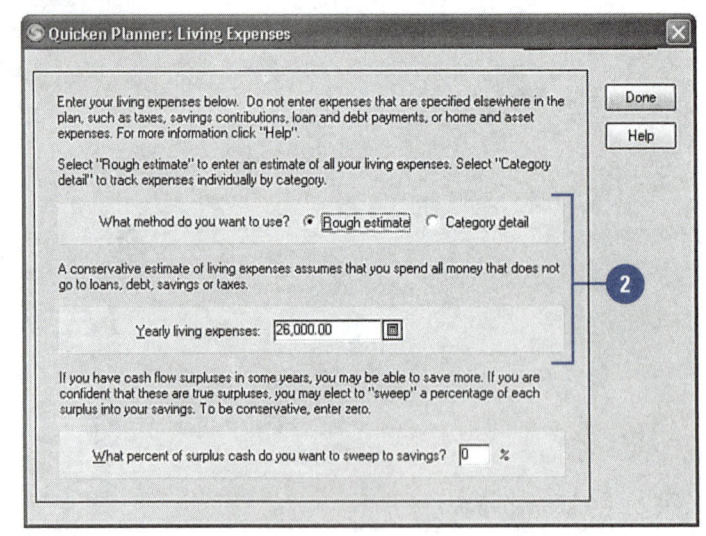

3. To use the total derived from amounts you enter for all expense categories, select Category detail and then click Details.

4. To specify the date range you want Quicken to use for category estimates, click Estimate.

5. Enter the new date ranges and click OK.

6. To view only living expense categories, select the Only show living expense categories check box.

7. To change the living expense amounts, click in the Monthly Amount column for each category and type the amount that you use each month. Then click OK.

8. Click Done.

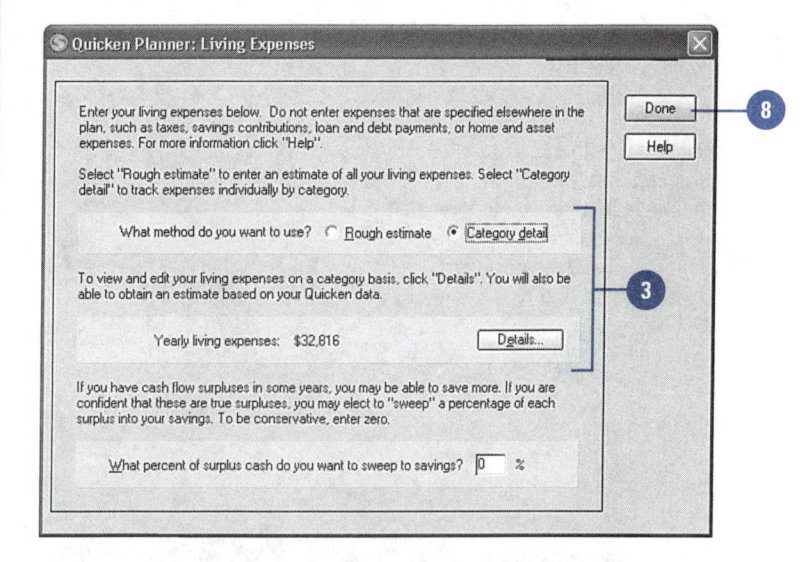

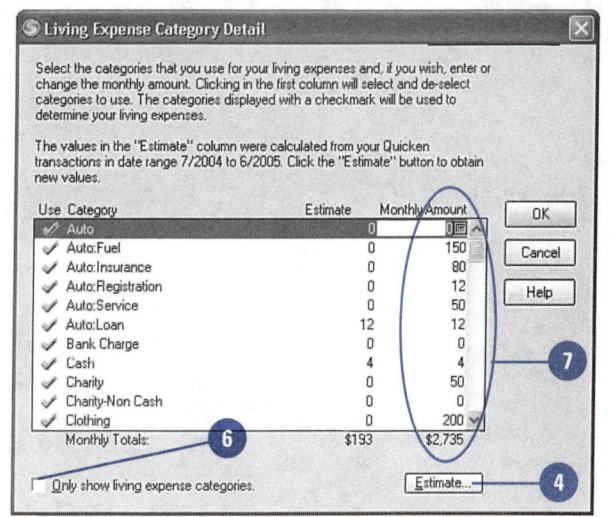

Planning for the Future **301**

Review and Change Adjusted Living Expenses

1. Scroll down to the Adjustments to living expenses section of the Planning assumptions window and review any adjustments you are planning to make to your yearly living expenses. To make changes, click Edit.

2. To add a life event, click New.

3. Select whether the event is for a specific person, complete the adjustment information, and click OK.

4. To update an adjustment, select it and click Edit.

5. To remove an adjustment, select it and click Delete.

6. To exclude an event from your plan, select the event and select the Exclude from plan check box.

7. When you have completed the adjustments, click Done.

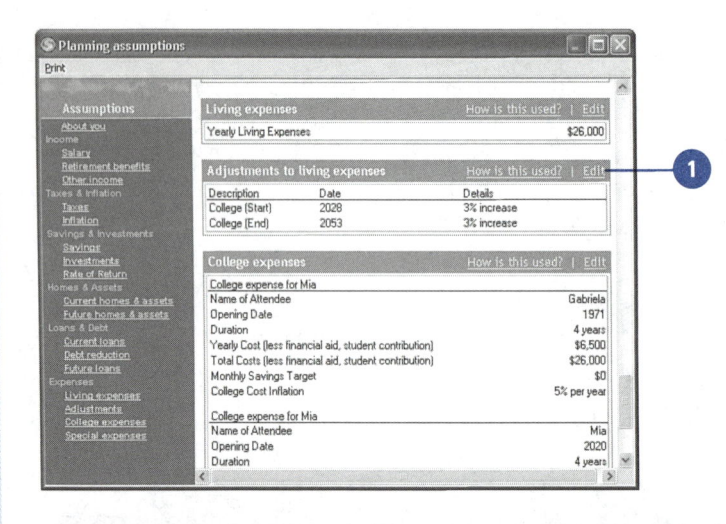

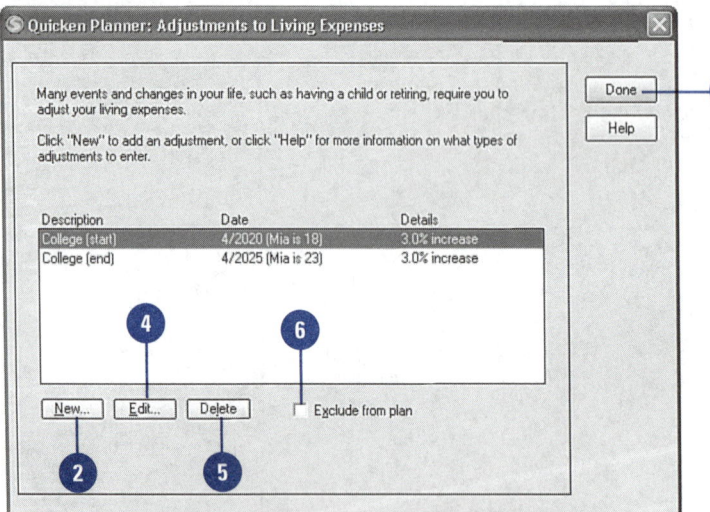

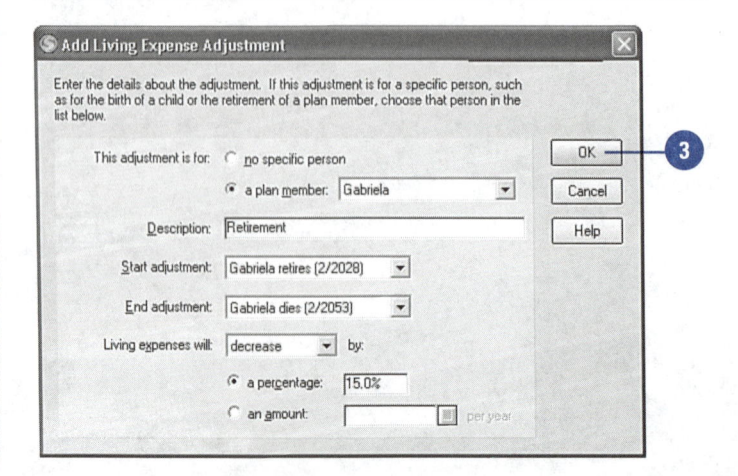

See Also

See "Planning for College" on page 312 for information on using the College Expenses section of the Planning Assumptions window.

Review and Change Special Expenses

1. Scroll down to the Special Expenses section of the Planning assumptions window and review any additional expenses you are planning. To make changes, click Edit.

2. To add a new expense, click New.

3. Select whether the expense is for a specific person, type a description for it, and then click Next.

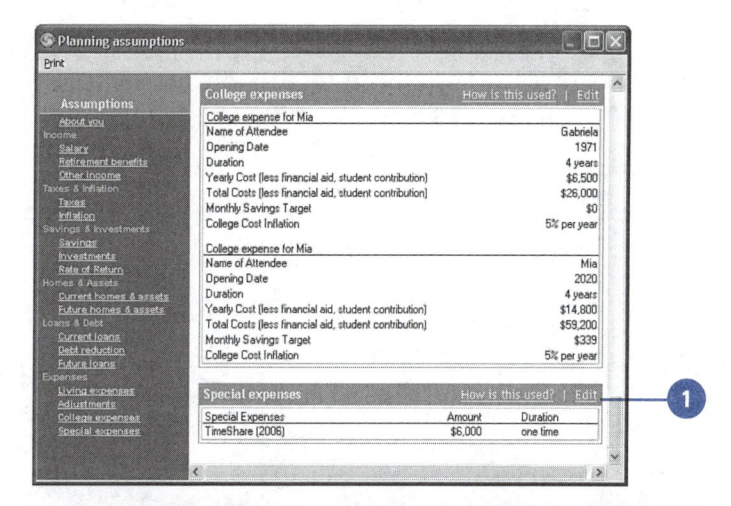

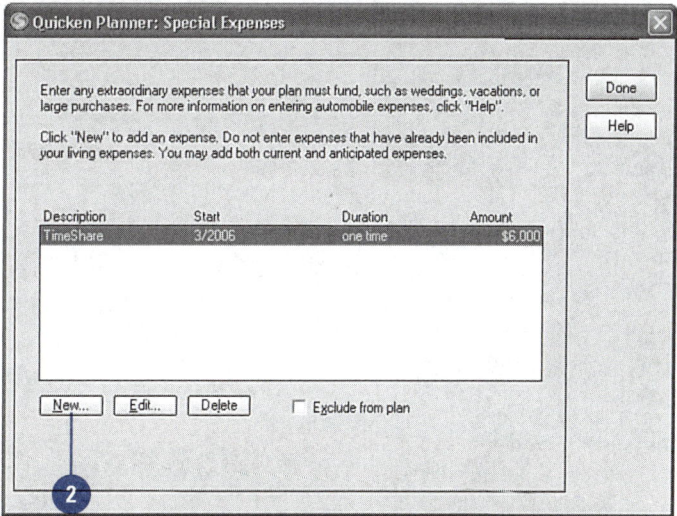

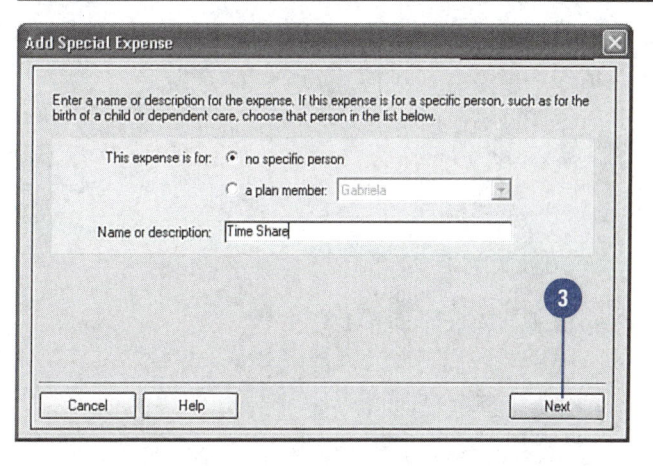

Planning for the Future **303**

4. Type the approximate date for the expense, the duration, and the expense amount and then click Next.

5. To select the accounts you plan to use to fund the expense (if any), click Choose accounts.

6. If you do not have a specific account to fund the expense, select General expenses; otherwise, select Specific accounts. The option you select determines what you see in the next step. This example uses the first option.

7. If you have money to apply toward the expense, enter that amount and type the date you expect to have the money. For example, if you selected Specific accounts in step 6, you would select the account you want to use in this step.

8. Click OK. Quicken fills in the top portion of the Add Special Expense dialog box with the account information.

9. In the Amount from loans box, enter the loan amount you want for the expense, if a loan will be used. The amount you need to save monthly to pay for the expense appears in the Monthly Savings Target box.

10. To change how you would like to fund the expense, repeat steps 5–9; otherwise, click Done.

11. You can edit, exclude, or delete special expenses just as you have for other expenses in the Planning assumptions planner.

12. Close the Special Expenses dialog box and the Planner assumptions window when you are finished.

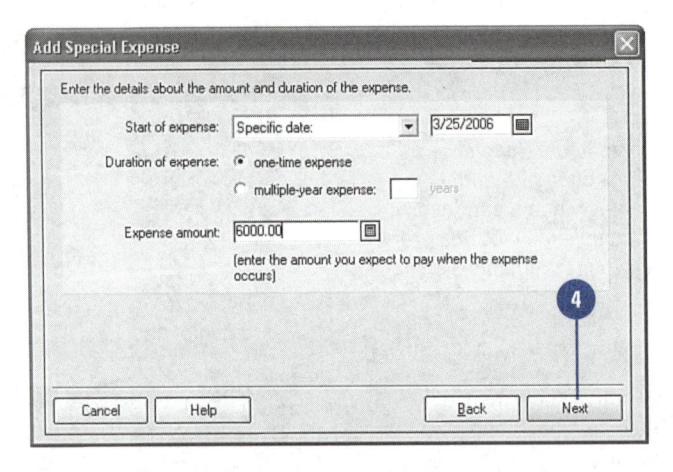

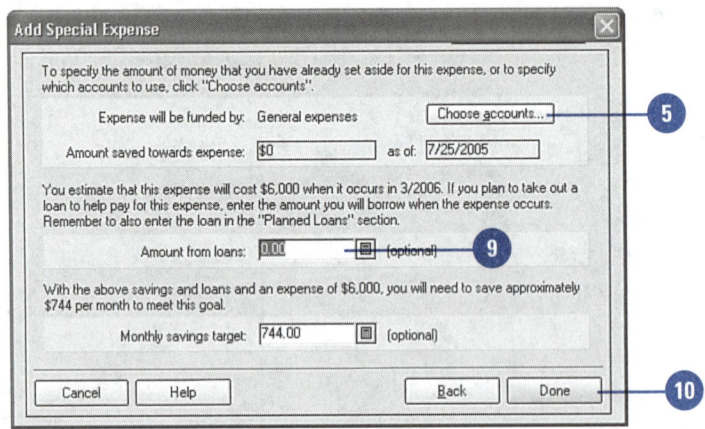

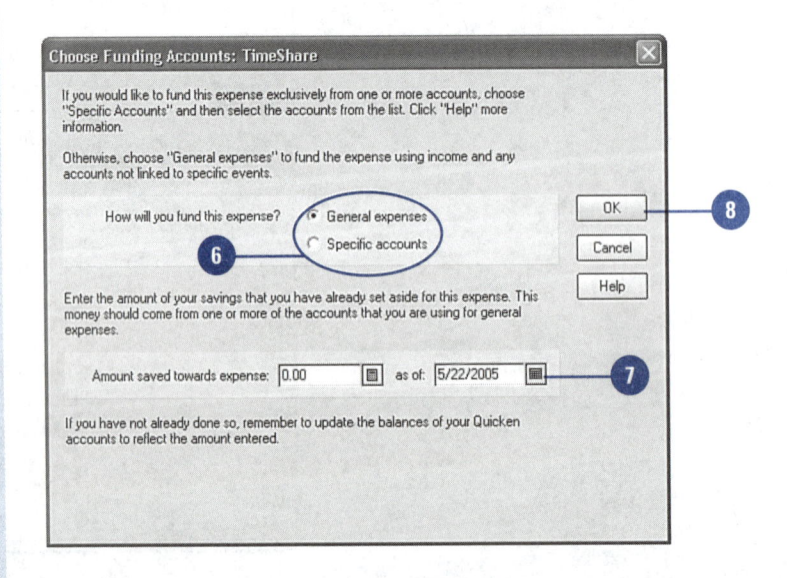

Review and Change Planner Assumptions and What-if Scenarios

1. If you don't already have the Planning tab open, from the Planning menu, click Go to Planning Center and then click the Planning tab.

2. Scroll down to the Plan Assumptions section and click Change Assumptions to open the Planning Assumptions window.

3. Click any of the sections to make changes and close the window when you are finished.

4. To explore different scenarios or situations to see how they change the outcome of your plans, click Explore What If's.

5. Select a what-if scenario, such as changing your retirement age.

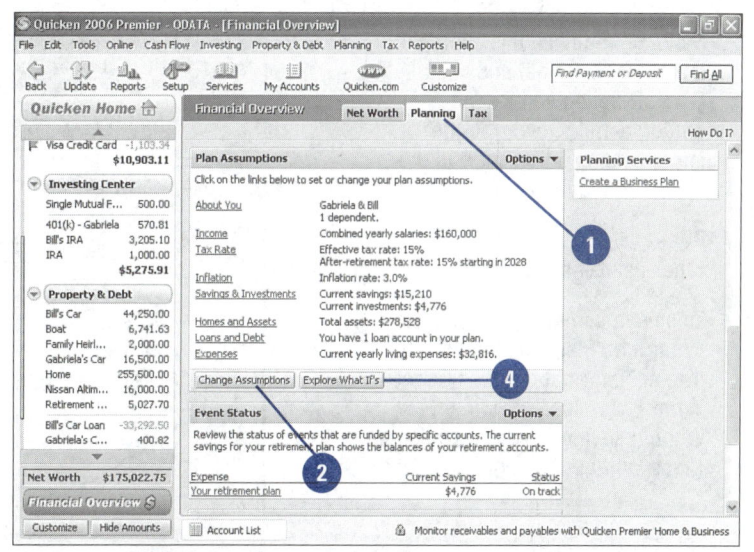

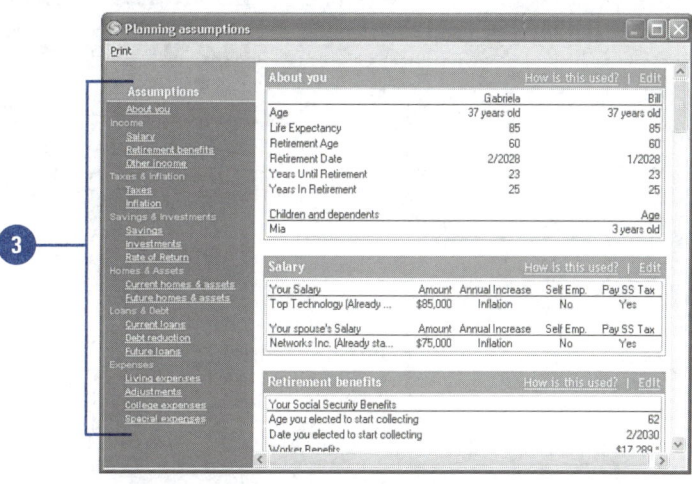

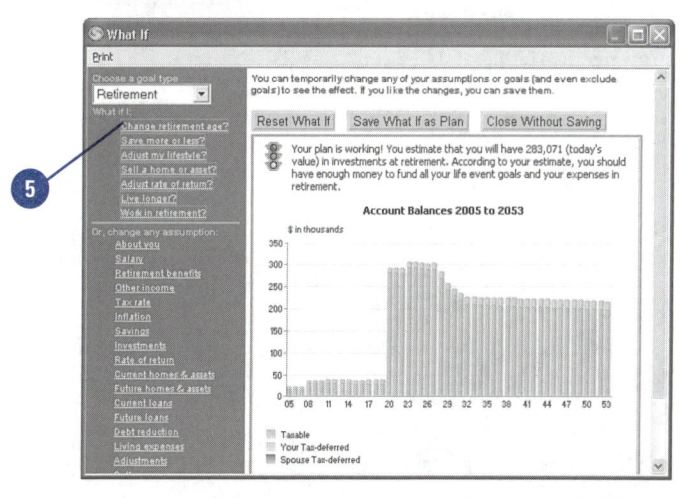

Planning for the Future 305

6 Make changes (in this example, the retirement age) and click Done. Quicken adjusts the outcome and shows you the impact, using a line chart in the What If window.

7 Repeat steps 5–6 to play with other what-if scenarios.

8 To save a scenario, click Save What If as Plan. To revert to the original information, click Reset What If. To close the window without saving anything, click Close Without Saving.

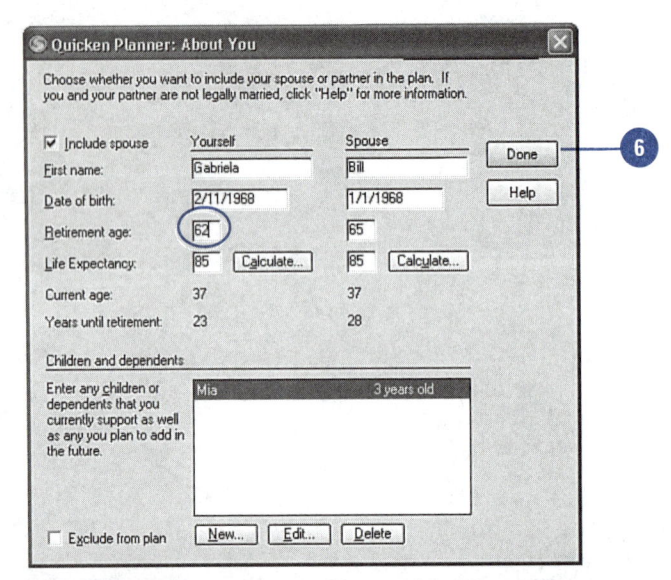

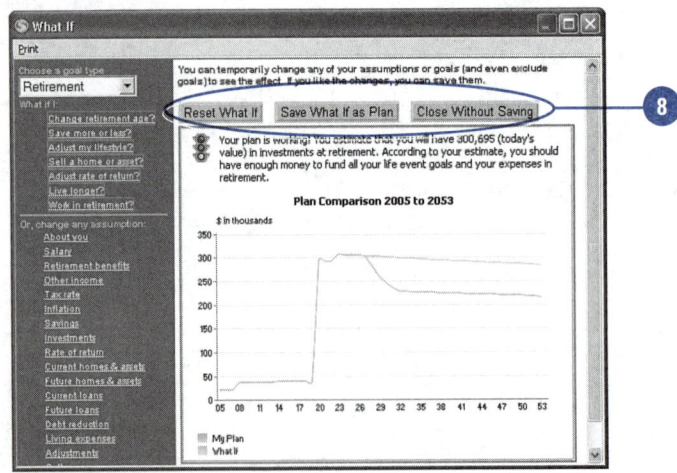

Using Calculators

The Calculators section of the Planning tab in the Financial Overview center provides a series of calculators that can help you crunch numbers for retirement, college, refinancing, savings goals, and loans. Each calculator is customized to determine the potential for the particular situation. For example, if you want to see whether it would be advantageous to refinance your home, you can use the Refinance Calculator to find out. Using the Refinance Calculator as an example, let's step through how the calculators work:

1. In the Calculators section of the Planning tab, click Refinance Calculator.

2. Type the current payment and escrow amounts for your existing mortgage.

3. Enter the principal amount, the length of the loan (in years), and the interest rate for the new mortgage.

4. Type any closing costs and points you will be charged.

5. Click Calculate.

6. If needed, change any of the information in steps 2–4 and click Calculate again to see how different figures affect the outcome.

7. When you are finished, click Done. You can use the other calculators in the same way.

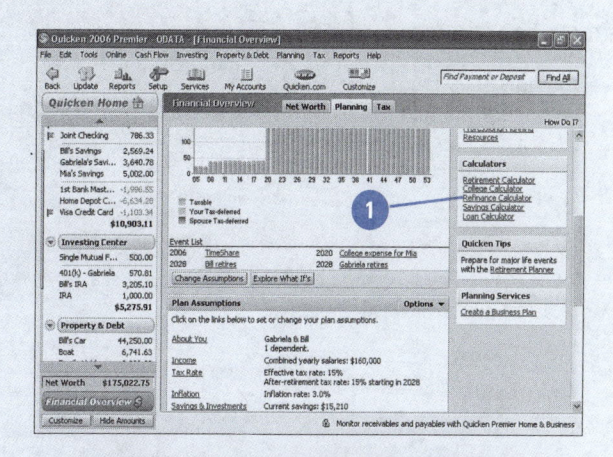

Planning for the Future 307

Planning for Retirement

No matter your age, it's never too early to plan for your retirement. One of the many great planners you can use in Quicken is the Retirement planner. You can set up a retirement plan to determine when you can retire and how much you need to start saving in order to retire and ensure you will be comfortable during that period of your life. The information contained in the retirement plan is derived from the assumptions you set up in the Planning assumptions planner window, so most of the information is already completed for you. You can, however, change it, if needed.

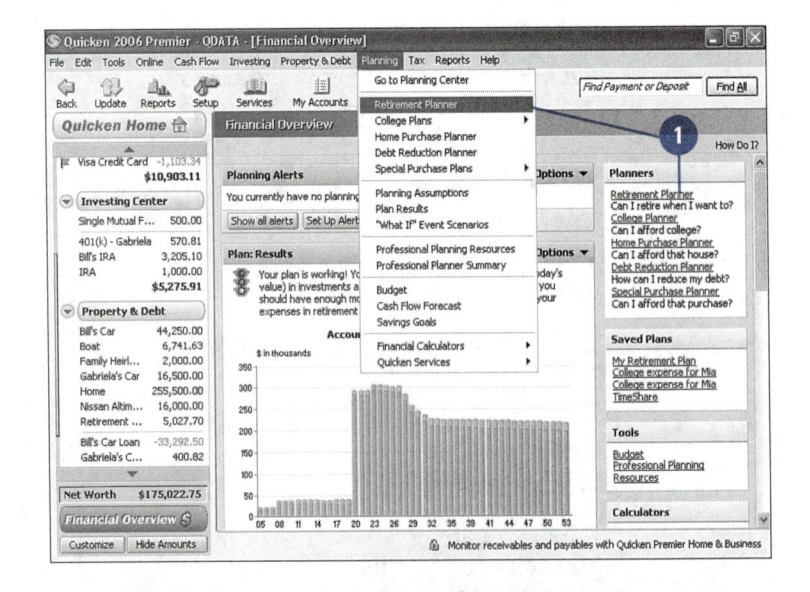

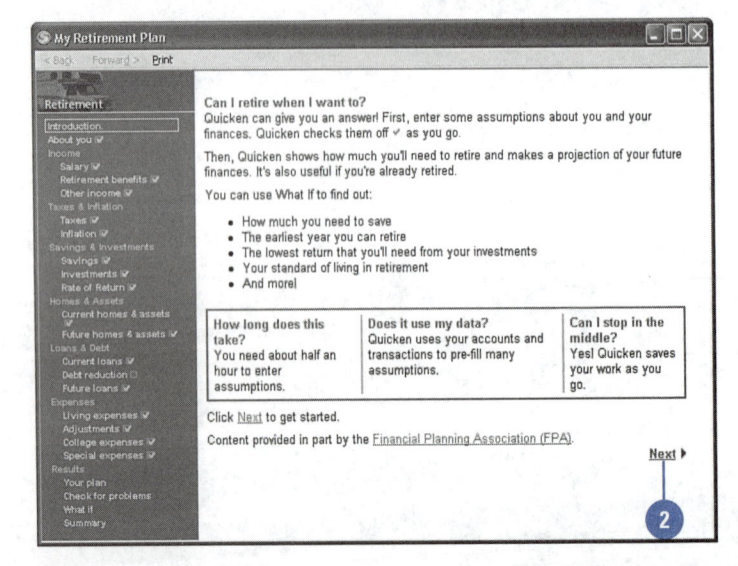

Plan for Retirement

1. From the Planning menu, select Retirement Planner. Or click the Retirement Planner link in the Planners section of the Planning tab. The My Retirement Plan window opens.

2. Review the introduction and click Next to get started with a plan.

3. Review the About you section. To change any of the information, click Edit.

4. Make any necessary changes and then click Next to move on.

5. Continue reviewing each section, making any changes, if needed, by clicking the Edit links. Click Next to proceed through the Retirement planner.

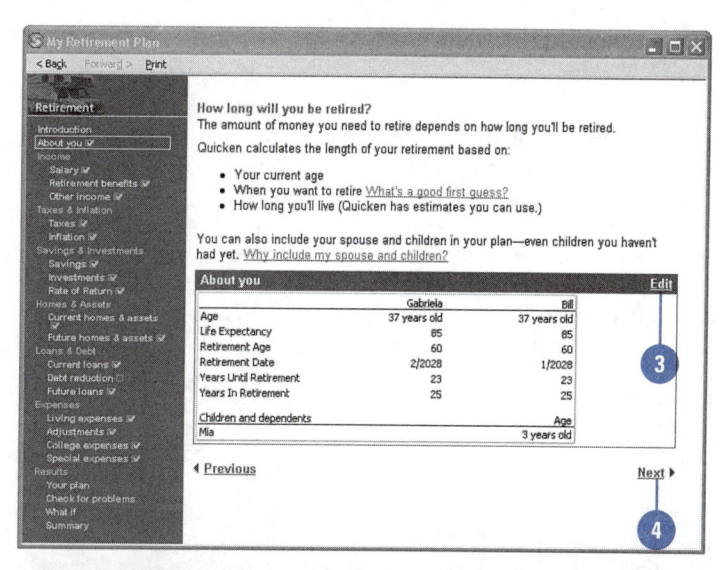

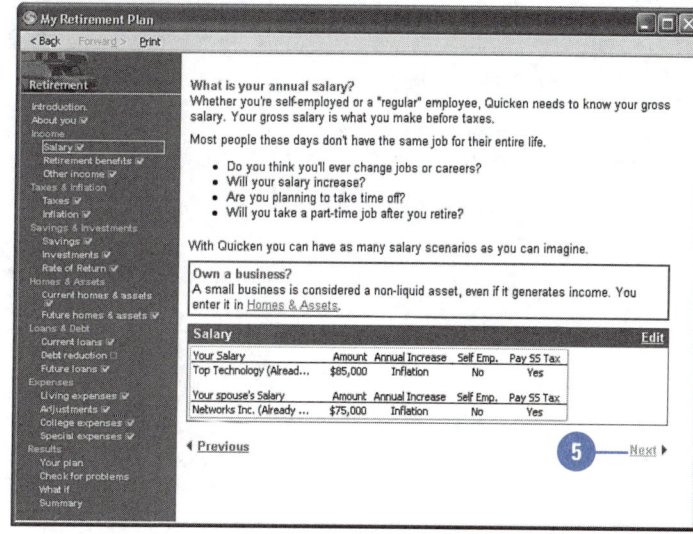

Planning for the Future 309

6 When you reach the Results section, Quicken shows you a bar graph of your account balances from the current year through the remainder of your life. In addition, Quicken lets you know if you will be able to retire when you want to. To make adjustments to your assumptions, click Change Assumptions.

7 To play with different scenarios to determine the impact to your retirement plan, click Explore What If's.

8 To have Quicken check for any potential weaknesses or problems with your plan, click Check for problems.

9 Review any potential problem areas and go back and make adjustments, if needed, by clicking the planner menu links or clicking the Previous link.

10 To review or change the what-if scenarios, click Next.

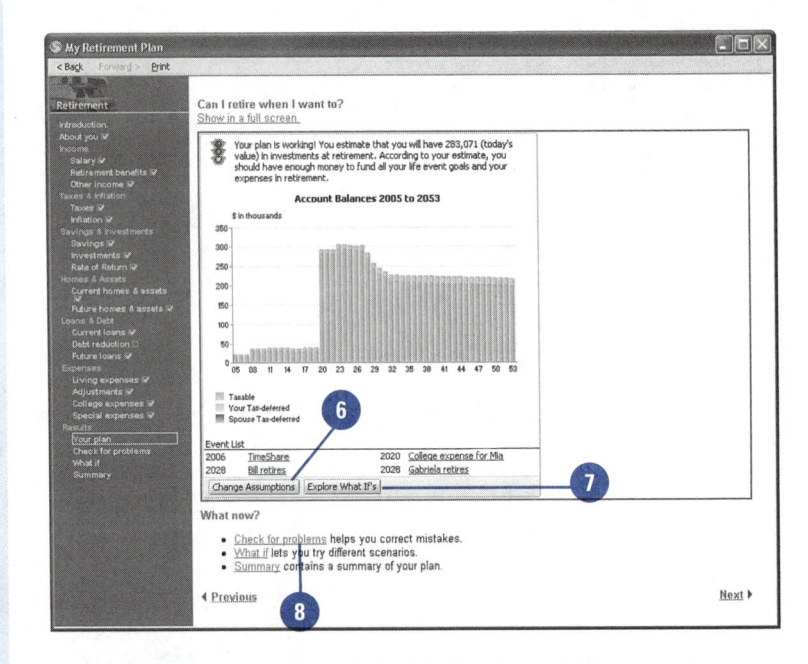

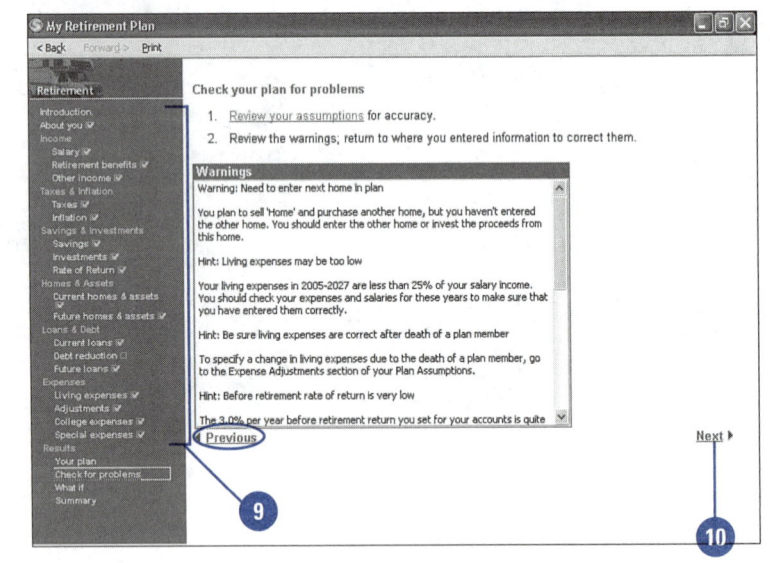

⑪ Click What If event scenarios to open the What If window, where you can explore what-if scenarios.

⑫ When you are satisfied with the plan, click Next to view the plan summary.

⑬ Review the plan summary, make changes, if needed, and then close the window when you are finished. The results of your retirement plan appear in the Plan: Results section of the Planning tab in the Financial Overview center.

> **See Also**
>
> See "Review and Change Planner Assumptions and What-if Scenarios" on page 305 for information on working with what-if scenarios.

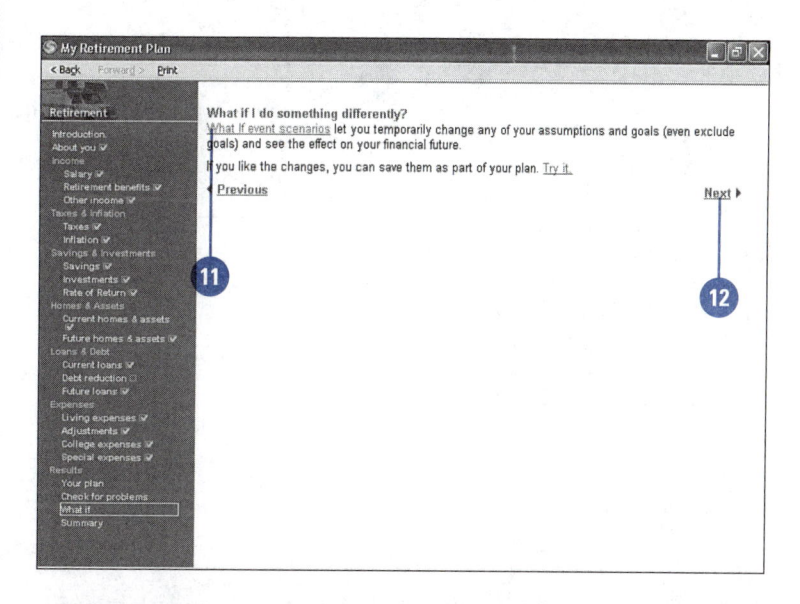

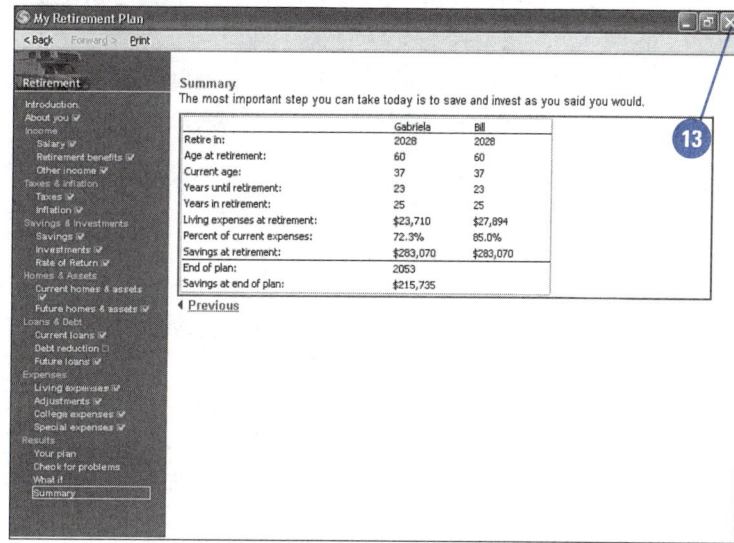

Planning for the Future **311**

Planning for College

Whether you are planning on going to college or have a family member you are sending or helping to send to college, the College planner can help you plan for it. With the rising costs of higher education, planning for college is getting tougher and tougher. By using the College planner, you can see exactly what you need to do to plan for college expenses.

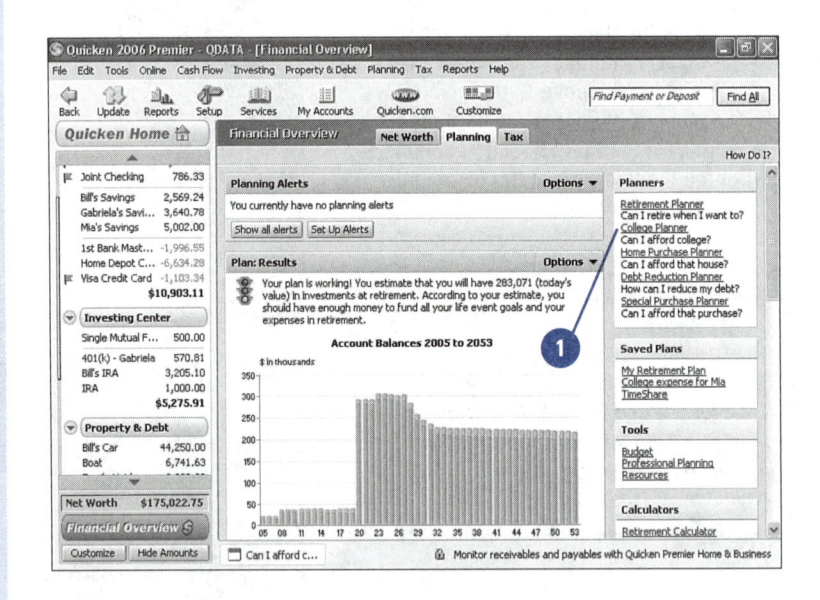

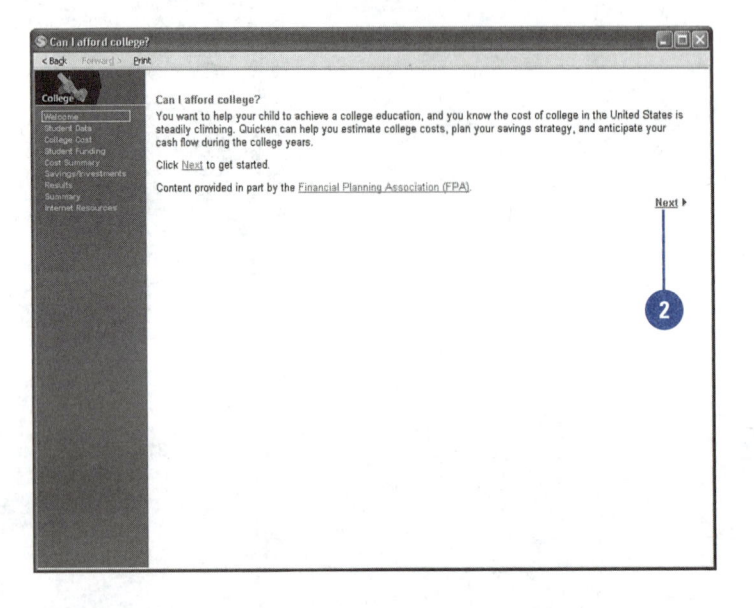

Plan for College

1. If you're not already there, open the Planning tab in the Financial Overview center and in the Planners section, click College Planner.

2. Review the introduction and click Next to get started with the plan.

312

Add or Edit Student Data

1. To add or change information about the person going to college, click Edit.

2. Select who is going to college, type a description, specify when the student is to begin college, enter the number of years he or she will attend, and click Done.

3. Click Next.

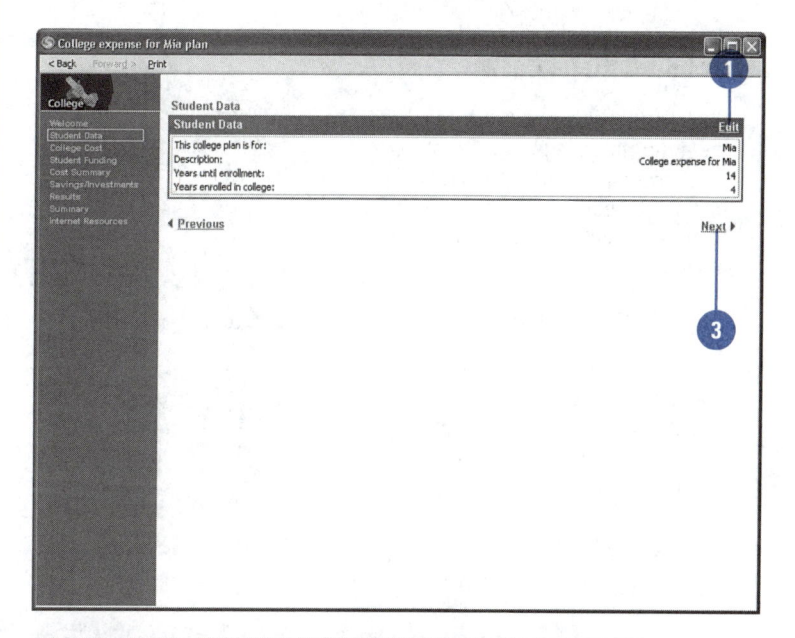

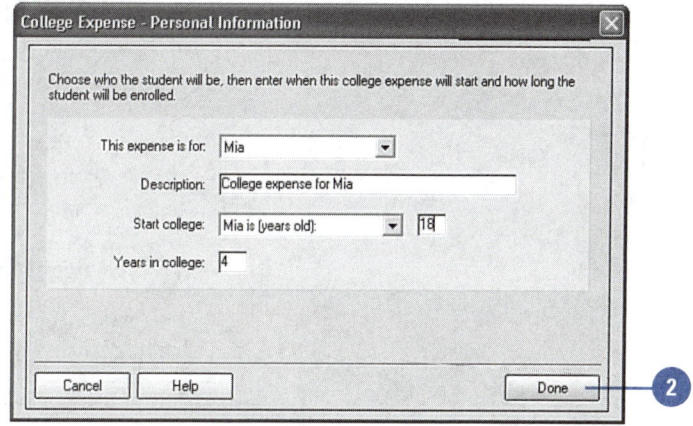

Add or Edit College Costs

1. Click the links to read more about the different college expenses. This will help you determine the costs you need to enter in the next step. Some links require Internet access.

2. Click Edit to add college expenses.

3. Enter the annual costs for tuition, any out-of-state fees, room and board, books and supplies, and other (personal) college expenses. Then click Done.

4. Click Next.

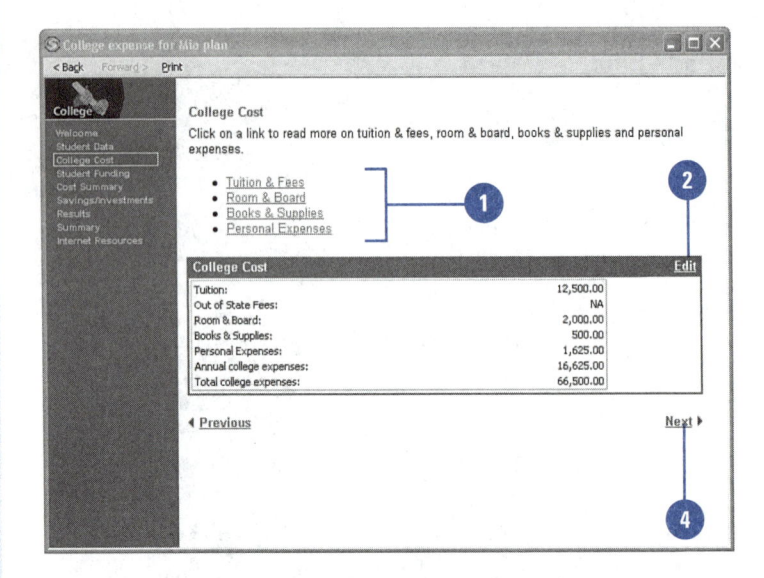

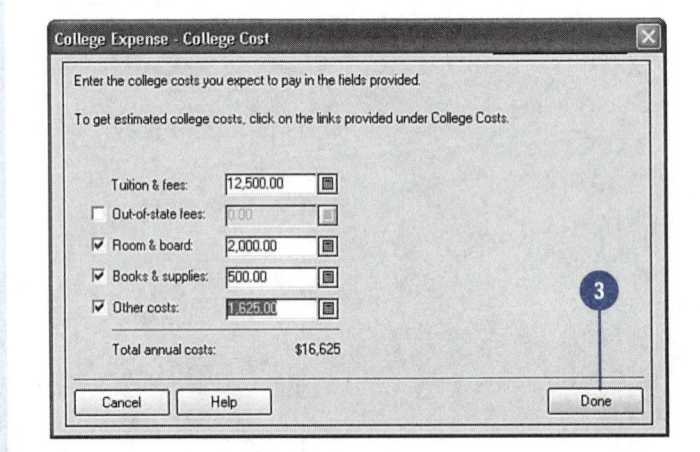

Add or Edit Student Funding Options

1. If you anticipate needing financial assistance to fund college expenses, review all the information about the different financial aid sources by clicking the links. Most sources require Internet access.

2. To add financial aid information, click Edit.

3. Type the potential funding amounts for all applicable types of financial contributions and click Done.

4. Click Next.

Did You Know?

You may make too much money to get financial aid. *Be aware that in a household with income more than $70,000 per year, a student most likely will not be eligible for financial aid.*

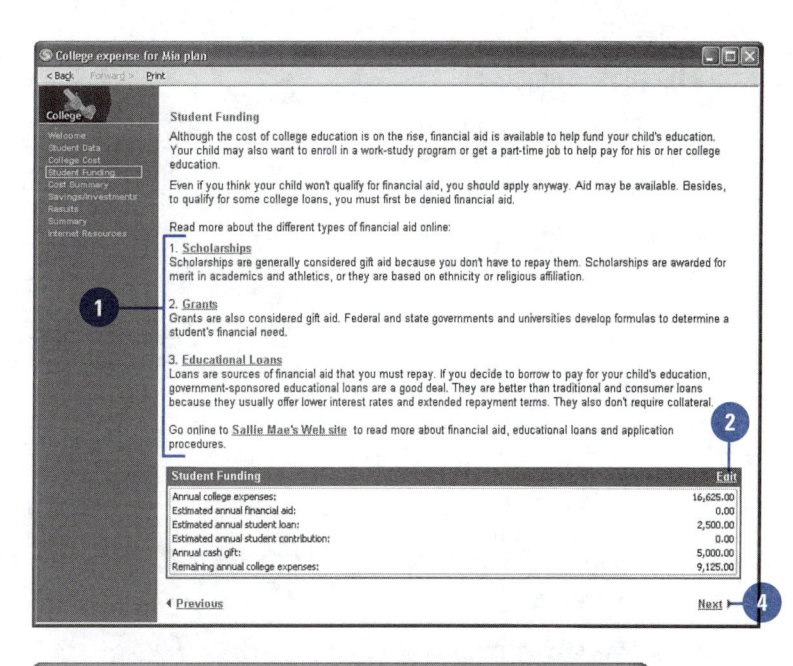

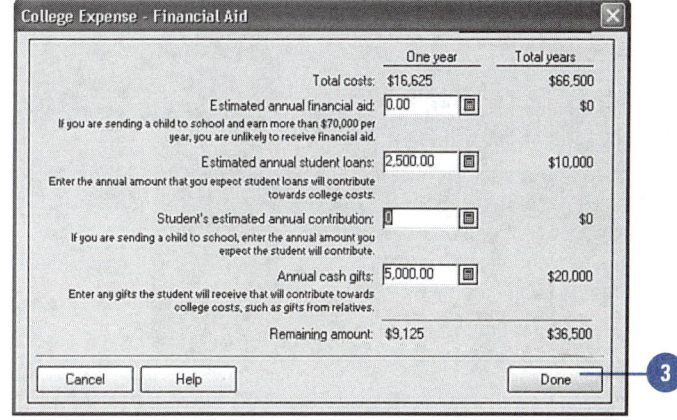

Planning for the Future **315**

Review the Cost Summary

1. Review the cost summary information. To go back and make any changes, click Previous.

2. When you are ready to proceed, click Next.

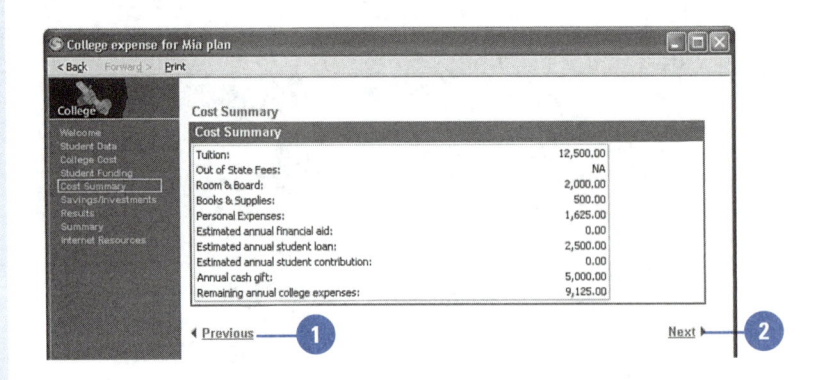

Review and Change Savings and Investment Information

1. Click the links to read more about saving for college expenses. Some links require Internet access.

2. Click Edit to set up a savings plan.

3. Use the default inflation rate and click Choose accounts to select the account to use to save for college expenseees. Quicken determines how much you need to save monthly.

4. Click Done.

5. Click Next.

Did You Know?

You can set up a plan to save for college. When you know how much you need to save for college, you can set up a savings plan by clicking the Schedule link at the bottom of the Savings and Investments window. You can also get help with setting up scheduled transactions by clicking the How do I fill out the Schedule Transaction Window?

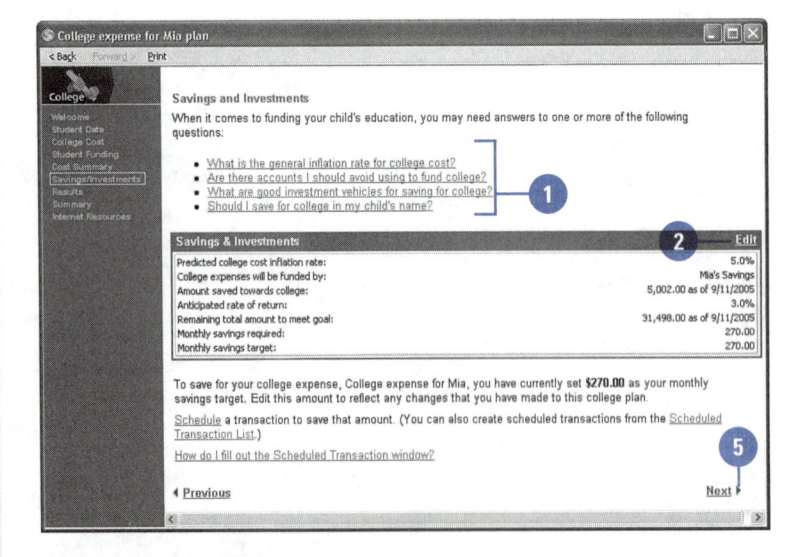

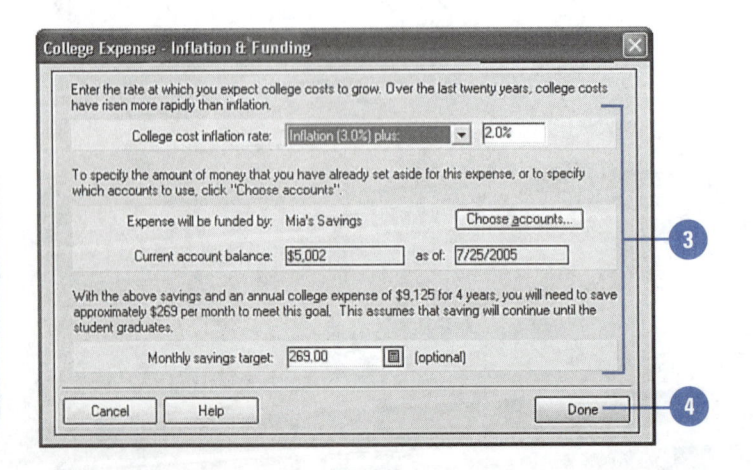

316

Review Plan Results

1. Review the results. To make changes, click Previous or the menu links.

2. To review the plans already in place, click one of the links.

3. To change your plan assumptions, click Change assumptions.

4. To change the what-if scenarios, click Explore What If's.

5. If you are not able to obtain or save the money required for college expenses, click the link What options should I consider if I can't fund this college goal?

6. Click Next to review the plan summary.

Review the Plan Summary and Internet Resources

1. Review the summary. To make changes, click Previous or the menu links.

2. Click Next to review the Internet resources.

3. Click any of the links to view helpful Internet resources related to preparing for college and its expenses.

4. When you are finished, close the planner. The plan results appear in the Plan: Results section of the Planning tab.

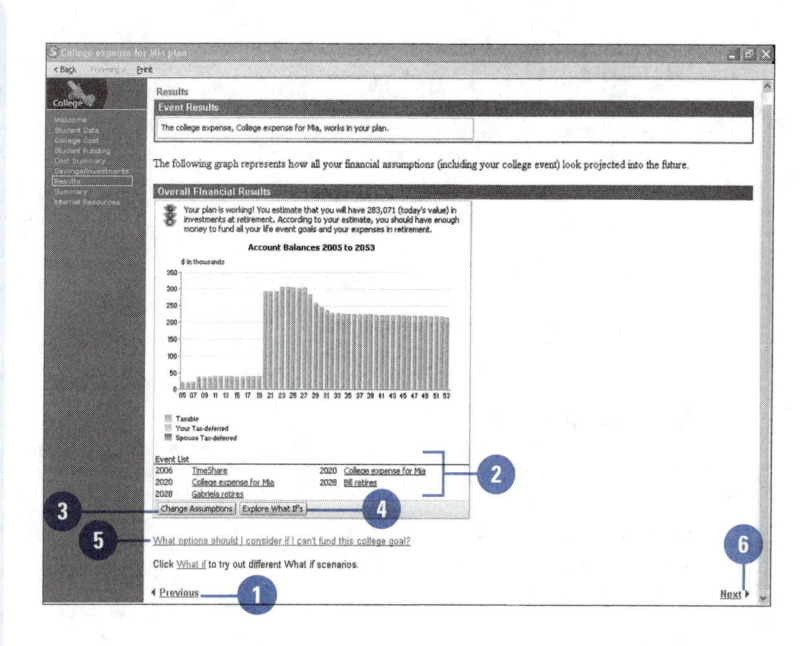

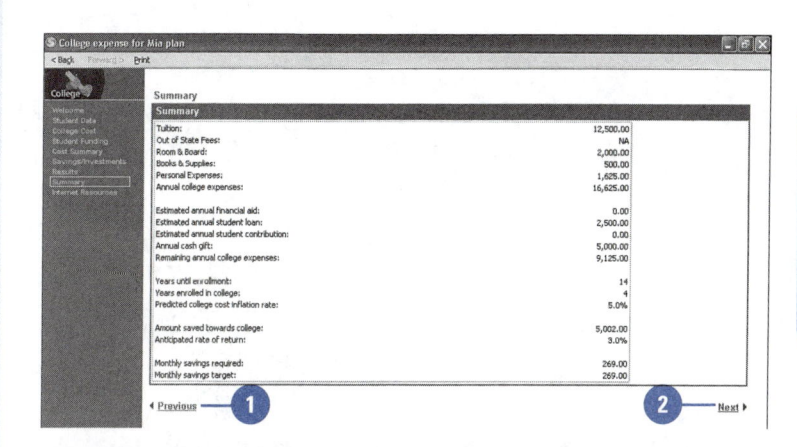

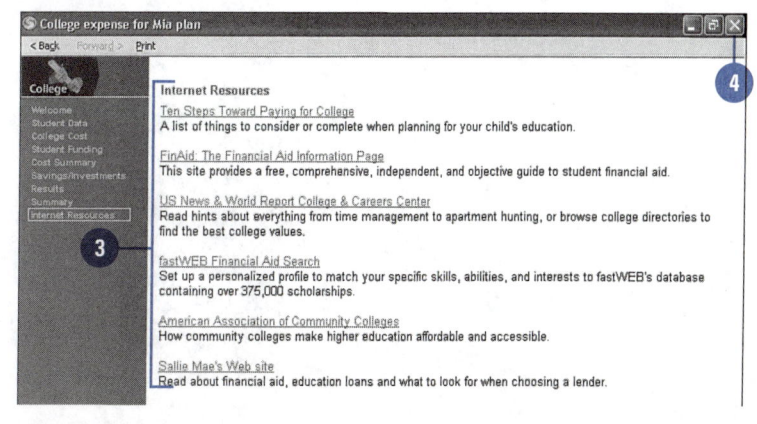

Planning for the Future **317**

Planning to Purchase a Home

One of the biggest milestones in a person's life is being able to buy his or her first home. It's an exciting and fulfilling time, but also a very serious time. How do you determine how much you can afford? How much will you need to put down? What type of home do you need? There are so many questions and concerns related to buying a home. No matter if this is your first home or your fifth home, the Home Purchase planner can help you prepare for purchasing a home. As soon as you're finished with the planner, you'll be able to see how much you can afford, how much you need to put down, and other important information you need when planning to purchase a home.

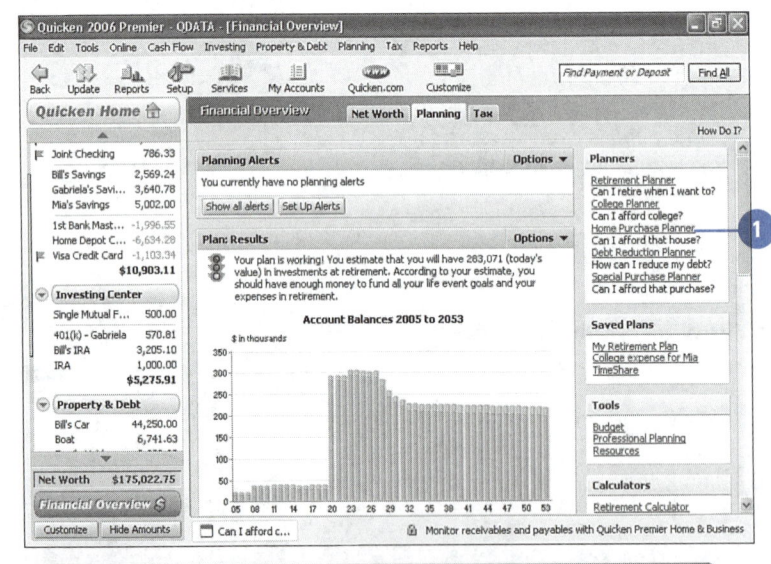

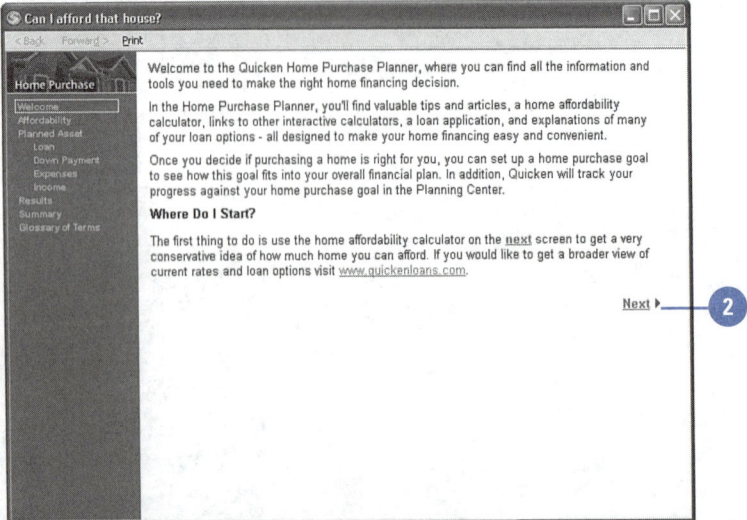

Plan to Purchase a Home

1. If you're not already there, open the Planning tab in the Financial Overview center and in the Planners section, click Home Purchase Planner.

2. Review the introduction and click Next to get started with the plan.

Determine How Much House You Can Afford

1 Enter your income or you and your spouse's combined gross income and from the drop-down menu select how often you receive this income.

2 Enter your total monthly debt payments, any cash that you can put down on a house, and the current interest rate.

3 Select the mortgage term you are considering and enter the maximum payment you want.

4 Click Calculate. Quicken calculates what you can afford and lists the information in the What a Lender would typically let you borrow section in the middle of the window.

5 To view information on how Quicken determines how much you can afford and other information to help you determine how much you should spend, click the links.

6 If needed, adjust the figures you entered in steps 1–3 to see how the changes affect the final outcome. When you are finished, click Next to proceed.

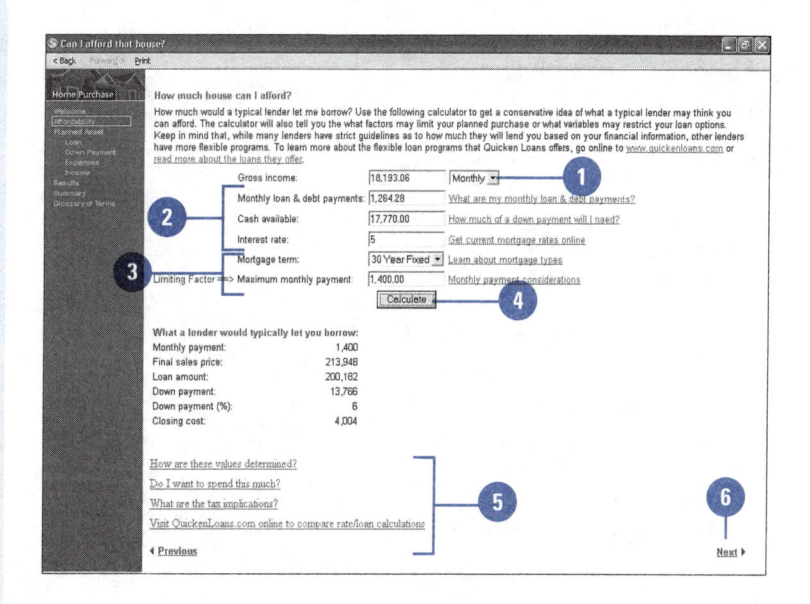

Did You Know?

You can use the Income and Expense Comparison by Category report to help complete the Affordability section of the planner. *To help determine what your gross income and monthly loan and debt payments are, you can run an income/expense report. To do this, from the Reports menu, select Comparison, Income and Expense Comparison by Category. The report is broken down into income and expense categories so that you can see what your monthly income and debt payments are. You can also use the links on the right of the How much house can I afford? section of the Home Purchase planner to get more information.*

Planning for the Future   **319**

Add or Edit Planned Asset Information

1. If you don't already have in mind a specific house at a specific price, go online to search for a home or click QuickenLoans.com to get help finding a home.

2. Click Edit to add information about the house you want to purchase.

3. Type a description, an approximate date you want to purchase the house, and an approximate amount. Leave the inflation percentage as it is. Click Next.

4. Select whether this house will be your primary residence and whether you plan to sell the home anytime soon and then click Done.

5. Click Next.

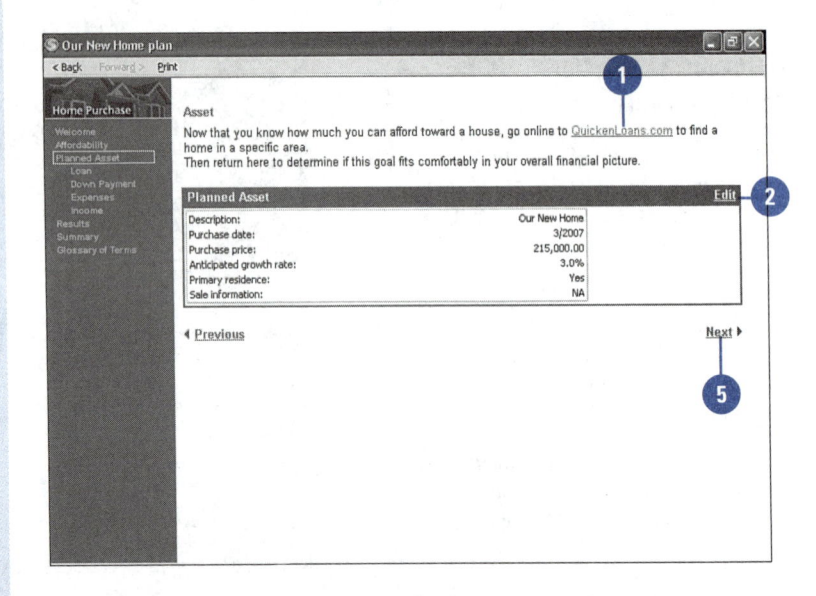

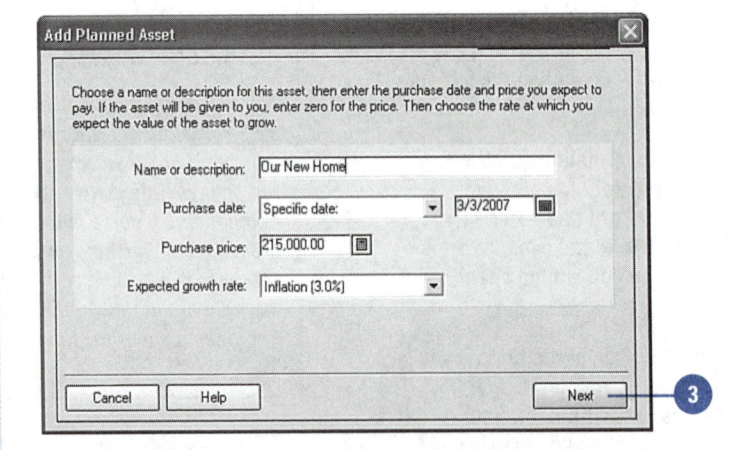

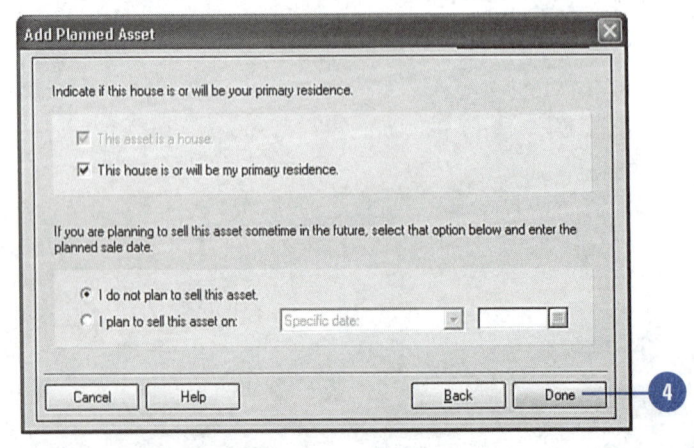

Add or Edit Loan Information

1. Click Edit to add estimated loan information.

2. Click New and complete the loan information on the Add Planned Loan dialog box.

3. To make changes to the loan, select it and click Edit.

4. To remove the loan, select it and click Delete.

5. To exclude the loan from your plan, select the loan and click the Exclude from Plan check box. If you exclude the loan, it does not show up on the Loan section in the Home Purchase planner.

6. When you are finished making changes to the loan information, click Done.

7. Click Next.

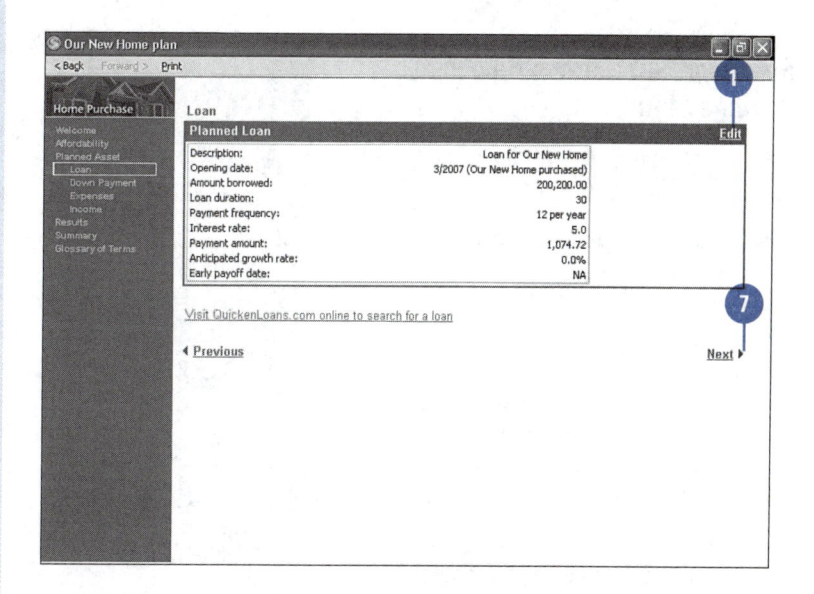

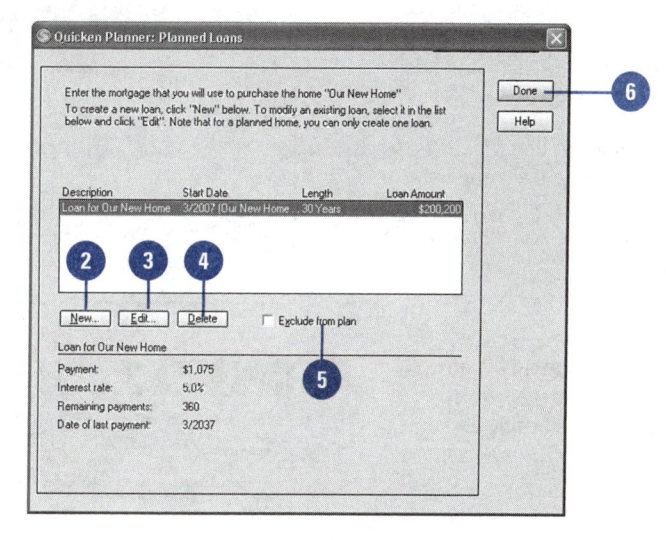

Planning for the Future

Set Up or Edit a Down Payment Savings Plan

① Click Edit to add down payment and savings information.

② Click Choose accounts to specify the accounts you want to use to save for the new home.

③ To use income and accounts not currently being used for special events, select General expenses. To specify the account(s) you want to use, select Specific accounts (as shown here).

④ If you use specific accounts (as shown here), select the account(s) you want to use. To use general expenses, type the amount you have saved and the date it is available (not shown).

⑤ Click OK. Quicken determines how much you need to save and lists the amount in the Monthly Savings Target box on the Asset Funding dialog box.

⑥ Click OK.

⑦ If needed, you can adjust any information in the planner by clicking Previous or any of the links in the menu. Otherwise, click Next to proceed.

Did You Know?

You can set up a plan to save for your new home. When you know how much you need to save for a new home, you can set up a savings plan by clicking the Schedule link at the bottom of the Down Payment section. To get help setting up scheduled transactions, click the How do I fill out the Schedule Transaction window?

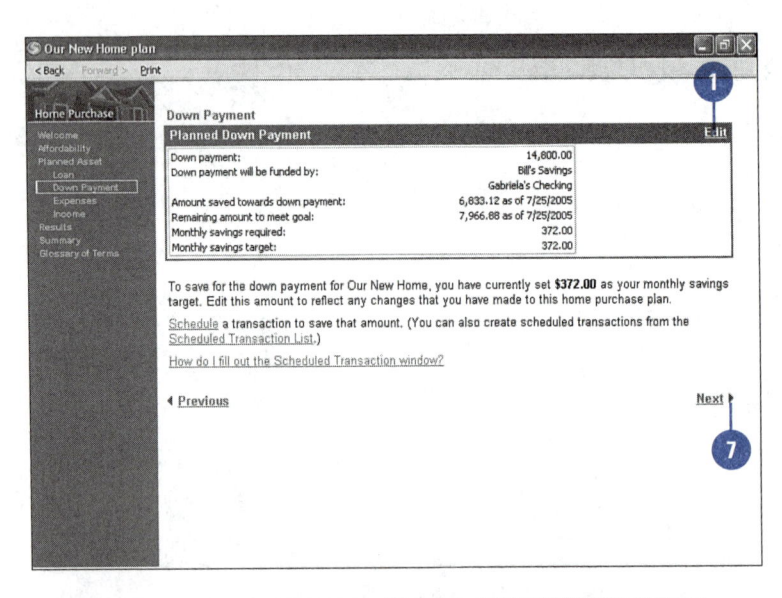

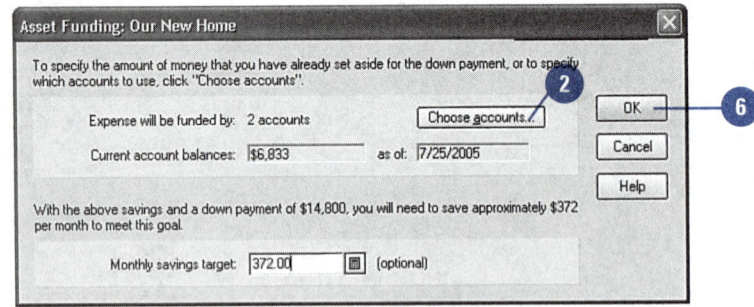

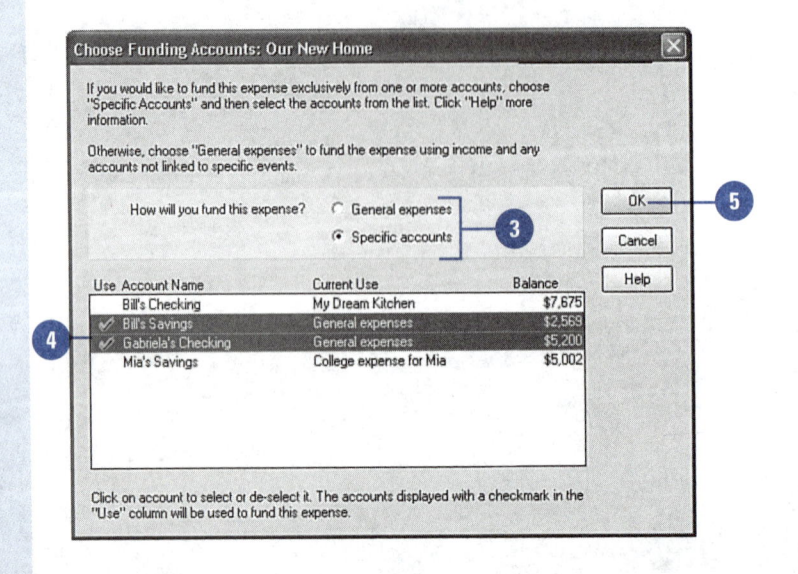

Add or Edit Expenses

1. Click Edit to add expense information for your new home.

2. Type the tax amount you expect to pay; if you are unsure, use the amount that Quicken has estimated for you in the intro paragraph.

3. To add new expenses (for example, for remodeling), click New and follow the prompts to enter the information.

4. To go back and make changes to an expense, select the expense and click Edit.

5. To remove an expense, select it and click Delete.

6. To exclude an expense from your plan, select the expense and click the Exclude from plan check box. If you exclude an expense, it does not show up in the Expenses section in the Home Purchase planner.

7. When you are finished, click Done.

8. Click Next.

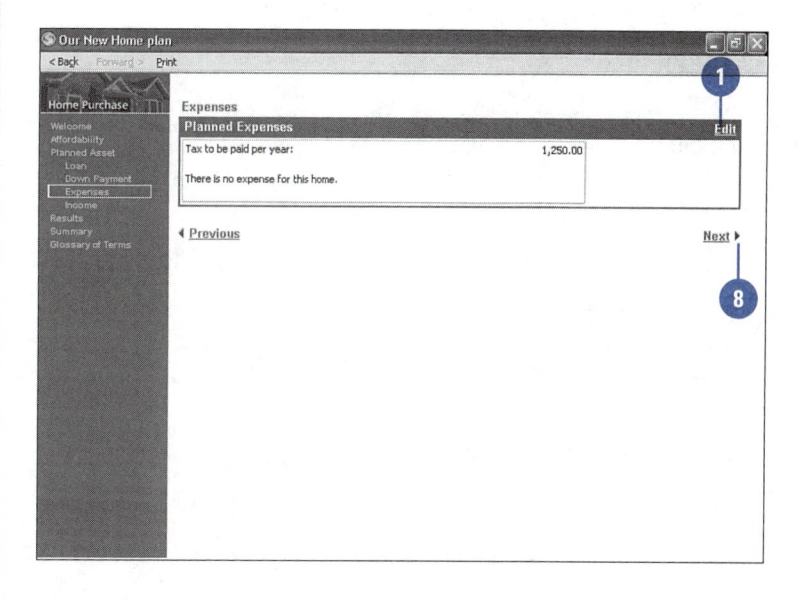

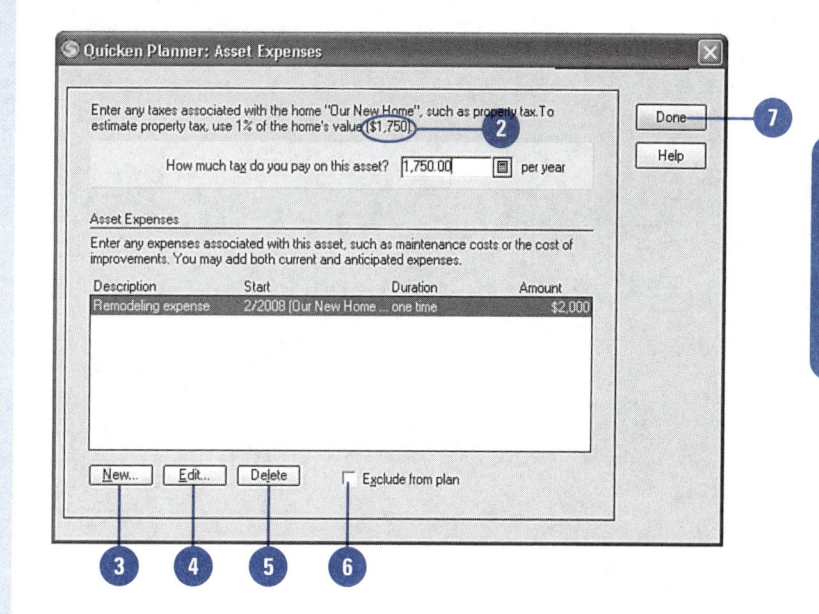

Planning for the Future **323**

Add or Edit Income

1. Click Edit to add income you expect to receive from the new property (for example, if it is a rental property). If you don't expect any income, skip this section and click Next.

2. If you expect to receive income from the house, click New and follow the prompts to add the income information.

3. When you are finished, click Done.

4. Click Next to review the results of the plan.

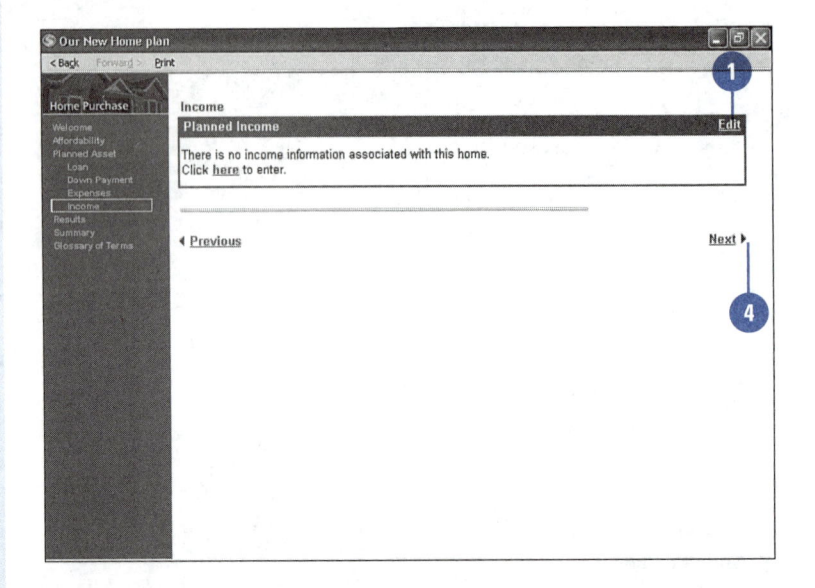

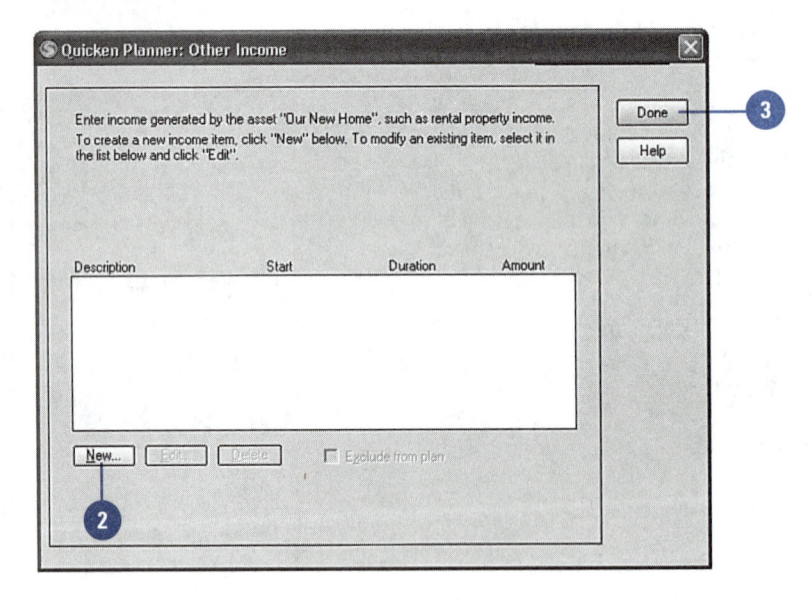

Review Plan Results

1. Review bar graph of your account balances to see if you afford the house. To make changes, click Previous or click any of the menu links.

2. To review the plans already in place, click one of the links.

3. To make adjustments to your assumptions, click Change assumptions.

4. To play with different scenarios to determine the impact to your home purchase plan, click Explore What If's.

5. When you are satisfied with the plan, click Next to view the plan summary.

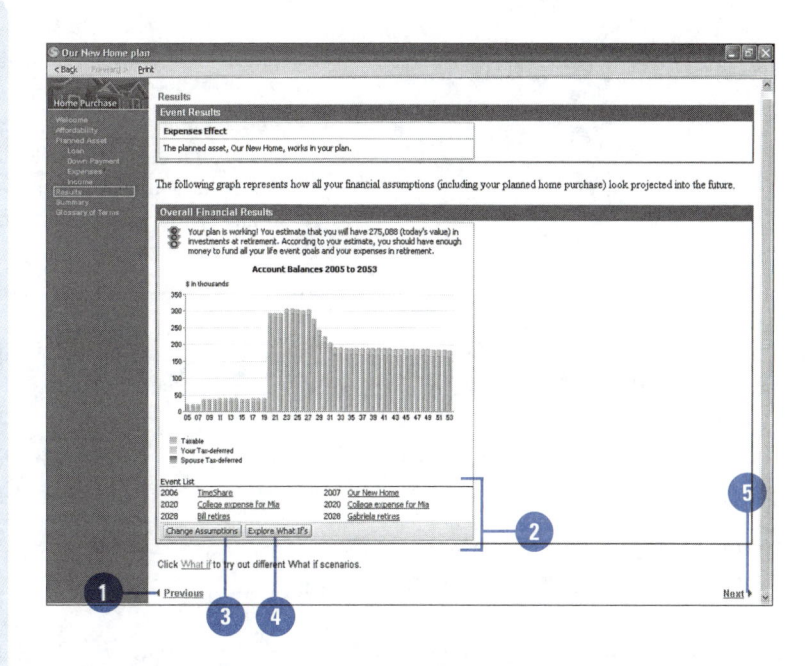

See Also

See "Review and Change Planner Assumptions and What If Scenarios" on page 305 for information on changing assumptions and what-if scenarios.

Review the Plan Summary

1. Review the summary. To make changes, click Previous or click any of the menu links.

2. To get information about home loans and mortgage rates, click a link.

3. To view a home buying glossary of terms, click Next.

4. When you are finished with the Home Purchase planner, close it. The results of your home purchase plan appear in the Plan: Results section of the Planning tab in the Financial Overview Center.

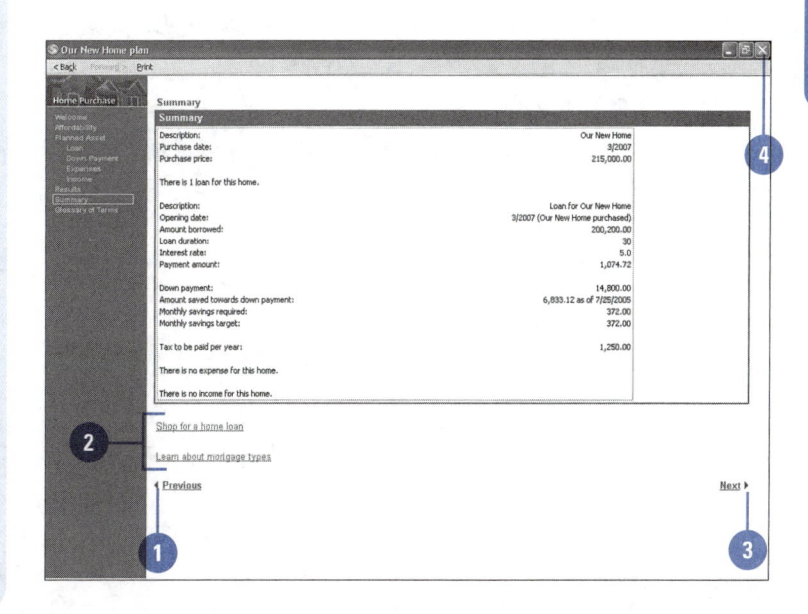

Planning for the Future **325**

Getting Out of Debt

Is it hard to breathe under all that debt? Don't despair; help is available. Quicken's Debt Reduction planner can help you create a plan to get yourself out of debt and, hopefully, stay out of debt. I know it's more fun to go shopping, but the Debt Reduction planner is easy to use and does a lot of the work for you by importing your debt information from your accounts in Quicken. You have nothing to lose but your debt, so follow the steps here to get started.

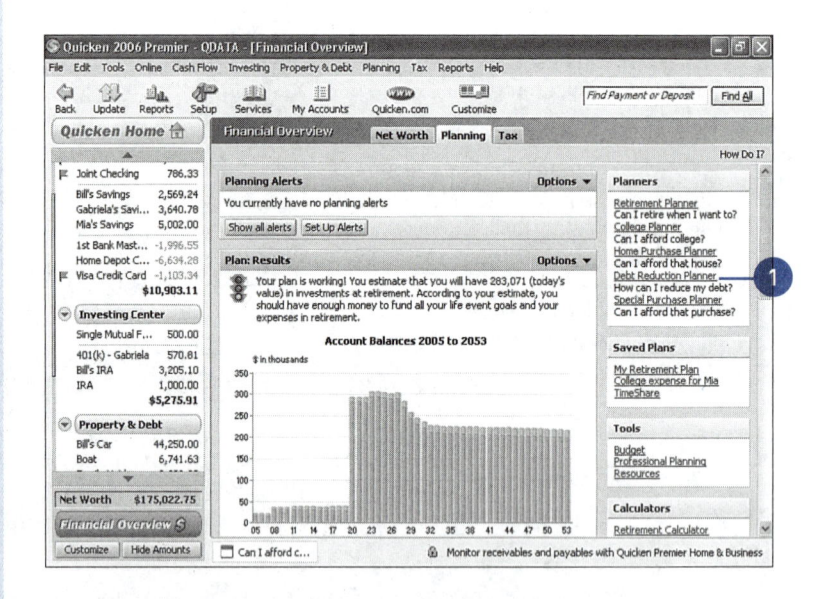

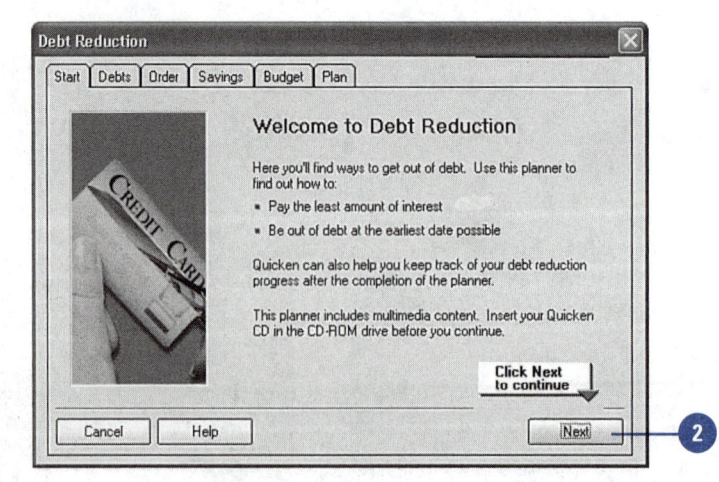

Get Out of Debt

1. If you're not already there, open the Planning tab in the Financial Overview center and in the Planners section, click Debt Reduction Planner.

2. Review the introduction and click Next to get started with the plan.

Did You Know?

You can view multimedia clips as you go through the Debt Reduction planner. *You can view multimedia clips as you create your debt reduction plan. However, you must insert your Quicken CD in your CD drive to view the clips. If you do not want to watch the clips or if you don't have your CD nearby, click Next two times on each tab to proceed through the planner and bypass the clips. This task does not show the multimedia clips.*

326

3. Review your debt accounts. You can add missing accounts, edit exiting ones, remove incorrect information by using the buttons. (Removing accounts does not remove them from Quicken—only from the Debt Reduction planner.)

4. Click Next. If a message appears, asking for more information about the debt accounts, complete the information and click OK.

5. Review your debt results and click Next.

6. Review the order in which you should pay off your debt. You can change the order, but doing so is not recommended. Quicken uses a specific order to ensure that you pay off your debt quickly and save as much money as possible. Click Next.

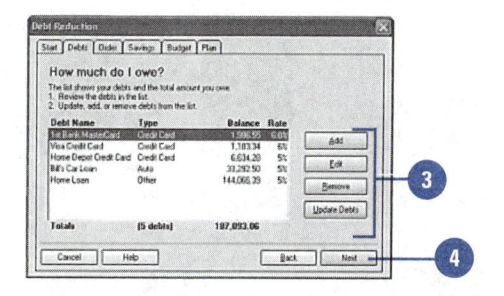

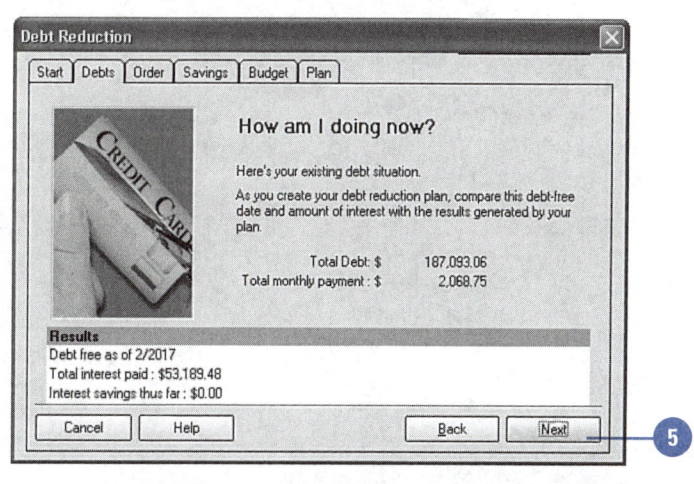

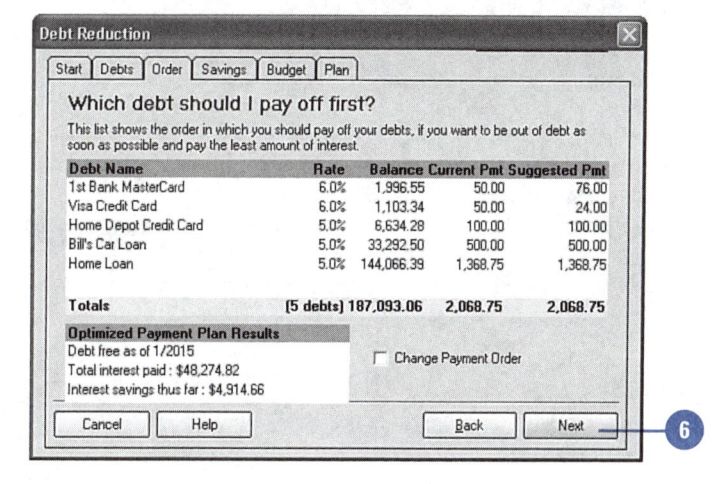

Planning for the Future 327

7 Type the amount you can put toward reducing your debt and click Recalculate. Your savings are listed to help you decide. You can change the amount and click Recalculate to see how the change affects your debt.

8 When you are finished, click Next.

9 From the drop-down menu in the Quicken Category column, select a category. The average spending amount for that category is listed in the Average Monthly spending column.

10 For each category, type the dollar amount you are willing to cut back for each category listed and then click Recalculate. You can change the amount and click Recalculate to see how the change affects your debt.

11 When you are finished selecting categories and entering the amount you are going to cut back, click Next.

12 Review your debt reduction plan of attack. You can print it by clicking Print this Action Plan, go back and make changes, or click Next to finalize the plan.

Did You Know?

The Results section provides a running tally of your plan. As you enter the amounts you are going to cut back, Quicken provides a running tally of when you will be debt free, how much you are currently paying in interest, and how much you will be saving in interest in the Results section of the Budget tab. A monthly amount that will be applied to your debt is provided just above the Results section.

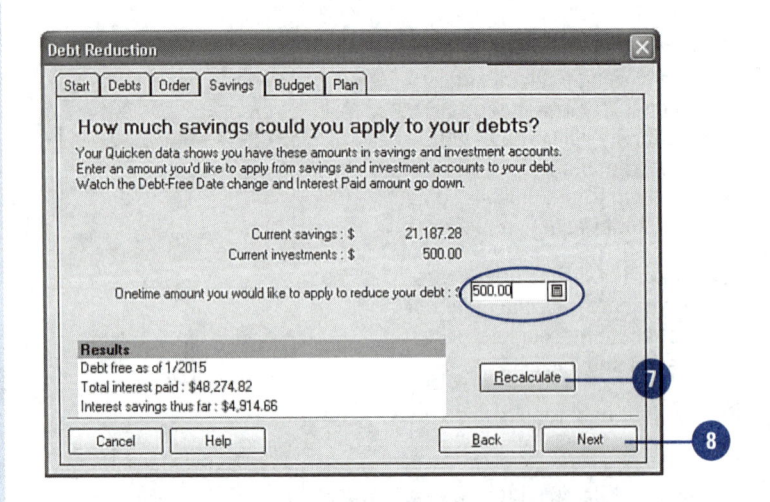

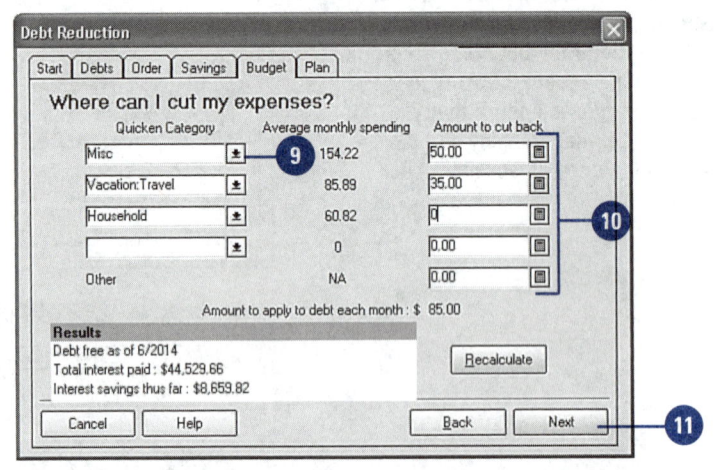

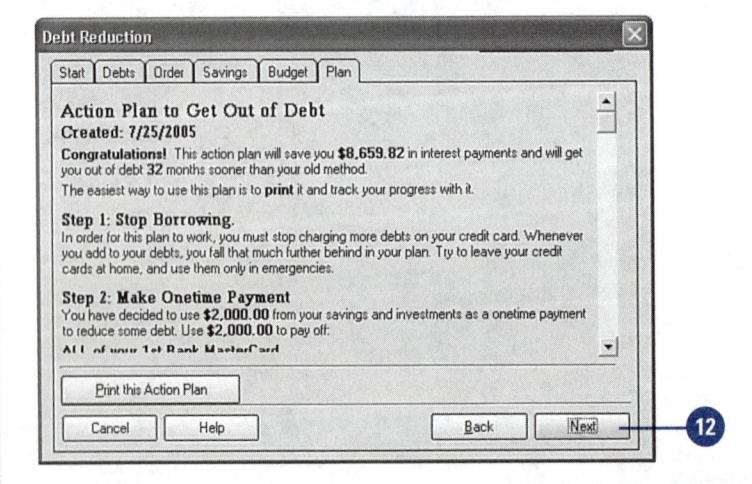

13 If you want to track your plan, select Alert me if I fall behind. If you want Quicken to automatically set up your scheduled transactions, select Set up scheduled transactions for my monthly payments. Then click Next and Done.

14 Review your plan and the steps you should take to update it. Close it when you are finished. The plan now appears in the Plan: Results section of the Planning tab in the Financial Overview center.

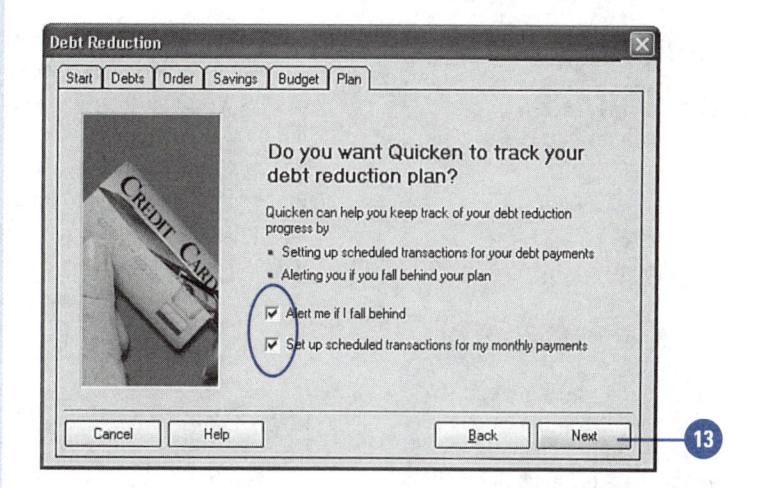

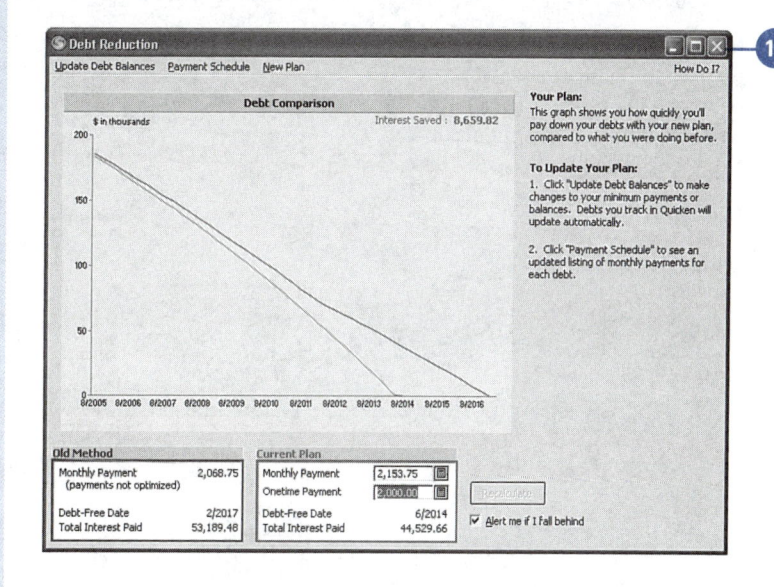

Planning for the Future **329**

Planning for a Special Purchase

Special life events from weddings to special projects such as remodeling your kitchen, periodically come up. And because such events are not always a regular fixture in your budget, it can be a daunting task to figure out how to pay for such expenses. That's where the Special Purchase planner can be of assistance. By using the Special Purchase planner, you can turn wishful thinking into a cohesive plan. Or you may find out that the new kitchen you want will have to remain wishful thinking for a little while longer. But without using the planner, you'll never know for sure, right?

Plan for a Special Purchase

1. If you're not already there, open the Planning tab in the Financial Overview center and in the Planners section, click Special Purchase Planner.

2. Review the introduction paragraph. To enter special purchase information, click Enter and complete the Add Special Expense dialog box.

3. Click Next.

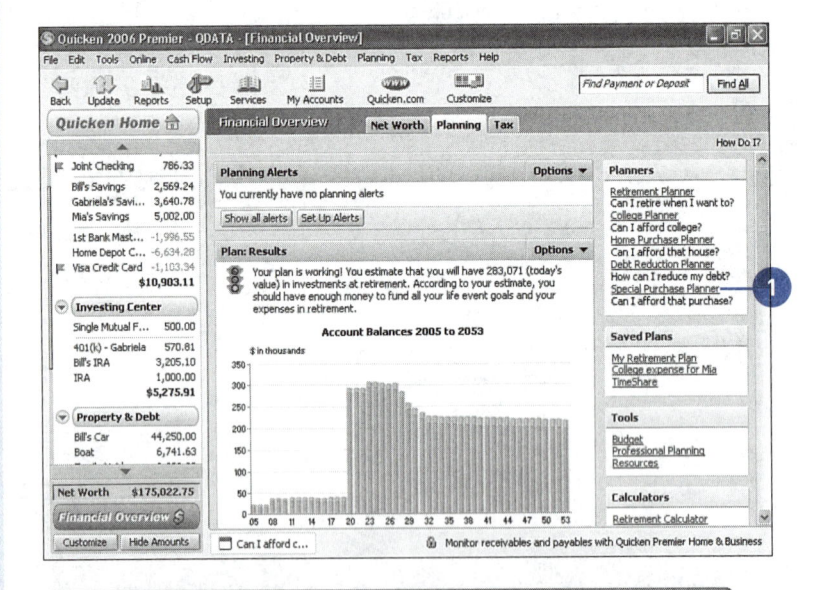

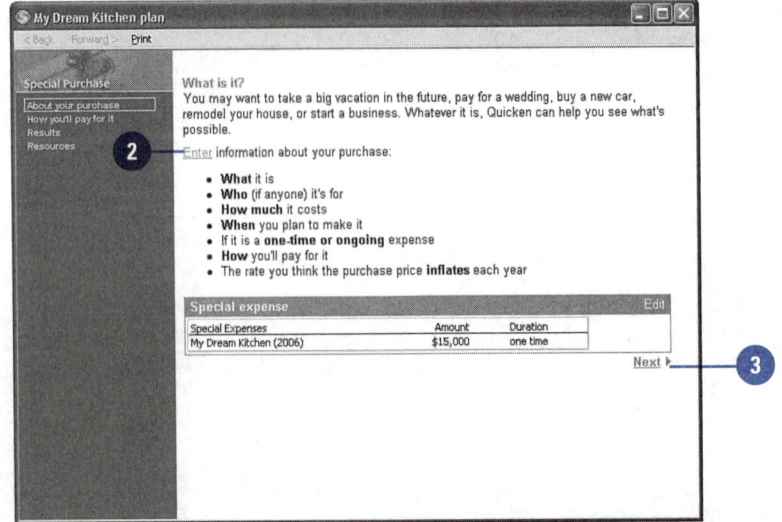

④ Review how you intend to pay for the special purchase. Click the Schedule link to set up a scheduled transaction or click the Enter a future loan if a loan link in step 2 is required to fund your special purchase.

⑤ To get more information about funding the purchase, click one of the links.

⑥ To make changes to the plan, click Previous or click Next to view the results of the plan.

⑦ Review the bar graph of your accoun balances to see if you can afford the special purchase. To make adjustments to your assumptions, click Change assumptions.

⑧ To play with different scenarios to determine the impact on your special purchase plan, click Explore What If's.

⑨ To view any of your other plans, click a link.

⑩ Click Create to create a new special purchase plan or click Delete to remove the plan.

⑪ When you are satisfied with the plan, click Next to view a list of resources to help you with your special projects and plans.

⑫ Click a link to view a resource. The resources that require Internet access are indicated by the word Internet in the Where column.

⑬ When you are finished, close the planner. The results of your special purchase plan appear in the Plan: Results section of on the Planning tab in the Financial Overview center.

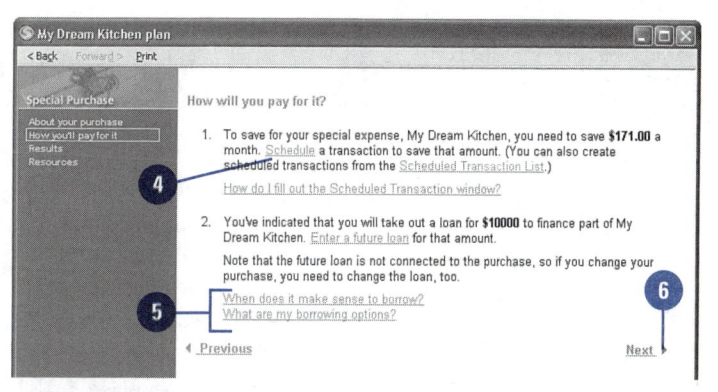

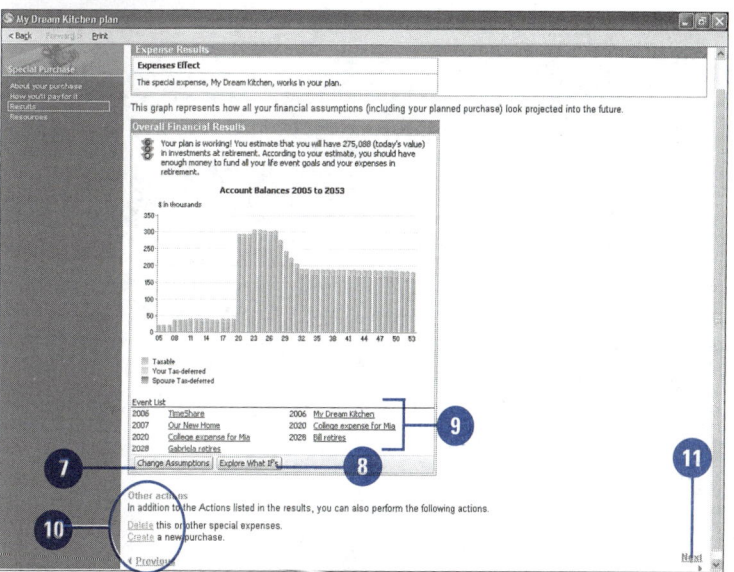

Did You Know?

You can set up a plan to save for your special purchase. *When you know how much you need to save for your special purchase, you can set up a savings plan by clicking the Schedule link in step 1 at the top of the How Will You Pay For It? section. To get help setting up scheduled transactions, click the How do I fill out the Schedule Transaction window?*

Planning for the Future **331**

Setting Up a Budget

If you have used any of the planners thus far, you've probably gotten the hang of using them. However, the Budget planner is completely different from the other planners. Creating a budget can be a time-consuming task. But Quicken provides a fast way of creating a budget for you. Sound good?

Quicken gives you choices on how you want to create your budget. You can either create one manually, one painstaking step at a time; you can let Quicken create one for you, using all your existing information; or you can import one that you've used in a previous version of Quicken. If you're like me, you want to see what's behind door number two and have Quicken create a budget for you. You can tweak it later if needed. To get started, you need to be on the Planning tab of the Financial Overview center.

Set Up a Budget

1. If you're not already there, open the Planning tab in the Financial Overview center and in the Tools section on the Planning tab, click Budget.

2. Select Automatic to have Quicken automatically create a budget for you and then click Create budget.

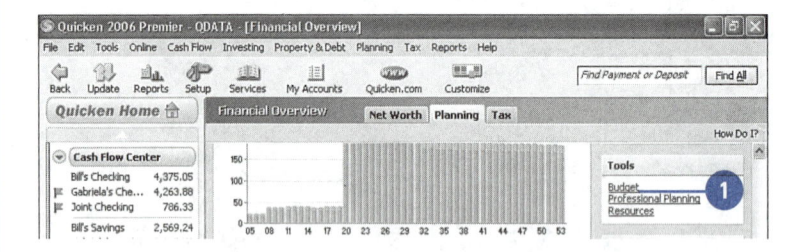

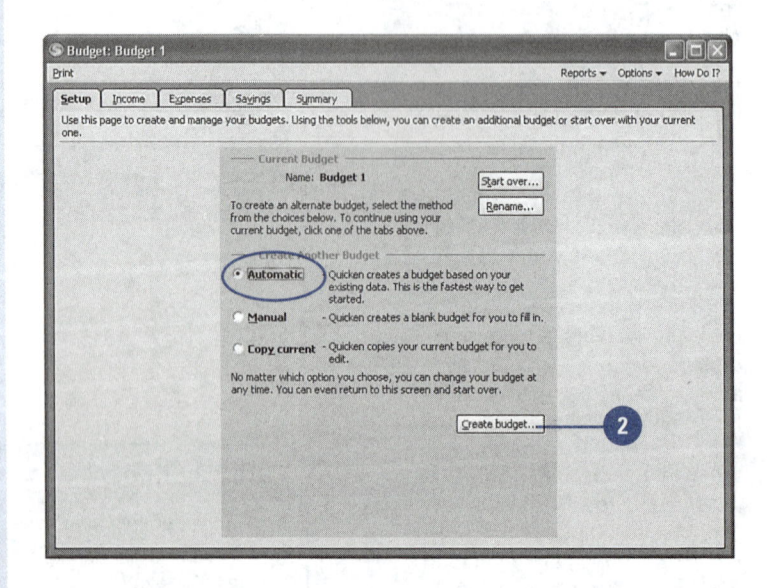

③ Type a name and description for the budget and select the date range that you want Quicken to use to scan your transactions. Quicken uses this information to create your budget.

④ If want to use another time frame besides monthly for your budget, select a different budget method. Click OK.

⑤ The Income tab contains all your income sources. To change any of the sources of income, from the Category/Account column on the Income tab, select a row and make your changes on the right.

⑥ To view a bar graph that shows averages for a specific income source, select the income and click Analyze.

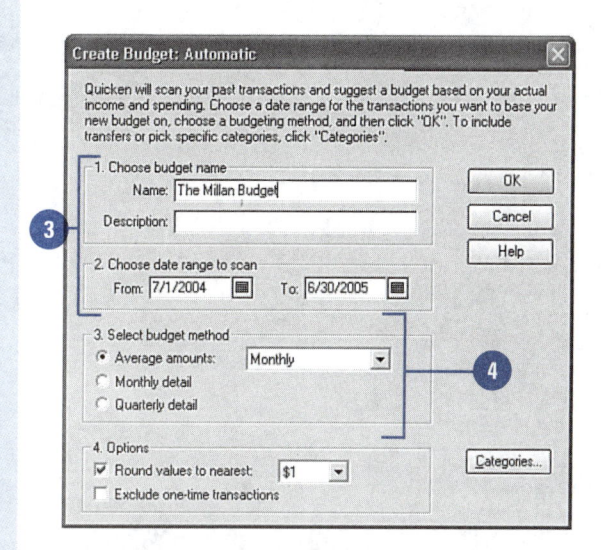

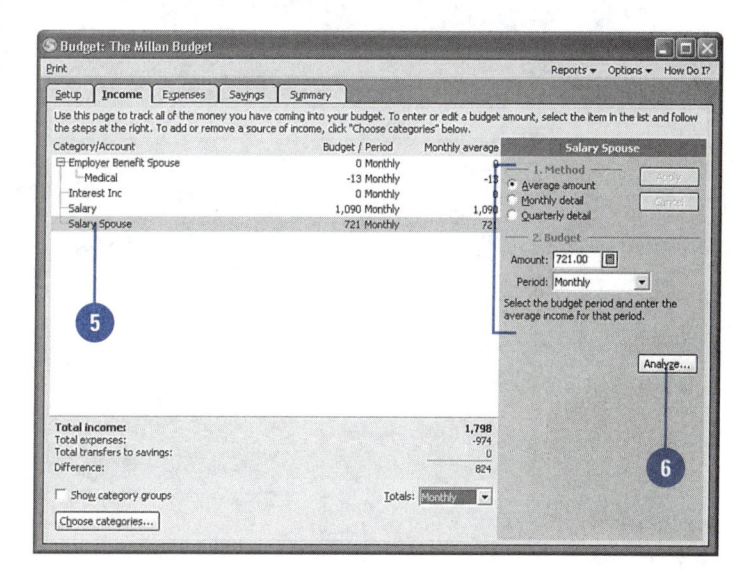

Planning for the Future 333

7 To review your expenses, budgeted amounts, and average spending, click the Expenses tab.

8 To change any of the information, from the Category/Account column, select a row, change the information on the right, and click Apply. Review all budget items and change them, if needed.

9 To view a bar graph that shows averages for a specific budgeted item, select the item and click Analyze.

10 To have Quicken notify you when you go over a budgeted amount, type or change the amount.

11 To add new categories to your budget, click Choose categories.

12 Select the categories you want to add. (Highlighted items are already included.) Then click OK.

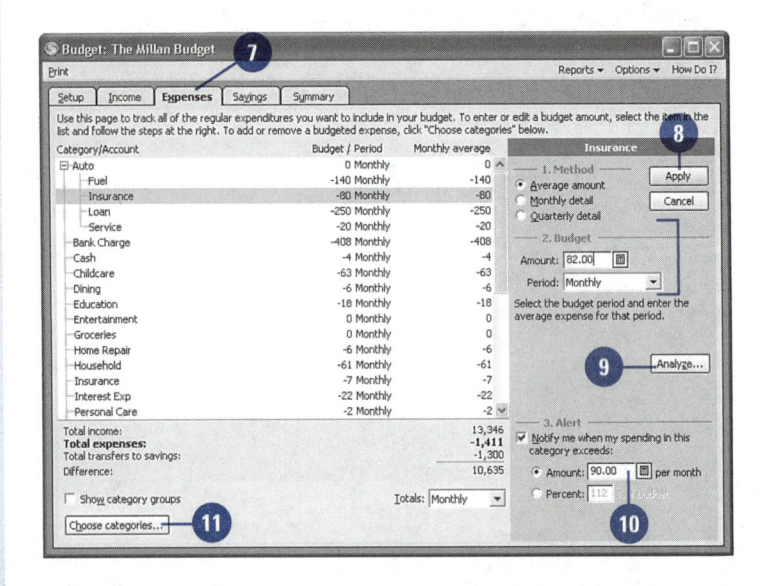

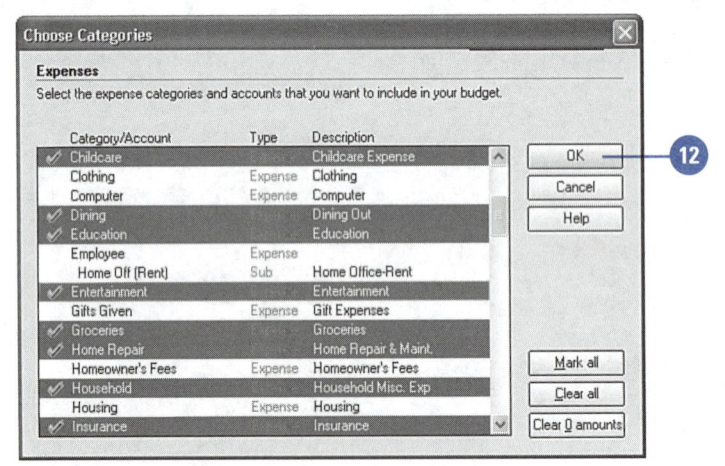

13. Click the Savings tab to review your savings, investment, and budgeted items. Make changes, add new accounts, or view analysis bar graphs, as you did for income and expenses.

14. Click the Summary tab to view your entire budget and see whether your budget works for you. The Monthly Budget Summary section provides a breakdown, by month, of your income and expenses. The pie chart shows a yearly view of how your budget breaks down.

15. You can go back and make changes by clicking the tabs, if needed, print the budget, and click the links at the bottom of the window to view a budget report or set savings goals. Close the budget when you are finished.

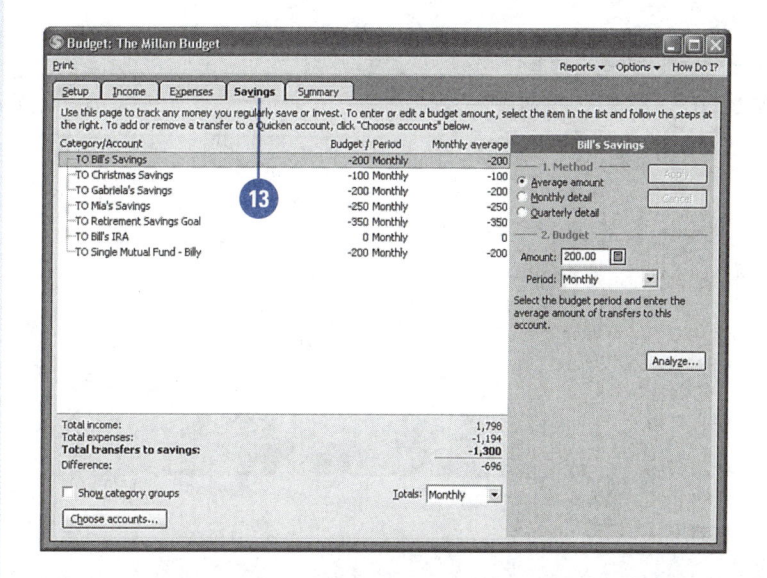

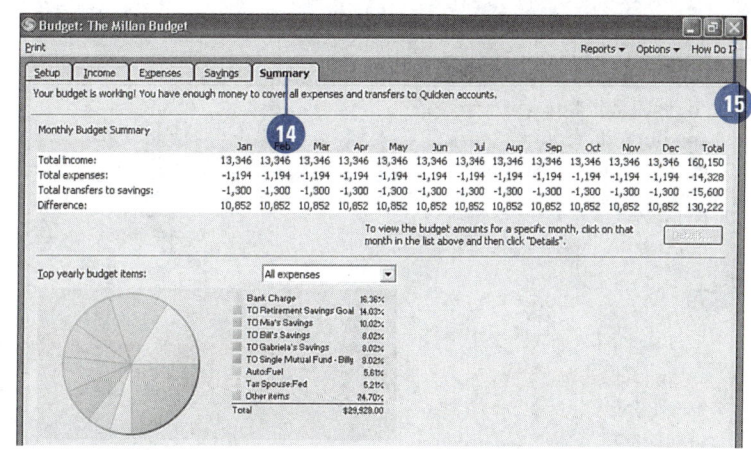

Getting Professional Financial Advice

Finding a trustworthy financial service can be risky and somewhat intimidating. The Professional Planning Resources guide provides sound financial advice, translations of financial jargon, and information on how to find help, where to look, what questions to ask, and much more. In addition, you can use it to create a financial planner to take to an advisor or keep for your records. Whether the information you seek is for your retirement, savings, or taxes, or if you're pondering the idea of starting your own business, hopefully the Professional Planning Resources guide can steer you in the right direction. To access this resource, from the Planning menu, select Professional Planning Resources.

Planning for the Future 335

Reviewing and Editing Your Plans

If you've set up plans, such as a retirement plan or debt reduction plan, you can conveniently manage all these plans on the Planning tab in the Financial Overview center. You can review your plans, make changes to them, and explore the what-if scenarios to determine whether they are still working for you over time. In addition, you can update assumptions on the Planning tab.

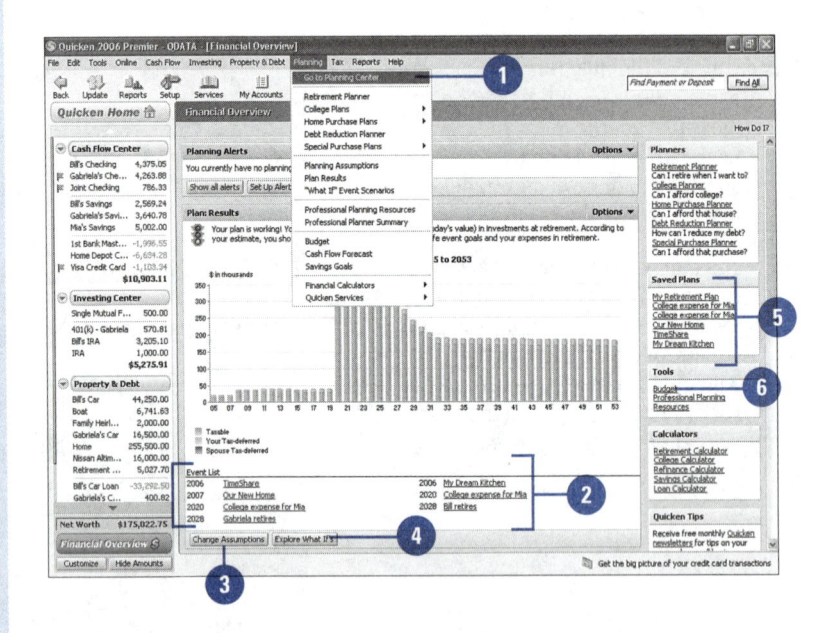

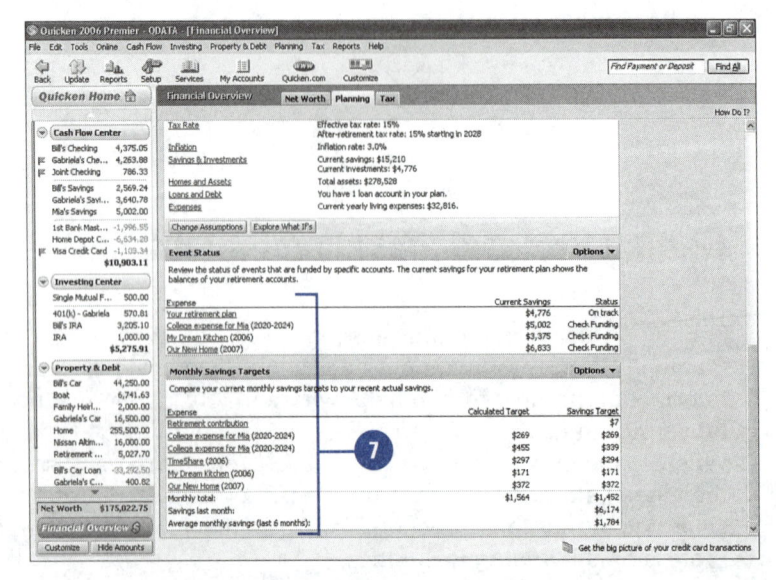

Review and Edit Your Plans

1. If you're not already on the Planning tab, from the Planning menu, select Go to Planning Center.

2. To review or update one of your plans, click a link to open the appropriate planner.

3. To review or update your assumptions, click Change Assumptions.

4. To play with different scenarios to see how they affect your plans, click Explore What If's.

5. If desired, access any of your plans in the Saved Plans section.

6. To review or update your budget, click Budget.

7. To see how your plans are doing, scroll down to the Event Status and Monthly Savings Targets sections. Then click any of the links to open the plan and make changes, if needed.

Managing Your Tax Information

Introduction

"The only difference between death and taxes is that death doesn't get worse every time Congress meets."—Will Rogers, 1879–1935, American humorist, actor

"It's getting so that children have to be educated to realize that 'Damn' and 'Taxes' are two separate words."—Unknown

"It is getting harder and harder to support the government in the style to which it has become accustomed."—Unknown

"Taxes and golf are alike: You drive your heart out for the green and then end up in the hole."—Unknown

"The difference between tax avoidance and tax evasion is the thickness of a prison wall."—Denis Healey, British labor politician

Dying and paying taxes are both givens in this life, so why not make preparing for and paying taxes as easy on yourself as possible? The Quicken Tax tab in the Financial Overview center provides many tax-related features to help you plan for and manage your tax information. You can to track tax-related expenses, estimate taxes for the current year, find tax deductions, create tax categories and tax line items, and lots more. In addition, you can import and export information to and from TurboTax, which saves you time and ensures that all your tax information is accurate and ready to use.

What You'll Do

Set Up New and Edit Existing Tax Alerts

Import and Export TurboTax Information

Create Year-End Files

Review and Edit Your Projected Tax Using the Tax Planner

Review and Edit Taxable Income

Assign or Edit Tax Categories

Estimate Capital Gains

Estimate Tax Withholding

Find Deductions

Setting Up New and Editing Existing Tax Alerts

As with the other centers in Quicken, on the Tax tab in the Financial Overview center you can set up alerts to remind or warn you of tax-related actions you need to take. For example, you can set up alerts that remind you to pay quarterly taxes or tell you if you are not saving enough to pay your taxes. Tax alerts are automatically turned on when you create a new Quicken file. Creating and editing tax alerts works the same as creating and editing alerts in the other centers.

Set Up New and Edit Existing Tax Alerts

1. From the Tax menu, select Go to Tax Center to open the Tax tab in the Financial Overview center.

2. To view all alerts, click Show all alerts.

3. To create or edit tax alerts, click Setup. You can also click Set Up Alerts in the Tax Alerts section of the Tax tab.

See Also

See "Using Alerts" on page 74 for more information on creating or changing alerts.

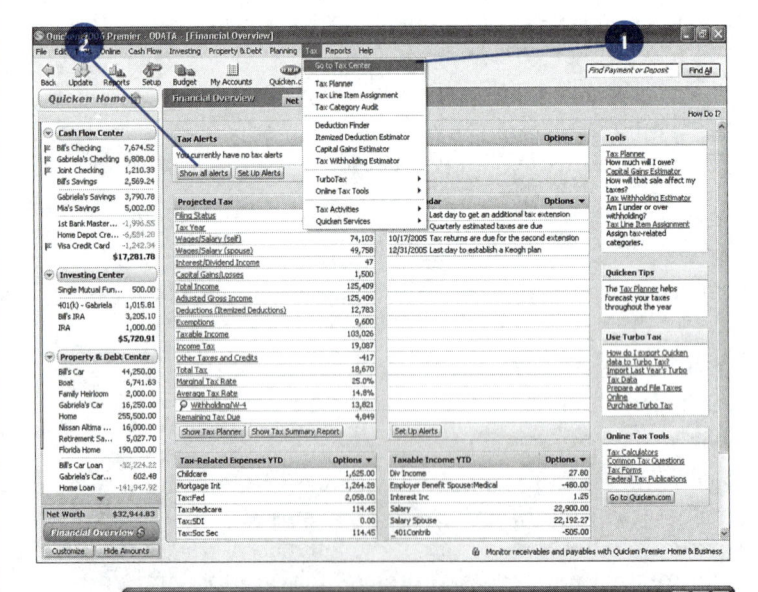

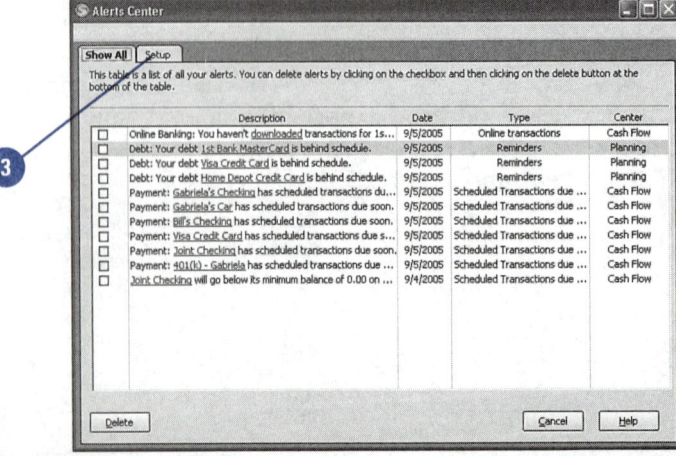

Importing and Exporting TurboTax Information

To get the most out of the Tax Planner and to ensure that the information you are using to estimate and plan for this year's taxes is as accurate as possible, you can import your TurboTax file from a previous year. However, because tax codes change frequently, Quicken allows only the current year or the previous year's tax files. If you do not use TurboTax to file your taxes, you can manually enter your tax information in Quicken and still benefit from using the Tax Planner. Whether you import the information or enter it manually, the first things you should do before using the Tax Planner, which is covered a little later in this chapter, is set up your tax information.

You can also export information from individual accounts in Quicken to use in TurboTax, such as transaction information that you can use when itemizing your taxes.

Import TurboTax Information

1. Click File, Import, TurboTax.

2. Click the Look in drop-down menu and locate and select the TurboTax file you want to import. The file should have a `.tax` extension (for example, `tax2005.tax`).

3. Click OK.

4. If the file is the one you want to import, click Continue. Otherwise, click Change File to locate the correct file.

5. When the file is finished importing, click OK. Quicken automatically updates the Tax tab with the tax information you imported.

Did You Know?

Import messages may differ. The messages you see when you import your tax information may differ from what you see here, depending on your filing status and the tax filing form you use.

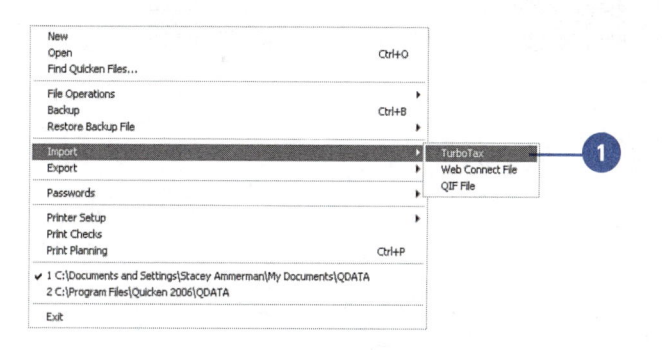

Did You Know?

You can export account information to use in TurboTax by selecting Export from the File menu. You then select the destination folder, the account you want to use, the transaction dates, and any additional transaction information you want exported. Quicken creates a .QIF file that you can then use to import into TurboTax to use for your taxes.

Managing Your Tax Information   339

Creating Year-End Files

At the end of the year, you can save a copy of the current year's information in a separate file (an archive) and continue using the file. You can then use the archived year-end file when preparing for tax time. You can have a year-end file contain all your financial information up to the date when you create the file, or you can select a specific time frame for the transactions that you want to include in the file. In future years, you can use this information for financial projections and reports.

Create a Year-End File

1. Select File, File Operations, Year-End Copy.

2. If you want to continue using the current Quicken file for the coming year, select Do Nothing. My Current Data File Will Remain Unchanged.

3. If you want to remove all information from your data file, with the exception of transactions dated from a specific date forward, select I only want transactions in my current data file starting with this date.

4. Type the date or select it by clicking the calendar icon.

5. Click Browse to locate the folder where you want to save your archive or copy of the current file.

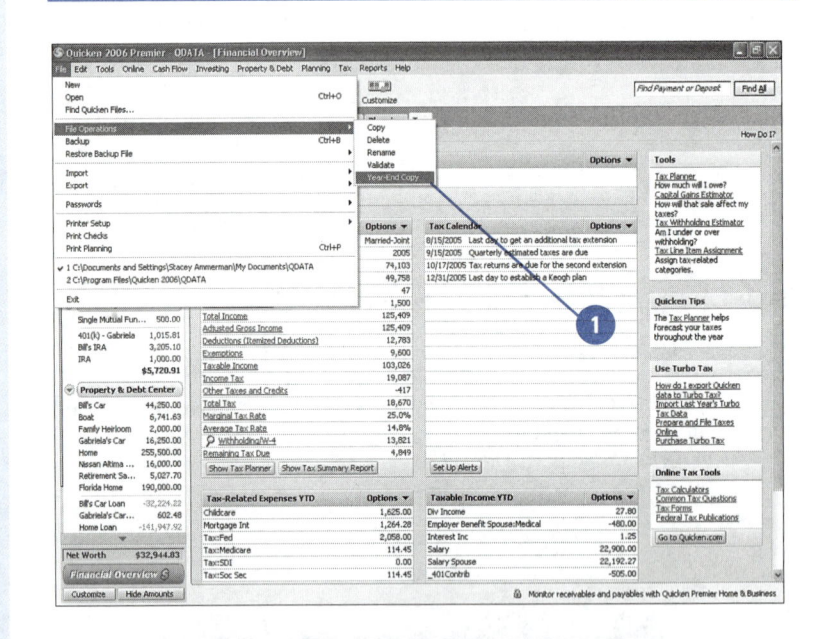

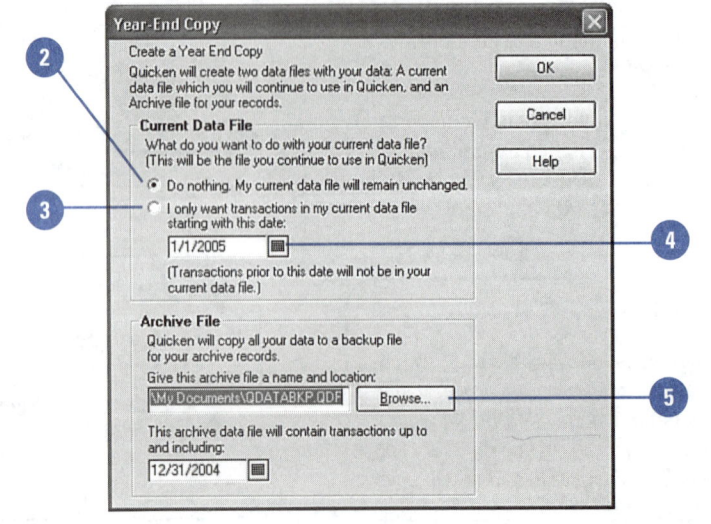

⑥ From the Save in drop-down menu, locate the folder where you want to save the file.

⑦ In File name, type the name of the archive file. You do not need to type the .QDF file extension; Quicken automatically does that for you.

⑧ Click Save.

⑨ To specify a date for the transactions to be included in the file, click in the box under This archive data file will contain Transactions up to and Including and type the date.

⑩ Click OK.

⑪ Select the file you want to work in. Select either Old file or File for New Year and click OK.

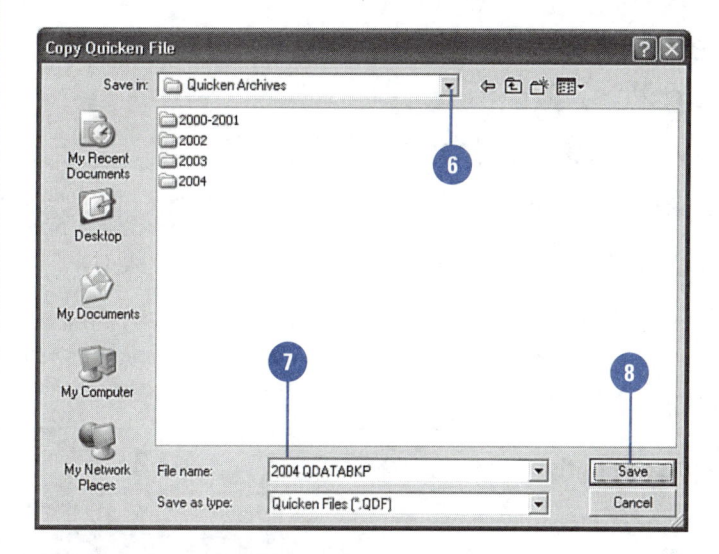

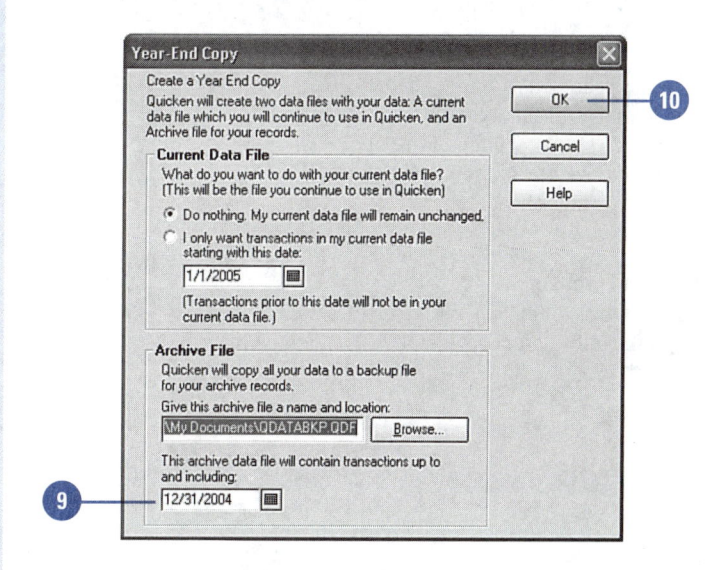

Managing Your Tax Information **341**

Reviewing and Editing Your Projected Tax by Using the Tax Planner

The Tax Planner helps you determine what you can expect to pay or get back in federal and/or state taxes, based on the financial and tax-related information you entered or imported into Quicken. Quicken also uses the most recent tax laws and inflation rates when calculating estimated taxes. Taking all this information into account, the Tax Planner can dissect your financial and tax situation, make certain assumptions, and provide projections on your return or payment probability for the current tax year. You can use the projections to help plan and make adjustments to your finances, if necessary. You can also change information in the Tax Planner to see how certain changes affect the projections. For example, you can create two different scenarios with different withholdings in each to see which scenario works to your advantage.

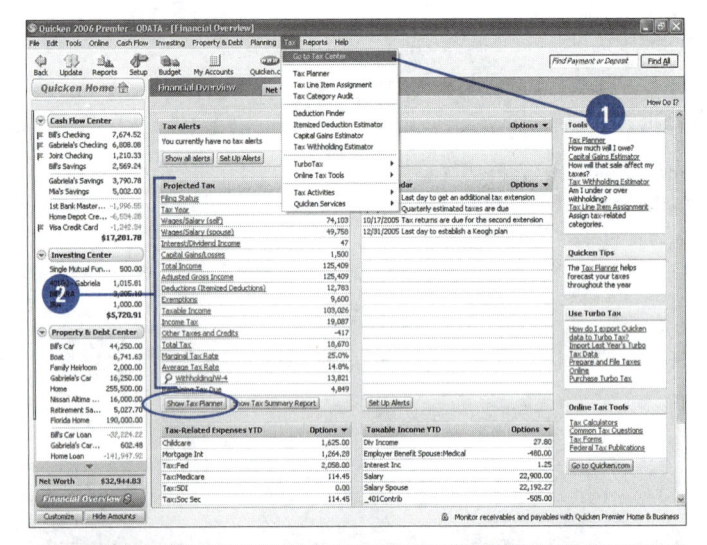

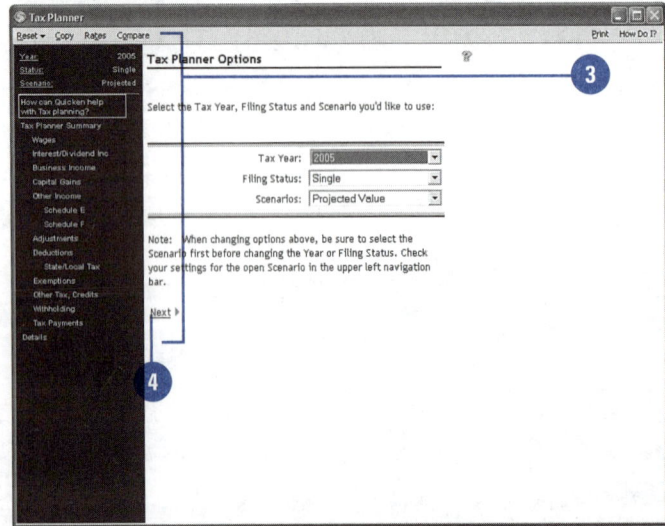

Get Started with the Tax Planner

1. If you're not already there, open the Tax tab in the Financial Overview center by clicking the Tax menu and selecting Go to Tax Center.

2. Click any of the links in the Projected Tax section or click Show Tax Planner to open the Tax Planner.

3. The tax filing year, your filing status, and the current tax scenario are listed at the top of the Tax Planner. Click any of the menu links to review and change your tax information.

4. Click Next to proceed. You can also click the next heading in the menu on the left to proceed.

5. Review the Tax Planner overview and click Let's Get Started.

6. The Tax Planner Summary lists all your basic tax information, such as your income sources, adjusted gross income, tax deductions, and so on. To review and/or change any of the information, click the links. To go through each category consecutively, click Next.

7. Complete or change all applicable information in the Tax Planner. When you reach the Estimated Tax Payments section, you can review the planner results, go back and make changes, or create another scenario, for comparison.

Did You Know?

You can create multiple scenarios. *A great way to decide what options work best for you is to create difference scenarios. For example, if you are married, you can create one scenario using a Married Filing Jointly status and another one using Married Filing Separately status. The outcome will show you which status you should use.*

Did You Know?

You cannot use foreign currency in the Tax tab. *Although you can use foreign currency in most other Quicken features, the Tax Planner and the other tax tools in the Tax tab support only U.S. currency. If you enter anything other than U.S. currency, those amounts are ignored and not included in your projections.*

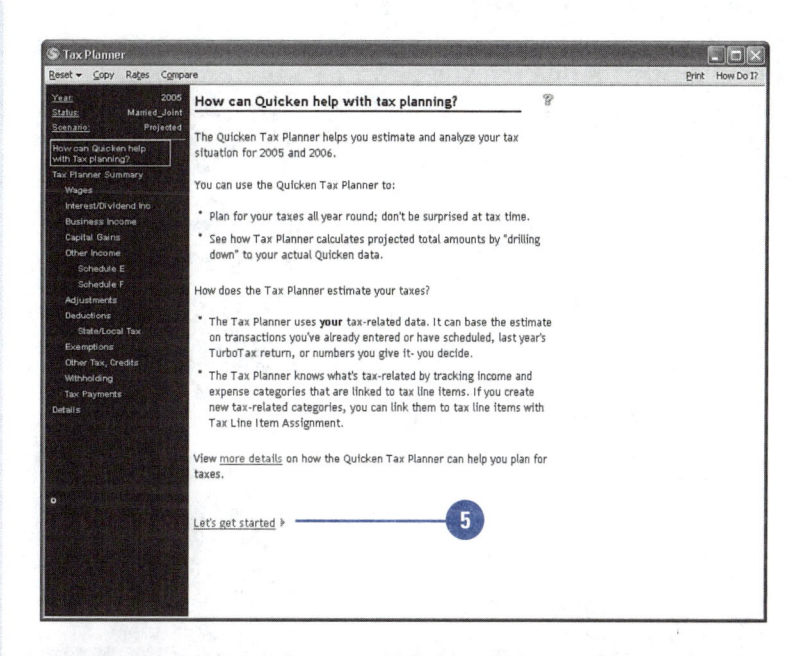

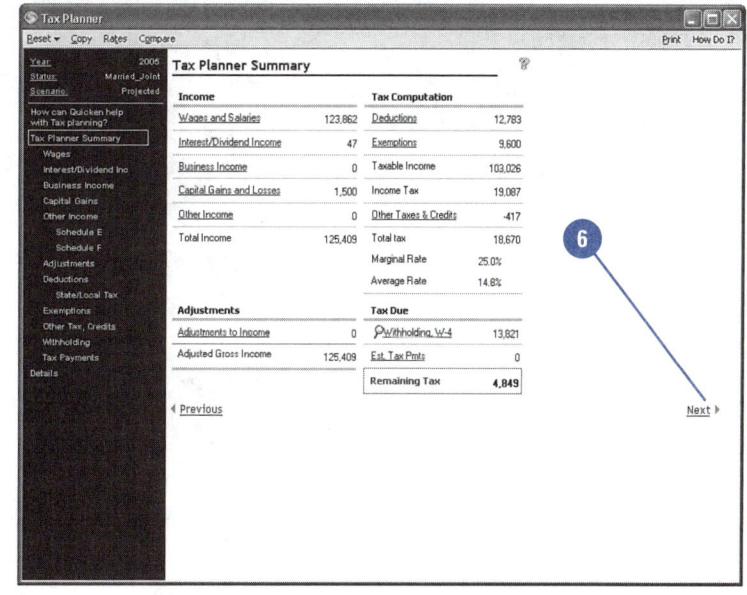

Managing Your Tax Information **343**

Determine Other Income and Losses

① If you have or expect to have income from sources that you have not already entered in Quicken, type those amounts in the correct boxes in the Other Income or Losses section in the Tax Planner.

② Click a link to see the details of that item in the table at the bottom of the window.

③ Select or type the data source and enter the amount, if applicable, you want to use for each item.

④ To enter income from rent, royalties, or partnerships, click Schedule E. To enter income from farming, click Schedule F.

⑤ Type the income you received for each item, a total for any depreciation, and your total expenses. Quicken calculates your net income/loss and adjusts your refund or tax due.

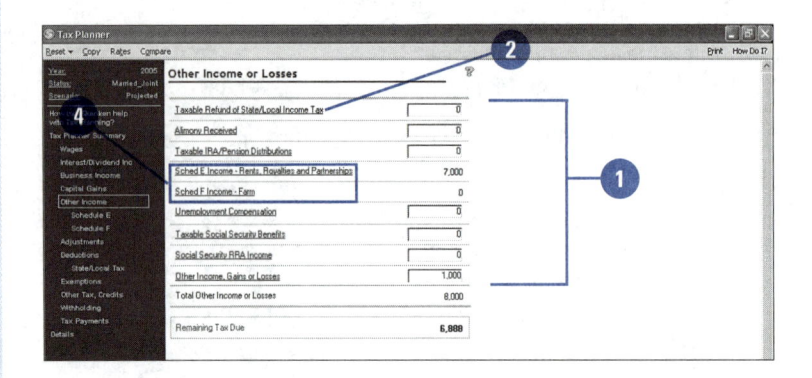

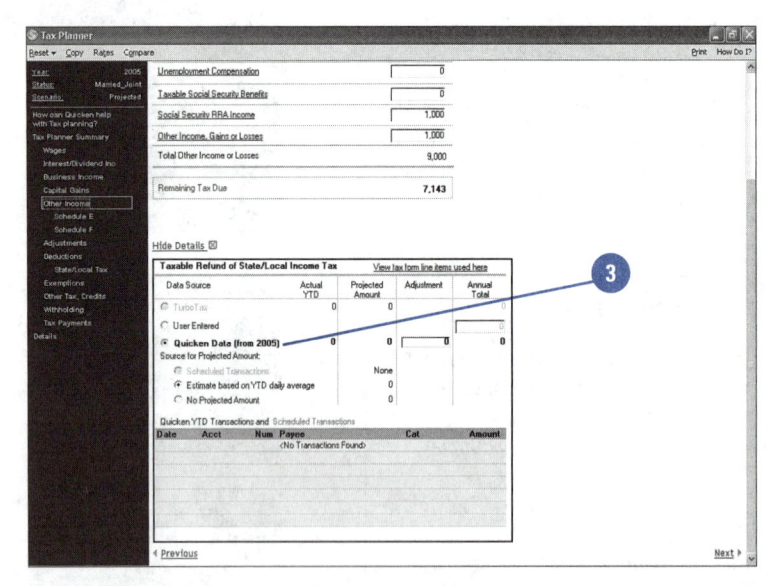

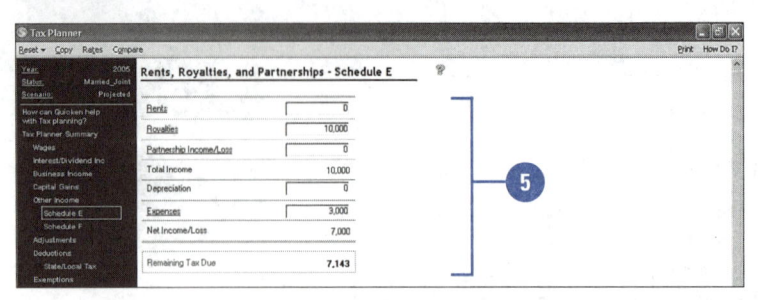

344

6. Select or type the data source and enter the amount, if applicable, you want to use for each item.

7. Scroll down and click Next to open the Farm Income—Schedule F section.

8. If you have income from a farm, enter the information at the top of the window and then select the data source, if needed, at the bottom of the window.

9. When you are finished entering all your other income and losses, scroll to the bottom of the window and click Next, or from the menu on the left side of the screen, click Adjustments.

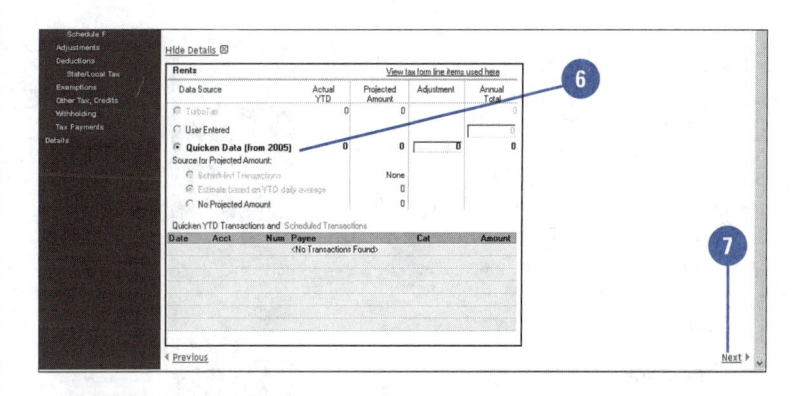

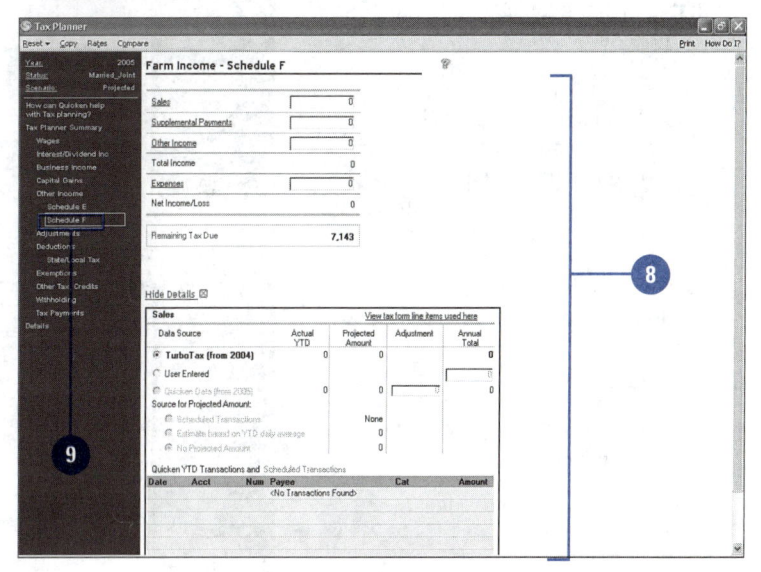

Managing Your Tax Information **345**

Determine Estimated Taxes

1. If you know what your estimated taxes may be, in the Estimated Tax Payments section, type the amounts in the Estimated Taxes (1040-ES) Paid to Date, Projected Future Estimated Tax Payments, and Refund Applied from Prior Year Federal Tax Return boxes.

2. Click a link to see the details of that item in the table at the bottom of the window.

3. Select or type the data source and enter the amount, if applicable, you want to use for each item. Quicken totals your estimated tax payments and adjusts your refund or tax due.

4. To view just the details for any of the Tax Planner sections, click Details.

5. From the Form and Item drop-down menus, select the sections you want to view.

6. Make adjustments, if needed, by typing new amounts.

7. To view the details for the next section in the planner, click Next Detail Item.

8. Click Return to Tax Planner Summary to review the outcome of the changes you have made.

9. Go back through the current scenario to make changes, if you like, by clicking any of the menu links. Then review how the changes affect the outcome.

10. To create a new scenario, click Scenario and select a new one.

11. When you are finished, close the window.

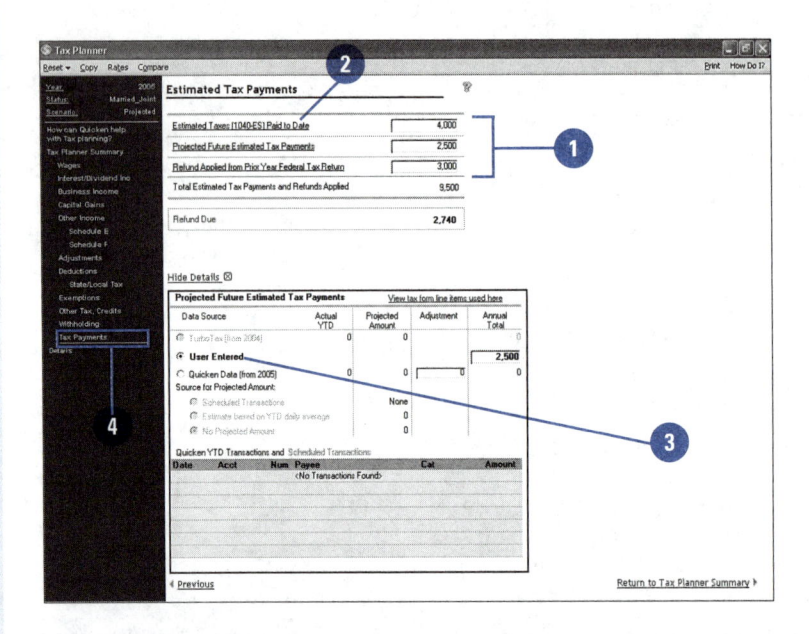

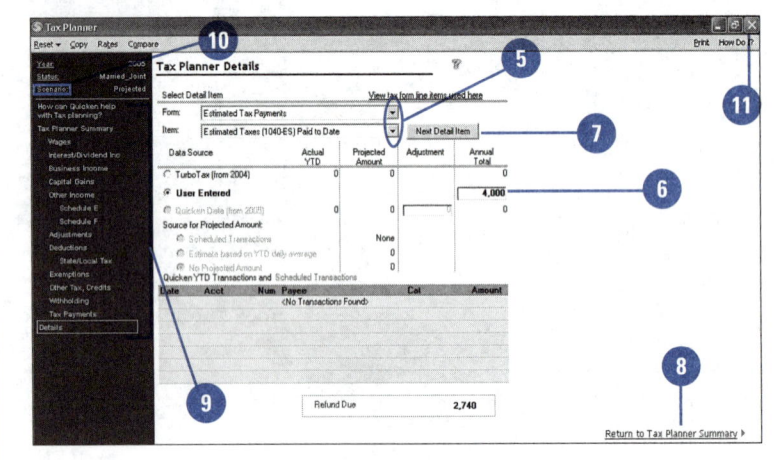

346

Reviewing and Editing Taxable Income

The Taxable Income YTD section of the Tax tab lists all your income that is taxable, such as your paychecks, interest income, bonuses, and so on. You can review the list, add paychecks, and change paycheck information in this section.

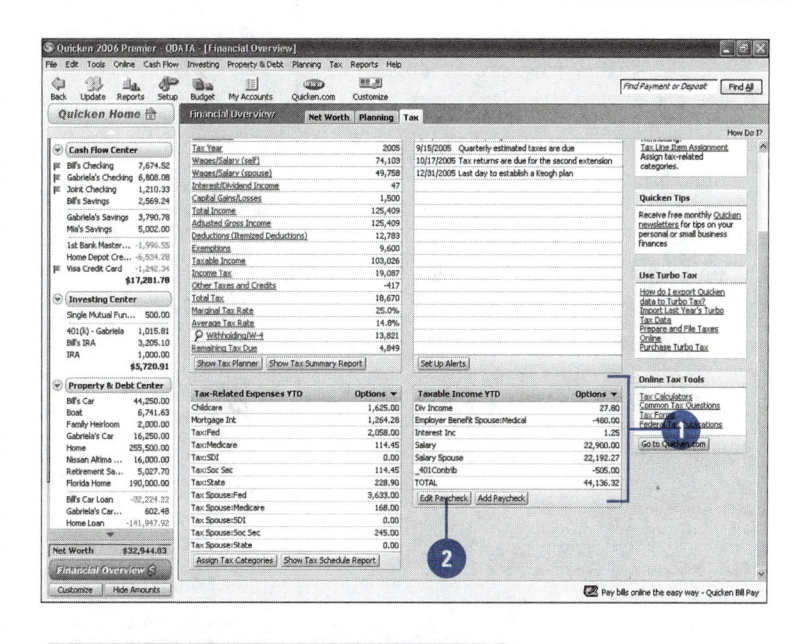

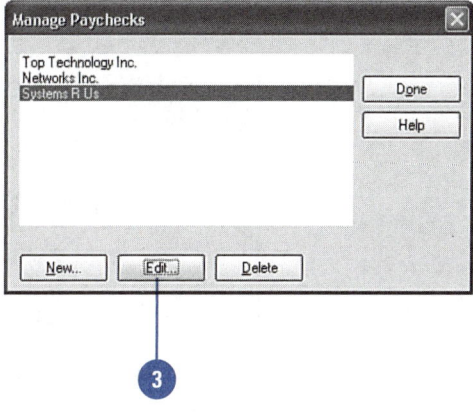

Review and Edit Taxable Income

1. If you're not already there, open the Tax tab and review the paycheck information listed in the Taxable Income YTD section.

2. To update a paycheck, click Edit Paycheck.

3. Select the paycheck you want to change and click Edit.

4. Make the applicable changes and click Done.

See Also

See *"Setting Up New and Edit Existing Tax Alerts"* on page 338 for information on accessing the Tax tab.

See Also

See *"Adding and Editing Information"* on page 166 for more information on updating paycheck details.

Did You Know?

You can view the Tax Summary Report. *A summary of all your tax-related information, such as income, transactions, and taxes, is available in the Tax Summary Report. You can view it by clicking the Show Tax Summary Report button in the Projected Tax section of the Tax tab.*

Managing Your Tax Information **347**

5. To add a paycheck, click New. You can also add paychecks from the Taxable Income YTD section on the Tax tab by clicking Add Paycheck.

6. Complete the paycheck setup by clicking Next to move through the setup and entering the paycheck information.

7. To delete a paycheck, select the paycheck and click Delete. A message appears, asking if you want to remove the paycheck.

8. Click Yes to delete it or click No to keep it.

9. When you are finished adding, updating, and deleting paychecks, click Done.

Did You Know?

See "Adding and Editing a New Paycheck" on page 166 for more information on creating a new paycheck.

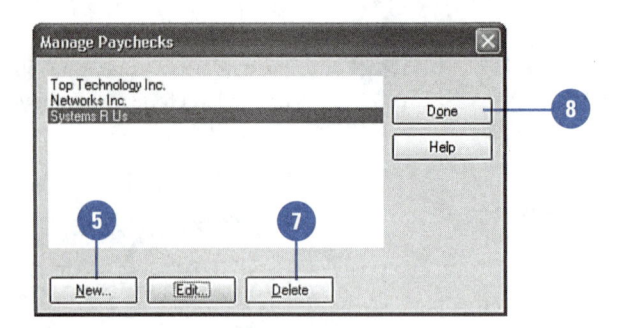

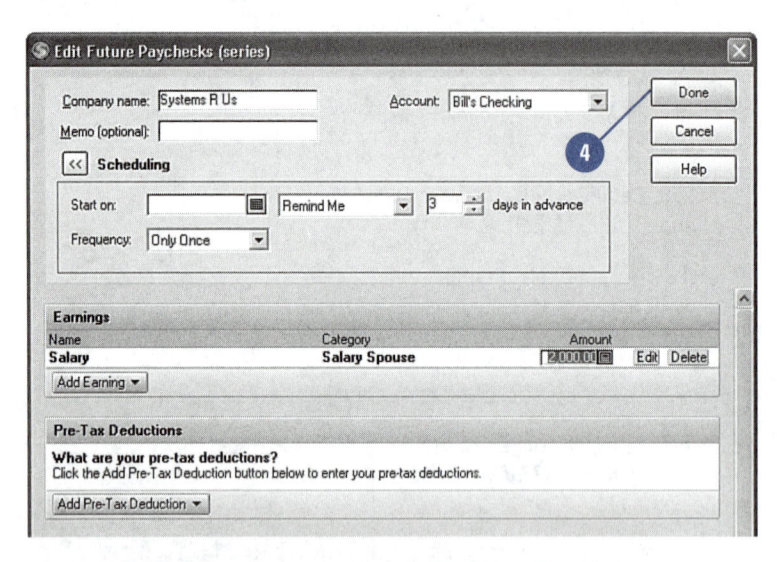

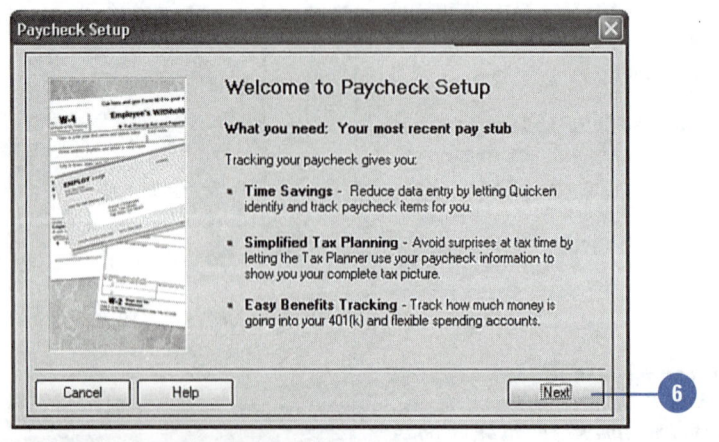

Assigning and Editing Tax Categories

The Tax-Related Expenses YTD section of the Tax tab lists all your current expenses that can be claimed on your taxes, such as childcare and taxes. To ensure that your expenses are marked and assigned correctly, you should review the list and the tax categories assigned to all your expenses and transactions. The transactions that are assigned to tax categories are tracked in Quicken, and each is assigned to a specific tax line item, which you can deduct on your taxes. This information is used to determine your estimated taxes liabilities, to project future liabilities, and to create reports. This information can also be exported to and used in TurboTax. In the Category List window, you can create categories, assign categories to tax line items, edit categories, and delete categories. The tax line items are predefined, but you can change them and add your own to meet your needs.

Review the Category List

1. Open the Tax tab and click Assign Tax Categories in the Tax-Related Expenses YTD section.

2. The category list contains every category and subcategory for your finances in Quicken. Each subcategory that is associated with a tax line item has a check mark in the Tax Line Item column.

3. Click a subcategory (a line item) to see a description in the Tax Line Item Assignments section.

4. To go to a specific tax line item, click the Tax Item drop-down menu and select the item.

5. To hide a category description in your register, select the check box next to that category in the Hide Description column.

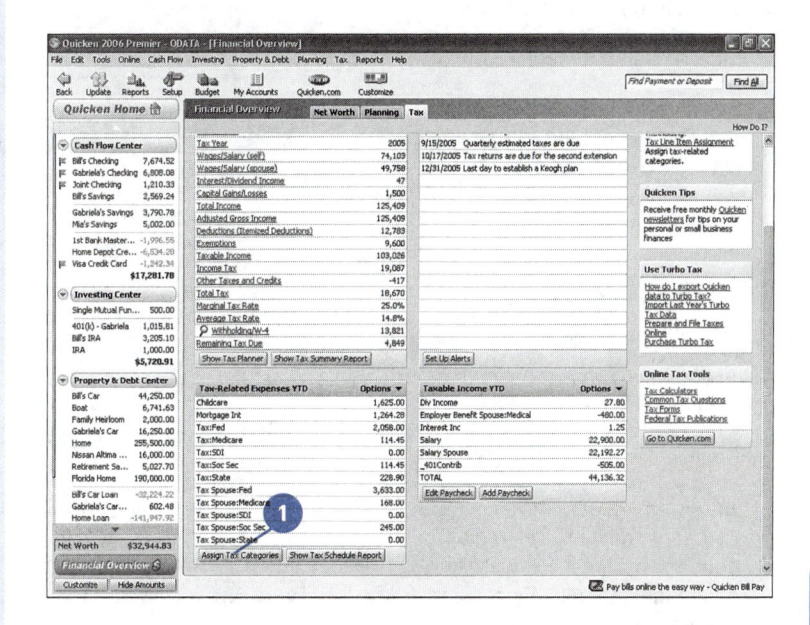

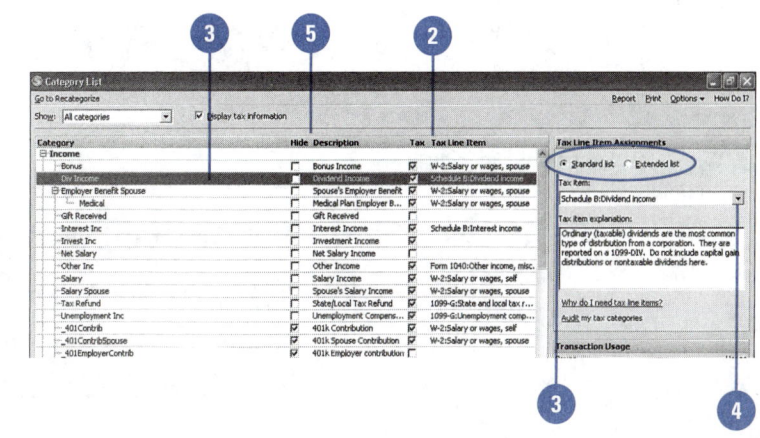

Managing Your Tax Information 349

Assign Category Groups

1. From the Options menu in the Category List window, select Assign category groups.

2. Review the list and if you see a category that you want to assign to a new category group, from the Category Name column, select the category. The group is automatically selected.

3. In the Category Group List column, select the new group you want to assign to the category name.

4. Click Assign Category to Group.

5. To remove a category group from a category, select the category and click Clear Assignment.

6. To create a new category, click New.

7. Type the category name and click OK.

8. To change a category name, select the category and click Edit.

9. Change the name and click OK.

10. To remove a category, select the category and click Del. A message appears, asking if you want to delete the category. Remember that deleting a category also deletes all subcategories.

11. Click Yes to delete it or click No to keep it.

12. When you are finished making changes, click OK.

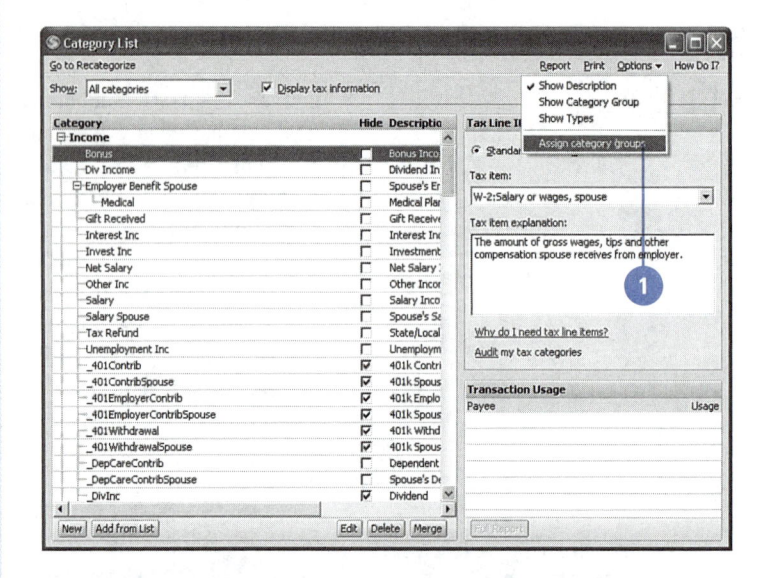

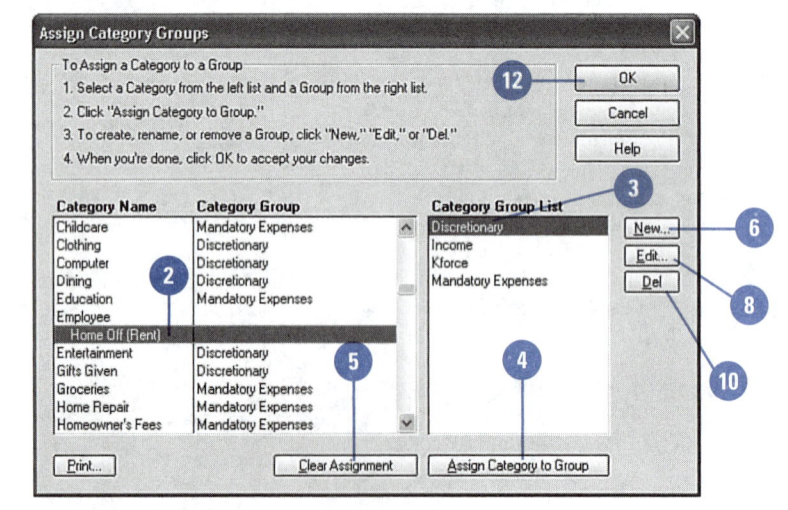

350

Add New Categories

1. To add a new category, in the Category List window, click New.

2. Type the name, enter a description, and select the group.

3. Select the type of category.

4. Select a tax line item, if applicable. If the new category is tax related, select Tax-related.

5. Click OK.

6. To add categories that are not currently in the category list, click Add from List in the Category List window.

7. From the Available Categories section, select the category from which to select the subcategories and then select each subcategory you want to add. Green check marks appear next to the items you select.

8. Click Add. The subcategories you selected appear in the Categories to Add section.

9. Click OK.

See Also

See "Assign Category Groups" on page 350 for information on adding new categories.

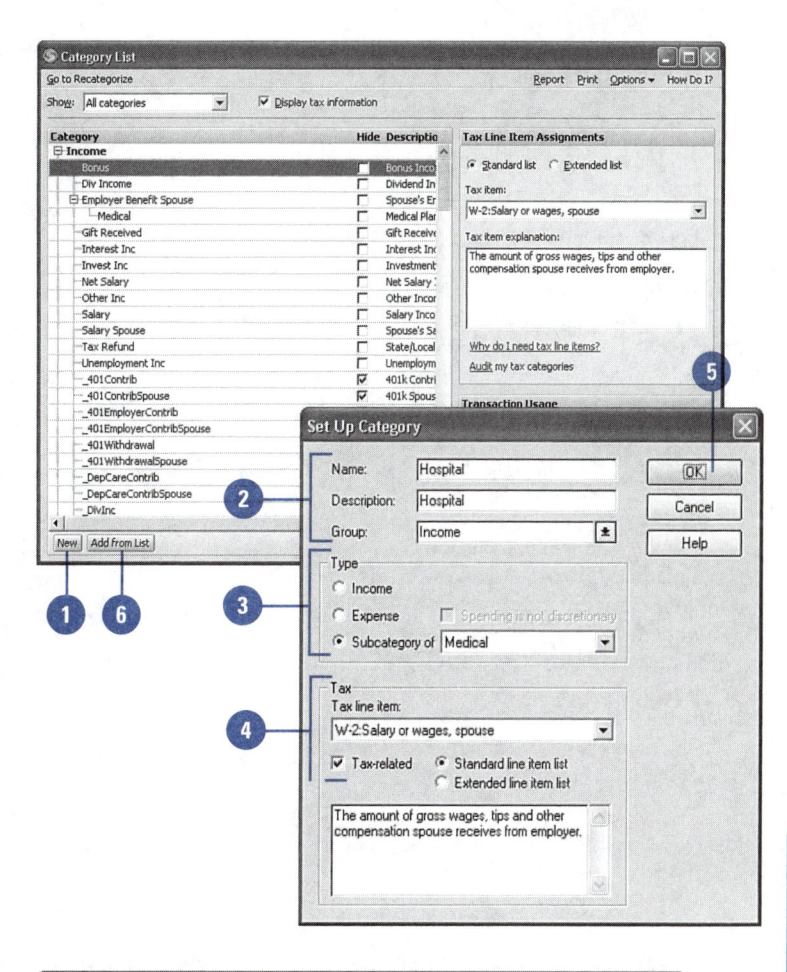

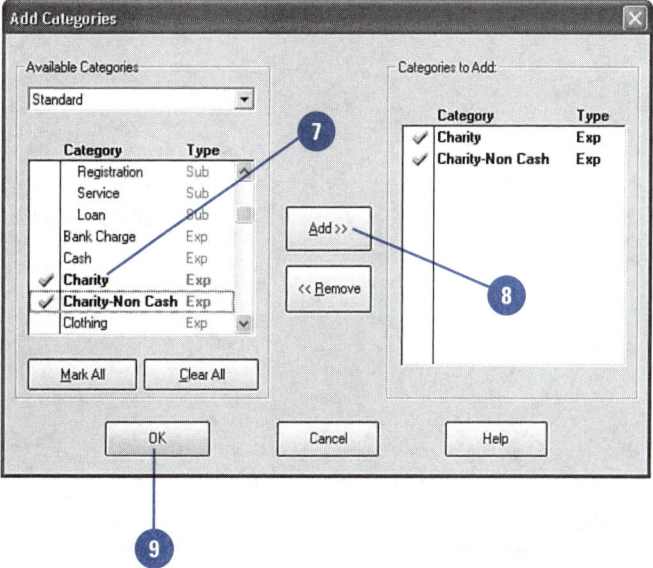

Managing Your Tax Information **351**

Edit or Delete Categories

1. To edit a category, in the Category List window, select the category and click Edit.

2. Make your changes and click OK.

3. To delete a category, select the category and click Delete. A message appears, asking if you want to delete the category and letting you know that deleting the category also deletes all subcategories.

4. If you are given the option to assign the transactions currently assigned to this category to another category, from the Recategorize Transactions To drop-down menu, select a new category.

5. Click OK to delete the category or click Cancel to keep it.

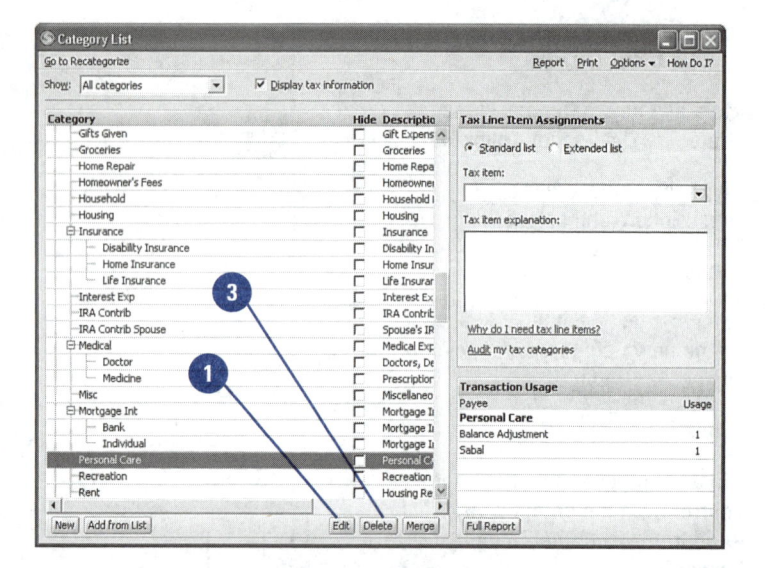

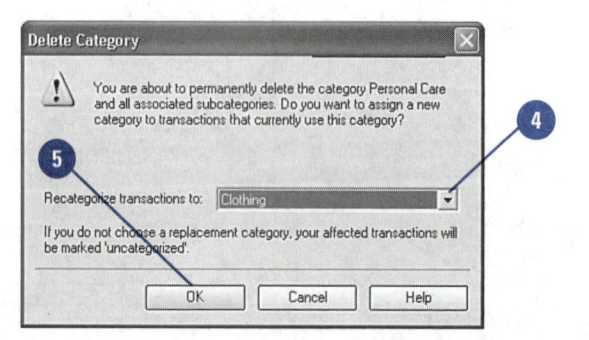

Move Categories

1. To move a category under another one, in the Category List window, select the category you want to move and click Merge.

2. Select the category you want to merge with the one you selected in step 1 and click OK.

Did You Know?

You can do an audit of your tax categories. To perform a quick audit of your tax categories to check for potential mistakes, click the Audit link. Quicken flags any potential mistakes, such as linking categories with incorrect tax line items, and lists them in the Tax Category Audit window. To fix a mistake, you can click Change, correct the mistake, and click OK.

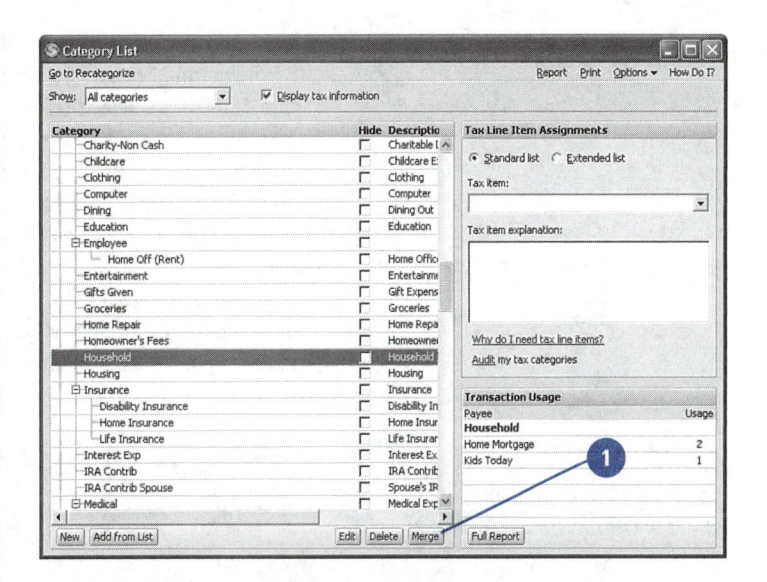

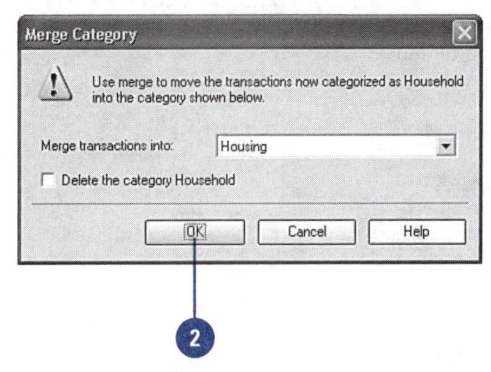

Managing Your Tax Information **353**

Estimating Capital Gains

If you sell an investment and the selling price exceeds the purchase price, that investment produces a profit for you. This profit is known as a *capital gain*. Quicken provides a feature, called the Capital Gains Estimator, to help you determine what your capital gain potential is, using your existing investments. Estimating your capital gains helps you determine whether it would be advantageous to sell an investment and what tax liability you could encounter. You can access the Capital Gains Estimator from the Investment and Tax menus, from the Tools section on the Tax tab in the Financial Overview center, from the Analysis tab in the Investing Center, and from the Portfolio Analyzer. For the purposes of this task, you will be accessing it from the Analysis tab.

Estimate Capital Gains

1. Open the Tax tab in the Financial Overview center and click Capital Gains Estimator.

2. Review the Welcome window and click Let's get started to proceed.

See Also

See "Setting Up New and Edit Existing Tax Alerts" on page 338 for information on accessing the Tax tab. See "Reviewing and Editing Your Projected Tax by Using the Tax Planner" on page 342 for information on determining tax liabilities and setting up your tax information by using the Tax Planner.

Did You Know?

You can use the Capital Gains Estimator menu to move through the Capital Gains Estimator. *You can click the menu options on the left side of the window or go to a specific place in the Capital Gains Estimator. If you have saved scenarios you are working with, you can click a scenario in the Scenarios section to go directly to it.*

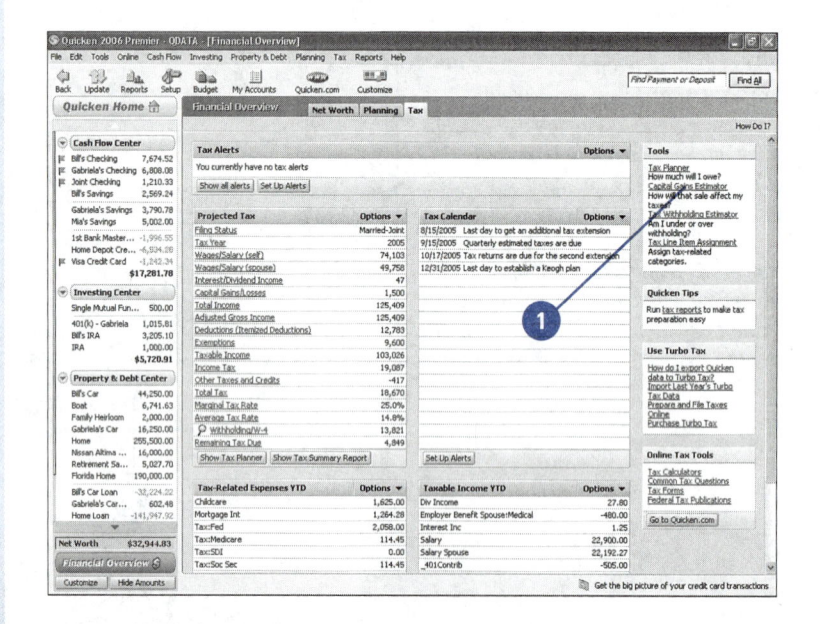

354

3. Select a scenario and then click Next. You can set up as many as three scenarios to compare and contrast situations. However, you have to create the scenarios one at a time.

4. Select the investments you want to include by clicking in the column next to the name of each investment you want to include. A green check mark means the investment is selected. Then click Next.

5. If you're sure of your federal tax rate, in the Federal Tax Rates section, select it from the list. Otherwise, use the rate that Quicken has selected for you.

6. If you want to enter a state rate, in the State Tax Rates section, select your state tax rate.

7. If you are unsure of what your tax rate is, click How do I find my State Tax rate? to get more information on how to determine the rate.

8. Click Next.

Did You Know?

The top of the Select Tax Rates window lists your estimated taxes. Quicken determines these taxes based on the information you have entered into Quicken about your investments and tax information. Setting up your tax information in the Tax Planner is not required, but doing so gives you a more accurate estimate.

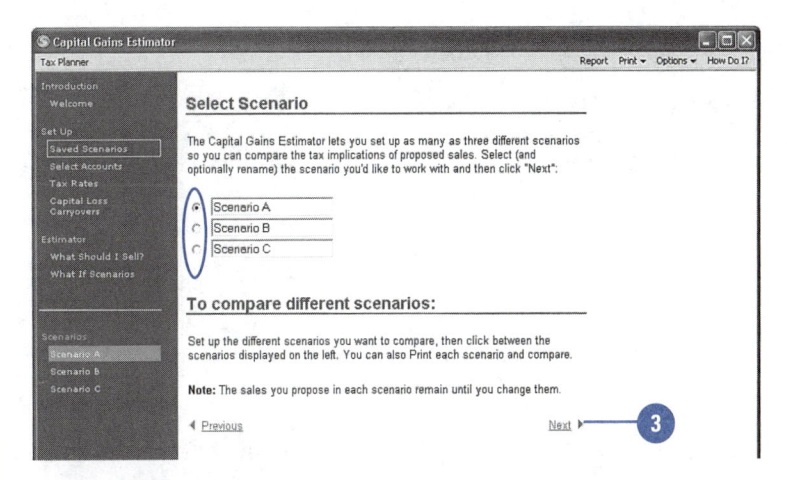

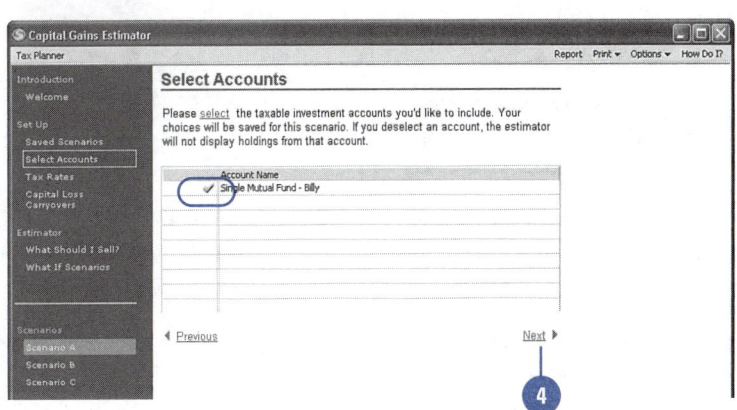

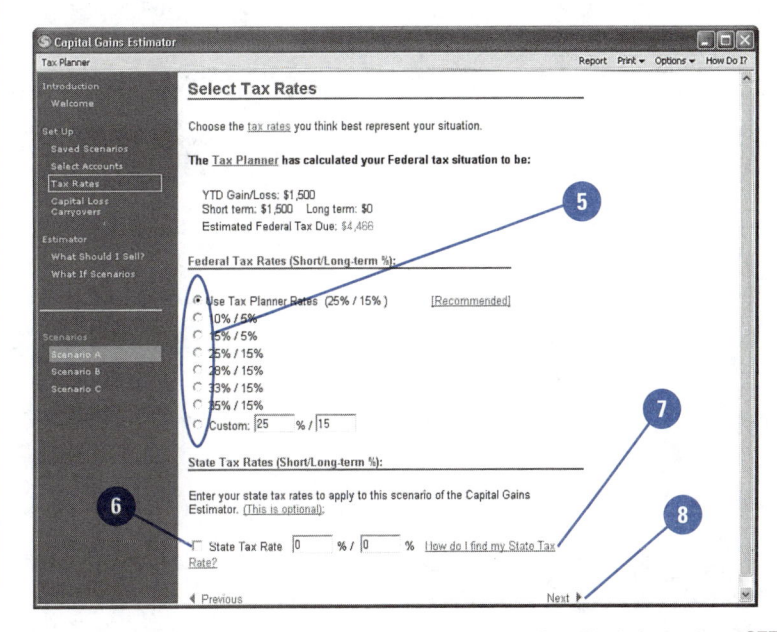

Managing Your Tax Information   355

⑨ To help offset your taxes, use losses from previous years by selecting Use Tax Planner Values to automatically fill in the figures from the Tax Planner or select Enter different values to enter them yourself.

⑩ Click Next.

⑪ If you know exactly how much you want to make, complete the What Should I Sell? section; otherwise, click Next to proceed.

Did You Know?

You can use the What Should I Sell? section to determine how you can make a specific amount of money. If you know how much money you want to make and want Quicken to determine what you should sell to make the money, in the What Should I Sell? section, enter the amount you want to make, select a goal, and click Search. From there, follow the instructions to get the results you want.

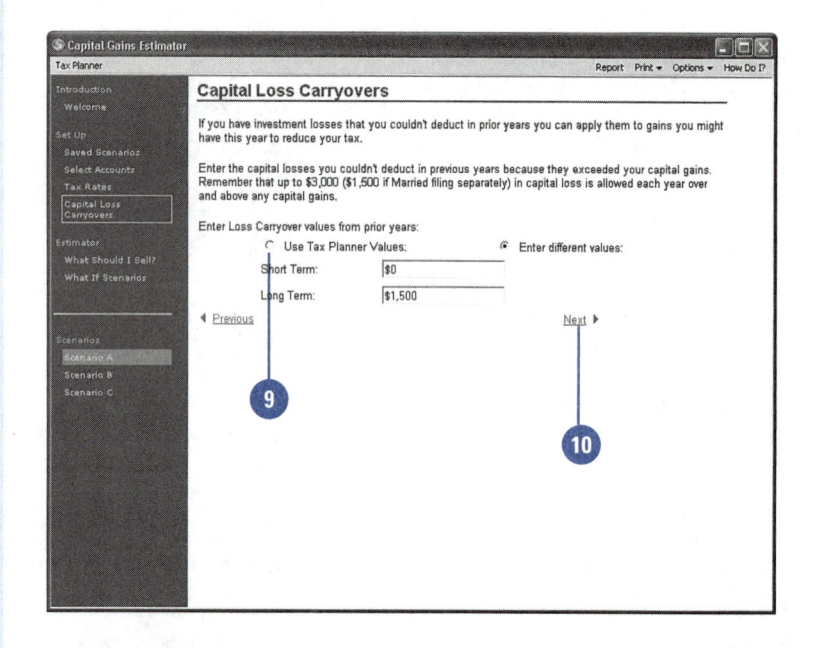

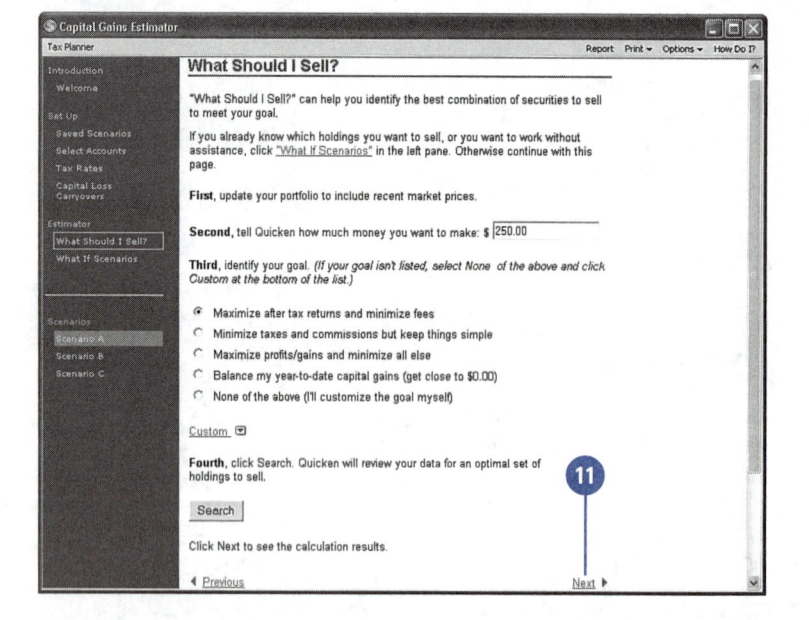

⑫ Select the security or lot that you are thinking of selling. The number of shares and selling price automatically update in the Proposed Sales table, based on the security or lot you select.

⑬ Click Shares to Sell or Sale Price to change the figures, if needed.

⑭ Any losses or gains are listed in the Taxable Gains from Proposed Sales table.

⑮ The potential total gross proceeds, total estimated taxes due or refund, and net proceeds are calculated and provided toward the bottom of the window.

⑯ If desired, go back through this scenario and make changes by clicking the menu links.

⑰ To set up another scenario repeat steps 1–15. However, be sure to select the next scenario—for example, Scenario B—in step 3.

⑱ When you are finished, close the window.

Did You Know?

You can compare taxes before and after sales. To see what your taxes would be before and after you sell an investment, you can click the links under Detailed Calculations at the bottom of the window.

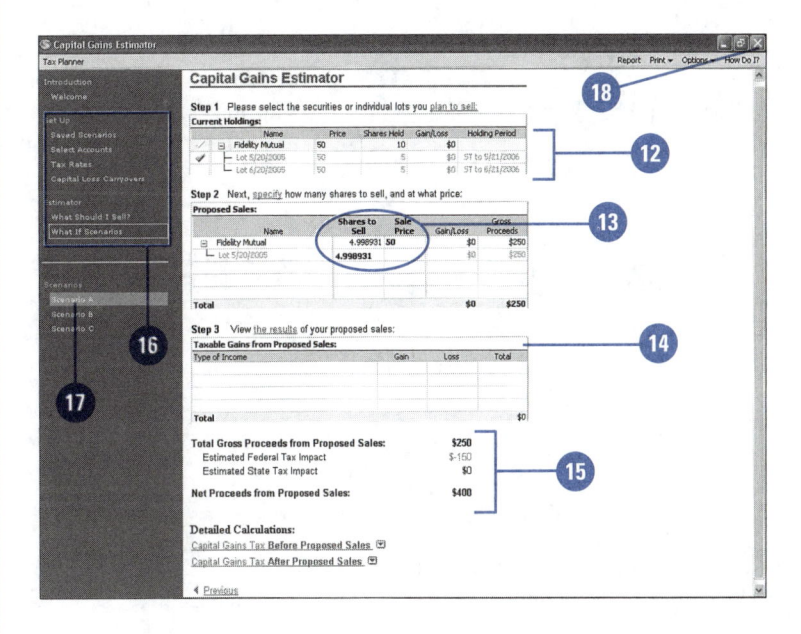

Managing Your Tax Information **357**

Estimating Tax Withholding

One of the simplest ways of planning for and managing your income and tax obligations is by changing your withholding. Quicken offers a tool to help you determine what your withholding should be: the Tax Withholding Estimator. You can access this tool from the Tax Planner or from the Tax tab.

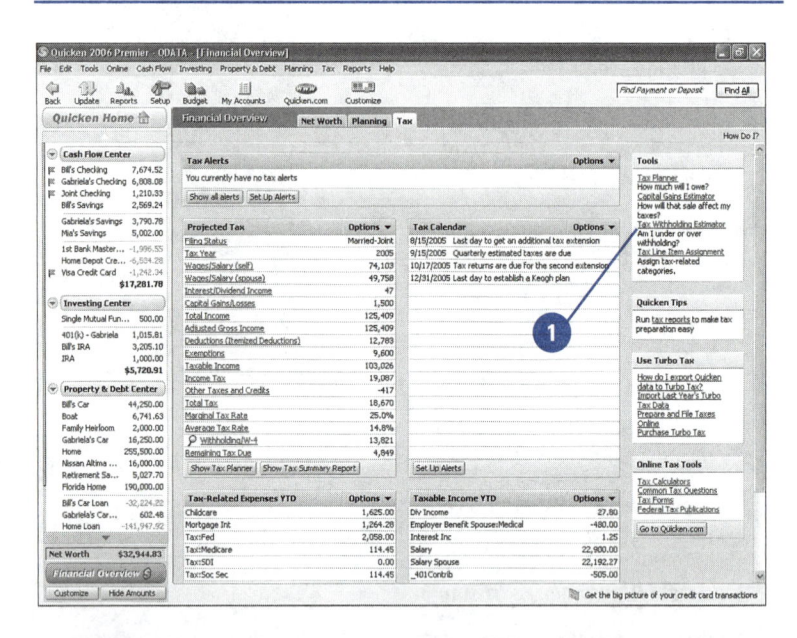

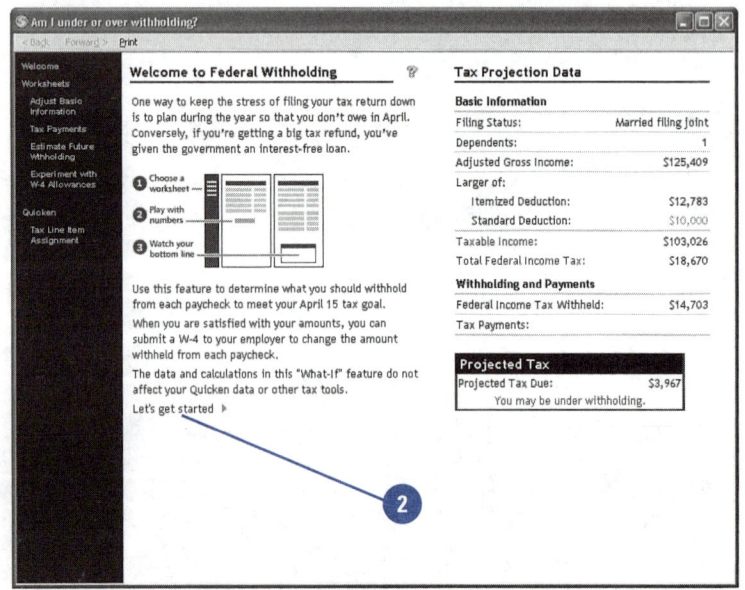

Estimate Tax Withholding

1. If you're not already there, open the Tax tab in the Financial Overview center and click Tax Withholding Estimator.

2. Review the Welcome window. Your basic tax information is listed, including your projected tax. Click Let's get started to proceed.

See Also

See "Setting Up New and Edit Existing Tax Alerts" on page 338 for information on accessing the Tax tab.

3. In the Adjust Basic Information section, if needed, select a different filing status, change or enter the number of dependents you have, change your adjusted gross income, and change your itemized deductions.

4. To use the information from the Tax Planner, click Reset to Tax Planner Values.

5. Click Next.

6. In the Tax Payments box, type the amount you expect to pay for the year, if any. To use the amount from the Tax Planner, click Reset to Tax Planner Values.

7. Click Next.

8. In the Estimate Future Withholding section, change or enter the amount of tax you've paid so far this year, any additional withholding, your next pay date, the amount of federal tax withheld for each of your paychecks, and your pay period.

9. If you are unsure of any of the information in step 8, use the amount from the Tax Planner by clicking Reset to Tax Planner Values and then click Next.

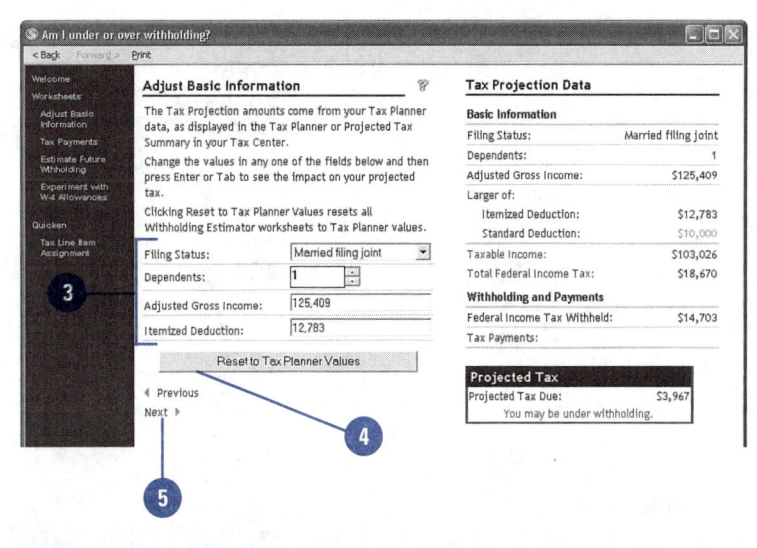

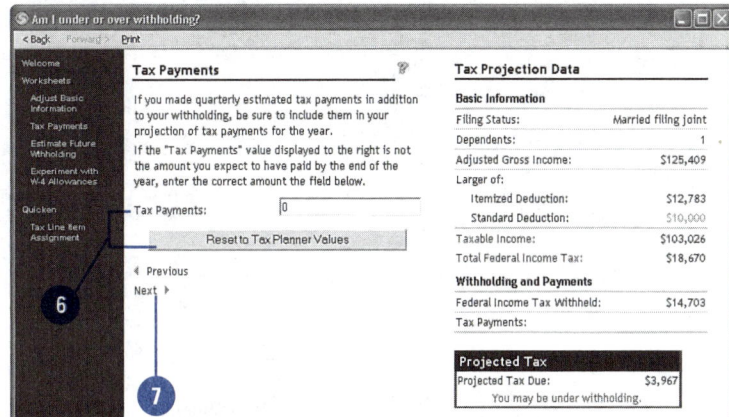

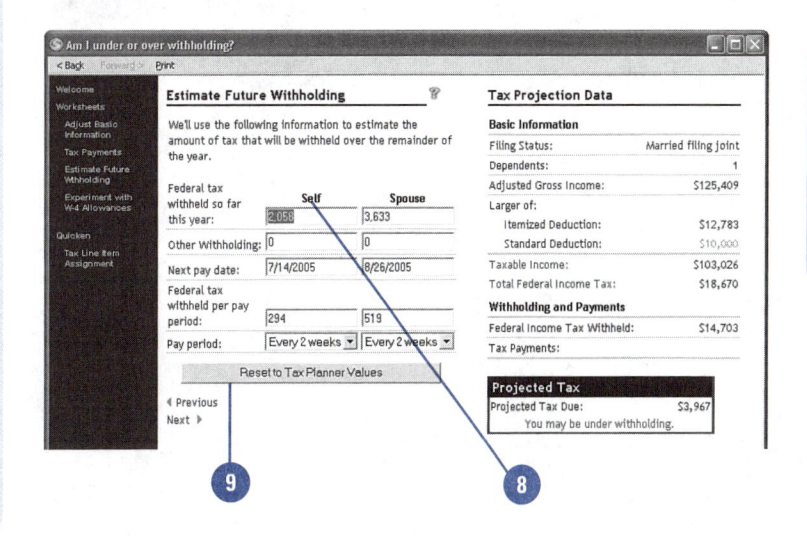

Managing Your Tax Information   359

10. In the Experiment with W-4 Allowances section, type the amount of your and/or your spouse's wages that are taxable and the number of allowances you want to take.

11. If you want to enter additional withholdings, in the Additional withholding per pay period box(es), type the additional withholdings for you and/or your spouse.

12. To use the wages amount from the Tax Planner, click Reset to Tax Planner Values.

13. Press Enter or Tab to calculate your withholding amount. Change the withholding to see how the withholding amount differs.

14. When you are satisfied with the amount, click Next.

15. In the Tax Line Item Assignment section, if needed, add or assign tax categories and link tax line items with categories.

16. If desired, go back through the worksheets and make changes to see how the changes affect the outcome by clicking the Previous link or selecting a link from the menu.

17. When you are finished, close the window.

See Also

See "Assigning and Editing Tax Categories" on page 349 for information on how to add tax categories and assign categories to tax line items.

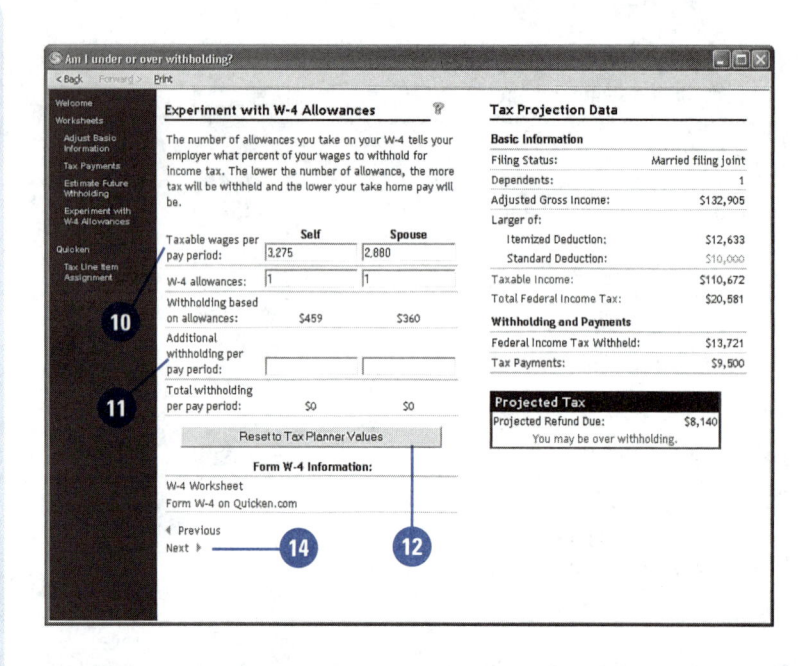

Finding Deductions

"Income tax time is when you test your powers of deduction." These are true words spoken by author Shelby Friedman. An important and easy way to help manage and plan for tax time is to determine which deductions you are eligible to take. The Deduction Finder helps you find deductions you might not otherwise have known about by stepping you through a questionnaire that asks you questions related to possible deductions. Your answers determine which deductions you are eligible for and, if there are no tax categories already set up for the deductions you qualify for, Quicken sets them up for you. You can even print a summary of the deductions you can use.

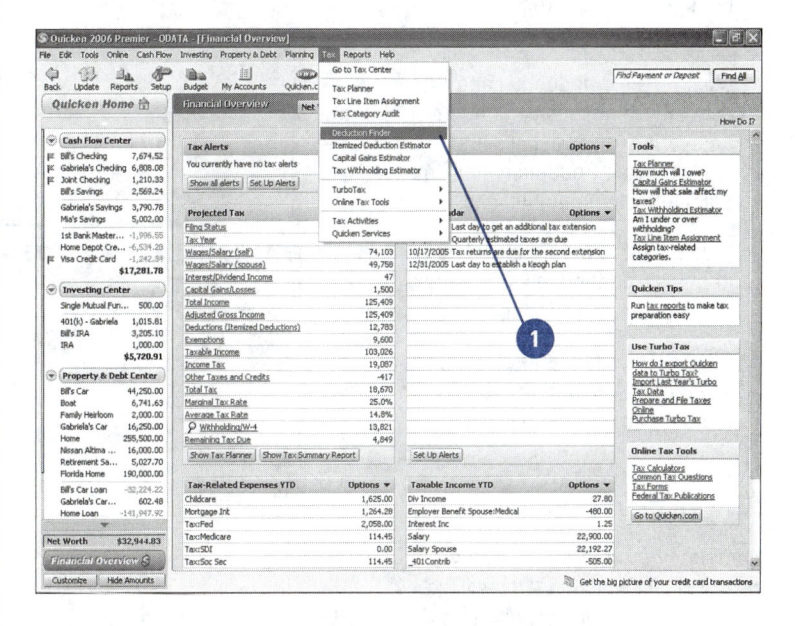

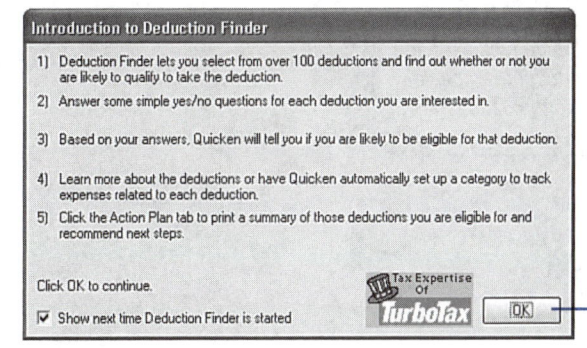

Find Deductions

1. From the Tax menu, select Deduction Finder.
2. Review the introduction information and click OK.

See Also

See "Assigning and Editing Tax Categories" on page 349 for information on tax categories.

Managing Your Tax Information **361**

3 From Choose a Deduction Type, select the type of deduction you want to explore.

4 In the Choose a Deduction column, select a deduction. The questions related to that deduction appear to the right.

5 Review each questions and select Y (yes) or N (no) for each question. When you are finished answering the questions, the result appears at the bottom of the window.

6 Click the next deduction and answer the questions. Continue answering the questions and clicking Next Deduction until you complete all the deductions.

7 If you want to create a tax line item for a deduction you qualify for, click Create a Category.

8 Click OK to add the new category. Categories you add now appear in the Choose a Deduction list.

Did You Know?

Your eligibility status is indicated next to each deduction. After you've answered the deduction questions, if you are not eligible for a deduction, an X appears next to the deduction. If you are eligible for a deduction, a check mark appears next to the deduction.

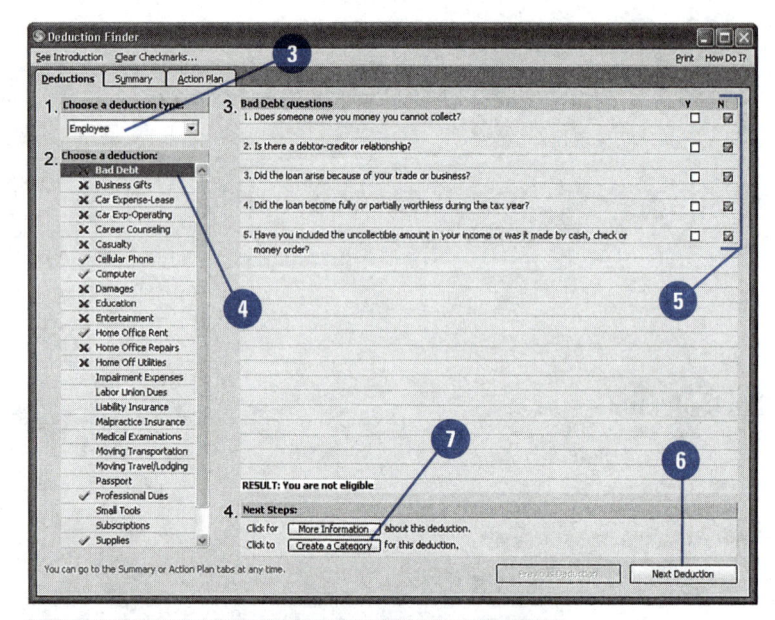

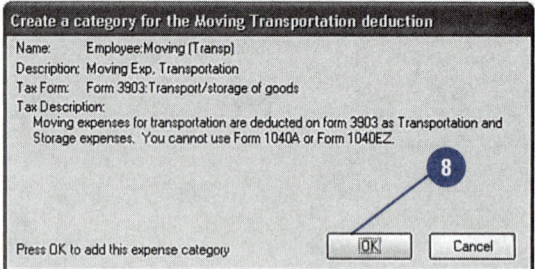

9. When you are finished answering all the questions for the deduction type, select another deduction type and answer all those questions. Repeat this for all deduction categories.

10. When you are finished answering all questions, click the Summary page to view a summary of all the deductions you are eligible for.

11. Click the Action Plan tab to view what you need to do to confirm your eligibility for the deductions and what you need to do in order to claim the deductions.

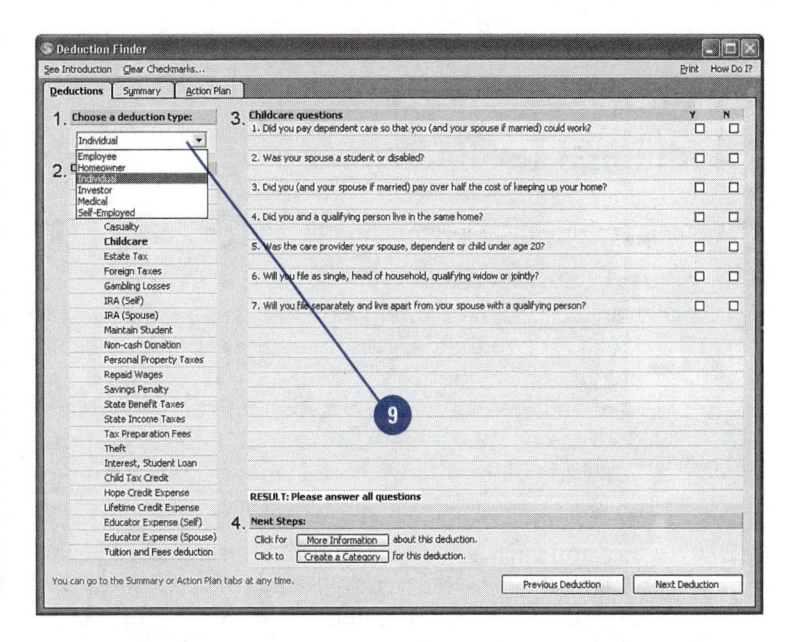

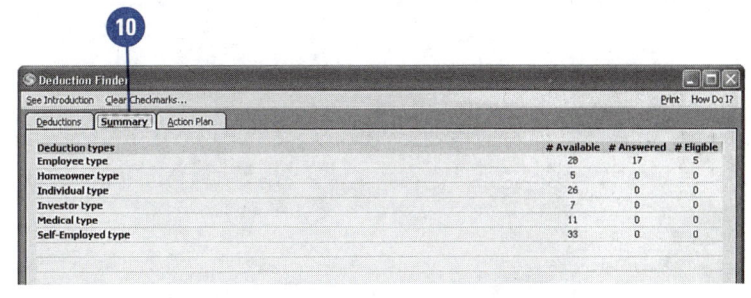

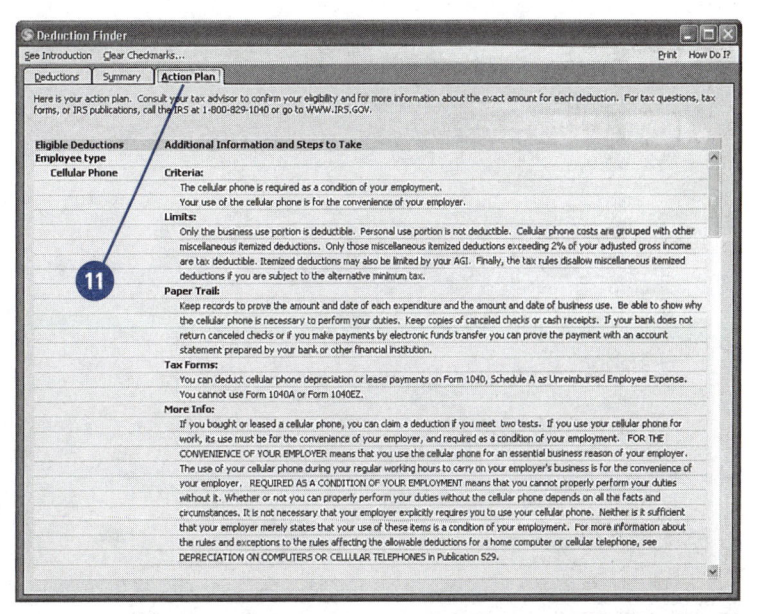

Managing Your Tax Information **363**

Additional Tax Resources

You can use the following tool and links to help prepare for and manage your taxes:

- **Tax Category Audit**—This tool audits the categories you currently have set up for all your transactions, and it flags potential problem areas. When Quicken scans your categories, it looks for two things: categories that are not linked to tax line items or are incorrectly linked and categories that you have created and that may need to be linked to different tax line items. By using this tool, you can avoid headaches later when you're preparing your taxes. When you run the audit and Quicken flags any potential problem categories, you can edit or remove the category directly from the Tax Category Audit.

- **Web links**—You can find links to additional tax resources on the Web in the Use Turbo Tax and Online Tax Tools sections in the lower-right section of the Tax tab. You can review these resources to find answers to questions that aren't answered in this chapter, get help preparing and filing your taxes, and access the latest federal tax publications.

Working with Reports

12

Introduction

Quicken provides a wide variety of reports for just about every aspect of your financial situation, for just about every scenario or combination of scenarios, and for many time periods (past, present, and future). And if you can't find a report to meet your exact needs, Quicken gives you the power of customizing reports so you can create and save your own reports. In addition, you can print reports and export them into another format—for example, to use in a Microsoft Excel spreadsheet so that you can share the information with others. You can use reports to analyze your financial condition, to shed light on how you're doing with a budget, a savings goal, or another financial concern.

In this chapter, you will learn how to view the standard reports that Quicken offers, such as the Cash Flow report, which shows you exactly where all your money is going for a specific period of time. Quicken offers several standard reports and graphs that you can customize to meet your specific needs; you can then save them and reuse them. You'll learn about all this in this chapter. In addition, you will learn how to set preferences, such as how to use a specific date range for all reports so that Quicken uses that date range each time you run a report or graph.

Using reports and graphs helps you manage your money so that you can clearly see exactly where your money is going and where it is coming from. This information can help you make decisions about your spending, budget, potential taxes, and much more. There are a host of uses for reports and graphs, and this chapter steps you through how to get the most out of reports and graphs, which will help you manage your finances.

What You'll Do

View Reports

Customize Reports

Set Report Preferences

Export Reports

Save and View Saved Reports

Viewing Reports

You can access reports from many places in Quicken, such as from some of the activity centers, from the Financial Overview center, and from the Reports menu. For the purposes of this task, we will access reports by using the Reports menu.

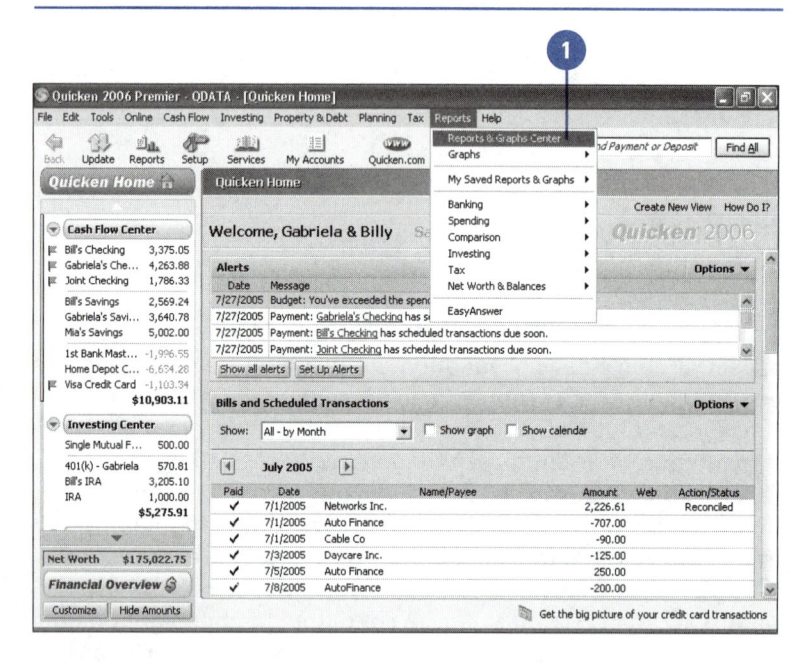

View a Report

① Click Reports, Reports & Graphs Center. Any reports that you have created and saved appear under the Saved Reports section.

② Click a report heading to view the available reports and graphs. A paper icon appears next to the reports, and a pie chart icon appears next to the graphs.

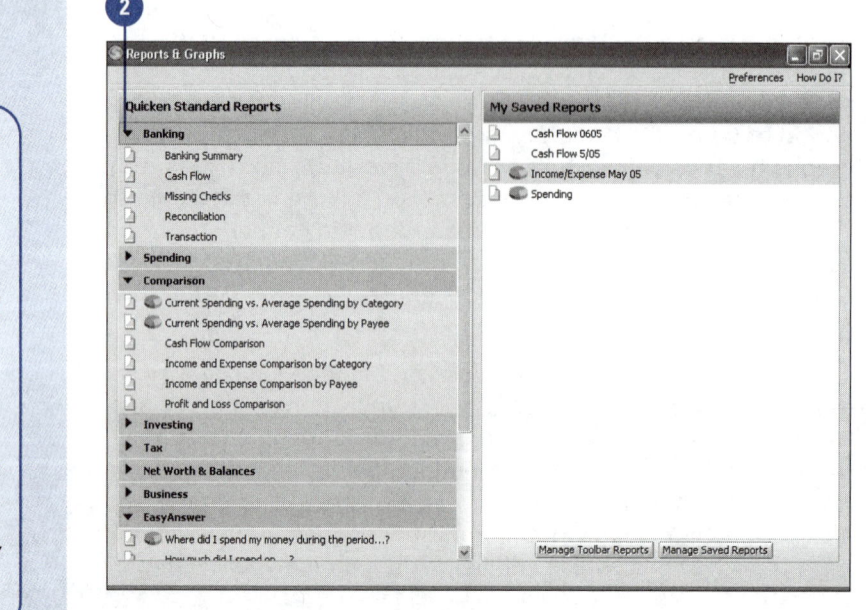

Did You Know?

You can use the Reports menu to create instant reports. *The quickest way to view a report, no matter where you are in Quicken, is to use the Reports menu. You can go into the Reports and Graphs window from here, but you don't even have to go that far to run a report. You can click Reports from the menu bar and then click a menu option, such as Banking. Each menu option contains reports that you can view directly from the menu. You can select a report from one of the options, and you get an instant report.*

③ Click a report to select it. The report criteria options that appear vary, depending on which report or graph you select.

④ Select or type the report criteria you want to view in the report. For example, for the Cash Flow report, I selected Last month from the Date range drop-down menu. Quicken automatically fills in the dates.

⑤ Click Show Report.

See Also

See the next task, "Customizing Reports," on page 368, to learn how to customize the information in the report. See "Saving and Viewing Saved Reports" on page 375 to learn how to save reports.

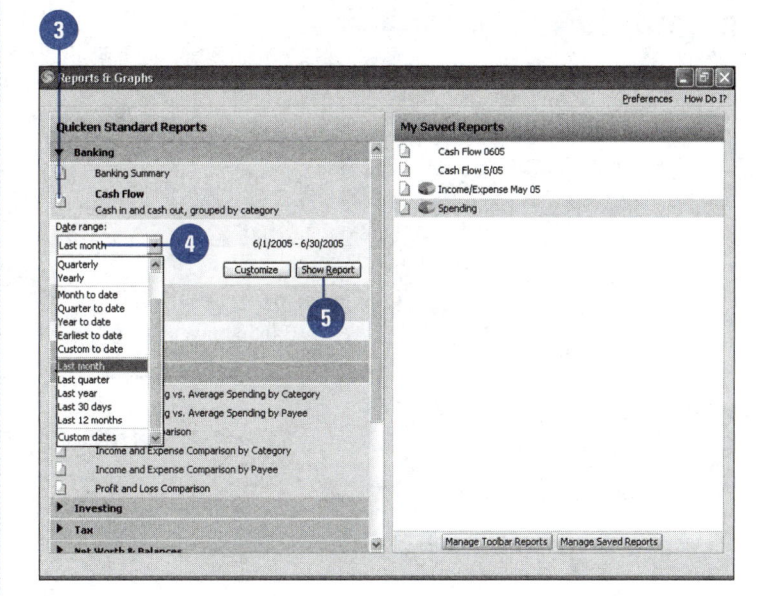

Did You Know?

You can use the Easy Answer reports and graphs to answer common financial inquiries. *The Easy Answer reports and graphs provide answers to some common questions about your finances, such as how much you've spent in gas over a month's time. You can use this information to help create or adjust your budget, or to make bigger decisions, such as whether to buy a car that gets better gas mileage.*

In order to take full advantage of this feature, you must assign a category to the expense when entering the transaction in your account register (for example, Auto: Fuel for gasoline expenses). Refer to the section "Using Bills and Scheduled Transactions" in Chapter 3 for more information on recording transactions in your register.

Working with Reports 367

Customizing Reports

Quicken provides many options for customizing reports. You can change the appearance of a report, weed out information that you don't want to see, add criteria that you do want to see, specify dates or time frames, or specify the category groups you want to include or not include. Remember that *categories* are the groups that you assign to a transaction when you enter it in your register, and they are used for tracking and reporting on those categories. Your options for customizing a report vary, depending on which report you are customizing. You can customize a report in the Reports & Graphs window before you view the report, or after the report opens, you can customize it from there as well. This task customizes the Cash Flow report after it has been opened.

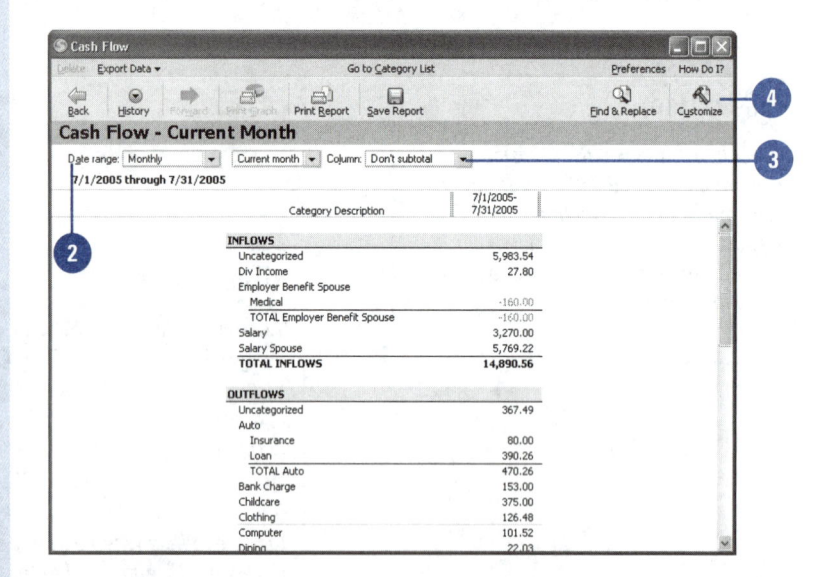

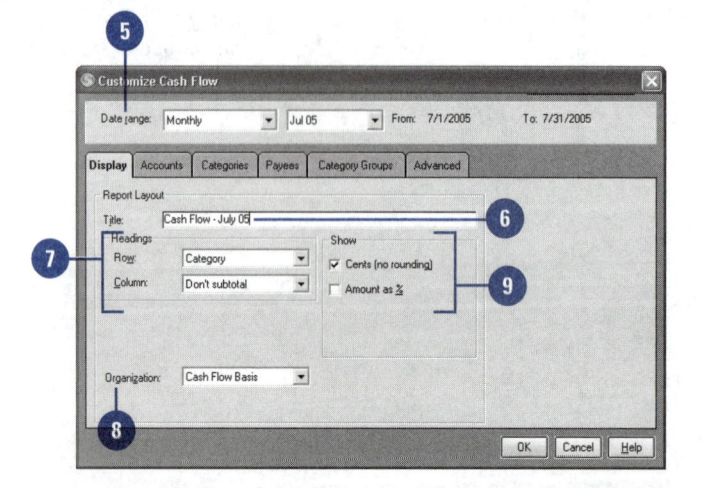

Customize a Report

1. Open a report, if you don't already have one open.

2. To view a different time period, click the Date Range drop-down menu and make a selection.

3. Click the Column drop-down menu to change the columns you want to see for the report.

4. To customize the report options, click Customize.

5. To change the standard time period for this report, from Date range drop-down menu, select the time period you want to use.

6. On the Display tab, if desired, change the title of the report so that it's more descriptive.

7. Set row and column headings by making selections from the drop-down menus.

8. Organize content by using the Organization options.

9. Select whether you want to see cents or percentages.

368

10. On the Accounts tab, click the box next to each account you want to include and clear the box to remove an account from the report or graph.

11. To include accounts from other account groups, click an account group and select the account(s) that you want. To select all accounts in an account group, click Mark All, or click Clear All to remove all selected accounts.

12. On the Categories tab, select or clear the categories that you want to include or not include in the report or graph. You can select all categories by clicking Select All or clear all categories by clicking Clear All.

13. From the Matching section, if desired, select a specific payee so that the report includes only transactions and categories assigned to that payee. Use the Category contains and Memo contains areas to enter specific category and transaction information that you want to see for that payee.

See Also

See "View Saved Reports" on page 376 to learn how to run reports.

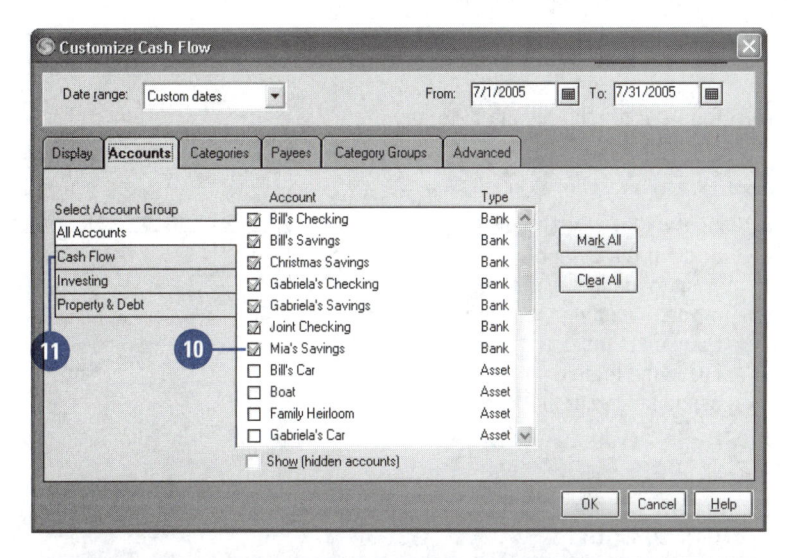

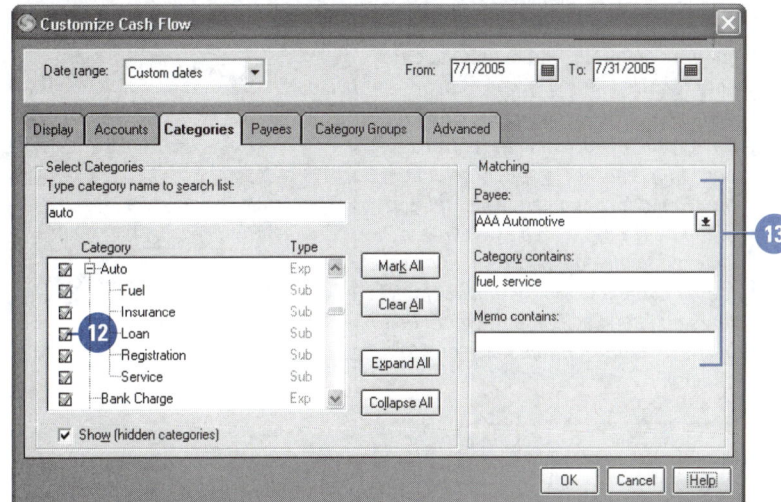

Did You Know?

You can quickly find the categories you want to include in a report or graph. *Rather than scrolling through the category list to find the category you want to include in a report, you can search for the category and ensure that hidden categories are shown. First, you select the Show (hidden categories) check box. Then you click in the box under the Type Category Name to Search list and type the name or partial name of the category you are looking for. Quicken locates or finds the closest match to the one you are looking for in the category list. You click the Expand All button to see all subcategories. To just view the top categories, you click Collapse All. You can then make your selection. If you want to include transactions that are not assigned to a specific category, from the top of the category list, select Not Categorized.*

Working with Reports **369**

14 On the Payees tab, select the payees you want to see in the report or graph. Use the Category contains and Memo contains areas.

15 On the Category Groups tab, select or clear the category groups you want to include in the report or graph. Selecting these groups tells Quicken to include transaction sums and totals that are associated with that category group.

Did You Know?

You can use the No Payee option to view transactions that match the category requirements. *If some transactions do not have payees assigned to them, you can still view those transactions in a report or graph by selecting the No Payee option shown at the top of the payee list in step 14. This tells Quicken to include all transactions that match the category requirements that you specified in the Category text box, even if they are not assigned to a specific payee.*

Did You Know?

You can use the Unassigned option to view transactions that match the category requirements. *To ensure that all the transactions that meet your requirements are included, you select the Unassigned option shown at the bottom of the Category Group list in step 15. This tells Quicken to include all transactions that match the requirements that you specified in steps 12 and 13, even if they are not assigned to a category group.*

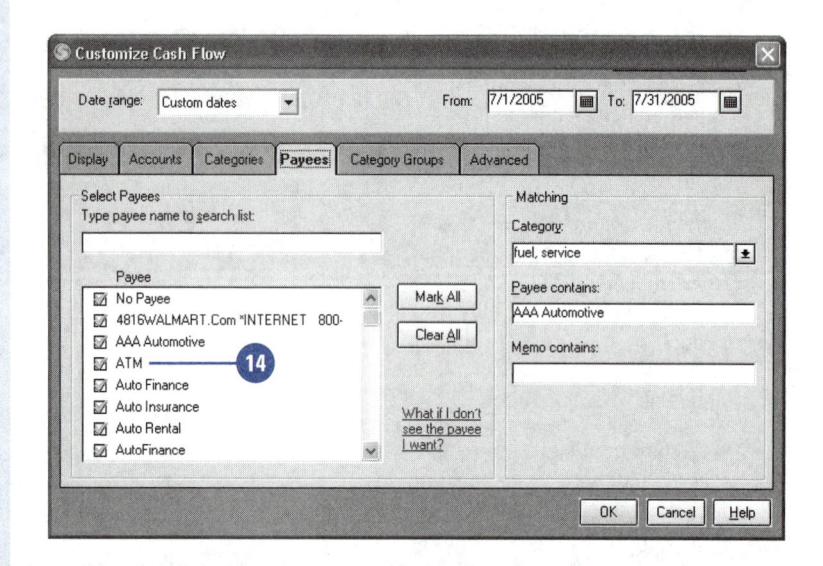

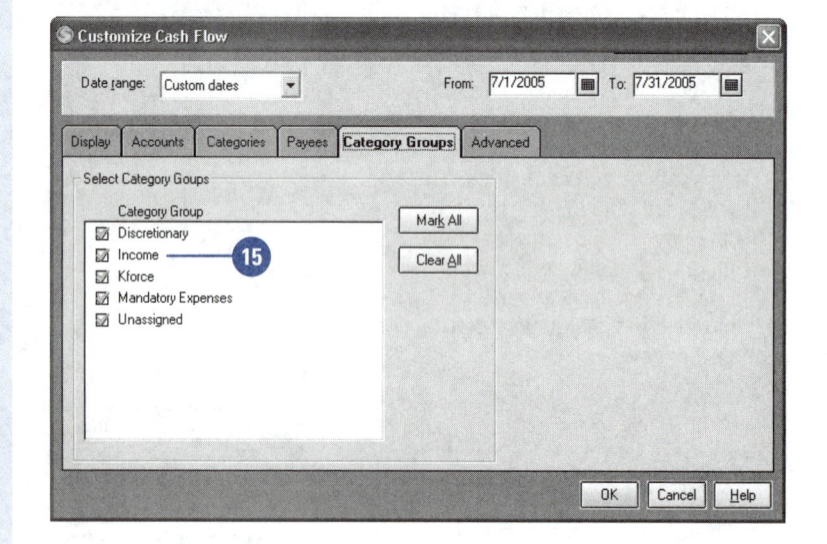

Did You Know?

You can use the Quicken taskbar to return to the Reports and Graphs window. *You can go back to the Reports & Graphs window to view and run other reports by clicking the Reports & Graphs icon on the Quicken taskbar (at the bottom of the Quicken main window). When you open a report, the Reports & Graphs window doesn't go away; it minimizes to the taskbar. The Quicken taskbar works just like the Windows taskbar. If you have more than one program open in Windows, the programs you are not using are minimized on your taskbar, next to the Start menu. Quicken works the same way.*

16 On the Advanced tab, select the transaction information you want to see. For example, to view all transaction amounts, select All from the Amounts drop-down menu. Or, to view amounts greater or less than a specific figure, select one of the other options and type the figure you want to use as the baseline.

17 Select include unrealized gains to show any investment transactions that reflect increases and/or decreases in security values.

18 Select Tax-related transactions only to show only transactions that are related to your taxes.

19 Select the type of transactions you want to view in the report or graph.

20 Select whether you want to view transfer transactions and subcategories in the report or graph.

21 Select the transaction statuses you want to view.

22 Click OK to save your changes.

23 To print the report, click Print.

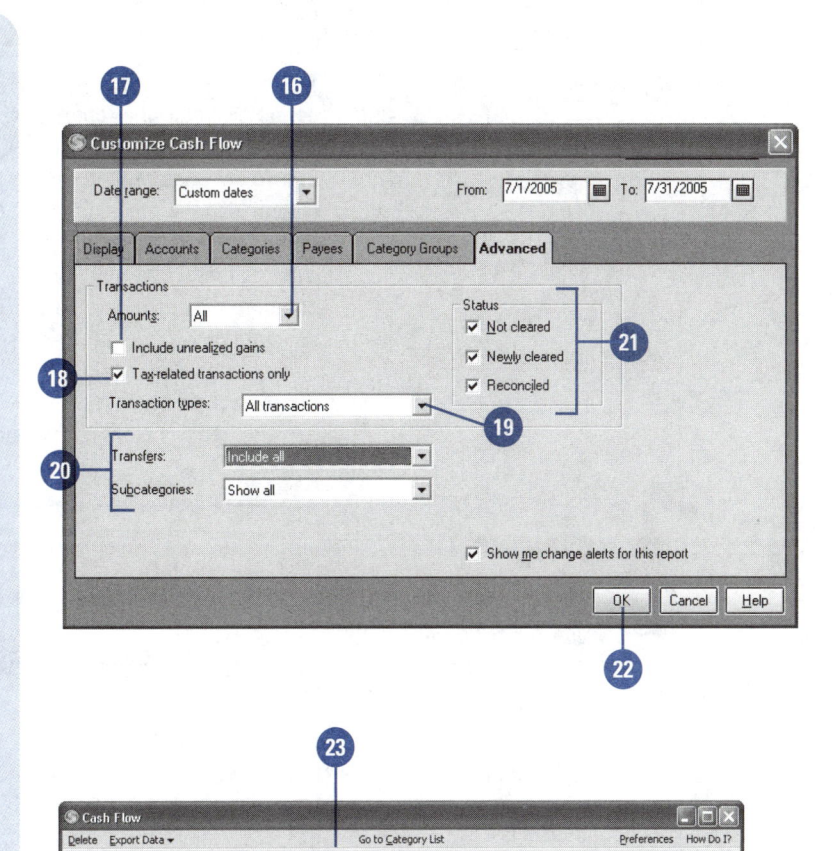

Did You Know?

You can set up a change alert for the report. *If you want to be notified when changes are made to categories, classes, or securities that affect a saved report, select Show me change alerts for this report. For example, after you set up all your customized changes to a report and save it, in the future, if you add new subcategories that affect the categories, classes, or securities that are included in the report, Quicken will notify you. If the report already includes all categories, classes, or securities by default, Quicken automatically updates the report without notifying you first.*

Working with Reports **371**

Setting Report Preferences

There are a few preferences or settings that you can tell Quicken to use each time you run a report or graph. For example, you can set default date ranges for custom dates so that when you run any of the reports or graphs and select Custom Date for the date range, Quicken always uses the dates specified in the preferences. You can also set a custom comparison date range for Quicken to use when viewing the comparison reports. You can use this feature so that each time you run comparison reports, you always compare the same time period. For example, if you set the default comparison date range from the beginning of a specific quarter to the end of a specific quarter, Quicken uses this date range as the default comparison date range each time you run it. In addition, you can set preferences for customizing reports and graphs, and you can set default settings for reports only.

Select Reports and Graphs Preferences

1. Open a report, if you don't already have one open, and click Preferences.

2. To set a default date for a specific time period, from the Default date range section, select the time period you want to use as the default. Then select the dates for the time period.

3. To set a date to use as the default for comparison reports, from the Default comparison date range section, select the time period for which you want to set the default. Then select the dates for the time period.

4. If you want to create a new report every time you customize a report, select Customizing creates new report or graph.

5. If you don't want to create a new report every time you customize a report, select Customizing modifies graph before creating.

6. If you would like to have the option to customize a report before you view it, select Customize report/graph before creating.

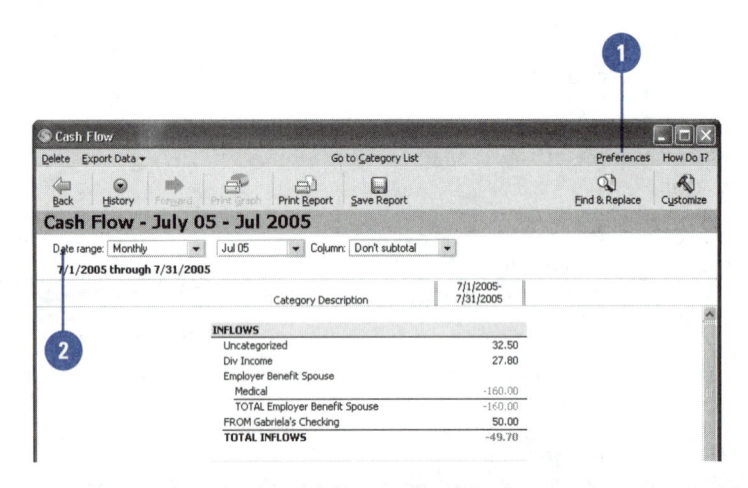

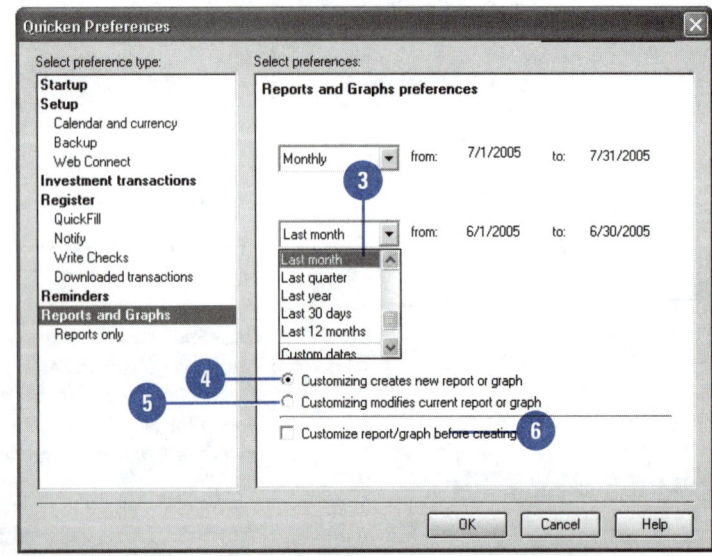

Select Report Preferences Only

1 To set preferences for reports, click Reports only.

2 To view only descriptions for every account or category that appears in reports, from either the Account display or Category display section, select Description. The descriptions come from the description that you entered, if at all, when you created the account.

3 To view just the names of the accounts or categories and not any descriptions in reports, select Name.

4 To view both the name and description for accounts or categories, select Both.

5 To view reports in color, instead of in black and white, select Use Color in Report.

6 To automatically open the appropriate investment form related to investment report transactions select QuickZoom to investment forms. Otherwise, clear from a transaction in an investment report to the appropriate transaction entry in your investment register.

7 To have Quicken ask if you want to save a report each time you close a report, select Remind me to save reports.

8 To change the decimal placement for figures, click the Decimal places for prices and shares box and type the number of decimal places you want to use. You can use from zero to six places.

9 Click OK to save all your preferences.

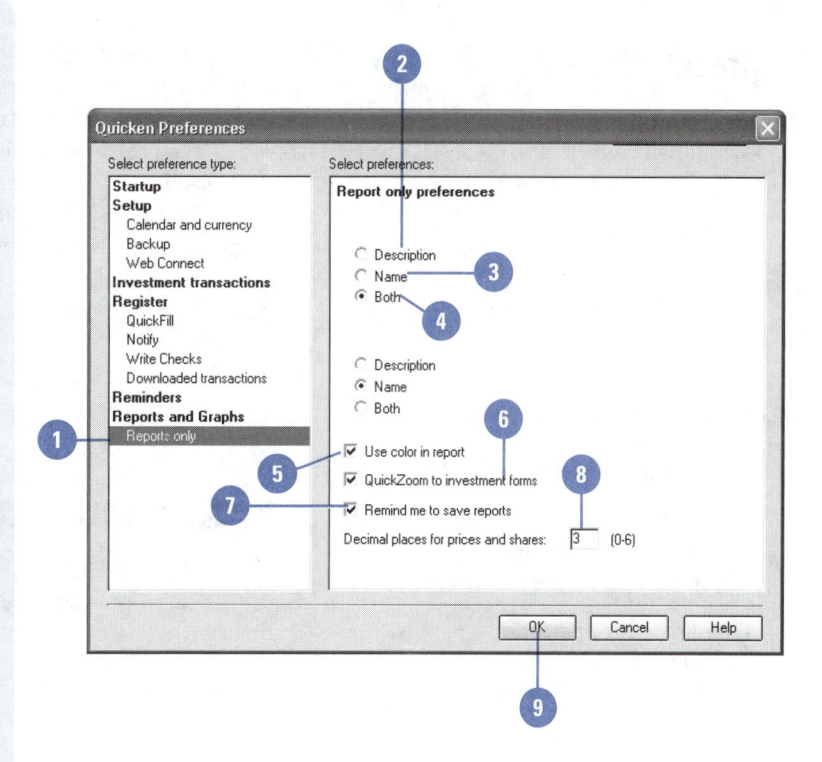

See Also

See "Setting Quicken Preferences" on page 53 for information on setting the other Quicken preferences. See "Saving and Viewing Saved Reports" on page 375 to learn how to run reports.

Working with Reports **373**

Exporting Reports

When you run a report, you have the option of exporting it or saving it in a separate file and in another format. The format that Quicken uses to export is a text file, which means that the report content is in plain text, without formatting, such as styles, tables, and so on. This makes the report content compatible with just about any other program, such as Microsoft Excel or Word. If you have specific information that you need to share with someone else—for example, your accountant, you can do so by exporting the report and saving it as a text file, and then you can either send the file as an email attachment, print it, or open it in Excel or another program to work with it further.

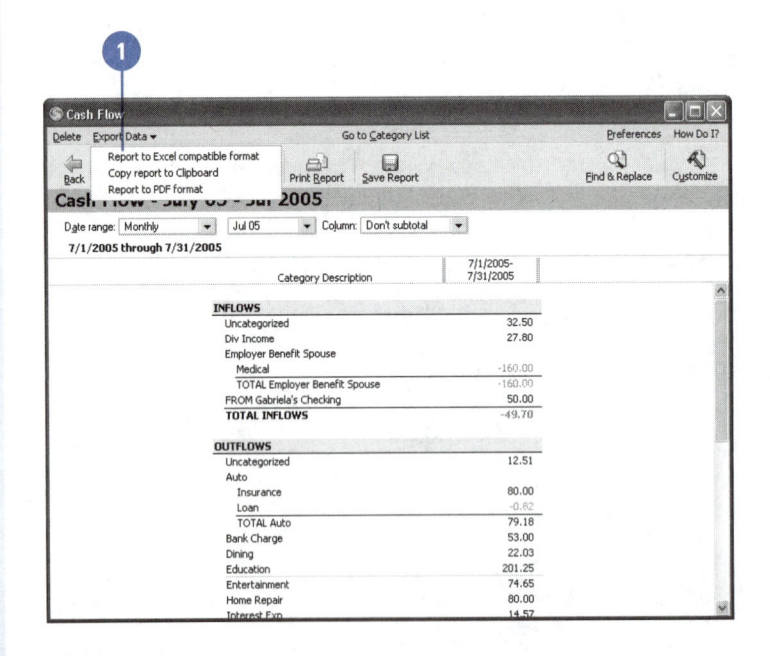

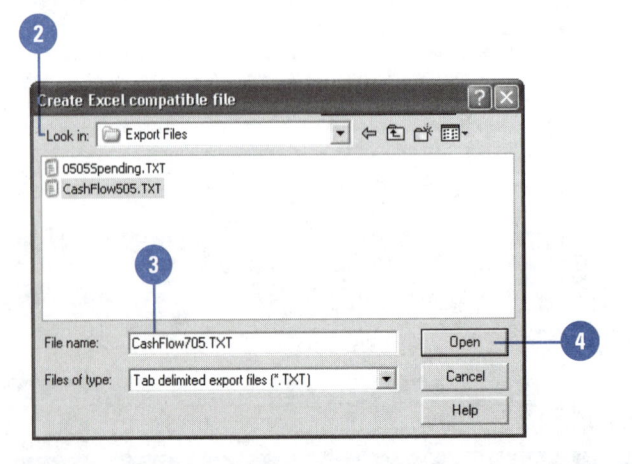

1. Open a report, if don't already have one open, and click Export Data, Report to Excel compatible format.

2. Click Look in to locate the folder where you want to save the file.

3. Click in the File name text box and type the name of the file (for example the report name).

4. Click Open. The file is saved with the name you gave it and a .txt extension (for example, CashFlow705.txt).

See Also

See "Setting Quicken Preferences" on page xx for information on setting the other Quicken preferences. See "Saving and Viewing Saved Reports" on page 375 to learn how to run reports.

Saving and Viewing Saved Reports

In previous tasks we spent some time talking about viewing, customizing, and exporting reports. After you spend so much time getting your report the way you want it, it would be a shame to let all that hard work go to waste by not saving the report. You can save a report and reuse it. For example, if you want to run a monthly expenditure report with specific criteria, after you get the report the way you want it, you can save it, and then the next month, you can open the saved report, select the month you want to view, run it, and save it. This saves you time and ensures that you get out of the report exactly what you want each time you run it.

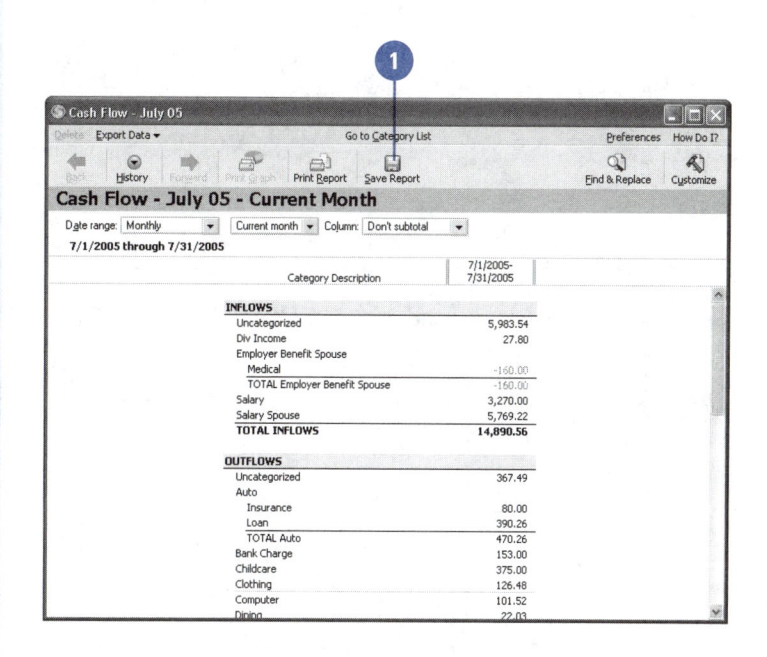

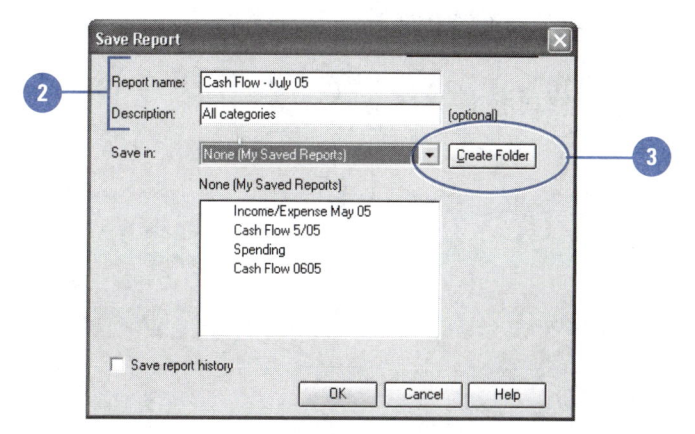

Save Reports

1. Run and customize a report the way you want and then click Save Report.

2. In Report name, type the name you want to use for this report. You can also type a description to provide more detail.

3. Select the center with which to associate the report. To create a folder for your customized reports, click Create Folder.

See Also

See "Customizing Reports" on page 368 for more information on running and customizing reports.

Working with Reports **375**

4. Type a name and click OK.

5. Click OK. The report now appears under My Saved Reports in the Reports & Graphs window.

View Saved Reports

1. To open a saved report, open the Reports & Graphs window, if you don't already have it open. All reports that you have saved so far appear under the My Saved Reports on the right.

2. Click a report to select it.

3. Click Show Report.

4. To create new, move existing, or rename existing folders for your saved reports, click Manage Saved Reports. You can also edit and delete saved reports from the Manage Saved Reports window.

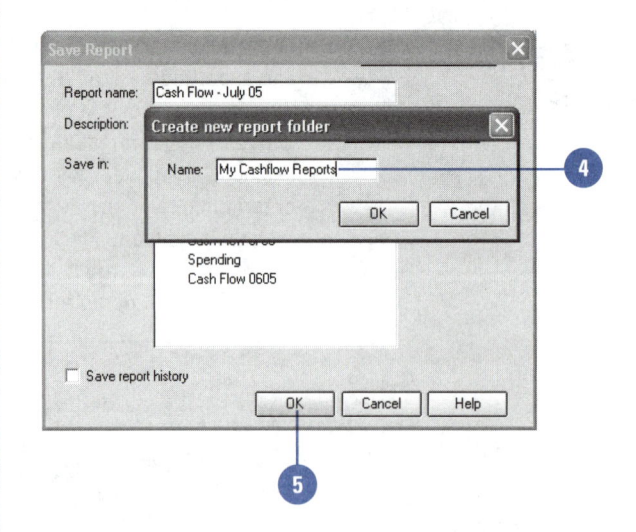

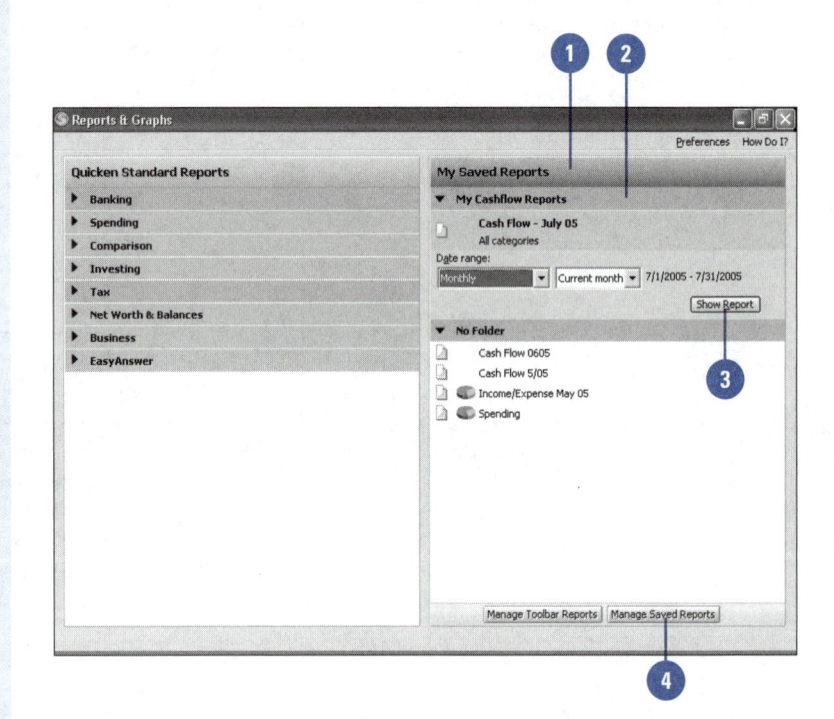

Index

A

About You section (Planning Center), reviewing/editing personal information, 286
Account Attachments section (Investment Center), 194, 253
Account Attributes section (Investment Center), 148, 193, 253
Account Balance section (Property & Debt Center, Overview tab), 253
account bar
    accounts, adding/removing, 68
    activity centers, 66-71
    Change Group button, 68
    Customize button, 67
    Financial Overview Center, 67-71
    hidden bars, displaying, 68
    Hide Amounts button, 67
    Investment Center, 66
    menu actions, viewing, 67
    Move Up/Down buttons, 68
    moving, 54
    Property & Debt Center, 66
    Remove from Bar column, 68
    removing, 54
    Show Amt. button, 67
Account Details window
    credit card accounts, deleting, 134
    debt accounts, deleting, 243
    investment accounts, deleting, 190
    min/max account balances, entering, 101
    property accounts, deleting, 243
    retirement accounts, deleting, 190
    spending/savings accounts, updating/deleting, 105-106
Account Holdings section (Investment Center), 194
Account List window
    account registers, opening, 194
    accounts
        adding, 194
        configuring online access, 62, 194
        updating, 104, 132, 190, 243
        printing, 194
    debt accounts, 243
    Don't Include in Totals column, 73
    functions of, 105
    help, accessing, 194
    Hide in Quicken column, 73
    Investing Accounts section, 188-189
    investment accounts, 190
    property accounts, 243
    retirement accounts, 190
    spending/savings accounts, 104-106
Account Location (Cash Flow Center), moving spending/savings accounts, 101
account registers, 56, 129
Account Status section (Investment Center), 148, 193, 253
Account Summary window (Cash Flow Center), updating credit card accounts, 151
Account Value vs. Cost Basis section (Investment Center), 202

accounts
- account bar, 68
- Account List window, adding in, 194
- asset accounts, 30-32, 264. *See also* property accounts
- auto property accounts, 25-29, 66
- balances
  - bar graph view, 158
  - hiding, 67
  - showing, 67
- brokerage accounts, 19-22
- car property accounts, 25-29, 66
- cash accounts, 18
- checking accounts, 13-18, 66
- creating, 9
- credit card accounts
  - adding attachments to transactions, 138-139
  - adding, downloading information, 131
  - adding, manual setups, 130, 140
  - adding notes to transactions, 140
  - adding paychecks, 145
  - adding scheduled transactions, 145
  - balancing manually, 149-151
  - balancing online accounts, 152-154
  - Cash Flow Center, 66
  - categorizing transactions, 136, 140
  - deleting, 134
  - deleting attachments from transactions, 139
  - deleting scheduled transactions, 145
  - deleting transactions, 137, 141
  - downloading transactions, 135-137
  - editing, 132
  - editing scheduled transactions, 145
  - editing transactions, 141
  - flagging transactions, 138-140
  - ID, 17
  - Quicken Guided Setup, 17-18
  - reviewing/changing tax schedules, 133
  - scheduled transactions, adding to account registers, 144
  - searching transactions, 142-143
  - skipping scheduled transactions, 145
  - sorting transactions, 143
  - updating, 132
  - viewing account overviews, 148
  - viewing transactions, 137
- debt accounts
  - adding, 240-241
  - adding scheduled transactions, 250
  - adding transactions, 245
  - deleting, 242-243
  - deleting scheduled transactions, 250
  - deleting transactions, 246
  - editing, 242
  - editing scheduled transactions, 249
  - editing transactions, 246
  - managing scheduled transactions, 252
  - Property & Debt Center, 66
  - reviewing, 239
  - reviewing scheduled transactions, 250
  - searching transactions, 247
  - sorting transactions, 247
  - tax-deferred accounts, 241
  - tax exempt accounts, 241
  - tax schedules, 242
  - transferring funds to property accounts, 248
  - updating, 242
  - updating balances, 244
  - viewing overviews, 253
  - viewing transaction calendars, 251
  - viewing transaction graphs, 252
- flagging, 67, 76, 116, 145
- home property accounts, 23-26, 66

investment accounts, 184-190, 202-206
liability accounts, 32
loan accounts, reviewing, 256
messages, viewing, 67
net worth, hiding from, 73
online accounts
    configuring access, 62, 194
    saving information, 55
    updates, 89
passwords, PIN vault, 90-92
payment methods, changing, 179
portfolio accounts, configuring Internet access, 61
printing from Account List window, 194
property accounts. *See also* car property accounts
    adding, 240-241
    adding transactions, 245, 250
    balancing, 254-255
    deleting, 242-243
    deleting transactions, 246, 250
    editing, 242
    editing transactions, 246, 249
    managing, 252
    Property & Debt Center, 66
    reviewing, 239
    reviewing transactions, 250
    searching transactions, 247
    sorting transactions, 247
    tax-deferred accounts, 241
    tax exempt accounts, 241
    tax schedules, 242
    transferring funds to debt accounts, 248
    updating, 242
    updating balances, 244
    viewing overviews, 253
    viewing transaction calendars, 251
    viewing transaction graphs, 252

red flags, 67
remote access, 9
retirement accounts, 66
    adding to Investment Center, 185-188
    balancing in Investment Center, 204-206
    configuring online access, 185
    deleting, 190
    editing in Investment Center, 188-189
    reviewing performance in Investment Center, 202-203
    reviewing summaries, 194
savings accounts
    Cash Flow Center, 66
    ID, 14, 17
    passwords, 14
    Quicken Guided Setup, 13-18
    statements, importing, 127
Accounts tab (Reports and Graphs window), selecting accounts for reports, 369
Actions for Performance section (Portfolio Analyzer), 230
activity centers, 66-71
Actual pie chart (Analysis tab), 208, 211
Add Account (Cash Flow Center), 102
Add Attachment (Cash Flow Center), 109
Add Follow-up Flag (Cash Flow Center), 109
Add from List command (Tax tab, Category List section), 351
Adjustments to Living Expenses section (Planning Center, Plan Assumptions section), 302
Advanced tab (Reports and Graphs window), 371
alerts, 57, 74. *See also* notifications; warnings
    Bill and Scheduled Transaction section (Cash Flow Center), 156
    Cash Flow Center alerts, configuring, 98
    change alerts, viewing in reports, 371

Credit Card Accounts section (Cash Flow Center), 126
duration of, selecting, 75
editing, 75
Investment Center alerts, configuring, 182
notifications, 74
Planning Center alerts, configuring, 284
Property & Debt Center alerts, configuring, 238
removing, 74-75
resolving, 98
reviewing, 74
Tax Center alerts, configuring, 338
type of, selecting, 75
uses for, 74
viewing, 98
Alerts section (Home page), 74-75
Allocation by Security section (Investment Center), 203, 214
allocations
asset classes, 216
percentages, determining, 231
amortized loans, 32
Analysis & Reports tab (Cash Flow Center), 168-169
Analysis tab (Investment Center)
Actual pie chart, 208, 211
Capital Gains Estimator
accessing, 218
Federal Tax Rates section, 220
investment scenarios, 219
navigating, 219
Proposed Sales table, 222
Search, 221
State Tax Rates section, 220
Taxable Gains from Proposed Sales table, 222
Use Tax Planner Values, 221

Choose Securities, 210
Mutual Fund Ratings section, 212-214
Show Accounts, changing account views, 210
Target pie chart, 208-209
asset accounts, 30-32, 264. *See also* property accounts
Asset Allocation Guide
accessing, 215
asset classes, 216
editing, 203
asset allocation reports, 203, 211
Asset Allocation section
Investment Center, 203
Portfolio Analyzer, 231
assets
allocation reports, 203, 211
classes, 216-217
information, editing, 297-298, 320
Assign Category Groups command (Tax tab, Category List section), 350
attachments, adding to/deleting from transactions, 109, 138-139
Auto Expenses section (Property & Debt Center), 269
auto property accounts, 25-29, 66
Average Tax Rate section (Planning Center, Plan Assumptions section), 291

B

Backup preference type (Preferences menu), 55
backups, 46-47, 55
Balance column (Property & Debt Center, Loan Accounts Summary section), 256
balances (accounts)
bar graph view, 158
credit card accounts, updating, 127
estimated balances, viewing, 147, 163

forecasting, Forecast Lowest Balance window (Bills and Scheduled Transactions section), 159

hiding, 67

showing, 67

balancing
    credit card accounts, 149-154
    debt accounts, 254-255
    investment accounts in Investment Center, 204-206
    property accounts, 254-255
    retirement accounts in Investment Center, 204-206
    spending/savings accounts, 120-124

bank accounts (checking/savings), 13-18, 66

bar graph view (account balances), 84, 158

Bill and Scheduled Transactions section (Cash Flow Center), configuring alerts, 156

Bill Inbox (Quicken Bill Pay), 175

bills
    online payments, 36
    Quicken Bill Pay, 170-175
    Quicken Guided Setup, entering in, 36-37
    registers, adding to/skipping instances in, 160

Bills and Scheduled Transactions section
    average transaction amounts, viewing, 157
    bar graph view, 84, 158
    bills, adding to register, 160
    Bills section, 159
    calendar view, 84
    Deposits and Other Scheduled Transactions section, 159
    estimated balances, viewing, 163
    Forecast Lowest Balance window, 159
    Lowest Balance section, 159
    opening, 157
    paychecks, adding/editing information, 166-167

    Show menu, 83-84
    transactions
        adding, 82
        Edit All Future Transactions window, 80
        editing, 79
        recording, 76-78, 159
        scheduled transactions, 80, 160-165
        skipping, 81
        sorting, 158
        viewing, 83-85

Bills section (Bills and Scheduled Transactions section), 159

black transactions, 76

Borrow Money option (Property & Debt Center, Loan Accounts Summary section), 257

brokerage accounts, 19-22

Budget section
    Analysis & Reports tab, 169
    Financial Overview Center, Planning tab, 332, 335

buttons (toolbar), 42-43

C

Calculators section (Financial Overview Center, Planning tab), 307

Calendar and Currency preference type (Preferences menu), 54

calendars
    day view, 84
    debt account calendars, viewing, 251
    month view, 84
    notes, adding to days 85
    property account calendars, viewing, 251
    selecting, 54
    transaction calendar, printing/viewing, 117-118, 146-147, 162-163
    transactions, viewing in, 84

How can we make this index more useful? Email us at indexes@quepublishing.com

canceling Quicken Bill Pay payments, 175
Capital Gains Estimator, 354
    accessing, 218
    Federal Tax Rates section, 220
    investment scenario, selecting, 219
    navigating, 219
    Proposed Sales table, 222
    Search, 221
    State Tax Rates section, 220
    Taxable Gains from Proposed Sales table, 222
    Use Tax Planner Values, 221
    What Should I Sell? section, 356
Capital Gains Report (Investment Center), 194
car property accounts, 25-29, 66
case-sensitivity (passwords), 51
cash accounts, 18
Cash Flow Center, 66
    Account Details window, 101, 105-106
    Account List window, 104-106
    Account Location, 101
    Account Summary window, 151
    Add Account, 102
    Add Attachment, 109
    Add Follow-up Flag, 109
    alerts, configuring, 98
    Analysis & Reports tab, 168-169
    Bills and Scheduled Transactions section
        adding transactions, 82
        average transaction amounts, viewing, 157
        bar graph view, 84, 158
        bills, adding to register, 160
        Bills section, 159
        calendar view, 84
        Deposits and Other Scheduled Transactions section, 159
        Edit All Future Transactions window, 80
        editing transactions, 79
        estimated balances, viewing, 163
        Forecast Lowest Balance window, 159
        Lowest Balance section, 159
        opening, 157
        paychecks, adding/editing information, 166-167
        recording transactions, 76-78, 159
        scheduled transactions, 80, 160-165
        Show menu, 83-84
        skipping transactions, 81
        sorting transactions, 158
        viewing transactions, 83-85
    Credit Card Accounts section
        Account Details window, 134
        Account List window, 129, 132-134
        account registers, viewing, 129
        account statements, importing, 127
        alerts, configuring, 126
        Credit Limit window, 129
        Download Transaction tab, 135-137
        estimated balances, viewing, 147
        Interest Rate window, 129
        manually adding transactions, 140
        Match If menu, 142
        One Step Update, 127
        Online Update Summary window, 128
        Quicken Account Setup window, 129-131
        scheduled transactions, 146-147
        Search menu, 142
    Find, transaction searches, 112
    Match If menu, transaction searches, 112
    One Step Update, updating spending/savings accounts, 99-100
    Online Update Summary window, 152-154

Overview tab, 148
Quicken Checks, 176-180
Scheduled Transactions tab, 115-116
Search menu, 112
Statement Summary window, 149-151
Transaction Attachments window, 109
Categories tab (Reports and Graphs window), 369
categorizing
   credit card transactions, 136, 140
   transactions, 80, 110
Category column (Mutual Fund Ratings section), 212
Category Groups tab (Reports and Graphs window), 370
Category List section (Tax tab, Tax-Related Expenses YTD section), 349-352
change alerts, 371
Change Group button (account bar), 68
charts (pie)
   Actual pie chart (Analysis tab), 208, 211
   asset allocation reports, deleting from, 211
   Asset Allocation section (Portfolio Analyzer), 231
   date ranges, changing, 214
   Holdings section (Portfolio Analyzer), 230
   printing, 211
   Target pie chart (Analysis tab), 208-209
checking accounts, 13-15, 66
checks (Quicken)
   cost of, 176
   entering payee information, 179
   Order Checks & Supplies option (Quicken Services), 93
   ordering, 176
   printing, 58, 178, 180
   selecting style, 180
   tear-off strips, 180

Choose Securities (Analysis tab), 210
College Planner, 312-317
   college costs, adding/editing, 314
   cost summary, reviewing, 316
   Internet resources, reviewing, 317
   investments information, reviewing, 316
   plans, reviewing, 317
   savings information, reviewing, 316
   student data, adding/editing, 313
   student funding options, adding/editing, 315
color keys (graphs), 69
Column menu (Reports and Graphs window), 368
comparing
   investment taxes before/after sales, 222
   mutual funds, 212
Compounding Period menu (Property & Debt Center), 260
continuous transactions, setting, 165
copying inventory items, 271
Create Scheduled Transaction window, 80, 165
credit card accounts
   account overviews, viewing, 148
   account registers, viewing, 129
   adding, 130-131, 140
   attachments, adding to/deleting from transactions, 138-139
   balancing
      manually, 149-151
      online accounts, 152-154
      updating balances, 127
   Cash Flow Center, 66
   credit limits, changing, 129
   deleting, 134
   editing, 132
   ID, 17
   interest rates, setting, 129

notes, adding to transactions, 140
paychecks, adding, 145
Quicken Guided Setup, 17-18
scheduled transactions, adding/deleting, 144-145
tax schedules, reviewing/changing, 133
transactions
    attachments, 138-139
    categorizing, 136, 140
    deleting, 134, 137, 141
    downloading, 135-137
    editing, 141
    flagging, 138-140, 145
    notes, 140
    scheduled transaction, 144-145
    searching, 142-143
    sorting, 143
    updating, 127
    viewing, 137
updating, 132, 151
Credit Card Accounts section (Cash Flow Center)
    Account Details window, 134
    Account List window, 129, 132-134
    account registers, viewing, 129
    account statements, importing, 127
    alerts, configuring, 126
    Credit Limit window, 129
    Download Transaction tab, 135-137
    estimated balances, viewing, 147
    Interest Rate window, 129
    manually adding transactions, 140
    Match If menu, 142
    One Step Update, 127
    Online Update Summary window, 128
    Quicken Account Setup window, 129-131
    scheduled transactions, 146-147
    Search menu, 142

Credit Limit window (Credit Card Accounts section), 129
credit limits, changing, 129
currency (foreign), tracking, 54
Current Balance Amount box (Property & Debt Center), 260
Current Homes & Assets section (Planning Center, Plan Assumptions section), 297-298
Current Loans section (Planning Center, Plan Assumptions section), 299
Customize button (account bar), 67
Customize This Graph option (Options menu), 214
Customize View (Portfolio tab), 228
customizing
    account registers, 56
    graphs, 59
    portfolio views, 228
    reports, 59, 368-371
    toolbar, 42-43

D

daily transaction graphs, viewing, 118, 147, 163
data entry, QuickFill option, 57
Date of Next Payment box (Property & Debt Center), 261
Date Range menu (Reports and Graphs window), 368
Day Gain/Loss column (Today's Data tab), 184
day view (calendars), 84
debt accounts.
    adding, 240-242
    balancing, 254-255
    deleting, 242-243
    liability accounts, Quicken Guided Setup, 32
    overviews, viewing, 253

Property & Debt Center, 66
reviewing, 239
scheduled transactions, 249-252
tax-deferred accounts, 241
tax exempt accounts, 241
tax schedules, changing, 242
transactions
    adding, 245, 250
    deleting, 246, 250
    editing, 246, 249
    managing, 252
    reconciling, 254-255
    reviewing, 250, 299
    searching, 247
    sorting, 247
    viewing transaction calendars, 251
    viewing transaction graphs, 252
transferring funds to property accounts, 248
updating, 242-244
Debt Reduction Planner, 326-328
Deduction Finder (Tax menu), 361-363
deductions, finding, 361-363
deleting
    account bar, 54
    accounts, 68, 190
    alerts, 74-75
    asset allocation reports, 211
    buttons from toolbar, 42
    categories in Category List section (Tax tab, Tax-Related Expense YTD section), 352
    credit card accounts, 134
    credit card transactions, 137, 141, 145
    debt accounts, 242-246
    dependent information in About You section (Planning Center), 286
    emergency records, 282
    home inventory claims/policies, 274-277
    inventory items, 271
    investment accounts from Investment Center, 190
    investment transactions from Investment Center, 199
    loan rates, 268
    passwords from files/transactions, 52
    pie charts from asset allocation reports, 211
    property accounts, 242-246, 250
    retirement accounts from Investment Center, 190
    retirement transactions from Investment Center, 199
    scheduled transactions, 116-117, 146, 162, 250
    spending/savings accounts, 106-108
    transactions, 111
    accounts with active transactions, 190
    attachments, 109
    debt accounts, 246
    portfolio transactions, 226
    property accounts, 246
dependents, editing/deleting information on, 286
Deposits and Other Scheduled Transactions section (Bills and Scheduled Transactions section), 159
displaying
    account balances, 67, 158
    account bars, 68
    active alerts, 74
    alerts, 98, 126, 156, 371
    all toolbar buttons, 42
    asset allocation reports, 211
    average transaction amount, 157
    button icons in toolbar, 43
    change alerts in reports, 371
    credit card account information, 129, 137, 148

daily transaction graphs, 147, 163
estimated balances, 118, 147, 163
net worth graphs, 70
net worth reports, 71
reports, 366, 376
securities, 210, 225
spending totals (spending accounts), 108
spending/savings account overviews, 119
transactions, 226, 371
    Bills and Scheduled Transaction section (Home page), 83-85
    calendar, 84, 117-118, 146, 162
    credit card account transactions, 137
    reports (spending accounts), 108
Don't Include in Totals column (Account List window), 73
down payment savings plans, editing in Home Purchase Planner, 322
Download Historical Prices (Portfolio tab), 223
Download Quotes (Portfolio tab), 223
Download Transaction tab (Credit Card Accounts section), 135-137
Download Transactions preference type (Preferences menu), 58
downloading
    asset classes, 216
    credit card account information, 131
    credit card transactions, 135-137
    online investment accounts, 183
    quotes, 62, 224
    spending/savings account information, 102-103
    transactions, 58, 135

E

e-bills, Quicken Bill Pay, 175
Easy Answer reports and graphs feature, 367

Edit All Future Transactions window (Bills and Scheduled Transactions section), 80
Edit Security Details (Portfolio tab), 225
editing
    alerts, 75, 126, 156
    Asset Allocation guide (Investment Center), 203
    asset information, 297-298, 320
    button order (toolbar), 43
    categories in Category List section (Tax tab, Tax-Related Expense YTD section), 352
    college costs in College Planner, 314
    credit card information, 132, 141, 145
    data, QuickFill option, 57
    debt information, 242, 246, 249, 299
    dependent information in About You section (Planning Center), 286
    down payment savings plans in Home Purchase Planner, 322
    expenses in Home Purchase Planner, 323
    home inventory claims, 277
    income information, 290, 324
    inflation rates in Planning Center, 291
    investment information, 188-189, 197-199, 294
    living expenses information in Planning Center, 300-302
    loan information, 267-268, 299, 321
    paycheck information, Bills and Scheduled Transactions section (Cash Flow Center), 166
    payee information, Quicken Checks, 179
    pension information in Planning Center, 289
    personal information in About You Section (Planning Center), 286
    planner assumptions, 285
    plans, 336

property information, 242, 246, 249, 297-298

Quicken Bill Pay payments, 175

Quicken Guided Setup information, 40

rate of return information in Planning Center, 296

retirement information, 188-189, 197-199, 288-289

salary information in Planning Center, 287

savings information in Planning Center, 292

scheduled transactions, 117, 146, 161-162, 249

securities, 62, 225

Social Security benefits information in Planning Center, 288

special expenses information in Planning Center, 303-304

spending/savings accounts, 104

student data in College Planner, 313

student funding options in College Planner, 315

tax rates in Planning Center, 291

taxable income information in Tax Planner, 347-348

transactions, 77-79, 111, 121, 226

what-if scenarios in Planning Center, 305

Emergency Records Organizer tool, 278-282

Enter Missing Transactions window (Portfolio tab), 226

Estimated Tax Payments section (Tax Planner), 346

estimating taxes, Select Tax Rates window, 355

Evaluate (Portfolio tab), 225

expenses, reviewing/editing
  in Home Purchase Planner, 323
  living expenses, 300-302
  special expenses, 303-304

Expenses section
  Analysis & Reports tab, 168
  Overview tab, 148

Explore What If's section (Planning Center, Plan Assumptions section), 305

exporting
  files, 50
  reports, 374

F

Federal Tax Rates section (Capital Gains Estimator), 220

files
  backups, 46-47, 55
  creating, 45
  exporting, 50
  importing, 48-49
  naming, 45
  opening quickly, 44
  organizing, 45
  passwords, assigning/removing, 51-52
  storing, 45-46

Financial Overview Center, 67
  Capital Gains Estimator
    accessing, 218
    Federal Tax Rates section, 220
    investment scenarios, 219
    navigating, 219
    Proposed Sales table, 222
    sales tax comparisons, 357
    Search, 221
    State Tax Rates section, 220
    Taxable Gains from Proposed Sales table, 222
    Use Tax Planner Values, 221
  Hide Graph button, 70
  net worth, 69-71

Planning tab
    Budget section, 332, 335
    Calculators section, 307
    College Planner, 312-317
    Debt Reduction Planner, 326-328
    Home Purchase Planner, 318-325
    Retirement Planner, 308
    Special Purchase Planner, 330-331
    Show Net Worth Report button, 71
financial websites, linking to, 95
Find (Cash Flow Center), transaction searches, 112
Find Top Funds (Mutual Fund Ratings section), 213
Finish Later button (Quicken Guided Setup), 12
firewalls, downloading transactions, 135
flagging transactions, 109-111
    credit card transactions, 138-140
    red flags, 67, 76, 145
    scheduled transactions, 116
Forecast Lowest Balance window (Bills and Scheduled Transactions section), 159
foreign currency, 54, 343
frequency of transactions, selecting, 165
funds transfers (spending/savings accounts), 113-114

G

Gain/Loss column (Today's Data tab, 184
gains, Capital Gains Estimator (Financial Overview Center), 354-357
Get Business Tools for Quicken option (Quicken Services), 93
Glossary (Portfolio tab), 223
goals (financial), entering in Quicken Guided Setup, 12
graphs
    bar graphs, viewing transactions as, 84
    color keys, 69
    daily transaction graphs, viewing, 118
    debt account graphs, viewing, 252
    Easy Answer reports and graphs feature, 367
    net worth graphs, 70
    preferences, setting, 59, 372
    property account graphs, viewing, 252
green transactions, 76
grouping listings (investments), 224

H

help, accessing from Account List window, 194
Hide Amounts button (account bar), 67
Hide Graph button (Financial Overview Center), 70
Hide in Quicken column (Account List window), 73
hiding
    account balances, 67
    account bars, 54, 68
    accounts from net worth, 73
    information in Category List section (Tax tab, Tax-Related Expenses YTD section), 349
    net worth graphs, 70
Holdings section (Investment Center), 193
Holdings section (Portfolio Analyzer), 230
home inventories
    inventory items
        adding, 270
        copying, 271
        deleting, 271
        entering information on, 272-273
        searches, 273
    policy management, 274-277
    reports, viewing, 277

Home page
    account bar, 66-68
    Alerts section, 74-75
    Bills and Scheduled Transactions section
        adding transactions, 82
        average transaction amounts, viewing, 157
        bar graph view, 84, 158
        bills, adding to register, 160
        Bills section, 159
        calendar view, 84
        Deposits and Other Scheduled Transactions section, 159
        Edit All Future Transactions window, 80
        editing transactions, 79
        estimated balances, viewing, 163
        Forecast Lowest Balance window, 159
        Lowest Balance section, 159
        opening, 157
        paychecks, adding/editing information, 166-167
        recording transactions, 76-78, 159
        scheduled transactions, 80, 160-165
        Show menu, 83-84
        skipping transactions, 81
        sorting transactions, 158
        viewing transactions, 83-85
    Next Steps to Meet Your Financial Goals section, 86-87
    online updates, 88-89, 92
home property accounts, 23-26, 66
Home Purchase Planner, 318
    affordability, determining, 319
    asset information, adding/editing, 320
    down payment savings plans, 322
    expenses, adding/editing, 323
    Income and Expense Comparison by Category reports, 319

    income, adding/editing, 324
    loan information, adding/editing, 321
    plans, reviewing, 325

I

icons (buttons), viewing in toolbar, 43
ID
    bank accounts, Quicken Guided Setup, 14, 17
    changing, Quicken.com, 64
    investments, Quicken Guided Setup, 21
    Quicken accounts, creating, 9
importing
    account statements, 127
    files, 48-49
    TurboTax information to Tax Planner, 339
income
    editing in Home Purchase Planner, 324
    miscellaneous income, Other Income and Losses section (Tax Planner), 344-345
    paycheck information, Quicken Guided Setup, 33
    taxable income information, reviewing/editing in Tax Planner, 347-348
Income and Expense Comparison by Category reports (Home Purchase Planner), 319
Income vs.. Expenses section (Analysis & Reports tab), 169
inflation rates, reviewing/editing in Planning Center, 291
Inflation section (Planning Center, Plan Assumptions section), 291
Ins/Policy menu (Quicken Home Inventory tool, Receipts & Records Section), 273
installing Quicken, 3-7
Int Rate column (Property & Debt Center, Loan Accounts Summary section), 256
Interest Pd column (Property & Debt Center, Loan Accounts Summary section), 256

Interest Rate box (Property & Debt Center, Loan Accounts Summary section), 262
Interest Rate window (Credit Card Accounts section), 129
interest rates, setting in credit card accounts, 129
Internet
    access, configuring, 61-63
    online updates, 88-89, 92
inventories (home)
    claims management, 275-277
    inventory items
        adding, 270
        copying, 271
        deleting, 271
        entering information on, 272-273
        searches, 273
    policy management, 274
    reports, viewing, 277
Investing Accounts section (Account List window), 188-189
Investing Activity section (Investment Center), 194
Investing menu
    Portfolio Analyzer, 229-232
    Portfolio Rebalancer, 233-236
investment accounts
    Investment Center
        adding to, 184-188
        balancing in, 204-206
        deleting from, 190
        editing in, 188-189
        reviewing in, 202-203
    configuring online access, 185
    deleting, 190
    online accounts, downloading, 183
    quotes, updating, 183
    reviewing, 184, 194, 202-203
    securities, reviewing, 214

transactions, Investment Center
    adding to, 195, 198
    deleting from, 199
    editing in, 197-199
    managing in, 200-201
views, changing, 210
Investment Center, 66
    Account Attachments section, 194
    Account Attributes section, 193
    Account Holdings section, 194
    Account Status section, 193
    Account Value vs. Cost Basis section, 202
    alerts, configuring, 182
    Allocation by Security section, 203
    Analysis tab, 208-214, 218-222
    Asset Allocation section, 203
    Capital Gains Report, 194
    Holdings section, 193
    Investing Activity section, 194
    investment accounts
        adding, 184-188
        balancing, 204-206
        configuring online access, 185
        deleting, 190
        editing, 188-189
        reviewing, 184, 202-203
        reviewing account summaries, 194
        updating quotes, 183
    investment transactions, 195-201
    online investment accounts, downloading, 183
    paychecks, adding, 199
    Performance & Analysis tab, 202-203
    Portfolio tab, 223-228
    Portfolio Value report, 184
    retirement accounts
        adding, 185-188
        balancing, 204-206

configuring online access, 185
deleting, 190
editing, 188-189
reviewing account summaries, 194
reviewing performance, 202-203
retirement transactions, 197-201
security quotes, updating, 183
Show Full Graph option, 202
Statement Summary window, 206
Today's Data tab, 184, 191-192
Investment Transactions preference type (Preferences menu), 56
investments
brokerage accounts, 19-22
College Planner, reviewing in, 316
federal tax rates, 220
ID, 21
listings, grouping, 224
quotes, updating, 223-224
securities, selling, 222
Planning Center, reviewing/editing in, 294
state tax rates, 220
taxes, estimating, 220-222
tracking, 61, 191-192
Investments section (Planning Center, Plan Assumptions section), 294

J – K – L

Keep the Alert in the List For menu (Home page, Alerts section), 75
keyboard shortcuts, table of, 96

liability accounts, 32. *See also* debt accounts
lightning bolt symbols, 225
links, financial websites, 95
Living Expenses section (Planning Center, Plan Assumptions section), 300-302

Loan Accounts Summary section (Property & Debt Center)
Borrow Money option, 257
Compounding Period menu, 260
Current Balance Amount box, 260
Date of Next Payment box, 261
Int Rate column, 256
Interest Pd column, 256
Interest Rate box, 262
loans
adding to, 257-259, 262
recording payments, 266
reviewing accounts, 256
Opening Date box, 258
Original Balance box, 258
Original Length box, 259
Payment Amount box, 261
Pmts Left column, 256
Principal Pd column, 256
refinanced loans, tracking, 265
Total row, 256
Loan Rate Changes window (Property & Debt Center), 268
loans
amortized loans, 32
asset accounts, creating, 264
editing, 267, 321
Loan Accounts Summary section (Property & Debt Center), adding to, 257-259, 262
Payment section (Property & Debt Center), setting up payments, 263
payments, recording/editing, 266-267
Planning Center, reviewing/editing in, 299
rate changes, editing/deleting, 268
refinanced loans, tracking, 265
losses, Other Income and Losses section (Tax Planner), 344-345
Lowest Balance section (Bills and Scheduled Transactions section), 159

M

managing
- debt account scheduled transactions, 252
- home inventories (claims/policies), 274-275
- investment transactions in Investment Center, 200-201
- property account scheduled transactions, 252
- retirement transactions from Investment Center, 200-201
- scheduled transactions, 117, 146-147, 162-163

Market Value column (Today's Data tab), 184
Match If menu, 112-114
Matching section (Reports and Graphs window), selecting payees, 369
maximum account balances (savings/spending accounts), entering, 101
messages (accounts), viewing, 67
minimum account balances (savings/spending accounts), entering, 101
miscellaneous income information
- Other Income and Losses section (Tax Planner), 344-345
- Planning Center, reviewing/editing in, 290

missing transactions
- portfolios, entering in, 226
- spending/savings accounts, adding to, 121

month view (calendars), viewing transactions in, 84
Monthly Avg column (Property & Debt Center, Auto Expenses section), 269
Morningstar mutual fund rating service, 213
Move Up/Down buttons (account bar), 68
moving
- account bar, 54
- accounts, 68, 101
- buttons in toolbar, 43

categories in Category List section (Tax tab, Tax-Related Expense YTD section), 353
MTD Expenses column (Property & Debt Center, Auto Expenses section), 269
Mutual Fund Ratings section (Analysis tab), 212-213
mutual funds
- comparing, 212
- evaluating, 225, 234
- rating, Morningstar rating service, 213
- researching, 213
- reviewing, 212
- ticker symbols, 235
- Yahoo! Finance web page, 213

My Web Links tool, 94-95

N

naming
- buttons (toolbar), 43
- files, 45
- reports, 368
- spending/savings accounts, 103

net worth
- accounts, hiding from, 73
- Financial Overview Center, 67-71
- graphs, opening/viewing, 70
- reports, opening, 70

Net Worth Allocation option (Financial Overview Center), 71
Net Worth by Year option (Financial Overview Center), 71
Net Worth Summary (Financial Overview Center), 71
new files, creating, 45
new Quicken installations, 3-5
newsletters (Quicken), subscribing to, 93
Next Steps to Meet Your Financial Goals section (Home page), 86-87

392

No Payee option (Payees tab), 370
notes
    calendar, adding to days, 85
    credit card transactions, adding to, 140
    payments, adding to (Quicken Bill Pay), 175
    transactions, 165
notifications/warnings, 57. *See also* alerts
Notify preference type (Preferences menu), warnings/notifications, 57

O

One Step Update
    Cash Flow Center, 99-100
    Portfolio tab, 223
online accounts, saving information, 55
online backups (Quicken files), 46
online bill pay, 36
Online Update Summary window (Cash Flow Center), 128, 152-154
online updates, 88-89, 92
Opening Date box (Property & Debt Center, Loan Accounts Summary section), 258
Options menu, Customize This Graph option, 214
Order Checks & Supplies option (Quicken Services), 93
Organization menu (Reports and Graphs window), 368
organizing files, 45
Original Balance box (Property & Debt Center, Loan Accounts Summary section), 258
Original Length box (Property & Debt Center, Loan Accounts Summary section), 259
Other Income and Losses section (Tax Planner), 344-345
Other Income section (Planning Center, Plan Assumptions section), 290

Overview tab
    Cash Flow Center, 148
    Property & Debt Center, 253

P

passwords
    bank accounts, 14, 17
    case-sensitivity, 51
    changing, 51, 64
    files, assigning to/removing from, 51
    investments, 21
    PIN vault, 90-92
    Quicken accounts, creating, 9
    transactions, assigning to/removing from, 52
paychecks
    adding to Investment Center, 199
    Bills and Scheduled Transactions section (Cash Flow Center), adding/editing information, 166-167
    credit card accounts, adding to, 145
    Quicken Guided Setup, entering in, 33
    spending/savings accounts, adding to, 116
payees
    Quicken Bill Pay, entering information in, 173
    Quicken Checks, entering information in, 179
    reports, selecting for, 369
    transaction information, entering in Bills and Scheduled Transactions section, 165
Payees tab (Reports and Graphs window), 370
paying bills online, 36
Payment Amount box (Property & Debt Center, Loan Accounts Summary section), 261

How can we make this index more useful? Email us at indexes@quepublishing.com

Payment section (Property & Debt Center), setting up loan payments, 263
payments
    home inventory claims, 277
    loan payments, 263, 266-267
    methods of, changing, 179
    Quicken Bill Pay, 170-175
    taxes, Estimated Tax Payments section (Tax Planner), 346
pensions, reviewing/editing information in Planning Center, 289
Performance & Analysis tab (Investment Center), 202
Performance section (Portfolio Analyzer), 229
Performance tab (Investment Center), 203
pie charts
    Actual pie chart (Analysis tab), 208, 211
    asset allocation reports, 211
    Asset Allocation section (Portfolio Analyzer), 231
    date ranges, changing, 214
    Holdings section (Portfolio Analyzer), 230
    Target pie chart (Analysis tab), 208-209
PIN vault, 90-92
Plan Assumptions section (Planning Center), 285
planners
    College Planner, 312-317
    Debt Reduction Planner, 326-328
    Home Purchase Planner, 318-325
    Retirement Planner, 308
    Special Purchase Planner, 330-331
    Tax Planner
        accessing, 342
        Estimated Tax Payments section, 346
        importing TurboTax information, 339
        Other Income and Losses section, 344-345
        Projected Tax section, 342
        summaries, 343
        Tax Withholding Estimator, 358-360
        Taxable Income YTD section, 347-348
        Wages section, 343
        Year-End files, 340-341
Planning Center
    About You section, 286
    alerts, configuring, 284
    Plan Assumptions section
        Adjustments to Living Expenses section, 302
        Average Tax Rate section, 291
        Current Homes & Assets section, 297-298
        Current Loans section, 299
        editing planner assumptions, 285
        Explore What If's section, 305
        Inflation section, 291
        Investments section, 294
        Living Expenses section, 300
        Other Income Section, 290
        Rate of Return section, 296
        Retirement Benefits Section, 288-289
        reviewing planner assumptions, 285
        Salary Section, 287
        Savings section, 292
        Special Expenses section, 303-304
Planning menu, 308, 335
Planning tab (Financial Overview Center)
    Budget section, 332, 335
    Calculators section, 307
    College planner, 312-317
    Debt Reduction Planner, 326-328
    Home Purchase planner, 318-325
    Retirement planner, 308
    Special Purchase Planner, 330-331
plans, editing/reviewing, 336
Pmts Left column (Property & Debt Center, Loan Accounts Summary section), 256

Portfolio Analyzer (Investing menu), 229-232
Portfolio Rebalancer (Investing menu), 233-236
Portfolio tab (Investment Center), 223-228
Portfolio Value report, opening in Investment Center, 184
portfolio view (Portfolio tab), 223
portfolios
    accounts, configuring Internet access, 61
    allocations, 231, 235
    custom views, creating, 228
    holdings, getting advice on, 230
    missing transactions, entering, 226
    mutual funds, evaluating, 234
    rate of return, 229-231
    rebalancing, 233-236
    risk, determining, 231
    securities, 229-230
    stocks, evaluating, 234
    taxes, 232
    transactions, editing/deleting, 226
preferences
    graphs, setting in, 372
    Internet connections, setting, 62-63
    Quicken, configuring, 53-59
    reports, setting in, 372-373
    saving, 60
Preferences menu
    Backup preference type, 55
    Calendar and Currency preference type, 54
    Download Transactions preference type, 58
    Investment Transactions preference type, 56
    Notify Transactions preference type, 57
    QuickFill preference type, 57
    Register preference type, 56
    Reminders preference type, 59
    Reports and Graphs preference type, 59
    Reports Only preference type, 60
    Setup preference type, 54
    Web Connect preference type, 55
    Write Checks preference type, 58
Principal Pd column (Property & Debt Center, Loan Accounts Summary section), 256
printing
    asset allocation reports, 211
    Auto Expenses reports, 269
    checks, setting preferences, 58
    Quicken Checks, 178-180
    transaction calendar, 118, 147, 163
    transactions, 76
Professional Planning Resources guide (Planning menu), 335
Projected Tax section (Tax Planner), 342
Property & Debt Accounts section (Property & Debt Center)
    debt accounts
        adding, 240-241
        adding transactions, 245
        changing tax schedules, 242
        deleting, 242-243, 246
        editing, 242, 246
        reviewing, 239
        searching transactions, 247
        sorting transactions, 247
        transferring funds to property accounts, 248
        updating, 242-244
    property accounts
        adding, 240-241
        adding transactions, 245
        changing tax schedules, 242
        deleting, 242-243, 246
        editing, 242, 246
        reviewing, 239

How can we make this index more useful? Email us at indexes@quepublishing.com

searching transactions, 247
sorting transactions, 247
transferring funds to debt accounts, 248
updating, 242-244
Property & Debt Center, 66
    alerts, configuring, 238
    asset accounts, creating, 264
    Auto Expenses section, 269
    debt accounts, 239-248, 254-255
        adding, 240-242
        adding transactions, 245, 250
        balancing, 254-255
        deleting, 242-243
        deleting transactions, 246, 250
        editing transactions, 246, 249
        liability accounts, Quicken Guided Setup, 32
        managing transactions, 252
        overviews, viewing, 253
        Property & Debt Center, 66
        reconciling transactions, 254-255
        reviewing, 239
        reviewing transactions, 250, 299
        scheduled transactions, 249-252
        searching transactions, 247
        sorting transactions, 247
        tax-deferred accounts, 241
        tax exempt accounts, 241
        tax schedules, changing, 242
        transferring funds to property accounts, 248
        updating, 242-244
        viewing transaction calendars, 251
        viewing transaction graphs, 252
    Loan Accounts Summary section
        adding loans to, 257-259, 262
        Borrow Money option, 257
        Compounding Period menu, 260
        Current Balance Amount box, 260
        Date of Next Payment box, 261
        Int Rate column, 256
        Interest Pd column, 256
        Interest Rate box, 262
        Opening Date box, 258
        Original Balance box, 258
        Original Length box, 259
        Payment Amount box, 261
        Pmts Left column, 256
        Principal Pd column, 256
        recording loan payments, 266
        refinanced loans, tracking, 265
        reviewing loan acounts, 256
        Total row, 256
    Loan Rate Changes window, 268
    Overview tab, 253
    Payment section, setting up loan payments, 263
    Property & Debt Accounts section, 239-248
    property accounts, 239-248, 254-255
    Scheduled Transactions tab, 249-252
    Search menu, 247
    To Account menu, 248
    Transfer Money From menu, 248
    View Loans dialog, 267
property accounts
    adding, 240-241
    asset accounts, 30-32
    auto property accounts, 27-29
    balancing, 254-255
    deleting, 242-243
    editing, 242, 297-298
    home property accounts, 23-26
    overviews, viewing, 253
    payment type, selecting, 25
    Property & Debt Center, 66

reviewing, 239, 297-298
tax exempt accounts, 241
tax schedules, changing, 242
tax-deferred accounts, 241
transactions
    adding, 245, 250
    deleting, 246, 250
    editing, 246, 249
    managing, 252
    reconciling, 254-255
    reviewing, 250
    searching, 247
    sorting, 247
    viewing transaction calendars, 251
    viewing transaction graphs, 252
transferring funds to debt accounts, 248
updating, 242-244
Proposed Sales table (Capital Gains Estimator), 222
Protect Your Quicken Data) option (Quicken Services), 93

Q

Quicken
    files
        backups, 46-47, 55
        creating, 45
        exporting, 50
        importing, 48-49
        naming, 45
        opening, quickly, 44
        organizing, 45
        passwords, 51-52
        storing, 45-46
    installing, 3-7
    registering, 8-9, 64
    remote access, 9

Quicken Account Setup window (Credit Card Accounts section), 129-131
Quicken Bill Pay, 170-175
Quicken Checks, 176-180
Quicken Guided Setup, 10
    asset accounts, 30-31
    auto property accounts, 25-29
    bill information, entering, 36-37
    brokerage accounts, 19-22
    cash accounts, 18
    checking accounts, 13-15
    completing, 39
    credit card accounts, 17-18
    editing information, 40
    exiting, 10
    financial goals, entering, 12
    Finish Later button, 12
    home property accounts, 23-26
    liability accounts, 32
    paycheck information, entering, 33
    personal information, entering, 11
    reviewing, 39
    savings accounts, 16
Quicken Home Inventory tool, 271-277
Quicken MasterCard option (Quicken Services), 93
Quicken Newsletters, subscribing to, 93
Quicken Services, 93
Quicken.com website, updates, 64
QuickFill preference type (Preferences menu), 57
quotes
    Download Historical Prices (Portfolio tab), 223
    downloading, 62, 224
    grouping, 224
    updating, 183, 223-224
Quotes view (Portfolio tab), 223

How can we make this index more useful? Email us at indexes@quepublishing.com

Index

R

Rank in Category column (Mutual Fund Ratings section), 212
Rate of Return section (Planning Center, Plan Assumptions section), 296
rate of return, determining (portfolios), 229-231
Rating column (Mutual Fund Ratings section), 212-213
rebalancing portfolios, 233-236
Receipts & Records section (Quicken Home Inventory tool), 272-273
recurring transactions, setting up, 34
red flags (accounts), 67, 76, 116, 145
refinanced loans, tracking, 265
Register preference type (Preferences menu), customizing account registers, 56
registering Quicken software, 8, 64
registers (account)
    Account List window, opening in, 194
    bills, adding to, 160
    credit card accounts, viewing, 129
    customizing, 56
    scheduled transactions, adding to, 115-116, 160
    transactions, recording, 159
Reminders preference type (Preferences menu), transaction reminders, configuring, 59
remote access
    accounts, 61-63
    Quicken, 9
Remove from Bar column (account bar), 68
removing. *See* deleting
renaming
    buttons in toolbar, 43
    reports, 368

reordering
    accounts in account bar, 68
    buttons in toolbar, 43
reports
    change alerts, viewing, 371
    creating, 366
    customizing, 368-371
    Easy Answer reports and graphs feature, 367
    exporting, 374
    net worth reports, 70-71
    preferences, setting, 59, 372-373
    renaming, 368
    saving, 375-376
    selecting, 367
    Tax Summary reports, 347
    viewing, 366
Reports and Graphs preference type (Preferences menu), 59
Reports and Graphs window
    Accounts tab, selecting accounts for, 369
    Advanced tab, 371
    Categories tab, selecting categories for, 369
    Category Groups tab, 370
    Column menu, 368
    Date Range menu, 368
    Matching section, selecting payees, 369
    Organization menu, 368
    Payees tab, 370
    Row menu, 368
    taskbar, accessing via, 370
Reports menu, 366
Reports Only preference type (Preferences menu), 60
Resale Value History dialog (Quicken Home Inventory tool, Receipts & Records Section), 272
researching mutual funds, 213

resolving alerts, 98
restoring backup files, 47
Results section (Debt Reduction Planner), 328
retirement accounts
    account summaries, reviewing, 194
    deleting, 190
    Investment Center, 66
        adding to, 185-188
        balancing in, 204-206
        editing, 188-189
        reviewing in, 202-203
    online access, configuring, 185
    securities, reviewing, 214
    views, changing, 210
Retirement Benefits section (Planning Center, Plan Assumptions section), 288-289
retirement information, reviewing/editing in Planning Center, 288-289
Retirement Planner, 308
retirement transactions, editing/managing in Investment Center, 197-201
Risk Profile section (Portfolio Analyzer), 231
risk, determining (portfolios), 231
Row menu (Reports and Graphs window), 368

S

Salary section (Planning Center, Plan Assumptions section), 287
sales taxes, comparing via Capital Gains Estimator (Financial Overview Center), 357
saving
    online account information, 55
    Quicken preferences, 60
    reports, 375-376

savings accounts
    adding, 102
    balancing, 99, 118-124
    Cash Flow Center, 66
    deleting, 106
    editing, 104
    funds transfers, 113-114
    ID, 14
    information, downloading, 102-103
    interest rates, entering, 101
    min/max balances, entering, 101
    moving, 101
    naming, 103
    online update summaries, turning off, 100
    overviews, viewing, 119
    passwords, 14
    paychecks, adding, 116
    Quicken Guided Setup, 16
    reviewing, 101, 292, 316
    tax schedules, reviewing, 105
    transactions
        adding, 110-111, 115-117, 121
        attachments, 109
        categorizing, 108, 110
        deleting, 111, 116-117
        editing, 111, 117, 121
        flagging, 109-111
        managing, 117
        printing transaction calendar, 118
        scheduling, 114
        searches, 112
        skipping, 116
        sorting, 112
        updating, 111, 117
        viewing daily transaction graphs, 118
        viewing transaction calendar, 117-118
    updating, 104

How can we make this index more useful? Email us at indexes@quepublishing.com

Savings section (Planning Center, Plan Assumptions section), 292
Schedule These? section (Scheduled Transactions tab), 116
scheduled transactions, 114
- Bills and Scheduled Transactions section (Cash Flow Center), adding to, 162-164
- continuous transactions, 165
- Credit Card Accounts section (Cash Flow Center), adding to, 146
- credit card transactions, 144-145
- daily transaction graphs, 147, 163
- debt account transactions, 249-252
- deleting, 116-117, 145-146, 162
- editing, 117, 145-146, 161-162
- flagging, 116
- frequency of, selecting, 165
- investment transactions, 198-201
- managing, 117, 146-147, 162-163
- notes, 165
- online updates, 89, 92
- payment methods, changing, 179
- property account transactions, 249-252
- registers, adding to, 160
- retirement transactions, 198-201
- setting up, 34
- skipping, 116, 145, 160
- transaction calendar, printing/viewing, 146-147, 162-163
- updating, 117

Scheduled Transactions tab
- Cash Flow Center, 115-116
- Property & Debt Center, 249-252

Search menu
- Cash Flow Center, 112
- Credit Card Accounts section, 142
- Property & Debt Center, 247

searching
- inventory item searches in Quicken Home Inventory, 273

transactions, 112
- credit card transactions, 142-143
- debt account transactions, 247
- property account transactions, 247

securities
- adding, 62
- Allocation by Security report (Investment Center), viewing, 203
- asset allocation reports, viewing detailed security breakdowns, 211
- asset classes, retrieiving information, 217
- details, editing/viewing, 225
- editing, 62
- Investment Center, 66
- market status, viewing, 225
- names, changing, 225
- performance analysis, 229
- portfolio securities, determining largest securities, 230
- reviewing, 214
- selling, Capital Gains Estimator (Analysis tab), 222
- symbols, viewing, 62
- viewing, 210
- Watch List folder (Portfolio tab), 223
- Watch List section (Today's Data tab), 191-192

security
- ID, Quicken.com, 64
- passwords, 51-52, 64, 90-92

security quotes, updating, 183
Select Tax Rates window, estimating taxes, 355
selling securities, Capital Gains Estimator (Analysis tab), 222
Services (Quicken), 93
Set Up Alerts button (Home page, Alerts section), 75
setup checklist (Quicken), 2

Setup preference type (Preferences menu), 54
share information, viewing, 61
shortcuts
- keyboard shortcuts table, 96
- toolbar buttons, assigning to, 43

Show Account (Analysis tab), changing account views, 210
Show All Alerts button (Home page, Alerts section), 74
Show Amt. button (account bar), 67
Show Full Graph option (Investment Center), 202
Show Me Change Alerts for This Report option (Advanced tab), 371
Show Me the Alert As menu (Home page, Alerts section), 75
Show menu (Bills and Scheduled Transactions section), 83-84
Show Net Worth Report button (Financial Overview Center), 71
skipping
- bill instances in register, 160
- transactions, 81, 116, 145, 160

Social Security benefits, reviewing/editing information in Planning Center, 288
sorting transactions, 56, 112, 143, 158, 247
special expenses information, reviewing/editing in Planning Center, 303-304
Special Expenses section (Planning Center, Plan Assumptions section), 303-304
special messages (accounts), viewing, 67
Special Purchase Planner, 330-331
spending accounts
- adding, 102
- balancing, 99, 118-124
- deleting, 106
- editing, 104
- funds transfers, 113-114
- information, downloading, 102-103
- interest rates, entering, 101
- min/max balances, entering, 101
- moving, 101
- naming, 103
- online update summaries, turning off, 100
- overviews, viewing, 119
- paychecks, adding, 116
- reviewing, 101
- spending totals, viewing, 108
- tax schedules, reviewing, 105
- transaction reports, viewing, 108
- transactions
  - accepting, 108
  - adding, 110-111, 115-117, 121
  - attachments, 109
  - categorizing, 108-110
  - deleting, 108, 111, 116-117
  - editing, 111, 117, 121
  - flagging, 109-111
  - managing, 117
  - printing transaction calendar, 118
  - scheduling, 114
  - searches, 112
  - skipping, 116
  - sorting, 112
  - updating, 111, 117
  - viewing daily transaction graphs, 118
  - viewing transaction calendar, 117-118
- updating, 104

Split Transaction window, tracking refinanced loans, 265
start page, changing, 53
State Tax Rates section (Capital Gains Estimator), 220
Statement Summary window
- Cash Flow Center, 149-151
- Investment Center, 206

statements (accounts), importing, 127
stocks, 225, 234-235
storing files, 45-46

T

target allocation preferences (portfolios), 235
Target pie chart (Analysis tab), 208-209
Tax Category Audit tool, 364
Tax Category Audit window, 353
Tax Center, configuring alerts, 338
tax exempt accounts, 241
tax-deferred accounts, 241
Tax Implications section (Portfolio Analyzer), 232
Tax menu, Deduction Finder, 361-363
Tax Planner
    accessing, 342
    Estimated Tax Payments section, 346
    Other Income and Losses section, 344-345
    Projected Tax section, 342
    summaries, 343
    Tax Withholding Estimator, 358-360
    Taxable Income YTD section, 347-348
    TurboTax information, importing to, 339
    Wages section, foreign currency, 343
    Year-End files, creating, 340-341
Tax-Related Expenses YTD section (Tax tab), Category List section, 349-353
Tax-Related Transactions Only option (Advanced tab), 371
Tax Summary Reports, 347
Tax tab, Tax-Related Expenses YTD section, 349-353
Tax Withholding Estimator (Tax Planner), 358-360
Taxable Gains from Proposed Sales table (Capital Gains Estimator), 222

Taxable Income YTD section (Tax Planner), 347-348
taxes
    credit card accounts, reviewing/changing tax schedules, 133
    Estimated Tax Payments section (Tax Planner), 346
    estimating, 220-222, 335
    foreign currency, 343
    investment taxes, estimating, 220-222
    portfolios, 232
    rates, reviewing/editing in Planning Center, 291
    resource web links, 364
    sales taxes, comparing via Capital Gains Estimator (Financial Overview Center), 357
    schedules, 105, 241-242
    tax-deferred accounts, 241
    taxable income information, reviewing/editing in Tax Planner, 347-348
    tax exempt accounts, 241
    Year-End files, 340-341
ticker symbols (stocks/mutual funds), 235
Time Period menu (Portfolio Analyzer), 229
time periods (customized reports), 368
Tips and Services, 93
To Account menu (Property & Debt Center), 248
Today's Data tab (Investment Center), 184, 191-192
toolbar, customizing, 42-43
Total row (Property & Debt Center), 256, 269
tracking
    emergency records, 278, 282
    investment performance, 191-192
    investments, 61
    loan rate changes, 268
    transactions, 80

Transaction Attachments window (Cash Flow Center), 109
transaction calendar, printing/viewing, 146-147, 162-163
transaction graphs, viewing, 147, 163
transactions
- attachments, 109, 138-139
- average amount of, viewing, 157
- Bills and Scheduled Transactions section (Home page), recording in, 76-78, 82, 159
- categorizing, 80, 108-110
- color designations, 76
- continuous transactions, 165
- credit card transactions, 127, 135-145
- daily transaction graphs, viewing, 118
- debt transactions, 245-247, 254-255
- deleting, 111
- downloading, 58, 135
- editing, 77-79, 111, 121
- flagging, 109-111, 116, 145
- frequency of, selecting, 165
- investment transaction, 195-201
- missing transactions, entering in
  - portfolios, 226
  - spending/savings accounts, 121
- multiple lines, selecting, 56
- notes, 165
- passwords, 52
- payment methods, changing, 179
- portfolio transactions, editing/deleting, 226
- property transactions, 245-247, 254-255
- Print button, 76
- recurring transactions, 34
- registers, recording in, 159
- reminders, configuring, 59
- retirement transactions, 197-201
- scheduled transactions, 114
  - adding, 115-117, 144-145, 160-165
  - deleting, 116-117, 145-146, 162
  - editing, 117, 145-146, 161-162
  - flagging, 116
  - managing, 117, 146-147, 162-163
  - online updates, 89, 92
  - printing calendar, 147, 163
  - setting up, 34
  - skipping, 116, 145, 160
  - updating, 117
  - viewing calendar, 146, 162
  - viewing daily transaction graphs, 147, 163
- searches, 112
- skipping, 81
- sorting, 56, 112, 158
- spending/savings accounts, 106-111
- tracking, 80
- transaction calendar, 117-118
- updating, 111
- viewing, 83-85, 226

Transfer Money From menu (Property & Debt Center), 248
TurboTax, importing information to Tax Planner, 339
tutorials, Quicken Bill Pay, 170

U

Unassigned option (Category Groups tab), 370
Unrealized Gains option (Advanced tab), 371
updates, 6-7
- asset classes, 216
- checking for, 5
- credit card accounts, 127, 132, 151
- debt accounts, 242
- investment quotes, 183
- online updates, 88-89, 92

How can we make this index more useful? Email us at indexes@quepublishing.com

Index **403**

online accounts, saving information, 55
property accounts, 242
Quick.com, 64
Quicken Guided Setup information, 40
quotes, 223-224
savings accounts, 99-100, 104
scheduled transactions, 117
security quotes, 183
spending accounts, 99-100, 104
transactions, 111
Use Tax Planner Values (Capital Gains Estimator), 221

V

vehicles, 269
View Loans dialog (Property & Debt Center), 267
viewing
  account balances, 67, 158
  account bars, 68
  account messages, 67
  active alerts, 74
  alerts, 98, 126, 156, 371
  all toolbar buttons, 42
  Allocation by Security report (Investment Center), 203
  asset allocation reports, 211
  average transaction amount, 157
  button icons (toolbar), 43
  change alerts, 371
  credit card account information, 129, 137, 148
  daily transaction graphs, 118, 147, 163
  debt account information, 251-253
  estimated balances, 118, 147, 163
  home inventory reports, 277
  net worth graphs, 70
  net worth reports, 71
  property account information, 251-253
  reports, 366, 376

  securities, 210, 225
  securities symbols, 62
  share information, 61
  spending totals (spending accounts), 108
  spending/savings account overviews, 119
  Tax Summary Reports, 347
  transactions, 226
    Bills and Scheduled Transactions section (Home page), 83-85
    calendars, 84, 117-118, 146, 162
    reports (spending accounts), 108, 371
  watch lists (investments), 61

W

Wages section (Tax Planner), foreign currency, 343
warnings/notifications, 57. *See also* alerts
Watch List folder (Portfolio tab), 223
Watch List section (Today's Data tab), 191-192
watch lists (investments), viewing, 61
Web Connect preference type (Preferences menu), 55
What Should I Sell? section (Capital Gains Estimator), 356
What to Look for in Performance section (Portfolio Analyzer), 230
what-if scenarios, reviewing/editing in Planning Center, 305
withholdings, Tax Withholdings Estimator (Tax Planner), 358-360
working calendars, 54
Write Checks preference type (Preferences menu), check printing, 58

X – Y – Z

Yahoo! Finance web page, 213
Year-End files (taxes), 340-341
YTD Expenses column (Property & Debt Center, Auto Expenses section), 269